剑桥应用语言学年度评论 2011
Annual Review of Applied Linguistics

第二语言教育研究
Topics in Second Language Pedagogy

主编 〔美〕Charlene Polio
导读 张琳

2016年·北京

Originally published by Cambridge University Press in 2011. This reprint edition is published with the permission of the Syndicate of the Press of the University of Cambridge, Cambridge, England.

原书由英国剑桥大学出版社于 2011 年出版。

本版经英国剑桥大学出版社授权出版。

This edition is licensed for sale in the People's Republic of China only (excluding Hong Kong SAR, Macao SAR and Taiwan Province). No part of this publication may be reproduced or distributed by any means, or stored in a database or retrieval system, without the prior written permission of the publisher.

本版仅限在中华人民共和国境内（不包括香港特别行政区、澳门特别行政区及台湾）销售。未经出版者书面许可，不得以任何方式复制或发行本书的任何部分。

剑桥应用语言学年度评论
专家委员会

主　任　胡壮麟
副主任　田贵森　朱永生
委　员　曹　进　何　伟　靳　琰　赖良涛　李战子
　　　　　彭宣维　齐振海　孙迎晖　王振华　辛志英
　　　　　杨信彰　于　晖　张　辉　张　琳　张　薇
　　　　　郑　萱

CONTENTS

总序 ·· 胡壮麟　1
导读 ·· 张　琳　11

Editor's Introduction
·· Charlene Polio　i

SECTION A: SECOND LANGUAGE INSTRUCTION IN DIFFERENT SETTINGS

Teaching Academic Language in L2 Secondary Settings
························· Mary J. Schleppegrell and Catherine L. O'Hallaron　3
Current Trends in Online Language Learning
··· Robert J. Blake　24
The Implementation of Communicative and Task-Based Language
  Teaching in the Asia-Pacific Region
··· Yuko Goto Butler　47
Enhancing Language Learning in Study Abroad
··· Celeste Kinginger　77
Teaching Second Languages for the Workplace
························· Jonathan Newton and Ewa Kusmierczyk　99

SECTION B: SECOND LANGUAGE INSTRUCTION FOR SPECIFIC LEARNERS

All Shades of Every Color: An Overview of Early Teaching
  and Learning of Foreign Languages
························· Marianne Nikolov and Jelena Mihaljević Djigunović　127

Teaching Adult Second Language Learners Who Are Emergent Readers
.... Martha Bigelow and Patsy Vinogradov   160

Teaching American Sign Language to Hearing Adult Learners
.... David Quinto-Pozos   183

SECTION C: TOPICS IN INTEGRATED APPROACHES

Research in Language-Literature Instruction: Meeting the Call for Change?
.... Kate Paesani   217

Content-and-Language Integrated Learning: From Practice to Principles?
.... Christiane Dalton-Puffer   246

Corpus Research Applications in Second Language Teaching
.... Ute Römer   278

Teaching Multimodal and Digital Literacy in L2 Settings:
New Literacies, New Basics, New Pedagogies
.... Heather Lotherington and Jennifer Jenson   306

SECTION D: INSTRUCTION IN SPECIFIC SKILL AREAS

Best Practices in Teaching Logographic and Non-Roman Writing
Systems to L2 Learners
.... Michael E. Everson   337

Collaborative Writing in L2 Contexts: Processes, Outcomes, and
Future Directions
.... Neomy Storch   372

Teaching Pragmatics: Trends and Issues
.... Naoko Taguchi   391

CONTRIBUTOR BIODATA

总　序

自2013年8月起,商务印书馆与剑桥大学出版社开始商洽在大陆出版《应用语言学年度评论》(Annual Review of Applied Linguistics)事宜,至2014年春末签约。此后,商务印书馆英语编辑室领导栾奇和马浩岚并责任编辑杨子辉博士先后来访,约我办三件事,一是代为组织国内学者为各卷写导读,二是承担导读的审稿任务,三是为商务版《应用语言学年度评论》写一个总序。作为对我的照顾,同意我邀请复旦大学朱永生教授[①]和北京师范大学田贵森教授[②]参加导读审定工作。就总序而言,多次思考之后,想谈以下四个方面。

一、刊物方针

《应用语言学年度评论》(以下简称《年度评论》)是美国应用语言

[①] 朱永生:复旦大学教授、博导,杭州师范大学钱塘学者,高校功能语言学研究会副会长,高校语篇分析研究会副会长,Linguistics and Human Sciences 编委及《中国外语》等杂志编委。曾任苏州大学外语系主任、复旦大学外文系主任和国际文化交流学院院长、国际系统功能语言学研究会执委、国务院学科评议组成员、全国高校外语教学指导委员会委员等职务。著有《系统功能语言学多维思考》《系统功能语言学再思考》《语境动态研究》《系统功能语言学概论》等。

[②] 田贵森:北京师范大学外文学院教授、博导,中国功能语言学学会常务理事、中国社会语言学学会理事。1976年河北师范大学外语系毕业后留校任教,1987年北京外国语大学硕士,1991年纽约市立大学硕士,1997年北京大学博士。曾任河北师大外国语学院院长,河北省高校外语教学研究会会长,中国教育学会外语教学专业委员会副理事长。著有《禁忌语的功能研究》《英语专业毕业论文写作教程》《新编英语词汇学教程》等。

学学会（American Association for Applied Linguistics，简称 AAAL）主办的一部书刊结合的出版物，自 1980 年起每年一卷，至 2014 年已出版 34 卷。该刊最初由 Newbury House 出版社出版，自第 5 卷起改为剑桥大学出版社出版，延续至今。美国南加州大学美国语言研究所主任 Robert B. Kaplan 教授筹划第 1 卷《年度评论》时，邀请犹他州布里格姆-扬大学日耳曼语系 Randall L. Jones 教授和华盛顿大学应用语言学中心主任 G. Richard Tucker 教授三人合作主编。在他们领导下的编委会对办刊宗旨确定这样一个基本认识：尽管 1941 年美国密执安大学率先成立了将语言学理论应用于语言教育的英语学院，1956 年英国爱丁堡大学成立了应用语言学系，1959 年美国华盛顿大学建立了应用语言学中心，1966 年 *TESOL Quarterly* 出版，1977 年美国应用语言学学会成立，《年度评论》编委会无意选定其中之一作为应用语言学界共同遵循的蓝图，而是决定走自己的路。在此基础上编委会确定的方针有如下特点：(1)《年度评论》不是杂志，因为它一年只出一本；它又被看作是一本杂志，因为它由出版社的杂志部负责编辑、发行事务。[①]（2）该出版物不对应用语言学做面面俱到的报道，而是对应用语言学学科的现状进行专题评论、综述和文献式的归纳。(3) 应用语言学具有高度的跨学科性，因此该刊重点结合双语教育、语言教育学、心理语言学和社会语言学四个方面进行选题。考虑到这四个学科枝叶蔓生，年刊会对一个学科的某一领域做全面的综述和评论。(4) 即使上述四个学科也不是应用语言学的唯一研究领域，因为该刊遵循美国应用语言学学会所倡导的功能导向，着眼于具体应用更甚于理论。(5) 所有的文章由编委会组织某一领域的专家撰写，不转载已在其他刊物上发表的文章，也不采用在某个学术会议上已经宣读的论文，更不对某一部具体的学术著作进行评论。因此，《年度评论》的主要任务是收集和突出被学术界很少报道或研究的领域，不重复已有工作，更不企图贬低某一

---

① 《应用语言学年度评论》问世后，受到国际学术界的高度重视，被权威的《社会科学引文索引》(SSCI)、《艺术和人文科学引文索引》(AHCI) 和《科学引文索引》(SCI) 所收录。

个方面,或对本学科内某项研究的价值进行排队。这样,《年度评论》对二语习得和语言干扰等内容谈得不多,因为这方面的研究成果已经发表很多。反之,微语言学、符号语言学、计算机辅助教学等受到重视。(6)《年度评论》本身应当正确面对来自不同领域实践者的认同或挑战。[①][②] 鉴于上述情况,《年度评论》每卷都有一个主题,如"语言和语言教育政策"(卷2)、"书面话语"(卷3)、"读写教育"(卷4)等。这些选题均具有学术性、实用性、时代性和独特性。与此同时,该刊每隔四五年会有一卷就应用语言学的整体研究从不同方面进行总结式的调研和讨论,内容涉及语言学习和教学、话语分析、教学创新、二语习得、计算机辅助教学、职场语境下的语言用途、社会语言学、语言政策和语言评估(如卷1、5、10、15、19等)。每年向读者提供500多个新的文献,以帮助本学科教学科研人员能深入掌握情况,点面结合。《年度评论》原计划的第1卷在1980年出版,由于组稿和印刷的原因,实际上在1981年问世。这一脱节现象直到1994年第14卷才得到扭转,即每卷标明的年度与出版年度取得一致。[③]

二、主编更迭

三十多年来,《年度评论》的总主编大约十年更换一次。美国南加利福尼亚大学美国语言研究所主任 Robert B. Kaplan 教授从创刊起任总主编,连续十年。Kaplan 曾任美国应用语言学会会长、英语作为第二语言教

---

① Rota, A. (1982). ANNUAL REVIEW OF APPLIED LINGUISTICS (ARAL). Robert B. Kaplan (Gen. Ed.); Randall L. Jones and G. Richard Tucker (Co-Eds.). *TESOL Quarterly*, 16, 398–404.

② Kaplan, Robert B. (1980). Introduction. *Annual Review of Applied Linguistics*, 1, vii–xi.

③ Kaplan, Robert B. and William Grabe. (2000). Applied Linguistics and the Annual Review of Applied Linguistics. in *Annual Review of Applied Linguistics*, 20, 3–17. Cambridge University Press.

学学会会长、《牛津应用语言学手册》总主编、《国际语言学百科全书》编委等。[1]在 Kaplan 主编的《牛津应用语言学手册》中,他认为应用语言学家至少应该具备以下领域的一些知识:人类学、社会学、经济学、政治学、教育学、老年入学、历史学、国际关系、语言学习和教学、词典编纂学、政策研究、心理学和神经科学、公共管理、教师培训和文本生成等。此外,每一位应用语言学家都应精于计算机使用,能够对数据进行统计分析。[2][3]

自第 11 卷起,William Grabe 任主编。Grabe 是美国北亚利桑那州大学负责科研的副校长,曾先后在该校英语系和应用语言学系任教。Grabe 认为应用语言学的核心是"试图解决人们在日常生活中遇到的与语言相关的问题",是一种"研究现实世界语言问题的、实践驱动的学科"。[4]鉴于这个原因,应用语言学必然是一个交叉学科,涉及许多其他领域。这可见之于他对每卷的选题,如"读写教育"(卷12)、"二语教学"(卷13)、"语言政策和规划"(卷14)、"技术和语言"(卷16)、"多语现象"(卷17)、"二语教育基础"(卷18)、"应用语言学的学科性"(卷19,20)。Grabe 任总主编至 2000 年卸任。在他最后一次负责的第 20 卷,他和 Robert Kaplan 合写了一篇回顾应用语言学和《年度评论》发展历程的总结性文章。

自 2001 年起任总主编的是北亚利桑那大学英语系的 Mary McGroarty 教授。她主要研究双语现象、语言政策、语言教育和课堂研究、社会语言学、二语教学的文化影响等。由于第一次出任主编,McGroarty 邀请了美

---

[1] Bruthiaux, Paul, Dwight Atkinson, William G. Egginton, William Grabe, Viadehi Ramanathan. Eds. (2005). *Directions in Applied Linguistics in Honour of Robert B. Kaplan.* Clevedon: Multilingual Matters Ltd.

[2] Kaplan, Robert B. (1999). *The Oxford Handbook of Applied Linguistics.* Edinburgh: Edinburgh University Press.

[3] 刘海涛. 从比较中看应用语言学. 北华大学学报(社会科学版),2007,8(2):4.

[4] Grabe, William. (2000). Introduction. *Annual Review of Applied Linguistics*, 20, 1–2. Cambridge University Press.

国著名外语教学法专家 Wilga M. Rivers 为第 21 卷"语言和心理学"写序，题为"沿着记忆巷道的漫长旅程"。此后，McGroarty 在她任期内主编了"话语和对话"（卷 22）、"语言接触和演变"（卷 23）、"语言教育学的进展"（卷 24）和"通用语语言"（卷 26）。《年度评论》第 27 和 28 卷的主题分别为"语言与科技"和"神经语言学和认知语言处理"，但未见到这两卷本应由总主编执笔的引言，在目录中也未出现，原因不详。作为总主编的 McGroarty 在第 29 卷"语言政策和语言评估"中再次出现，不过她邀请了著名学者 Bernard Spolsky 作为客座主编。Spolsky 教授长期在以色列的 Bar-Ilan 大学任教，曾任该校人文学院院长，并创建语言政策研究中心。在编辑业务方面，他曾任国际刊物 *Language Policy*（《语言政策》）的总主编，*Asia TEFL*（《亚洲英语作为外语教学》）杂志的出版部主任和总编辑。Spolsky 的专著都与语言政策和语言教育有关，如《教育语言学导论》（1978）、《二语学习的条件》（1991）、《社会语言学》（1998）、《以色列诸语言：政策、意识和实践》（1999）、《语言政策》（2004）、《语言管理》（2009）等。[1] 由此看来，Spolsky 无力全心投入《年度评论》的编辑工作，这次只是扮演一次客串角色而已。

自第 30 卷起，总主编一职由美国密执安州立大学的 Charlene Polio 教授担任。Polio 的主要研究领域为二语写作、二语习得、外语课堂话语、新技术和有经验教师之间的行为差异。她在编辑工作上有较多经验，除接受《年度评论》的总主编任务外，也是 *Modern Language Journal*（《现代语言杂志》）的编辑，此前曾为 *Journal of Second Language Writing*（《二语写作杂志》）和 *TESOL Quarterly* 杂志编委会委员。[2] Polio 为《年度评论》各卷确定的选题为"应用语言学专题"（卷 30）、"第二语言教育研究"（卷 31）、"公式化语言研究"（卷 32）、"多语现象研究"（卷 33）、"研究方法专题"（卷 34）。这体现了她作为总主编延续了该刊创办时的主导思

---

[1] Spolsky, Bernard. Homepage. http://www.biu.ac.il/faculty/spolsky/. 2015.1.3.
[2] Polio, Charlene. http://www.wsu.edu/~oikui/. 2015.1.5.

想,即每卷的稿子都是就某一领域的特定问题而精选的。

为《年度评论》写稿的作者中不乏名人,如 Henry G. Widdowson、James R. Martin、Bernard Spolsky、Alan Davies 等都是国际著名语言学家。

三、国人参与

我国大陆、港台地区和国际华人圈对《应用语言学年度评论》很为重视。

台湾学者郑锦全(Chan-chuan Cheng)在第 7 卷上发表"语言和计算机"一文。郑当时任台湾师范大学华语文教学研究所讲座教授、台湾地区研究院语言所研究员和人文社会科学研究中心通信研究员(Cheng,2014)。① 另一位是台湾清华大学培养的许静芬(Ching-fen Hsu)博士,现在台湾华梵大学人文学院师资培养研究中心工作,专攻威廉姆斯综合征(Williams Syndrome)发育障碍的语言习得研究,是第 28 卷"威廉姆斯综合征:基因型和认知表型描述"一文的第一作者。② 香港教育学院语言教学研究中心主任的李楚成(David C. S. Li)教授在第 26 卷上发表"作为大中华通用语的汉语"一文。③ 在《年度评论》第 30 卷独立发表有关传承语学习的社会文化维度一文的何纬芸(Agnes Weiyun He)教授,早期毕业于北京外国语大学,现为 Stony Brook 大学应用语言学和亚洲研究专业的教授,筹建了该校多语和跨文化交际中心。何纬芸主要研究语言语境和语篇的结合,人们如何通过日常互动逐步构建和重构概念、社团和文化。近十年来,她专门研究不同时期和不同背景下汉语作为传承语的社会化。④ 在《年度评论》第 27 卷与 John Flowerdew 联名发表"多语制和二语写作在电

---

① Cheng, Chan-chuan(郑锦全). http://doc88. com/P-795557797523. html. 2014. 12. 9.
② Hsu, Ching-fen(许静芬). http://www. docin. com/p-2898691. html & key. 2015. 1. 5.
③ Li, David, C. S.(李楚成). http://dfl. shufe. edu. cn/structure/ xueshu-com-142410-1. htm. 2014. 12. 9.
④ He, Agnes Weiyun(何纬芸). http://www. stonybrook. edu/commcms/asian/PROGRAMS. html. 2014. 12. 9.

子时代的关系"一文的李咏燕博士（Yongyan Li）任教于香港大学教育学院英语教育系，其研究范围包括专业写作、多语学者的研究和发表实践、言而有据的写作、科学文章的整篇抄袭现象、在职教育等。^① 令人瞩目的是，上述学者与大陆高校和研究单位保持良好的学术联系，如郑锦全教授曾担任四川大学文学与新闻学院兼职教授、厦门大学嘉庚学院中文系兼职教授、北京大学汉语语言学研究中心兼职研究员；李楚成教授曾在上海财经大学举行关于中国外语学习者和使用者常见错误的纠正讲座；何纬芸教授与上海交通大学苗瑞琴副教授合作编写了"继承语之习得及其社会化"一文。[②]

大陆学者对《年度评论》也做出了应有的反应和贡献。早在 1981 年《年度评论》第 1 卷问世后，我国学者左焕琪教授便在国内语言学权威刊物《当代语言学》上作了报道，既介绍了编者 Kaplan 的背景，也对该卷四个部分作了近似导读的介绍。作者当时就以敏锐的眼光指出这是"近年来美国应用语言学领域引人瞩目的新刊物"。[③] 较近的可举 2012 年方秀才的"程式语面面观介绍"一文，对《年度评论》第 32 卷从认知视角、教学应用、社会学进展和未来展望四个部分深入介绍。作者特别注意到，为了从多种视角讨论程式语这一主题，总主编没有限定程式语的定义、内涵，也没有统一术语，让每篇文章的作者采用自己认同的术语和定义，[④] 这表明《年度评论》并没有因为总主编的变动而放弃原有的风格。

行文至此，有必要提一下以 Charlene Polio 为首的新编委会所作的一个重大决定，那就是她代表编委会聘请了我国广东外语外贸大学王初明教授从第 31 卷起任《年度评论》顾问委员会的委员。这是对我国应用语言

---

① Li, Yongyan（李咏燕）. http://www_researchgate. net/profile/Yongyan_Li/publications. 2014.12.9.
② 何纬芸，苗瑞琴. 继承语之习得及其社会化. 载姬建国，蒋楠主编：应用语言学（西方人文社会科学前沿述评）. 北京：中国人民大学出版社，2007. 239–255.
③ 左焕琪. 应用语言学年度评述（1980）.《国外语言学》，1983，（3）：46–49.
④ 方秀才.《程式语面面观》介绍.《当代语言学》，2013，15（4）：492–495.

学研究发展和水平的肯定。我与王初明教授结识于 1995 年 9 月，当时我是香港中文大学的访问学者，他是英语系的博士生。我们经常一起讨论学术问题。长江后浪推前浪，2011 年我从北京外国语大学中国外语教育研究中心学术委员会主任退下后，他接替了此职。王初明教授现在的学术兼职有国务院学位委员会外国语言文学学科评议组成员、中国高等教育学会外语教学研究分会副会长。他的主要研究方向为第二语言习得研究及其在外语教学中的应用，主要学术创见有外语写长法、语境补缺假说、外语语音学习假设、外语学习的学伴用随原则、读后续写的理论和应用价值。

四、"商务"特色

除保留剑桥版《应用语言学年度评论》的原有特色外，商务版《应用语言学年度评论》有它自己的特色。

商务版《年度评论》从第 20 卷开始，而不是从第 1 卷开始。我认为商务印书馆此举着眼于让读者以更多的精力把握应用语言学在新世纪的发展，急读者之所急。我们还应该看到，《年度评论》第 20 卷实际上起到承前启后的作用。在该卷中，为上世纪创刊时立下汗马功劳的 Robert Kaplan、William Grabe 和 G. Richard Tucker 分别对应用语言学和《年度评论》在二十年中的发展作了系统的总结，帮助读者对前二十年有个总体了解，又寄厚望于这门新学科在新世纪、新千年的发展，把握前进的方向。其次，商务版《年度评论》增加了满足中国读者需求的新内容，那就是每卷都有一篇 1.5 万字左右的中文导读。这便于帮助读者掌握每卷的基本内容和背景材料，特别是汉语界的教师、研究者和学生。

参与此任务的导读作者有国内外语界著名学者，也有新生代的中青年学者。这些专家学者对自己撰写的内容比较熟悉。作为此项目的组织者，我没有向他们摊派任务，而是让各位学者根据自己熟悉的领域自由选题。对各位作者的努力我在此谨表谢意。如前所述，导读初稿完成后均由上海复旦大学朱永生教授和北京师范大学田贵森教授分别先行审读。对两位教授退休后仍能不辞辛苦、鼎力相助的感激之情,难以言表。

由于《年度评论》涉及多个学科和领域,各卷原版的体例不全相同,而各位导读作者的学术生涯也不尽相同,我们对导读编写体例上只作大致要求,不强调绝对统一。总的印象是,每位导读作者对本卷各章内容都能做提纲挈领的介绍和解释,帮助读者理解和抓住要点,这是共同的优点。导读作者各自的特色则表现在:(1)能在正文之前对本卷的总主编、客座编辑做介绍,并对总主编的引言深入分析,起到画龙点睛的作用;(2)对本卷主题进行了解释;(3)对有关主题在20世纪的研究状况或《年度评论》已经发表过的专辑作必要回顾;(4)对每卷论文内容进行归纳,指出其特点;(5)坦率指出某卷内容的不足之处;(6)结合国内现状进行讨论,并进行反思;(7)在讨论中,引入当代先进理论;(8)向我国学界和领导部门提出今后有待深入展开研究的问题。

在结束本序之际,再次感谢各位导读作者,以及永生教授和贵森教授的共同努力,使本项艰巨任务得以顺利完成;祝贺商务版《应用语言学年度评论》正式出版;祝愿商务印书馆今后在应用语言学和理论语言学等领域为外语教育界和学术界做出更多更大贡献!

北京大学蓝旗营寓所
2015年元月

导　　读[1]

张琳[2]

全球化和网络的发展改变了人们的沟通习惯和方式，也对语言教学提出了更高的要求；语言学、二语习得理论、心理学以及社会学等理论的加入，也为第二语言教育提供了更多理论支持和发展空间，二语教育越来越引起研究者、教育家和一线教师的重视。进入新世纪的二语教学有什么新的特点？当前的研究热点是什么？二语教学未来的发展方向在哪里？这卷《第二语言教育研究》为我们较为系统全面地呈现了当前二语教学的新热点和发展趋势。

剑桥大学出版社的《应用语言学年度评论》（*Annual Review of Applied Linguistics*, ARAL）是美国应用语言学协会的官方刊物，其第二语言教育专题每五年出版一次，邀请第二语言教学领域的专家学者就最近几年该领域的研究动态和发展趋势进行回顾总结。本卷是 2011 年第 31 卷《年度评论》的第二语言教育专题，由密歇根州立大学 Charlene Polio 教授主编。Polio 教授多年从事二语写作教学与研究，在二语习得、外语课堂语篇分析以及教师行为研究方面颇有建树。在本年度的二语教育专题中，Polio 教授共邀请了 20 位专家学者通过 15 篇专题文章就二语教学领域中一些热点问题的现状及发展进行梳理和展望。全卷内容丰富，涵盖面

---

[1] 感谢解放军国际关系学院李战子教授对本文撰写提供的悉心指导。
[2] 作者简介：张琳，女，解放军国际关系学院英美语言文学专业硕士、英国威斯敏斯特大学 TESOL 专业硕士，现为解放军国际关系学院讲师。主编教辅类书籍 8 部，参加各类科研立项 7 个，其中包括教育部重点课题。

广，是二语教学领域的研究者和一线教师了解该领域前沿理论和研究动态的窗口，也有助于外语教师和研究学者扩大视野，开阔思路，切实提高二语教学的理论水平和实践能力。在进入对本卷各篇文章介绍之前，我对二语（外语）教学的发展进行简要梳理和回顾。

1. 二语教学及研究发展综述

1.1 "第二语言"与"外语"

在语言教学中，经常提到"第二语言"（简称二语，L2）和"外语"，两者都是相对于"第一语言"或"母语"而言，但彼此又存在区别，因此有必要对这两个概念进行厘清。联合国教科文组织对"第二语言"的定义是"母语以外的其他语言"[①]。这一定义最为宽泛，既指母语以外的本国通用语，也指国外语言，将"外语"涵盖在"二语"范畴之内，这一定义被Ellis[②]所采纳。Stern[③]和Cook[④]则给出了相对狭义的定义，认为第二语言是在本国国内通用的语言，而外语则是在本国之外使用。Stern还进一步指出，第二语言往往是官方语言或官方认可使用的语言，而外语则不是。束定芳等[⑤]综合两种定义认为，"第二语言"有两种理解：一是泛指母语之外的任何一种其他语言（包括外语）；二是区别于"外语"的语言，即在本国内作为通用语或其他民族用语的语言，与母语有同等重要的地位，是日常生活中被大量使用的语言。20世纪70年代以前，语言教学领域普遍使

[①] 参见 Vivian Cook, *Second Language Learning and Language Teaching* (4th edition), London, UK: Hodder Education, 2008, p.2.

[②] Rod Ellis, *The Study of Second Language Acquisition*, 上海：上海外语教育出版社，1999, p. 22.

[③] H. H.Stern, *Fundamental Concepts of Language Teaching*, 上海：上海外语教育出版社，1983. p.16.

[④] Vivian Cook, *Second Language Learning and Language Teaching* (4th edition), London, UK: Hodder Education, 2008, p.11.

[⑤] 束定芳、庄智象，《现代外语教学》，上海：上海外语教育出版社，1996年版。

用"外语"一词,但70年代之后随着二语习得理论的兴起,"外语"逐渐被"第二语言"所替代。

本书中的"第二语言"或L2采用UNESCO的广义定义,即母语以外的其他语言(包括外语),它可能是学习者学习的第二门,也可能是第三门、第四门语言。此外,本书中的二语还指学习者在二语环境(周围人都使用目标语言)和非二语环境(周围人不使用目标语言)以及介乎两者之间的环境中学习的语言。

1.2 第二语言教学研究发展回顾

语言教学有着悠久的历史。早在一千九百多年前的文献中就有关于古希腊时期的教育家Marcus Fabius Quintilianus(A.D.35—95)关于如何讲授希腊语的记载[①]。纵观近两千年的二语教学的发展历程,根据其教学内容、方法及研究的侧重点大致可以划分为以下四个阶段:

(1)前方法时代:20世纪以前

早期的二语教学主要是外语教学。Quintilianus在讲授希腊语时以伊索寓言为主体进行词汇和句子的讲解,这一做法流传了很长时间。到了18、19世纪,欧洲主要通过文献和经典著作来学习拉丁语和希腊语,逐渐形成了语法—翻译法(Grammar-Translation Method,GT),其特点是背诵语法规则和机械地翻译。这一做法很快被其他语种教学所采纳,成为主流的语言教学方式,成为当时运用最广泛、时间最长的教学方法。纵观这一千多年的早期外语教学,传统的语法—翻译法一统天下,这与20世纪方法时代的"各法纷呈"局面截然不同,因而可以称之为"前方法时代"。

(2)改革时代:20世纪初至20世纪中期

19世纪末20世纪初,西方的工业化进程对外语人才的培养提出了新的要求,传统的语法—翻译法已经不能适应时代的需求。在英国语言学家

---

① Aubrey S.J. Gwynn, *Roman Education from Cicero to Quintilian*, New York: Teachers College Press, 1926, p.139.

斯威特（Henry Sweet）为代表的改革派的推动下，教育领域开始了语言教学的改革运动（the Reform Movement），矛头直指语法—翻译法在培养学习和口头表达能力方面的不足，强调口语和语音训练的重要性以及课堂教学中口语的重要性[①]。1870年法国人Sauveur提出了自然法（Natural Approach），教育家伯里兹（Maximilian Berlitz）在此基础上进一步提出了直接法（Direct Method），将儿童母语习得的经验运用于二语（外语）教学，并流传广泛，这也是语言教学借鉴语言学理论的首次尝试。

20世纪40年代，美国在结构主义语言学和行为主义心理学的基础上逐渐形成听说法（Audio-Lingualism），主张外语教学听说为主、读写为辅，成为首个综合运用语言学理论和心理学理论的教学方法；而在英国，Palmer和Hornby等人提出了口语教学法（Oral Method）作为对直接法的补充[②]，并逐渐发展成后来的情景教学法（Situational Method）。然而，这些语言教学就其理论本身而言，仍主要停留在经验总结的基础上，对语言本质的认识还不够深刻，尚未形成系统全面的理论学科。

（3）方法时代：20世纪中期至20世纪末

20世纪60年代一批语言教学机构相继成立，从制度上确立了外语教学的学科地位：1966年教师联盟（Teachers of English to Speakers of Other Languages, TESOL）在美国成立；次年，英语教师联盟（Association of Teachers of English as a Foreign Language）在英国成立[③]。随着外语教学学科的建立和相关领域研究的深入，20世纪后半叶二语教学开始发生巨大而深刻的转变。

1966年社会语言学家Hymes提出了"交际能力（Communicative

[①] A. P. R. Howatt, *A History of English Language Teaching*, 上海：上海外语教育出版社, 1984, p.295.

[②] Jack C. Richards and Theodore S. Rodgers, *Approaches and Methods in Language Teaching*, Cambridge: Cambridge University Press, 1986, p.33.

[③] A. P. R. Howatt, *A History of English Language Teaching*, 上海：上海外语教育出版社, 1984, p.303.

Competence)"的概念,在二语教学领域引起了强烈的反响,交际法（Communicative Approach）教学随即兴起并被广泛接受,至今仍具有极大影响力。同样在60年代,分别在语言学和心理学领域占据主导地位的两大理论——生成转换语法理论和认知学派——相结合产生了一门新的学科:心理语言学,运用到二语教学领域便产生了认知教学法,这一教学法以乔姆斯基（Chomsky）关于"语言能力"（Language Competence）的基本观点与认知心理学有关认知过程的理论为二语教学的指导原则。认知法和交际法的产生改变了语言教学的方向,语言教学开始从传统的以教师为中心转向以学习者为中心。认知法和交际法从思维和功能角度凸显了语言教学的心理属性和社会属性,在这种从语言本质出发指导二语教学的启发下,涌现了一批新的二语教学法,例如任务型教学法（Task-Based Approach）、内容教学法（Content-Based Approach）、多元智能教学法（Multiple-Intelligence Approach）、全身反应法（Total Physical Response, TPR）、沉默法（Silent Way）、整体语言教学法（Whole Language Approach）等。

与此同时,经过数十年的发展,二语习得理论形成了一系列理论和假说,例如Selinker的中介语理论（Interlanguage）,Krashen的学习-习得理论（Acquisition-Learning Hypothesis）、监控假说（Monitor Hypothesis）、输入假说（Input Hypothesis）和情感过滤假说（Affective Filter Hypothesis）,等等。二语习得研究的深入和发展也为二语教学的研究提供了一个新的理论支撑和发展方向,许多关于学习者学习动机、自我认同、学习者策略、特殊用途外语（英语）教学（ESP）等领域的教学研究纷纷涌现。20世纪后半叶各类流派纷呈,多元并举,Rogers[①]（2000）将这段时期称为二语教学的"方法的时代"。

到了20世纪末,随着语言学和二语习得研究的不断发展深入,二语

---

① Ted Rogers, Methodology in the New Millennium, *English Teaching Forum*, 2000, April, pp.2–13.

教学开始受到如心理语言学、社会语言学、语用学、跨文化交际等新兴学科的影响，研究不再局限于语言本身，而是扩大到教学的各个环节和各个方面，例如学习者个体差异、二语教学环境、教师培训等领域。二语教学逐渐成为一门多学科交叉，以语言学和二语习得理论为基础，涉及心理学、教育学、社会学等相关领域的综合学科。

回顾整个20世纪，语言教学告别了传统教学单维度的发展轨迹，现代意义上的二语教学真正出现，语言学、应用语言学和二语习得等理论的加入让二语教学呈现出蓬勃发展的态势，二语教学开始"在经验积累的基础上，系统地寻求自己的理念、原则和方法"，二语教学正从一个"单向地依赖相关领域研究的应用学科，逐渐发展成一个立足于本学科特点，积极而审慎地从相关学科研究中吸取营养的学科"[1]。

（4）后方法时代：21世纪至今

进入21世纪，二语教学实践与研究呈现出一些新的特点和发展趋势。

首先，二语教学从过去追求单一的方法体系向综合方向发展。回顾二语教学研究的发展历程不难发现，在漫长的发展过程中，语言教学历经了纷繁复杂的历史演变，语言教育者在教学方法上始终孜孜不倦，"找寻一种语言教学的最佳方法"[2]。然而二语教育是一个极为复杂的、立体的系统工程，涉及的因素众多，例如教育政策、教学大纲、测试与评估、教材编撰、教师因素、学习者情感、年龄、文化因素等。由于二语教学的复杂性，对单一的"最佳教学法"的片面追求会导致人们忽视语言教学中的各种外部因素，从而影响人们对语言教学的理解。Kumaravadivelu[3]更是提出二语教学已经进入了"后方法时代"（Post-Method Era），认为以往单

---

[1] 吴一安，"导读"，《语言教学的原则》（第3版），北京：外语教学与研究出版社，2002年版，第F30页。

[2] H. Douglas Brow, *Teaching by Principles: An Interactive Approach to Language Pedagogy* (3rd edition), 北京：外语教学与研究出版社，2002年版，p.14.

[3] B. Kumaravadivelu, *Beyond Methods: Macro-strategies for language teaching*, Yale University, 2003.

一的方法体系已经不能满足二语教学与研究的需求。早在20世纪70、80年代便已出现但当时并未引起重视的"折中主义"(Eclecticism)重新引发了人们的关注。Larsen-Freeman[①]和Mellow[②]在折中主义的基础上提出了"有原则的折中主义"(Principled Eclecticism),认为各类教学法或理论是相互包容而非排斥的,在实际教学过程中,以语言学、心理学、教育学等学科作为理论基础,根据教学对象、教学环境、教学目标等变量的实际情况出发,从各种二语教学理论和方法中选取适用部分综合运用。例如,在中国、日本等亚洲国家的二语教学中,采取交际法与传统的语法—翻译法相结合的方式,而不是用交际法完全取代语法—翻译法。当然,作为一种新兴的实践方法,折中法仍处于实践摸索阶段,尚缺乏系统深入的研究,但这种兼容并蓄、博采众长的"折中法"或"综合法"(Eclectic Teaching Approach, ETA)在后方法时代正引起越来越多的学者和教育者的关注。

其次,二语教学和研究重点发生转变。二语教学不再以语言知识和技能为主。回顾语言教学的历史,无论是早期Marcus Fabius Quintilianus的希腊语教学法,还是到19世纪的语法—翻译传统教学法,还是后来的听说法、交际法,都是以发展语言知识和技能作为教学内容和重点。然而"语言从来就不是一个纯粹的语言问题",而是与政治、文化、主体性、民族认同等等因素相关[③]。随着人们对语言及文化的认识逐渐深入,语言的功能性和社会性日益引起人们的重视,语言教学的内容和重点不以语言知识的讲解和技能训练为主,作为教育的组成部分,语言教学也开始关注

---

① Diane Larsen-Freeman. *Techniques and Principles in Language Teaching* (2nd edition), Oxford: Oxford University Press, 2000.
② J. Dean Mellow, 'Western influences on indigenous language teaching', in J. Reyhner, J. Martin, L. Lockard, & W. Sakiestewa Gilbert (eds.), *Learn in beauty: Indigenous education for a new century*, Flagstaff, AZ: Northern Arizona University, 2000, pp.102-113.
③ 王守仁,"关于学术英语教学的几点思考",《中国外语》,2013年第5期,第7页。

个人能力的发展（包括交际能力、批判性思维能力、文化意识、社会公民意识等）①。例如欧洲理事会文化合作教育委员会制定的《欧洲语言共同参考框架》②就对语言能力提出了明确要求并制定了明确的标准。与此同时，二语教学研究的重点也不再以语言本身为主。语言教学是一个复杂的教学活动，Larsen-Freeman 将语言教学相关因素归纳为三个大领域，即语言学习者/学习——语言/文化——教师/教学；Stern③ 提出了语言教学四要素，即语言、学习、教学和环境。越来越多的教学者和研究者将目光投向英语教学场所等语言以外的其他要素④，例如从二语学习者的个体差异、教学大纲、教材编选、不同环境下的语言指导、教师自身发展等角度研究二语教学。

再次，科学技术和网络技术的发展让语言教学的呈现方式发生了变化。越来越多的课堂教学采用多媒体等技术，在线语言学习（OLL）、慕课（MOOC）等一批新的语言教学形式和手段不断涌现。语言教学告别了传统的线性思维，呈现出超文本的特性⑤。语言教学打破了时空局限，教学的内容、目标、形式、媒介、参与方、教师职责等都发生了变化，传统以读写为主的语言识读能力在多媒体时代已不够用⑥。计算机辅助语言教学（CALL）、多模态教学等教学方法正日益获得越来越多的关注。

---

① 李战子，"英语教育：知识与话语的汇集点"，《外语研究》，2002 年第 6 期，第 74–75 页。
② 欧洲理事会文化合作教育委员会，刘骏、傅荣译，《欧洲语言共同参考框架：学习、教学、评估》，北京：外语教学与研究出版社，2008 年版。
③ H. H. Stern, *Fundamental Concepts of Language Teaching*, 上海：上海外语教育出版社，1983, p.83.
④ 李战子，"英语教育：知识与话语的汇集点"，《外语研究》，2002 年第 6 期，第 74–75 页。
⑤ 胡壮麟，"外语教学理念的发展"，《基础教育外语教学研究》，2005 年第 1 期，第 21–25 页。
⑥ 胡壮麟，"社会符号学研究中的多模态化"，《语言教学与研究》，2007 年第 1 期，第 1–9 页。

另一大趋势是二语教学的研究方法更趋科学规范。以往研究主要采取基于课堂观察或经验总结的定性研究，由于缺乏信度和效度，其科学性和准确性往往受到质疑。随着应用语言学和二语教学的不断融合发展，越来越多的专家学者和教育研究者开始关注语言教学的研究方法，如 Eli Hinkel 的 *Handbook of Research in Second Language Teaching and Learning*、Rod Ellis 的 *Language Teaching Research and Language Pedagogy*，刘润清的《外语教学中的科研方法》等。人们对研究方法的认识愈趋理性科学，实证研究方法被越来越多地运用于二语教学研究，量化研究引起了研究者的重视。当然，人文科学不同于自然科学，并非所有变量都可以如同在实验室般进行量化和控制，质化研究在人文科学研究中依然有着不可取代的优势和必要性，因此二语教学研究呈现出量化研究与质化研究相结合的趋势，即注重规范性（normative）研究和解释性（interpretive）研究相结合（例如在课堂环境下进行小型研究时采取观察法、访谈与问卷相结合的方式），二语教学的研究方法更趋理性、多元、科学[①]，研究结果的科学性和可信度得以增强。

2. 全卷结构及内容

由 Charlene Polio 任总主编的第 31 卷《年度评论》共包含 15 篇论文，主要关注近五年（2006—2011）二语教学领域新的发展动态和研究成果。全书根据研究类别的不同共分为四大部分：

1）不同环境下的二语教学（Second Language Instruction in Different Settings），包括中学阶段的二语教学、网络语言教学、职场语言培训、亚太国家和地区的二语教学以及海外留学环境下的二语教学；

2）针对特定学习者的二语教学（Second Language Instruction for

---

① 高一虹、吴红亮、李莉春，"关于外语教学研究方法的调查"，《外国语》，2000年第 1 期，第 65-72 页。

Specific Learners),分别就青少年/儿童学习者、成人学习者和非听障碍学习者的二语教学研究进行总结回顾;

3)融合教学法专题(Topics in Integrated Approaches),即语言教学与其他学科或方法相结合的做法,如语言文学教学、内容与语言相融合的教学、在语言教学中的语料库运用以及多模态读写能力的培养;

4)语言技能教学(Instruction in Specific Skill Areas),针对非罗马字母书写系统(如中文、日文和埃及文字等)、协同写作和语用学的教学进行分析研究。

2.1 不同环境下的二语教学

语言教学是一个情景化的教学活动,不能脱离具体语境而独立存在,因此第一部分的五篇论文分别就五个不同环境下(中学、网络、亚洲地区、海外留学以及职场)的二语教学进行探讨。

(1)以英语为第二语言的中学学术语言教学(*Teaching academic language in L2 secondary settings*)

Schleppegrell 和 O'Hallaron 选取二语为英语的中学阶段的学术语言教学作为研究对象,对过去五年间(2006—2011年)关于中学阶段学术语言教学的英文研究进行了梳理总结。学术语言教学是近年来二语教学的一个新热点。在我国以英语为主的外语教学中"学术语言/英语"通常指的是 EAP(English for Academic Purposes),准确地说应当是"以学业用途为目的的英语"。而国外的"学术语言"是指 Academic Language,即教师和学生在课程教学过程中所使用的语言,它具有与学科相关的语言特点。这一概念有别于我国针对通用外语而言的"学术语言"(EAP)。Schleppegrell 和 O'Hallaron 的研究对象是国外定义的"学术英语"(Academic Language)。两作者发现尽管近年来基于内容的二语教学获得了越来越多的关注,但实际情况是许多中学教师通常认为自己是学科专业教师,认为语言教学不属于自己的授课范畴,因此不愿在课程教学过程中融入语言指导。然而随着中学阶段课程内容的深入,学术语言愈趋复杂专业，课堂教学必须对学生提供语言指导。文章介绍了有关如何让学科教师掌握学术语言并在课堂教学中融入语言指导，从而为学生提供语言与内容相结合的学习环境的实践和研究，例如，在历史课中帮助学生理解历史学家如何评判历史人物和事件，文学课中让学生学会如何从文学角度描述并评价一个文学人物，以及在生物、化学等课程中使用相关术语。Schleppegrell 和 O'Hallaron 在这些研究的基础上提出中学阶段有效的学术语言教学取决于三个因素：1）教师必须对所授学科的学术语言有深刻的认识和了解；2）宏观层面的课程设计必须对学生的二语能力发展予以长期支持和引导；3）微观层面的课堂教学中，教师必须让学生积极参与课堂活动，通过任务型活动鼓励学生用学术语言，从而实现语言和专业知识的同步提高。然而实际教学中，学术语言的教学效果并不理想，其主要原因在于中学教师培训很少涉及课程专业语言学习，因此教师自身对学术语言及如何进行语言教学缺乏必要了解。此外，中学课堂教学中小语种学生往往被边缘化，针对这一群体的二语教学必须考虑语言身份和学习者认同等问题，同时，应用语言学和二语教学、青少年学习者语言教学和学科专业教学之间也应当加大融合与研究。Schleppegrell 和 O'Hallaron 以英语作为二语研究对象，其结论是否适用于二语为其他语种尤其是非印欧语系学术语言教学有待进一步研究。但论文提出的三点建议对教学存在指导意义。

（2）在线语言学习的发展趋势（*Current trends in online language learning*）

新世纪语言教学的变化之一是教学内容呈现手段发生改变。在数字网络化语境下的今天，在线语言学习（Online Language Learning, OLL）的出现为学习者和教师教学提供了新的语言教学环境，大大地改变了传统的语言教学模式。OLL 是借助网络在半虚拟或全虚拟的课堂中进行教学的模式。它突破了时空限制，学习者在语言学习过程中可以拥有更大的主动性和灵活性。自诞生以来，尤其是进入 21 世纪以来，网络课程便呈现出快速增长的趋势：2002 年到 2008 年，美国秋季入学的大学及研究生课程中网络课程平均增幅超过 19%，网络课程在总课程中所占比重增加了 16%（见 Blake 表 1），网络课程的快速发展也引发了教育界的关注和热议，国内外有关 OLL 的研究都呈现上升趋势。具体到语言教学领域，计算机辅助语言学习（Computer-Assisted Language Learning，CALL）是 OLL 与语言教学结合的主要形式。近年来随着人工智能技术、数字化技术和信息网络技术的发展，计算机辅助交际（Computer-Mediated Communication，CMC）和语言游戏也逐渐兴起并获得越来越多的关注。在我国，近年来网络课程数量日益增加，授课对象范围不断扩大，在线语言教学也日益引起研究者和学者的关注。CNKI 数据库显示，过去五年（2010—2014 年）共有 204 篇关于在线语言教学的研究文章，大大多于上一个五年（2005—2009 年）84 篇的数量。

本文作者 Robert J. Blake 聚焦 OLL 这一新兴模式对语言教学的影响，对有关在线语言学习研究的现状进行了回顾，并对 CALL、CMC 和语言学习游戏三种主要的在线语言教学形式的发展进行了分析与展望。Blake 在回顾有关 OLL 的研究后发现，国际上针对中小学阶段的网络教学研究仍属空白，而针对大学及研究生阶段的研究一致认为在线学习效果好于传统的课堂教学，但 Blake 指出这些研究并未考虑学习者的时间投入因素，因此只能作为参考。具体到二语教学领域，尽管近年来 CALL 在素材累计和课程设计方面都取得了显著进展，但针对在线二语教学进行的比较研究却依然几乎空白。

作为 CALL 的分支，近年来教师指导下的 CALL（Tutorial CALL）和 CMC 获得了较大关注和发展，一些研究者主张在语言教学中通过计算机游戏对两者进行融合。因此 Blake 对教师指导下的 CALL、CMC 和语言学习游戏近年来的发展进行了逐一回顾。教师指导下的 CALL 主要提供语法及词汇练习，许多研究者认为这一方式能有效增加学习者的词汇量，但缺点是学习者之间缺乏互动。此外，有学者（Sykes 和 Cohen）还尝试通过 CALL 来提高学习者的语用能力，Blake 认为这将是未来 CALL 的一个新的研究领域。在近年来人工智能技术发展推动下，教师指导下的 CALL 出现了另一大新兴领域——CALL 智能系统（iCALL）。该系统能够对自然语言进行加工处理,记录、跟踪甚至预见学习者的错误,并对学习者在线学习的信息进行反馈,提供个性化的教学指导。这一智能系统弥补了传统CALL与学习者之间缺乏互动的不足,具有良好的发展前景。

社交媒体和即时通信技术的发展与普及推动了CMC的发展,也改变了人们的社交模式。许多研究者从互动主义角度或Vygotsky的社会文化角度,尤其是最近发展区理论(proximal development)对CMC进行了研究。社会媒体方兴未艾,CMC仍将是未来研究的热点。

基于语言学习的计算机游戏的出现能够通过"寓教于乐"的方式激发学习者的学习热情,通过有效的游戏环境设计,语言游戏可以作为一种可行的语言学习途径。在游戏虚拟环境中,学习者通过扮演角色、团队协作完成任务的方式提高语言能力。

Blake认为三个领域在现代语言教学中将日趋融合。近年来一些研究人员已经开始尝试通过计算机游戏将CALL教程与CMC进行整合。这种让学习者独自或使用文字或音视频交流的方式和以团队协作的方式完成游戏任务是很好的尝试,也是在线语言教学的未来发展趋势,但同时他也指出了一些影响语言学习效果的因素,例如游戏设计、学习者角色扮演、游戏价格等。总体而言,OLL目前仍处于起步摸索阶段,一方面针对OLL的相关研究不足,在线学习的效果缺乏科学可信的统计结果;另一方面,OLL软件面临开发成本高、设计周期长以及学习者接受度等风险因素;再者,OLL如何通过设计避免游戏成为语言学习的干扰因素也有待进一步研究。但相较传统的语言教学模式,OLL具有不可比拟的优势和良好的发展前景,未来将获得越来越多研究者和教师的关注。

(3)在亚太地区语言教学中运用交际教学法和任务型教学法(*The implementation of communicative and task-based language teaching in the Asia-Pacific region*)

交际法教学(Communicative Language Teaching, CLT)和任务型教学法(Task-Based Language Teaching, TBLT)自20世纪70、80年代引入亚洲以来便受到了许多研究者和教师的关注。由于东西方文化传统、教育理念等方面均存在差别，尽管 CLT 和 TBLT 在西方国家被广泛接受并取得了较好效果，但它们在亚洲国家是否可行？如何运用？效果如何？实际教学过程中遇到什么样的问题？诸多学者和教师对此展开了相关研究和探讨。Yuko Goto Butler 总结了亚太地区语言教学中运用交际法和任务型教学法的情况、存在的困难并提出了针对性建议。有关在亚洲地区二语课堂教学中 CLT 和 TBLT 运用情况的实证研究显示，两种教学法在从小学到大学的各级二语教学中的效果并不尽如人意，研究认为 CLT 和 TBLT 在亚洲水土不服的根源主要来自三方面的限制：

1）观念上的限制。CLT 和 TBLT 的主要教学理念与亚洲地区的传统教学理念（例如许多亚洲国家信奉的儒家思想）存在差异，另一个局限是亚洲师生对这两种教学法存在误解，尤其是教师对 communicativeness 和 task 的理解不充分；

2）课堂层面的限制。主要表现在缺乏有效的课堂管理（学生在课堂活动中的参与度不够、过多使用母语）、教材不适用（教材的真实性不够）以及教学安排不合理（例如课堂人数太多）等方面；

3）体制层面的限制。最大的阻力来自于课程设置和考试制度，例如学生在课后缺乏二语氛围，课时不足，考试仍主要考查语法—翻译等传统内容。

对此，Butler 提出了三点建议，即：

1）入乡随俗，对 CLT 和 TBLT 做出契合实际的变通，例如可以在 TBLT 中保留一定 P-P-P 的做法；

2）在教育体制方面，既要有自上而下的指导，也要赋予自下而上的灵活性，例如对考试制度进行改革、赋予教师更多自主权、注重教师培训等；

3）打造课外学习环境，鼓励学生使用目标语。CMC 可以为学生提供一个良好的学习平台。

必须指出的是，Butler 回顾的英文文献绝大部分来自中国、日本和韩国，东南亚国家和地区的研究涉及较少，因此论文结论存在一定局限性。

尽管如此，Butler较为全面地展现了亚太地区语言教学中CLT和TBLT的实际情况和面临的问题，其建议或对亚洲地区，尤其是中、日、韩等东亚国家和地区的二语教学实践具有指导意义。

（4）海外留学环境对提高二语能力的影响（*Enhancing language learning in study abroad*）

海外学习环境一直被认为有助于提高二语能力，本文作者Celeste Kinginger就海外留学这一有别于传统课堂的特殊环境与学习者的二语能力的发展进行探讨。有关海外留学环境对二语学习影响的研究可以分为以下四类：

1）基于学习者的语言输出对其二语整体能力及交际能力进行的研究；

2）对与语言能力发展相关的学习者行为变量（如学习时间）进行的量化研究；

3）个案研究；

4）质的研究与理论研究相结合的多方法综合研究。

Kinginger对四类研究逐一进行了回顾后指出，理论上海外留学环境有助于学习者总体二语水平的提高，尤其是交际能力和社会语言能力，但对语法能力的帮助不是特别明显。然而一些研究同时也显示，海外留学对学习者二语水平提高的实际效果因人而异，原因主要在于：1）学习者没有很好地融入当地社会；2）学习者跨文化交际意识和语用知识不足，缺少相关指导。例如在新西兰学习的日本学生因为害羞等原因多选择与本国留学生来往，不愿与当地民众和寄宿家庭打交道。对此，Kinginger认为，语言教育者应当发挥更大作用，包括为学习者提供文化和语用方面的指导，帮助学习者更好地融入当地社会。在出国前、留学期间和回国后通过专门的语言教学活动帮助学习者更好地利用海外留学环境，切实提高二语水平。近些年来，我国每年赴海外求学的人数越来越多，然而正如研究所显示的，并非所有海外留学生的二语能力都能突飞猛进。本文对相关语言教学机构，尤其是各类留学语言辅导班具有现实指导意义，相关语言教育者可以从中获得如何在出国前、留学期间和回国后各个阶段对学生进行针对性的语言及文化辅导的有益启示。

同样值得指出的是，Kinginger 在回顾多方法综合研究时对研究方法进行了阐述，尤其是对研究方法中常见的量和质的研究进行了客观评述，这不仅反映了二语教学研究方法的发展趋势，同样也对我国相关研究者和学者具有重要的启迪和指导意义。此外，Kinginger 所回顾的研究不仅仅局限于以英语为二语的学习者，还包含了西班牙语等其他语言学习者为对象的研究，因而能较为客观全面地反映该研究领域的全貌。随着我国外国留学生人数的日益增长，从事对外汉语教学研究的学者可以针对这一群体的二语学习进行更多研究，也是对该研究领域构成重要补充。

（5）职场二语教学（Teaching second languages for the workplace）

随着全球化和科技水平的快速发展，职场语言的本质和要求不断变化，职场语言培训和相关研究日益引发关注。在本文中，Jonathan Newton 和 Ewa Kusmierczyk 对职场二语培训进行了相关研究，尤其是从人类学和语言社会化角度进行的研究进行了总结，对当前职场语言培训的现状及问题进行了综述。当前的职场二语教学研究呈现出四大趋势：

1）越来越多的研究采用情景化的人类学研究方法以了解特定情景下的职场话语；

2）越来越多的研究关注职场的非正式人际交流，这与专门用途语言（language for specific purpose，LSP）注重讲授工作相关技术用语或职场正式用语不同，此外它还涉及跨文化交际研究；

3）研究如何提高学习者语言意识（如批评语言意识（critical language awareness））以及特定职场语境下的社交语用意识；

4）聚焦面试情景中的语言运用，以及多元文化语境下面试所面临的挑战。

研究显示，早期的职场培训存在教学内容与实际工作脱节，不能满足工作对语言的要求。目前越来越多的职场语言培训采取结合工作实习和实地培训的方式进行教学，不刻意区分教学与工作的界限，具有便于安排、教学内容与实际工作密切相关等优势，但也存在一些问题，例如学习者往往对语言发展抱有不切实际的期望、教师必须掌握丰富的专业知识、许多培训不颁发证书等。早期的职场语言培训研究大多从需求分析和课程评价角度进行研究,而当前研究则更多从就业技能、人际沟通、跨文化与批判性语言意识、求职面试培训等四个方面进行研究。研究显示,职场语言培训必须贴合工作实际需求,在职场文化和语言日趋多元的背景下,语言培训还需注重提高学习者的交际能力和文化意识。此外 Newton 和 Kusmierczyk 还指出,语言能力的标准测试与职场语言教学的目标并不一致,因此不适用于职场语言培训的评估,目前职场语言培训仍缺乏科学有效的评估。

2.2 针对不同学习者的二语教学

学习者是二语教学的主体,第二部分(本卷第6—8篇)就近年来针对三类学习者(儿童、成人和非听障手语学习者)的二语教学及研究进行回顾。

(6)儿童早期外语教学综述(*All Shades of Every Color: An overview of early teaching and learning of foreign languages*)

Marianne Nikolov 和 Jelena Mihaljević Djigunović 回顾了最近五年(2006—2011)儿童早期二语教学的相关研究(包括非英语文献),从教学课程设计、儿童学习者、教师以及评估四个方面较为全面呈现了当前儿童外语教学与研究的发展状况。Nikolov 和 Djigunović 发现,关于儿童二语教学的研究不再仅仅以儿童语言能力发展为研究重点,越来越多的研究开始关注儿童语言教学的各方参与者(例如教师和家长)。影响儿童二语教学的因素包括:来自母语或 L1 及身份与文化认同的影响、来自学习者社会经济地位的影响,以及多数早期教育教师缺乏专业培训的事实。从学习者角度进行的研究主要关注儿童语言的相互影响(如 L2 与 L1、双语儿童的 L3 与 L1 和 L2),学习者的个体差异(情感、认知和学习策略等)对二语学习的影响,以及儿童早期二语学习可能遇到的困难,如注意力缺陷和诵读困难等。值得注意的是,某些研究的结论并不一致,甚至完全相反，例如日本的一项研究认为只有获得大量的二语输入（input）之后学习者的年龄因素差异才会显现，但匈牙利的研究却得出了截然相反的结论。教师视角研究主要针对教师在课堂中的作用、教师语言水平和教学理念进行，结果发现非母语教师往往认为自身语言水平不够，有待提高；教师的二语教学理念和实际课堂教学并不一致。在语言评估方面，研究表明由于儿童在背景知识、认知能力、情感、动机等方面均不同于成人，因此必须对两者加以区分，对儿童进行学习性评估（assessment for learning）。在总结回顾的基础上，Nikolov 和 Djigunović 就未来的儿童二语教学和研究提出了建议。作者认为未来的儿童二语教学必须注重内容与语言的融合，并注重提高教师的语言水平和专业素养。与此同时，作者认为关于如何在课堂教学中体现课程要求，如何对儿童二语能力进行评估，以及儿童早期二语学习如何影响其青少年甚至成人阶段的二语学习等，这些领域有待进一步研究。

（7）针对成人萌发读者的二语教学（*Teaching adult second language learners who are emergent readers*）

本篇两作者 Martha Bigelow 和 Patsy Vinogradov 关注的是成人二语学习者中一个较为特殊的群体——成人萌发读者（emergent reader）。他们往往文化层次不高，从未受过或仅受过有限的学校教育，或会说第二语言却不会读写，但因为种种个人、经济、历史或政治原因开始学习二语（例如难民、移民）。研究显示可以从两方面提高这类学习者的二语读写能力：一是教学中利用口语与书面语互惠的方法，即通过口语来促进学习者的读写能力；二是利用社会及文化因素帮助其发展读写能力。研究还指出，针对这一群体的教学必须给予与其年龄和语言水平相匹配的情景教学，例如语言经验教学法（language experience approach, LEA），即将学习者熟悉的生活场景作为教学内容。Bigelow 和 Vinogradov 还将成人萌发读者的二语学习与儿童二语学习及成人 L1 读写能力发展进行了对比，发现三者存在异同，儿童二语习得理论并不能完全适用于成人。此外，政策、传统、观念、社会经济地位等一系列外部因素也会影响甚至阻碍成人萌发读者的二语学习。Bigelow 和 Vinogradov 对成人萌发读者的二语教学提出了三点建议：1）成人二语萌发读者作为较为特殊的二语学习者群体必须引起重视，并在教师培训的内容中有所体现；2）可以考虑针对这一群体单独开设课程并调整评估方法；3）对政策中针对成人教育的部分进行调整，为成人提供受教育机会（例如中学不允许学生工作，这一规定可能将有求学需求的成人拒之门外）。

（8）针对非听障人士的美国手语教学（*Teaching American Sign Language to hearing adult learners*）

本篇作者 David Quinto-Pozos 关注的是另一群特殊的成人学习者——学习美国手语的非听障人士。美国手语（American Sign Language, ASL）是一个完整且复杂的语言体系，它结合了手势、面部表情和肢体动作的综合运用，主要为北美听障人士所使用。Quinto-Pozos 就美国手语教学的发展现状、存在问题、课程及教材改革等问题进行了回顾。近年来美国越来越多的大学将 ASL 纳入外语范畴，学习 ASL 的学生人数日益增长，2009 年美国秋季入学统计显示，ASL 已经成为第四大热门外语。尽管如此，在研究领域，鲜有研究者将二语习得理论运用于 ASL 的教学研究。ASL 具有独特的语言特点，也由此对教学构成了挑战：例如 ASL 没有统一的文字系统，如何布置并检查课后作业存在困难；手势配合面部表情或肢体动作可同时表达多种含义，这与口语/书面语的顺序表达不同；ASL 属于一种视觉-空间语言，是融合视觉、手势等多种表意方式的多模态话语。实际教学中，ASL 遇到来自师生两方面的困惑：许多非听障学生对 ASL 存在误解，认为它比其他语言（如英语、法语、葡语等）容易，但事实并非如此。在教师方面，课堂教学是否允许使用口语也一直是一个争论焦点。最后 Quinto-Pozos 指出关于 ASL 的教学研究较少，许多领域尚待进一步深入，例如社会文化因素（例如听障人文化）如何影响 ASL 教学；课堂教学中是否以及如何允许学生使用 L1（包括口语和书面语）；以及视频及计算机技术如何有效辅助 ASL 教学等。

2.3 融合教学法专题

第三部分讨论二语教学与其他学科领域相结合的尝试。这部分从第 9 篇到第 12 篇的四篇文章分别就语言文学教学、内容与语言相融合的教学、在语言教学中运用语料库以及培养学习者多模态读写能力进行分析。

（9）外语与文学融合教学法研究：顺应改革的呼声？（*Research in language-literature instruction: Meeting the call for change?*）

一个多世纪以来，文学始终是美国大学外语课程中的一个重要部分，文学课程与外语课程是两个独立的课程，语言课程重交际，文学课程重读写。然而 2007 年美国现代语言学会外语特别委员会的报告建议将外语与文学相融合，取代以往双轨制的课程结构。与此同时，有学者对 CLT 提出质疑，认为仅仅具备交际能力不足以让学生对外文高阶作品（如外国文学作品）进行纯文学解读。在此背景下，许多专家学者就在美国大学外语教学中将语言与文学融合的做法进行了大量研究和分析。作者 Kate Paesani 回顾了语言与文学课程分分合合的历史，对在文学课程中加入语言教学，以及语言教学中加入文学教学的相关实证研究和课堂实践研究进行了梳理。研究显示，传统外语课本中语言形式与意义之间缺乏系统联系，有必要在基础阶段将文学文本引入外语教学；另一方面，文学课程几乎不涉及语言教学，但学生能力尚不足以进行纯文学分析，这凸显出文学课程中加入语言教学的必要性，因此在理论上有必要对大学阶段的文学和语言课程进行融合。在制度上，有学者指出美国《21 世纪外语学习标准》（*Standards for Foreign Language Learning in the 21st Century*）针对文学制定的要求措辞模糊，这为在文学课程中融入语言文化内容提供了空间。Paesani 还指出了当前研究的不足：现阶段研究都基于对某一堂课的观察与分析，缺乏科学长效的研究；由于多数教师并未就语言文学融合教学接受正式培训，因此有必要对教师能力进行研究；此外，新技术对语言文学教学的影响也不容忽视。Paesani 认为关于语言文学融合教学的讨论仍将持续，文学与语言课程也将在课程和教学法改革的呼声中越走越近。

（10）内容与语言整合学习：从实践到理论？（*Content-and-language integrated learning: From practice to principles?*）

内容与语言整合学习（Content-and-Language Integrated Learning，CLIL）是指将外语作为数学、地理等非语言课程的教学语言，是一种兼顾学科知识和外语学习的具有双重教学目的的教育模式。作者 Christiane Dalton-Puffer 对过去五六年间（2005—2011）针对 CLIL 的研究（以欧洲国家开展的研究为主）进行了回顾总结。研究显示，尽管根据 CLIL 的定义任何外语均可以成为教学语言，但由于英语的通用语地位，英语仍是 CLIL 课堂教学主要使用的教学语言，多数 CLIL 其实是 CEIL（Content and English Integrated Learning）。Dalton-Puffer 在回顾相关研究的基础上对 CLIL 在语言、教师、课程及实施条件等方面的特点进行了总结。之后，Dalton-Puffer 根据近年来 CLIL 相关研究从政策、学习效果、课堂研究和理论支撑四个角度对 CLIL 进行了介绍。在政策方面的研究显示，CLIL 得到了教师和家长以及政策层面的认可和接受，欧盟的多元语言政策对 CLIL 在欧洲的推广起到了推动作用和政策支撑，但也引发了一些争议和担忧。在亚洲等其他国家和地区 CLIL 也获得了广泛认可。针对 CLIL 学习效果的研究主要聚焦学习者的语言能力。研究显示学习者在词汇、句法、语用意识、口语、学习策略等方面均有明显提高。一些研究还发现教育者和家长的担忧以及 CLIL 存在的问题，例如担心学生外语水平会影响课程知识的理解和学习，非英语国家学生的课堂参与度下降，无法用英语准确表述思维过程等。课堂研究与实践显示了教师二语能力、课堂设计以及课程教学传统都会对学生产生影响。在理论方面，Dalton-Puffer 从 Krashen 的监视理论、Long 的互动理论、Swain 的语言输出假设以及 Lyster 倡导的意义与形式并重的平衡教学法（Counter-balanced Approach）等角度对 CLIL 进行分析并指出了 CLIL 存在的不足。Dalton-Puffer 认为未来需对以下领域做进一步研究：1）母语或 L1 对学生课程学习的影响，2）与 CLIL 并行的外语课程教学，3）教师的语言能力以及让母语人士担任专业课程教师的可行性。此外，Dalton-Puffer 也指出以英语作为教学语言进行的 CLIL（CEIL）研究结果是否适用于其他语种也有待进一步论证。

（11）语料库研究在二语教学中的运用（*Corpus research applications in second language teaching*）

语料库是基于大量书面或口语素材，通过计算机存储及处理，用于语言研究和教学的数据库。语料库的出现不仅大大改变了语言学的研究方式，为词典及各类教材编撰提供了丰富的语料源泉，同时也对二语教学产生了影响。作者 Ute Römer 对语料库在二语教学中的运用情况以及近年来有关语料库语言学和语言教学的文献进行了回顾。相关研究显示，过去十几年间，语料库及语料库工具的发展不仅改变了语言学研究的方式，同时也对二语教学产生了影响。COBUILD、DDL 等语料库以及 BNC MICASE、ICLE 等学习者语料库为工具书及教材编撰提供了丰富而真实的语料。在教学方面，尽管越来越多的研究者和教师意识到了语料库及语料库语言学对语言教学的促进作用，但在实际教学中语料库面临着推广普及不够、教师对其普遍缺乏了解等问题。Römer 认为语料库可以从诸多方面参与二语教学，未来语料库的发展必须考虑以下三方面的问题：

1）注重学习者和教师需求，例如了解学习者的语言水平、课程类型、学习目标等，为教师提供在线教学资源；

2）推动二语教学间接使用语料库，例如为师生提供更多基于语料库的语言素材。目前的语言素材主要存在两个问题，一是语言素材多为通用语言，而学术英语或商务英语等专业素材相对缺乏；二是语言素材大多为书面语，不利于培养学习者的交际能力。Römer 认为未来的语料库建设应当考虑学习者及教师需求，尤其是学习者的交际需求。

3）推动语料库在二语教学中的直接运用，例如在二语教学中更多地运用 DDL 方法，让语料库直接参与教学活动，例如在教学资料编纂和制定语言测试中引入像定位索引（concordance）这样的语料库检索手段等。Römer 还指出必须研发易于使用的语料库工具并提供相关教师培训。关于外语教学中运用语料库的研究仍有待深入，两大领域必须进一步融合，才能让语料库真正走进课堂。

Römer 的回顾与介绍显示，国外有关语料库学与语言教学的研究主要集中在教学资源开发、学习任务研究和教学语料库建立等方面。我国真正将语料库学运用于语言教学始于 20 世纪 80 年代，虽然起步晚于国外，但经过三十多年的发展已经取得了令人瞩目的成绩，建立了一批颇具影响力的语言数据库，例如中文语言资源联盟（Chinese Linguistic Data Consortium，CLDC），英汉双语平行语料库、中国学习者英语语料库（CLEC）等。与此同时，许多学者还就语料库语言学在中国外语教学中的运用进行了思考与研究，也获得了许多学者的关注（如桂诗春、冯志伟、杨惠中、何安平等）[①]，从双语平行语料库、口语语料库、行业语料库等学习者语料库的建设与共享、语料库纳入语言教学整体框架的"教学加工"等方面进行了有益思考与探索，我国学者的研究方向基本与 Römer 提出的研究热点相一致，可见我国的语料库教学运用研究基本与国外同步，但正如 Römer 指出的，我国研究同样缺乏相关实证研究和对比研究，这将是未来的研究方向和热点。

（12）**在二语教学中培养学习者多模态识读和数字识读能力：新能力、新素养、新方法**（*Teaching multimodal and digital literacy in second language settings: New literacies, new basics, new pedagogies*）

全球化和数字化技术的飞速发展和语言及文化的日趋多元在改变人们沟通交流方式的同时，也对语言教学产生了影响。传统的语言文字不再是唯一的信息载体，越来越多的多模态（multimodal）信息走入课堂。

Healther Lotherington 和 Jennifer Jenson 两位作者聚焦多模态对二语教学的影响，就近年来有关二语教学中培养多模态识读（Multimodal Literacy）和数字识读（Digital Literacy）能力的研究和文献进行了总结。多模态识读超越了书面或口头的传统信息输出方式，它利用各种媒

[①] 桂诗春、冯志伟、杨惠中、何安平、卫乃兴、李文中、梁茂成，"语料库语言学与中国外语教学"，《现代外语》，2010 年第 4 期，第 419–426 页。

体和模态来传递视觉、听觉、手势、空间及触觉等信息。文章回顾了多模态理论的产生与发展,从多模态读写能力、教学要素以及教学法等方面对各类多模态二语教学实践进行了介绍分析。1996年新伦敦小组(New London Group)提出了"多模态识读能力"(multimodal literacies)这一概念,以凸显信息时代下阅读各类媒体和各种模态所呈现的信息的能力,包括语言的、视觉的、听觉的、肢体的、空间的等多模态信息。此后,许多学者从不同角度,包括系统功能语法学角度,对多模态教学进行了理论探索和实践。与此同时,数字技术也推动了多模态信息的传递,数字技术对多模态教学的影响也引起了一些学者的关注。多模态及数字识读能力的出现也改变了语言教学的要素,Sinclair提出了数字时代教育的4R新理论——即再使用(reuse)、再调整(revise)、再混合(remix)以及再发布(redistribute)——以取代传统教育的3R理论,即读(reading)、写(writing)、算(arithmetic)。有关多模态教学的研究发现多模态识读在二语教学中主要存在以下几个问题:1)教师思想观念尚未转变,多数仍固守传统教学模式,不愿接受多模态化的语言教学;2)实际运用中教师缺乏专业指导;3)教学条件的限制,硬件设施跟不上。Lotherington和Jenson认为多模态二语教学的发展必须注重提供教师培训、对多模态教学实践提供支持、并在实际运用中考虑学习者语言能力差异等问题。

随着网络和多媒体技术在外语课堂中的逐渐普及,我国的多模态教学也日益受到越来越多教师和研究者的关注。然而正如有学者指出的,多模态就像一把双刃剑,"处理好可以把学习者的注意力真正集中在知识点上,以达到强化记忆的作用,从而提高学习效率;处理不好相反会分散学习者的注意力,发生对知识点记忆的干扰"[①]。如何科学有效地运用新技术手段和教学方法,培养学习者的多模态识读能力和数字识读能力有待我们进行更多的研究和探索,Lotherington和Jenson在总结回顾的基础上指出的多模态二语教学所面临的问题与困难也值得我们深思。

---

① 顾曰国,"多媒体、多模态学习剖析",《外语电化教学》,2007年第2期,第9页。

2.4 语言技能教学

第四部分包含本卷第 13 到第 15 的三篇文章,分别就表意文字教学、协同写作和语用学教学等语言特殊技能教学进行分析研究。

(13)二语教学中表意文字和非罗马拼音文字的教学法探索(*Best practices in teaching logographic and non-Roman writing systems to L2 learners*)

近数十年来,国外越来越多的人选择汉语、阿拉伯语等语言作为第二外语,许多中学和大学也都开设了相应的语言课程。以汉语为例,我国教育部数据显示,目前全球通过各种方式学习汉语的人数超过 3000 万人,100 个国家超过 2500 余所大学在教授中文,越来越多的中小学开始开设汉语课程,各种社会培训机构不断增加,发展势头迅猛[①]。汉语学习人数的快速增长也推动了对外汉语教学研究的发展。作者 Michael E. Everson 聚焦这类语言文字,以中文、日文、阿拉伯文和希伯来文四种文字为例,探讨二语教学中有关表意文字和非罗马拼音文字的教学。

Everson 首先回顾了有关表意文字和非罗马拼音文字的研究。有研究认为语言存在难易之分,对于美国学习者而言,阿拉伯语、汉语或韩语等语言就难于西欧国家语言(例如法语或西班牙语)。关注学习者母语对二语学习影响的研究认为 L1 和 L2 文字书写差异的大小会影响学习者的学习成效。此外还有研究者从正字法、学习者学习策略、学习者差异等方面对这类文字的教学进行研究。

Everson 在回顾相关研究与文献的基础上分别阐述了四种文字(中文、日文、阿拉伯文和希伯来文)的特点、与英语等拼音文字的区别、学习难点和对教学的启示,例如让学习者能够从偏旁部首推断字意,了解汉字构造是学习汉字的有效方式。以中文为例,McGinnis 针对学习者策

---

① 国外汉语教学情况简介,中华人民共和国教育部网站,http://www.moe.edu.cn/publicfiles/business/htmlfiles/moe/moe_1017/200507/10584.html,访问日期:2014 年 12 月 15 日。

略进行的研究发现学习汉字构词法有助于学习者记忆汉字，Wang、Liu 和 Perfetti 的研究同样显示学习者可以通过偏旁部首推断词义。另一些研究者（Everson，DeFrancis 等）则研究汉字发音对学习汉字这种象形文字的影响，结果显示字音也同样有助于学习记忆汉字。对于中等水平的学习者而言，研究显示学习者普遍认为中文字与字之间没有空格而难以确定意群是他们阅读文本时的一大难点，而母语也往往影响他们对汉字的理解。

在教学方面，Everson 从不同角度介绍了四种文字的教学方法，包括拼音等辅助系统教学、学习者母语对二语学习的影响、教学材料的选择、文字书写及默写练习、文字教学中纳入文化内容、口语学习对文字学习的影响等。例如，有关中文和日文的教学法研究中一直存在争议的一个问题是，何时开始进行文字教学。一种观点认为，应当先学拼音，待打牢基础后再学习汉字或日文；另一种观点认为学习者应当从一开始就学习文字，但这可能会令学习者产生畏难情绪。最新的研究认为文字教学必须让学习者形成一套对目标语的元语言认识，因此初学者的教学材料不一定必须采用真实语篇，那些专为初学者设计、让其能用口语表达的阅读材料同样适用。尽管文章主要以中文、日文、阿拉伯文和希伯来文为例，但对其他表意文字和非罗马拼音文字的教学也同样具有一定理论指导和启迪意义，对我国对外汉语教学也具有指导意义。

（14）二语教学中的协同写作：过程、结果及发展趋势（*Collaborative writing in L2 contexts: Processes, outcomes, and future directions*）

协同写作（Collaborative Writing）是指由两人或两人以上共同合作完成文本创作。Neomy Storch 聚焦协同写作在二语教学中的实践与研究，探讨协同写作对二语写作教学的影响及未来发展方向。本文作者 Storch 从认知和社会文化角度对协同写作进行了简要的理论阐述，他谈到 Swain 的语言输出假设和言说（languaging）理论以及在此之前的 Vygotsky 的社会文化理论都对协同写作提供了理论支撑。上世纪 90 年代，受 Vygotsky "社会文化心理理论" 和 "语言社会化理论" 的影响，二语习得研究出现了"社会转向"，二语习得开始关注"语言调节行为"。在此背景下 Swain 提出了"languaging"（言说）这一概念，以体现学习者为表意而使用语言的过程。"Languaging"是调节复杂的认知任务的重要工具之一，它一方面强调语言输出，另一方面又体现个体用语法调节认知的过程，其目的是构建意义，本身就是自我支架。Swain 认为 languaging 往往是不发声的，是个体内在的认知过程，然而在进行协同写作时，学习者会注重自己的语言表达，从而实现言说过程的外在化，即协同写作是关于如何使用语言的语言交流（language about language）。

Storch 认为这些理论都对协同写作提供了理论支撑，但他同时指出，目前针对二语教学中协同写作的研究非常有限。仅有的少量研究主要集中在三个方面：1）协同写作中学习者的认知过程；2）协同写作结果分析；3）计算机辅助下的协同写作，尤其是 wiki 词条编辑。因为任何访问者都可以对 wiki 站点进行编辑和维护，每个人都可以发表自己的意见，或者对共同的主题进行扩展或者探讨，因此 wiki 既为知识共享提供了高效平台，实现了快速广泛的信息整合，同时也为语言教学提供了支持面向社群的协同写作平台。这些研究证实了协同写作对二语教学的促进作用，同时也指出了影响教学效果的因素，如任务类型、学习者彼此之间的关系、学习者二语水平、学习者的交流方式（面对面交流或计算机辅助交流）等。Storch 认为协同写作可以成为二语教学的有效模式，通过 wiki 进行在线协同写作是未来发展的新方向，他同时也指出了具体实践时必须注意的问题，如布置任务前对学习者进行相关培训，密切关注学习者的写作过程等。

我国的二语教学研究学者同样也对协同写作/协作学习进行了有益探索，例如胡壮麟教授从课程教学要求的角度探讨了外语教学中的协作化理念[1]；更多学者则聚焦协作学习在各类语言课程中的运用，例如有学者对英语专业大二学生进行协同写作的教学实践效果进行了实证研究[2]，还

---

[1] 胡壮麟，"大学英语教学的个性化、协作化、模块化和超文本化"，《外语教学与研究》，2004 年第 5 期，第 345–350 页。
[2] 张晓兰，"合作学习在英语专业写作教学中运用的实验研究"，《四川外语学院学报》，2006 年第 3 期，第 137–140 页。

有学者从内涵、学习策略、施行条件等方面对协作学习进行理论探讨，这些都促进了协同写作/协作学习理论与实践的发展，然而可以看出，我国的协同写作/写作学习研究大多聚焦理论本身和课堂实践，而 Storch 在回顾近年来国外相关研究的基础上指出，针对学习者认知过程、基于计算机及网络的协同写作以及结果分析等领域的研究偏少，未来我国学者不妨在这些领域进行更多探索和研究。

（15）语用教学：发展趋势及问题（*Teaching Pragmatics: Trends and issues*）

Naoko Taguchi 探讨了二语教学中培养学习者语用能力的问题。有关培养二语学习者语用能力的理论研究、实证研究及实践大致可分为两大类：一是检验各类语用教学方法效果的实验性研究，即语用能力培养中教学干预效果研究；二是探索培养二语学习者语用能力的最佳课堂教学实践和教学资源的研究。文章分别对近年来两大领域的研究及文献进行了回顾。在教学干预方面，Taguchi 简要回顾了"语用能力是否可教"这一争论的由来与发展。1997 年 Gabriele Kasper 在美国佛罗里达州奥兰多召开的 TESOL 国际会议上发表了题为"语用能力是否可教？（*Can Pragmatic Competence Be Taught?*）"的主旨发言，从而引发了关于语用能力教学的论战。上世纪 90 年代进行的研究显示大部分语用能力是可教的，于是语用能力教学研究从是否可行转向如何教，开始关注不同教学方式的教学效果。其中 Schmidt 的注意假说（noticing hypothesis）为二语教学中的语用教学提供了主要的理论支撑。Schmidt 认为只有那些被学习者注意到并经学习者理解、融合后的输入才有可能转化为内在知识。基于这一理论，语用教学主要通过提供显性的元语用信息、提升学习者的语用意识等方式来引起学习者对目标语的注意。最近针对显性（explicit）与隐性（implicit）教学效果的对比研究（Alcon-Soler 和 Takahashi 的研究）证实了显性教学的效果，显示元语用能显著提高学习者的语用能力，研究同时显示学习者 L2 水平、教学内容、时间、方式都会对教学效果产生影响。

尽管Schmidt的注意假说及相关理论对语用学教学影响颇大，但近年来语际语用学（Interlanguage Pragmatics）的兴起为语用学教学提供了新的理论框架——Van Patten的语言输入加工理论（input processing）和Dekeyser的技能习得理论（Skill Acquisition Theory, SAT）。Taguchi分别从这两个框架对语用教学效果进行探讨，同时指出未来该领域的研究热点：1）针对学习能力、教学内容、教学方法和学习效果的动态研究；2）既得语用知识的迁移，即已经掌握的语用知识是否有助于学习者掌握新的语用能力。在教学实践与教学资源方面，本文作者从三个方面——教学材料及教师培训、学习者策略及自主学习、课堂教学中附带语用教学——回顾了该领域的研究现状、不足与发展方向。

文章最后讨论了后结构主义和多元文化语境下语用教学所面临的机遇和挑战。Taguchi指出，文化和语言的日趋多元化对语用标准构成了挑战。正如House指出的，非母语人士在交往时可能会建立一套自己的语用标准，在这种情况下，目标语的语用标准不再是单一标准。此外，一些最新研究还显示有些学习者希望保持其母语文化身份，因而不愿遵从目标语的语用规范。例如David发现澳大利亚的韩国学生更倾向于美式英语而不是澳大利亚英语的语用规范，因为韩国受美国文化影响较深；Ishihara和Tarone的研究同样发现因受母语文化影响而信奉社会平等的澳大利亚学习者在学习日语时，往往会拒绝使用日语中的敬语或性别语言。这些研究从另一个侧面凸显了语用教学的独特性，学习者母语和二语的文化差异会对其二语学习产生影响，因此二语教学中的语用教学应当考虑学习者的母语文化因素。文章还从后结构主义角度探讨了语用教学，并指出应当以动态发展的眼光看待语用能力。Taguchi最后指出未来语用教学的实践与研究应当对这些新领域和新挑战予以更多关注。

我国关于语用教学的研究大致与国外相同，主要集中在外语教学是否有助于语用能力的提高（语用是否可教），以及各类教学法对提高外语语用能力的效果两大领域，还有一些学者注意到了不同语境下的语用教学并进行了相关探索，例如段玲琍就对中国外语教学语境下的语用教学进行了实证研究[①]，这也是 Taguchi 在总结近年来语用教学相关研究后指出的未来研究的新热点和发展方向，即多元文化语境下，针对不同文化背景的学习者进行的动态研究。

3. 评介

2011 年剑桥大学出版社出版的第 31 卷《剑桥应用语言学年度评论：第二语言教学研究》较为系统、全面地呈现了近年来二语教学领域的研究热点和发展趋势。本书在内容撰写和体例编排上有以下几个特色：

（1）新旧结合，脉络清晰。本书所介绍的均是近年来，尤其是近五年来（2006—2011）二语教学领域最新的理论及实践动态，但这些新内容均建立在对以往相关理论与研究进行回顾的基础上，并对关键术语及概念进行了定义和解释，为读者尤其是对该领域了解不多的读者提供了相关研究的理论依据和发展脉络，便于读者准确理解和把握二语教学的发展动态。

（2）选题恰当。二语教学是一门跨多领域的学科，涉及面广，理论繁多。然而本卷篇幅有限，不可能做到包罗万象，面面俱到。本卷从众多研究问题中进行筛选，合理编排，所选取的 15 个选题具有以下两个特点。首先，契合二语教学研究的发展趋势。正如上文提到的，新世纪以来二语教学的研究重点发生了变化。本文所选取的这些选题充分体现了这些变化和发展趋势。全卷一改以往探讨语言技能教学为主的传统，将目光拓宽到技能以外的教学环境、学习者和教学方法等因素，四大专题与 Stern[②] 提出的语言教学四要素（语言、学习、教学和环境）完全契合，更加系统、全面地呈现二语教学研究与实践的现况。其次，选题重点突出，兼顾热点。全书不求面面俱到，只选取二语教学研究领域的要点问题（如 OLL、多模

[①] 段玲琍，"中国外语教学语境下语用能力可教性的实证研究"，《天津外国语学院学报》，2009 年第 4 期，第 67-74 页。
[②] H. H. Stern, Fundamental Concepts of Language Teaching, 上海：上海外语教育出版社，1983 年版。

态教学、语料库教学等），同时兼顾近年来逐渐引发关注的热点（如职场语言培训、手语教学、表意文字教学等），范围涵盖了课堂教学和课外教学、成人教学与儿童教学、小语种教学与非文字语言教学、学校教育与职场培训，视野广阔，对现实更具指导意义。

（3）严谨客观，兼容并蓄。每一篇论文都介绍并回顾了某一领域近年来的理论探索和实践研究。论文主要选取有代表性的、能反映该领域研究热点及趋势的研究，同时注重研究方法的科学性，许多论文还对研究方法进行专门分析评论。此外，作者采取兼容并蓄的开放态度，不仅介绍各类最新研究，对于结论不同甚至完全相左的研究也予以客观呈现，并对结果差异进行客观分析、梳理和评述，尽可能客观全面地呈现各领域的研究概貌。

（4）理论与实践相结合，研究与教学并重。每一篇论文都从基本理论入手，以相关实践与研究为主体，既有理论阐述，又有具体案例分析，理论与实践紧密结合。研究者可以了解二语教学领域最新的前沿理论和相关研究结论；一线教师不仅可以为自身教学实践找到理论支撑，更可以获得具体的实践指导，了解最新教学法的发展动态。因此本书对二语教学研究者及教师具有理论指导和实践提高的双重指导意义。

由于二语教学所涉学科领域众多，理论繁杂，内容广泛，尽管全书选题已经尽量兼顾要点和热点问题，但毕竟很难在一本书的有限篇幅中做到面面俱到，因此本书内容全面性上存在些许不足。例如，尽管聚焦的是二语教学，大多数论文（除了 Quinto-Pozos 的手语教学和 Everson 的表意文字教学）所回顾的都是英文文献，且研究大部分是以英语作为二语，这在一定程度上影响了结论的普及性。当然，这也反映出当前二语教学领域英语依然是主要目标语言的事实。然而随着选择汉语、阿拉伯语等非英语语言作为第二外语的学习者人数日益增多，非英语的二语教学与研究也应当获得更多关注，我国的研究者和学者可以也应当在此领域有更多贡献。

本书是一本介绍二语教学最新理论与实践的专著。它聚焦二语教学领域的最新热点和焦点问题，较为系统全面地呈现了二语教学的最新发展动态。语言教育问题成为越来越多的专家学者、高校教师和研究机构的关注重点。国内的二语教学研究仍有很大的发展空间,将二语习得理论指导与二语教学改革与实践相结合的著作仍不多见。本书不仅可以让国内研究学者和教师了解掌握该领域国外最新发展动态,对我国二语教学的改革与实践也具有实际指导意义。

参考书目

Brow, H. Douglas. *Teaching by Principles: An Interactive Approach to Language Pedagogy* (3rd edition), 北京: 外语教学与研究出版社, 2002 年版。

Ellis, Rod. *The Study of Second Language Acquisition*, 上海: 上海外语教育出版社, 1999年版。

Gwynn, Aubrey. (1926). *Roman Education from Cicero to Quintilian*. New York: Teachers College Press.

Howatt, A.P.R. *A History of English Language Teaching*, 上海: 上海外语教育出版社, 1984 年版。

Kumaravadivelu, B. (2003). *Beyond Methods: Macro-strategies for language teaching*. New Haven: Yale University Press.

Larsen-Freeman, Diane. (2000). *Techniques and Principles in Language Teaching* (2nd edition). Oxford: Oxford University Press.

Mellow, J. Dean. (2000). Western influences on indigenous language teaching, in J. Reyhner, J. Martin, L. Lockard, & W. Sakiestewa Gilbert (eds.), *Learn in beauty: Indigenous education for a new century*, Flagstaff, AZ: Northern Arizona University, pp. 102–113.

Richards, Jack C. and Theodore S. Rodgers. (1986). *Approaches and Methods in Language Teaching*, Cambridge: Cambridge University Press.

Rogers, Ted. Methodology in the New Millennium, *English Teaching Forum*, 2000, April, pp. 2–13.

Spolsky, B. (1988). Bridge the Gap: A General Theory of Second Language Learning. *TESOL Quarterly, 22*(3): pp 377–396.

Stern, H. H. *Fundamental Concepts of Language Teaching*, 上海: 上海外语教育出版社, 1983 年版。

Vivian, Cook. (2008). *Second Language Learning and Language Teaching* (4th edition), London, UK: Hodder Education.

高一虹, 吴红亮, 李莉春, "关于外语教学研究方法的调查",《外国语》, 2000 年第 1 期, 第 65–72 页。

胡壮麟, "外语教学理念的发展",《基础教育外语教学研究》, 2005 年第 1 期, 第 21–25 页。

胡壮麟, "社会符号学研究中的多模态化",《语言教学与研究》, 2007 年第 1 期, 第 1–9 页。

胡壮麟,《胡壮麟英语教育自选集》, 北京: 外语教学与研究出版社, 2008 年。

李战子,"英语教育:知识与话语的汇集点",《外语研究》,2002年第6期,第74—75页。
李战子,《跨文化自传与英语教学》,北京:高等教育出版社,2007年。
欧洲理事会文化合作教育委员会,刘骏、傅荣译,《欧洲语言共同参考框架:学习、教学、评估》,北京:外语教学与研究出版社,2008年版。
束定芳,庄智象,《现代外语教学》,上海:上海外语教育出版社,1996年版。
王守仁,"关于学术英语教学的几点思考",《中国外语》,2013年第5期,第4—10页。

Editor's Introduction

With this volume of the *Annual Review of Applied Linguistics* (*ARAL*), I continue the tradition of my predecessors of producing a volume on the topic second language pedagogy about every five years. Although applied linguistics encompasses more than the teaching and learning of second languages, articles on these topics tend to be among the most downloaded from the *ARAL* web site. I decided, however, to break with the tradition of focusing mostly on specific skill areas. Because language teaching is a situated activity that cannot be separated from its contexts and learners, the first section is devoted to language learning in or for specific contexts (secondary school settings, online, the workplace, the Asia-Pacific region, and study abroad), and the second section focuses on specific learners (young learners, adult emergent readers, and hearing learners of sign language). These are followed by a section on integrated approaches and includes articles on language-literature instruction, content and language integrated learning, the application of corpus research to language teaching, and multimodal literacy. The final section includes articles on more specific skill areas including teaching non-Roman writing systems, collaborative writing, and pragmatics.

Note that the term second language or L2 is used throughout this volume to refer to the learning of an additional language be it the second, third, or so on. It also refers to learning in second language settings, where the language being learned is spoken in the environment, as well as in foreign language settings, where it is generally not spoken, and every context in between.

As in the past, review articles in *ARAL* tend to focus on recent research, but because the reviews need to be comprehensible to nonspecialists in each area, the authors often need to refer to older research to define terms and explain concepts or set the context for more current research. Although each of these articles reports on research, each author has tried to keep in view the goal of facilitating language learning through instructional practices.

All of the articles in this volume were invited, but each was reviewed by a member of the board and/or outside reviewer. I am extremely grateful to my colleagues, who responded cheerfully and promptly to my requests for reviews. In particular, I thank Yuko Bulter, David Carless, Nobuko Chikamatsu-Chandler, Andrew Cohen, Senta Goertler, Greg Kessler, Eva Lam, Roy Lyster, Hiram Maxim, Kim McDonough, Yoshiko Mori, Joy Peyton, Randi Reppen, Rusty Rosen, Ann Snow, Janet Swaffar, Julie Sykes, Linda Yates, Martha Young-Scholten, Eve Zyzik, and four anonymous reviewers. All of their reviews improved the final versions of the articles. The editorial directors, too, responded promptly to requests for reviewing and, of course, contributed greatly to this volume with their suggestions of topics and authors.

In addition, I would like to thank, from Cambridge University Press, Morrell Gillette, the production manager, who responds quickly and cheerfully to emails, and Laura Etheredge, our new editor, who took off running in her new position. Finally, I thank my former graduate student, Sally Behrenwald, who kindly agreed to stay on to help edit despite now having a full-time job and despite having had to adapt to the sixth edition of the APA manual after having literally memorized parts of the index to the fifth edition. I could not do this job without any of you all.

Charlene Polio,
East Lansing, MI

SECTION A: SECOND LANGUAGE INSTRUCTION IN DIFFERENT SETTINGS

Teaching Academic Language in L2 Secondary Settings

Mary J. Schleppegrell and Catherine L. O'Hallaron

Research on instruction in academic language in second language (L2) secondary settings is currently emerging as a focus in applied linguistics. Academic language refers to the disciplinary registers that students encounter in the secondary years, and using academic language calls for advanced proficiency in complex language across subject areas, posing challenges for teacher preparation. In this article we summarize recommendations from syntheses of research on adolescent L2 learners and then present reports of recent studies that describe instructional approaches that illuminate the recommended practices in contexts where students who speak languages other than English are learning school subjects in English. Three key instructional dimensions are highlighted: that teachers need knowledge about how language works in their subject areas, that academic language development calls for careful planning across a unit of instruction, and that students need support for engagement in classroom activities that promote the simultaneous learning of language and content. To prepare teachers for this work, secondary teacher education needs to incorporate a focus on language-content relationships in each disciplinary area. More research is needed to better understand and support academic language development, and we call for collaboration and dialogue between educational researchers and applied linguists concerned with these issues.

Second language (L2) learners in secondary schools are quite diverse, as they come from different linguistic and cultural backgrounds, have varying levels of proficiency, and differ in the knowledge of school subjects they have developed in their first languages. But regardless of their backgrounds, they are expected to engage with challenging school subjects across a range of disciplines. This means that the language they most need to develop is what is referred to as *academic language*, the language through which school subjects are taught and assessed. While researchers debate definitions of academic language and even raise questions about the value or utility of this construct (for different perspectives, see, Bunch, 2006; Cummins & Man, 2007), the fact that secondary students need to engage with a range of registers—oral and written, formal and informal, in a range of subject areas—means that second language learning presents great challenges for this population. Our definition of academic language comes from work in systemic functional linguistics (SFL), a linguistic theory that enables language forms to be linked with their contexts of use (e.g., Halliday & Matthiessen, 2004). Description of academic language focuses on the discourse, lexical, and grammatical challenges of the tasks students are asked to engage in across school subjects (Schleppegrell, 2004; Snow & Uccelli, 2009). Learning to read, write, and interact using academic language requires support for language development that assists students in engaging with the communicative and literacy demands of disciplinary learning.

Many secondary-level language learners continue to struggle with academic language and academic subjects even after several years in the new language environment. Newly arrived immigrants of secondary school age with little or no proficiency in the L2 need intensive support for language development and are often served in classrooms specially dedicated to their instruction. In many cases, however, adolescent students who are still developing proficiency in the language of instruction are placed directly in mainstream classrooms for most subject-area learning.[1] This has major implications for the contributions that applied linguists and language teachers can make in regard to this population, as much of these students' language learning will take place in mainstream classrooms without continued support from language specialists. Teachers in all disciplinary areas need to be supported in providing opportunities for continuing language development for their L2 students, many of whom may speak the second language with colloquial fluency even while they still have much work to do to develop the reading, writing, and academic language needed for full participation and success in academic subject areas. This means that applied linguists and L2 educators need to engage more closely with content-area teachers and develop new paradigms for L2 instruction in secondary school, with greater attention to preparing teachers to support L2 development across school subjects.

To prepare this review, we surveyed research published in English over the past 5 years to identify work that reports on teaching and learning academic language in L2 secondary contexts. Several recent research reports have synthesized recommendations for instruction in academic language for L2 students at the secondary level, and we begin our review with a summary of these reports. In general, the empirical research in this area is sparse. Most of the research on academic language in secondary schooling uses qualitative methods such as ethnography and discourse analysis to report on case studies and small-scale interventions.[2] In the latter part of this article we draw on these studies to describe instructional approaches that exemplify recommended practices.

Our focus is on secondary school settings where students are learning English in English-speaking contexts, and we do not review work from foreign language instruction contexts, such as CLIL (content-and-language integrated learning) in Europe (but see Dalton-Puffer, 2011–this volume) or foreign language instruction in English-speaking contexts (see Paesani, 2011–this volume). We do not discuss research pertaining to the identities of adolescent ELLs (English language learners) and literacy practices or instruction that does not specifically address academic language development.

RECOMMENDATIONS FROM RESEARCH SYNTHESES FOR INSTRUCTION IN ACADEMIC LANGUAGE AT THE SECONDARY LEVEL

Several recently published reviews help us summarize current recommendations for instruction that supports the development of academic language at the secondary level. Roessingh (2004) developed a synthesis and meta-analysis of 12 studies of effective high school English as a second language (ESL) programs over two decades in Canada and the United States. Meltzer and Hamann (2005) surveyed the research literature on adolescent learners of English and synthesized research-based literacy strategies for this population. Téllez and Waxman (2006) completed what they called a "meta-synthesis" of the results of 25 studies of effective teaching practices for ELLs, including some studies at the secondary level. Although not specifically focused on the secondary context, Lindholm-Leary and Borsato (2006) synthesized recommendations from five studies of instructional strategies for teaching content, a focus relevant to secondary teaching. Francis, Rivera, Lesaux, Kieffer, and Rivera (2006) synthesized findings from a range of research reports to suggest what newcomers require for effective instruction. Short and Fitzsimmons (2007) reviewed research studies on adolescents learning English, convened a panel of experts to offer instructional recommendations, conducted site visits to three programs that they deemed promising, and synthesized recommendations from these activities. Cumming (2008) presented a review of recommendations from five recent books on literacy development in secondary contexts, and Jiménez and Teague (2009) reviewed seven studies of secondary-age students learning English over the past 10 years. Finally, although they did not focus specifically on adolescent students, we include the recommendations of Anstrom et al. (2010), who reviewed literature on academic English teaching practices in U.S. K–12 contexts, and Goldenberg and Coleman (2010), who presented a synthesis of research-supported instructional practices for academic instruction in a second language. Table 1 summarizes the recommendations from these reports.

The research summarized in Table 1 highlights three points: that all teachers need knowledge about academic language in their content areas (foundational knowledge), that they need to build in support for students' L2 development at the planning stages (macro-scaffolding), and that they need strategies for engaging students in robust ways in exploring language and content in the moment-to-moment unfolding of instruction in the classroom (micro-scaffolding). In particular:

- Language instruction at the secondary level should be situated in the subject areas, supported by teachers with deep understanding of the language challenges of their content areas. With such understanding, teachers can support language learning in content instruction and develop students' metalinguistic awareness about how language works in the disciplinary

Table 1. Recommendations from Recent Research Syntheses on Instruction in Academic Language at the Secondary Level

Instructional recommendation	Sources
Knowledge about academic language in the content areas—Support learning about academic language in all subjects: Incorporate language development in the content area; organize content thematically; provide explicit instruction in academic language, including vocabulary, text structures and discourse features; develop metalinguistic knowledge; develop critical literacy.	Anstrom et al. (2010); Francis et al. (2006); Jiménez & Teague (2009); Lindholm-Leary & Borsato (2006); Meltzer & Hamann (2005); Roessingh (2004); Short & Fitzsimmons (2007)
Macro-scaffolding—Plan challenging work that develops language and content over time and involves students in learning: Set high expectations; offer challenging and motivating contexts; have clear goals and learning objectives; share language objectives with students; teach learning strategies and have students reflect on their own learning; use a "balanced approach" to literacy, teaching all four skills from the beginning; use multiple forms of assessment; provide opportunities to apply new knowledge; review and practice.	Cumming (2008); Francis et al. (2006); Goldenberg & Coleman (2010); Jiménez & Teague (2009); Meltzer & Hamann (2005); Roessingh (2004); Short & Fitzsimmons (2007)
Micro-scaffolding—Support students' engagement with language and content: Create an atmosphere for trust and risk-taking within a small community of learners; support group/collaborative work; engage students in protracted language events and authentic communication tasks that motivate them and give them choices; ask high-level questions that enable students to apply new knowledge; encourage participation; provide clear instructions, modeling, and presentation of new information; use visual/multiple/multimodal representations; use appropriate technology; build on prior knowledge; bridge between everyday and academic language; use slower, flexible pacing; give effective feedback.	Anstrom et al. (2010); Cumming (2008); Goldenberg & Coleman (2010); Jiménez & Teague (2009); Lindholm-Leary & Borsato (2006); Meltzer & Hamann (2005); Roessingh (2004); Short & Fitzsimmons (2007); Téllez & Waxman (2006)

contexts. As we discuss later, this implies the development of teachers' knowledge about language in ways that currently rarely occur and that offer new opportunities for applied linguists to contribute to teacher preparation.

- Embedding language instruction in a challenging and motivating curricular context with high expectations for students' performance requires careful planning over a unit of instruction and over the school year. This planning should consider how the content and language will be developed simultaneously over time, as well as how individual lessons will present and scaffold new knowledge and provide practice. It needs to address oral and written language development, teaching strategies that involve students in their own learning.
- Academic language instruction occurs in the moment-to-moment work of teaching, and students need to support engagement with content in multiple ways. Teachers can support this by connecting with the language students bring to school, whether from first language contexts or from contexts of informal interaction that draw on everyday registers, and by creating classroom contexts where all students are able to participate in cognitively challenging work. In addition, academic language development requires flexible pacing that responds to students' needs and growth in both language and content, and students need regular feedback that focuses on meaning as well as form.

These key recommendations from research syntheses are stated in very general terms in Table 1. In the next sections we report on studies that illustrate what implementation of these recommendations looks like in L2 secondary settings.

RESEARCH ON FOUNDATIONAL UNDERSTANDING OF LANGUAGE IN THE CONTENT AREAS

One way to improve instruction for secondary L2 learners is to prepare their teachers with greater knowledge about language in their content areas and strategies for supporting language development as students learn new content. It may seem obvious, in light of decades of applied linguistics work on content-based teaching (e.g., Mohan, 1986; Stoller, 2004), that instruction in secondary schools should be content-embedded. However, this recommendation has tremendous implications for teacher development that have not yet been realized. The culture of secondary school positions teachers as disciplinary experts, leading them in many cases to resist taking on instructional responsibility for issues such as language development that may seem to fall outside of their disciplinary mandate (for discussion, see, Arkoudis, 2006). In a recent review of programmatic issues for ESL in secondary social studies classrooms, Duff (2005) noted:

> Explicitly combined [language and content] instruction is less frequently found in mainstream content courses unless major reforms initiated by ESL specialists have been successfully implemented, often because of a lack of coordination between ESL and content specialists, little or no applied linguistics training among the latter, and the (misguided) notion that ESL students' needs are not the responsibility of content specialists, even though they may constitute more than half the students in a course. (p. 49)

Secondary teachers are, understandably, highly focused on teaching their subject areas. At the same time, as the academic language that students must master becomes increasingly complex and specialized, and as L2 learners are increasingly served in mainstream classrooms, content-area teachers are best positioned to provide effective instruction in the uses of language specific to the disciplines. This means that research on effective ways to do this and to prepare teachers for this work is a current imperative. It is essential for teachers to develop an understanding of the language demands of common genres and tasks in their subject areas as well as to learn strategies for making that knowledge available to students.

A current focus of research is to provide support for teachers by developing their understanding about how language works in their subject areas. A major theoretical framework informing this research on discipline-specific language features is SFL. Systemic functional (SF) linguists have analyzed and described the features of language in secondary content areas across disciplines (for a review, see Christie & Derewianka, 2008; Unsworth, 2000), and currently many researchers are using this framework to enable teachers to understand the challenges of disciplinary language in their fields.

One such context is work in the California History Project, where SF linguists worked with teachers to develop what was called a *literacy in history* approach to professional development (e.g., Schleppegrell, 2011). Teachers learned about linguistic features of the language of history and prepared teaching activities that engaged students in analysis of texts, linked with a grade-level California history standard and supported by a guiding question that became a focus of discussion. Students worked in groups to analyze the ways their textbooks and primary source documents used language in presenting historical content, followed by whole-class discussion of the language and meaning and individual writing tasks that enabled students to try out new ways of writing about what they had learned.

Schleppegrell and de Oliveira (2006) described California History Project workshops in which mainstream teachers with large numbers of students learning English in their classrooms engaged in analyses of the ways that historians used different language choices to represent historical actors, position an actor as agentive, and report on causes and effects. The teachers then designed instructional units to engage in similar activities with their students, breaking down sentences into meaning-based elements that facilitated examination of "what happened, who did it and to whom, and under what circumstances" (p. 259). The authors reported that teachers found that their students gained a greater understanding of the texts' embedded meanings—in other words, of the content—through this guided deconstruction, and also gained deeper understanding about how English works in presenting knowledge about history. Achugar, Schleppegrell, and Oteíza (2007) and Schleppegrell, Greer, and Taylor (2008) offered further descriptions of this work in action in the classroom with teachers' comments on the ways it supported their students' learning. (For background on functional language analysis for secondary school instruction across disciplines, see Fang & Schleppegrell, 2008, 2010).

Another SFL-based professional development program was designed by Aguirre-Muñoz, Park, Amabisca, and Boscardin (2008), who worked with 21 mainstream middle school English language arts teachers in California to improve their understanding of academic language. In particular, they helped teachers analyze and respond to students' academic writing about literature, using SFL concepts to consider how protagonists/antagonists and events in the texts are described, how authors ascribe attributes to and evaluate characters, and how cohesion is achieved across a text. The researchers analyzed how training in recognizing the linguistic features that enable students to accomplish these goals influenced the teachers' evaluation of student work and its impact on instructional practices. They reported that "the training helped to support and develop teachers' understanding of the linguistic features of academic language in a manner that focused their analysis of ELL writing on meaning and providing feedback and instruction to students centered on developing their linguistic resources for improving clarity in their writing" (pp. 14–15). Specifically, teachers provided more genre-specific feedback on features of academic language and were better able to scaffold expansion of noun groups, effective use of conjunctions and transitions, and greater sentence variety. Through enhanced knowledge about the linguistic features of academic writing in language arts, teachers were able to give their students more explicit instruction about language to support their disciplinary goals.

Mohan and Slater (2006) illustrated how linguists, using a functional perspective, can identify how effective teachers use language to present disciplinary concepts and interact with students in ways that develop their subject-area knowledge. Reporting on a ninth-grade mainstream science class with diverse learners, they tracked the learning path from the teacher's introduction of concepts and new language through students' use of that language in problem-solving activities that gave students practice. They suggested that work that analyzes what effective teachers do is needed to help all teachers engage students more effectively in linking theory and practice in science.

A key implication of this functional linguistics research is that although secondary teachers may not initially see language instruction as their purview, they can be motivated to learn to talk about discipline-specific language tied to achieving their broader instructional goals, and when they do so, they are able to offer their L2 students opportunities to learn language and content simultaneously. Helping students understand historians' interpretations of historic events and actors and see how authors construe agency in language, helping students learn how to present and evaluate characters in a literary review, or helping students develop and use technical language in science are key goals of secondary teachers. Greater understanding of language and how to use it to scaffold learning offers teachers new ways of accomplishing these goals.

RESEARCH ON MACRO- AND MICRO-SCAFFOLDING OF STUDENTS' LANGUAGE AND CONTENT DEVELOPMENT

The research summarized in Table 1 highlights the need for teachers to consider L2 development both at the planning stage, as they take into account students' developmental trajectories over time (macro-scaffolding); and in the moment-to-moment unfolding of instruction in the classroom (micro-scaffolding). While we present these as distinct considerations, in successful classrooms they tend to function together as part of a comprehensive instructional approach. Several studies have described instructional practices that enrich understanding of these recommendations.

One study that exemplifies the kind of comprehensive approach to instruction for secondary-level English learners called for in the recommendations outlined in Table 1 is Kramer-Dahl, Teo, and Chia (2007), who presented a case study of an upper secondary social studies teacher in Singapore who participated in professional development through their expanding textual repertoires (ETR) framework. ETR is based on the principles of intellectual quality, connected learning, and explicit instruction: dimensions of an overarching belief that higher order academic learning, in contexts where the majority of students do not come from English-speaking backgrounds, is contingent upon focused and coherent instructional talk. Among the instructional practices highlighted as effective was macro-scaffolding that considered the whole sequence of lessons that make up a unit, helping the teacher develop coherence across activities and lessons and build in recursivity through review and practice. Teachers who participated in an intervention project planned ways of moving students from relating to content on the basis of everyday experience to acquiring and using the specialized knowledge and language of the subject area. Specifically, lesson sequences were designed to foster the use of literate talk, "planned, elaborated language in which the students engaged constructively and critically with each others' and their teachers' ideas and developed principled, deep understandings of the concepts and skills taught" (p. 169).

This macro-scaffolding then provided a framework for the micro-scaffolding that occurs in the "moment-by-moment unfolding of the classroom talk" (p. 179), as the focal teacher supported linguistic and cognitive growth through structuring of in-class discussions. Transcripts of classroom interaction showed that the teacher regularly encouraged students to give more information, make deeper connections, and actively participate in the class's collaborative construction of knowledge. In this way the students' academic language was developed through regular practice coupled with the teacher's use of modeling and scaffolding.

A prominent approach to teaching language in content areas that addresses both the macro- and micro-scaffolding needs is the Sheltered Instruction Observation Protocol (SIOP) model (Echevarria, Vogt, & Short, 2000). Developed in conjunction with an observation instrument (for the latest iteration, see Echevarria, Vogt, & Short, 2007), the SIOP model focuses teachers on specific practices that they can build into their lesson plans to support language learning in subject-area teaching. These practices include explicitly specifying language objectives, slower pacing, connecting with students' background knowledge, making language comprehensible, and supporting interaction, among others. Echevarria, Short, and Powers (2006) reported on a study in which middle school teachers were trained in SIOP strategies and given feedback on how they engaged in these activities in practice. When compared with students of teachers who were not trained in SIOP techniques, students of the intervention teachers achieved greater improvement in their writing.

This dual focus on scaffolding at the macro- and micro-levels is a prominent feature of other reports on effective discipline-specific secondary school language teaching. Hammond (2006), for example, described instruction in a seventh-grade English literature classroom in Australia where academically gifted ESL students were taught in a class designed to provide ongoing language-learning support. Drawing on SFL and Vygotsky's sociocultural theory, the teacher designed a unit on *Romeo and Juliet* that had both curricular and language goals: to develop understanding and appreciation of the text as well as to support students' learning of the language features that would enable their full participation in the English curriculum. As the class studied the Shakespeare play over 8 weeks, their reading was supported by frequent discussion of and about language, including the rhetorical structures and language features of written genres that the teacher used to engage them in analysis of the text, attention to abstract concepts such as voice, and support for students to shift between informal and specialist registers. The teacher assisted the students in developing metalanguage that they used to talk about writing as well as abstract technical terms commonly used in the specialist domain of literary analysis. Hammond described this approach as "high challenge, high support" (p. 269) and argued that the purposeful interweaving of content and academic language offered a positive alternative to well-meaning teachers' inclination to accommodate the needs of their English-learning students by modifying the curriculum to make it less challenging.

Spycher (2007) presented a case study that reported on explicit teaching of academic language to 11th-grade students with early intermediate proficiency in an English language development class. As the classroom teacher, Spycher drew on an SFL framework to identify language features that students were attempting to use in their expository writing, but found challenging. These included establishment of an authoritative stance through nominalization, modality, and less use of "I"; use of conjunctions to concede points relevant to the developing argument; and effective use of lexical, rather than pronominal, reference. She reported on a focal student's development of proficiency in persuasive writing, both organizationally and in the use of specific language features, through a cycle of explicit teacher modeling and explanation about how to deconstruct text, practice in deconstructing, and opportunities for peer collaboration and independent practice. Spycher's approach departed from the conventional wisdom that says students need to control foundational skills before engaging with more advanced language features, as she employed supportive scaffolding techniques to engage the learners in high-level academic writing tasks.

Both written and oral academic language development need to be supported in secondary classrooms. Zwiers (2006) reported on an action research study carried out with the 60 seventh-through ninth-grade English learners who were his students in a 5-week history-based English language development summer program. His course emphasized the development of historical thinking and academic language, culminating in the writing of a persuasive essay. Scaffolding at the macro-level included the design of mini-lessons built around each of the six historical thinking dimensions (background knowledge, cause, effect, bias, empathy, and application). Careful planning around multiple micro-level supports was also evident. The class discussed and practiced perspective-taking and the use of academic transitions through spoken language that served as a bridge to more formal oral language and then academic writing. Students studied professional models of persuasive essays, identifying and discussing the important features and the functions they served, and then drafted and revised their own essays, using graphic organizers and peer and teacher feedback. Reporting on his analysis of the essays, classroom audio recordings, student logbooks, and his own notes, Zwiers concluded that modeling and scaffolding and frequent informal assessment had played important roles in encouraging historical thinking and academic language use, and that authentic communication tasks that fostered genuine desire to communicate ideas were essential in motivating students to use the more academic features of language.

Bunch (2006) highlighted the need to focus on academic language in the spoken language tasks that secondary students engage in. He reported on a social studies curriculum developed to engage students in linguistically and academically heterogeneous classrooms in intellectually challenging tasks as they worked with authentic historical documents. Students participated in a series of group work tasks that enabled them to draw on their more informal oral registers as they developed more academic language for the presentations they were preparing. Bunch suggested that our understanding of academic language needs to be enhanced through more research on the role of oral language in developing academic language proficiency, and in a recent study (Bunch, 2009), he described the particular features students used in their classroom presentations, including the self-mention and engagement markers used to present information to multiple audiences and verbal frame markers used to transition between phases of their presentations.

Gibbons (2007) also identified and illustrated what students are doing when they engage in highly demanding intellectual practices, drawing on her research in seventh-grade English, science, and history classrooms with linguistically and culturally diverse students. Key practices included engaging students with the ideas and concepts of the discipline, engaging them in transforming what they learned into a different form or presenting it to a different audience, helping them move between concrete and abstract knowledge, engaging in substantive conversation about what they were learning, making connections between the spoken and written practices and the semiotic artifacts of the discipline, and problematizing knowledge and questioning accepted wisdom. Based on her extensive ethnographic work in science classrooms with language learners (e.g., Gibbons, 2006a), Gibbons (2006b) offered three principles for curriculum planning: use of authentic curriculum contexts, assignment of tasks that are intellectually and cognitively challenging, and provision of support through scaffolding. She urged that teachers analyze the language demands of each topic, select focus language on this basis, and design activities to teach the focus language. Drawing on SFL, she illustrated how this is done by focusing first on the larger context: moving from the text to specific language features, from meaning in context to language form, and from what is known to what is new.

CONCLUSIONS

Our research review suggests that effective instruction for L2 students at the secondary level takes shape along three dimensions—it is grounded in teachers' understanding of how language functions in a particular content area; supported by macro-level curricular planning; and implemented through effective micro-level, moment-to-moment interactions during challenging curricular tasks. Taking into account the combined implications of the studies discussed in this article, we can conclude that effective teachers of ELLs at the secondary level draw on knowledge about how language is used to achieve the specific purposes of discourse in their disciplines to integrate language and content in their teaching, have a long-term plan for development of academic language proficiency over time, have high expectations for their students, build bridges between students' prior knowledge and experience and what is being learned, scaffold students' moves from simple to complex understanding and expression of ideas, emphasize higher order thinking, and promote the use of related academic language through meaningful tasks that engage students in content and language learning simultaneously.

We are still far from this goal, as secondary-level teacher preparation seldom helps teachers learn about the linguistic challenges of their content areas. Content-area teachers need to understand the language demands of the genres of their subject and learn to analyze the texts, assignments, and assessments they plan to use with this understanding in mind. They also need to develop the metalanguage that enables them to discuss language features with their students. In implementing this knowledge and metalanguage, they need to offer their L2 students a challenging and motivating curriculum. This may mean modifying prepackaged curricula in light of the needs of a particular group of students without reducing the cognitive demand of the curriculum. As teachers consider the developmental trajectories of their students' learning over time, their planning should take into account not only individual lessons but also how a sequence of lessons can be constructed to support the meeting of specific language and content goals over time. Teachers need strategies for involving and engaging students in protracted, high-level written and oral exchanges with their instructors as well as their peers. These strategies should include specific discussion about language itself and the development of metalinguistic awareness about the demands of the subject area, as the teacher uses a variety of scaffolding techniques to build on students' prior knowledge and bridge between everyday and academic language (e.g., see Walqui, 2006). L2 students in English-speaking contexts are often learning in mainstream subject-area classrooms where many of their peers also need to develop academic registers, and so preparing teachers to focus on language can benefit not only these learners but also other students who struggle to engage with the specialized content of secondary school subjects. Despite the potential for both ELLs and non-ELLs to benefit from teachers' increased attention to discipline-specific academic language demands, however, we caution against reducing these recommendations to a matter of "just good teaching" (de Jong & Harper, 2005, p. 102).

Although many mainstream content-area teachers do not see themselves as language teachers, at the secondary level it is they who are likely to have the deepest content-area knowledge and who are therefore best positioned to support students' academic language development. Unfortunately, teacher education programs currently seldom prepare teachers to assume that role, and in-service teachers are unlikely to receive ongoing support for working with L2 learners at the secondary level (Lucas & Grinberg, 2008; Maxwell-Jolly, Gándara, & Méndez Benavídez, 2007). Without adequate preparation, teachers may be limited to instruction in vocabulary or decontextualized language features. Teachers need strategies embedded in a rich curricular context in order to adequately address the complexities of language learning and teaching in secondary school subjects; vocabulary instruction, while necessary for academic language development, does not provide enough support for learning in the secondary content areas (Bruna, Vann, & Escudero, 2007; Zwiers, 2007). Applied linguists can make major contributions by identifying the particular challenges of different secondary subject areas and developing support for teachers to help students make sense of what they read and help them participate in the spoken and written language tasks that they are asked to do.

Of course, classroom instruction is only one aspect of the experience of secondary school students. Various reports suggest that language minority students are often provided with inferior academic opportunities and are positioned as marginal participants in secondary schools (Callahan, 2005; Coulter & Smith, 2006; Haneda, 2008; Reeves, 2006), and that addressing their instructional needs calls for systemwide efforts. It also calls for understanding the complexity of the designation *English language learner* and addressing the identity issues that are even more complex for these students than for the average adolescent (Harklau, 2007).

More research in a range of contexts is needed to inform these issues. In particular, we call for increased dialogue between applied linguists and education researchers. Work being done by the educational research community on adolescent literacy and disciplinary literacy teaching (see, e.g., Fagella-Luby, Ware, & Capozzoli, 2009; Moje & Speyer, 2008) has the potential to inform and enhance research on how best to serve adolescent ELLs. Such dialogue can support a comprehensive approach to these students, who, despite their additional language-based educational needs, are still shaped and inspired by the same forces affecting their native-speaking peers.

NOTES

1 Immigrant students with interrupted schooling and low levels of proficiency in the new language face particular challenges, but little research has focused on that population (but see Francis et al., 2006).

2 We identified one report on a vocabulary intervention using experimental methods (Townsend & Collins, 2009) and one report on a sentence-combining intervention with a small group of students (Shin, 2009).

ANNOTATED BIBLIOGRAPHY

Johns, A. M., & Snow, M. A. (2006). Editorial: Introduction to special issue: Academic English in secondary schools. *Journal of English for Academic Purposes, 5*, 251–253.

Johns and Snow introduced a special issue of the journal that includes many of the articles cited in this chapter. The volume represents a range of disciplinary contexts and approaches to academic language development in secondary classrooms.

Fagella-Luby, M., Ware, S., & Capozzoli, A. (2009). Adolescent literacy—Reviewing adolescent literacy reports: Key components and critical questions. *Journal of Literacy Research, 41,* 453–475.

Fagella-Luby et al. reviewed and synthesized a number of recent reports on adolescent literacy. The review provides an overview of recommendations for improving literacy for all adolescent learners by identifying key components and questions common among the reports. This offers an introduction to educational research of interest to applied linguists.

Hammond, J. (2008). Challenging pedagogies: Engaging ESL students in intellectual quality. *Australian Journal of Language and Literacy, 31,* 101–105.

Hammond introduced a thematic issue on the challenges and opportunities that linguistically, culturally, and socioeconomically diverse students and their teachers face, mainly focused on middle school contexts. The articles describe innovations that emphasize the importance of intellectual challenge for all students.

REFERENCES

Achugar, M., Schleppegrell, M. J., & Oteíza, T. (2007). Engaging teachers in language analysis: A functional linguistics approach to reflective literacy. *English Teaching Practice and Critique, 6,* 8–24.

Aguirre-Muñoz, Z., Park, J.-E., Amabisca, A., & Boscardin, C. K. (2008). Developing teacher capacity for serving ELLs' writing instructional needs: A case for SFL. *Bilingual Research Journal, 31,* 295–322.

Anstrom, K., DiCerbo, P., Butler, F., Katz, A., Millet, J., & Rivera, C. (2010). *A review of the literature on academic language: Implications for K–12 English language learners.* Arlington, VA: George Washington University Center for Equity and Excellence in Education.

Arkoudis, S. (2006). Negotiating the rough ground between ESL and mainstream teachers. *International Journal of Bilingual Education & Bilingualism, 9,* 415–433.

Bruna, K. R., Vann, R., & Escudero, M. P. (2007). What's language got to do with it? A case study of academic language instruction in a high school "English Learner Science" class. *Journal of English for Academic Purposes, 6,* 36–54.

Bunch, G. (2006). "Academic English" in the 7th grade: Broadening the lens, expanding access. *Journal of English for Academic Purposes, 5,* 284–301.

Bunch, G. (2009). "Going up there": Challenges and opportunities for language minority students during a mainstream classroom speech event. *Linguistics and Education, 20,* 81–108.

Callahan, R. (2005). Tracking and high school English learners: Limiting opportunity to learn. *American Educational Research Journal, 42,* 305–328.

Christie, F., & Derewianka, B. (2008). *School discourse: Learning to write across the years of schooling.* London, UK: Continuum.

Coulter, C., & Smith, M. L. (2006). English language learners in a comprehensive high school. *Bilingual Research Journal, 30,* 309–335.

Cumming, A. (2008). Research for and within literacy instruction in secondary schools. *Curriculum Inquiry, 38,* 401–416.

Cummins, J., & Man, E. Y.-F. (2007). Academic language: What is it and how do we acquire it? In J. Cummins & C. Davison (Eds.), *International handbook of English language teaching* (vol. 2, pp. 797–810). New York, NY: Springer.

Dalton-Puffer, C. (2011). Content and language integrated learning: From practice to principles? *Annual Review of Applied Linguistics, 31,* this volume.

de Jong, E. J., & Harper, C. A. (2005). Preparing mainstream teachers for English-language learners: Is being a good teacher good enough? *Teacher Education Quarterly, 32,* 101–124.

Duff, P. A. (2005). ESL in secondary schools: Programs, problematics, and possibilities. In E. Hinkel (Ed.), *Handbook of research in second language teaching and learning* (pp. 45–63). Mahwah, NJ: Erlbaum.

Echevarria, J., Vogt, M. E., & Short, D. J. (2000). *Making content comprehensible for English language learners: The SIOP model.* Newton, MA: Allyn & Bacon.

Echevarria, J., Vogt, M. E., & Short, D. J. (2007). *Sheltered Instruction Observation Protocol (SIOP)* (3rd ed.). Boston, MA: Pearson Education.

Echevarria, J., Short, D. J., & Powers, K. (2006). School reform and standards-based education: A model for English language learners. *Journal of Educational Research, 99,* 195–210.

Fagella-Luby, M., Ware, S., & Capozzoli, A. (2009). Adolescent literacy—Reviewing adolescent literacy reports: Key components and critical questions. *Journal of Literacy Research, 41,* 453–475.

Fang, Z., & Schleppegrell, M. J. (2008). *Reading in secondary content areas: A language-based pedagogy.* Ann Arbor: University of Michigan Press.

Fang, Z., & Schleppegrell, M. J. (2010). Disciplinary literacies across content areas: Supporting secondary reading through functional language analysis. *Journal of Adolescent & Adult Literacy*, *53*, 587–597.

Francis, D. J., Rivera, M., Lesaux, N., Kieffer, M., & Rivera, H. (2006). *Practical guidelines for the education of English language learners: Research-based recommendations for serving adolescent newcomers*. Houston, TX: Center on Instruction, University of Houston.

Gibbons, P. (2006a). *Bridging discourses in the ESL classroom: Students, teachers, and researchers*. London, UK: Continuum.

Gibbons, P. (2006b). Steps for planning and integrated program for ESL learners in mainstream classes. In P. McKay (Ed.), *Planning and teaching creatively within a required curriculum for school-age learners* (pp. 215–233). Alexandria, VA: TESOL.

Gibbons, P. (2007). Mediating academic language learning through classroom discourse. In J. Cummins & C. Davidson (Eds.), *International handbook of English language teaching* (pp. 701–718). New York, NY: Springer.

Goldenberg, C., & Coleman, R. (2010). *Promoting academic achievement among English learners: A guide to the research*. Thousand Oaks, CA: Corwin.

Halliday, M. A. K., & Matthiessen, C. (2004). *An introduction to functional grammar* (3rd ed.). London, UK: Arnold.

Hammond, J. (2006). High challenge, high support: Integrating language and content instruction for diverse learners in an English literature classroom. *Journal of English for Academic Purposes*, *5*, 269–283.

Hammond, J. (2008). Challenging pedagogies: Engaging ESL students in intellectual quality. *Australian Journal of Language and Literacy*, *31*, 101–105.

Haneda, M. (2008). Contexts for learning: English language learners in a US middle school. *International Journal of Bilingual Education & Bilingualism*, *11*, 57–74.

Harklau, L. (2007). The adolescent English language learner: Identities lost and found. In J. Cummins & C. Davison (Eds.), *International handbook of English language teaching* (vol. 2, pp. 639–653). New York, NY: Springer.

Jiménez, R. T., & Teague, B. L. (2009). Language, literacy, and content: Adolescent English language learners. In L. M. Morrow, R. Rueda, D. Lapp, & E. W. Gordon, (Eds.), *Handbook of research on literacy and diversity* (pp. 114–134). New York, NY: Guilford Press.

Johns, A. M., & Snow, M. A. (2006). Editorial: Introduction to special issue: Academic English in secondary schools. *Journal of English for Academic Purposes*, *5*, 251–253.

Kramer-Dahl, A., Teo, P., & Chia, A. (2007). Supporting knowledge construction and literate talk in secondary social studies. *Linguistics and Education*, *18*, 167–199.

Lindholm-Leary, K., & Borsato, G. (2006). Academic achievement. In F. Genesee, K. Lindholm-Leary, W. M. Saunders, & D. Christian (Eds.), *Educating English language learners: A synthesis of research evidence* (pp. 176–222). New York, NY: Cambridge

University Press.

Lucas, T., & Grinberg, J. (2008). Responding to the linguistic reality of mainstream classrooms: Preparing all teachers to teach English learners. In M. Cochran-Smith, S. Feiman-Nemser, D. J. McIntyre, & K. E. Demers (Eds.), *Handbook of research on teacher education: Enduring questions in changing contexts* (pp. 606–636). New York, NY: Routledge.

Maxwell-Jolly, J., Gándara, P., & Méndez Benavídez, L. (2007). *Promoting academic literacy among secondary English language learners: A synthesis of research and practice*. Davis: University of California, Linguistic Minority Research Institute.

Meltzer, J., & Hamann, E. T. (2005). *Meeting the literacy development needs of adolescent English language learners through content area learning, part two: Focus on classroom teaching and learning strategies*. Providence, RI: Northeast and Islands Regional Educational Laboratory (LAB) at Brown University.

Mohan, B. A. (1986). *Language and content*. Reading, MA: Addison-Wesley.

Mohan, B. A., & Slater, T. (2006). Examining the theory/practice relation in high school science register: A functional linguistic perspective. *Journal of English for Academic Purposes, 5*, 302–316.

Moje, E. B., & Speyer, J. (2008). The reality of challenging texts in high school science and social studies: How teachers can mediate comprehension. In K. A. Hinchman & H. K. Sheridan-Thomas (Eds.), *Best practices in adolescent literacy instruction* (pp. 185–211). New York, NY: Guilford Press.

Paesani, K. (2011). Research in language-literature instruction: Meeting the call for change? *Annual Review of Applied Linguistics, 31*, this volume.

Reeves, J. (2006). Secondary teacher attitudes toward including English-language learners in mainstream classrooms. *Journal of Educational Research, 99*, 131–142.

Roessingh, H. (2004). Effective high-school ESL programs: A synthesis and meta-analysis. *Canadian Modern Language Review, 60*, 611–636.

Schleppegrell, M. (2004). *The language of schooling*. Mahwah, NJ: Erlbaum.

Schleppegrell, M. J. (2011). Supporting disciplinary learning through language analysis: Developing historical literacy. In F. Christie & K. Maton (Eds.), *Disciplinarity: Functional linguistic and sociological perspectives*. London, UK: Continuum.

Schleppegrell, M., & de Oliveira, L. C. (2006). An integrated language and content approach for history teachers. *Journal of English for Academic Purposes, 5*, 254–268.

Schleppegrell, M. J., Greer, S., & Taylor, S. (2008). Literacy in history: Language and meaning. *Australian Journal of Language and Literacy, 31*, 174–187.

Shin, S. (2009). Negotiating grammatical choices: Academic language learning by secondary ESL students. *System, 37*, 391–402.

Short, D. J., & Fitzsimmons, S. (2007). *Double the work: Challenges and solutions to acquiring language and academic literacy for adolescent English language learners—A report to Carnegie Corporation of New York.* Washington, DC: Alliance for Excellent Education.

Snow, C. E., & Uccelli, P. (2009). The challenge of academic language. In D. R. Olson & N. Torrance (Eds.), *The Cambridge handbook of literacy* (pp. 112–133). New York, NY: Cambridge University Press.

Spycher, P. (2007). Academic writing of adolescent English learners: Learning to use "although." *Journal of Second Language Writing, 16,* 238–254.

Stoller, F. (2004). Content-based instruction: Perspectives on curriculum planning. *Annual Review of Applied Linguistics, 24,* 261–283.

Téllez, K., & Waxman, H. C. (2006). A meta-synthesis of qualitative research on effective teaching practices for English learners. In J. M. Norris & L. Ortega (Eds.), *Synthesizing research on language learning and teaching* (pp. 245–277). Amsterdam, The Netherlands: John Benjamins.

Townsend, D., & Collins, P. (2009). Academic vocabulary and middle school English learners: An intervention study. *Reading and Writing: An Interdisciplinary Journal, 22,* 993–1019.

Unsworth, L. (Ed.). (2000). *Researching language in schools and communities: Functional linguistic perspectives.* London, UK: Cassell.

Walqui, A. (2006). Scaffolding instruction for English language learners: A conceptual framework. *International Journal of Bilingual Education and Bilingualism, 9,* 159–180.

Zwiers, J. (2006). Integrating academic language, thinking, and content: Learning scaffolds for non-native speakers in the middle grades. *Journal of English for Academic Purposes, 5,* 317–332.

Zwiers, J. (2007). Teacher practices and perspectives for developing academic language. *International Journal of Applied Linguistics, 17,* 93–116.

Current Trends in Online Language Learning

Robert J. Blake

Online language learning (OLL) can take place in Web-facilitated, hybrid, or fully virtual classes. These formats are beginning to attract serious attention from the language profession and, in particular, the field of computer-assisted language learning (CALL). This article traces recent studies of online learning and then focuses in on its application to language learning through tutorial CALL, social computing, and games for language learning. I strive to show that tutorial CALL and computer-mediated communication can complement each other in the service of modern language instruction, along with the inclusion of language games. Although assessment studies of OLL remain sparse, the evidence is steadily mounting that shows that these new formats can provide learning environments conducive to successful second language development when properly integrated into the curriculum.

As a language learning environment, online instruction is just beginning to enjoy the same popularity already experienced within other disciplines for some time now (Goodfellow & Lamy, 2009; Lamy & Hampel, 2007; Meskill & Anthony, 2010). The term *online language learning* (OLL) can refer to a number of learning arrangements: a Web-facilitated class, a blended or hybrid course, or a fully virtual or online course. These delivery formats, along with the mix of the technological tools employed therein, overlap in many cases with the differences in nomenclature having more to do with the percentage of content that is delivered online (for a detailed classification, see Kraemer, 2008). Fully online language courses might have students never meeting with each other in a face-to-face context. To add to the confusion, the term *distance learning* has also been used to refer to some of these online learning environments as well as to the mix of more traditional methods such as correspondence courses and teleconferencing, teaching techniques long employed in the U.S. educational system. In this study, I focus on online language courses as previously defined here—Web-facilitated, hybrid, or totally virtual—although these three formats can also incorporate desktop videoconferencing or audioconferencing as well, as will be examined more fully.

Table 1. Postsecondary Total and Online Enrollments for Fall 2002 Through Fall 2008 (*Adapted from Allen & Seaman, 2010*)

Fall Term	Total Enrollment	Annual Growth Rate Total Enrollment	Students Taking at Least One Online Course	Annual Growth Rate Online Enrollment	Online Enrollment as a Percent of Total Enrollment
Fall 2002	16,611,710	NA	1,602,970	NA	9.6%
Fall 2003	16,911,481	1.8%	1,971,3976	23.0%	11.7%
Fall 2004	17,272,043	2.1%	2,329,783	18.2%	13.5%
Fall 2005	17,487,481	1.2%	3,180,050	36.5%	18.2%
Fall 2006	17,758,872	1.6%	3,488,381	9.7%	19.6%
Fall 2007	17,975,830	1.2%	3,938,111	12.0%	21.9%
Fall 2008	18,199,920	1.2%	4,606,353	16.9%	25.3%

Recent trends in online learning are sparking a lively debate in educational circles. In the period from 2002 to 2008, postsecondary online course enrollments reached 4.6 million, mostly as a result of undergraduate offerings, which were 82% of the total online offerings (Allen & Seaman, 2010). The growth rate for online courses averaged 19% over this last decade, while total enrollments have only grown by 1.5%; these trends in favor of online learning show no signs of abating. As can be seen in Table 1, online enrollments in 2008 represented approximately a quarter of the U.S. total postsecondary fall enrollment figures, mostly as a result of courses offered by large, public universities and junior colleges.

PREVIOUS STUDIES ON EFFICACY OF ONLINE LEARNING

Some educators and parents worry that these trends in increased online learning will degrade educational quality, represented for many by the gold standard of traditional face-to-face instruction (e.g., see concerns expressed in the report, "Remote and Online Learning in the University of California System," 2010; also Sanders, 2006). Ironically, few people stop to reflect on the fact that traditional classroom practices can vary widely with respect to techniques, class sizes, individual student attention, and teacher talents in ways that can often tarnish the privileged status normally accorded to the face-to-face classroom experience. By the same token, online courses also differ wildly not only in terms of their format but also in terms of their use of particular technological tools and pedagogies, making comparisons with other online courses or other traditional courses extremely difficult (with reference to language comparisons, see discussion in Blake, Wilson, Pardo Ballester, & Cetto, 2008). Duly noting these research problems, the Department of Education recently engaged SRI International to do a meta-analysis of the reported results concerning online learning (U.S. Department of Education, 2009). Surprisingly, researchers for this meta-study found almost no studies that rigorously compared online learning with face-to-face instruction at the K–12 level, but there did exist a basis of comparison with postsecondary courses. The authors concentrated on post-secondary Web-based courses ($N = 51$ effect sizes drawn from 46 separate studies) and eliminated from consideration other video- or audio-based courses and stand-alone computer materials. The findings showed that students who took all or part of their classes online performed better than those in traditional face-to-face learning environments ($p < .01$); furthermore, students involved in blended/hybrid learning environments did better than those in purely online courses ($p < .001$). The authors concluded that online learning offered a modest advantage over traditional classroom instruction, but the results appeared to be highly sensitive to the amount of time on task and did not directly address the issue of OLL. Not surprisingly, learners taking online courses who spent more time working on their own did better than those in a face-to-face situation (with respect to language study only, see the online Iowa State database compiled by Grgurovic, 2007).

  Perhaps this last factor alone constitutes the most important value added with respect to online learning: The medium stimulates students to spend more time engaged with the second language (L2) materials, which ultimately promotes greater learning. The U.S. Department of Education report (2009) stated, "one should note that online learning is much more conducive to the expansion of learning time than is face-to-face instruction" (p. xvii).

With reference to OLL and L2 learning, again few comparative studies exist (for a brief review, see Blake, 2009; Blake et al., 2008; Sanders, 2005), despite the clear progress made in the area of materials creation and course design within the field of computer-assisted language learning (CALL). With respect to CALL design, two areas have flourished: tutorial CALL and social computing or computer-mediated communication (CMC). Only recently have OLL practitioners begun to think in terms of integrating both tutorial CALL and CMC together. Some CALL researchers have advocated the mixing of these two types of materials through a computer gaming approach to language learning. In what follows, each of these themes will be reviewed separately: tutorial CALL, social computing CALL, and CALL gaming.

TUTORIAL CALL

Exercises for Grammar, Vocabulary, Pronunciation, and Beyond

The name *tutorial CALL* is very often associated with grammar exercises of the mechanical type or what people have often referred to in pejorative terms as *drill-and-kill*. These exercises offer language students a relatively low level of interactivity and a limited ability to construct meaning independently (Blake, 2009; Garrett, 1991). Nevertheless, mechanical grammar exercises also have a place in the L2 curriculum (Hubbard & Bradin Siskin, 2004), especially when one contemplates the importance of time on task, as has already been discussed here in connection with the U.S. Department of Education meta-analysis report (2009). Peters, Weinberg, and Sarma (2009) have shown in their study of students learning languages in five Canadian universities that the students themselves appreciated the more individually oriented tutorial CALL approach over the social computing activities that involve newer Web 2.0 technologies such as blogs, wikis, and online chatting (Warschauer & Grimes, 2007).

Fortunately, language instructors now have at their disposal a plethora of tools to help them create or customize these types of exercises for online postings, such as *Quia* (http://www.quia.com/) and *Hot Potatoes* (http://hotpot.uvic.ca/), to name only a few. Commercial publishers for the more commonly taught languages are increasingly catering to market demands by providing extensive online grammar exercises as part of their regular textbook packages.

Although grammar may continue to be the principal teaching focus for many language instructors, L2 researchers have shown that lexical issues are just as important, if not more so, when it comes to reading and listening comprehension, especially as students progress beyond the novice level of about 1,000 to 2,000 words (Chun 2006; Cobb, 2007; Nation, 2001; Nation & Waring, 1997). From the students' perspective, then, developing an adequate L2 lexicon will not happen without some form of explicit instruction or graded reading program (Cobb, 2008). This viewpoint contradicts Krashen's (1989) insistence that incidental vocabulary learning from extensive amounts of reading will suffice. As explained by Cobb (2007), the computer can play a pivotal role in L2 lexical acquisition by tracking students' lexical problems and providing them with multiple exposures to new words through graded texts, glossing, or explicit instruction:

> The key problems of learning through extensive reading are clear. Corpus analysis shows that words beyond the 2,000 most frequent are unlikely to be encountered in natural reading in sufficient numbers for consistent learning to occur. Lexical profile analysis shows that the amount of new vocabulary in natural texts is at odds with both the lexical level and learning capacity of most learners. Text comparison analysis further shows that the rate of new word introduction in a text designed for native speakers is far more than most L2 learners will be able to cope with. And yet these same tools can also be employed positively to multiply learning opportunities, whether by facilitating the adaptation of texts that learners can read and learn from, or by habilitating unadapted texts through external resourcing. (Cobb, 2007, p. 60)

CALL researchers have long been convinced that multimedia word glosses make a difference in L2 lexical growth, as can be seen in Chun's (2006) excellent overview of previous research on this topic. Chun is careful to distinguish between lexical knowledge and reading comprehension, the latter being affected by many additional factors. She asserts that lexical knowledge, rather than grammatical knowledge, is significantly related to both reading and listening comprehension.

The research shows that explicit instruction, including tutorial CALL (see Lafford, Lafford, & Sykes, 2007; Ranalli, 2009), has a significant impact on vocabulary acquisition, but reading comprehension is more complicated and subject to a number of additional factors, including prior or background knowledge of the topic at hand. For example, Fukkink, Hulstijin, and Simis (2005) have demonstrated that L2 learners retrieve unfamiliar words faster and with less variation when they are dealing with words they have trained on. In the same vein, Yanguas (2009) found that students with access to multimedia glosses (i.e. text plus picture) outperformed all other groups, including those with only textual glosses, on measures testing reading comprehension. (For a review of work done on listening or video comprehension and with bimodal input, i.e., subtitles in the target language, see Sydorenko, 2010).

With respect to commercial applications and glossing, LeLoup and Ponterio (2005) reviewed two free Internet software programs, *WordChamp* and *UltraLingua*, which allow users to control their word searches while reading on the Web for a large number of languages. The user rolls the cursor over a word on the Web or any textual passage pasted into their special text field in order to look up the words and, in most cases, hear them pronounced correctly. *WordChamp* allows students to assemble a list of difficult words in flashcard fashion in order to continue practicing them. An interesting line for the design of future tools would be to connect the learner not only with lexical entries but also with corpora data that offer collocation information, too.

In a similar fashion to the benefits cited earlier for vocabulary growth, computer programs that focus on improving L2 pronunciation have shown some promise. Cucchiarini, Neri, & Strik (2008) examined the effectiveness of using an automatic speech recognition (ASR) system to give feedback on L2 Dutch pronunciation. Thirty immigrants studying Dutch were assigned to three groups that had access to (a) an ASR-based system for pronunciation training with automatic feedback, (b) an ASR-based system without feedback, or (c) no computer-assisted pronunciation training whatsoever. According to the human experts who evaluated overall segmental quality, the first group, which received ASR-based feedback, posted the largest mean improvement, although overall the means for these three groups did not differ significantly. The group receiving ASR-based feedback showed a significantly larger improvement than the no-feedback group in terms of the segmental quality of the problematic phonemes targeted.

Many commercially available language programs tend to include a section dedicated to pronunciation along with exercises, with the program *Tell Me More* from Auralog being one of the leading contenders because of its ASR-based feedback (see review by Lafford, 2004). This program is organized into 12 lessons, each with an abundant array of activities and exercises that deal with vocabulary development and pronunciation that can be undertaken in three modes: guided, free-to-roam, and dynamic (which promotes or demotes the students according to their progress). The program's oral workshop provides waveforms and pitch contours for both words and sentences based on the correct native speaker forms that serve as a basis of comparison for the learner's own speech production. In the phonetics exercises, the program offers learners not only waveforms and pitch curves but also a 3-D animation of the correct pronunciation that focuses on the action of the lips and tongue. Both the "Picture-Word Association" and "Word Order" exercises both employ the Auralog ASR-tool where students can compare their pronunciation contours with those of native speakers.

CALL programs that tackle teaching pragmatics are relatively rare, with the notable exception being the work of Sykes and Cohen (2009) and Sykes (2009). These researchers have created CALL materials for teaching Spanish pragmatics on the Web called *Dancing with Words* (http: //www.carla.umn.edu/speechacts/sp_pragmatics/home.html). The Web site is organized by pragmatic functions such as expressions of gratitude, leave-takings, requests, apologies, invitations, advice, suggestions, complaints, and reprimands. Each topic provides a detailed pragmatic explanation, a possible situation, video illustrations that provide a correct model, and self-correcting activities. The site is designed with both teachers and students in mind.

They have also collaborated to produce a synthetic immersive learning environment called *Croquelandia* to teach pragmatics that will be examined in the next section on games. However, progress in pragmatic knowledge for students using these materials appears to have been rather modest by the authors' own admission (Cohen & Sykes, 2010). Clearly, this will remain an active and promising area for future CALL research.

Intelligent CALL (iCALL)

Another avenue within tutorial CALL employs the use of natural language processing and a modicum of artificial intelligence in order to enhance the type of feedback provided to the student working alone online (Nerbonne, 2003). This approach is known as intelligent CALL, or iCALL, because it seeks to individualize instruction by providing a system of responses and interactions based on an extensive record of each user's exchanges with the tutorial CALL system (Heift, 2010a). iCALL systems should be designed to anticipate students' mistakes, offer helpful suggestions, and keep track of their behavior while using the program. Accordingly, one of the key features of an iCALL system resides in the detailed and individualized level of feedback that the program offers the student, along with keeping track of each student's most common mistakes.

To date, only three iCALL systems have been fully implemented with similar types of activities: *E-Tutor* for German, described earlier (Heift, 2010a); *Tagarela* for Portuguese (Amaral & Meurers, 2009); and *Robo-Sensei* for Japanese (Nagata, 2010). One of the advantages of an iCALL approach to language learning is that the increased level of feedback significantly raises the students' grammatical awareness, sometimes by providing preemptive feedback (Ellis, Basturkmen, & Loewen, 2001).

In the specific case of *E-Tutor* (Heift, 2010a), the program logs have compiled a learner corpus over 5 years that has tracked over 5,000 students. Each of the 15 chapters includes 70 to 80 individual exercises that practice grammar, vocabulary, listening and reading comprehension, and cultural knowledge. Sentence building is one of *E-Tutor's* trademark activities because of the extensive feedback offered to each student response. Not only can students access and compare their own interlanguage with that of their peers, but instructors can also use these logs to guide the design of the L2 curriculum with an increased sensitivity to what constitutes difficulty for the L2 learner. Such an L2 learning corpus has allowed Heift (2010a, 2010b) to discover that the more specific the feedback— and, possibly, the easier it is to correct an error—the more likely students are to engage in the error-correction process by showing an increase in learner uptake. Clearly, the iCALL approach holds great promise for the CALL field, but the time it takes to develop such a system in not significant by any means.

SOCIAL COMPUTING CALL

Textual-Based Chat, Asynchronous and Synchronous CMC

For several decades now (see Garrett, 1991), CALL researchers have joined other educators in demanding a more learner-centered classroom where students can exercise their own agency. Without a doubt, social computing and other forms of CMC constitute the single most influential technological response to this call for more learner control, because CMC gives both the instructors and students the ability to direct the conversational flow (Chapelle, 2008; Kern & Warschauer, 2000). Not all researchers regard the terms *CMC* and *social computing* as synonymous, because the latter implies the idea of social networks and a greater communicative depth (Brown & Adler, 2008; Warschauer & Grimes, 2007).

CMC, however, is a broad term that could refer to asynchronous CMC (ACMC) using e-mails, forums, blogs, wikis, or synchronous CMC (SCMC) such as instant messenger programs or Skype, with or without voice or video (for a review of CMC tools, see Lafford & Lafford, 2005). Some CMC formats, such as *Wave* (soon to be abandoned by Google), are hard to categorize, but still belong somewhere in the mix of social computing tools. *Chat* is another slippery term that is often used to refer to just textual exchanges, but it also is used to refer to more elaborate audio and video exchanges such as with Skype. This array of tools has made social computing providers such as Facebook, MySpace, and LinkedIn an integral part of our society, especially among our youth, by facilitating the growth of social networks via the computer. A Wikipedia search for social networking sites yields a staggering list of servers aimed at all age groups and interests.

With respect to L2 instruction, CMC allows instructors and learners to engage in meaningful negotiations with all of the positive benefits associated with scaffolding that have been reported in the literature for face-to-face exchanges (Smith, 2009). Typically, foreign language teachers have set up tasks that their students accomplish by helping each other in pairs through CMC chat, with or without sound or video. As the participants encounter linguistic structures that they fail to understand, they may request the assistance of their partner in order to continue working on a common solution to the assigned task. This type of CMC-assisted curriculum has been employed with native speakers and learners, as well as peer groups of learners, with proven benefits for all parties concerned. Some teachers have even used Facebook to stimulate their students to interact with each other, but not without awakening certain concerns about mixing personal networks with more academic ones. But as mentioned earlier, there are many CMC tools to choose from that do not invade the more personal realm of social networking while still allowing teachers to take advantage of the power of social computing.

RESEARCH ON CMC USE AND EFFECTIVENESS

Recently, the CALL field has witnessed a veritable explosion in the number of studies examining the use and effectiveness of CMC (e.g., Hample & Hauck, 2004; Lomicka & Lord, 2009; Meskill, 2009). Researchers have analyzed the use of CMC from either an interactionist (Smith, 2009) or sociocultural perspective (Belz & Thorne, 2006; Lomicka, 2006). Both approaches have their roots in Vygotsky's (1962) notions of scaffolding or, to be more precise, the zone of proximal development, which refer to the difference between what learners can do with or without assistance.

The interactionist approach has focused more on how L2 learners negotiate meaning with their peers or with more expert interlocutors (i.e., advanced learners or native speakers) in the course of carrying out meaningful exchanges of information, especially jigsaw tasks. In general, researchers within this paradigm have followed a coding system developed more than 20 years ago by Varonis and Gass (1985) that labels the scaffolding that occurs as part of the negotiations of meaning according to the following sequence: <trigger→indicator→response →reaction to the response>. Earlier CMC interactionist studies found that negotiations of meaning occurred in ACMC in ways similar to those exhibited in face-to-face exchanges and with the same learning outcomes (Blake 2000; de la Fuente, 2003; Pellettieri, 2000; Smith, 2003; Sotillo, 2000). More recently, Yanguas (2010) has provided data to support the notion that SCMC with video capabilities also allows students to carry out negotiations of meaning with the same success as students working in a face-to-face format. Smith (2009), however, has urged researchers to improve their methodology by supplementing text logs with video recordings in order to capture the dynamics of these online exchanges, especially with an eye to revealing students' self-initiated repairs. Sauro (2009) reported that metalinguistic feedback given during CMC session had a positive effect on grammatical accuracy, at least in the short run—results that concur with the findings from Heift's (2010b) longitudinal study (see also Lee [2007] for a more sociocultural approach).

Finally, Sauro's (2008) case study of dyad online communication showed how one student preferred to use textual chat as opposed to voice chat as a means of regaining control of the conversational dynamics as a way to equalize the power relationships in play during the completion of the task. Clearly, interactionist CMC studies still have more to say to the CALL field in the future, especially with respect to tracking the effect of feedback and charting the preferred CMC tools and their respective affordances.

Researchers using sociocultural theory (SCT) have focused on CMC more by looking at how L2 learners participate in new communities of practice—with different levels of success in using the target language and gaining an understanding of the new culture. In many cases, the central issue within SCT deals with the construction of an emerging L2 identity within a learning environment that provides interpersonal and interactive scaffolding (Kramsch, 2009). Some instructors use telecollaborations or teleconferenced tandem learning with students from different countries who are learning each other's language and culture (Darhower, 2007; O'Dowd, 2006; Ware & Kramsch, 2005). The Massachusetts Institute of Technology project *Cultura* (Furstenberg, Levet, English, & Maillet, 2001) is perhaps the most widely known application of this concept of tandem learning where German, French, or Spanish students from an overseas L2 English class carry out a discussion of cultural topics in conjunction with a corresponding group of American L2 language learners. Students share their opinions on broad cultural issues using their native language to leverage maximum expressiveness and clarity, but then use their counterparts' comments phrased in the target language as classroom linguistic fodder to further their knowledge of new L2 vocabulary and structures. Understandably, these tandem exchanges will sometimes produce a number of cultural misunderstandings, precisely because L2 learners have an incomplete knowledge of the target culture. These types of electronic exchanges provide a forum to expand cultural awareness, provided that the teacher is skillful enough to keep students from becoming bogged down in cultural and ethnic stereotypes (Belz & Thorne, 2006).

Within the same classroom, Oskoz (2009) has explored how learner-learner exchanges can foster the students' linguistic improvement (i.e., microgenetic growth) as a result of the shared performance that takes place while working together on an assigned task. Lee (2007) explored a similar theme with a variety of tasks: jigsaw, spot-the-differences, and open-ended questions.

Both CMC approaches, interactionist and sociocultural, promise a rich line of investigation for the future since social computing shows no sign of losing its importance in our society.

GAMES FOR LANGUAGE LEARNING

The Nature of Language Learning Games

CALL researchers and curriculum developers have recently begun to turn to the gaming environment and the notion of play as a viable way to stimulate learning a second language (Gee, 2007; Peterson, 2006, 2010; Sørensen & Meyer, 2007; Thorne & Black, 2007). Games have the potential to combine the best of what has been developed over recent years in tutorial CALL programs with the attractive affordances provided by social computing (Thorne, 2008). Accordingly, students can work individually but also share their results by working in teams using chat programs to facilitate textual and/or audio exchanges. Usually, the visual representation of the students' personae is mediated through the use of an avatar (Peterson, 2010). Games are always task oriented or focused on play and often are accomplished by working in groups. For instance, in *World of Warcraft* (whether in Spanish, French, English, or another language), online players navigate through a fantasy world of beasts and warriors in pursuit of different quests or battle goals. In *Second Life* (*SL*), people dress in whimsical costumes in order to pursue their own social or academic agendas. In the *Forgotten World*, English learners participate in an online comic-strip drama that develops new linguistic skills while helping to solve the adventure story at hand.

Understandably, then, not all games are the same: There are single-player games, cooperative or two-player games, and massively multiplayer online role-playing games (MMOs). Each has its own rhythms, affordances, and dynamics. Multiple-player games often provide online chat during play, either through textual and/or audio exchanges. Thorne, Black, and Sykes (2009) used a tripartite classification: (a) social virtualities, such as *Second Life or Active Worlds* (Peterson, 2006, 2010); (b) commercial MMOs, such as *World of Warcraft* (Soares, 2010; Thorne, 2003); and (c) made-for-education synthetic immersive environments, such as *Croquelandia* (Sykes, 2011; Sykes, Oskoz, & Thorne, 2008). These different gaming platforms are all part of the virtual environment and gaming spaces that can be harnessed in the service of OLL.

What do games do that might assist students in learning in general (Gee, 2007; Prensky 2000; Squire & Jenkins, 2004; Steinkuehler, 2004, 2006) and in language learning in particular? First and foremost, games allow people to play, and language games are no exception. But games are not entirely free or unstructured play; they are *designed experiences*, as Squire (2006) described them, with defined goals and rules. Learners submit to these goals, but only if they can continue to be playful (Klopfer, Osterweil, & Salen, 2009). Playfulness itself is rather like an act of faith that invests the game with special meaning. Players accept the rules of the designed experience just as people accept the protocols of the live stage, thereby allowing the game to have verisimilitude along with variety. Verisimilitude constitutes the very essence of play—the game has to seem real, feel real, or at least allow us to pretend it is real in order to suspend disbelief.

Role-playing is another way to think about play and verisimilitude; games allow students to explore new identities in a unique state of relative pseudonymity in a persistent or ever-present game world. This quality parallels what language instructors are trying to get their students to do when they learn a second language: Expand into a new bilingual or multilingual self, something akin to what Kramsch (2009) has described with references to the multilingual subject.

The environment of *Second Life* constitutes a good example of a learning environment where play-acting can take place, although *SL* play may not constitute a game in the strict sense of the term. All this play-acting, however, has an effect on language as well. Yee and Bailenson (2007) have called this the "Proteus effect": An individual's verbal behavior is affected by his or her digital self-presentation. In other words, the ways in which students play crucially affect how they learn.

Second, and closely related to the idea of role-playing, games foster agency, allowing players to do something and construct meaning. Games make the users feel that they are being competent and independent problem solvers. Games encourage a participatory culture with different rates and learning paths in response to the gamers' interests and abilities. Within these designed experiences, the participants enjoy the freedom to fail with low risks, experiment, fashion identities, exert varying degrees of effort, and interpret. Gee (2007) concluded that games let players be producers, not just consumers, by promoting agency, control, and ownership. Game players have to think like scientists because they must hypothesize, probe the micro world, get a reaction, reflect on the results, and then probe again in order to get better results.

This last phase of the process really is a reference to practice. Purushotma, Thorne, and Wheatley (2008) insisted that game design must dedicate at least as much thought about failure states as to success states—a trait that shares much in common with the stated goals of iCALL programs. In other words, repetitive practice, with instructive feedback, has to be an integral part of the game design and the learning cycle. Again, this sounds very similar to what students need to go through when learning a second language and should be part of any CALL design.

Language Games, Language Play: Research, Caveats

To date, there have been few experimental studies that examine how L2 learners fare within a virtual learning environment. Soares (2010) has begun the exploration of *World of Warcraft* as a learning platform for Spanish, using an ethnographic approach that looks at her own behavior and that of a friend. Peterson (2010) reported on six studies dealing with a German-language multiuser object-oriented domain (MOO), an English-language *SimCopter*, an ESL-based *SimCity*, a Japanese-based application programmed in *Active Worlds*, an ESL (English as a second language) example realized in *World of Warcraft*, and an Arabic language multimedia tutorial/simulation called *Tactical Iraqi*. Peterson described these six gaming experiences in positive terms, especially because they helped learners increase their target language production, negotiations of meaning, and good learner reception. Ranalli (2008) used *SimCity* to teach vocabulary and included a rigorous set of assessment measures, but only nine students participated. The use of *Croquelandia* as a learning medium has already been discussed here (Thorne et al., 2009), but Cohen and Sykes (2010) reported limited progress in developing strategic competence in L2 pragmatics competence or students working in this medium.

Curriculum development for language learning games is proceeding ahead on many fronts. With their online publication of the *Forgotten World* <http: //www.theforgottenworld.net> and the *Xenos* platform, the Learning Games Network (http://www.learninggamesnetwork.org) has effectively employed games in China to teach ESL online, with an eye to expanding this environment to other languages in the near future. Languagelab.com has an extensive ESL presence in *Second Life* and has also launched *Ciudad Bonita* as a locus for teaching Spanish. Likewise, there are other locations in *SL* where speaking in languages other than English can take place spontaneously (e.g., Barcelona, *SL* coordinates: 169, 68, 23).

Without a doubt, using games for learning languages opens up an exciting new area for future research but its curricular development faces serious caveats. The literature often refers to environments such as *Second Life* as "digital dollhouses," where people just dress up and act out without much significant learning taking place. Likewise, the school-age population is increasingly intolerant of unsophisticated graphics, which increases the possibility that incursions into the gaming curriculum will become an expensive proposition. Pedagogically sound games should be able to exist in black-and-white or color, with more or fewer pixels, but ultimately, the students themselves will have to determine the limits of visual acceptability. Finally, programming games, whether stand-alone or online, such as for an adventure in *Croquelandia* or *SL*, remain a thoroughly time-consuming and, consequently, expensive endeavor for most, leaving the development process accessible only to well-financed commercial ventures that have little stake in the educational curriculum or highly collaborative research groups, which are hard to maintain.

Clearly, more research is needed with respect to using games for OLL, but the fact that $125 million was spent on the first day of the release of *Halo 2* on November 9, 2004, should give our profession reason alone to be interested in games for the purposes of language learning (Squire, 2006). Games have captured the attention of today's students and, to a greater degree, the new generation coming up from the elementary ranks, as has been well documented in the forward-looking recommendations contained in the federal report *Transforming American Education* from the U.S. Department of Education (2010).

CONCLUSIONS

Fortunately, the CALL field has matured beyond the dilemma of choosing either tutorial CALL or social computing, as long as the curricular choices support activities that contribute to L2 learning (Chapelle, 2009). Both types of CALL have their place in the OLL curriculum. No doubt, the role of explicit feedback either through iCALL or CMC will continue to be a major focus for CALL researchers.

The gaming world, as described here, has not been burdened with this traditional dichotomy and simply employs both techniques when warranted in order to maintain student interest. Perhaps therein lies the importance of all activities carried out through OLL: These learning environments and tools help students maintain their interest in learning a language over a long period of time. And like it or not, learning another language to a minimal professional level (i.e., level 3 on the Interagency Linguistic Roundtable scale) is a very time-consuming activity (Blake, 2008).

Given the enthusiasm with which today's young people engage in social networking, it is quite possible that language students feel particularly comfortable connecting digitally with members of the target culture, which would enhance their digital communicative competence at the very least. The same channel might also be leveraged to connect the language classroom with other language-use areas, so that L2 students can become lifelong language learners, rather than dead-end students, at the completion of the language requirement.

ANNOTATED BIBLIOGRAPHY

Allen, I. E., & Seaman, J. (2010). *Learning on demand: Online education in the United States, 2009*. Retrieved from the Babson Survey Research Group Web site: http://www.sloan-c.org/publications/survey/index

This survey-based study of online learning in U.S. institutions of higher education (2,500 colleges and universities) was supported by the Sloan Foundation and constitutes the seventh annual report on this topic. The authors documented the proportional increase in the online delivery of the postsecondary curriculum over the last decade, ending in 2008, when 25% of all course enrollments were carried out through an online format, mostly in large public institutions. Ironically, the acceptance of online learning by faculty and administrators has not changed since first measured in 2002 and only garners the approval of about 33% of faculty. Similarly, training for faculty wishing to adapt their courses in an online format has not significantly increased. When compared to face-to-face learning, more than 50% of those surveyed felt that online courses produced similar learning outcomes. A more negative vision emerged when participants were asked about the quality of complete online degree programs.

Heift, T. (2010a). Developing an intelligent language tutor. *CALICO Journal, 27*, 443–459.

Few iCALL systems have been implemented that benefit students, teachers, and researchers, and *E-Tutor* for the German language is one of them. The author described the *E-Tutor* features in clear, understanding terms so that all parties can evaluate its importance for the language curriculum. That fact that *E-Tutor* has traced the L2 interlanguage of more than 5,000 students over a period of five years establishes its value in both theoretical and practical terms.

Kramsch, C. (2009). *The multilingual subject.* Oxford, UK: Oxford University Press.

This new book from Claire Kramsch will become essential reading for anyone in the language teaching profession because she probed the essence of what it means to learn a second language from the students' perspective (e.g., emotions, memories, and perceptions) or what she called the "subjective dimensions of language." She meditates, in particular, on how language students construct a new L2 identity, drawing on the following sources: published testimonies or memoirs, learner journals, oral interviews, personal essays on what it means to be bilingual, and online chat transcripts. For the CALL field, her reflections in Chapter 6, "The Virtual Self," are particularly insightful.

Thorne, S. L., Black, R., & Sykes, J. (2009). Second language use, socialization, and learning in Internet interest communities and online games. *Modern Language Journal, 93*, 802–821.

Much research has been carried out to determine how technology can be used to teach language in an institutional setting. As a complement to this more formal learning environment, the authors concentrated on how learners use technology to learn languages outside of classroom via fan fiction communities, online games, global social networks, and other virtual realities. In broad terms, the discussion is informed by sociocultural theory and the notion of participating in communities of practice.

REFERENCES

Amaral, L., & Meurers, D. (2009). Little things with big effects: On the identification and interpretation of tokens for error diagnosis in iCALL. *CALICO Journal, 26,* 580–591.

Belz, J., & Thorne, S. L. (Eds.). (2006). *Internet-mediated intercultural foreign language education.* Boston, MA: Thomson Heinle.

Blake, R. (2000). Computer mediated communication: A window on L2 Spanish interlanguage. *Language Learning & Technology, 4,* 120–136.

Blake, R. (2008). *Brave new digital classroom: Technology and foreign language learning.* Washington, DC: Georgetown University Press.

Blake, R. (2009). The use of technology for second language distance learning. *Modern Language Journal, 93,* 822–835.

Blake, R., Wilson, N., Pardo Ballester, C., & Cetto, M. (2008). Measuring oral proficiency in distance, face-to-face, and blended classrooms. *Language Learning and Technology, 12,* 114–127.

Brown, S., & Adler, R. P. (2008). Minds on fire. Open education, the long trail, and learning 2.0. *Educause, 43,* 17–32.

Chapelle, C. A. (2008). Technology and second language acquisition. *Annual Review of Applied Linguistics, 27,* 98–114.

Chapelle, C. A. (2009). The relationship between second language acquisition theory and computer-assisted language learning. *Modern Language Journal, 93,* 741–753.

Chun, D. (2006). CALL technologies for L2 reading. In L. Ducate & N. Arnold (Eds.), *Calling on CALL: From theory and research to new directions in foreign language teaching* (pp. 81–98). CALICO Monograph Series (Vol. 5). San Marcos, TX: CALICO.

Cobb, T. (2007). Computing the vocabulary demands of L2 reading. *Language Learning & Technology, 11,* 38–63.

Cobb, T. (2008). Commentary: Response to McQuillan and Krashen (2008). *Language Learning & Technology, 12,* 109–114.

Cohen, A., & Sykes, J. (2010). Language learner strategies and their effect on speech act performance. *Applied Linguistics Forum, 30.* Retrieved from http: //www.tesol.org//s_tesol/article.asp?vid=142&DID=13196&sid=1&cid=695&iid=13190&nid=2857

Cucchiarini, C., Neri, A., & Strik, H. (2008). The effectiveness of computer-based corrective feedback for improving segmental quality in L2-Dutch. *ReCALL, 20,* 225–243.

Darhower, M. (2007). A tale of two communities: Group dynamics and community building in a Spanish-English telecollaboration. *CALICO Journal, 24,* 561–589.

de la Fuente, M. J. (2003). Is SLA interactionist theory relevant to CALL? A study of the effects of computer-mediated interaction in L2 vocabulary acquisition. *Computer Assisted Language Learning, 16,* 47–81.

Ellis, R., Basturkmen, H., & Loewen, S. (2001). Preemptive focus on form in the ESL classroom. *TESOL Quarterly, 35,* 407–432.

Fukkink, R. G., Hulstijn, J., & Simis, A. (2005). Does training of second language word recognition skills affect reading comprehension? An experimental study. *Modern Language Journal, 89,* 54–75.

Furstenberg, G., Levet, S., English, K, & Maillet, K. (2001). Giving a virtual voice to the silent language of culture: The *Cultura* Project. *Language Learning & Technology, 5,* 55–102.

Garrett, N. (1991). Technology in the service of language learning: Trends and issues. *Modern Language Journal, 75,* 74–101.

Gee, J. P. (2007). *What video games have to teach us about learning and literacy* (2nd ed.). New York, NY: Palgrave Macmillan.

Goodfellow, R., & Lamy, M-N. (Eds.). (2009). *Learning cultures in online education.* London, UK: Continuum Books.

Grgurovic, M. (2007). Research synthesis: CALL comparison studies by language skills/ knowledge. Retrieved from http: //tesl.engl.iastate.edu: 591/comparison/ synthesis.htm

Hample, R., & Hauck, M. (2004). Towards an effective use of audio conferencing in distance language courses. *Language Learning & Technology, 88,* 166–182.

Heift, T. (2010b). Prompting in CALL: A longitudinal study of learner uptake. *Modern Language Journal, 94,* 198–216.

Hubbard, P., & Bradin Siskin, C. (2004). Another look at tutorial CALL. *ReCALL, 16,* 448–461.

Kern, R. G., & Warschauer, M. (2000). Theory and practice of network-based language teaching. In M. Warschauer & R. Kern (Eds.), *Network-based language teaching: Concepts and practice* (pp. 1–19). Cambridge, UK: Cambridge University Press.

Klopfer, E., Osterweil, S., & Salen, K. (2009). Moving learning games forward: Obstacles, opportunities & openness: An educational arcade paper. Retrieved from http: //education.mit. edu/papers/MovingLearningGamesForward_EdArcade.pdf

Kraemer, A. (2008). Formats of distance learning. In S. Goertler & P. Winke (Eds.), *Opening doors through distance language education: Principles, perspectives, and practices* (pp. 11–42). CALICO Monograph Series (Vol. 7). San Marcos, TX: CALICO.

Krashen, S. (1989). We acquire vocabulary and spelling by reading: Additional evidence for the input hypothesis. *Modern Language Journal, 73,* 440–464.

Lafford, B. (2004). Review of *Tell Me More. Language Learning & Technology*, 8, 21–34.

Lafford, B., Lafford, P., & Sykes, J. (2007). Entre el dicho y hecho . . . : An assessment of the application of research from second language acquisition and related fields to the creation of Spanish CALL materials for lexical acquisition. *CALICO Journal*, 24, 497–529.

Lafford, P., & Lafford, B. (2005). CMC technologies for teaching foreign languages: What's on the horizon? *CALICO Journal*, 22, 679–710.

Lamy, M.-N., & Hampel, R. (2007). *Online communication in language learning and teaching.* Basingstoke, UK: Palgrave Macmillan.

Lee, L. (2007). Focus-on-form through collaborative scaffolding in expert-to-novice online interaction. *Language Learning & Technology*, 12, 53–72.

LeLoup, J. W., & Ponterio, R. (2005). On the net: Vocabulary support for independent online reading. *Language Learning & Technology*, 9, 3–7.

Lomicka, L. (2006). Understanding the other: Intercultural exchange and CMC. In L. Ducate & N. Arnold (Eds.), *Calling on CALL: From theory and research to new directions in foreign language teaching* (pp. 211–236). CALICO Monograph Series (Vol. 5). San Marcos, TX: CALICO.

Lomicka, L., & Lord, G. (Eds.). (2009). *The next generation: Social networking and online collaboration in foreign language learning.* CALICO Monograph Series (Vol. 8). San Marcos, TX: CALICO.

Meskill, C. (2009). CMC in language teacher education: Learning with and through instructional conversations. *Innovation in Language Learning and Teaching*, 3, 51–63.

Meskill, C., & Anthony, N. (2010). *Teaching languages online.* Bristol, UK: Multilingual Matters.

Nagata, N. (2010). Some design issues for an online Japanese textbook. *CALICO Journal*, 27, 460–476.

Nation, P. (2001). *Learning vocabulary in another language.* Cambridge, UK: Cambridge University Press.

Nation, P., & Waring, R. (1997). Vocabulary size, text coverage and word lists. In N. Schmitt & M. McCarthy (Eds.), *Vocabulary: Description, acquisition, and pedagogy* (pp. 6–19). Cambridge, UK: Cambridge University Press.

Nerbonne, J. A. (2003). Computer-assisted language learning and natural language processing. In R. Mitkov (Ed.), *The Oxford handbook of computational linguistics* (pp. 670–698). Oxford, UK: Oxford University Press.

O'Dowd, R. (2006). The use of videoconferencing and e-mail as mediators of intercultural student ethnography. In J. Belz & S. L. Thorne (Eds.), *Internet-mediated intercultural foreign language education* (pp. 86–119). Boston, MA: Thomson Heinle.

Oskoz, A. (2009). Learners' feedback in online chats: What does it reveal about students' learning? *CALICO Journal, 27,* 48–68.

Pellettieri, J. (2000). Negotiation in cyberspace: The role of chatting in the development of grammatical competence. In M. Warschauer & R. Kern (Eds.), *Network-based language teaching: Concepts and practice* (pp. 59–86). Cambridge, UK: Cambridge University Press.

Peters, M., Weinberg, A., & Sarma, N. (2009). To like or not to like! Student perceptions of technological activities for learning French as a second language at five Canadian institutions. *Canadian Modern Language, 65,* 8679–8896.

Peterson, M. (2006). Learner interaction management in an avatar and chat-based virtual world. *Computer Assisted Language Learning, 19,* 79–103.

Peterson, M. (2010). Computerized games and simulations in computer-assisted language learning: A meta-analysis of research. *Simulation & Gaming, 41,* 72–93.

Prensky, M. (2000). *Digital game-based learning.* New York, NY: McGraw-Hill.

Purushotma, R., Thorne, S. L., & Wheatley, J. (2008). *10 Key principles for designing video games for foreign language learning.* Paper produced for the Open Language & Learning Games Project, Massachusetts Institute of Technology Education Arcade. Retrieved from http: //knol.google.com/k/10-key-principles-for-designing-video-games-for-foreign-language-learning#

Ranalli, J. (2008). Learning English with *The Sims*: Exploiting authentic computer simulation games for L2 learning. *Computer Assisted Language Learning, 21,* 441–455.

Ranalli, J. (2009). Prospects for developing L2 students' effective use of vocabulary learning-strategies via Web-based training.*CALICO Journal, 27,* 161–186.

Remote and online instruction at the University of California: A report from the Academic Senate Special Committee on remote and online instruction and residency. (2010). Retrieved from http: //www.universityofcalifornia.edu/senate/reports/ HP_MGYreRpt_Spec_Cte_ Online_Remote_Instruction_FINAL.pdf

Sanders, R. (2005). Interaction and online learning communities. In C. Crawford, D. Willis, R. Carlsen, I. Gibson, K. McFerrin, J. Price, & R. Weber (Eds.), *Proceedings of Society for Information Technology and Teacher Education International Conference, 2005* (pp. 2320–2325). Chesapeake, VA: Association for the Advancement of Computing in Education.

Sanders, R. (2006). The "imponderable bloom" : Reconsidering the role of technology in education. *Innovate,* 2. Retrieved from http: //www.innovateonline.info/index. php?view=article&id=232

Sauro, S. (2008). Strategic use of modality during synchronous CMC. *CALICO Journal, 27,* 101–117.

Sauro, S. (2009). Computer-mediated corrective feedback and the development of L2 grammar. *Language Learning & Technology, 13,* 96–120.

Smith, B. (2003). Computer-mediated negotiated interaction: An expanded model. *Modern*

Language Journal, 87, 38–58.

Smith, B. (2009). Revealing the nature of SCMC interaction. In A. Mackey & C. Polio (Eds.), *Multiple perspectives on interaction* (pp. 197–225). Mahwah, NJ: Erlbaum.

Soares, D. (2010). *Second language pragmatic socialization in World of Warcraft.* Unpublished doctoral dissertation, University of California, Davis.

Sotillo, S. (2000). Discourse functions and syntactic complexity in synchronous and asynchronous communication. *Language Learning & Technology, 4,* 82–119.

Sørensen, B. H., & Meyer, B. (2007). Serious games in language learning and teaching: A theoretical perspective. In *Proceedings of the 2007 Digital Games Research Association Conference* (pp. 559–566). Tokyo, Japan: Digital Games Research Association.

Squire, K. (2006). From content to context: Videogames as designed experience. *Educational Researcher, 35,* 19–29.

Squire, K., & Jenkins, H. (2004). Harnessing the power of games in education. *Insight, 3,* 5–33.

Steinkuehler, C. A. (2004). Learning in massively multiplayer online games. In Y. B. Kafai, W. A. Sandoval, N. Enyedy, A. S. Nixon, & F. Herrera (Eds.), *Proceedings of the Sixth International Conference of the Learning Sciences* (pp. 521–528). Mahwah, NJ: Erlbaum.

Steinkuehler, C. A. (2006). Why game (culture) studies now? *Games and Culture, 1,* 97–102.

Sydorenko, T. (2010). Modality of input and vocabulary acquisition. *Language Learning & Technology, 14,* 50–73.

Sykes, J. M. (2009). Learner requests in Spanish: Examining the potential of multi-user virtual environments for L2 pragmatic acquisition. In L. Lomika & G. Lord (Eds.), *The next generation: Social networking and online collaboration* (pp.199–234). CALICO Monograph Series (Vol. 8). San Marcos, TX: CALICO.

Sykes, J. M. (2011). Multi-user virtual environments: User-driven design and implementation for language learning. In G. Vincenti & J. Braman (Eds.), *Teaching through multi-user virtual environments: Applying dynamic elements to the modern classroom* (pp. 283–305). Hershey, PA: IGI Global.

Sykes, J. M., & Cohen, A. D. (2009). Learner perception and strategies for pragmatic acquisition: A glimpse into online learning materials. In C. Dreyer (Ed.), *Language and linguistics: Emerging trends* (pp. 99–135). Hauppauge, NY: Nova Science.

Sykes, J., Oskoz, A., & Thorne, S. L. (2008). Web 2.0, synthetic immersive environments, and mobile resources for language education. *CALICO Journal, 25,* 528–546.

Thorne, S. L. (2003). Artifacts and cultures-of-use in intercultural communication. *Language Learning & Technology, 7,* 38–67.

Thorne, S. L. (2008). Transcultural communication in open Internet environments and massively multiplayer online games. In S. Magnan (Ed.), *Mediating discourse online* (pp. 305–327). Amsterdam, The Netherlands: John Benjamins.

Thorne, S. L., & Black, R. (2007). Language and literacy development in computer-mediated contexts and communities. *Annual Review of Applied Linguistics, 27*, 133–160.

Thorne, S. L., Black, R., & Sykes, J. (2009). Second language use, socialization, and learning in Internet interest communities and online gaming. *Modern Language Journal, 93*, 802–821.

U.S. Department of Education, Office of Educational Technology. (2010). *Transforming American education: Learning powered by technology.* Retrieved from http: //www2.ed.gov/about/offices/list/os/technology/netp.pdf

U.S. Department of Education, Office of Planning, Evaluation, and Policy Development. (2009). *Evaluation of evidence-based practices in online learning: A meta-analysis and review of online learning studies.* Retrieved from http: //www2.ed.gov/rschstat/eval/tech/evidence-based-practices/finalreport.pdf

Varonis, E. M., & Gass, S. M. (1985). Non-native/non-native conversations: A model for negotiation of meaning. *Applied Linguistics, 6*, 71–90.

Vygotsky, L. (1962). *Thought and language.* Cambridge, MA: MIT Press

Ware, P., & Kramsch, C. (2005). Toward an intercultural stance: Teaching German and English through telecollaboration. *Modern Language Journal, 89*, 90–105.

Warschauer, M., & Grimes, D. (2007). Audience, authorship, and artifact: The emergent semiotics of Web 2.0. *Annual Review of Applied Linguistics, 27*, 1–23.

Yanguas, I. (2009). Multimedia glosses and their effect on L2 text comprehension and vocabulary learning. *Language Learning & Technology, 13*, 48–67.

Yanguas, I. (2010). Oral computer-mediated interaction between L2 learners: It's about time. *Language Learning & Technology, 14*, 72–79.

Yee, N., & Bailenson, J. (2007). The Proteus effect: The effect of transformed self-representation on behavior. *Human Communication Research, 33*, 271–290.

The Implementation of Communicative and Task-Based Language Teaching in the Asia-Pacific Region

Yuko Goto Butler

Communicative language teaching (CLT) and task-based language teaching (TBLT) have been widely adopted in the Asia-Pacific region, with a number of Asian countries strongly promoting CLT and TBLT in their curricula and English language education policies. Despite their popularity, a number of challenges have arisen in connection with implementing CLT and TBLT in Asian classrooms. The challenges that have emerged include (a) conceptual constraints (e.g., conflicts with local values and misconceptions regarding CLT/TBLT); (b) classroom-level constraints (e.g., various student and teacher-related factors, classroom management practices, and resource availability); and (c) societal-institutional level constraints (e.g., curricula and examination systems). These constraints have led some to argue that successfully implementing CLT and TBLT in Asia requires adaptation to local environments, such that CLT and TBLT become embedded in local practices. Although there have been a growing number of reports of various CLT/TBLT implementation efforts in different Asia-Pacific regions, we still have only a limited understanding of how best to achieve contextually embedded adaptations and how they affect students' English learning. After reviewing relevant studies, this article suggests potential options for moving forward, including (a) employing more contextually feasible and flexible interpretations of CLT and TBLT, (b) implementing decentralized or innovative language-in-education policies, and (c) creating communities of learning outside of the classroom as well as in the classroom.

Communicative language teaching (CLT) and task-based language teaching

(TBLT) have influenced English language teaching worldwide, and Asia is no exception to this trend. In many parts of Asia, there has been mounting criticism of the traditional approaches to English language teaching, such as the grammar-translation and audio-lingual methods. These traditional ways of teaching can be characterized as synthetic approaches, and a common critique of such approaches is that they fail to help students develop a high level of communicative ability. In the synthetic approach, the target language is broken down into constituent parts in various ways, and such parts are then presented to learners in a linear fashion (e.g., grammar rules, words, phonemes, structures, functions; see Wilkins, 1976). Long and Robinson (1998) argued that such approaches, labeled *focus on forms*, lead to instruction that isolates linguistic forms from their meaning.

To provide an alternative to synthetic approaches, various governments in Asia established CLT and TBLT as major components of their English language curricula and instruction programs. Despite their popularity, however, there are a number of reports that point to challenges that have arisen in connection with implementing CLT and TBLT in Asian classrooms. This review attempts to expand our understanding of the implementation of CLT and TBLT in the Asia-Pacific region and to present a number of instructional and policy-related suggestions.

Although there are extensive publications on CLT and TBLT in local Asian languages as well as unpublished documents including master's theses and doctorial dissertations, the review here only includes published articles in English and excludes opinion papers that do not offer any empirical, theoretical, or policy analyses to support their claims.

I begin with a description of the educational and policy backgrounds that underlie the adoption of CLT and TBLT in the Asia-Pacific region. Since CLT was introduced in the region before TBLT, I review the initial concerns cited regarding implementing CLT in classrooms in the region. Next, I review more recent implementation efforts in various parts of the Asia-Pacific region, with a particular focus on TBLT, and identify potential options for moving forward with such implementations. The article concludes with a number of suggestions for policy, research, and instruction. As shown later in the article, the majority of the published studies on this topic have came from scholars in China (including Hong Kong), Japan, and South Korea, and a smaller number of studies have come from authors in Southeast Asian countries (e.g., Malaysia, Singapore, Thailand, and Vietnam). Therefore, the discussion is inevitably somewhat limited (and possibly skewed) to countries generating more frequent reports in Asia. For the rest of this article, "Asia" is used to refer to the broader Asia-Pacific region (i.e., East and Southeast Asia).

THE INTRODUCTION OF CLT AND TBLT IN ASIA

The premise of CLT is to develop learners' communicative competence in social interactions, as opposed to focusing primarily on linguistic forms (e.g., Richards & Rodgers, 2001; Savignon, 2005). Meaningful communication is considered to be both the means as well as the goal in CLT. Learners in the classroom should therefore be given opportunities to receive meaningful input and to use language meaningfully through interactive works (Brown, 2001). CLT is broadly based on theories of communicative competence and second language learning. However, this theoretical broadness has invited various interpretations of CLT and led to some variety in its realization in practice. The strong version of CLT is based on the assumption that language acquisition is a natural process where learners self-analyze the language; this version holds that this process cannot be directly controlled by the teacher. The teacher's role is thus to facilitate this process, rather than to teach the learner pre-analyzed linguistic knowledge. Weaker versions of CLT, while keeping the same ultimate objective, see a more direct role of the teacher in this process and suggest that the teacher should introduce structured, meaningful communicative activities in a controlled manner in the classroom so that learners can gradually and autonomously express meaning in more naturalistic settings (Klapper, 2003). X. J. Li (1984) suggested that there are three conditions that activities must satisfy in order to be classified as communicative: (a) they must be embedded in real situations; (b) they have purpose and convey substance in communication; and (c) they contain a certain level of freedom and unpredictability.

The term *task* was increasingly used as a replacement for *communicative activity* during the 1980s (Skehan, 2003), and in this respect, TBLT can be considered as "an offset of CLT" (Kumaravadivelu, 2006, p. 66). It is important to note, however, that the definition of a task itself has been a matter of some debate. Tasks can be considered, for example, to be "things people will tell you they do" (Long, 1985, p. 89) in which the connection with the real world's activity is emphasized. Another definition that has been offered focuses on the cognitive process, defining a task as "an activity which required learners to arrive at an outcome from given information through some process of thought and which allowed teachers to control and regulate that process" (Prabhu, 1987, p. 24). Researchers such as Ellis (2003) and Samuda and Bygate (2008) have tried to synthesize the essential characteristics of tasks, defining them as follows: "[a] task is a holistic activity which engages language use in order to achieve some non-linguistic outcome while meeting a linguistic challenge, with the overall aim of promoting language learning, through process or product or both" (Samuda & Bygate, 2008, p. 69). In addition, some authors view the precise features of tasks as varying depending on the pedagogical and research purposes, as well as depending on users and contexts (teachers, learners, and assessments) (Bygate, Skehan, & Swain, 2001).

Similarly, researchers have also debated how tasks should be used in instruction. A number of different versions of TBLT have been proposed, ranging from a strong version (*task-based teaching*; see Willis, 1996) to a weaker version (*task-supported teaching*; see Ellis, 2003). Whereas the former sees tasks as the central component of syllabus design, the latter uses tasks for communicative practice in conjunction with a grammar- or function-based syllabus. As with CLT, however, such varied approaches in TBLT have invited substantial confusion at the practice level in Asia, as we shall see later.

CLT was introduced in Asia in the 1970s, but it took some time to gain widespread attention in the region. For example, in China, there was a strong resistance among teachers to employing CLT in classrooms, and a heated debate arose over its applicability and effectiveness (Hu, 2002a, 2005; Yu, 2001). In Japan and Korea, the importance of communicative ability in language education had been recognized among innovative English language teaching professionals and in the private sector, but it was not until the late 1980s and the early 1990s that CLT became the center of attention among general English language educators and policy makers (Butler & Iino, 2005; Y.-H. Choi, 2007).

With the rapid expansion of international exchanges via business, technology, and communication, the governments of various Asian countries became increasingly concerned about insufficient communication skills in English among their population. CLT quickly gained further recognition and became a central component of their national curricula and syllabi. In China, the State Education Development Commission (SEDC) introduced a CLT-based syllabus in 1992. The SEDC's 2001 syllabus required implementing TBLT at the secondary school level, and a number of textbooks for TBLT have been published since then (Liao, 2004). CLT was at the forefront of South Korea's *7th National Curriculum* announced in 1997 (Y.-H. Choi, 2007). The National Curriculum in Japan, *The Course of Study*, introduced "communication abilities" as the central premise of foreign language education in 1999 (Butler & Iino, 2005, p. 34). Singapore's 1991 *English Language Syllabus* reflected the rapid advance of CLT and gave teachers greater flexibility in fostering students' communicative skills as facilitators rather than as knowledge providers. The syllabus also promoted theme- and topic-based instruction (L. J. Zhang, 2006). Hong Kong adopted TBLT officially in its syllabus in 1997 at the primary school level and in 1999 at the secondary school level (Carless, 2007). Other Asian countries surveyed in Nunan (2003), including Malaysia, Taiwan, and Vietnam, all adopted CLT and/or TBLT in their curricula.

INITIAL CONCERNS REGARDING CLT

As already mentioned, CLT became a slogan for English language teaching in many Asian countries. However, since the late 1980s and early 1990s, a growing number of studies have reported various concerns and difficulties in implementing CLT in Asian language teaching contexts (for China: Anderson, 1993; Burnaby & Sun, 1989; Hu, 2002a, 2002b; Penner, 1995; Rao, 1996, 2002; Sun & Cheng, 2002; for China and India: Holliday, 1997b; for Hong Kong: L. Miller & Aldred, 2000; for Japan: Gorsuch, 2000; Nishino, 2008; Sakui, 2004; Samimy & Kobayashi, 2004; Sano, Takahashi, & Yoneyama, 1984; for the Philippines: Gonzalez, 1985; for Singapore: Kirkpatrick, 1984; for South Korea: S. Choi, 2000; D. Li, 1998; for Thailand: Prapaisit de Segovia & Hardison, 2008; for Vietnam: Pham, 2007; Sullivan, 2000). The majority of these studies were survey, interview, or classroom observation studies (or a combination). According to these studies, three types of constraints limit effective CLT implementation in English as a foreign language (EFL) contexts in Asia: (a) conceptual constraints, (b) classroom-level constraints, and (c) societal-institutional level constraints.

Conceptual Constraints

Conceptual constraints stem from the differences between the principal concepts of CLT and those of the traditional view of learning and teaching in Asia. From the earliest stages of the implementation of CLT in Asia, observers of Asian classrooms questioned the universality of the features considered as communicative in nature (e.g., oral-focused activities, the importance of group work, and teachers as facilitators of communication). Considering these features to be the hallmarks of communicativeness can be ethnocentric; what accounts for so-called good communication is often based on particular cultural values. Many have argued that being sensitive to local cultural norms and beliefs is necessary if CLT is to be successfully implemented (Anderson, 1993; Holliday, 1997a, 1997b; Sullivan, 2000). Cameron (2002) went a step further; she expressed concern over the "obsession with 'communicative skills' and 'communication problems'" (p. 67) in contemporary language teaching and warned of the dangers of imposing Anglocentric ideologies on genres and styles of communication. Bax (2003) expressed concerned over CLT's hidden assumption that CLT is the only modern and progressive solution for language learning irrespective of context, and proposed a context approach that allowed various ways for learning a language based on context.

In Asia, a common discourse is about the conflict between the Western premises of CLT instruction and the Confucian norms that conceptualize learning as the acquisition of knowledge residing mainly in books (e.g., Cortazzi & Jin, 1996; Hu, 2002a, 2002b; T. Miller, 1995; Rao, 1996). Traditionally, a literary education was considered important, and little value was placed on the acquisition of knowledge for practical purposes. The teacher was seen as the possessor and messenger of profound knowledge, and the student as the recipient of that authoritative knowledge. Under such a view, literacy-focused and teacher-centered teaching was a natural consequence. According to these authors, such a mismatch in cultural values regarding teaching and learning makes it difficult for teachers in Asia to implement CLT in their classrooms.

However, this cultural value-based explanation itself has come under criticism for presenting an oversimplified view of culture and ignoring diversity within cultures (McKay, 2002). Indeed, it has been documented that there are substantial differences in school practices and cultures across Asia as well as within each country. The stereotypical view of Asian students as more passive, less vocal, and preferring lecture-style instruction does not always accurately describe students in Asia. For example, Kubota (1999) observed considerable differences in classroom cultures between elementary schools and secondary schools in Japan. In Savignon and Wang (2003), Taiwanese college students, and those who had had early English education in particular, showed a preference toward meaning-based communicative activities in class. Taiwanese high school students in Chung and Huang (2009) showed positive attitudes toward CLT. Similarly, the stereotypical view of Asian teaching as being authoritarian and teacher-centered does not always seem to reflect reality. Stevenson and Stigler (1992) found that elementary school teachers in Japan and Taiwan spent little time lecturing compared with U.S. teachers. Vietnamese teachers in Ha (2004) used a variety of communicative-based instructional techniques in order to give their students autonomy in their English classes and objected to the stereotypical views commonly imposed on Asian teachers. It is thus potentially misleading to overemphasize the role of traditional cultural values (such as Confucian values) in shaping Asian classroom practices at all grade levels across Asia.

Another conceptual difficulty with implementing CLT stems from teachers' and students' "misconceptions" about CLT and how CLT might be adopted (D. Li, 1998, p. 687). One can argue that this is partially because CLT itself is open to interpretation, as we have seen already. Moreover, since CLT was employed as an alternative to the grammar-translation method in many countries in Asia, it was often interpreted as synonymous with the natural approach or what Long and Robinson (1998) would call "instruction with a 'focus on meaning'" (p. 18). In this interpretation, L2 learning should take place with sufficient input through natural exposure to the target language, and the learner should subconsciously and inductively analyze such input. Without receiving sufficient training, it was not uncommon to find Asian English teachers who believed that CLT focused only on oral language, ignoring grammar instruction and the accuracy of language use (D. Li, 1998; Sato & Kleinsasser, 1999). In response to the prevailing so-called misconceptions of CLT, Savignon (2005) devoted a section to clarifying "what CLT is not" (p. 645). According to Savignon, CLT is not exclusively meant for oral interaction, does not necessarily require small group work, and it does not exclude the role of conscious knowledge of the structure of language (e.g., grammar instruction). Unfortunately, many countries in Asia started implementing CLT in their curricula before providing their teachers with sufficient training (Kam & Wong, 2004). This appears to be particularly evident in English education at the primary school level, where policy decisions have frequently been hastily made without providing teachers with sufficient training (e.g., Butler, 2004).

Classroom-level Constraints

The second set of constraints relate to various contextual constraints at the classroom level. Such constraints include the lack of human resources and material, structural challenges (e.g., large class sizes, limited number of instructional hours), and issues with classroom management. Nonnative English-speaking teachers in EFL contexts often do not feel confident that they possess sufficient sociocultural and strategic competencies to introduce communicative activities in their classes or to assess students' communicative competence (Burnaby & Sun, 1989; Butler, 2004; D. Li, 1998; Nishino, 2008; Pham, 2007; Prapaisit de Segovia & Hardison, 2008; Rao, 1996; Sakui, 2004; Samimy & Kobayashi, 2004; Sun & Cheng, 2002). Teachers may not understand how to actually implement CLT in their classrooms. A number of observational studies have reported that what were called communicative activities introduced in class were not in fact communicative and were often found to be mixed with an audio-lingual approach and/or an explicit form-focused approach (Lee, 2002; Prapaisit de Segovia & Hardison, 2008; Yukawa, 2002).

Although various types of materials have increasingly been introduced in Asia, Asian teachers have often found it difficult to choose meaningful materials that are appropriate for their students (e.g., Butler, 2005a). Reliable and effective authentic assessments are still largely limited in number. Furthermore, teachers often do not have enough resources, assistance, or time to develop materials and assessments by themselves. It is also important to keep in mind that the concept of authenticity is ambiguously understood in many Asian EFL contexts. What is perceived to be authentic often means materials and activities that accurately reflect the actual use of language and activities in English-speaking countries. One can find numerous types of materials and activity books that have been imported from the inner circle (Kachru, 1992) to Asia. However, such materials may or may not relate to Asian students' daily lives or correspond to the kinds of language that they would use in real communicative contexts as a means of global communication.

In addition, large class sizes and limited instructional hours have been frequently mentioned as major obstacles for implementing CLT in Asia (e.g., D. Li, 1998; Nishino, 2008; Sakui, 2004). In large classes, teachers sometimes find it a challenge to introduce interactive activities and to ensure that everybody participates. Performance-based assessments tend to be time-consuming in such large classrooms. Group work may invite excessive discussions unrelated to the objectives of a given activity, often in the students' first language. Such activity-irrelevant discussions may make it difficult to keep the class in order in such a way that is culturally perceived as desirable (e.g., Butler, 2005a).

Societal-Institutional Level Constraints

The third set of constraints identified in prior studies consists of structural constraints at the societal-institutional level. The most significant constraints in this category include grammar-translation-oriented college exams and the limited opportunity to use English outside of the classroom. The grammar-translation-oriented college exam system is considered to be a major structural constraint prevalent in Asia in general (e.g., Kam & Wong, 2004). According to previous studies, with an already limited number of hours allocated to English in the curriculum, teachers and students have tended to think that CLT might not be the most efficient way to teach or acquire grammar and reading/writing proficiency, particularly with the added pressure of college exams. It is interesting to note, however, that a number of Asian countries have recently attempted to include communicative components in their college entrance exams (e.g., incorporating listening tasks and writing tasks). While teachers may be fully aware of such attempts, studies have often failed to find the intended washback effects in teaching methodologies in classrooms (e.g., for Hong Kong: L. Cheng, 2004; for Japan: Gorsuch, 2000; for China: Qi, 2007).

Last, it has been claimed that there are still relatively few opportunities for the majority of Asian students to use English communicatively outside of their classrooms (e.g., Rao, 2002). This factor has been of particular concern among educators who teach English in areas in the expanding circle (Kachru, 1992).

However, it is also worth noting that there is much variability with respect to learners' opportunities to use English outside of the classroom even within these regions.

In sum, while CLT has substantially influenced the curricula and syllabus designs in English language teaching in Asia, there exists a substantial discrepancy between policies and actual practices at the classroom level. Although the importance of acquiring what is perceived to be communicative competence is generally acknowledged, researchers have reported a number of constraints that work against implementing CLT in Asia, and they have questioned whether or not the currently specified features of CLT are universally effective across cultures and across contexts. As Mitchell and Lee (2003) have demonstrated in their comparative study of Korea and the United States, it is often very challenging (and sometimes may not be appropriate) to directly transfer what has been identified as an effective pedagogy in one context to another. It has been repeatedly claimed that the acquisition of communicative competence needs to be achieved in contextually appropriate ways. The empirical question thus remains as to how best to do so in Asian contexts.

FROM ADOPTION TO ADAPTATION: INCREASING INTEREST IN TBLT

Given the various challenges it faces in its implementation, CLT has gradually lost its popularity to TBLT among TESOL professionals, according to Kumaravadivelu (2006). The exact relationship between CLT and TBLT is still debatable. Kumaravadivelu's position is that TBLT is not associated with a particular method but rather should be considered as a "curricular content" (p. 65); that is, Kumaravadivelu argued that TBLT should be considered as encompassing tasks that form part of a different method that leads to different learning goals. Others argue that TBLT is "the latest methodological realization of CLT" (Nunan, 2003, p. 606). In whatever way we might characterize the relationship between CLT and TBLT, as Kumaravadivelu has observed, there have been a growing number of publications in Asia since the mid-2000s that specifically focus on TBLT. Two special volumes dedicated to TBLT in Asia were published in the late 2000s: One was in *The Asian EFL Journal Quarterly* in 2006, and the other was in *Asia Journal of English Language Teaching* in 2009. As we have seen before, tasks can range from more structured-based to more communicative-based tasks (Skehan, 2003). Such flexibility with regard to the definition of TBLT seems to be appealing to TESOL professionals in Asia.

Studies investigating the early stages of TBLT implementation in Asia revealed similar challenges to those seen in the implementation of CLT as already discussed here. For example, Carless (2002, 2004) examined the implementation of TBLT in Hong Kong elementary schools through a series of interviews with teachers and classroom observations and identified three major problems: (a) difficulties in maintaining discipline, (b) students' excessive use of their mother tongue, and (c) substantial variability among students with respect to their production of the target language. Carless (2003) also identified six preclass planning issues: (a) a lack of belief among teachers in the benefits of the tasks they were overseeing; (b) teachers' understanding of the tasks at hand, (c) time constraints, (d) the relevancy of topics covered in textbooks versus the tasks being designed, (e) resource availability in the preparation of tasks, and (f) students' proficiency levels. Tong, Adamson, and Che's (2000) classroom observation at an elementary school in Hong Kong revealed that most activities were not fully communicative. Instead they could be characterized as somewhere between what Ellis (2003) called an *exercise* and a *task*, in both English classes and Chinese classes. Jeon's (2006) survey found that one of the biggest obstacles for secondary school teachers in South Korea was their lack of confidence in conceptualizing TBLT and implementing it in their own classrooms.

Based on his extensive experience working with teachers in East Asia, Littlewood (2004, 2007) proposed a five-level model in order to respond to the need among teachers for a finer-grained framework for communicativeness in activities. His model describes the degrees of communicativeness along a continuum that ranges from activities that focus on forms to those that focus on meaning. Littlewood's (2004) continuum included noncommunicative learning, precommunicative language practice, communicative language practice, structured communication, and authentic communication. Littlewood (2007) suggested that teachers who are used to form-oriented activities in class "can maintain their base in activities represented in the first and second categories, but gradually expand their repertoire into the other three" (p. 247).

The Adaptation of TBLT: Flexibility in Context

Recently, there have been a growing number of case studies that have tried to identify how best to adapt TBLT in various contexts, as opposed to solely addressing the difficulties with its implementation. At the national level, Singapore provides us with an example of such efforts. L. J. Zhang (2006) found that Singapore's national syllabus of English language in 1991 was influenced by the CLT movement and therefore viewed language as a meaning-making system, had a strong emphasis on fluency rather than accuracy, marginalized grammar teaching, and promoted a holistic approach to language teaching. However, "to pacify the outcry from the general English-speaking public," the revised syllabus in 2001 placed "grammar in the text type" (p. 4) as a central component and integrated reading/writing and oral communication, while heavily emphasizing literacy development among children. The 2001 syllabus also considered Singapore's sociocultural factors seriously and set the acquisition of a standard variety of English (as opposed to a certain native-model of English) as its target.

Case studies from classrooms in various countries and at various grade levels all address the important role that context plays in implementing TBLT. Many of these studies dismiss the strong version of TBLT (Willis, 1996) and suggest flexibility in its implementation within a given context. In other words, the discussions centered around how a weaker version of TBLT, or what Ellis called *task-supported language teaching* (2003), can be implemented in classrooms.

At the elementary and secondary school levels, where TBLT is often introduced as part of an officially mandated curriculum, studies frequently have found that TBLT is not implemented in classrooms as the policy intended and have suggested that major adaptations are necessary if TBLT is to be implemented effectively. In Hong Kong, several case studies have revealed a number of key components for the potential adaptation of TBLT based on teachers' experiences and insights (e.g., Carless, 2007, 2008, 2009; Luk, 2009; Tinker Sachs, 2007, 2009). For example, Carless (2007), through his interview with secondary school teachers, identified three major areas for adaptation: (a) granting a greater role to grammar instruction in TBLT, (b) incorporating TBLT with due attention paid to the students' examination requirements, and (c) employing a greater emphasis on reading and writing tasks. Carless (2007) also suggested a flexible approach toward the use of students' first language (L1) during tasks, including the possibility of using L1 for language-analysis tasks. Given the fact that there is a strong and prevailing preference toward the traditional presentation-practice-production (P-P-P) approach over TBLT among teachers, Carless (2009) further suggested that it may be possible to productively combine P-P-P with TBLT in such a way that the teachers can minimize the limitations that P-P-P may have, instead of completely dismissing it.

Similarly, Deng and Carless (2009) conducted a series of interviews and classroom observations at an elementary school in Guangdong, China, and found that most activities were low in communicativeness (i.e., less focused on meaning); they were classified as either noncommunicative learning or precommunicative language practice using Littlewood's framework (2004, 2007). Similar to what we saw in Hong Kong, the TBLT mandated by the state in Guangdong was also not implemented in classrooms. Moreover, teachers showed a preference toward activities with lower communicativeness. While the interview data of Deng and Carless reveal that the implementation of TBLT was largely constrained by the teachers' limited understanding of tasks and examination factors in China, the authors also suggested that Littlewood's framework should not be considered as a barometer of the desirability of activities. That is, we should not consider activities with higher communicativeness as always being "desirable" (p. 131). According to Deng and Carless, depending on various contextual factors—such as the students' proficiency levels and age—activities with different degrees of communicativeness should be chosen and combined.

Case studies at the college level also cite similar findings when it comes to adaptation, though college teachers are usually granted more autonomy in adapting curricula when compared to their elementary and secondary school counterparts. As a result, various examples of actual adaptations have been cited in the literature (Lingley, 2006; McDonough & Chaikitmongkol, 2007; Muller, 2006; Nunn, 2006; Rivers, 2008; Watson Todd, 2006). For instance, Watson Todd (2006) examined the implementation of a task-based curriculum at a Thai university and analyzed how and why changes were made by the instructors during the first 4 years of its implementation. Based on interviews with the instructors, three major changes were revealed: (a) reducing the number of tasks introduced in class, (b) placing greater emphasis on explicit grammar instruction, and (c) granting greater roles to summative examinations in the courses examined. With these changes, the revised curriculum looked more like "a mixed methodology" rather than "a pure version" of TBLT (Watson Todd, 2006, p. 9).

Lingley (2006) described a case where a task-based approach was implemented in a content-based course (a Canadian Studies course) in a Japanese university. Content-based instruction (CBI) aims to develop students' content knowledge and second language skills and is increasingly popular across Asia (Butler, 2005b). In Lingley's study, when teachers were observed developing material, the notion of authentic material was redefined in order to respond to the needs of students who did not have sufficient language skills or content knowledge. The original texts were simplified while attempting to keep the language natural. Form-focused activities such as vocabulary instruction were considered as "a necessary foundation step in working through the staged progression of tasks that become more meaning focused" (p. 131). Teachers had to play various roles during the tasks. When the students were not capable of completing the tasks, it was found that the teachers inevitably became heavily involved in the students' tasks in order to assist them to engage in meaningful activities. In sum, previous case studies have all stated in one form or another that flexibility and attention to the context in which instruction takes place is the key component for the successful implementation of TBLT in Asia.

UNSOLVED ISSUES AND CONCERNS

There is indeed "emerging evidence of successful, grass-roots implementation of task-based teaching in Asia" (Adams & Newton, 2009, p. 1), but a number of unsolved issues and concerns remain. Some of the most prominent issues and concerns include (a) how best to implement tasks in an exam culture (Hamp-Lyons, 2007), (b) when and how best to include grammar instruction in TBLT, (c) students' use of their L1 in TBLT, and (d) the difficulty of top-down policy implementations.

The first and perhaps most serious concern with respect to the implementation of TBLT in Asia is how to implement communicative tasks and task-based assessments in an exam culture where norm-referenced classic testing has exerted so much influence on teaching and learning practices (e.g., Carless, 2007; D. Li,

1998; Littlewood, 2007). In such environments, syllabi and teaching methods are strongly influenced (or sometimes determined) by the contents of assessments, and teachers often "feel powerless" over instructional and assessment-related decisions (Hamp-Lyons, 2007, p. 498). In order to implement tasks and task-based assessments, not only are changes in the exam system required, but also drastic conceptual changes toward learning and assessment in general in society are necessary. This is unlikely to happen easily because the exam culture is so deeply rooted in sociocultural history in Asia. For example, referring to the situation in China, Y. Cheng (2010) stated that certain merits of the exam system (such as being considered a fair selection device) and some of its harms are both recognized and accepted by Chinese society.

If the government sets the goal of language learning as acquiring communicative competence, and tasks are used to achieve this goal, one could easily say that assessment goals should reflect this and that task-based assessments should be used. However, it is much more complicated than it may at first seem. Long and Crookes (1992) indicated that in TBLT assessment should be conducted "by way of task-based criterion-referenced tests" (p. 45). However, a number of issues still remain to be solved, including how the criteria are determined (e.g., linguistic performance vs. task-completion), how and by whom tasks are developed and/or selected to correspond to such criteria, and how and by whom can student performance be rated validly and reliably. Adding to the complexity of the last point, traditional psychometric notions of validity and reliability may not be applicable depending on how task-based assessment is employed. Inevitably, teachers need to play a critical role in many of these processes. And without empowering teachers, it would not be a surprise to see TBLT winding up being a mere policy slogan.

Hong Kong has been innovative in that it has implemented a school-based assessment (SBA) as part of the Hong Kong Certificate of Education Examination (HKCEE) in English since 2005. SBA is a task-based in-class performance assessment and accounts for 15% of the students' final English scores on the HKCEE. In SBA, the students are assessed against criteria, and the teachers can adjust the assessment tasks according to individual students' levels and needs. Various concerns were initially raised regarding the implementation of SBA (e.g., fairness issues, concerns regarding teachers' increased workloads, and teachers' qualifications as assessors; Davison, 2007). However, teachers were given substantial support and thereafter appeared to gain more confidence and control; the result has been that "SBA is beginning to take hold in the English language curriculum" (Davison & Hamp-Lyons, 2010, p. 261). Although this is certainly a very promising move, some difficulties remain. For example, Luk (2010) closely examined students' group interactions in SBA and found that the students were making a "collective attempt to present a best impression of themselves as well as the whole group through ritualized, institutionalized, and colluded talk" (p. 46). The students usually prepared a speech in their group discussion in SBA in advance, even though this behavior was discouraged, and some students might have even rehearsed these ahead of the assessment. According to a participating teacher, in order for everybody to display their abilities fully, the students did not challenge others while they were talking and took turns mechanically, and as a result, the interaction became unauthentic. Luk's case study elegantly illustrates the complexity of task-based assessment when contradictory roles are imposed on it (namely, the dual purposes of being both a showcase for learner performance and being a venue for authentic communication).

A second concern, which is partially related to the assessment issues already discussed, is when and how best to incorporate form-focused instruction in TBLT. Although most TBLT methodologists see the importance of form-focused instruction in TBLT (Skehan, 2003), they do not have a clear consensus about when and how best to incorporate this in task-based lessons. It has been generally suggested that focus on form is necessary during the posttask phase, but not the pretask or during-task phases, because the latter two options could make a given task an exercise of preidentified vocabulary and structures (Ellis, 2003). However, teachers who are comfortable with the traditional P-P-P approach have often indicated that this suggestion is counterintuitive or inappropriate. As we have seen already, recommendations for implementing TBLT in Asia often include some type of form-focused instruction at the pretask phase due to the students' needs or institutional requirements (such as the requirement to use prescribed textbooks). A critical question that remains is the extent to which such adapted implementations of form-focused instruction at the pretask phase are effective in Asian classrooms. Muller's (2006) small-scale case study at a Japanese junior college showed that his students with lower English proficiency could use words beyond the prescribed ones introduced at the pretask phase but could not creatively use grammatical forms beyond those introduced in the textbook during the task. One can assume that various student-related and contextual factors may have influenced the effectiveness of such adapted versions of TBLT in complicated ways. Luk's (2009) case study of a secondary school teacher in Hong Kong indicates that teachers' notions of form-focused instruction may be limited to lexical and structural components, and that they may not include discourse or genre awareness. Both of these latter components could potentially help students to use language more meaningfully. Such limited perceptions among teachers can also affect results. In any case, unfortunately, we have very little empirical information to provide teachers with useful guidance on this matter.

A third issue relates to the use of students' L1 in TBLT in foreign language contexts. In a teaching context where students share the same L1, an excessive use of L1 is a frequently articulated concern among teachers. The excessive use of L1 also often relates to teacherss' concerns with classroom management. While the potential benefit of L1 in second and foreign language learning has increasingly been acknowledged, it is not easy to for teachers to make judgments about when and how much L1 the students are allowed to use (or encouraged to use on certain occasions) in TBLT. Carless (2007) addressed one significant dilemma between L1 and TBLT, noting that "the more absorbing the task, the greater is the risk of student use of MT [mother tongue]" (p. 335). Eguchi and Eguchi (2006) found that, while their college students in Japan enjoyed a project-based lesson (composed of a series of tasks), this was largely due to their excessive use of L1, and as such they found that the tasks performed had little effect on their English learning. The more meaning-focused the task becomes, the greater the incentives that students need to perceive in order to complete the task at hand with their fellow students in their foreign language. As Eguchi and Eguchi commented, "Speaking English is like using an old computer when a new one is available. Why use English when they can finish the job in their native language in a snap?" (p. 221). This raises a fundamental question with regard to what counts as authentic and meaningful language use in a foreign language context. Again, we still have little information to use to find an answer to this question.

Finally, various studies have repeatedly found difficulty in implementing top-down, mandatory TBLT implementations. Based on extensive interviews with stakeholders, classroom observations, and document analyses in Shenzhen, China, E. Zhang (2007) described how the original intentions of curriculum policies were transmitted, understood or misunderstood, and changed by agents at different levels in its implementation. Individual teachers implemented the curriculum (the enacted curriculum) differently, and accordingly these versions of the curriculum were experienced by their students (the experienced curriculum) differently. Complicated power relationships within schools and institutions also may not allow individual teachers to exercise their knowledge and beliefs (Tsui, 2007). Examining the complicated process of top-down curriculum implementation and understanding the substantial role that teachers play in the process, it is not too surprising that the intended TBLT is not found at the classroom level.

The four concerns described in the preceding paragraphs are just a few of the major concerns that many teachers face in adapting TBLT in their teaching contexts. There is a lack of studies that have systematically examined the effectiveness of various adaptations of TBLT. The overwhelming majority of studies conducted so far on this topic have employed interviews with teachers and/or classroom observations. In order to understand both the psycholinguistic and sociolinguistic effectiveness of various adaptations tried out in Asian contexts, more diverse research approaches are necessary.

POTENTIAL OPTIONS FOR MOVING FORWARD

Based on the information drawn from previous studies, a number of potential alternatives to enable English teaching in Asia to move forward are indicated. Such alternatives include (a) employing more contextually feasible and flexible interpretations of CLT/TBLT, (b) implementing decentralized or innovative language-in-education policies, and (c) creating communities of learning outside of classrooms as well as in classrooms, including using new technologies to enable this.

First, more flexible conceptualizations and methodologies for CLT/TBLT appear to be necessary. As we have seen here, several constraints in the implementation of CLT/TBLT in Asia have been identified. However, we may need to consider them as positive forces, rather than constraints, that help teachers and learners to develop approaches that maximize their teaching and learning.

Depending on the context, drills may be suggested or even highly effective in combination with other strategies. Ding (2007), for instance, found that text memorization and imitation were the most effective strategies identified by competent Chinese learners of English. It may be possible to pursue teacher-fronted but communicative activities in crowded classrooms. As Carless (2009) suggested, incorporating certain aspects of P-P-P in TBLT may be more adaptable or appropriate in some contexts.

As already mentioned, CLT and TBLT were introduced as counter-approaches to the traditional synthetic approach in Asia, but they were not easily adapted to Asian classrooms. What we have seen is that teachers have struggled to incorporate such innovative approaches into their specific teaching contexts. It seems that CLT and TBLT have gradually spread throughout Asia, mostly in their weak formats, but that they are often greatly compromised, modified, tailored, and even changed outright in order to work in a given context. Some may say that what we see currently in many Asian classrooms is not CLT or TBLT in their original sense. However, one could also argue that the CLT or TBLT used in Asian classrooms should be considered as an outcome of the natural consequence of searching for localized task-supported teaching, rather than treated as poorly implemented or lost-in-translation versions of the original forms. In my interpretation of the studies reviewed in this article, researchers and theorists can provide teachers with a basic recipe of the tasks that are performed in TBLT. However, depending on the context, teachers may want to change some of the ingredients or add some local elements. In negotiating their local environments, teachers should be given great autonomy to decide how best to synthesize and digest the tasks of TBLT in order to maximize the effectiveness of their teaching.

Second, more decentralized and flexible language policies may be advisable. Traditionally, educational policies in Asian countries often have been carried out in a strong top-down manner, and thus, without having a top-down push, any substantial changes in practice are perhaps unlikely in many Asian contexts. However, as we have seen here, implementations of CLT/TBLT that have been mandated from the top down have been difficult to implement in many classrooms, particularly when teachers and students have less autonomy in its adaptation. Therefore, it is important to have a balanced combination of top-down direction and bottom-up flexibility in order to implement CLT/TBLT successfully. A critical component of the top-down direction is to ensure that teachers receive sufficient training and support so that they will understand the purpose of the new policy and have the resources to implement it. Other-wise, a lack of support may end up generating little change in practice, or it could accelerate widening gaps in resource availability (e.g., Hu, 2005, which describes the environment in China), and this in turn may contribute to socioeconomic divisions by English proficiency levels within a given country. It also appears that the top-down direction needs to be accompanied by drastic reforms in the exam system. Although the washback effects of testing are not as straightforward as one might expect (L. Cheng & Watanabe, 2004), there is little room for teachers to develop bottom-up influence or control under the current exam culture that prevails in Asia. Though it will not be easy to change societal attitudes toward exams, it also does not appear to be an impossible task to cause some changes, as we have seen here in the case of SBA in Hong Kong. In sum, a top-down implementation of TBLT has to be accompanied by sufficient teacher training and various other forms of support for teachers and schools, as well as reforms in the exam system, while at the same time allowing a greater degree of bottom-up flexibility in the implementation process.

Third, we need to develop communities of learning outside of the classroom, as well as inside it, in order to implement CLT/TBLT. This may be particularly important for contexts where learners see limited opportunities to use the target language in their real-life situations or where learners share the same L1 and see little relevancy in engaging in tasks with their peers in a foreign language. In major cities in China, one can often find English corners or English clubs where students create spaces to use English among themselves outside of the classroom. According to Gao (2008), such spaces not only provide participants with opportunities to practice English but also serve as a means of bringing together a supportive community that grants learners greater autonomy in their learning.

New technology has tremendous potential to provide learners with new and greater opportunities to use English across geographies. Recently, there has been emerging interest in computer-mediated communication (CMC) in TBLT (Levy & Stockwell, 2006; Thomas & Reinders, 2010), and Asia is no exception to this trend (e.g., Alwi & Adams, 2009; Greenfield, 2003; Hwang, 2008; Kiernan & Aizawa, 2004; Murray, 2007; Stockwell, 2010). CMC can provide authentic interactional spaces within and across classrooms that may promote a community of learning.

In addition, in CMC, students' output can be easily collected and monitored by teachers, and this can be an attractive feature for teachers in crowded classrooms. At this point, however, research concerning how best to introduce CMC as part of TBLT in specific teaching contexts in Asia is very limited. In Greenfield (2003), 11th-grade Hong Kong students and U.S. students collaboratively produced an anthology through CMC. The results indicated that the Hong Kong students found the project enjoyable and helpful when it came to gaining confidence in English and computational skills as well as improving their speaking and writing skills. However, the Hong Kong students felt "ambivalent" (p. 46) about improving skills directly related to the standardized exam (HKCEE) such as grammar and discourse skills. It appears that we need more research on the use of new technology; however, technology is certainly a promising tool for TBLT in Asia.

CONCLUSION

Although CLT and TBLT have gained substantial popularity in language-in-education policies in many countries in Asia, a number of constraints on the implementation of CBI/TBLT in Asia have been reported. The importance of considering the context in which education takes place has also been emphasized repeatedly. More recently, we can see a shift in focus from CBI to TBLT. A growing number of case studies have also indicated that innovative approaches have been experimented with in various parts in Asia, especially in contexts wherein teachers have greater autonomy over the implementation of TBLT. These studies consistently emphasize the importance for having flexibility in implementing TBLT.

Prabhu (1990) stated more than 20 years ago that there seems to be no single golden method that works well for everybody regardless of context. Similarly, for a specific context, there is no single method that works best all the time. Whether or not we are in the state of the "postmethod" era (Kumaravadivelu, 2006, p. 66) perhaps depends on how we define "methods" (Bell, 2003). Similarly, whether or not CLT/TBLT works in Asia depends on how flexibly we can conceptualize CLT/TBLT. However, it is perhaps safe to say that effective practice, whatever that denotes conceptually, is grounded in context and has never been static. Indeed, a historical analysis indicates that various types of methods and approaches have been widely exercised, dismissed, and revitalized across time and regions (Fotos,

2005). This recursive journey in search of effective practice may simply be a result of the complex relationship between teaching/learning and contexts. This journey is likely to continue, with new and different challenges, in order to respond to rapidly changing teaching/learning environments and the diversifying needs of learners.

ANNOTATED BIBLIOGRAPHY

Two special volumes on TBLT in Asia were published in the late 2000s: One was in the *Asian EFL Journal Quarterly* in 2006 and the other was in *Asia Journal of English Language Teaching* in 2009.

Adams, R., & Newton, J. (Eds.). (2009). TBLT in Asia: Constraints and opportunities. *Asia Journal of English Language Teaching, 19*.

Following an introduction by its guest editors, Adams and Newton, this special volume consists of seven empirical studies: one from China (Chunrao Deng & David Carless), two from Japan (Michael Hood, James Elwood, & Joseph Falout; Eriko Ishii), three from Hong Kong (David Carless; Jasmine Luk; Gertrude Tinker Sachs), and one from Malaysia (Nik Aloesnita Nik Hohd Alwi & Rebecca Adams). While these case studies illustrate the challenges that teachers face when implementing TBLT, they also indicate the various possible ways one may adapt task-based instruction in context. Though sometimes provocative, the insights and suggestions addressed in these case studies will stimulate any current discussion of how TBLT can be implemented in contextually appropriate ways.

Littlewood, W. (2007). Communicative and task-based language teaching in East Asian classrooms. *Language Teaching, 40*, 243–249.

This article is based on Littlewood's plenary speech delivered at the International Conference of the Korean Association for Teachers of English in Seoul in June 2006. In this article, he reintroduced a five-level framework indicating the communicativeness of activities that he had developed over the prior years. The framework explains the degree of communicativeness along a continuum from more form-focused activities to more meaning-based activities. Although this framework, as we almost always see with any newly developed model, is not free from criticism (e.g., Bruton, 2007), it has been widely used in research as well as professional development in Hong Kong and other Asian regions.

Robertson, P., & Jung, J. (Eds.). (2006). Special conference proceedings volume: Task-based learning in the Asian context. *Asian EFL Journal Quarterly, 8*. This special volume is a collection of papers which were originally presented as part of the Annual Asian EFL Journal Conference held in Pusan, South Korea, in March 2006. The volume includes general theoretical and methodological issues on TBLT contributed by leading TBLT researchers including David Nunan, Rod Ellis, Francis Mangubhai, and Rebecca Oxford. Other papers in this volume include case studies from different regions in Asia (i.e., four papers from Japan by Roger Nunn, Darren Lingley, Theron Muller, and Mariko Eguchi & Keiichi Eguchi; one paper from South Korea by In-Jae Jeon; and one paper from India by Meena Lochana & Gitoshree Deb). Many of these case studies dealt with the issue how best to strike a balance between form-focused and meaning-focused instruction in context. The volume also includes a paper from Ahmet Acar that addresses the importance of the perspective of English as an international language in task design and implementation.

REFERENCES

Adams, R., & Newton, J. (2009). TBLT in Asia: Constraints and opportunities. *Asian Journal of English Language Teaching, 19*, 1–17.

Alwi, N. A. N. M., & Adams, R. (2009). TBLT and SCMC: How do students use communication strategies? *Asian Journal of English Language Teaching, 19*, 135–157.

Anderson, J. (1993). Is a communicative approach practical for teaching English in China? Pros and cons. *System, 21*, 471–480.

Bax, S. (2003). The end of CLT: A context approach to language teaching. *ELT Journal, 57*, 278–287.

Bell, D. M. (2003). Method or postmethod: Are they really so incompatible? *TESOL Quarterly, 37*, 325–336.

Brown, H. D. (2001). *Teaching by principles: An interactive approach to language pedagogy.* Upper Saddle River, NJ: Prentice Hall Regents.

Bruton, A. (2007). Description or prescription for task-based instruction?: A reply to Littlewood. *Asian EFL Journal Quarterly, 9*, 227–235.

Burnaby, B., & Sun, Y. (1989). Chinese teachers' views of Western language teaching: Context informs paradigm. *TESOL Quarterly, 23*, 219–238.

Butler, Y. G. (2004). What level of English proficiency do elementary school teachers need to attain in order to teach EFL?: Case studies from Korea, Taiwan, and Japan. *TESOL Quarterly, 38,* 245–278.

Butler, Y. G. (2005a). Comparative perspectives towards communicative activities among elementary school teachers in South Korea, Japan, and Taiwan. *Language Teaching Research, 9,* 423–446.

Butler, Y. G. (2005b). Content-based instruction in foreign language contexts: Considerations for effective implementation. *JALT Journal, 27,* 227–245.

Butler, Y. G., & Iino, M. (2005). Current Japanese reforms in English language education: The 2003 "Action Plan." *Language Policy, 4,* 25–45.

Bygate, M., Skehan, P., & Swain, M. (Eds.). (2001). *Researching pedagogic tasks, second language learning, teaching, and testing.* Harlow, UK: Longman.

Cameron, D. (2002). Globalization and the teaching of "communication skills." In D. Block & D. Cameron (Eds.), *Globalization and language teaching* (pp. 67–82). London, UK: Routledge.

Carless, D. (2002). Implementing task-based learning with young learners. *ELT Journal, 56,* 389–396.

Carless, D. (2003). Factors in the implementation of task-based teaching in primary schools. *System, 31,* 485–500.

Carless, D. (2004). Issues in teachers' re-interpretation of a task-based innovation in primary schools. *TESOL Quarterly, 38,* 639–662.

Carless, D. (2007). The suitability of task-based approaches for secondary schools: Perspectives from Hong Kong. *System, 35,* 595–608.

Carless, D. (2008). Student use of the mother tongue in the task-based classroom. *ELT Journal, 62,* 331–338.

Carless, D. (2009). Revisiting the TBLT versus P-P-P debate: Voices from Hong Kong. *Asian Journal of English Language Teaching, 19,* 49–66.

Cheng, L. (2004). The washback effect of a public examination change on teachers' perceptions towards their classroom teaching. In L. Cheng & Y. Watanabe (Eds.), *Washback in language testing: Research contexts and methods* (pp. 147–170). Mahwah, NJ: Erlbaum.

Cheng, Y. (2010). The history of examinations: Why, how, what and whom to select? In L. Cheng & A. Curtis (Eds.), *English language assessment and the Chinese learner* (pp. 13–25). New York, NY: Routledge.

Cheng, L., & Watanabe, Y. (Eds.). (2004). *Washback in language testing: Research contexts and methods.* Mahwah, NJ: Erlbaum.

Choi, S. (2000). Teachers' beliefs about communicative language teaching and their classroom teaching practices. *English Teaching, 55,* 3–32.

Choi, Y.-H. (2007). The history and the policy of English language education in Korea. In Y. H. Choi & B. Spolsky (Eds.), *English education in Asia: History and policies* (pp. 33–66). Seoul, South Korea: Asia TEFL.

Chung, I.-F., & Huang, Y.-C. (2009). The implementation of communicative language teaching: An investigation of students' viewpoints. *The Asia-Pacific Education Researcher, 18*, 67–78.

Cortazzi, M., & Jin, L. (1996). Cultures of learning: Language classrooms in China. In H. Coleman (Ed.), *Society and the language classroom* (pp. 169–206). Cambridge, UK: Cambridge University Press.

Davison, C. (2007). Views from the chalkface: English language school-based assessment in Hong Kong. *Language Assessment Quarterly, 4*, 37–68.

Davison, C., & Hamp-Lyons, L. (2010). The Hong Kong certificate of education: School-based assessment reform in Hong Kong English language education. In L. Y. Cheng & A. Curtis (Eds.), *English language assessment and the Chinese learner* (pp. 248–266). New York, NY: Routledge.

Deng, C., & Carless, D. (2009). The communicativeness of activities in a task-based innovation in Guangdong, China. *Asian Journal of English Language Teaching, 19*, 113–134.

Ding, Y. (2007). Text memorization and imitation: The practices of successful Chinese learners of English. *System, 35*, 271–280.

Eguchi, M., & Eguchi, K. (2006). The limited effect of PBL on EFL learners. *Asian EFL Journal, 8*, 207–225.

Ellis, R. (2003). *Task-based language learning and teaching*. Oxford, UK: Oxford University Press.

Fotos, S. (2005). Traditional and grammar translation methods for second language teaching. In E. Hinkel (Ed.), *Handbook of research in second language teaching and learning* (pp. 653–670). Mahwah, NJ: Erlbaum.

Gao, X. (2008). The "English corner" as an out-of-class learning activity. *ELT Journal, 63*, 60–67.

Gonzalez, A. (1985). Communicative language teaching in the rural areas: How does one make the irrelevant relevant? In B. K. Das (Ed.), *Communicative language teaching* (pp. 84–105). Singapore: Singapore University Press.

Gorsuch, G. J. (2000). EFL educational policies and educational cultures: Influences on teachers' approval of communicative activities. *TESOL Quarterly, 34*, 675–710.

Greenfield, R. (2003). Collaborative e-mail exchange for teaching secondary ESL: A case study in Hong Kong. *Language Learning Technology, 7*, 46–70.

Ha, P. L. (2004). University classrooms in Vietnam: Contesting the stereotypes. *ELT Journal, 58*, 50–57.

Hamp-Lyons, L. (2007). The impact of testing practices on teaching: Ideologies and alternatives. In J. Cummins & C. Davison (Eds.), *The international handbook of English language teaching*. (Vol. 1, pp. 487–504). Norwell, MA: Springer.

Holliday, A. (1997a). The politics of participation in international English language education. *System*, *25*, 409–423.

Holliday, A. (1997b). Six lessons: Cultural continuity in communicative language teaching. *Language Teaching Research*, *1*, 212–238.

Hu, G. (2002a). English language teaching in the people's republic of China. In R. E. Silver, G. Hu, & M. Iino (Eds.), *English language education in China, Japan, and Singapore* (pp. 3–77). Singapore: National Institute of Education, Nanyang Technological University.

Hu, G. (2002b). Potential cultural resistance to pedagogical imports: The case of communicative language teaching in China. *Language, Culture and Curriculum*, *15*, 93–105.

Hu, G. (2005). Contextual influences on instructional practices: A Chinese case for an ecological approach to ELT. *TESOL Quarterly*, *39*, 635–660.

Hwang, P.-A. (2008). Linguistic characteristics in synchronous and asynchronous CMC. *English Language & Literature Teaching*, *14*, 47–66.

Jeon, I.-J. (2006). EFL teachers' perceptions of task-based language teaching: With a focus on Korean secondary classroom practice. *Asian EFL Journal*, *8*, 192–206.

Kachru, B. B. (1992). Teaching world Englishes. In B. B. Kachru (Ed.), *The other tongue: English across cultures* (pp. 355–365). Urbana: University of Illinois Press.

Kam, H. W., & Wong, R. Y. L. (Eds.). (2004). *English language teaching in East Asia today: Changing policies and practices*. Singapore: Eastern Universities Press.

Kiernan, P., & Aizawa, K. (2004). Cell phones in task based learning: Are cell phones useful language learning tools? *ReCALL*, *16*, 71–84.

Kirkpatrick, T. A. (1984). The role of communicative language teaching in secondary schools: With special reference to teaching in Singapore. In B. K. Das (Ed.), *Communicative language teaching* (pp. 171–191). Singapore: Singapore University Press.

Klapper, J. (2003). Taking communication to task? A critical review of recent trends in language teaching. *Language Learning Journal*, *27*, 33–42.

Kubota, R. (1999). Japanese culture constructed by discourse: implications for applied linguistic research and ELT. *TESOL Quarterly*, *33*, 9–36.

Kumaravadivelu, B. (2006). TESOL methods: Changing tracks, challenging trends. *TESOL Quarterly*, *40*, 59–81.

Lee, K.-M. (2002). Investigation into teacher proficiency for communicative English teaching in elementary schools. *Primary English Education*, *8*, 235–264.

Levy, M., & Stockwell, G. (2006). *CALL dimensions: Options and issues in computer assisted language learning*. Mahwah, NJ: Erlbaum.

Li, D. (1998). "It's always more difficult than you plan and imagine" : Teachers' perceived difficulties in introducing the communicative approach in South Korea. *TESOL Quarterly, 32,* 677–703.

Li, X. J. (1984). In defense of the communicative approach. *ELT Journal, 38,* 2–13.

Liao, X. (2004). The need for communicative language teaching in China. *ELT Journal, 58,* 270–273.

Lingley, D. (2006). A task-based approach to teaching a content-based Canadian studies course in an EFL context. *Asian EFL Journal, 8,* 122–139.

Littlewood, W. (2004). The task-based approach: Some questions and suggestions. *ELT Journal, 58,* 319–326.

Littlewood, W. (2007). Communicative and task-based language teaching in East Asian classrooms. *Language Teaching, 40,* 243–249.

Long, M. H. (1985). A role for instruction in second language acquisition: Task-based language teaching. In K. Hylstenstam & M. Pienemann (Eds.), *Modeling and assessing second language acquisition* (pp. 77–99). Clevedon, UK: Multilingual Matters.

Long, M. H., & Crookes, G. (1992). Three approaches to task-based syllabus design. *TESOL Quarterly, 26,* 27–56.

Long, M. H., & Robinson, P. (1998). Focus on form: Theory, research and practice. In C. Doughty & J. Williams (Eds.), *Focus on form in classroom second language acquisition* (pp. 15–41). Cambridge, UK: Cambridge University Press.

Luk, J. (2009). Preparing EFL students for communicative task performance: The nature and role of language knowledge. *Asian Journal of English Language Teaching, 19,* 67–90.

Luk, J. (2010). Talking to score: Impression management in L2 oral assessment and the co-construction of a test discourse genre. *Language Assessment Quarterly, 7,* 25–53.

McDonough, K., & Chaikitmongkol, W. (2007). Teachers' and learners' reactions to a task-based EFL course in Thailand. *TESOL Quarterly, 41,* 107–132.

McKay, S. L. (2002). *Teaching English as an international language.* Oxford, UK: Oxford University Press.

Miller, L., & Aldred, D. (2000). Student teachers' perceptions about communicative language teaching methods. *RELC Journal, 31,* 1–22.

Miller, T. (1995). Japanese learners' reactions to communicative English lessons. *JALT Journal, 17,* 31–53.

Mitchell, R., & Lee, J. H. W. (2003). Sameness and difference in classroom learning cultures: Interpretations of communicative pedagogy in the US and Korea. *Language Teaching Research, 7,* 35–63.

Muller, T. (2006). Researching the influence of target language on learner task performance. *Asian EFL Journal, 8,* 165–173.

Murray, D. E. (2007). Teaching and learning communicative competence in an e-era. In J. Liu (Ed.), *English language teaching in China: New approaches, perspectives and standards* (pp. 75–90). London, UK: Continuum.

Nishino, T. (2008). Japanese secondary school teachers' beliefs and practices regarding communicative language teaching: An exploratory survey. *JALT Journal, 30,* 27–50.

Nunan, D. (2003). The impact of English as a global language on educational policies and practices in the Asia-Pacific region. *TESOL Quarterly, 37,* 589–613.

Nunn, R. (2006). Designing holistic units for task-based instruction. *Asian EFL Journal, 8,* 69–93.

Pham, H. H. (2007). Communicative language teaching: Unity within diversity. *ELT Journal, 61,* 193–201.

Prabhu, N. S. (1987). *Second language pedagogy.* Oxford, UK: Oxford University Press.

Prabhu, N. S. (1990). There is no best method—why? *TESOL Quarterly, 24,* 161–76.

Prapaisit de Segovia, L., & Hardison, D. M. (2008). Implementing education reform: EFL teachers' perspectives. *ELT Journal, 63,* 154–162.

Penner, J. (1995). Change and conflict: Introduction of the communicative approach in China. *TESL Canada Journal, 12,* 1–17.

Qi, L. (2007). Is testing an efficient agent for pedagogical change? Examining the intended washback of the writing task in a high-stakes English test in China. *Assessment in Education, 14,* 51–74.

Rao, Z. (1996). Reconciling communicative approaches to the teaching of English with traditional Chinese methods. *Research in the Teaching of English, 30,* 458–471.

Rao, Z. (2002). Chinese students' perceptions towards communicative and non-communicative activities in EFL classroom. *System, 30,* 85–105.

Richards, J. C., & Rodgers, T. S. (2001). *Approaches and methods in language teaching: A description and analysis.* New York, NY: Cambridge University Press.

Rivers, D. J. (2008). Task design to task enactment: How teacher interpretations of a given task manipulate its evolution as a pedagogical construct. *Journal of Asia TEFL, 5,* 31–54.

Sakui, K. (2004). Wearing two pairs of shoes: Language teaching in Japan. *ELT Journal, 58,* 155–163.

Samimy, K. K., & Kobayashi, C. (2004). Toward the development of intercultural communicative competence: Theoretical and pedagogical implications for Japanese English teachers. *JALT Journal, 26,* 245–261.

Samuda, V., & Bygate, M. (2008). *Tasks in second language learning.* New York, NY: Palgrave Macmillan.

Sano, M., Takahashi, M., & Yoneyama, A. (1984). Communicative language teaching and local needs. *ELT Journal, 38,* 170–177.

Sato, K., & Kleinsasser, R. C. (1999). Communicative language teaching (CLT): Practical understandings. *Modern Language Journal, 83*, 494–517.

Savignon, S. J. (2005). Communicative language teaching: strategies and goals. In E. Hinkel (Ed.), *Handbook of research in second language teaching and learning* (pp. 635–651). Mahwah, NJ: Erlbaum.

Savignon, S. J., & Wang, C. (2003). Communicative language teaching in EFL contexts: Learner attitudes and perceptions. *IRAL, 41*, 223–249.

Skehan, P. (2003). Task-based instruction. *Language Teaching, 36*, 1–14.

Stevenson, H. W., & Stigler, J. W. (1992). *The learning gap: Why our schools are failing and what we can learn from Japanese and Chinese education.* New York, NY: Touchstone.

Stockwell, G. (2010). Effects of multimodality in computer-mediated communication tasks. In M. Thomas & H. Reinders (Eds.), *Task-based language learning and teaching with technology* (pp. 83–104). London, UK: Continuum.

Sun, G., & Cheng, L. (2002). From context to curriculum: A case study of communicative language teaching in China. *TESL Canada Journal, 19*, 67–86.

Sullivan, P. N. (2000). Playfulness as mediation in communicative language teaching in a Vietnamese classroom. In J. P. Lantolf (Ed.), *Sociocultural theory and second language learning* (pp. 115–131). Oxford, UK: Oxford University Press.

Thomas, M., & Reinders, H. (Eds.). (2010). *Task-based language learning and teaching with technology.* London, UK: Continuum.

Tinker Sachs, G. (2007). The challenging of adopting and adapting task-based cooperative teaching and learning in an EFL context. In K. Van den Branden, K. Van Gorp, & M. Verhelst (Eds.), *Task-based language education from a classroom-based perspective* (pp. 235–264). Newcastle, UK: Cambridge Scholars.

Tinker Sachs, G. (2009). Taking risks in task-based teaching and learning. *Asian Journal of English Language Teaching, 19*, 91–112.

Tong, A. S., Adamson, B., & Che, M. A. (2000). Tasks in English language and Chinese language. In B. Adamson, T. Kwan, & K. Chan (Eds.), *Changing the curriculum: The impact of reform on primary schooling in Hong Kong* (pp. 145–173). Hong Kong: Hong Kong University Press.

Tsui, A. B. M. (2007). Complexities of identity formation: A narrative inquiry of an EFL teacher. *TESOL Quarterly, 41*, 657–680.

Watson Todd, R. (2006). Continuing change after the innovation. *System, 34*, 1–14.

Wilkins, D. (1976). *National syllabuses.* Oxford, UK: Oxford University Press.

Willis, J. (1996). *A framework for task-based learning.* London, UK: Longman.

Yu, L. M. (2001). Communicative language teaching in China: Progress and resistance. *TESOL Quarterly, 35*, 194–198.

Yukawa, E. (2002). Inside the classroom: Interaction in elementary school English lessons in Japan. *Japan Journal of Multilingualism and Multiculturalism, 8*, 1–25.

Zhang, E. Y. F. (2007). TBLT—Innovation in primary school English language teaching in mainland China. In K. Van den Branden, K. Van Gorp, & M. Verhelst (Eds.), *Tasks in action: Task-based language education from a classroom-based perspective* (pp. 68–91). Cambridge, UK: Cambridge Scholars.

Zhang, L. J. (2006, November). *The ecology of communicative language teaching: Reflecting on the Singapore experience.* Paper presented as plenary keynote speaker at the 2006 Annual China English Language Education Association (CELEA) International Conference. Guangdong University of Foreign Studies, Guangdong, China. Retrieved from http: //www. eric.ed.gov/ERICDocs/data/ericdocs2sql/content_storage_01/0000019b/80/2b/65/ba.pdf

Enhancing Language Learning in Study Abroad

Celeste Kinginger

Research demonstrates that study abroad can have a positive impact on every domain of language competence, and that it is particularly helpful for the development of abilities related to social interaction. However, some results suggest that study abroad intensifies individual differences in achievement: Certain students thrive while others founder. Qualitative studies provide insight into the sources of these differences both in the stances that students adopt toward their host communities and in the ways in which they are received. Overall, the research points to a need for language learners' broader engagement in local communicative practices, for mindfulness of their situation as peripheral participants, and for more nuanced awareness of language itself. This article offers a rationale, based on the current state of the art in research, for including the expertise of language educators in the choice and design of study abroad programs. Students will benefit from programs specifically designed to foster language learning through observation, participation, and reflection.

In the United States particularly, both professional and lay folklore encourage a view of study abroad as a magical formula for the development of language ability, an effortless process of "easy learning" (DeKeyser, 2010, p. 89). Study abroad has occasionally been interpreted as a cure-all for language problems, as a rationale for neglecting students' language-related needs (Polio & Zyzik, 2009), and even as an excuse not to teach languages at all (Coleman, 1997). The growing research base on this topic, however, presents a very different picture: If indeed study abroad holds the potential to enhance students' language ability in every domain examined thus far, this enhancement requires effort and engagement on the part of all concerned, including students, teachers, host families, and program administrators. When students cultivate language abilities in their host communities, the qualities and outcomes of this process emerge from a complex interplay of students' dispositions, features of their environments, and host communities' stances toward their guests.

This article first outlines major findings of contemporary research following an array of traditions within applied linguistics. Ranging from investigations focusing strictly on outcomes, where study abroad is to be interpreted as a form of experimental treatment, to in-depth qualitative and hybrid studies, this research offers considerable insight for pedagogy. Specifically, research findings point to (a) the need for greater and more qualitatively meaningful engagement of students in the practices of their host communities and (b) closer attention to students' preparation for language learning abroad. Having established a rationale for recruiting the expertise of language educators in the design and best use of study abroad programs, we move on to consider an array of illustrative projects and suggestions for enhancing study abroad as an environment for language learning.

OVERVIEW OF RECENT RESEARCH

As outlined in Kinginger (2009a), the research on language learning in study abroad generally follows overall trends in the applied linguistics literature. This research may be divided into four broad categories. The earliest and most prominent efforts focused on the outcomes of study abroad in terms of language, variously defined. A number of projects have attempted to measure or predict the development of general proficiency as operationalized in tests, whereas other studies have pinpointed outcomes defined as components of communicative competence (grammatical, sociolinguistic, discourse, or strategic abilities). Although carefully designed outcomes-based inquiry does demonstrate that study abroad can enhance every aspect of language ability, it also reveals that outcomes are occasionally lackluster in comparison to the expectations held by teachers and students. Further, many studies find significant individual differences in outcomes, leading one researcher (Huebner, 1995) to speculate that study abroad intensifies these differences.

Why do some students register impressive gains in proficiency scores or documented communicative abilities, whereas others do not, and some may even appear to have forgotten some of what they knew of the language before their sojourn abroad (Kinginger, 2008)? When students are supposedly surrounded by a constant stream of "high quality, contextualized exposure" to language (Isabelli, 2007, p. 333), how can we explain their occasionally quite undistinguished achievement? This mystery drives investigations of a second type, namely, studies attempting to specify independent behavioral variables, such as time-on-task, that correlate with linguistic gains. Much of this research retains a deterministic outlook, searching for the causes of success or failure in quantitative accounts of students' activities, such as diaries reporting amounts of time spent using the language in question, or the Language Contact Profile (Freed, Dewey, Segalowitz, & Halter, 2004) documenting student activities and accompanying language use. Sometimes this approach yields interpretable results, as in the case of Freed, Segalowitz, and Dewey's (2004) investigation of fluency development in French under three conditions: study abroad, domestic immersion, and classroom learning. Using data from the Language Contact Profile, these researchers were able to show that the domestic immersion learners' superior fluency development took place in a context where students used significantly more French than did their counterparts both at home and abroad. On the other hand, Ginsburg and Miller (2000) reported with astonishment that their calendar diary data appeared to shed no light on students' proficiency scores in Russian.

It would appear that a purely quantitative approach to understanding students' use of time may not suffice if the goal is to understand how and why language learning does or does not take place in study abroad. Thus, researchers began to pursue a third type of empirical investigation, this time seeking to understand the qualities of the in-country sojourn, mainly from the perspective of students. The qualitative research on language learning in study abroad has included ethnographies of cohorts and settings, such as the homestay or the classroom; case studies of individuals; and close, detailed study of language socialization as it takes place in host family interactions. This research clearly demonstrates that language learning in study abroad is a dialogic and situated affair whose success depends on not only the attributes and intentions of the student but also the ways in which the student is received within his or her host community. A student who is mindful of his or her role as a peripheral participant (Lave & Wenger, 1991); who actively seeks access to learning opportunities; and who is welcomed as a person of consequence, worthy of the hosts' time and nurture, is likely to succeed. Conversely, achievement may be more modest for a student who interprets study abroad as a parenthetical diversion from serious study (Gore, 2005), who avoids contact with local people (Feinberg, 2002), or who is received with indifference. This research also illuminates the role of identity, and particularly gender, in shaping the study abroad experience. When students are framed by their interlocutors in unfamiliar ways, as representatives of a category, much depends on their ability to choose unbiased analysis over judgmental rejection of these practices.

Since the mid-2000s, researchers have continued to develop the three strands of inquiry outlined earlier. They have refined these approaches and explored the intersections between them. Gaining in prominence is a fourth type of study in which researchers combine in-depth qualitative study of student experiences and documentation of learning outcomes. In the following section, I will present examples of the most recent research in each of these categories: (a) outcomes-based research on general proficiency development and on aspects of communicative competence; (b) studies of specific learner activities believed to correlate with language development; (c) ethnographies and case studies; and (d) mixed-method studies combining qualitative inquiry with measurement or other documentation of language learning. This review is by no means comprehensive or exhaustive, but instead examines selected studies illustrating both the potential benefits of study abroad for language learning and issues of concern to language educators.

Proficiency and Communicative Competence

As already noted, the contemporary literature includes both studies of general proficiency development and investigations of particular components of communicative competence: grammatical, sociolinguistic, discourse, and strategic abilities (e.g., Savignon, 1983). In the first category, the most robust and well-regarded U.S.-based study, sponsored by the American Council on the Teaching of Russian (ACTR), examined predictors of gain scores on a variety of holistic proficiency tests. When data for 658 participants had been gathered between 1984 and 1990, Brecht, Davidson, and Ginsburg (1995) reported that the major predictors of gain in Russian oral proficiency were experience in learning another language, command of reading and grammar skills, and gender, with men more likely than women to reach the Advanced (2) level on the ACTFL (American Council on the Teaching of Foreign Languages) Oral Proficiency Interview.[1]

A replication of this study by Davidson (2010) involved 1,881 U.S.-based students of Russian who had participated in ACTR programs of various durations between 1994 and 2009. For this cohort, results pertaining to reading ability and structural control replicated the findings of the earlier study. In addition, duration of the program was correlated with gain in speaking, reading, and listening. In the case of gender, however, the earlier correlation with gain scores was no longer in effect. Davidson interpreted this finding in terms of changes in gender roles since the collapse of the Soviet Union and also mentioned "dedicated training in self-management and strategy selection provided by ACTR to its departing groups with special attention to female participants" (p. 20). In concluding the report, Davidson noted the "remarkable" (p. 23) levels of individual variation in outcomes. He argued that language learning in study abroad holds "enormous potential for meeting the needs of education in the 21st century" (p. 23), but that this potential would not be realized until study abroad was integrated into the curriculum and enjoyed strong support from all stakeholders.

The uniqueness of study abroad as an environment for language learning is illustrated in the work of scholars examining particular modalities of language use or features of communicative competence. For example, the role of study abroad in the development of writing ability is illustrated in Sasaki's (2009) exploration of the long-term effects of Japanese students' sojourns in English-speaking environments. In a study examining changes in second language writing ability and related motivation as they evolved over a period of 3.5 years, Sasaki found a predictable significant effect for writing practice and metaknowledge of English. More compelling are the results of her qualitative inquiry into the motivation potentially underlying efforts at writing improvement: Only those students who had spent some time abroad formed a second-language-related "imagined community" (p. 71) to inspire and inform these efforts.

In the case of grammatical ability, the distinctive advantages of a sojourn abroad have not always been easy to prove, particularly when the construct under study is broadly defined. The findings of some studies have suggested that students abroad gain in fluency at the expense of accuracy (e.g., Walsh, 1994), or that academic or classroom learning may be equal to or better than study abroad in this domain (Collentine, 2004). When researchers narrow their focus to particular grammatical features, the picture becomes more complex; though the findings of some studies suggest that study abroad leads to modest gains in grammatical competence, others offer no such evidence. Isabelli and Nishida (2005), for example, examined modality in Spanish through the use of the subjunctive by U.S.-based participants in a 9-month program of study abroad. In comparison with their peers at home, some of these students produced more complex syntax requiring the subjunctive and more actual tokens of verbs in the subjunctive. Although they did not master this aspect of Spanish grammar in its entirety, they demonstrated readiness for further learning that offered a clear advantage in subsequent classroom instruction (Isabelli, 2007). Similarly, study abroad participants in an investigation by Howard (2005) were shown to have advanced in the long-term process of learning to mark past tense and aspect in French. In comparison to their peers at home, these participants possessed an expanded repertoire for autonomous use of this grammatical system. On the other hand, Isabelli-García (2010) found no difference between study abroad and at-home learners in the acquisition of gender agreement in Spanish.

It is in the investigation of abilities related to social interaction that the most significant advantages of study abroad become evident. Whereas classroom interaction is most often limited to the theatrical use of sanitized, preselected language forms, study abroad participants may become engaged in a wide range of communicative settings where their interlocutors' purposes and intentions may vary significantly, and their own language use becomes consequential. This participation may enhance students' communicative repertoires through the development of sociolinguistic, discourse, and pragmatic abilities.

Regan, Howard, and Lemée (2009) investigated the development of sociolinguistic competence in study abroad from a variationist perspective. They found that although classroom learning is useful for acquiring the categorical features of a language, a key advantage of the study abroad context is in providing exposure to that which is variable in the speech of expert users. Regan et al. scrutinized the performance of Irish advanced learners of French who had studied in France to show that these learners developed nativelike ability to manipulate certain variable features (e.g., deletion or retention of "ne" in negation, or choice of "nous" versus

Enhancing Language Learning in Study Abroad   83

"on" to index the first person plural). According to these authors, sociolinguistic competence is a crucial aspect of second language ability, because it allows learners to signal their integration into the host community. Furthermore, they argued that study abroad is the optimum context for this domain of second language acquisition.

Similar findings emerged from Iwasaki's (2010) study of style shifting in the Japanese of American learners. Choice of plain or polite style is obligatory in Japanese, and difficulty in learning to speak appropriately as a second language learner is widely attested in the literature. Iwasaki's study showed not only that study abroad participants learned these forms, but also that they learned to use and mix them as a resource for the creation of interactional contexts (e.g., to express emotion), just as expert speakers of Japanese do.

The most prevalent focus of study abroad research on social interactive abilities is the speech act, that is, how students "do things with words" (Austin, 1975) such as requesting and apologizing. Schauer (2009), for instance, examined the performance and awareness of English-language requests by a group of German sojourners in Britain, showing that the students' ability to craft appropriate requests and to recognize pragmatically inappropriate requests were both enhanced by study abroad. Magnan and Back (2007a) showed that American learners of French whose proficiency increased during an in-country stay also developed greater ability to balance direct and indirect requests, although some of the baseline native request features they collected were not represented in the learner data. Taguchi (2008) focused on comprehension of direct and indirect opinions and refusals in American English by a cohort of Japanese students. Although only modest gains were made for comprehension of indirect opinions, Taguchi found that study abroad improved accuracy in assessing the implied meaning of indirect refusals. Thus, the results of current research on speech act performance and comprehension mirrors earlier finding: Students abroad make gains in this domain but do not become simulacra of native speakers.

The most compelling study of speech acts, and the one that most convincingly demonstrates the unique nature of learning in study abroad, remains Shardakova's (2005) examination of American students' apologies in Russian. Shardakova argued that it is not only the performance of speech acts that must be studied in relation to that of native speakers but also their interpretation. According to the author, speakers of Russian evaluate situations involving intimacy, unfamiliarity, or hierarchy in ways that are distinct from Americans' perceptions of the same situations. Using a research design involving native speakers and four groups of learners, with intermediate and advanced proficiency, with and without study abroad in Russia, Shardakova provided evidence that only a sojourn in-country would allow learners to "see things from the point of view of a Russian" (p. 445) and choose (or not) to apologize accordingly.

In summary, the contemporary research on outcomes of study abroad highlights a number of themes. First is the sheer power of a sojourn abroad, given adequate institutional and pedagogical support, to further language proficiency. Second is the subtlety of some language-related development, particularly in the domain of grammatical competence. Third is the unique potential of study abroad to enhance social interactive language abilities. Finally, if one goal of language learning is to see things from the point of view of others, that is, to develop true intercultural understanding, then study abroad has much to be recommended. This research also shows, however, that a sojourn in-country does not guarantee language learning, that outcomes for individual learners are highly variable, and that student performance often does not approximate that of expert speakers.

Correlating Students' Activities With Linguistic Gains

The search for an explanation of individual differences in the linguistic outcomes of study abroad has led some researchers to question the extent to which students actually do enjoy "high quality, contextualized exposure" to language (Isabelli, 2007, p. 333) and unlimited access to expert speakers while abroad. Tanaka (2007), for example, interviewed a cohort of Japanese students about their contact with English during a 3-month sojourn in New Zealand. Many of these students confessed that they preferred to construct a "cozy Japanese environment" (p. 50) over seeking out opportunities to interact with local people. Due to insecurity about their language proficiency or shyness, they avoided interactions with their host families.

Magnan and Back (2007b) designed an investigation of proficiency gain in French in relation to housing (with or without native speakers of French) and reported activities such as reading local newspapers, watching films, and speaking French with American compatriots versus local people. Beginning their semester-long sojourns with intermediate level proficiency, the majority (12 of 20) registered gains on the ACTFL Oral Proficiency Interview, but eight maintained their predeparture score. Echoing the findings of an earlier study (Ginsburg & Miller, 2000), the researchers found no significant correlations between housing type and reported activity, with the exception of a negative correlation with the amount of French spoken with American classmates against level of improvement. A post hoc test of the relationship among age, gender, and level of previous coursework revealed an effect only for the latter variable, where advanced studies predicted gain. Magnan and Back suggested that students with intermediate proficiency may not be prepared to engage in extensive interactions with native speakers, but that readiness for learning may be enhanced by prior academic experience. They further suggested that American students in programs of one semester's duration may be returning home just as their self-confidence increases to the point where "ability to maneuver in academic and social spheres permits them to form the bonds with native speakers that will lead to increased proficiency" (Magnan & Back, 2007b, p. 53).

Ethnographies and Case Studies

Although studies of language contact attempt to link language proficiency gains to quantitative accounts of time-on-task of various kinds, case studies and other ethnographic works portray the qualities of study abroad sojourns, usually without external assessment of language development. These studies reveal that language learning in study abroad is a complex, dialogic, situated affair in which the subjectivities of students and hosts are deeply implicated. Jackson (2008) followed a cohort of Hong Kong-based Chinese university students as they traveled to Britain for a short-term intensive English language immersion experience, including homestays with local families. While these students recounted similar experiences of perceived racism and linguistic insecurity, their developmental trajectories were highly individualized. The amount and quality of dialogic interaction and mutual interest in the homestay settings varied considerably, as did the students' own openness to change, investment in language learning, and ethnocentric versus ethnorelative frames of mind. For example, one student perceived her host family as dismissive both of her identity as a Hong Konger (they referred to her as Japanese) and of her anxiety about safety. Her emotional detachment from her hosts limited the quality of her interactions at home, and she never overcame feelings of inferiority when speaking English. Another participant, however, chose to persevere in her efforts to build local relationships and lived with a family eager to spend time with her and to engage in multiple forms of dialogic interaction. By the end of the sojourn, she had learned to value English as a living language rather than as a mere academic object of primarily utilitarian value.

A diary study by Hassall (2006) illustrated the struggles of learners abroad as they attempt to work out pragmatic meanings within the languages they are learning. Hassall documented his own efforts to develop competence in leave-taking while studying in Indonesia. In the absence of pedagogical materials or empirical data to describe leave-taking formulae and clarify their uses in context, Hassall was obliged to garner this knowledge on his own, through cycles of observation, testing in interpersonal interactions, and reflection. The story of this effort unfolds in episodes of triumph, when Hassall's experiments are successful, and in defeat and embarrassment, when he applies a leave-taking formula in a way that is clearly, yet still mysteriously, wrong. Hassall concluded that acquiring pragmatic knowledge in a study abroad context is a "major task" (2006, p. 53).

A number of studies have scrutinized the role of gender in shaping the qualities of study abroad, normally focusing on the experiences of American women. These studies routinely show that U.S.-based female students interpret other societies as sexist, and many of their interactions as constituting or bordering on harassment (e.g., Polanyi, 1995; Talburt & Stewart, 1999). Two recent studies shed new light on this phenomenon. Churchill (2009) portrayed the uniquely positive experience of a male Japanese high school student during an English immersion program in the United States. At home, Churchill's participant was among the least successful learners in the cohort, isolated by his gender in a predominantly female class. In the study abroad context, however, he rapidly gained access to a broad social network through participation in sports. He was interpreted as a person of consequence, recruited as a broker of relationships with the female members of the group, and included in conversations on many topics relevant to adolescent boys: music, hobbies, and girls. An analysis of spoken narratives at the end of the program showed that, when compared to female students with similar initial proficiency scores, he made the most progress.

While it may appear that, as a general rule, male students enjoy enhanced status and greater language learning opportunities than do females abroad, a study by Patron (2007) offers some evidence to suggest that this finding may be in part an artifact of the U.S.-based cultural contexts under study. Patron investigated the experiences of French students on a yearlong study away program in Australia. In the initial phase of their sojourn, many of these students experienced culture shock as they encountered the everyday and academic practices of Australians. Among the more troubling issues, for the female students, was the absence of practices interpretable by American students as harassment. That is, these students reported feeling insecure in their gender identity because they received no compliments on their appearance and observed few instances of flirtation or gentility. Thus it may be that a true understanding of cultural practices in study abroad contexts will require true ethnographic studies that include the perspectives of students and their hosts.

Mixed Methods Research

In terms of research methodology, the most recent development in the study abroad research is the rise to prominence of studies combining in-depth, qualitative study with assessment of language development. Isabelli-García (2006), for example, tracked the social networks of four U.S.-based students enrolled in a semester-long Spanish language program in Argentina and interpreted Simulated Oral Proficiency Interview scores and a more fine-grained measure of proficiency development in relation to students' engagement with these networks. The highest achieving student, a young man, gained immediate access to a broad social network through a friend of a friend and became actively involved in this group's social and travel activities. The only female whose case was presented made no measureable proficiency gain. This student was initially placed with a family demonstrating no interest in interacting with her, then moved twice before settling with an acceptable family. She was distressed by the gender-related *piropos* (catcalling) she encountered in the streets. By mid-semester, her social network was limited to the host family, program staff, and an American friend with whom she spent most of her free time.

Kinginger (2008) offered case studies of a cohort and six individual American students enrolled in semester-long programs in France. In this study, a primarily qualitative focus was enhanced by measurement of overall proficiency (via the *Test de Français International*) and assessment of language awareness (via the

Language Awareness Interview designed for the project). Individual differences in proficiency and awareness gains were interpreted in light of each student's reported experiences and dispositions toward their host community. The profiles of three of the most successful students were presented. One young man was an avid reader and writer of literary French who also became involved in voluntary service at a local soup kitchen. Another participated in an internship and in multiple campus-based associations, and he was housed with a family who actively pursued his language development in lengthy, routine dinner table conversations. A young woman viewed her study abroad experience as serious preparation for a career in international business or the Foreign Service. Students whose achievement was more modest, all of them female, retreated from engagement with their local hosts, albeit in different ways. After a series of uncomfortable discussions about American foreign policy and the war in Iraq, one student became alienated from her host family. Another viewed her sojourn abroad as a modern-day Grand Tour intended primarily to mix entertainment with the accumulation of highly regarded cultural experiences, and so spent most of her time traveling to European capital cities with other Americans. Yet another reattached herself to her home social networks, via the Internet, and screened herself from local reality to the best of her ability. Thus, to understand the sources of individual variation in outcomes, it is important to understand that the study abroad experience is highly variable.

DeKeyser (2010) proposed a closer look at the struggles of students, such as the participants in Magnan and Back's (2007b) study, who arrived in programs abroad with intermediate proficiency. Participants in the study were 16 U.S.-based learners of Spanish in a sheltered program in Argentina, which included a homestay component. Data included interviews in Spanish with stimulated recall sessions, questionnaires, and observation. DeKeyser's interest was in the process of monitoring, that is, the process of drawing on explicit conscious knowledge of grammar and vocabulary during communicative events. DeKeyser's findings paint a bleak picture of students in a "valiant struggle in a battle for which they were ill-equipped" (2010, p. 81). These students began their program with high motivation and belief in their ability to make dramatic strides in speaking proficiency, but quickly became discouraged. For DeKeyser, the culprit here is the students' inability to monitor the accuracy of their speech due to limited declarative knowledge of grammar and very little prior practice that might have helped to convert declarative to procedural knowledge. When faced with the cognitive challenges associated with social interaction in Spanish, many students simply opted out. They spent their time "reinventing the elementary grammar wheel in their classes and avoiding practice opportunities with native speakers because they were too painful" (DeKeyser, 2010, p. 89).

The findings of contemporary research on language learning in study abroad demonstrate, first of all, that study abroad holds great potential for students' intellectual growth through integrated language and culture learning. However, the outcomes and qualities of student experience are highly variable. These findings also suggest that when students do not make dramatic gains in language ability or intercultural awareness despite a professed desire to do so, it is because they do not become sufficiently or meaningfully engaged in the practices of their local host communities or because they lack guidance in interpreting their observations. The reasons for this lack of engagement are myriad; they can include, for example, (a) students' or programs' de-emphasis on language learning in favor of other goals, such as the accumulation of symbolic capital through tourism; (b) a retreat into national superiority based on observations about gender-related or other cultural practices; (c) increasingly, the tendency to remain virtually "at home," tied to an electronic umbilical cord or an immense personal library of home-based media; (d) inadequate preparation to practice the language, to understand the nature of language learning, and to observe and reflect upon their experiences in an unbiased manner.

PROMOTING ENGAGEMENT IN LANGUAGE LEARNING ABROAD

Clearly, studentss' interest and investment in language learning is not guaranteed, and there will always be a variety of ways in which study abroad is approached and interpreted. In the interest of students who truly desire language competence, however, it follows from the preceding findings that language educators have a number of crucial roles to play: promoting educationally relevant engagement in the practices of host communities, providing guidance in the interpretation of these practices, and preparing students to take specific advantage of language learning opportunities.

Before students go abroad, they can be guided toward the practice of unbiased observation, participate in informal dialogs with members of their host communities, articulate appropriate goals, and prepare to make the most of their sojourn. While students are abroad, they can engage in informal ethnographic inquiry through tasks and projects, and they can participate in service learning, internships, or independent research. When students return from their in-country experience, much depends on how their experience is received within their home institution: whether or not it is integrated into the curriculum, with ongoing attention to their need for instruction in language and advanced literacy practices.

Preparing Students for a Sojourn Abroad

There are several ways in which language educators can help students to prepare for a language-focused sojourn abroad. First among these is the provision of guidance in selecting a program prioritizing language learning. Subsequently, students may benefit from enhanced understanding of both what and how they may learn while they are abroad. Concerning the former, many students may hold "folklinguistic theories" (Miller & Ginsburg, 1995, p. 293), in which, for example, language is analogous to architecture, with words as building blocks and grammar as mortar. Absent from such portrayals are the social interactive abilities (sociolinguistic, discourse, or pragmatic) best learned in extensive interactive contact with expert speakers (Miller & Ginsburg, 1995). A short course in language awareness, such as the one outlined in Kinginger (2009b) or participation in an online pragmatics course (e.g., Ishihara, 2007; Sykes & Cohen, 2010; see also Shively, 2010) might help students to recognize and cultivate these abilities.

Kinginger (2009b) also noted the commonalities between the goals of language learners abroad and those of scholars in the ethnography of communication (see also Cain & Zarate, 1996; Jackson, 2008; Jurasek, Lamson, & O'Maley, 1996; Roberts, Byram, Barro, Jordan, & Street, 2001). Observation, participation, and reflection or introspection are among the main modes of learning languages in study abroad settings, as revealed in the Hassall (2006) study already reviewed here. These modes are also the key techniques used by ethnographers of communication as they attempt to understand what a speaker needs to know in order to communicate appropriately within a given community, and as they carry out field work "observing, asking questions, participating in group activities, and testing the validity of one's perceptions against the intuitions of natives" (Saville-Troike, 2003, p. 3). Kinginger (2009b) and Jackson (2008) offered suggested tasks for training in ethnographic observation for the predeparture stage.

Through computer-mediated communication, it is possible to offer students occasions to practice informal, intercultural dialog (Tudini, 2007), virtual visits to their future host country (Pertusa-Seva & Stewart, 2008), and telecollaborative exchanges in which they interact directly with their peers at institutions abroad (Kinginger & Belz, 2005). Telecollaborative exchanges provide a sheltered opportunity to participate in socially consequential interactions, discover the social significance of linguistic choices, and begin crafting an appropriate foreign-language-mediated identity.

Finally, the findings of DeKeyser's (2010) study suggest careful consideration and cultivation of students' predeparture language proficiency. Other studies, including Kinginger (2008), offer evidence for the benefit of study abroad to students of quite varied initial proficiency. However, if students' aspiration is to quickly and efficiently develop speaking ability while abroad for a typical sojourn of a semester or less, guidance in preparing for this challenge is in order.

Engagement in Host Communities

The contemporary literature on language learning in study abroad includes a number of practical suggestions for enhancing student participation and engagement in local communities. In addition to training and practice in ethnographic inquiry (Jackson, 2008), there have been proposals for various kinds of tasks and projects. Knight and Schmidt-Rinehart (2010), for example, found that a curriculum requiring students to initiate structured conversations with their host families offered considerable benefit. The structured conversations led to impromptu discussions and generally upgraded both the quantity and the quality of dialogic interaction in the homestay. Kinginger (2009b) proposed a number of larger language-related projects designed to foster focused observation of a specific phenomenon (e.g., the language of service encounters or of publicity) followed by interaction with members of the host community around culturally unique artifacts. Streitwieser and Leephaibul (2007) described a program offering training and support for undergraduate research for American students in Germany. Student research projects, often on topics of contemporary relevance, facilitated a "more intensive immersion into the local culture" (p. 169).

In addition to tasks or projects, engagement in host community practices may be furthered through service learning and internships. Ducate (2009), for example, reported on a program involving U.S.-based study abroad participants in teaching English at a German elementary school. This program offered students opportunities to participate in a variety of communicative settings, including their own classrooms and the homes of their hosts, away from their American peers. Kurasawa and Nagatomi (2006) discussed the language learning experiences of American undergraduate interns in Japanese. Although these interns contributed to the companies or institutions they joined through their expertise in English, they also participated in casual conversations in Japanese.

Technology also has strong potential to further students' involvement in their host communities, for example, in the creation of thematic digital video projects (Goulah, 2007) or in the use of e-journals (Stewart, 2010) and mobile blogs (Comas-Quinn, Mardomingo, & Valentine, 2009) to promote documentation of experiences, reflection on their meaning, and guidance from language educators or other experts.

Integrating Study Abroad Into the Curriculum

Although the integration of study abroad into the language curriculum remains a rare consideration in many institutions of higher learning, there is some indication that this issue is attracting professional attention. Moreno-Lopez, Saenz-de-Tejada, and Smith (2008), for example, described a project designed to integrate foreign language study abroad into the curriculum of a small liberal arts college with a mandate to educate students as global citizens. The project involved designing coherent sequences of courses cotaught by language and discipline specialists and including a service learning experience abroad. Within this program and others like it, the discipline-specific language needs of the students may be cultivated throughout their studies.

CONCLUSION

This article has reviewed the contemporary literature on language learning in study abroad for its pedagogical implications. Whereas off-campus experiences are often considered to be outside the purview of language programs, findings of research provide a strong rationale for including the expertise of language educators in the choice, design, and use of study abroad. Every effort should be made to ensure that language learners abroad enjoy access to—and engagement in—the practices of their host communities as well as guidance in their efforts to learn and to interpret their experiences. Based on this need, language educators have recently proposed a number of suggestions for enhancing study abroad as a language-learning experience, but clearly, there is room for continued investment in this worthy endeavor.

NOTE

1 According to the guidelines provided by the ACTFL for rating the Oral Proficiency Interview, a speaker possessing Advanced (level 2) ability can participate actively in conversations and can narrate and describe in the past, present, and future.

ANNOTATED BIBLIOGRAPHY

DuFon, M., & Churchill, E. (Eds.). (2006). *Language learners in study abroad contexts*. Clevedon, UK: Multilingual Matters.

This edited volume illustrates the theoretical and methodological diversity of contemporary approaches to language learning in study abroad. The introductory essay provides a useful and comprehensive overview of research on second language acquisition, development of pragmatic competence, and documentation of individual differences. Highlights include Hassall's diary study of learning to take leave in Indonesian, Churchill's investigation of Japanese students in the United States, and three studies, based on micro-analysis of recorded interactions, of language socialization at host family dinner tables in Indonesia (DuFon) and Japan (Cook & Iino).

Jackson, J. (2008). *Language, identity and study abroad: Sociocultural perspectives*. London, UK: Equinox.

This ethnographic study, grounded in socially and critically oriented theory, followed a cohort of Chinese students studying in Britain. The core of the volume is a series of four case studies or "journeys" following individual students throughout their experiences, from the pre- through the postsojourn stage. These cases demonstrate that even when students benefit from the prevision of expert guidance, the process of identity negotiation remains complex and unpredictable. Readers are provided an overview of a curriculum designed to train students as ethnographers.

Kinginger, C. (2009a). *Language learning and study abroad: A critical reading of research.* Basingstoke, UK: Palgrave Macmillan.

This book outlines the history and current state of the knowledge base in applied linguistics research on language learning in study abroad. Following an overview of related language-in-education policy, the author surveyed the literature on measurement of language ability and research on components of communicative competence. Research on settings for language learning (the classroom, the homestay, and informal encounters) was also reviewed along with studies of language socialization and identity.

REFERENCES

Austin, J. L. (1975). *How to do things with words.* Cambridge, MA: Harvard University Press.

Brecht, R., Davidson, D., & Ginsburg, R. (1995). Predictors of foreign language gain during study abroad. In B. Freed (Ed.), *Second language acquisition in a study abroad context* (pp. 37–66). Philadelphia, PA: John Benjamins.

Cain, A., & Zarate, G. (1996). The role of training course in developing openness to otherness: From tourism to ethnography. *Language, Culture, and Curriculum, 9,* 66–83.

Churchill, E. (2009). Gender and language learning at home and abroad. *JALT Journal, 32,* 141–158.

Coleman, J. (1997). Residence abroad within language study. *Language Teaching, 30,* 1–20.

Collentine, J. (2004). The effects of learning contexts on morphosyntactic and lexical development. *Studies in Second Language Acquisition, 26,* 227–248.

Comas-Quinn, A., Mardomingo, R., & Valentine, C. (2009). Mobile blogs in language learning: Making the most of informal and situated learning opportunities. *ReCALL, 21,* 96–112.

Davidson, D. (2010). Study abroad: When, how long, and with what results? New data from the Russian front. *Foreign Language Annals, 43,* 6–26.

DeKeyser, R. (2010). Monitoring processes in Spanish as a second language during a study abroad program. *Foreign Language Annals, 43,* 80–92.

Ducate, L. (2009). Service learning in Germany: A four-week summer teaching program in

Saxony-Anhalf. *Die Unterrichtspraxis/Teaching German, 41,* 32–40.

Feinberg, B. (2002, May 3). What students don't learn abroad. *Chronicle of Higher Education.* Retrieved from http: //chronicle.com/weekly/v48/i34/34b02001.htm

Freed, B. F., Dewey, D., Segalowitz, N., & Halter, R. (2004). The language contact profile. *Studies in Second Language Acquisition, 26,* 349–356.

Freed, B. F., Segalowitz, N., & Dewey, D. (2004). Contexts of learning and second language fluency in French: Comparing regular classrooms, study abroad, and intensive domestic programs. *Studies in Second Language Acquisition, 26,* 275–301.

Ginsburg, R. B., & Miller, L. (2000). What do they do? Activities of students during study abroad. In R. D. Lambert & E. Shohamy (Eds.), *Language policy and pedagogy: Essays in honor of A. Ronald Walton* (pp. 237–261). Philadelphia, PA: John Benjamins North America.

Gore, J. E. (2005). *Dominant beliefs and alternative voices: Discourse, belief, and gender in American study abroad.* New York, NY: Routledge.

Goulah, J. (2007). Village voices, global visions: Digital video as a transformative foreign language learning tool. *Foreign Language Annals, 40,* 62–78.

Hassall, T. (2006). Learning to take leave in social conversations: A diary study. In M. DuFon & E. Churchill (Eds.), *Language learners in study abroad contexts* (pp. 31–58). Clevedon, UK: Multilingual Matters.

Howard, M. (2005). On the role of context in the development of learner language: Insights from study abroad research. *ITL Review of Applied Linguistics, 148,* 1–20.

Huebner, T. (1995). The effects of overseas language programs: Report on a case study of an intensive Japanese course. In B. Freed (Ed.), *Second language acquisition in a study abroad context* (pp. 171–193). Philadelphia, PA: John Benjamins.

Isabelli, C. A. (2007). Development of the Spanish subjunctive by advanced learners: Study abroad followed by at-home instruction. *Foreign Language Annals, 40,* 330–341.

Isabelli, C. A., & Nishida, C. (2005). Development of the Spanish subjunctive in a nine-month study abroad setting. In D. Eddington (Ed.), *Selected Proceedings of the 6th Conference on the Acquisition of Spanish as First and Second Languages* (pp. 78–91). Somerville, MA: Cascadilla Press.

Isabelli-García, C. L. (2006). Study abroad social networks, motivation, and attitudes: Implications for SLA. In M. DuFon & E. Churchill (Eds.), *Language learners in study abroad contexts* (pp. 231–258). Clevedon, UK: Multilingual Matters.

Isabelli-García, C. L. (2010). Acquisition of Spanish gender agreement in two learning contexts: Study abroad and at home. *Foreign Language Annals, 43,* 289–303.

Ishihara, N. (2007). Web-based curriculum for pragmatics instruction in Japanese as a foreign language: An explicit awareness-raising approach. *Language Awareness, 16,* 21–40.

Iwasaki, N. (2010). Style shifts among Japanese learners before and after study abroad in Japan:

Becoming active social agents in Japanese. *Applied Linguistics, 31*, 45–71.
Jackson, J. (2008). *Language, identity and study abroad: Sociocultural perspectives*. London, UK: Equinox.
Jurasek, R., Lamson, H., & O'Maley, P. (1996). Ethnographic Learning While Studying Abroad. *Frontiers: The Interdisciplinary Journal of Study Abroad*, Retrieved June 17, 2011, from http://www.frontiersjournal.com/back/two/voltwo.htm
Kinginger, C. (2008). Language learning in study abroad: Case studies of Americans in France [Monograph]. *Modern Language Journal, 92*.
Kinginger, C. (2009a). *Language learning and study abroad: A critical reading of research*. Basingstoke, UK: Palgrave Macmillan.
Kinginger, C. (2009b). *Contemporary study abroad and foreign language learning: An activist's guidebook*. University Park, PA: Center for Advanced Language Proficiency Education and Research (CALPER).
Kinginger, C., & Belz, J. (2005). Sociocultural perspectives on pragmatic development in foreign language learning: Case studies from telecollaboration and study abroad. *Intercultural Pragmatics, 2*, 369–421.
Knight, S., & Schmidt-Rinehart, B. (2010). Exploring conditions to enhance student/host family interaction abroad. *Foreign Language Annals, 43*, 64–71.
Kurasawa, I., & Nagatomi, A. (2006). Study-abroad and internship programs: Reflection and articulation for lifelong learning. *Global Business Languages, 11*, 23–30.
Lave, J., & Wenger, E. (1991). *Situated learning: Legitimate peripheral participation*. Cambridge, UK: Cambridge University Press.
Magnan, S., & Back, M. (2007a). Requesting help in French: Developing pragmatic features during study abroad. In S. Wilkinson (Ed.), *Insights from study abroad for language programs AAUSC Issues in Language Program Direction* (pp. 22–44). Boston, MA: Thomson Heinle.
Magnan, S., & Back, M. (2007b). Social interaction and linguistic gain during study abroad. *Foreign Language Annals, 40*, 43–61.
Miller, L., & Ginsburg, R. (1995). Folklinguistic theories of language learning. In B. Freed (Ed.), *Second language acquisition in a study abroad context* (pp. 293–315). Amsterdam, The Netherlands: John Benjamins.
Moreno-Lopez, I., Saenz-de-Tejada, C., & Smith, T. (2008). Language and study abroad across the curriculum: An analysis of course development. *Foreign Language Annals, 41*, 674–686.
Patron, M.-C. (2007). *Culture and identity in study abroad contexts: After Australia, French without France*. Bern, Switzerland: Peter Lang.
Pertusa-Seva, I., & Stewart, M. (2008). Virtual study abroad 101: Expanding the horizons of the Spanish curriculum. *Foreign Language Annals, 33*, 438–442.

Polanyi, L. (1995). Language learning and living abroad: Stories from the field. In B. Freed (Ed.), *Second language acquisition in a study abroad context* (pp. 271–291). Amsterdam, The Netherlands: John Benjamins.

Polio, C., & Zyzik, E. (2009). Don Quixote meets *ser* and *estar*: Multiple perspectives on language learning in Spanish literature classes. *Modern Language Journal, 93*, 550–569.

Regan, V., Howard, M., & Lemée, I. (2009). *The acquisition of sociolinguistic competence in a study abroad context.* Clevedon, UK: Multilingual Matters.

Roberts, C., Byram, M., Barro, A., Jordan, S., & Street, B. (2001). *Language learners as ethnographers.* Clevedon, UK: Multilingual Matters.

Sasaki, M. (2009). Changes in English as a foreign language students' writing over 3.5 years: A sociocognitive account. In R. M. Manchón (Ed.), *Writing in foreign language contexts: Learning, teaching, and research* (pp. 49–76). Clevedon, UK: Multilingual Matters.

Savignon, S. (1983). *Communicative competence: Theory and classroom practice.* Reading, MA: Addison-Wesley.

Saville-Troike, M. (2003). *The ethnography of communication: An introduction.* Oxford, UK: Blackwell.

Schauer, G. (2009). *Interlanguage pragmatic development: The study abroad context.* London, UK: Continuum.

Shardakova, M. (2005). Intercultural pragmatics in the speech of American L2 learners of Russian: Apologies offered by Americans in Russian. *Intercultural Pragmatics, 2*, 423–454.

Shively, R. (2010). From the virtual world to the real world: A model of pragmatics instruction for study abroad. *Foreign Language Annals, 43*, 105–137.

Stewart, J. A. (2010). Using e-journals to assess students' language awareness and social identity during study abroad. *Foreign Language Annals, 43*, 138–159.

Streitwieser, B., & Leephaibul, R. (2007). Enhancing the study abroad experience through independent research in Germany. *Die Unterrichtspraxis/Teaching German, 40*, 164–170.

Sykes, J., & Cohen, A. (2010). *Dancing with words: Strategies for learning pragmatics in Spanish.* Retrieved from http://www.carla.umn.edu/speechacts/sp_pragmatics/home.html

Taguchi, N. (2008). Cognition, language contact, and the development of pragmatic comprehension in a study abroad context. *Language Learning, 58*, 33–71.

Talburt, S., & Stewart, M. A. (1999). What's the subject of study abroad? Race, gender and "living culture." *Modern Language Journal, 83*, 163–175.

Tanaka, K. (2007). Japanese students' contact with English outside the classroom during study abroad. *New Zealand Studies in Applied Linguistics, 13*, 36–54.

Tudini, V. (2007). Negotiation and intercultural learning in Italian native speaker chat rooms. *Modern Language Journal, 91*, 577–601.

Walsh, R. (1994). The year abroad—A linguistic challenge. *Teanga, 14*, 48–57.

ACKNOWLEDGMENT

This research was supported by a grant from the United States Department of Education (CFDA 84.229, P229A020010) to the Center for Advanced Language Proficiency Education and Research at the Pennsylvania State University. However, the contents do not necessarily represent the policy of the Department of Education and one should not assume endorsement by the Federal Government.

Teaching Second Languages for the Workplace

Jonathan Newton and Ewa Kusmierczyk

Workplace culture and organization are evolving as they adapt to globalization and rapid technological development. Likewise, the nature and role of workplace language and the literacy demands of work are changing in the face of increasingly multicultural workplaces and global communication networks. Among these changes, recent research has highlighted the role that informal modes of interpersonal communication play in the functioning of the modern workplace. Successful participation in such interactions is seen as not just a question of fitting in socially, but of doing work through talk. Ethnographic research in the workplace has stressed the importance of understanding language by viewing it within its social setting and understanding the interactional norms of particular communities of practice. Research into language programs for the workplace reflects this shift in emphasis. In contrast to research in the field of language for specific purposes on the specialized vocabulary and formal registers of particular professions, a growing body of research focuses on teaching and learning the language of routine workplace interactions. This article reviews current research into the nature of workplace language, noting in particular the contributions from ethnographic and language socialization research. It then discusses research into four aspects of the content of language programs for the workplace: employability skills, interpersonal communication, intercultural and critical language awareness, and teaching focused on the employment interview.

In writing this review article we find ourselves working in a somewhat crowded space between the two related fields of language for specific purposes (LSP) and language socialization. Our review foregrounds language socialization perspectives (Duff, 2005, 2008; Roberts, 2005, 2010) because much teaching for the workplace occurs within or in close alliance with workplaces and so lends itself to the socially situated orientation that this field provides. We also focus on recent research into the nature of workplace language, especially research pursued for the explicit purpose of informing language teaching for the workplace.

We see four interconnected trends emerging from recent research on language teaching for the workplace, each of which we address in this review. First, a growing body of research uses situated, ethnographic methods of data collection for the purposes of describing workplace discourses in particular settings, understanding the social processes typical of these settings (e.g., Franklin, 2007), and highlighting the experiences of new workers in the workforce (e.g., Warriner, 2010). Second, research increasingly focuses on interpersonal, informal workplace communication (e.g., Yates, 2008). This reflects an awareness of how important but challenging the language of routine interactions is for those seeking to participate in workplaces in which they are seen to be culturally or linguistically peripheral (Holmes, 2005b). Such an emphasis stands in stark contrast to a traditional LSP focus on the technical, formal language of particular jobs or professions. It also lends itself to a focus on issues of language and power (Fairclough, 2001) and the intercultural dimensions of interaction (Tomalin, 2009). The third trend, and one that mirrors the attention to interpersonal communication in the workplace noted earlier, is toward pedagogic approaches that prioritize awareness raising (Newton, 2007), including critical language awareness (Guo, 2009) and development of analytic skills for unpacking and of sensitivity to the sociopragmatic dimensions of communication in particular workplace settings (Holmes, 2005a; Riddiford & Newton, 2010; Yates, 2008). It should be noted that such developments aim to complement rather than replace learning of the specialized vocabulary and formal registers of a chosen vocation. The fourth and final trend involves research into the discursive requirements of the employment interview and the challenges that intercultural interviews pose, particularly interviews involving migrants or ethnic minority candidates. The growing body of research in this area is informed by critical perspectives (Roberts & Campbell, 2006) and both draws on and contributes to all four of the trends just described here.

LANGUAGE, LITERACY, AND THE CHANGING NATURE OF WORK

Rapid social and technological change is transforming the face of work in Western societies. As Roberts (2005) noted, this transformation includes a move toward high-technology manufacturing; service-oriented industries; and new forms of organization such as self-directed teams, more flexible work practices, more multitask working, and flatter organizational structures. These changes in turn produce new forms of workplace communication as people are required to adopt new ways of writing, speaking, and making meaning through multimedia and through an ever diversifying range of electronic communication tools (Vertovec, 2007). An increasingly common feature of new electronic literacies is highly intertextual texts involving bits of text from different sources (Duff, 2005) and linkages across different media. Duff (2008) saw implications for language and communication in which

> new forms and means of (tele)communication in the service industries and other professions, coupled with intensive globalization, migration, and market pressures, are associated with the development of new literacies, new measures of sociolinguistic control and new expectations about language learning and use. (p. 268)

Contradictions emerge as workplaces become increasingly multicultural and multilingual (Vertovec, 2007), while simultaneously experiencing the homogenizing pressure of English as a lingua franca. Many multinationals have adopted a policy of using English for company communication, a policy that has had a marked impact on demand for workplace language programs (Chivers, 2010). For example, Rakuten, Japan's top online shopping site, switched its in-house language from Japanese to English, a decision explained in the following way by Chief Executive Hiroshi Mikitani:

> The language used for the process of sharing information internationally is something everyone in the world can understand, which is not Japanese, unfortunately. If you cannot follow internationalization and a language shift to

English, you will find no place to work in Rakuten. (Wallace, 2010, p. 24)

Indeed, as Duff (2005) has noted, English is now the international norm for electronic intercultural communication among nonnative users of English. These changes, coupled with an increasingly globally mobile workforce across all sectors of the economy, ensure growing demand for workplace training and language courses. In many cases these link directly to the workplace through job internships and integrative cooperative experiences, on-site training, and professional development, all of which reflect a trend toward what Vertovec (2007) described as a blurring of distinctions between (higher) education and work. This trend is particularly important for the teaching of language for the workplace. As Roberts (2005) noted,

> Although thousands of English language courses have been run in workplaces, it is the opportunity to *use* the workplace environment as a continuing site of language development that is central to most workplace projects. . . . The "novice" English speaker learns to use language as a social practice and through language learns the sociocultural knowledge that is "wired into" language use. (p. 118)

Burt and Mathews-Aydinli (2007) identified a number of potential advantages of in-situ learning including ease of scheduling, authenticity of content, and cultivation of a positive work environment. They also noted significant challenges, including unrealistic expectations about language development, learner discomfort when classes are viewed as projecting a deficit attitude, demands on teachers to be knowledgeable about both language pedagogy and workplace-specific tasks, tension between training and education goals, and lack of opportunities for gaining credentials.

EVIDENCE-BASED WORKPLACE LANGUAGE TEACHING

Research into workplace discourse is increasingly focused on the workplace as a holistic communicative environment and on the communicative ideology of the workplace, rather than on needs analysis and course evaluations as in earlier studies (Roberts, 2005). This change reflects the influence of the growing field of language socialization research focused on the workplace (Duff, 2008). The range of settings being researched in this way has expanded to include physics labs, hospitals, legal practices, hairstyling salons, call centers, manufacturing plants, professional workplaces, and government and civil service (Duff, 2008). This trend for situated research dovetails nicely with a call from applied linguists for content in workplace language programs based more firmly on empirical and ethnographic description and analysis of patterns of actual language use in specific workplaces and sectors (Duff, 2005; Holmes, 2005b; Holmes & Riddiford, 2009; Newton, 2007; Yates, 2010b). It also concurs with the opinions of employers according to a recent study involving a survey of 245 supervisors and executives in 24 U.S. manufacturing companies with at least 150 employees. The study found that a number of companies were dissatisfied with the results of English language classes because the classes focused too much on decontextualized language study and failed to address language needs directly relevant to the workplace (Duval-Couetil & Mikulecky, 2006, cited in Burt & Mathews-Aydinli, 2007).

Yates (2010b) called for "an approach to instruction that draws on empirical evidence from a range of perspectives so that non-native speakers can understand patterns of language use, how these relate to cultural values, and how individuals actually draw on them in context" (p. 109). Similarly, Duff (2005) argued for shaping workplace literacy education through "situated research," which seeks to understand the social practices accompanying texts and that exposes students to "the specific genres that fulfill particular communicative functions within particular settings" (p. 358). For example, research by Waldvogel (2005) has shown how the conventions for e-mail correspondence, including level of formality, times when e-mail is used in preference to face-to-face conversation, and ways of signing off an e-mail, vary tremendously across workplaces. Similarly, Holmes and Stubbe (2003) showed how humor and small talk are used differently across workplace communities of practice and how these and other features of workplace talk reflect and construct social values such as those concerning power and status. Duff (2005) eloquently outlined the purpose and vision underlying this approach:

Examining the contextualized experience of individuals interacting in different languages (L1, L2, or L3) in work environments and closely examining the new literacies and competencies required for work provides a basis for improving work conditions, productivity, mutual understanding, and, it is hoped, cooperation within and among employees and management teams. (p. 346)

Ethnographic approaches to data collection serve this purpose well, as reflected in some recent studies (Arakelian, 2009; Franklin, 2007; Vickers, 2007; Warriner, 2010). These studies share a commitment to understanding the experience of new workers in specific multicultural and multilingual work settings in order to assist them to participate fully in their chosen places of work. Warriner (2010), for example, used ethnographic methods such as participant observation, interviews, and document collection to explore the relationship between work processes and learning processes in the lives of three refugee women transitioning from an adult ESL (English as a second language) program into work in a North American city. She found that while the women successfully entered the workforce and moved from peripheral to legitimate membership of the communities of practice, their low-skill menial jobs were likely to exclude and marginalize them from participation in other more economically and socially advantageous workplace communities.

Transition into full participation in the workplace is also investigated by Vickers (2007). She carried out a detailed analysis of the interactions that led to the socialization of a peripheral, nonnative speaker member (named Ramelan) of a team of engineering students in a capstone design course into core membership of the team. Socialization relied on three main factors: access to observation of core members interacting; guidance from core members both in the lab and in the team meetings; and opportunities for successful participation in the work of the team. Vickers argued that Ramelan's language behavior changed (i.e., he adopted the team's way of talking) as a "product of learning to think, design, and talk like a competent engineer" (p. 637).

A related approach, *appreciative inquiry* (Hammond, 1996), acknowledges that the precise form that effective communication takes depends on who is talking to whom, and in what kind of context; it depends on what each is trying to achieve in the interaction; and it depends on their workplace culture or the interactional norms of their particular community of practice. As its name suggests, appreciative enquiry focuses on the skills and strategies that underpin successful communication. Holmes et al. (2011) reported on a research project being carried out by the Wellington Language in the Workplace Project using this approach to identify features of successful communication at work. When workers from different social and cultural backgrounds engage in workplace interaction, there is considerable potential for mismatches in their assessments of the relative importance of some of these components, which can result in misunderstandings, including unintended offence (Clyne, 1994; Holmes, 2005a). This research has led quite naturally toward an exploration of the lessons that could be learned about successful interaction for the benefit of new employees in a workplace, especially those who may be fundamentally disadvantaged when they join a new society because of their lack of social power as well as their unfamiliarity with societal norms. Consequently, this kind of approach is designed to explore ways to empower these people, rather than attempt to make them fit (cf., Eades, 2004; Pennycook, 2001; Rampton, 2001). Such approaches help people to undertake their own sociolinguistic analyses of the relative weight of dimensions such as power, social distance, and formality, for example, in order to decide how to relate comfortably to others at work. Let us give an example of how this might be applied to classroom practice. A class is given in which a challenging workplace scenario is created that requires the students, in a particular work-place role, to respond to a situation via e-mail. In their roles, the students each craft and send an e-mail to their teacher. The replies are collated by the teacher and shared with the students in a subsequent class along with the teacher's response to the same scenario and perhaps responses from others beyond the class. These are discussed and compared with the purpose of identifying different language choices, why these were made, and what impact they might have. From this discussion, students develop awareness of the repertoire of discursive options available to them and what impact these options are likely to have. And so rather than describing and learning to replicate workplace genres as in a more traditional LSP approach, this approach encourages a critical and constructivist engagement with the process of learning ways of communicating at work.

WHAT IS BEING TAUGHT?

The following sections survey scholarship on four aspects of the content of workplace language courses: employability skills, interpersonal communication, intercultural and critical language awareness, and teaching focused on the employment interview. This list is necessarily selective. We think, however, that it captures the more important and interesting areas addressed in recently published research in this area.

Teaching and Learning Employability Skills

Employability skills come under a variety of guises, referred to as *core* or *key skills* in the United Kingdom; *workplace competencies* in the United States; *essential skills* in Canada; *core competencies* in New Zealand; and *key competencies, generic skills,* or *employability skills* in Australia. Broadly speaking, these skills include basic numeracy and literacy, use of technology, communication and people skills, thinking skills such as problem-solving skills, and personal skills and attributes such as responsibility and time management (Yates, 2008). The overlap with language, literacy, and communication skills makes these skills an important component of many workplace-based language/skills programs. As Yates (2008) noted, English requirements are no longer based on proficiency only; they contain a range of other skills such as sociopragmatic competencies, flexibility, and ability to communicate in diverse settings:

> New arrivals entering the job market face the challenge of not only having English language and literacy skills commensurate with technical demands of the job, but also of understanding how to operate in a new work culture where the norms and expectations relating to good communication and how teams work together may be very different. (p. 13)

Employability skills are frequently seen by employers as at least as important if not more so than job-specific technical skills (Yates, 2008). Those seeking employment, or in the early stages of new employment, also appear to value employability skills. Knight (2009) carried out a small-scale study on the effectiveness of a business internship program in preparing a small group of six students for participating in the global workforce. The internship took place within a mock domestic business company set up in a Japanese university. Reponses to a 43-item questionnaire showed that while most of the students ranked such employability skills as teamwork, interpersonal skills, problem solving, marketing expertise among the five most valuable benefits of the internship, only one identified improved English proficiency. This low ranking for English was despite the fact that all meetings in the internship were conducted in English.

Yates (2010c) investigated the experience of newly arrived migrants to Australia in the community and in the Adult Migrant English Program (AMEP) with the aim of identifying the English language needs typical of early settlement. The findings of this research highlight the need for programs to link language instruction to generic workplace skills training, and for program content to be based on the specific language requirements of particular occupations or industries.

TEACHING AND LEARNING SOCIAL, INTERACTIONAL TALK

The second trend is that research into language teaching for the workplace is focusing on the nature and roles of informal, interpersonal workplace communication. This reflects a trend toward less formal forms of discourse in Western workplace contexts and a shift in focus in language programs from front-of-house communication (such as service encounters and doctor-patient interactions) to nontechnical, social, interpersonal behind-the-scenes talk (such as on the factory floor or in an office) (Yates, 2010a). More than ever in the workplace, success depends not only on the ability to perform work but also on managing social aspects of interaction at work in order to participate fully in the life of the workplace (Holmes, 2005a). As Myles (2009) noted, "the formal systems of command with written memos, formal letters and supervisors' orders have been replaced by multidiscipline or multi-function teams, which is much more dependent on informal, oral and interpersonally sensitive written forms, such as email messages" (p. 4). This trend is reflected in research on private discourse in the workplace, such as research on language in routine interactions (Holmes, 2005b), on the discourse of particular workplace communities of practice (Myles, 2009), and on speech acts (Yates, 2010b; Yates & Springall, 2010).

Three small-scale studies have shown that a focus on informal, oral communication is also seen as a priority by those required to use a second language at work. Myles (2009) interviewed four ESL interns (engineering graduates) and their associates (e.g., tutors, trainers, employers) over 6 months at a large computer software company. The workplace was described as having an "intensely oral culture" (p. 60) that required participation in social talk and the ability to use and understand colloquial expressions, cultural connotations, and different styles. Not surprisingly, the interns all reported that oral communication was the most challenging aspect of language use at work. Similarly, Qian (2009) found that novice engineers in Hong Kong viewed the need to improve their oral English as more important than the need to improve their writing skills for technical report writing (see also Cooper, 1998). Wood (2009) also reported how engineering students from non-English-speaking backgrounds often struggle to cope with the communication demands of an English-speaking workplace. By chance rather than design these three studies all focus on the engineering profession. Whether other professions manifest the same priorities is a matter for further research.

As this research shows, the sociopragmatic dimension of talk at work is particularly challenging for migrants or people functioning in a second language and culture. For instance, choosing an appropriate level of directness in status-differentiated interactions involving requests and refusals (Holmes & Stubbe, 2003) or participating in small talk (Holmes, 2005b) requires sensitivity to cross-cultural differences in the way talk functions in different work settings. In the case of small talk, Holmes suggested analyzing small talk in local soap television shows (presumably focusing on workplace interactions in these shows) and performing role-plays as a way to sensitize new migrants in some of the ways that small talk functions in a particular cultural setting.

One approach to researching the sociopragmatic dimension of talk at work is to focus on particular speech acts, with requests being a particular favorite in recent research. Riddiford and Joe (2010) tracked the development of request strategies in English by skilled migrants enrolled in a blended classroom-internship workplace training program. Data collection involved pretest, midpoint, and posttest assessment using discourse-completion tests (DCTs) and role-plays; recordings of participants interacting in workplaces; and final interviews. The study found that both awareness of aspects of the sociopragmatics of requests in New Zealand

English and communicative behaviors showed marked development over the 12 weeks. End-point DCTs revealed greater use of internal and external modifiers (e.g., openers such as *I wonder if you could . . . ?* and preparators such as *Can I have a quick word*). End-point role-plays showed greater responsiveness to addressees through small talk, increased use of personal names, and more turn-taking. Riddiford and Joe argued that these gains point to the benefits of three salient features of the program: (a) explicit pragmatic instruction alongside workplace placement, (b) opportunities to analyze recordings of authentic workplace conversations, and (c) sufficient time to develop awareness of sociopragmatic features of workplace communication in a particular setting.

Also focusing on request speech acts, Wigglesworth and Yates (2007) investigated how native English speakers (NESs) in Australia and nonnative English speakers (NNESs) enacted a range of complex role-play requests. The aim was to identify the pragmalinguistic devices and sociopragmatic values underpinning NESs' performance, to identify what learners find problematic about the task, and, from both these sources, to suggest priorities for teachers preparing learners for similar complex request situations in the workplace. The authors found that in contrast to the NNESs, the NESs "asserted solidarity rather than acknowledged hierarchy" (p. 793) in their request strategies. They did this through, for example, using down toners (e.g., "This is *bit of* a problem."); hedges (e.g., "*I could be wrong*, but I think it's a bad idea."); and other pragmatic devices to establish rapport, informality, and apparent egalitarianism. The value of this research is that it offers insights that can assist both native and nonnative English speakers in hierarchical workplace relationships to understand and adapt to differences in each other's discourse style in relation to this important and potentially face-threatening speech act.

Speech acts have also been a focus of materials developed for teaching workplace communication in English to migrants from non-English-speaking backgrounds. Yates and Springall (2010) drew on Wigglesworth and Yates's (2007) research, discussed earlier, to propose an approach to designing materials for the purpose of equipping adult learners of English with successful request strategies for the workplace. Request speech acts warrant this attention because not only are they pervasive in the workplace, but they are also quite risky to perform (because they involve asking someone to do something) and, in English, involve a wide range of devices and strategies for mitigating imposition and building rapport. Riddiford and Newton (2010) also focused on speech acts in a book of teaching materials designed to prepare migrant professionals for a work placement and for eventual employment in their chosen professions (see also Holmes & Riddiford, 2009). The book focuses on face-threatening speech acts such as requests, refusals, disagreements, complaints, and apologies. A unique feature of this book—and one that connects it closely to research—is that it incorporates (re)recordings and transcriptions of naturalistic, authentic interactions from various workplaces. This is different from the usual practice in workplace communication textbooks of using made-up or elicited samples of workplace communication. The process of obtaining and transcribing authentic workplace talk and selecting and adapting samples for use in a workplace language program is challenging. This is because, as Newton (2007) observed, the situated nature of workplace conversations makes for "complex, idiosyncratic, unruly conversational artifacts that belie the perceived ease with which we all carry out conversations in our native language" (p. 520).

But drawing on naturalistic data is not the only way of ensuring fidelity in materials design. Yates (2008) reported on a detailed and rigorous research project on the teaching of employability communication skills to adult migrants in Australia for the AMEP settlement program, out of which four sample teaching units were developed. In each unit, the samples of workplace language provided were based around role-plays carried out by NESs. Yates argued that this approach allowed the materials writers to maintain some control over the content of the dialogues, while also ensuring that the features they were interested in were included. Whether the data are naturalistic or elicited, a common feature of materials design in both approaches is a commitment to authenticating the language models being used and providing opportunities for learners to analyze, reflect on, and try out what they have learned. A contentious issue is the extent to which these approaches treat NES interactions as prototypical. How does this align with the increasingly multilingual and multicultural workplace (Kramsch & Whiteside, 2008)? Does it assume that NESs are fully pragmatically competent, in contrast to NNESs, who might actually be fully proficient and even more pragmatically capable in some cases? And to what extent are NES interactional norms preferred or even achievable targets? Such issues are central to the critical and intercultural approaches to workplace language teaching discussed in the following section.

Teaching and Learning for Intercultural and Critical Language Awareness

Awareness raising is important both as a process and goal of language teaching designed to prepare learners for the workplace (e.g., Arakelian, 2009; Guo, 2009; Newton, 2007; Roberts, 2007; Yates, 2008) and especially in teaching focused on intercultural and critical language awareness. As Yates (2010a) argued, language teaching for the workplace needs to "equip learners with the analytic tools to research interactive practices for themselves" (p. 110). Holmes et al. (2009) described an ongoing project looking at just this. The project tracked the sociopragmatic skills of professional migrants transitioning from a workplace language course into internships and then into full participation in the workplace. In the course and internship, authentic interactional data and critical internship incidents were used to develop the analytical skills that enabled the migrants to select linguistic forms that enacted an authoritative identity when required, and to be supportive, collaborative, and collegial when they judged it appropriate.

Cross-cultural and intercultural workplace training is a large field in its own right, and one with obvious overlaps with language teaching and applied linguistics. A focus on intercultural awareness in workplace language programs naturally follows from a focus on social and interpersonal workplace discourse. Communication is replete with culturally shaped expectations and communicative norms (Kramsch, 2004); indeed, as Kramsch (1993) argued, every time we speak, we perform a cultural act. Intercultural competence is a key component of the influential Common European Framework of Reference (Council of Europe, 2001) and is now a major component of adult education (Feng, Byram, & Fleming, 2009) and healthcare education. A number of recent studies and publications in this area focus on materials design and training implementation. Utley (2004) presented materials designed to encourage reflection on cultural differences in communication and on the underlying causes of these differences. Utley explicitly sought to raise learners' awareness of latent ethnocentrism by exploring their own culturally shaped values, assumptions, and beliefs. Guilherme, Glaser, and Méndez García (2009) described the development and evaluation of materials prepared as part of a pan-European project targeting adult learners in multicultural, professional workplaces. They also incorporated critical reflection, with a strong emphasis on dialogue and holistic, experiential learning. A reflective approach is also advocated by Tomalin (2009), who outlined a rationale for intercultural materials based on experiential learning and critical incident methodology. This approach is well suited to workplace-based training and education programs in which participants are able to reflect on critical incidents from their own recent work experience. Such reflective processes would ideally also involve managers and co-workers whose own workplace pragmatics may give rise to some of the critical incidents that this approach draws on.

Franklin (2007) sought to test the assumption underlying culture-general training that a contrastive approach to broad cultural differences (e.g., Hall, 1959; Hofstede, 2001) provides an appropriate basis for cross-cultural training. To do so, he used a case study involving self-report data from 26 German and British managers working together after a postmerger company integration. Franklin found that contrary to predictions based on cross-cultural studies, cultural differences were not necessarily experienced as difficult, and, overall, the difficulties that the managers did experience in their intercultural interactions could not be easily predicted or explained by a traditional cross-cultural analysis. Instead, Franklin argued for an emic approach that "examines one culture or pair of cultures, studies behavior in the culture from within the system using structures discovered by the analyst, the absence of an overall framework thus allowing cultures to be studied in their own right" (p. 278). Franklin proposed that this approach would provide authentic data that applied linguists and cross-cultural trainers could use to directly address the communication difficulties typical of particular situations.

Finally, Arakelian (2009) described an intercultural communication skills program delivered in 16 UK hospitals. The program aimed to facilitate integration of skilled migrant workers into work in the UK health sector. Arakelian argued that existing diversity-based training approaches (which involve sharing information about different ethnic and religious groups) are ineffective in changing attitudes and behavior because they are too information-focused and essentializing about broad-brush cultural differences. In contrast, the program advocated by Arakelian is skills-based and avoids a "rule-based performative model" (p. 175). Program methods include reflective diaries for structured reflection, ethnography, role-playing practice scenarios (critical incidents as the basis for role-play and scenario-based learning), and workplace-based assignments.

The few studies surveyed in the preceding paragraphs are part of a growing literature on interculturally focused workplace language teaching. They all share a reflective, awareness-raising pedagogy, and all but Utley (2004), which is designed as a generic resource, advocate experiential learning as a way of tapping into the language and practices of particular workplaces and communities of practice. Here again we see a marked shift away from teaching normative generic discourse patterns and toward developing sensitivity to communication patterns in particular workplace settings.

Closely allied to intercultural awareness is critical language awareness. A critical stance on teaching language for the workplace focuses on hegemonic processes and outcomes implicit in the competition between languages and in discriminatory employment practices based on linguistic difference (Guo, 2009; Warriner, 2010). Roberts (2005) highlighted the tension between approaches to training driven by the productivity goals typical of management and approaches focused on emancipatory goals. Ultimately, this is an issue of whether work related English Language training functions to benefit migrant workers or merely to corner them in low-paid unskilled jobs, Roberts argued that "if language training is only part of the hegemonic process that gives English absolute dominance and further marginalizes limited speakers of English, then it needs to be challenged" (p. 126). Similarly McAll (2003) claimed that

> language competence . . . comes to be a convenient tool for discriminating against other language groups in an apparently "legitimate" way, since no one can deny the importance of language in order to function in areas of the labour market where language is necessary to the work process. (p. 249)

A critical perspective was taken by Guo (2009), who employed a qualitative, interpretative paradigm to examine data collected through interviews and naturalistic observation into the ways in which immigrant professionals are prepared for employment in Canada through an ESL program. Guo showed how an emphasis in the program on acquiring accentless pronunciation, anglicizing given names, and adopting aspects of the dominant Canadian culture all reflect a deficit, subtraction model of the immigrants' own cultures and languages. Guo argued that such employment preparation programs should move away from narrowly linguistic training and focus more on the language required in the workplace. Guo also called for a critical multiculturalism that challenges the deficit model of cultural difference and encourages immigrants to "develop critical language awareness in order to contend and change practices of domination and institutional racism" (p. 31).

Teaching and Learning for Employment Interviews

A critical perspective is particularly relevant to the employment interview. The discourse requirements of interviews have been identified as resulting in "persistent but intangible barriers" for ethnic minority groups (Roberts, Campbell, & Robinson, 2008, p. 9). Research within this area has focused on identifying the highly specialized discursive requirements of the job interview and problems stemming from the gap between those requirements and performance by migrant/ethnic minority candidates. For example, in a two-part study on employment and promotion interviews, Roberts and Campbell (2006) and Roberts et al. (2008) showed how a disjunction between the discursive requirements of interviews and on-the-job language use and the practice of othering migrant identity both impede access to employment and promotion for ethnic minority candidates.

Problems in discursive performance are also the main focus of Sarangi and Roberts's (2004) study on interviews and exams in medical settings. They showed how the failure of an international candidate in an oral exam resulted not from professional competence but from misalignment in the way three modes of talk (professional, institutional, and personal experience) were managed by participants in the interview. The authors focused on different uses of contextualization cues by the interlocutors to signal and interpret the ongoing activity (Erickson & Schultz, 1982). The problem was illustrated with an example of an exam with a Spanish candidate who failed to respond to signals that conveyed dissatisfaction of the interviewers with her answers. A similar, problem-identification approach was taken by Birkner and Kern (2004), who reported on differences in impression management leading to unsuccessful outcomes for the Eastern candidates in job interviews in Western Germany. These differences include self and other perspectives in talk and discursive organization of agreement and disagreement, which are subsumed under "different understandings of the genre" (p. 244).

Not all research in this area has taken a critical perspective. An alternative approach based on "appreciative inquiry" (Hammond, 1996) has been adopted in a small number of studies that focus on the skills and strategies used by interview participants to shape the dynamics of the interview and to bring about positive outcomes. These studies have focused on, for example, discourse features that indicate co-membership and an analysis of how expertise and trust is negotiated between the candidate and the interviewer. For example, Kerekes (2006) examined successful interviews where potentially problematic moves were mitigated by compensatory strategies used by the candidates to build the interviewers' trust. Factors that appeared crucial for determining the outcome of the interaction for both majority group and minority group candidates included positive self-presentation and establishing solidarity and rapport with interviewers. What distinguishes Kerekes's approach is the notion of success as achieving an agreeable outcome to both participants rather than merely matching their cultural and linguistic backgrounds (p. 29). When operationalizing the notion of success, Kerekes pointed to the inaccurate assumption made in cross-cultural studies that in order to be successful, a second language speaker needs to resemble the native speaker (NS) in performance. Indeed, Kerekes (2007) argued that it is not important whether they perform similarly to successful NSs, but "that they perform in such ways as to have similarly successful results to those of their successful NS counterparts" (p. 1945).

The creation of co-membership was also discussed by Lipovsky (2006, 2008), who examined how NES candidates negotiated their skills and professional experience in interviews carried out in Australia in French for an academic post in France. Lipovsky showed how the candidates' lexicogrammatical choices contributed to the construction of solidarity between the interview participants and influenced the interviewers' positive or negative impressions of the answer, and thus of the candidate. In a small-scale study focusing on the interviewer, Lim, Winter, and Chan (2006) investigated the ways that interviewers could mitigate negative bias in their own judgments in intercultural interviews. These included interviewers developing rapport with candidates prior to the formal beginning of an interview and discussing their different experiences and expectations concerning interviews. Both strategies led to more successful interview outcomes. The Lim et al. recommended that candidates prepare for interviews by making explicit comparisons between cultures in order to highlight the implicit demands of interviews in the target cultural setting. Similarly, Louw, Derwing, and Abbott (2010) provided an example of a training module that highlights aspects of pragmatic performance for helping migrants in Canada to improve their interview skills. They stressed the need for access to authentic models that provide learners with examples of successful communication strategies. Although they did not expect learners to imitate NS pragmatic behaviors, they nevertheless argued that such models are important because learners "are expected to communicate according to established conventions, and knowledge of those conventions should be made available to them" (Louw et al., p. 754).

The literature on interviews reviewed in the preceding paragraphs highlights the need for both critical and appreciative perspectives and for both candidates and interviewers or employers to work on reducing barriers to success in intercultural interviews. From a critical perspective, those involved in teaching interview skills can focus on power inequalities and implicit forms of discrimination in intercultural interviews. At the discursive level, guided analysis of the conventional interview schema in the target setting and the candidate's culture offers a way of highlighting differences and similarities and of identifying interview strategies which promote positive interview outcomes. A blend of critical and appreciative approaches acknowledges the unique character of an intercultural job interview in which the candidate does not necessarily have to imitate the native performance in order to win the interview game.

EVALUATING WORKPLACE LANGUAGE PROGRAMS

A number of studies have investigated the effectiveness of workplace language teaching (Arakelian, 2009; Benseman, 2010; Ekkens & Winke, 2009; Guilherme et al., 2009; Riddiford & Joe, 2010; Yates, 2010a). Only one of these, Ekkens and Winke (2009), focused explicitly on the nature of evaluation of workplace language programs. Ekkens and Winke investigated the efficacy of standardized tests and alternative assessment in the form of learning journals for measuring learning in a 10-week workplace English language program. In this program 21 learners took the standardized tests (pre and post) and kept learning journals. Results of the two tests stood in stark contrast. Whereas the standardized tests showed marginal nonsignificant gains, the learning journals reported gains in listening and reading and demonstrated improvements in a range of other areas including performance on job-related English tasks, self-confidence, willingness to communicate, and motivation. This study highlights the mismatch between standardized tests of generic language proficiency and the goals of workplace courses, which are very often customized to address quite specific job requirements in particular workplaces. It also highlights the value of nonstandard forms of assessment for revealing a broader view of the learning outcomes of such programs.

Other studies focusing on the effectiveness of programs in delivering intended outcomes have been discussed elsewhere in this review. Two that have not been discussed warrant mention here. Yates (2010a) reported on an extensive investigation into the fit between the goals of an Australian migrant on-arrival settlement program and migrants' real-world experiences. The research involved multiple forms of ethnographic data collection over a 12-month period, including interviews, classroom observation, analysis of classroom materials, samples of assessment, and recordings of participants in a range of settings outside the classroom. Yates found a generally good fit between the program goals and participants' needs, as well as generally successful uptake of skills necessary for settlement and work in Australia.

Finally, Benseman (2010) provided a short report on the effect of a language, literacy, and numeracy program in a New Zealand factory setting. Self-report data indicated transfer of skills was taking place through the program not only in terms of the improved ability of participants managing paperwork and accuracy and efficiency with measurements and calculations, but also in terms of oral communication at work, and beyond the workplace. Among the factors that contributed to these results, Benseman identified the priority given to teaching content based on both the company's and individual's needs analysis, and opportunities to contextualize the teaching content, use realia, and make concrete links between skills being taught and their application.

CONCLUSIONS

The workplace itself does not always deliver the opportunities for language socialization that might be expected. In blue collar workplaces, noisy working environments, isolation, and clustering of first language culture groups—in particular workplaces and in teams within these workplaces—all constrain language learning opportunities (Duff, 2008; Yates, 2010b). Even in the increasingly globally mobile professional sector (Guo, 2009), evidence suggests that intercultural and sociopragmatic skills in multilingual contexts are difficult to acquire without explicit, guided attention (Franklin, 2007; Guilherme et al., 2009; Guo, 2009; Holmes, 2005b). Workplace programs that couple work and education can address these gaps. Such a coupling offers the obvious advantages of teaching the specific language needed for successful participation in particular workplaces and using the experience of learners in that workplace as an instructional resource. Furthermore, such an approach creates a congruence between the worlds of workplace language teachers and applied linguistics researchers. Both share an interest in the way language is used in particular workplace settings. For both, ethnographic methods offer a valuable tool for accessing and understanding this language. Both also share an emancipatory vision—a vision that, on the one hand, seeks to empower and equip people for fuller participation in work in multilingual and multicultural workplaces and, on the other, to challenge hegemonic processes and discourses in the workplace. In its groundbreaking work, the New London Group (2000) expressed this vision: "The role of pedagogy is to develop an epistemology of pluralism that provides access without people having to erase or leave behind different subjectivities" (p. 18). As highlighted in this review, recent research drawing on language socialization and intercultural and critical language awareness perspectives offers pedagogic tools and insights that can help the teaching of second languages in and for the workplace to achieve these important multicultural objectives.

ANNOTATED BIBLIOGRAPHY

Duff, P. A. (2008). Language socialization, higher education, and work. In P. A. Duff & N. H. Hornberger (Eds.), *Encyclopedia of language and education: Vol. 8. Language socialization* (pp. 257–270). Boston, MA: Springer Science+Business Media.

Although only 14 pages long, this chapter is a highly informative overview of language socialization in work and higher education. Duff described recent trends in work practices and the changing discourse demands of work. She looked at the implications of these changes for the multicultural workplace, the induction into the workplace by immigrants, and the transition from education to work. The insights into workplace socialization offered by this chapter make it a valuable read for teachers, trainers, and course designers.

Feng, A., Byram, M., & Fleming, M. (Eds.). (2009). *Becoming interculturally competent through education and training*. Bristol, UK: Multilingual Matters.

This edited collection describes research on interculturally informed training and teaching in a range of workplace settings, mostly within the European context. The chapters offer a wealth of examples of intercultural training in practice and bring to the fore the voices of teachers and learners. The book also explores the theoretical debates and conundrums that emerge within and between education and training, not least when culture is addressed.

Yates, L. (2008). The not-so generic skills: Teaching employability communication skills to adult migrants. North Ryde, NSW, Australia: AMEP Research Centre, Macquarie University on behalf of the Department of Immigration and Citizenship.

This publication reports on research conducted into preparation for the workplace through the Australian Adult Migrant English Program (AMEP), which provides English language instruction for newly arrived migrants to Australia. The research involved two projects. The first project, Employability Skills for Professional Workers, investigated the employment-related needs and experiences of learners who had completed an AMEP course and found work. The project investigated the particular skills and knowledge that helped project participants to get and keep their jobs, as well as areas of difficulty they experienced in the workplace. The second, the Communication Skills Project, investigated the nature of routine workplace interactions and drew on insights and data from this research for developing and trialing classroom materials for language teaching relevant to the workplace. This report demonstrates effective synergies between research into workplace language and classroom practice.

REFERENCES

Arakelian, C. (2009). Professional training: Creating intercultural space in multi-ethnic workplaces. In A. Feng, M. Byram, & M. P. Fleming (Eds.), *Becoming interculturally competent through education and training* (pp. 174–193). Bristol, UK: Multilingual Matters.

Benseman, J. (2010). Transferring literacy skills in the workplace. *Reflect, 13*, 9–11.

Birkner, K., & Kern, F. (2004). Impression management in East and West German job interviews. In H. Spencer-Oatey (Ed.), *Culturally speaking* (pp. 255–271). London, UK:

Continuum.
Burt, M., & Mathews-Aydinli, J. (2007). Workplace instruction and workforce preparation for adult migrants. Retrieved from CAELA Web site: http: //webdev.cal.org/ development/ CAELA/esl_resources/briefs/WorkplacePrep.pdf
Chivers, N. (2010). Tap a well of opportunities in Baku. *EL Gazette, 369*, 13.
Clyne, M. G. (1994). *Inter-cultural communication at work: Cultural values in discourse.* Cambridge, UK: Cambridge University Press.
Cooper, A. (1998). Mind the gap! An ethnographic approach to cross-cultural workplace communication research. In M. Byram & M. Flemming (Eds.), *Language Learning in Intercultural Perspective: Approaches through drama and ethnography* (pp. 119–142). Cambridge, UK: Cambridge University Press.
Council of Europe. (2001). *Common European framework of reference for languages.* Cambridge, UK: Cambridge University Press.
Duff, P. A. (2005). Thinking globally about new literacies: Multilingual socialization at work. In J. Anderson, M. Kendrick, T. Rodgers, & S. Smythe (Eds.), *Portraits of literacy across families, communities, and schools* (pp. 341–362). Mahwah, NJ: Erlbaum.
Duff, P. A. (2008). Language socialization, higher education, and work. In P. A. Duff & N. H. Hornberger (Eds.), *Encyclopedia of language and education: Vol. 8. Language socialization* (pp. 257–270). Boston, MA: Springer Science+Business Media.
Eades, D. (2004). Understanding Aboriginal English in the legal system: A critical sociolinguistics approach. *Applied linguistics, 25*, 491.
Ekkens, K., & Winke, P. (2009). Evaluating workplace English language programs. *Language Assessment Quarterly, 6*, 265. doi: 10.1080/15434300903063038
Erickson, F., & Schultz, J. J. (1982). *The counselor as gatekeeper: Social and cultural organization of communication in counseling interviews.* New York, NY: Academic Press.
Fairclough, N. (2001). *Language and power* (2nd ed.). Harlow, UK: Longman.
Feng, A., Byram, M., & Fleming, M. (Eds.). (2009). *Becoming interculturally competent through education and training.* Bristol, UK: Multilingual Matters.
Franklin, P. (2007). Differences and difficulties in intercultural management interaction. In H. Kotthoff & H. Spencer-Oatey (Eds.), *Handbook of intercultural communication* (pp. 263–284). New York, NY: Mouton de Gruyter.
Guilherme, M., Glaser, E., & Méndez García, M. (2009). The pragmatics of intercultural competence in education and training: A cross-national experiment on "diversity management." In A. Feng, M. Byram, & M. Fleming (Eds.), *Becoming interculturally competent through education and training* (pp. 193–210). Bristol, UK: Multilingual Matters.
Guo, Y. (2009). Racializing immigrant professionals in an employment preparation ESL program. *Cultural and Pedagogical Inquiry, 1*, 40–54.

Hall, E. T. (1959). *The silent language.* New York, NY: Anchor.

Hammond, S. A. (1996). *The thin book of appreciative inquiry.* Plano, TX: Thin Book.

Hofstede, G. (2001). *Cultures consequences: International differences in work-related values (Abridged).* Newbury Park, CA: Sage.

Holmes, J. (2005a). Socio-pragmatic aspects of workplace talk. In Y. Kawaguchi, S. Zaima, T. Takagaki, K. Shibano, & M. Usami (Eds.), *Linguistic informatics—State of the art and the future: The first international conference on linguistic informatics* (pp. 196–220). Amsterdam, the Netherlands: John Benjamins.

Holmes, J. (2005b). When small talk is a big deal: Sociolinguistic challenges in the workplace. In M. H. Long (Ed.), *Second language needs analysis* (pp. 344–372). Cambridge, UK: Cambridge University Press.

Holmes, J., Joe, A., Marra, M., Newton, J., Riddiford, N., & Vine, B. (2011). Applying linguistic research to real world problems: The case of the Wellington Language in the Workplace Project. In C. Candlin & S. Sarangi (Eds.), *Handbook in applied linguistics: Communication in the professions* (pp. 533–549). Berlin: Mouton de Gruyter.

Holmes, J., Marra, M., Newton, J., Joe, A., Riddiford, N., & Vine, B. (2009). Enhancing sociopragmatic skills among professionally qualified workers. *New Zealand Studies in Applied Linguistics, 15,* 38–46.

Holmes, J., & Riddiford, N. (2009). Talk at work: Interactional challenges for immigrants. In V. K. Bhatia, W. Cheng, & B. Du-Babcock (Eds.), *Language for professional communication: Research, practice & training.* Hong Kong: Asia-Pacific LSP and Professional Communication.

Holmes, J., & Stubbe, M. (2003). *Power and politeness in the workplace: A sociolinguistic analysis of talk at work.* London, UK: Longman.

Kerekes, J. (2006). Winning an interviewer's trust in a gatekeeping encounter. *Language in Society, 35,* 27–57. doi: 10.1017/S0047404506060027

Kerekes, J. (2007). The co-construction of a gatekeeping encounter: An inventory of verbal actions. *Journal of Pragmatics, 39,* 1942–1973.

Knight, K. (2009). Business internship program development in light of professional communication research: Kevin's company at Kanda University of International Studies. In V. K. Bhatia, W. Cheng, B. Du-Babcock, & J. Lung (Eds.), *Language for professional communication: Research, practice & training* (pp. 235–249). Hong Kong: Asia-Pacific LSP and Professional Communication.

Kramsch, C. (1993). *Context and culture in language teaching.* Oxford, UK: Oxford University Press.

Kramsch, C. (2004). Language, thought and culture. In A. Davies & C. Elder (Eds.), *The handbook of applied linguistics* (pp. 235–261). Malden, MA: Blackwell.

Kramsch, C., & Whiteside, A. (2008). Language ecology in multilingual settings. Towards a theory of symbolic competence. *Applied Linguistics*, *29*, 645–671. doi: 10.1093/applin/amn022

Lim, C. H., Winter, R., & Chan, C. C. (2006). Cross-cultural interviewing in the hiring process: Challenges and strategies. *Career Development Quarterly*, *54*, 4.

Lipovsky, C. (2006). Candidates' negotiation of their expertise in job interviews. *Journal of Pragmatics*, *38*, 1147–1174.

Lipovsky, C. (2008). Constructing affiliation and solidarity in job interviews. *Discourse & Communication*, *2*, 411–432. doi: 10.1177/1750481308095938

Louw, K. J., Derwing, T. M., & Abbott, M. L. (2010). Teaching pragmatics to L2 learners for the workplace: The job interview. *Canadian Modern Language Review [La Revue canadienne des langues vivantes]*, *66*, 739–758. doi: 10.3138/cmlr.66.5.739

McCall, C. (2003). Language dynamics in the bi- and multilingual workplace. In R. Bayley & S. Schecter (Eds.), *Language socialization in bilingual and multilingual societies* (pp. 235–250). Clevedon: Multilingual Matters.

Myles, J. (2009). Oral competency of ESL technical students in workplace internships. *TESL-EJ*, *13*, 1–24.

New London Group. (2000). Introduction. In B. Cope & M. Kalantzis (Eds.), *Multiliteracies: Literacy learning and the design of social futures* (pp. 9–37). London, UK: Routledge.

Newton, J. (2007). Adapting authentic workplace talk for workplace communication training. In H. Kotthoff & H. Spencer-Oatey (Eds.), *Handbook of intercultural communication* (pp. 519–537). New York, NY: Mouton de Gruyter.

Pennycook, A. (2001). Critical applied linguistics: A critical introduction. In A. Davies & C. Elder (Eds.), *Handbook of applied linguistics* (pp. 784–807). Malden, MA: Blackwell.

Qian, D. D. (2009). Using English for workplace communication: A study of novice professionals. In V. K. Bhatia, W. Cheng, B. Du-Babcock, & J. Lung (Eds.), *Language for professional communication: Research, practice, and training* (pp. 270–285). Hong Kong: Asia-Pacific LSP and Professional Communication.

Rampton, B. (2001). Language crossing, cross-talk, and cross-disciplinarity in sociolinguistics. In N. Coupland, S. Sarangi, & C. Candlin (Eds.), *Sociolinguistics and social theory* (pp. 261–296). London, UK: Pearson.

Riddiford, N., & Joe, A. (2010). Tracking the development of sociopragmatic skills. *TESOL Quarterly*, *44*, 195–205. doi: 10.5054/tq.2010.215252

Riddiford, N., & Newton, J. (2010). *Workplace talk in action: An ESOL resource*. Wellington, New Zealand: Victoria University of Wellington.

Roberts, C. (2005). English in the workplace. In E. Hinkel (Ed.), *Handbook of research in second language teaching and learning* (pp. 117–136). Mahwah, NJ: Erlbaum.

Roberts, C. (2007). Multilingualism in the workplace. In P. Auer & L. Wei (Eds.), *Handbooks of applied linguistics: Vol. 5. Handbook of multilingualism and multilingual communication* (pp. 405–422). New York, NY: Mouton de Gruyter.

Roberts, C. (2010). Language socialization in the workplace. *Annual Review of Applied Linguistics 30*, 211–227.

Roberts, C., & Campbell, S. (2006). Talk on trial: Job interviews, language and ethnicity. Research *Report-Department for Work and Pensions, 344*. Retrieved from http: //research.dwp.gov.uk/asd/asd5/rports2005-2006/rrep344.pdf

Roberts, C., Campbell, S., & Robinson, Y. (2008). *Talking like a manager: Promotion interviews, language and ethnicity (Research Report No. 510)*. London, UK: Department for Work and Pensions.

Sarangi, S., & Roberts, C. (2004). Discoursal (mis)alignments in professional gatekeeping encounters. In C. J. Kramsch (Ed.), *Language acquisition and language socialization*. New York, NY: Continuum International.

Tomalin, B. (2009). Applying the principles: Instruments for intercultural business training. In A. Feng, M. Byram, & M. Fleming (Eds.), *Becoming interculturally competent through education and training* (pp. 115–131). Bristol, UK: Multilingual Matters.

Utley, D. (2004). *Intercultural resource pack*. Cambridge, UK: Cambridge University Press.

Vertovec, S. (2007). Super-diversity and its implications. *Ethnic and Racial Studies, 30*, 1024. doi: 10.1080/01419870701599465

Vickers, C. H. (2007). Second language socialization through team interaction among electrical and computer engineering students. *Modern Language Journal, 91*, 621–640. doi: 10.1111/j.1540-4781.2007.00626.x

Wallace, R. (2010, July 8). Japan lost in translation. *Australian, 24*.

Waldvogel, J. (2005) *The role, status and style of workplace email: A study of two New Zealand workplaces* (Unpublished doctoral dissertation). Victoria University of Wellington, Wellington, New Zealand.

Warriner, D. S. (2010). Competent performances of situated identities: Adult learners of English accessing engaged participation. *Teaching and Teacher Education, 26*, 22–30.

Wigglesworth, G., & Yates, L. (2007). Mitigating difficult requests in the workplace: What learners and teachers need to know. *TESOL Quarterly, 41*, 791–803.

Wood, D. (2009). Preparing ESP learners for workplace placement. *ELT Journal, 63*, 323–331.

Yates, L. (2008). *The not-so generic skills: Teaching employability communication skills to adult migrants*. North Ryde, NSW, Australia: AMEP Research Centre, Macquarie University on behalf of the Department of Immigration and Citizenship.

Yates, L. (2010a). *Language training and settlement success: Are they related?* North Ryde, NSW, Australia: AMEP Research Centre, Macquarie University.

Yates, L. (2010b). Speech act performance in workplace settings. In A. M. Martinez Flor & E. U. Juan (Eds.), *Speech act performance: Theoretical, empirical and methodological issues* (pp. 109–126). Amsterdam, the Netherlands: John Benjamins.

Yates, L. (2010c). Welcome to Australia: Social inclusion, opportunities for interaction and investment in English language learning for migrants. Paper presented at the 35th Applied Linguistics Association of Australia (ALAA) Congress, Queensland University, Brisbane, Australia.

Yates, L., & Springall, J. (2010). Soften up! Successful requests in the workplace. In D. Tatsuki & N. Houck (Eds.), *Pragmatics from research to practice: Teaching speech acts* (pp. 67–86). Alexandria, VA: TESOL.

SECTION B: SECOND LANGUAGE INSTRUCTION FOR SPECIFIC LEARNERS

All Shades of Every Color: An Overview of Early Teaching and Learning of Foreign Languages

Marianne Nikolov and Jelena Mihaljević Djigunović

The paper analyzes research published over the last five years. The first part looks into policy documents, types of programs, and surveys to identify (a) reasons why an early start to learning languages is seen as beneficial and under what conditions; (b) possible threats; and (c) the aims and expected outcomes that are predicted by various models. The second part discusses studies on learners, including what they do in classrooms, how they perform on tasks, how their languages interact, and how they develop in different skills. A separate section reviews individual differences in the affective, cognitive, and strategic domains, as well as the role of learners' socioeconomic status and their learning difficulties. In the third part, we draw on classroom observation and interview studies to discuss teachers' roles, proficiency and uses of languages, and beliefs and practices. In the fourth part, we focus on the assessment of young learners; more specifically, we review what the construct of assessment is, what various assessment frameworks include, what international and national examinations exist, and what assessment for learning involves. Finally, in the last section we review implications for further research.

ALL SHADES OF EVERY COLOR: AN OVERVIEW OF EARLY TEACHING AND LEARNING OF FOREIGN LANGUAGES

In recent years, there has been an unprecedented increase not only in the number of young learners (YLs) and their teachers, but also in the quantity of language policy documents, teachers' handbooks, teaching materials, and empirical studies devoted to the topic of early foreign language learning. In addition, several conferences have been held on YLs and their teachers, and a number of surveys have either been published (e.g., Edelenbos, Johnstone, & Kubanek, 2007; Nikolov & Mihaljević Djigunović , 2006; Rhodes & Pufahl, 2008) or are in progress. Furthermore, several handbooks for teachers have been produced (e.g., Curtain & Dahlberg, 2010; Hood & Tobutt, 2009; Pinter, 2006a; Szpotowicz & Szulc-Kurpaska, 2009), as have a number of volumes on empirical research (e.g., Enever, Moon, & Raman, 2009; Kawahara, 2008; Muñoz, 2006; Nikolov, 2009a, 2009b; Nikolov, Mihaljević Djigunović , Mattheoudakis, Lundberg, & Flanagan, 2007; Peng & Zhu, 2010). Finally, the variety of studies in refereed journals is also remarkable.

The aim of this paper is to show the most important trends by critically reviewing recent publications and projects in progress. As will be shown, although the most frequently researched target language (L2) is English, other target languages have also been researched. Interestingly, in some studies, bilingual children are exposed to a third language, thus providing a new perspective.

Early language learning and teaching has become one of the key areas in applied linguistics and language pedagogy characterized by multiple research methods (Nikolov, 2009c). Studies have moved away from a narrow focus on language gains or other discrete aspects of second language acquisition; many current inquiries involve various stakeholders and apply mixed methods thus documenting the complexity of issues far beyond the-earlier-the-better stand-point. Therefore, it is difficult to discuss studies under single headings. Another important point concerns where studies are conducted. Most importantly, Asian countries have moved to the foreground, and research has increased in English speaking countries as well.

POLICY DOCUMENTS AND EARLY FOREIGN LANGUAGE PROGRAMS

Language Policy Documents

Many language policy documents explicitly state the advantages of early language learning. The Commission of the European Communities (2003) defined them in a broad sense (e.g., better L1 skills, and favorable attitudes to other languages, people, and cultures) and listed conditions under which they can be beneficial (e.g., trained teachers, small classes, enough time devoted to languages). As for which language to teach, the European standpoint is clear. The Council of Europe (2007) language policy document listed several reasons why it does not matter what language YLs study. A recent resolution passed by the European Parliament (2009) stated that "Europe's linguistic diversity constitutes a major cultural asset and it would be wrong for the European Union to restrict itself to a single main language" (n.p.).

The Position Statement on Teaching English as a Foreign or Additional Language to Young Learners (TESOL, 2009), for instance, emphasizes that "age alone does not determine success in learning a foreign language" and "there is no single best way to implement" (p. 1) such programs. The strengthening of YLs' own cultural values and identities is also often stressed, as in some contexts early English is often perceived not only as a blessing, but also as a threat.

The particular age range considered *young* varies to a great extent. In the European context, a working group of the European Union member states agreed that pre-school children between the ages of three to six are called *very young learners*, whereas primary-school pupils between seven to twelve are *young learners*, although in certain contexts even 14-year-olds are included in the YLs' group. Practices regarding when early language learning starts in national curricula also vary along a similar continuum.

Types of Early Programs

Much variation characterizes early language learning programs according to when they start, how much time they allocate to early language learning, what type of curriculum they apply, who the teachers are, and how the programs are implemented. A review of European countries found that time devoted to ELL ranges between about one hour (in awareness-raising and language-focused programs) and several hours per week (in content and language integrated learning [CLIL] programs; for details, see Edelenbos, Johnstone, & Kubanek, 2007; Dalton-Puffer, this volume).

Johnstone (2009a) describes four models of early language learning. In the first, some general topics are used for teaching the foreign language (e.g., colors, parts of the body), whereas in the second model the topics are borrowed from other curricular areas (e.g., animals and their habitat). In both models about one hour per week is devoted to language learning. The third approach seeks to sensitize children to languages, often those in the local community. Finally, the fourth model is immersion, in which a significant part of the curriculum is taught through the medium of the additional language "with a correspondingly large increase in the time made available over the other three models" (p. 35). The first two models are the most widely applied and their common characteristics include (a) a fairly limited amount of time is dedicated to instruction per week; (b) teachers are homeroom teachers, that is, generalists, rather than language specialists; and (c) teachers' proficiency in the foreign language (FL) often falls short of native speaker level. In many studies reviewed in this paper, the time devoted to ELL ranges between one to three sessions per week in the first two models. However, no comparative study was found on how weekly exposure impacts on outcomes.

Research has been conducted on all of these four models, although most typically the first two are referred to as ELL. Little research is available on awareness raising programs (type three, but see Horst, White, & Bell, 2010) and especially on how children benefit from them over time. Our understanding of the main issues is that many findings may be relevant across these models. As Harris (2009) argues, "we are focusing so much on the 'foreign' in language learning that we overlook language contexts that actually have quite rich comparative potential" (p. 351). Based on findings of the Irish language primary school program, he claims that FL learning is not really that different from minority, heritage, or regional language learning. Similarly, a lot of the methodological issues are in common between the first two and the fourth model where curricular content is delivered in the FL.

The specific type of program has important implications for general aims and achievement targets in the L2. Overall, the achievements tend to be modest: YLs are not expected to achieve native levels of proficiency (e.g., Curtain, 2009; Haenni Hoti, Heintzmann, & Müller, 2009; Inbar-Lourie & Shohamy, 2009; see also the section on testing in this paper) and achievement targets reflect developmental stages in early language learning as children gradually shift from prefabricated utterances to more analyzed language use (Johnstone, 2009a). In most contexts, programs also aim to develop favorable attitudes towards languages and language learning, and YLs' own culture and identity (e.g., Prabhu, 2009; Vickov, 2007).

The concern worded by Prabhu (2009) resonates in many educational contexts in relation to English as a lingua franca: "we would like this to lead to an enlargement of the linguistic repertoire and cultural horizons of many different communities, not a substitution of English for all or many other languages accompanied by a loss of different cultures" (p. 43).

Therefore, it is not by coincidence that results of many studies enquiring into how children benefit from different types of programs are evaluated as "no loss to L1" (e.g., Johnstone, 2009b). The worry about the potential negative impact on first language development has led to several studies looking into how YLs' languages interact in the early language learning process, and many of these document that exposure to a new language may favorably impact L1 development– a most desirable and fascinating outcome. Besides linguistic and socio-affective aims, metacognition and learning strategies are also often among the explicit aims of early language learning programs and how they interact with the learners' L1 in complex ways. How awareness towards learners' own culture and their identity are shaped by early language learning is another area, besides the ones above, where more longitudinal research is necessary in all types of programs.

Large-Scale Projects

A national survey conducted in the U.S. (Rhodes & Pufahl, 2008) revealed both positive and negative trends in enrollment between 1997 and 2008. Most importantly, a significant decrease was found in the percentage of elementary and middle schools offering FL instruction. The decline occurred mainly in public elementary schools, whereas the percentage of private elementary schools teaching languages remained about the same.

Survey results revealed issues of unequal access to FL instruction. Students attending rural or low socioeconomic status (SES) schools were less likely to learn a FL. A disparity was found between public and private elementary schools: the latter offered languages at much higher rates. As for the target languages offered, the most popular language was Spanish; the teaching of French, German, Japanese, and Russian decreased, whereas Arabic and Chinese increased. More than one quarter of all elementary school FL teachers were not certified at all, and schools found it difficult to find qualified teachers.

A working group of the EU member states has conducted a survey on early language learning at a very early age in a project called Early Language Learning at Pre-primary Level in Europe: Current Situation and Future Perspectives. Data were collected with the help of a questionnaire and case studies of good practice from national ministries. The findings are expected to be published in a policy guidebook in 2011 (Hartung, personal communication, July 7, 2010). The main challenges were that the type and amount of data available vary a lot in different countries and ministries are not aware of what goes on in the private sector, a major issue in equity. One finding is clear: few teachers and staff are trained to work with this particular age group in most educational contexts; thus, teacher education is the main stumbling block of meeting parental needs.

A global project funded by the British Council (Investigating Global Practices in Teaching English to Young Learners) using a questionnaire and case studies is also in progress. So far over 4,000 teachers have filled in questionnaires in over 130 countries providing insights into classroom practices in local contexts (Garton, personal communication, July 6, 2010).

An innovative EU-sponsored longitudinal project called Early Language Learning in Europe (ELLiE, http: //ellieresearch.eu) was launched in 2007. The main aim was to find out what European YLs can achieve by learning a FL in state schools, where the FL is just one of many school subjects and where a limited amount of time is devoted to FL instruction. During the three years of this seven-country project the same investigations were carried out in England, Italy, the Netherlands, Poland, Spain, Sweden, and Croatia (sponsored by the British Council) using a mixed-method approach. The progress of around 1,200 children was followed along three specific foci: policy implementation in each of the seven contexts, factors that contribute to the effectiveness of early language learning, and learning outcomes (both linguistic and non-linguistic). The role of the teacher and the impact of digital media on early language learning were two special investigation strands within the project. Some findings are discussed in the sections below.

RESEARCH ON YOUNG LEARNERS

One of the recent developments in ELL studies concerns the use of multiple methods. Researchers make sure that each method of data collection is complemented by other types of or sources of data to allow for triangulation. This is a welcome development, as studies become more reliable and valid. However, this development also makes studies more difficult to classify.

Classroom Observation Studies

Investigations within the ELLiE project included classroom observation of learners' linguistic and non-linguistic behavior during FL lessons focusing on learners' attention, participation, relationship to teacher and classmates, language comprehension, and production. Findings of the Croatian cohort learning English in Grades 1 and 2 (Mihaljević Djigunović , 2009b) showed how students' engagement in pair work increased significantly and how interest, attention and engagement, and shyness and anxiety interacted in complex ways. Lundberg and Lindgren (2008) reported that YLs can pick up on formal aspects of language when focus is on meaning, and that spontaneous production emerges very slowly in the first two years.

Besides observing classroom processes and how children behave, some studies focus on how YLs perform certain tasks. These studies provide valuable insights into what actually happens, how children comprehend and complete tasks, which language they use for what purposes, and how they benefit from participating in them. In an in-depth observation study on classroom tasks implemented in early English classrooms in China (Peng & Zhang, 2009a, Peng & Zhang, 2009b), students responded to teachers' fast questions in English exclusively. Practice was done in drill-like sequences in a lockstep fashion in huge classes, and the drills seemed to provide most of the learners with a feeling of success and allowed them to practice what they experienced as English.

Ten-year-olds' peer-peer interactions on spot-the-difference tasks were analyzed by Pinter (2007a, b). After the task, the students were invited to watch their first and last performances and comment on the changes they noticed. Findings clearly indicated that peer-peer interactions at a very low level of competence brought various benefits. When asked what they thought about task repetition, children could clearly see the advantages: they learned from one another, noticed gaps in their own performances, and their anxiety also decreased.

Interaction of Learners' Languages

An important development in language pedagogy concerns the revival of studies looking into how learners' languages interact with one another as they develop multi-competence (e.g., Cook, 1991). Recent studies tend to focus not only on how L1 impacts on L2 but also on interrelationships between languages shifting from transfer to access (Walter, 2007). This means a more general approach to transfer: it is bidirectional and draws on all kinds of resources (skills, knowledge, and strategies) available to learners.

Another emerging trend is marked by the number of YLs' languages: several studies involve bilingual children developing in three languages. For example, learners of English as a FL were bilingual in Catalan and Spanish (Muñoz, 2006), Basque and Spanish (García Mayo & García Lecumberri, 2003), Dutch and various other languages (Goorhuis-Brouwer & de Bot, 2010), and Hungarian and Ukrainian (Huszti, Fábián, & Bárányné Komári, 2009). These studies document that the learners' three languages develop in harmony, and there is no loss of L1 due to early exposure to a new language.

Standardized tests were used in an innovative way in a study in the Netherlands involving four cohorts of young (age 4+) Dutch and non-Dutch learners of English. Goorhuis-Brouwer and de Bot (2010) tested participants' development over two years in English and Dutch with the help of Dutch and English versions of the Reynell test for language development. Their findings refuted arguments against early language learning assuming a negative impact on learners' L1 and L2 development. Lower language ability children benefited more from early language learning than their peers with average skills.

One of the focal points, transfer, was similar in a small-scale correlational study conducted by Larson-Hall (2008). Japanese college students who started studying English early were examined on a phonemic discrimination and a grammaticality judgment task. Modest relationships were found and age effects seemed to emerge after a substantial amount of input had been gained, a finding in line with what Muñoz (2006) has repeatedly pointed out. YLs tend to develop at a slow rate compared to their peers who start at a later point in time.

Chinese EFL learners in an immersion program from kindergarten to Grade 3 were compared with YLs learning English for fewer hours (Knell et al., 2007). In the experimental group, YLs studied half of the curriculum in English in groups of 50. They were assessed on a number of measures in Chinese and English. Although the immersion students outperformed their non-immersion peers on most measures, a special finding emerged: pinyin contributed to better results in both Chinese and

English.

Early and late EFL beginners' achievements were compared at age 14 in listening, reading, and writing in Croatian (L1) and English (L2) in a cross sectional study (Mihaljević Djigunović , 2010a). The degree of interdependence between the two languages varied among the three skills: reading in L1 and L2 were the most strongly connected; the relationship between writing in L1 and L2 was the weakest. Correlations across L1 and L2 skills indicated stronger relationships in the case of earlier beginners than for their later starting peers. The emerging patterns of multi-competence developed by the age of 14 indicated different interactions between YLs' L1 and L2.

Reading comprehension in L1 and L2 was compared in a complex study on sixth and eighth graders (Nikolov & Csapó, 2010) to explore the relationships between YLs' reading comprehension in English and Hungarian. Moderate significant relationships were found between students' performances in the two languages in both grades; variance explained by a subtest of verbal analogies was similar (sixth grade) or higher (eighth grade) than in the case of L1 reading as an independent variable. The underlying aptitude construct impacted reading comprehension in the two languages in different ways, and correlations were stronger between L2 scores.

An international comparative study examined the levels of achievement of 8th grade learners of English in listening, reading, writing, and pragmatics in Croatia and Hungary (Mihaljević Djigunović, Nikolov, & Ottó, 2008). Earlier starters were slightly, but significantly better on all measures; the correlations between skills were stronger in Hungary. Croatian learners outperformed their Hungarian peers despite the fact that they tended to start English later, in larger groups, and for fewer hours—a thought provoking result in light of what is generally expected in more intensive programs. A comparison of the two contexts suggested that out of class exposure to English and quality of EFL teaching were more favorable in Croatia.

Individual Differences

The misconception that children are so similar to one another that there is no real need to focus on individual differences in the field of early language learning is widespread (Mihaljević Djigunović, 2009a). We argue for the importance not only of attitudes, motivation, learning strategies, and aptitude, but also of language anxiety, something that has only recently been recognized as worth researching in YLs. What is, however, highlighted is the need for investigating interactions of individual differences. Instead of single individual differences variable, it is their interactions that can meaningfully inform early language learning processes. Another valuable perspective is an analysis of interactions between individual differences variables and contextual factors (Mihaljević Djigunović & Szpotowicz, 2008).

Affective Development

Students' motivation is an extremely popular research area, and fortunately a number of recent longitudinal studies have allowed researchers to examine how attitudes and motivation change over time. The time periods studied range from one to several years, and some studies compare and contrast different groups; a few inquiries compare what students claim happens in their classrooms versus what actually does and to what extent they enjoy them.

A national sample of Hungarian eighth graders (age 14) was involved in a longitudinal questionnaire study conducted by Dörnyei, Csizér, and Németh (2006) in 1993, 1999 and 2004. The results document the larger picture, namely, how students' language learning attitudes and motivation changed in a dynamic way reflecting globalization processes, but do not explore the classroom level.

An exceptionally long period of time was covered in a study conducted in the U. S. Heining-Boyton and Haitema (2007) combined a large-scale longitudinal survey and retrospective interviews with a few participants after ten years on attitudes towards early language learning. The inquiries were unique because the students were followed not only in elementary school, but also for years after their foreign language in the elementary school (FLES) experiences. In corroboration of the quantitative data, a qualitative analysis revealed that, for a majority of the students, FL study was viewed positively, as were FL speakers and their cultures.

Japanese elementary school pupils' intrinsic and extrinsic motivation for learning English was the focus of a study by Matsuzaki Carreira (2006). The author investigated how third and sixth graders' motivation changed with age. A steady developmental decline was found in both types of motivation for learning English. The author attributed it to a general fall in children's motivation in all subjects in Japanese elementary school pupils and found considerable room for improvement in early language learning in Japan.

Declining language learning motivation, however, is not limited to the above contexts. A comparative analysis of data on the motivation of YLs in the ELLiE project involving learners from six countries showed that initial motivation was very high and that girls were more motivated than boys (Szpotowicz, Mihaljević Djigunović, & Enever, 2009). An inspection of what participants found most inspiring showed that it was learning new words. This suggested that, at the start, YLs perceived language learning as vocabulary building. Analysis of motivation in the subsequent years is still under way but preliminary findings indicated a slow decrease in motivation (Lopriore, 2009; Mihaljević Djigunović , 2010b). Another study of 36 Croatian ELLiE participants (Mihaljević Djigunović & Letica Krevelj, 2010) confirmed that YLs started their L2 learning with positive attitudes toward classroom activities. However, under less than ideal conditions (large groups, two lessons per week, unqualified teachers), which was the current reality in many European contexts, some YLs soon started to develop negative attitudes to L2 learning. Also, children started L2 learning with overly favorable perceptions of their abilities and achievements. However, as their early language learning experience developed they soon started building their self-perceptions more realistically, and metacognition developed quite quickly with some young L2 learners.

In a different comparative study involving Croatian and Italian YLs (N = 91), Lopriore and Mihaljević Djigunović (in press) conducted a mixed methods investigation of their initial attitudes to learning English and attitudinal development over two years. In both cohorts, initial attitudes of YLs to EFL learning were mostly positive. In the second year, some YLs' attitudes continued to be positive, but many of them thought English was more difficult. Others liked it even more because they felt successful in classes.

The popular belief that YLs are anxiety-free is the reason that there have been few studies on language anxiety in early language learning. However, anxiety has been observed in YLs as well. In his comparative study of monolingual and bilingual YLs of English, Legac (2007) found that bilingual (Croatian-Albanian, Croatian-Czech, and Croatian-Italian) learners experienced lower levels of both listening anxiety and overall language anxiety than their monolingual peers. In another study, Mihaljević Djigunović and Legac (2008) compared mono- and bilingual seventh graders' anxiety during the three stages of the EFL learning process (input, processing and output). They found that bilinguals had lower anxiety in all three stages. The authors proposed that bilinguals, thanks to their more extensive experience in using two languages in everyday life, developed higher linguistic self-confidence, which contributed to lower language anxiety.

Academic Achievement and Cognitive Development

The relationship between general academic achievement and learning French and Spanish in FLES groups was explored in an impressive large-scale longitudinal study by Taylor and Lafayette (2010). Remarkable findings emerged from the examination of continued learning of FLs over a period of three years from Grade 3 to Grade 5 in Louisiana public schools. Participants' achievements were tested with the help of standardized tests in a variety of domains (English language arts, mathematics, science, and social studies). Students learning a FL significantly outperformed their peers who did not study a new language both in English as well as the other subjects. This result provides a very strong argument for early exposure to a FLES: the benefits transferred to general school achievements and the learners' L1.

Other studies have researched language learning aptitude, an under-researched area in the case of YLs, exploring how cognitive skills impact early language learning in two countries characterized by a tradition of streaming learners according to their learning abilities—a reason why placement is an issue from an early age. Greek learners were examined in a study involving five- to nine-year-old learners' cognitive abilities and their learning of English vocabulary in Greece. Significant relationships were found between YLs' aptitude and their vocabulary development in EFL (Alexiu, 2009).

Three independent studies explored how YLs' aptitude contributed to their achievements in FLL. In Hungary, where streaming has been typical for many decades and English tends to be provided for the more able learners, whereas learners of German lag behind their peers, one study (Kiss & Nikolov, 2005) involved over 400 sixth graders. Results showed that 22% of the variation in English performances was explained by participants' aptitude. An even younger age group was involved in a similar project piloting an aptitude test for 8-year-olds (Kiss, 2009). The test was found to discriminate well among learners.

The role of inductive reasoning was explored in a large-scale longitudinal study on representative samples of Hungarian learners of English and German (ages 12, 14, 16, and 18). Learners' scores on an inductive reasoning test predicted a large portion of the variance in their performances in reading (e.g., 14% in English at age 12). In the younger age groups inductive reasoning explained larger portions of the variance than in the older cohorts. The relationships between the cognitive variable, L1 reading, and other factors were stronger than in the case of older learners; relationships between L2 skills weakened over time (Csapó & Nikolov, 2009).

How Young Learners Use Strategies

YLs' learning and communication strategies were examined by either focusing on how they perform certain tasks or by examining their classroom behavior in larger groups. Intervention studies are the exception in researching YLs' strategies. In tasks based on interaction between peers on spot-the-difference tasks Pinter (2006b) analyzed what strategies 10-year-olds used and how, and compared them to adults on similarly low levels of English working on the same tasks. She found that YLs used similar strategies to adults: they were able to respond to each other, clarify messages, keep tally of the differences, and they interacted confidently. However, the adult learners used the strategies more often.

A study carried out by Tragant and Victori (2006) found that in the early stages of learning children used predominantly memorization strategies and generally relied on external resources. Focusing on the use of vocabulary, pronunciation, spelling, reading, and writing strategies by YLs of differing start ages (8, 11, and adults) who had the same amount of instruction, Tragant and Victori found evidence for age-dependent developmental stages in strategy use that were, however, independent of proficiency level or stage of learning. In contrast to older learners, YLs very rarely used varied and complex strategies at the beginning of learning.

Two studies compared reading strategies of more and less successful EFL learners. Šamo (2006) found that more successful learners used 11 reading strategies with a significantly higher frequency than their less successful peers. Quite a few of the strategies were metacognitive; thus, they involved monitoring the process of reading. Nikolov (2006) compared the use of reading and writing test-taking strategies of young top achievers and low achievers. Her study indicated variable frequency and types of strategies used by YLs of both groups; thus the author challenged the widely accepted assumption that good language performance necessarily implies using more and varied strategies.

Greek sixth graders' writing strategies were examined with the help of questionnaires, think-aloud protocols, and interviews. Griva, Tsakiridou, and Nihoritou (2009) found both similarities and differences between boys and girls as well as between more and less successful learners. Generally, all learners considered writing a difficult skill, and sometimes revised and proofread their drafts, translated, and used bilingual dictionaries. Differences between more and less successful writers were observed in the perception and use of metacognitive strategies: the former used more strategies and employed higher-level processing during writing.

An intervention study was implemented by Macaro and Erler (2008) aiming to raise the achievement of young-beginner readers of French through strategy instruction in England. A sample of 62 learners aged 11–12 participated in a program of reading strategy instruction lasting 14 months. Measures were taken of French reading comprehension, reading strategy use, and attitudes towards French before and after the intervention, and the findings were compared with a control group. Strategy instruction improved comprehension of both simple and more elaborate texts, brought about changes in strategy use, and improved attitudes towards reading.

A classroom observation study examined Chinese learners of EFL. Peng and Zhang (2009b) analyzed the classroom discourse data of fifth graders and found that although the most frequently applied communication strategies were L1-based ones when students asked for clarifications in Chinese and tried to cooperate with their peers, there were few examples of strategy use. According to their explanation, in large classes of 50–60 learners, teachers insisted on repetition mostly and thus prevented learners from applying strategies creatively.

Social Background and Equity

Socioeconomic status (SES) is a widely accepted variable contributing to school success in educational research; however, it is rarely addressed explicitly in studies on early language learning. In educational contexts where the private sector offers a range of early programs, socio-economically advantaged children's parents are more able to afford early English or other languages. Thus, issues of equity and diversity are often entangled in early language learning programs, as, for example Butler (2007) argues in the case of Japan, or Feng (2009) when discussing convergence and divergence in policy and practice in China, or Moon (2009) in Vietnam. Studies are not limited to Asia, however. SES was found to be an important and worrying factor in the U.S. survey cited above (Rhodes & Pufahl, 2008), but it is also often mentioned in many other contexts (see e.g., national case studies in Enever, Moon, & Raman, 2009 and European contexts below). As Johnstone (2009b) noted, learners' SES may impact on the generalizability and sustainability of national policy initiatives, as was documented in his discussion of an early French program in Scotland.

SES was addressed in several studies involving nationally representative samples of Hungarian learners studying English and German (Csapó & Nikolov, 2009; Nikolov, 2009d). The findings showed the larger picture: significant relationships were found between learners' SES and their language proficiency, language learning plans, and motivation, and SES was also related to language choice: more children with higher SES backgrounds tended to study English than their peers, who studied German.

Greek learners participated in an innovative study examining the relationships between YLs' SES and language development in English in a particular town in Greece (Mattheoudakis & Alexiou, 2009). Interestingly, all learners, irrespective of their SES, received private tutoring in addition to learning English at school. Although their families' SES significantly impacted the participants' level and progress in English, no such relationship was found for their motivation, a finding in contrast with the previously discussed studies.

A different approach was used by Carmel (2009). She applied critical discourse analysis to English for YLs. She found that English for young language learnersit was seen as a valuable asset and a widely spread socio-cultural phenomenon in Israel, and documented it as a social, educational and economic divider in parents', stakeholders' and pupils' discourses she analyzed. She found three main discourses: Americanization and internationalism, good parenting, and consumers. Similar analyses could cast light on how early language learning is perceived in other contexts.

Learning Difficulties in Early Language Learning

Due to the growing number of learners and teachers involved in early language learning, a variety of problems has emerged. Challenges caused by individual differences and special needs may make teachers' jobs demanding. Many teachers find it hard to work with children at risk or suffering from attention deficit (e.g., Ferrari & Palladino, 2007; Morrissette, 2009). A full volume edited by Kormos and Kontra (2008b) focused on learners with special educational needs, most importantly dyslexic YLs. Ndlovu and Geva (2008) stressed the importance of an early diagnosis of learning disability; Sparks, Ganschow, and Patton (2008) claimed that L2 learners with learning disabilities need support in both L1 and L2. Smith (2008) pointed out the lack of adequate language teacher preparation for working with such learners, whereas Helland (2008) provided an insight into characteristic patterns of spelling errors made by dyslexics, and showed clearly the importance of an interdisciplinary approach to problems.

RESEARCH ON TEACHERS

Teachers are key players in early language learning: they are not only the main sources of input and motivation, but they are also responsible for what happens in classrooms (e.g., Butler 2004, 2005; Inbar-Lourie, 2010; Johnstone, 2009a; Moon, 2009; Nikolov, 2008; Wang, 2009). Recent studies have explored teachers' classroom practices, their uses of language, their beliefs, and their development.

There are certain quality measures all teachers of YLs should meet (e.g., Curtain & Dahlberg, 2010; Johnstone, 2009a). They are expected to be (a) proficient in their pupils' L1 as well as in the L2, (b) familiar with the content and methodology of the general curriculum, and (c) the principles of how children learn in general and languages in particular. Teachers often fall short of these criteria (e.g., Butler, 2007; Lugossy, 2007; Moon, 2009; Nikolov, 2008). In most educational contexts, teachers are either generalist homeroom teachers or language specialists. In the first case teachers are familiar with the curriculum; thus, they can embed the L2 in the content children are familiar with, and can manage YLs well, but their proficiency may not be very good. In the second case teachers may be proficient in the L2 but less skilled in implementing age-appropriate methodology.

In a third scenario, homeroom teachers with limited or no English co-teach with native speakers (e.g., in Japan, see Aline & Hosoda, 2006).

Classroom Observation Studies on Teachers

Teachers' roles vary to a great extent in the YL classrooms. A study in Japan (Aline & Hosoda, 2006) explored team teaching participation patterns of homeroom teachers in interaction with native speaker teaching assistants in English activities classes in Japanese public elementary schools. Four patterns were observed in homeroom teachers' behavior: they acted as (a) a bystander, (b) a translator, (c) a co-learner of English, or (d) a co-teacher. The participation patterns affected the classroom interaction in distinct ways.

In a very different EFL context, a study combining classroom observations and follow-up interviews documented that many Hungarian teachers of YLs felt that the role of a caretaker was demanding and keeping children on task required a lot of energy and special pedagogical skills (Nikolov, 2008). Many of them wished that they could teach older learners, insisted on streaming YLs into ability groups, and preferred teaching more able ones. They lacked not only proficiency and pedagogical skills, but also a desire to improve their practice. Many teachers perceived games and storytelling as a waste of time, and looked forward to what they perceived to be proper teaching in later years.

In a study on pre-service teachers' teaching practice, very young children in kindergartens were found unpredictable and presented a challenge to novice English teachers in Poland (Szulc-Kurpaska, 2007). They found it difficult to evoke YLs' interest, involve them in carefully designed tasks, and manage their activities in English.

Teachers' proficiency in the target language and its impact on children's development is usually seen as a delicate issue. Inbar-Lourie (2010) explored the instructional linguistic choices of EFL teachers in the Israeli context. She examined how teachers adhered to English or incorporated it with the learners' L1. The study involved six teachers and 285 young EFL learners aged 6–8 whose L1 was either Hebrew or Arabic. Data were collected with observations and interviews to explore teachers' classroom practice, beliefs about their learners' needs, and how their use of L1 contributed to development in English. Teachers were conscious about their L1 use and their decisions concerning when and how to apply L1 and L2 were based on principles they worded in terms of learners' needs.

Looking into YLs' exposure to L2, Mihaljević Djigunović (2010b) found that teachers of YLs perceived their L1 use to be lower than observation data showed. However, when learner achievement was entered into the equation, it turned out that learners in teachers' classes who used the least L1 in their English classes did not score the highest on receptive and productive tasks. An analysis of classroom teaching that the highest-scoring group was exposed to suggested that it was not the amount of L1 versus L2 use that was decisive. Rather, it was when and why the L1 and L2 were used that was most important.

Data were collected from classrooms and interviews by Nagy (2009) focusing on the amount and function of mother tongue use (Hungarian) by teachers working in early and later start fourth grade EFL groups. According to the teachers, their practice was constrained by various factors: children's aptitude, proficiency in English, and the teachers' preference for using grammar, translation, and memorization to prepare the children for examinations.

Interview and Survey Studies on Teachers

How teachers think about their practices, YLs', and their own needs is an area where important insights have been gained. As teaching children tends to be a relatively new challenge in many contexts, the introduction of early language learning often happens overnight without appropriate teacher education. Problems are related not only to teachers' proficiency and new methodologies reflecting how children learn an L2, but also to what the use of a communicative methodology involves.

Butler (2005) explored teachers' views on communicative methodology in Korea, Japan, and Taiwan and found that they were concerned about using communicative activities for a number of good reasons. In a different study, Butler (2004) asked early language learning teachers to reflect on their own language proficiency and learned that they felt their productive skills lagged behind their receptive skills and they needed to improve their English to be able to implement programs they were involved in (Butler, 2004). A similar picture emerged from Moon's (2009) study on Vietnamese teachers. Her case studies cast light on teachers' needs and how such needs might be met. She also demonstrated how training in communicative language teaching, course materials and local traditions interact in teachers' beliefs and daily classroom practices, which generally reflected a behaviorist model of language learning and teaching.

The contradictions revealed between teachers' stated beliefs and their actual classroom practices are typical in other countries as well. Lugossy (2007) explored how in-service teachers implemented new ideas in a picture book project. She asked them to use storybooks with their YLs and to reflect on their own practice. She compared what teachers knew and believed, and what they actually did with their YLs of English. She found that very few teachers changed their practice over time.

The findings of a large-scale questionnaire survey in China are more positive. Wang (2009) surveyed 1,000 primary teachers of English in urban and rural schools and found teachers' beliefs with regard to early English and learner-centered teaching to be supportive and in line with the central curriculum. Teachers' self-reported classroom practices reflected that they implemented learner-centered teaching, with the exception of frequent drills. The overall findings showed teachers' enthusiastic support for implementing the new curriculum involving not only teaching YLs, but also documented a major shift towards learner-centered teaching – a relatively new concept in the Chinese context. It is to be seen, however, how teachers implement meaning-focused tasks in learner-centered ways on a daily basis.

In-depth semi-structured interviews with seven Croatian EFL teachers of YLs (Mihaljević Djigunović, 2010b) offered evidence of a range of teachers' beliefs. All believed that children learn FLs through games, songs, and role-plays; some thought that YLs need a leader and the teacher needs to take this role. Interestingly, none of the teachers believed that four weekly hours instead of the two prescribed by the national curriculum would contribute essentially to success in early language learning. As for the use of the L1 in the L2 classroom, all shared the belief that L1 was necessary to make sure that YLs could understand what went on and what they were learning.

The role of awareness-raising in the YL classroom is rarely focused on; thus, an exploratory research study conducted by Horst, White, and Bell (2010) in Canada is an exception. They examined how instruction could be designed so that learners build on their L1 knowledge in acquiring a new language. They involved two teachers, one of French (L1) and another of English (L2), and their 9–10-year-old francophone learners of English in cross-linguistic awareness raising activities to explore how certain themes in their L1 syllabus could be exploited in their L2 classes. The results showed how differently the two teachers applied the special pilot activities designed to draw learners' attention to a variety of specific L1 features.

ASSESSMENT OF YOUNG LEARNERS

The Construct: What Children Can Do

The dynamic spread of early language learning has brought about increased interest in testing YLs' proficiency and how they progress in their new language over time (McKay, 2006). The main issue in testing YLs concerns the construct. As Inbar-Lourie and Shohamy (2009) framed it, early language learning programs vary to a great extent from awareness raising to language focus programs, and from content-based curricula to immersion. They argued that testing must be in line with "the assessment constructs along with the language-content program continuum, particularly within the current integrated or embedded models in YL classrooms given its current status and use in diverse contexts" (p. 93). They demonstrated how the reflective process they applied to various tests and exams illustrated "the dynamics of testing construction and validation which need to be constantly rethought and revised" (p. 94).

Challenges in testing YLs are manifold. Low proficiency levels need to be defined and described along a continuum in small steps so that children's relatively slow development can be documented. This is important for their teachers, parents, and YLs themselves so that they feel that they are making progress. Also, the earlier instruction starts, the more probable it is that YLs are at the early stages of literacy development; what is typical for older learners cannot be automatically applied to YLs in the four skills. Teachers and test developers must bear in mind that YLs are different from older ones not only in their background knowledge of the world and other factors discussed in previous sections, but assessment may impact attitudes, motivation and anxiety in more important ways than in the case of older learners. Therefore, besides considering assessment of learning, a focus on assessment for learning is of crucial importance.

Assessment Frameworks and Exams

The need to quantify what children can do in terms of proficiency outcomes has resulted in various documents. In the U.S., the aim was to provide various types of programs with a profession-wide scale. For this purpose, several proficiency-based language assessment instruments were developed for early language learning. Curtain (2009) provided a detailed comparative analysis of various proficiency standards, performance guidelines as well as assessment instruments reflecting what YLs are expected to be able to do in various target languages. Work in Europe has focused on adapting Common European Frame-work of Reference for Languages descriptors (CEFR, Council of Europe, 2001; Figueras & Noijons, 2009; Jones, & Saville, 2009; Little, 2007) to YLs' needs and examinations (e.g., Hasselgreen, 2005; Papp & Salamoura, 2009; Pižorn, 2009).

Presently, to our knowledge, four international exams are available to provide YLs and their parents with a certificate on children's proficiency in English–for money (Pearson Test of English Young Learners, www.pearsonpte.com/PTEYoungLearners; Cambridge Young Learners English Tests, www.cambridgeesol.org/exams/young-learners; Integrated Skills in English, www.trinitycollege.co.uk; City & Guilds ESOL for Young Learners, www.cityandguilds.com). A detailed analysis is beyond our scope, but there appear to be some factors in common. In all four exams the construct is more towards the middle of the language-content continuum with a focus on some typical topics which YLs can be realistically expected to be familiar with, and the levels cover A1 and A2 in the CEFR (Council of Europe, 2001). No research is available on how taking exams impacts on children's motivation, anxiety and later progress. Several in-house publications are available on how Cambridge Young Learners English Tests were developed and validated (e.g., see special issue 28, 2007 at http: //www.cambridgeesol.org/rs_notes/rs_nts28.pdf), but no such information is available for the other three exams.

As early language learning programs become part of national curricula, more and more countries develop and publish their achievement targets and introduce national exams for an increasingly younger age group. In Switzerland, for example, a three-year longitudinal study was implemented on YLs development (Haenni Hoti, Heinzmann, & Müller, 2009). In Slovenia, research into what YLs can do resulted in validated national tests for sixth graders (Pižorn, 2009).

Assessment For Learning

Recent research into educational assessment has emphasized how dynamic testing can boost learning potential (Sternberg & Grigorenko, 2002) and a shift away from assessment of learning to assessment for learning has been observed. The emphasis is on how children benefit from classroom testing and feedback from teachers (Assessment Reform Group, 2002; Black & Wiliam, 1998; Davison & Leung, 2009; Leung & Scott, 2009; McKay, 2006; Teasdale & Leung, 2000). As McNamara and Roever (2006, pp. 251–252) argued, assessment should be sensitive to the issue of readiness to develop and there should be more research on learners' ability to profit from instruction and different kinds of interaction. In most of the cases in early language learning classrooms, interaction takes place between teachers and YLs, as well as between peers. Some studies discussed earlier provided insights into how task repetition and peer interaction contributed to better oral performance (e.g., Peng & Zhang, 2009a, 2009b; Pinter, 2007a), but a lot more similar studies are needed to find out more about the way feedback scaffolds learning.

How Teachers Assess Young Learners

There is not enough research on how teachers assess YLs. Butler (2009a) provided an overview of studies on teacher-based assessment in three Asian countries. She found that Korean and Taiwanese teachers faced a number of difficulties. They had to cope with large classes and lacked knowledge about teacher-based assessment, sufficient time to administer tests, and information on how best to use information gained through teacher-based assessment for formative and summative purposes. In Japan, teachers were not required to assess their YLs; however, they did use some self-assessment. In a different study, South Korean elementary and secondary school EFL teachers were asked to assess videotapes of sixth-grade students' group activities (Butler, 2009b). The teachers varied substantially in their overall evaluations.

The first findings of an exploratory study involving EFL teachers in Hungary showed that they applied two types of classroom assessment practices (Hild & Nikolov, 2010). First, they gave rewards for best performances on tasks; rewards were cumulative in nature. Good performers earned small rewards on a regular basis, whereas their less successful peers felt that they deserved nothing. This practice meant that able and more motivated learners got positive feedback and the lack of reward functioned as negative feedback for their less successful peers. Second, the other type of assessment teachers applied involved achievements on classroom tests, most frequently in reading and writing. This dual practice reflected what teachers saw as the aim of assessment: motivation and feedback on actual development in English.

Portfolios and self-assessment may contribute to autonomy and better learning. Some experts advocate the use of portfolios, especially in Europe. Hasselgreen (2005) considered what the CEFR (2001) and the European Language Portfolio offered to YLs. She explored ways in which they were applied in Norway. However, as Little (2007) stated, portfolio assessment was often seen by teachers and learners as extra work. Overall, not enough is known about actual uses of portfolios in YLs'classrooms.

Two studies looked into YLs'self-assessment in Korean elementary schools (Butler & Lee, 2006, 2010). The first one examined the validity of students' self-assessments of their oral performance in EFL in two types of assessments; whereas the second study explored the effectiveness of self-assessment on a regular basis for a semester during English classes.

The above discussions on teacher-based assessment lead to an important point connected to assessing YLs. Edelenbos and Kubanek-German (2004) coined the term *diagnostic competence*. In their view, it is "the ability to interpret students' FL growth, to skillfully deal with assessment material and to provide students with appropriate help in response to this diagnosis" (p. 260). This is a definite challenge in the YL classroom, especially in contexts where huge classes are typical, as in diagnostic assessment teachers are expected to work in one-on-one contact with the children rather than in a whole class.

MOVING FORWARD

The state of the art of early language learning is definitely a colorful tapestry. As more and more learners start learning FLs at an earlier age in different educational contexts and under so many varying conditions, many of the issues identified in previous studies are still on the agenda, but new ones have also surfaced. One of the obvious consequences is that early starters may achieve levels their peers used to achieve later; therefore, there must be new strategies for building on what they can do and for maintaining their motivation over an extended period of time. The most widely applied early language learning models may turn out to be less motivating and cognitively challenging after a few years. The integration of content and language at an early stage may help learners progress, but teacher education must keep in line with emerging needs.

Realistic aims and achievement targets must be continuously reexamined in specific educational contexts to meet local needs and reflect local realities. One of the most encouraging results of research in this review concerns the complex relationships between early language learning and learners' development in their academic, affective, strategic, and other domains of school curricula. Interactions of children's languages and various skills can give insight into the multi-competence that YLs start building up from the very beginning of their foreign language learning.

Obviously, the academic discussions and research have moved beyond unrealistic expectations of native speaker levels, both in the case of YLs and their teachers. Most studies explore realities of daily work with YLs. Teacher education in general, and teachers' age-appropriate methodology and proficiency in the target language in particular, however, are high on the global agenda, despite the fact that we did not cover this domain explicitly. Preparing enough teachers who are motivated and able to work efficiently with YLs in good quality programs is the way to move forward.

As was shown, dealing with growing diversity is a challenge for teachers in many contexts and equity is a recurring issue. Most importantly, the implications of English being the world's most important lingua franca are related to who has access to this currently precious commodity at the earliest possible time. Interestingly, hardly any studies are available on the private sector (but see Butler & Takeuchi, 2008), though it is widely known that private enterprises, including examination boards and publishers, definitely profit from the increased interest in early start programs.

More studies are needed on how teachers implement curricula in their classrooms, how they assess and scaffold their learners' development over an extended period, how YLs benefit from early exposure to their new language in other domains, and as adolescents and adults. Perhaps an integration of local and trans-contextual research that approaches early language learning from different perspectives is the most promising in the globalized world in which YLs live.

ACKNOWLEDGEMENT

Marianne Nikolov was a fellow at the Center for Advanced Study in the Behavioral Sciences at Stanford University at the time of writing this paper.

ANNOTATED BIBLIOGRAPHY

Enever, J., Moon, J., & Raman, U. (Eds.). (2009). *Young learner English language policy and implementation: International perspectives.* Reading, UK: Garnet Education Publishing.

The volume includes 28 chapters selected from papers presented at the international conference "The way forward: Learning from international experience of TEYL", held in Bangalore, India in January 2008. The contributions, from four continents, include keynote talks, national case studies, and chapters focusing on various innovations, experiments, and projects on teaching English to young learners.

Nikolov, M. (Ed.). (2009a). *Early learning of modern foreign languages: Processes and outcomes.* Clevedon, UK: Multilingual Matters.

This edited volume comprises 16 chapters on how children learn a variety of different languages including. The contexts include China, Croatia, Greece, Hungary, Ireland, Norway, Poland, Ukraine, and the United Kingdom, where the status of the target language is a foreign, second or third language. The studies represent a variety of research methods: enquiries apply qualitative, quantitative, and mixed methods.

Taylor, C., & Lafayette, R. (2010). Academic achievement through FLES: A case study for promoting greater access to foreign language study among young learners. *The Modern Language Journal, 94,* 22–42.

This is a thought-provoking study on how the benefits of early language learning contribute to general curricular domains. The authors explored whether FL study of first-year Grade 3 students who continued their FL study through Grade 5 in Louisiana public schools contributed to their academic achievement in curricular areas tested on the Iowa Tests of Basic Skills and the Louisiana Educational Assessment Program for the 21st Century Test. FL learners significantly outperformed their peers not learning a language on every test.

REFERENCES

Alexiou, T. (2009). Cognitive skills in young learners and their implications for FL learning. In M. Nikolov (Ed.), *Early learning of modern foreign languages: Processes and outcomes* (pp. 46–61). Clevedon, UK: Multilingual Matters.

Aline, D., & Hosoda, Y. (2006). Team teaching participation patterns of homeroom teachers in English activities classes in Japanese public elementary schools. *JALT Journal, 28*, 5–22.

Assessment Reform Group. (2002). Assessment for learning. 10 principles. Retrieved from www.assessment-reform-group.org

Black, P., & Wiliam, D. (1998). Assessment and classroom learning. *Assessment in Education, 5*, 7–71.

Butler, Y. G. (2004). What level of English proficiency do elementary teachers need to attain to teach EFL? Case studies from Korea, Taiwan, and Japan. *TESOL Quarterly, 38*, 245–287.

Butler, Y. G. (2005). Comparative perspectives towards communicative activities among elementary school teachers in South Korea, Japan, and Taiwan. *Language Teaching Research, 9*, 423–446.

Butler, Y. G. (2007). Foreign language education at elementary schools in Japan: Searching for solutions amidst growing diversification. *Current Issues in Language Planning, 8*, 129–147.

Butler, Y. G. (2009a). Issues in the assessment and evaluation of English language education at the elementary school level: Implications for policies in South Korea, Taiwan, and Japan. *The Journal of Asia TEFL, 6*, 1–31.

Butler, Y. G. (2009b). How do teachers observe and evaluate elementary school students' foreign language performance? A case study from South Korea. *TESOL Quarterly, 43*, 417–444.

Butler, Y. G., & Lee, J. (2006). On-task versus off-task self-assessment among Korean elementary school students studying English. *The Modern Language Journal, 90*, 506–518.

Butler, Y. G., & Lee, J. (2010). The effects of self-assessment among young learners of English. *Language Testing, 27*, 5–31.

Butler, Y. G., & Takeuchi, A. (2008). Variables that influence elementary school students' English performance in Japan. *The Journal of Asia TEFL, 5*, 61–91.

Carmel, R. (2009). English for young learners (EYL) in grades 1 and 2 in Israel. A critical discourse analysis. In M. Nikolov (Ed.), *The age factor and early language learning* (pp. 403–422). Berlin, Germany: Mouton de Gruyter.

Commission of the European Communities. (2003). *Promoting language learning and linguistic diversity: An action plan 2004–2006.* Retrieved from www.eu.int/comm/ education/doc/ official/keydoc/actlang/act_lang_en.pdf

Cook, V. J. (1991). The poverty-of-the-stimulus argument and multi-competence. *Second Language Research, 7,* 103–117.

Council of Europe. (2001). *Common European framework of reference for languages: Learning, teaching, assessment.* Cambridge, UK: Cambridge University Press.

Council of Europe. (2007). *From linguistic diversity to plurilingual education: Guide for the development of language education policies in Europe Main version.* Strasbourg, France: Council of Europe, Language Policy Division. Retrieved from http: //ec.europa. eu/ education/doc/official/keydoc/actlang/act_lang_en.pdf

Csapó, B., & Nikolov, M. (2009). The cognitive contribution to the development of proficiency in a foreign language. *Learning and Individual Differences, 19,* 203–218.

Curtain, H. (2009). Assessment of early learning of foreign languages in the USA. In M. Nikolov (Ed.), *The age factor and early language learning* (pp. 59–82). Berlin, Germany: Mouton de Gruyter.

Curtain, H. A., & Dahlberg, C. A. (2010). *Languages and children-making the match: New languages for young learners* (4th edition). Needham Heights, MA: Pearson Allyn & Bacon.

Davison, C., & Leung, C. (2009). Current issues in English language teacher-based assessment. *TESOL Quarterly, 43,* 393–415.

Dörnyei, Z., Csizér, K., & Németh, N. (2006). *Motivation, language attitudes and globalisation: A Hungarian perspective.* Clevedon, UK: Multilingual Matters.

Edelenbos, P., Johnstone, R., & Kubanek, A. (2007). *Languages for the children in Europe: Published research, good practice and main principles.* Retrieved from http: //ec.europa. eu/ education/policies/lang/doc/youngsum_en.pdf

Edelenbos, P., & Kubanek-German, A. (2004). Teacher assessment: The concept of 'diagnostic competence'. *Language Testing, 21,* 259–283.

Enever, J., Moon, J., & Raman, U. (Eds.). (2009). *Young learner English language policy and implementation: international perspectives.* Reading, UK: Garnet Education Publishing.

European Parliament. (2009). *Multilingualism: An asset for Europe and a shared commitment.* Retrieved from http: //www.europarl.europa.eu/sides/getDoc.do?pubRef = -//EP// TEXT+TA+P6-TA-2009–0162+0+DOC+XML+V0//EN

Feng, A. (2009). English in China: Convergence and divergence in policy and practice. *AILA Review, 22,* 72–84.

Ferrari, M., & Palladino, P. (2007). Foreign language learning difficulties in Italian children.

Journal of Learning Disabilities, 40, 256–269.
Figueras, N., & Noijons, J. (Eds.). (2009). *Linking to the CEFR levels: Research perspectives.* Arnhem, the Netherlands: Cito, EALTA.
García Mayo, M. P., & García Lecumberri, M. L. (Eds.). (2003). *Age and the acquisition of English as a foreign language.* Clevedon, UK: Multilingual Matters.
Goorhuis-Brouwer, S., & de Bot, K. (2010). Impact of early English language teaching on L1 and L2 development in children in Dutch schools. *International Journal of Bilingualism, 14*, 289–302.
Griva, E., Tsakiridou, H., & Nihoritou, I. (2009). A study of FL composing process and writing strategies employed by young learners. In M. Nikolov (Ed.), *Early learning of modern languages. Processes and outcomes* (pp. 132–148). Bristol, UK: Multilingual Matters.
Haenni Hoti, A., Heinzmann, S., & Müller, M. (2009). "I can you help?" Assessing speaking skills and interaction strategies of young learners. In M. Nikolov (Ed.), *The age factor and early language learning* (pp. 119–140). Berlin, Germany: Mouton de Gruyter.
Harris, J. (2009). Expanding the comparative context for early language learning: From foreign to heritage and minority language programmes. In M. Nikolov (Ed.), *The age factor and early language learning* (pp. 351–376). Berlin, Germany: Mouton de Gruyter.
Hasselgreen, A. (2005). Assessing the language of young learners. *Language Testing, 22*, 337–354.
Heining-Boynton, A., & Haitema, T. (2007). A ten-year chronicle of student attitudes toward foreign language in the elementary school. *The Modern Language Journal, 91*, 149–168.
Helland, T. (2008). Second language assessment in dyslexia: Principles and practice. In J. Kormos & E. Kontra (Eds.), *Language learners with special needs. An international perspective* (pp. 63–85). Bristol, UK: Multilingual Matters.
Hild, G., & Nikolov, M. (2010, June). *Teachers' views on tasks that work with primary schools EFL learners.* University of Pécs Round Table: Empirical Studies in Applied Linguistics Conference, University of Pécs, Hungary.
Hood, P., & Tobutt, K. (2009). *Modern languages in the primary school.* London, UK: Sage.
Horst, M., White, J., & Bell, P. (2010). First and second language knowledge in the language classroom. *International Journal of Bilingualism, 14*, 331–349.
Huszti, I, Fábián, M., & BáránynéKomári, E. (2009). Differences between the processes and outcomes in 3rd graders' learning English and Ukrainian in Hungarian schools in Beregszász. In M. Nikolov (Ed.), *Early learning of modern foreign languages: Processes and outcomes* (pp. 166–180). Clevedon, UK: Multilingual Matters.
Inbar-Lourie, O. (2010). English only? The linguistic choices of teachers of young EFL learners. *International Journal of Bilingualism, 14*, 351–367.
Inbar-Lourie, O., & Shohamy, E. (2009). Assessing young language learners: What is the

construct? In M. Nikolov (Ed.), *The age factor and early language learning* (pp. 83–96). Berlin, Germany: Mouton de Gruyter.

Johnstone, R. (2009a). An early start: What are the key conditions for generalized success? In J. Enever, J. Moon, & U. Raman (Eds.), *Young learner English language policy and implementation: international perspectives* (pp. 31–42). Reading, UK: Garnet Education Publishing.

Johnstone, R. (2009b). Review on research on language teaching, learning and policy published in 2007. *Language Teaching, 42*, 287–315.

Jones, N., & Saville, N. (2009). European language policy: Assessment, learning and the CEFR. *Annual Review of Applied Linguistics, 29*, 51–63.

Kawahara, T. (Ed.). (2008). *Shogakusei ni eigo wo oshierutowa? Ajia to nihon no kyouiku genba kara* [What is the meaning of teaching English to elementary school children?]. Tokyo, Japan: Mekong Publishing.

Kiss, C. (2009). The role of aptitude in young learners' foreign language learning. In M. Nikolov (Ed.), *The age factor and early language learning* (pp. 253–276). Berlin, Germany: Mouton de Gruyter.

Kiss, C., & Nikolov, M. (2005). Preparing, piloting and validating an instrument to measure young learners' aptitude. *Language Learning, 55*, 99–150.

Knell, E., Haiyan, Q., Miao, P., Yanping, C., Siegel, L., Lin, Z., & Wei, Z. (2007). Early English immersion and literacy in Xi'an, China. *The Modern Language Journal, 91*, 395–417.

Kormos, J., & Kontra, E. (2008a) Hungarian teachers' perceptions of dyslexic language learners. In J. Kormos & E. Kontra (Eds.), *Language learners with special needs. An international perspective* (pp. 189–213). Bristol, UK: Multilingual Matters.

Kormos, J., & Kontra, E. (Eds.). (2008b). *Language learners with special needs. An international perspective.* Bristol, UK: Multilingual Matters.

Larson-Hall, J. (2008). Weighing the benefits of studying a foreign language at a younger starting age in a minimal input situation. *Second Language Research, 24*, 35–63.

Legac, V. (2007). Foreign language anxiety and listening skill in Croatian monolingual and bilingual students of EFL. In J. Horváth & M. Nikolov (Eds.), *UPRT 2007: Empirical research in English applied linguistics* (pp. 217–243). Pécs, Hungary: Lingua Franca Csoport.

Leung, C., & Scott, C. (2009). Formative assessment in language education policies: Emerging lessons from Wales and Scotland. *Annual Review of Applied Linguistics, 29*, 64–79.

Little, D. (2007). The common European framework of reference for languages: Perspectives on the making of supranational language education policy. *The Modern Language Journal, 91*, 645–653.

Lopriore, L. (2009, March). *Development of young learners' perception of foreign language learning and teaching*. Paper presented at the American Association of Applied Linguistics conference, Denver, Colorado.

Lopriore, L., & Mihaljević Djigunović, J. (in press). Attitudinal aspects of early EFL learning. *UPRT 2009: Empirical research in English applied linguistics*. Pécs, Hungary: Lingua Franca Csoport.

Lugossy, R. (2007). Authentic picture books in the lives of young EFL learners and their teachers. In M. Nikolov, J. Mihaljević Djigunović, M. Mattheoudakis, G. Lundberg, & T. Flanagan (Eds.), *Teaching modern languages to young learners: Teachers, curricula and materials* (pp. 77–90). Strasbourg, France: Council of Europe.

Lundberg, G., & Lindgren, E. (2008, September). *Tracing young learners' foreign language development*. Paper presented at the British Association of Applied Linguistics Conference, Swansea, UK.

Macaro, E., & Erler, L. (2008). Raising the achievement of young-beginner readers of French through strategy instruction. *Applied Linguistics, 29*, 90–119.

Matsuzaki Carreira, J. (2006). Motivation for learning English as a foreign language in Japanese elementary schools. *JALT Journal, 28*, 135–158. Retrieved from http: //www.jalt-publications.org/archive/jj/2006b/art2.pdf

Mattheoudakis, M., & Alexiou, T. (2009). Early foreign language instruction in Greece: Socioeconomic factors and their effect on young learners' language. In M. Nikolov (Ed.), *The age factor and early language learning* (pp. 277–252). Berlin, Germany: Mouton de Gruyter.

McKay, P. (2006). *Assessing young language learners*. Cambridge, UK: Cambridge University Press.

McNamara, T., & Roever, C. (2006). *Language testing: The social dimension*. Oxford, UK: Blackwell Publishing.

Mihaljević Djigunović, J. (2009a). Individual differences in early language programmes. In M. Nikolov (Ed.), *The age factor and early language learning* (pp. 199–226). Berlin, Germany: Mouton de Gruyter.

Mihaljević Djigunović, J. (2009b). *Learner behavior and learning outcomes: Insights from the YL classrooms*. Paper presented at the American Association of Applied Linguistics conference, Denver, Colorado.

Mihaljević Djigunović, J. (2010a). Starting age and L1 and L2 interaction. *International Journal of Bilingualism, 14*, 303–314.

Mihaljević Djigunović, J. (2010b). *Classroom discourse as input in early SLA*. Paper presented at the Croatian Applied Linguistics Society Conference, Osijek, Croatia.

Mihaljević Djigunović, J., & Legac, V. (2008). Foreign language anxiety and listening comprehension of monolingual and bilingual EFL learners. *SRAZ, 53*, 327–347.

Mihaljević Djigunović , J., & Letica Krevelj, S. (2010). Instructed early SLA: Development of attitudes. *SRAZ, 54*, 127–146.

Mihaljević Djigunović , J., Nikolov, M., & Ottó, I. (2008). A comparative study of Croatian and Hungarian EFL students. *Language Teaching Research, 12*, 433–452.

Mihaljević Djigunović , J., & Szpotowicz, M. (2008, September). Interaction of contextual and individual variables in instructed early SLA. Paper presented at the EUROSLA Conference, Aix-en-Provence, France.

Moon, J. (2009). The teacher factor in early foreign language learning programmes: The case of Vietnam. In M. Nikolov (Ed.), *The age factor and early language learning* (pp. 311–336). Berlin, Germany: Mouton de Gruyter.

Morrissette, C. (2009). Challenges in teaching foreign languages to at-risk K-12 learners. *The Delta Kappa Gamma Bulletin, Spring*, 21–26.

Muñoz, C. (Ed.). (2006). *Age and the rate of foreign language learning*. Clevedon, UK: Multilingual Matters.

Nagy, K. (2009). English language teaching in Hungarian primary schools with special reference to the teacher's mother tongue use. (Unpublished doctoral dissertation). University of Stirling, Scotland. Retrieved from https: //dspace.stir.ac.uk/dspace/ handle/1893/1688

Ndlovu, K., & Geva, E. (2008). Writing abilities in first and second language learners with and without reading disabilities. In J. Kormos & E. Kontra (Eds.), *Language learners with special needs. An international perspectiv*e (pp. 36–62). Bristol, UK: Multilingual Matters.

Nikolov, M. (2006). Test-taking strategies of 12–13-year-old Hungarian learners of EFL: Why whales have migraine. *Language Learning, 57* , 1–51.

Nikolov, M. (2008). "Az általános iskola, az módszertan!" Alsó tagozatos angolórák empirikus vizsgálata ["Primary school means methodology!" An empirical study of lower-primary EFL classes]. *Modern Nyelvoktatás, 10*, 3–19.

Nikolov, M. (Ed.). (2009a). *Early learning of modern foreign languages: Processes and outcomes*. Clevedon, UK: Multilingual Matters.

Nikolov, M. (Ed.). (2009b). *The age factor and early language learning*. Berlin, Germany: Mouton de Gruyter.

Nikolov, M. (2009c). The age factor in context. In M. Nikolov (Ed.), *The age factor and early language learning* (pp. 1–38). Berlin, Germany/New York, NY: Mouton de Gruyter.

Nikolov, M. (2009d). Early modern foreign language programmes and outcomes: Factors contributing to Hungarian learners' proficiency. In M. Nikolov M. (Ed.), *Early learning of modern foreign languages: Processes and outcomes* (pp. 90–107). Clevedon, UK: Multilingual Matters.

Nikolov, M., & Csapó, B. (2010). The relationship between reading skills in early English as a foreign language and Hungarian as a first language. *International Journal of Bilingualism*,

14, 315–329.

Nikolov, M., & Mihaljević Djigunović , J. (2006). Recent research on age, second language acquisition, and early foreign language learning. *Annual Review of Applied Linguistics, 26*, 234–260.

Nikolov, M., Mihaljević Djigunović , J., Mattheoudakis, M., Lundberg, G., & Flanagan, T. (Eds.). (2007). *Teaching modern languages to young learners: Teachers, curricula and materials*. Strasbourg, France: Council of Europe.

Papp, Sz., & Salamoura, A. (2009). An exploratory study into linking young learners' examinations to the CEFR. *Research Notes, 37*, 15–22. Cambridge: Cambridge ESOL.

Peng, J., & Zhang, L. (2009a). An eye on target language use in elementary English classrooms in China. In Nikolov M. (Ed.): *Early learning of modern foreign languages* (pp. 212–228). Bristol, UK: Multilingual Matters.

Peng, J., & Zhang, L. (2009b). Chinese primary school students' use of communication strategies in EFL classrooms. In M. Nikolov (Ed.), *The age factor and early language learning* (pp. 337–350). Berlin, Germany: Mouton de Gruyter.

Peng, J. & Zhu, K. (2010).《小学英语学科发展研究》[A study on development of primary school English]. Chongqing, China: Chongqing University Press.

Pinter, A. (2006a). *Teaching young language learners*. Oxford, UK: Oxford University Press.

Pinter, A. (2006b). Verbal evidence of task-related strategies: Child versus adult interactions. *System, 34*, 615–630.

Pinter, A. (2007a). Benefits of peer-peer interaction: 10-year-old children practicing with a communication task. *Language Teaching Research, 11*, 189–207.

Pinter, A. (2007b). What children say: Benefits of task repetition. In K. Van den Branden, K. Van Gorp, & M. Verhelst (Eds.), *Task-based language education from a classroom-based perspective* (pp. 126–149). Cambridge, UK: Cambridge Scholars Publishing.

Pižorn, K. (2009). Designing proficiency levels for English for primary and secondary school students and the impact of the CEFR. In N. Figueras & J. Noijons (Eds.), *Linking to the CEFR levels: Research perspectives* (pp. 87–102). Arnhem, the Netherlands: Cito, EALTA.

Prahbu, N. S. (2009). Teaching English to young learners: The promise and the threat. In J. Enever, J. Moon, & U. Raman (Eds), *Young learner English language policy and implementation: international perspectives* (pp. 43–44). Reading, UK: Garnet Education Publishing.

Rhodes, N. C., & Pufahl, I. (2008). *Foreign language teaching in U.S. Schools: Results of a national survey*. Retrieved from http: //www.cal.org/projects/Exec%20Summary_111009.pdf

Šamo, R. (2006). Analiza strategija čitanja uspješnih i manje uspješnih učenika engleskog kao stranog jezika [Analysis of reading strategies used by more and less successful EFL learners]. (Unpublished doctoral dissertation). University of Zagreb, Croatia.Smith, A.M.

(2008). Teachers' and trainers' perceptions of inclusive education within TEFL Certificate courses in Britain. In J. Kormos & E. Kontra (Eds.), *Language learners with special needs. An international perspective* (pp. 214–233). Bristol, UK: Multilingual Matters.

Sparks, L. R., Ganschow, L., & Patton, J. (2008). L1 and L2 literacy, aptitude and affective variables as discriminators among high- and low-achieving L2 learners with special needs. In J. Kormos & E. Kontra (Eds.), *Language learners with special needs. An international perspective* (pp. 11–35). Bristol, UK: Multilingual Matters.

Sternberg, R. J., & Grigorenko, E. L. (2002). *Dynamic testing: The nature and measurement of learning potential.* Cambridge, UK: Cambridge University Press.

Szpotowicz, M., Mihaljevic Djigunovic, J., & Enever, J. (2009). Early language learning in Europe: A multinational, longitudinal study. In J. Enever, J. Moon & U. Raman (Eds.), *Young learner English language policy and implementation: International perspectives* (pp. 141–147). Reading, UK: Garnet Publishing.

Szpotowicz, M., & Szulc-Kurpaska, M. (2009). *Teaching English to young learners.* Warsaw, Poland: Wydawnictwo Naukowe PWN.

Szulc-Kurpaska, M. (2007). Teaching and researching very young learners: "They are unpredictable". In M. Nikolov, J. Mihaljević Djigunović, M. Mattheoudakis, G. Lundberg, & T. Flanagan (Eds.), *Teaching modern languages to young learners: Teachers, curricula and materials* (pp. 35–46). Strasbourg, France: Council of Europe.

Taylor, C., & Lafayette, R. (2010). Academic achievement through FLES: A case study for promoting greater access to foreign language study among young learners. *The Modern Language Journal, 94,* 22–42.

Teasdale, A., & Leung, C. (2000). Teacher assessment and psychometric theory: A case of paradigm crossing. *Language Testing, 17,* 163–184.

TESOL. (2009). Position statement on teaching English as a foreign or additional language to young learners. Retrieved from http: //www.artesol.org.ar/bin.pdf

Tragant, E., & Victori, M. (2006). Reported strategy use and age. In C. Muñoz (Ed.), *Age and the rate of foreign language learning* (pp. 208–236). Clevedon, UK: Multilingual Matters.

Vickov, G. (2007). Learners' own cultural identity in early language learning. In M. Nikolov, J. Mihaljević Djigunović , M. Mattheoudakis, G. Lundberg, & T. Flanagan (Eds.), *Teaching modern languages to young learners: Teachers, curricula and materials* (pp. 105–120). Strasbourg, France: Council of Europe.

Walter, C. (2007). First- to second-language reading comprehension: Not transfer, but access. *International Journal of Applied Linguistics, 17,* 14–37.

Wang, Q. (2009). Primary English in China: Policy, curriculum and implementation. In M. Nikolov (Ed.), *The age factor and early language learning* (pp. 277–310). Berlin, Germany: Mouton de Gruyter.

Teaching Adult Second Language Learners Who Are Emergent Readers

Martha Bigelow and Patsy Vinogradov

Some second language (L2) learners are unique in that they bring low print literacy and limited formal schooling to the language learning enterprise. A range of personal, economic, historical, and political circumstances bring them to highly literate, industrialized societies where print literacy becomes not only desirable but necessary to earn a living and participate in a range of everyday activities. This article is a review of current research related to this population of learners for the purpose of informing educators about their particular teaching and learning needs. While the emphasis is on scholarship focused on adult L2 emergent readers, attention is also given to related research with bi- and multilingual children and monolingual adults who are not print literate. Finally, sociopolitical and historical issues are touched upon with regard to broader policy matters that may have contributed to or perpetuate low print literacy.

Illiteracy is not a permanent condition or characteristic of adolescent or adult second language (L2) learners. Most people can become literate in any script, at any age, and when they do, this descriptor simply disappears. In this sense, illiteracy is different from other individual differences commonly explored in second language acquisition (SLA) research such as sex, age of arrival in a country, or mother tongue, none of which change. Educators working with students from different countries are typically trained and accustomed to teaching students with many proficiency levels, learning preferences, and aspirations, but they are generally less familiar with teaching learners who have not had formal schooling or are learning an L2 without being print literate in any language (Vinogradov & Liden, 2008). Furthermore, most educators became print literate when they were children and cannot recall the experience easily or relate to what it is like to become literate beyond childhood. More importantly, the educational and literacy experiences resulting in differences between teachers and adult students without print literacy can create a profound gap in the assumptions about how languages are taught and learned.

One of the challenges of writing about adolescents and adults without print literacy is finding the appropriate language to do so. Adjectives such as *illiterate*, *nonliterate*, and *preliterate*, while commonly used by educators, delimit individuals according to something they lack. Like others, individuals without print literacy have a range of attributes that may better characterize them than one quality that they lack. This article, however, necessarily characterizes them by what they lack because it focuses on the literature, particularly from the past 5 years, that addresses lack of print literacy as a particular learner characteristic. As our title suggests, we propose using the term *emergent reader*, which expresses the sense of becoming literate. For more nuance regarding terminology of this nature, see Burt, Peyton, and Adams (2003).

It is also necessary to offer a brief definition of literacy, however complex this may be. All of the research we are aware of to date regarding literacy development among adult L2 emergent readers focuses on the encoding and decoding of text, in other words, basic reading and writing skills. The studies we know of typically do not take a critical literacy (e.g., Morgan & Ramanathan, 2005) or multiple literacies (e.g., Street, 2003) stance. We are well aware of the both the breadth and the depth of how researchers define literacy beyond (basic) skills and the ideological debates related to how literacy is defined (Lewis & del Valle, 2009; Papen, 2005). Literacy, writ broadly, is complex and profoundly dependent on context; yet, in much of the L2 research related to adult emergent readers, literacy is still framed as a set of skills: alphabetics, vocabulary, fluency, and comprehension (e.g., Curtis & Kruidenier, 2005). In this article, we attempt to strike a balance between the recognition that adult L2 learners must learn to decode words and the need they have to learn these skills through meaningful and authentic instruction. In this article, we explore the nature of what it means to become literate for the first time in a new language as an adolescent or adult, and what sorts of teaching and learning opportunities may help students become literate, on their own terms, as quickly as possible.

TEACHING ADULT L2 LEARNERS WITH BEGINNING LITERACY

A number of scholarly articles describe instruction that works with emergent readers who are adult L2 learners (Birch, 2007; Condelli, Wrigley, & Yoon, 2008; Freeman & Freeman, 2001; Mace-Matluck, Alexander-Kasparik, & Queen, 1998). A professional organization named LESLLA (Low-Educated Second Language and Literacy Acquisition, www.leslla.org), focuses on adult L2 learners from around the world who begin their formal learning without or with limited print literacy (Faux, 2007; Young-Scholten, 2008). The professional meetings organized by LESLLA and the subsequent publications have yielded a wealth of knowledge about this population (e.g., Condelli & Wrigley, 2006; Faux, 2006; Geudens, 2006; Kurvers, 2007; Kurvers, Vallen, & van Hout, 2006; Kurvers, van Hout, & Vallen, 2007; Peyton et al., 2007; Tarone, Bigelow, & Hansen, 2007; Van de Craats, 2007; Van de Craats, Kurvers, & Young-Scholten, 2006a, 2006b; Young-Scholten & Strom, 2006).

While it is important to examine the emerging body of research with adult English language learners who are emergent readers, many of the findings from research with children who are becoming literate in an L2 may apply to adults, assuming the content and presentation are adjusted accordingly. Just like children becoming literate in an L2, older learners at the same level must also learn the basics of literacy (i.e., alphabetic, fluency, vocabulary, comprehension). It must be cautioned, however, that understanding L2 adult emergent readers through research done with children (often in their first language [L1]) is bound to result in misapplications of findings. With this caveat in mind, this article reviews recent research on adults, then turns to examples of research conducted with children who are emergent readers in the L2, and finally reviews some of the main findings from research conducted with monolingual adults who are not print literate in their L1.

Research With Adult Emergent Readers

Many adolescents and adults who are new to reading bring with them rich oral traditions from their past. Scholars have long known this and have also recognized that the transition to writing is a process often fraught with struggle and sacrifice, as well as empowerment and emancipation (Cook-Gumperz & Gumperz, 1981; Freire,

1970; Goody, 1987; McLuhan, 1964/1994; Olson, 2006; Ong, 1982; Rubin, 1980; Tannen, 1982). A recent dissertation by Watson (2010) explores in extraordinary depth the phenomenon of moving from orality to literacy. Drawing from a range of disciplines, Watson described the distance between the lifeworlds of indigenous cultures and those of cultures of high literacy as a semiotic abyss. This highly charged and politically oriented research reveals much in terms of what educators must understand about how to teach adolescents and young adults who come to class as emergent readers. Watson argued for "a pedagogy of reciprocity between orality and literacy" (p. v) in which primarily oral and primarily literate societies share the strengths of each other's ways of being in the world. This reciprocity, Watson reasoned, may be a path to the survival of both societies.

The research literature offers studies in which oral traditions grounded in historical, cultural roots are incorporated into teaching activities. For example, in qualitative research carried out with Sudanese families, Perry explored how personal stories and folktales can be used to teach literacy skills in English (Perry, 2007, 2008). Creating classroom activities that truly embrace the oral literacies of refugee adolescents and adults can be constructive avenues into print literacies in the L2. Similarly, in ethnographic work with Somali adolescent girls, Bigelow (2010) found that one participant was powerfully motivated to convey her favorite Somali folktales to English speakers so that they could learn from them and be entertained by them. She also understood that her folktales, originally told in oral modes in Somali, needed to be carefully written and edited in English for her readers to want to read them. Her motivation to share her stories resulted in many revisions that attended to both meaning and form. This research linking L1 oral traditions to L2 literacy offers new pedagogies within Western schooling practices that break down barriers to literacies needed in the new, literate society. That is, by building on community cultural wealth through use of oral traditions, new epistemologies and pedagogies can emerge (Yosso & García, 2007), which can include learners' histories of migration and traditional ways of relaying information, teaching, and entertaining.

Other studies uncover ways in which cultural strengths within immigrant and refugee families can also support educational aims. For example, in a mother-daughter qualitative case study, Espinoza-Herold (2007) described how the cultural *dichos* (sayings) used by a Mexican immigrant mother with little formal schooling supported her adolescent daughter in achieving her educational goals. Similarly, Bigelow (2007) found that a Somali mother with limited formal schooling, low levels of English language proficiency, and low native language literacy was able to do many things to help her children succeed in U.S. public schools. She would facilitate her children getting help with projects by releasing them from household chores to attend bilingual homework help programs or simply to work quietly at the public library. She would also take friends to help her interpret conversations with teachers about how her children were doing in school, who their friends were, and if they were doing their homework. In another study with Sudanese families, Walker-Dalhouse and Dalhouse (2009) learned, through conversations with parents, that there were many ways teachers could link to the students' home languages and cultures. Such studies illuminate how learners' social and cultural characteristics can inform and enrich instruction in powerful ways. Instead of reducing literacy to a set of skills to be mastered, teachers can take into account the complex processes at work in the classroom and within and among their learners.

Instruction for emergent adult/adolescent readers must fulfill two needs: Adults need contextualized, meaningful instruction that is age and level appropriate, and this instruction needs to be explicit and systematic, focusing on phonemic awareness, phonics, and word recognition. Whole-part-whole instruction is a balanced approach to teaching literacy (see Trupke-Bastidas & Poulos, 2007; Vinogradov, 2008). While focusing first on a meaningful story and establishing meaning, instructors using whole-part-whole instruction then move to specific parts (sounds, sight words, word families, etc.), before returning to the entire story for further study. This way the components or parts of language are never taught without being located within a memorable, interesting, meaningful context. Examples of such instruction for teacher-training purposes can be found in a brief video from New American Horizons (www.newamericanhorizons.org) and also in a publication from the Center for Applied Linguistics (Vinogradov & Bigelow, 2010).

This section explores some of the well-documented principles related to teaching adults without prior schooling who are emergent readers. We focus on principles because not all of the practices have a robust research base. DeCapua and Marshall (2011) have developed an approach to teaching learners with limited formal education they call the mutually adaptive learning paradigm (MALP). This paradigm asks educators to (a) understand and accept the unique cognitive and social orientations of learners without prior schooling; (b) creatively combine processes characteristic of these learners and those of U.S. schools; and (c) focus on U.S. learning activities with familiar language and content. This section explores examples from research that follow this approach.

One of the principles of teaching adults new to literacy that has persisted over time is the importance of using content from students' lives to develop basic literacy through balanced literacy instruction (Auerbach, 1992; Condelli et al., 2008; Crandall & Peyton, 1993; Weinstein, 2006). The use of learner-generated texts, a slightly more specific method that is widely known as the language experience approach (LEA), allows students and teachers together to tap into learners' often more developed listening and speaking skills to build literacy (Geva & Zadeh, 2006). Oral processing skills and print literacy skills are interconnected and interdependent (Tarone, Bigelow, & Hansen, 2009), and as learners practice and build their oral abilities, learner-generated texts provide a means to connect these skills and to present oral language on paper. The result is an array of rich and interesting readings for students.

In LEA, for example, students first share a common experience, perhaps a field trip or an experience like making a cup of tea in the classroom. Then, the teacher guides them to retell the experience aloud. Students recall what happened to a teacher or another scribe who writes down their words. Later, these words are used as reading texts. From here, a number of bottom-up techniques can be used to focus on word analysis and particular sounds and structures. Then, students revisit the entire text they have created and perhaps add to it. LEA is an efficient technique in working with emergent readers as it connects what they are able to communicate orally to what they are learning to do in print (Crandall & Peyton, 1993; Vinogradov, 2010).

Research with Children

The process of becoming literate for adults, it has been argued, is different from that of children. For example, adults have different strategies to draw upon to learn, and they have more life experience to bring to their comprehension of text (Weinstein, 2006). Adults may take longer and have different emotional reactions to learning to read, depending on how much they have been stigmatized for not knowing how to read during their lives (Bartlett, 2007). Adults may also approach learning literacy and language with a sense of urgency, as their family's well-being depends on their ability to find and maintain employment and provide life's basic necessities. Unlike children, adults have many responsibilities outside of school, and attending literacy and language classes is often a luxury of time and resources. However, although adults and children learn differently, adult emergent readers must also acquire the same skills and fulfill the same cognitive stages as children learning to read. Although this process looks different for adults and instruction must also differ, we do not recommend ignoring all research or instructional materials created for emergent L2 readers who are children. For example, Gardner (2008) designed her playful phonological awareness curriculum for young emergent readers with the following principles in mind:

1. Teachers should check comprehension because learners may decode, or pronounce text, but not comprehend it. Decoding which results in comprehension is essential.
2. Students should complete tasks and teachers should maintain high expectations of students' work, particularly their discussion about text.
3. Students should become accustomed to justifying answers to questions about text.
4. Teachers should expect that discussions about texts are designed to be meaningful.
5. Teachers should use formative assessment to monitor progress. (pp. 265–266)

A detailed examination of a short lesson using a prescriptive curriculum showed that these principles resulted in instruction that had a range of features including language play, whole-class shared imaging of the text, valuing the children's thoughts, opening up the communication to a two-way process where there is space for learning, connecting learning to students' lives, and legitimizing home languages and cultures. Even in the unlikely context of a prescriptive phonics lesson, this transformative, meaningful, and contextualized language instruction was possible. These outcomes are certainly what we hope can occur for adults who are also learning skills such as sound-letter correspondence.

Other research with children is relevant to consider when devising instruction for adult L2 learners without print literacy. For example, ways that oral language development assists in literacy development is another area that has been explored with children acquiring an L2 (e.g., August & Shanahan, 2006; de la Piedra, 2006; Geva & Zadeh, 2006; Gonzalez & Uhing, 2008). Teachers should work to develop L2 oral skills while developing literacy skills; language skills are interdependent, and oral skills pave the way for literacy. Likewise, reading skills transfer between L1 and L2(s) among children (Bialystok, 2007; Bialystok, Luk, & Kwan, 2005). The skills related to grapheme-phoneme correspondence can be applied to any alphabetic language. We believe that this phenomenon of transfer occurs among adolescent and adult language learners as well, although this assumption must be empirically verified. Work exploring the parallels and differences between emergent writing in L1 children and emergent writing in L2 adults without print literacy was recently done by Kurvers et al., (2007). Their study implies that while preliterate adults and children appear to follow similar stages as they learn to write, adults bring a different kind of print awareness to the classroom. Although the adults in the study were able to recognize many words on sight (they had lived in a print-rich environment for many years), they still needed direct instruction to connect oral language to writing and to access the "inside of the written code" (Kurvers et al., 2007, p. 885). However, the adult emergent readers had knowledge of print, and they brought to instruction knowledge of the functions and uses of print that the children did not. Adult literacy teachers need to keep in mind that learners are not naïve about writing and literacy instruction does not need to begin "from scratch" (Kurvers et al., 2007, p. 885). Such studies comparing the literacy acquisition of L2 adult emergent readers and L1 children are rare, although there is much to learn. Research with monolingual students is much more common, and we examine such learners next.

Research with Monolinguals

In the same way we can turn to research with bi- or multilingual children in an effort to understand the processes adult L2 learners go through to become literate, we can also turn to research done with monolingual adults in their L1. This work makes few and broad explicit links to teaching, but we believe that it is beneficial for educators to be aware of it to understand three main points: (a) The human brain in normal adults changes with the advent of specifically alphabetic (not logographic) print literacy; (b) these changes have been explored with research methodologies that measure a narrow range of language processing skills; and (c) the knowledge produced within these lines of research suggests that educators of adolescent and adult L2 learners should challenge the popular and well-documented assumption in research with children that phonemic awareness (e.g., the ability to distinguish sounds, syllables, and rhymes) must come before the ability to read. In recent years, the field has moved to accept that the relationship of phonemic awareness and achievement in reading appears to be reciprocal (Yopp, 1992). The literature relevant to adult emergent readers regarding brain changes and alphabetic literacy development, language processing, and phonemic awareness is summarized briefly here, because it has already appeared elsewhere in greater detail (Bigelow & Watson, 2011; Tarone & Bigelow, 2005; Tarone et al., 2009).

Cognitive scientists have provided a fascinating and relevant body of research that explores how lack of alphabetic print literacy affects how adults perceive, repeat, and manipulate oral language. This research has been done with monolingual adults in their L1s (Adrian, Alegria, & Morais, 1995; Bramão et al., 2007; Dellatolas et al., 2003; Reis & Castro-Caldas, 1997; Reis et al., 2007; Reis, Guerreiro, & Petersson, 2003). It suggests that even a small amount of literacy can make a difference in the performance of certain oral tasks. In these studies adults with some print literacy could manipulate language units such as phonemes and syllables, while adults without print literacy performed significantly worse on these oral skills. Dropping the first sound from a word (e.g., take /ka/ off /kade/) and flipping syllables in a word (e.g., /keda/ becomes /dake/) was much harder for illiterate adults than it was for those with alphabetic print literacy. On the other hand, participants performed similarly on oral tasks involving rhyming or generating lists of semantically related words. It seems that basic alphabetic literacy offers adults a strategy for visualizing encoded oral language in order to manipulate it phonemically.

Research carried out with Chinese-speaking participants corroborates independently the findings of the previous research. Charles Read and his colleagues (Read, Zhang, Nie, & Ding, 1986) found that individuals who were literate only in the logographic Chinese script, not the Romanized script, performed similarly to adults without alphabetic print literacy. This suggests that there is something unique about becoming literate in an alphabetic script, as opposed to a logographic, or character-based, script. Interesting, too, are the results obtained from de Gelder,

Vroomen, and Bertelson (1993), who studied bilingual Chinese adults residing in the Netherlands who were all able to read Chinese logograms. The group was divided into two groups: those who could read an alphabetic language (Dutch) and those who could not. There were significant differences between the groups in terms of the ability to delete word-initial consonants (e.g., /stan/ becomes /tan/) but no difference in rhyming tasks, similar to the studies described earlier. Researchers also tried to teach participants without alphabetic print literacy how to segment speech, but participants were not able to do so after the instruction. Again, alphabetic print literacy seems to promote awareness that utterances can be segmented and promote the skills to do this sort of task.

The cognitive neuroscience research done in Olhão, a fishing village in southern Portugal, warrants some elaboration here. (See Petersson, Ingvar, & Reis, 2009, for a recent summary.) This robust and active research program spans more than a decade in its attempts to isolate the cognitive processes that are consequences of literacy among adults, albeit in their L1, not an L2. Findings support the idea that formal schooling and alphabetic literacy acquisition is not only a process for cultural transmission but also a mechanism that changes the physical makeup of the human brain and the way the brain processes oral language.

The context of this research in Portugal is a socioculturally homogeneous community with low mobility. Causes of illiteracy in this context were due to sociocultural circumstances, not individual causes such as a learning disability or brain injury. In this village it was common to find families in which the older daughters did not attend school and the younger children did, although only for approximately 4 years. Researchers observed that illiteracy was not understood as problematic socially, and literate and illiterate individuals led similar lives working in agriculture or fishing. Therefore, it was possible to match participants who were literate with those who were not.

In one study, literate and illiterate participants from Olhão were asked to repeat words and pseudowords, because this task is a good measure of phonological processing. PET (positron-emission tomography) scans showed that literate participants had much more brain activation, occurring in more regions of the brain, during pseudoword repetition than did illiterate participants. Researchers explain this phenomenon as being in part due to the notion that verbal working memory is supported by the ability to store visuospatial information. In other words, the way that oral language is processed and stored is influenced by alphabetic literacy and aspects of subsyllabic phonological structures within literate participants. In another study by Reis et al. (2007) and a following study by Kolinsky, Cary, and Morais (1987), literate and illiterate participants were asked to listen to words and pseudowords during a task in which they had to decide which word of a pair was the longest (e.g., /stan/ or /tan/). The literate participants showed no difference between their ability to determine phonological length of words and pseudowords. The illiterate participants, on the other hand, performed better when identifying the length of pseudowords than words. The researchers explain these apparently contradictory results by arguing that illiterate participants struggled more to inhibit the influence of semantic interference in their decision of which word or pseudoword was longer. In other words, when illiterate participants were able to concentrate only on length (not the meanings of words they knew), they were better able to discern word length.

This team of researchers has carried out numerous other studies exploring the role of alphabetic literacy in phonological processing. For example, they explored the role of literacy in processing lexical items within a sentence context and found that explicit knowledge of words as independent units is dependent on literacy. Emergent readers may not be able to identify closed-class words or words without semantic content (determiners, prepositions, pronouns) as easily as adults with literacy. In another study, they explored the role of literacy in identifying black and white photographs versus colored drawings, with the literate group outperforming the illiterate group. Color, the researchers argue, is related to the semantic value of the images. Color and realistic images enhance the interpretation for adults without formal schooling. Researchers are quick to admit that it is problematic to use tasks that resemble those commonly performed in classroom settings, because the literate group would be advantaged. This problem was described in Luria's (1976) foundational research with illiterate adults in Russia.

The idea that even a very low level of alphabetic print literacy may facilitate performance on some phonemic awareness tasks has implications for teaching and learning. For example, teachers must know that it is entirely normal for adult emergent readers to have much more difficulty manipulating phonemes in oral language than adults with even minimal alphabetic print literacy. Likewise, some phonemic awareness skills may come after learners have begun to acquire basic literacy concepts, rather than before, an order that is assumed by many scholars of child L1 literacy. If being able to perceive phonemes in the speech stream depends on literacy, perhaps those with low literacy will not be able to use corrective feedback related to the manipulation of phonemes as efficiently as those with more print literacy. Teachers may also take from this research that it is very important to reduce the level of abstraction of materials—visually and linguistically. Images should be discussed to establish meaning within them (e.g., discuss how the pictures of the peach and the apple differ with students). Pictures should align with real life as much as possible (e.g., pictures of foods should closely resemble what they supposedly represent and ideally appear in color). Finally, authentic instruction that relates to learners' lives and does not depend on knowing how to do activities learned in school (e.g., multiple choice questions accompanying a reading) will help those who have not had formal schooling stay engaged. It will also make them feel capable as they embark on L2 initial literacy.

EDUCATIONAL POLICY AND L2 LEARNERS WITH LIMITED LITERACY

There are always larger social structures and policies that impact education across contexts. Adult L2 emergent readers' opportunities to learn may be facilitated or hindered by factors far beyond their control. Menard-Warwick (2005) explained the low print literacy of her participants (Central American immigrant women). She found that immigration laws, welfare status, and the economy impeded participants' ability to sustain their enrollment in literacy programs. The women's motivation was also influenced by their parents' views of education and their experiences, such as having the opportunity to attend school. An example of a literacy campaign initiated at the national level is offered by Warsame (2001). He explained how the Somali government promoted literacy by dictatorial mandate in the 1970s. This effort, under the mandate that everyone should be either teaching or learning, increased literacy among both rural and urban populations enormously. These efforts were dismantled by the civil war in Somalia and resulted in widespread inaccessibility to formal schooling and basic literacy and numeracy.

In some immigrant communities, adults may be hesitant to attend literacy classes, because doing so may jeopardize their status in their family or cultural community. For example, the religious beliefs of the Kurdish Yezidis, according to Sarroub (2008), advocate avoiding print literacy. Similarly, Levinson (2007) described resistance to literacy among English Gypsies (Roma). Saki, a participant in Levinson's study, lamented, "Education has divorced me from my community" (p. 30). Saki reported that his older brother said that he had betrayed all that his family stood for by becoming educated. Other participants said that if they wished to attend adult literacy classes, these classes must be outside their community, so that even their closest relatives would not know they were attending class.

Classrooms and programs are not neutral actors in the process of building literacy among adult L2 learners. Warriner (2007) demonstrated how the transnational movement is "conflated with bureaucratic sorting mechanisms that result in heightened surveillance and arbitrary distinctions that have lasting material consequences . . ." (p. 323). Warriner's analysis of students in an adult ESL (English as a second language) literacy program shows that although programs may be unfolding exactly as planned (i.e., to train low-wage workers), they may inadvertently construct the labor that students do as contributing to the global economy with little benefit to the workers themselves. In this sense, programs and even educators participate in a sort of policymaking enterprise that in turn plays into larger socioeconomic structures. For example, by teaching so-called survival English, programs may be contributing to learners' economic marginalization (Tollefson, 2006). Menken and Garcia (2010) illustrated how educators in particular are important actors in the implementation of or resistance to educational and political policy.

In sum, there is ample research showing how understanding literacy in its social context can contribute to a more complete understanding of literacy across cultures and contexts (Reder & Davila, 2005). Research also shows that adult L2 learners without print literacy are diverse and that reasons for lacking print literacy vary widely among individuals.

CONCLUSION

Educating adult L2 learners who are emergent readers requires paradigm shifts in a number of areas. First, preservice teacher education programs must recognize that these learners exist, that educating them is important, and that their needs require teachers prepared to reach across the experiential and literacy abyss to educate them in ways that are thoughtful and effective. Second, programs must attend to the needs of practicing teachers who wish to create separate curricula for adult emergent readers, revamp their assessment and placement procedures, or make their literacy curriculum more balanced between top-down and bottom-up reading processes. Third, there is a need for better educational policies worldwide that do not stand in the way of adults who are seeking print literacy. There are still many contexts in which children do not have access to primary schooling, which leads to projections that in 2015 there will be 29 million school-age children who will still be out of school. Nigerian and Pakistani children are projected to have particularly slim changes of attending school in 2015, with 7.6 and 3.7 million out-of-school children, respectively (UNESCO, 2009). While we hope that lack of print literacy does not persist until adolescence or adulthood, any learner should have the opportunity to become literate through high-quality formal instruction.

The ways adult emergent readers differ also requires the examination of educational policies and possibly advocacy for recognition of this population. For example, it is common to find state policies in which students enrolled in high school programs are not permitted to continue working toward graduation because of their age. Then, paths to adult diploma programs are unavailable or difficult to access. Typical educational policy simply does not afford them enough time in school to build the literacy needed to finish all of their high school requirements. Another common policy problem is adequate federal and state allocation of funding to programs for emergent readers, adult diploma programs for learners who started high school late, and adult basic education programs for English learners who may need instruction that will continue to develop their everyday English proficiency or vocational English skills.

This review has outlined the issues in educating L2 adolescent and adult emergent readers by exploring relevant scholarship (studies as well as articles suggesting promising practices) on this unique population. We have expanded the review to include a wide range of studies done with children who are becoming bi- or multilingual, and monolingual adults who are not literate in their home language. We hope to have shown, however, that this is a heterogeneous population with a unique set of strengths and needs that require a range of educational approaches. Finally, this is a population that requires advocacy—advocacy for appropriate instruction and advocacy for educational policies that allow them to pursue unconventional paths to employment and productivity.

ANNOTATED BIBLIOGRAPHY

Bigelow, M., & Watson, J. (2011). Educational level and L2 learning. In S. Gass & A. Mackey (Eds.), *The Routledge handbook of second language acquisition*. New York, NY: Routledge.

This book chapter offers a comprehensive survey to date of research, programs, and issues related to educational level and second language learning. The authors not only called attention to the body of current research findings and the need for increased focus on older ELLs (English language learners) with limited formal schooling and low print literacy but also began to frame the issue in its epistemological and ethical dimensions. By taking this critical approach, the authors asked readers to consider both the instructional needs of learners who have come of age in orality and also the deeper cultural and epistemological characteristics and implications of orality and the way of life that often accompanies orality. Specifically, the authors recognized that the presence of many of the refugees and immigrants in many industrialized countries such as the United States is the result of political and military might and that the judgment placed upon their lack of print literacy is evidence of privileging certain ways of being in the world.

Birch, B. (2007). *English L2 reading: Getting to the bottom* (2nd ed.). Mahwah, NJ: Erlbaum.

Birch's book offers a compelling argument for balanced literacy instruction that includes both top-down (focus on meaning and comprehension) as well as bottom-up (focus on smaller linguistic units such as letters and words) approaches. However, this book focuses on bottom-up strategies because this knowledge base and skill set are so often neglected in adult ESL teacher preparation. Birch delved into topics such as writing systems (logographic vs. alphabetic) and phonics instruction and offered a number of teaching ideas for each skill area. This book is best suited to teachers with some background in linguistics and language teaching, but for those who need more guidance, there are diagrams, ample examples, prereading questions, and study guide questions built into the structure of the book as learning aids.

DeCapua, A., & Marshall, H. (2011). *Breaking new ground: Teaching students with limited or interrupted formal schooling in secondary schools.* Ann Arbor: University of Michigan Press.

This book explores the cognitive and social profile of students from oral traditions and offers specific instructional approaches based on that profile. The authors were careful to distinguish between Western values such as individual autonomy, abstraction, and the primacy of literacy and the common orientations of oral societies such as face-to-face communication. This work emphasizes the fact that older students who are new to formal schooling and print literacy have different ways of understanding the world and asks educators to develop intersubjective understanding with regard to how they approach such learners. The authors introduced an intervention they call the mutually adaptive learning paradigm (MALP).

Reder, S., & Bynner, J. (Eds.). (2009). *Tracking adult literacy and numeracy skills: Findings from longitudinal research.* New York, NY: Routledge.

This book is a comprehensive collection of outstanding chapters that explore a wide range of issues related to adult literacy and numeracy across many different countries and educational settings. The research presented in this volume is not limited to L2 learners, but much of it is highly relevant to L2 teaching and learning. For example, the book includes chapters on the development of literacy and numeracy, teacher attitudes, workplace teaching and learning, identity and literacy, and the evaluation of programs. As the title suggests, the research presented in this volume is longitudinal. Some of the important and much needed issues explored include how adults' educational development interacts with their social and economic performance as well as how their private and social situation in the family and community may enhance or obstruct their progress.

Tarone, E., Bigelow, M., & Hansen, K. (2009). *Literacy and second language oracy.* Oxford, UK: Oxford University Press.

This book examines the relationship between low alphabetic print literacy and L2 oral language process. Findings, which are mainly based on a partial replication of Philp's (2003) study, show that some of the language-processing abilities that have been considered inherent, universal human abilities may actually be the specific consequences of alphabetic print literacy. These include the ability to notice oral recasts and the accuracy of recall on elicitation/imitation tasks involving grammatical correction. Another chapter of the book finds that certain morphosyntactic characteristics of learner interlanguage are used more with participants with higher levels of print literacy. This book offers a theoretical rationale for including learners with low print literacy in SLA research and sets out a thorough list of questions to develop this research agenda.

REFERENCES

Adrian, J. A., Alegria, J., & Morais, J. (1995). Metaphonological abilities of Spanish illiterate adults. *International Journal of Psychology, 3*, 329–353.

Auerbach, E. (1992). *Making meaning, making change: Participatory curriculum development for adult ESL literacy.* Washington, DC: Center for Applied Linguistics.

August, D., & Shanahan, T. (Eds.). (2006). *Developing literacy in second-language learners: Report of the National Literacy Panel on language-minority children and youth.* Mahwah, NJ: Erlbaum.

Bartlett, L. (2007). Literacy, speech, and shame: The cultural politics of literacy and language in Brazil. *International Journal of Qualitative Studies in Education, 20*, 547–563.

Bialystok, E. (2007). Acquisition of literacy in bilingual children: A framework for research. *Language Learning, 57*, 45–77.

Bialystok, E., Luk, G., & Kwan, E. (2005). Bilingualism, biliteracy, and learning to read: Interactions among language and writing systems. *Scientific Studies of Reading, 9*, 43–61.

Bigelow, M. (2007). Social and cultural capital at school: The case of a Somali teenage girl with limited formal schooling. In N. R. Faux (Ed.), *Low-Educated Second Language and Literacy Acquisition: Research, Policy and Practice: Proceedings of the Second Annual Forum* (pp. 7–22). Richmond: Literacy Institute at Virginia Commonwealth University.

Bigelow, M. (2010). *Mogadishu on the Mississippi: Language, racialized identity, and education in a new land.* New York, NY: Wiley-Blackwell.

Bigelow, M., & Watson, J. (2011). Educational level and L2 learning. In S. Gass & A. Mackey (Eds.), *The Routledge handbook of second language acquisition.* New York, NY: Routledge.

Birch, B. (2007). *English L2 reading: Getting to the bottom* (2nd ed.). Mahwah, NJ: Erlbaum.

Bramão, I., Mendonça, A., Fáısca, L., Ingvar, M., Petersson, K. M., & Reis, A. J. (2007). The impact of reading and writing skills on a visuomotor integration task: A comparison between illiterate and literate subjects. *International Neuropsychological Society, 13*, 359–364.

Burt, M., Peyton, J. K., & Adams, R. (2003). *Reading and adult English language learners: The role of the first language.* Washington, DC: Center for Applied Linguistics. Retrieved from http: //www.cal.org/caela/esl_resources/digests/reading.html

Condelli, L., & Wrigley, H. S. (2006). Instruction, language and literacy: What works study for adult ESL literacy students. In I. Van de Craats, J. Kurvers, & M. Young-Scholten (Eds.), *Low-Educated Adult Second Language and Literacy Acquisition: Proceedings of the Inaugural Symposium* (pp. 111–133). Utrecht, The Netherlands: LOT.

Condelli, L., Wrigley, H. S., & Yoon, K. S. (2008). "What works" for adult literacy students of English as a second language. In S. M. Reder & J. Bynner (Eds.), *Tracking adult literacy and numeracy skills: Findings from longitudinal research* (pp. 132–159). New York, NY: Routledge.

Cook-Gumperz, J., & Gumperz, J. J. (1981). From oral to written culture: The transition to literacy. In M. F. Whitehead (Ed.), *Variation in writing: Functional and linguistic-cultural differences* (pp. 89–109). Norwood, NJ: Ablex.

Crandall, J., & Peyton, J. (1993). *Approaches to adult ESL literacy instruction.* Washington, DC: Center for Applied Linguistics and Delta Systems.

Curtis, M. E., & Kruidenier, J. R. (2005). *Teaching adults to read: A summary of scientifically based research principles.* Washington, DC: National Institute for Literacy. Retrieved from http: //www.nifl.gov/publications/pdf/teach_adults.pdf

DeCapua, A., & Marshall, H. (2011). *Breaking new ground: Teaching students with limited or interrupted formal schooling in secondary schools.* Ann Arbor: University of Michigan Press.

de Gelder, B., Vroomen, J., & Bertelson, P. (1993). The effects of alphabetic-reading competence on language representation in bilingual Chinese subjects. *Psychological Research/Psychologische Forschung, 55,* 315–321.

de la Piedra, M. T. (2006). Literacies and Quechua oral language: Connecting sociocultural worlds and linguistic resources for biliteracy development. *Journal of Early Childhood Literacy, 6,* 383–406.

Dellatolas, G., Braga, L. W., Souza, L. d. N., Filho, G. N., Queiroz, E., & Deloche, G. (2003). Cognitive consequences of early phase of literacy. *Journal of International Neuropsychological Society, 9,* 771–782.

Espinoza-Herold, M. (2007). Stepping beyond *sí se puede: Dichos* as a cultural resource in mother-daughter interaction in a Latino family. *Anthropology & Education Quarterly, 38,* 260–277.

Faux, N. (2006). Preparing teachers to help low-literacy adult ESOL learners. In I. Van de Craats, J. Kurvers, & M. Young-Scholten (Eds.), *Low-Educated Adult Second Language and Literacy Acquisition: Proceedings of the Inaugural Symposium* (pp. 135–142). Utrecht, The Netherlands: LOT.

Faux, N. (Ed.). (2007). *Low-Educated Second Language and Literacy Acquisition: Research,*

Policy and Practice: Proceedings of the Second Annual Forum. Richmond: Literacy Institute at Virginia Commonwealth University.

Freeman, Y. S., & Freeman, D. E. (2001). Keys to success for bilingual students with limited formal schooling. *Bilingual Research Journal, 25*, 203–213.

Freire, P. (1970). *Pedagogy of the oppressed*. New York, NY: Continuum.

Gardner, S. (2008). Transforming talk and phonics practice: Or, how do crabs clap? *TESOL Quarterly, 42*, 261–284.

Geudens, A. (2006). Phonological awareness and learning to read in a first language: Controversies and new perspectives. In I. Van de Craats, J. Kurvers, & M. Young-Scholten (Eds.), *Low-Educated Adult Second Language and Literacy Acquisition: Proceedings of the Inaugural Symposium* (pp. 25–44). Utrecht, The Netherlands: LOT.

Geva, E., & Zadeh, X. Y. (2006). Reading efficiency in native English-speaking and English-as-a-second-language children: The role of oral proficiency and underlying cognitive-linguistic processes. *Scientific Studies of Reading, 10*, 31–57.

Gonzalez, J. E., & Uhing, B. M. (2008). Home literacy environment and young Hispanic children's English and Spanish oral language: A communality analysis. *Journal of Early Intervention, 30*, 116–139.

Goody, J. (1987). *The interface between the written and the oral*. Cambridge, UK: Cambridge University Press.

Kolinsky, R., Cary, L., & Morais, J. (1987). Awareness of words as phonological entities: The role of literacy. *Applied Psycholinguistics, 8*, 223–232.

Kurvers, J. (2007). Development of word recognition skills of adult L2 beginning readers. In N. R. Faux (Ed.), *Low-Educated Second Language and Literacy Acquisition: Research, Policy and Practice: Proceedings of the Second Annual Forum* (pp. 23–44). Richmond: Literacy Institute at Virginia Commonwealth University.

Kurvers, J., Vallen, T., & van Hout, R. (2006). Discovering features of language: Metalinguistic awareness of adult illiterates. In I. Van de Craats, J. Kurvers, & M. Young-Scholten (Eds.), *Low-Educated Adult Second Language and Literacy Acquisition: Proceedings of the Inaugural Symposium* (pp. 69–88). Utrecht, The Netherlands: LOT.

Kurvers, J., van Hout, R., & Vallen, T. (2007). Literacy and word boundaries. In N. R. Faux (Ed.), *Low-Educated Second Language and Literacy Acquisition: Research, Policy and Practice: Proceedings of the Second Annual Forum* (pp. 45–64). Richmond, VA: Literacy Institute at Virginia Commonwealth University.

Levinson, M. P. (2007). Literacy in English Gypsy communities: Cultural capital manifested as negative assets. *American Educational Research Journal, 44*, 5–39.

Lewis, C., & del Valle, A. (2009). Literacy and identity: Implications for research and practice. In L. Christenbury, R. Bomer, & P. Smagorinsky (Eds.), *Handbook of adolescent literacy* (pp. 307–322). New York, NY: Guilford.

Luria, A. (1976). *Cognitive development: Its social and cultural foundations* (M. Cole, Ed.; M. Lopez-Morillas & L. Solataroff, Trans.). Cambridge, MA: Harvard University Press. (Original work published in Russian, 1974)

Mace-Matluck, B. J., Alexander-Kasparik, R., & Queen, R. M. (1998). *Through the golden door: Educational approaches for immigrant adolescents with limited schooling.* McHenry, IL: Center for Applied Linguistics and Delta Systems.

McLuhan, M. (1994). *Understanding media: The extensions of man.* Cambridge, MA: MIT Press. (Original work published 1964)

Menard-Warwick, J. (2005). Intergenerational trajectories and sociopolitical context: Latina immigrants in adult ESL. *TESOL Quarterly, 39,* 165–185.

Menken, K., & Garcia, O. (2010). *Negotiating language policies: Educators as policymakers.* New York, NY: Routledge.

Morgan, B., & Ramanathan, V. (2005). Critical literacies and language education: Global and local perspectives. *Annual Review of Applied Linguistics, 25,* 151–169.

Olson, D. R. (2006). Oral discourse in a world of literacy. *Research in the Teaching of English, 41,* 136–143.

Ong, W. J. (1982). *Orality and literacy: The technologizing of the word.* London, UK, and New York, NY: Routledge.

Papen, U. (2005). *Adult literacy as social practice: More than skills.* New York, NY: Routledge.

Perry, K. H. (2007). Sharing stories, linking lives: Literacy practices among Sudanese refugees. In V. Purcell-Gates (Ed.), *Cultural practices of literacy: Case studies of language, literacy, social practice, and power* (pp. 57–84). Mahwah, NJ: Erlbaum.

Perry, K. H. (2008). From storytelling to writing: Transforming literacy practices among Sudanese refugees. *Journal of Literacy Research, 40,* 317–358.

Petersson, K. M., Ingvar, M., & Reis, A. (2009). Language and literacy from a cognitive neuroscience perspective. In D. R. Olson & N. Torrance (Eds.), *The Cambridge handbook of literacy* (pp. 152–182). Cambridge, UK: Cambridge University Press.

Peyton, J. K., Burt, M., McKay, S., Schaetzel, K., Terrill, L., Young, S., et al. (2007). Professional development for practitioners working with adult English language learners with limited literacy. In N. R. Faux (Ed.), *Low-Educated Second Language and Literacy Acquisition: Research, Policy and Practice: Proceedings of the Second Annual Forum* (pp. 213–225). Richmond: Literacy Institute at Virginia Commonwealth University.

Philp, J. (2003). Constraints on "noticing the gap" : Nonnative speakers'noticing of recasts in NS-NNS interaction. *Studies in Second Language Acquisition, 25,* 99–126.

Read, C., Zhang, Y., Nie, H., & Ding, B. (1986). The ability to manipulate speech sounds depends on knowing alphabetic spelling. *Cognition, 24,* 31–44.

Reder, S., & Davila, E. (2005). Context and literacy practices. *Annual Review of Applied Linguistics, 25,* 170–187.

Reis, A., & Castro-Caldas, A. (1997). Illiteracy: A cause for biased cognitive development. *Journal of International Neuropsychological Society, 3,* 444–450.

Reis, A., Fáısca, L., Mendonça, S., Ingvar, M., & Petersson, K. M. (2007). Semantic interference on a phonological task in illiterate subjects. *Scandinavian Journal of Psychology, 48,* 69–74.

Reis, A., Guerreiro, M., & Petersson, K. M. (2003). A sociodemographic and neuropsychological characterization of an illiterate population. *Applied Neuropsychology, 10,* 191–204.

Rubin, A. (1980). A theoretical taxonomy of the differences between oral and written language. In R. Spiro, B. Brice, & W. Brewer (Eds.), *Theoretical issues in reading comprehension: Perspectives from cognitive psychology, linguistics, artificial intelligence, and education* (pp. 411–438). Hillsdale, NJ: Erlbaum.

Sarroub, L. K. (2008). Living "glocally" with literacy success in the Midwest. *Theory into Practice, 47,* 59–66.

Street, B. (2003). What's "new" in new literacy studies? Critical approaches to literacy in theory and practice. *Current Issues in Comparative Education, 5,* 1–14.

Tannen, D. (Ed.). (1982). *Spoken and written language: Exploring orality and literacy.* Norwood, NJ: Ablex.

Tarone, E., & Bigelow, M. (2005). Impact of literacy on oral language processing: Implications for second language acquisition research. *Annual Review of Applied Linguistics, 25,* 77–97.

Tarone, E., Bigelow, M., & Hansen, K. (2007). The impact of alphabetic print literacy level on oral second language acquisition. In N. R. Faux (Ed.), *Low-Educated Second Language and Literacy Acquisition: Research, Policy and Practice: Proceedings of the Second Annual Forum* (pp. 99–122). Richmond: Literacy Institute at Virginia Commonwealth University.

Tarone, E., Bigelow, M., & Hansen, K. (2009). *Literacy and second language oracy.* Oxford, UK: Oxford University Press.

Tollefson, J. (2006). Critical theory in language theory. In T. Ricento (Ed.), *An introduction to language policy: Theory and method* (pp. 42–60). Malden, MA: Blackwell.

Trupke-Bastidas, J., & Poulos, A. (2007). Improving literacy of L1-non-literate and L1-literate adult English as a second language learners. *MinneWITESOL Journal, 25,* http://www.minnewitesoljournal.org

UNESCO. (2009, November). Inequality undermining education opportunities for millions of children. (Press release no. 2008–115). Retrieved from http://www.unesco.org/education/gmr2009/press/GMR2009_pressrelease_EN.pdf

Van de Craats, I. (2007). Obstacles on highway L2. In N. R. Faux (Ed.), *Low-Educated Second Language and Literacy Acquisition: Research, Policy and Practice: Proceedings of the Second Annual Forum* (pp. 149–163). Richmond: Literacy Institute at Virginia Commonwealth University.

Van de Craats, I., Kurvers, J., & Young-Scholten, M. (Eds.). (2006a). *Low-Educated Adult Second Language and Literacy Acquisition: Proceedings of the Inaugural Symposium.* Utrecht, The Netherlands: LOT.

Van de Craats,, I., Kurvers, J., & Young-Scholten, M. (2006b). Research on low-educated second language and literacy acquisition. In I. Van de Craats, J. Kurvers, & M. Young-Scholten (Eds.), *Low-Educated Adult Second Language and Literacy Acquisition: Proceedings of the Inaugural Symposium* (pp. 7–24). Utrecht, The Netherlands: LOT.

Vinogradov, P. (2008). "Maestra! The letters speak." Adult ESL students learning to read for the first time. *MinneWITESOL Journal, 25.* Retrieved from www. minnewitesoljournal.org

Vinogradov, P. (2010). Balancing top and bottom: Learner-generated texts for teaching phonics. In T. Wall & M. Leong (Eds.), *Low-Educated Second Language and Literacy Acquisition: Proceedings of the 5th Symposium* (pp. 3–14). Retrieved from http: //www.leslla.org/files/resources/Conference_Proceedings_FINAL_Aug12.pdf

Vinogradov, P., & Bigelow, M. (2010). *Using oral language skills to build on the emerging literacy of adult English learners.* Washington, DC: Center for Applied Linguistics. Retrieved from http: //www.cal.org/caelanetwork/resources/using-oral-language-skills.html

Vinogradov, P., & Liden, A. (2008). Principled training for LESLLA instructors. In I. Van de Craats & J. Kurvers (Eds.), *Low-Educated Adult Second Language and Literacy Acquisition: Proceedings of the Fourth Symposium* (pp. 133–144). Utrecht, The Netherlands: LOT.

Walker-Dalhouse, D., & Dalhouse, A. D. (2009). When two elephants fight the grass suffers: Parents and teachers working together to support the literacy development of Sudanese youth. *Teaching and Teacher Education, 25,* 328–335.

Warriner, D. S. (2007). "It's just the nature of the beast" : Re-imagining the literacies of schooling in adult ESL education. *Linguistics and Education, 18,* 305–324.

Warsame, A. A. (2001). How a strong government backed an African language: The lessons of Somalia. *International Review of Education, 47,* 341–360.

Watson, J. (2010). *Interpreting across the abyss: A hermeneutic study of initial literacy development by high school English language learners with limited formal schooling* (Unpublished doctoral dissertation). University of Minnesota, Minneapolis, MN.

Weinstein, G. (2006). "Learners' Lives as Curriculum" : An integrative project-based model for language learning. In G. H. Beckett & P. Chamness Miller (Eds.), *Project-based second and foreign language education: Past, present, and future* (pp. 159–165). Greenwich, CT: Information Age.

Yopp, H. (1992). Developing phonemic awareness in young children. *Reading Teacher, 45,* 696–703.

Yosso, T. J., & García, D. G. (2007). "This is no slum!" : A critical race theory analysis of community cultural wealth in culture clash's Chavez Ravine. *Aztlán: Journal of Chicano Studies, 32,* 145–179.

Young-Scholten, M. (Ed.). (2008). *Low-Educated Adult Second Language and Literacy Acquisition: Proceedings of the Third Annual Forum.* New Castle upon Tyne, UK: Newcastle University.

Young-Scholten, M., & Strom, N. (2006). First-time L2 readers: Is there a critical period? In I. Van de Craats, J. Kurvers, & M. Young-Scholten (Eds.), *Low-Educated Adult Second Language and Literacy Acquisition: Proceedings of the Inaugural Symposium* (pp. 45–68). Utrecht, The Netherlands: LOT.

Teaching American Sign Language to Hearing Adult Learners

David Quinto-Pozos

American Sign Language (ASL) has become a very popular language in high schools, colleges, and universities throughout the U.S., due, in part, to the growing number of schools that allow students to take the language in order to fulfill a foreign or general language requirement. Within the past couple decades, the number of students enrolled in ASL classes has increased dramatically, and there are likely more instructors of ASL at the present time than ever before. ASL and spoken language instruction are similar in some aspects; however, there are also differences between the two (e.g., modality differences involving visual rather than auditory perception and processing, no commonly used writing system in ASL, and the socio-cultural history of deaf-hearing relations). In spite of these differences, minimal research has been done on ASL learning and classroom pedagogy—especially in recent years. This article reports on studies that have been performed recently and it also suggests various themes for future research. In particular, three main areas of research are proposed: the possible role of the socio-political history of the Deaf community in which ASL teaching is situated, linguistic differences between signed and spoken languages, and the use of video and computer-based technologies.

TEACHING AMERICAN SIGN LANGUAGE TO HEARING ADULT LEARNERS

American Sign Language (ASL), the language of Deaf[1] communities throughout the United States and parts of Canada, is regularly taught in high schools, colleges, and universities throughout the United States, though this was not generally the case a few decades ago.² A Modern Language Association report of Fall 2009 foreign language enrollments in higher education claimed that ASL was the fourth most commonly studied language at colleges and universities in the United States and that there were nearly 92,000 students enrolled in ASL courses during the semester for which the numbers were reported (Furman, Goldberg, & Lusin, 2010). This represented a 30 percent increase in enrollment in comparison with figures reported for 2002.³ It was also reported in the 2009 data that the vast majority of ASL courses are introductory in focus rather than advanced, with a ratio of 11 to 1, respectively.⁴ The increase in ASL enrollments may be due in part to a trend in universities to accept ASL courses in fulfillment of a student's foreign language requirement, with the number of those schools totaling more than 160, as documented by one website (Wilcox, 2010). Rosen (2008) also reported that in 2005, ASL was being taught at 701 public high schools throughout the country and being accepted as a foreign language, a figure which represents more than a 4,000 percent increase since 1987, when only 17 secondary schools reported the offering of ASL in their language programs. Clearly, ASL is a popular language for L2 learners.⁵

Notwithstanding its popularity as a language, it seems to be the case that, over the years, there has not been substantial dialogue between ASL teaching professionals and educators and researchers from other foreign language units. There are few journal articles that can be found concerning ASL pedagogy, models and theories of second language acquisition (SLA) and language teaching have primarily focused on the teaching of spoken and written languages, and SLA-focused conferences have mostly not included representation of the teaching of ASL or other sign languages.⁶ This may due, in part, to common job requirements of ASL instructors and administrators; there may not be enough time for these pedagogy experts to engage in research because teaching is a primary focus—even for administrators—and tenure-track jobs with research components are still the minority of the positions in institutions of higher education (Cooper, Reisman, & Watson, 2008). In spite of the lack of ASL representation in SLA writings, ASL curricula have, to varying extents, incorporated aspects of various theories of spoken language instruction.

It appears that the teaching of ASL has been informed, in large part, by the linguistic intuitions and cultural beliefs of its instructors and curricula developers

—most of whom are members of the Deaf community. Some instructors are deaf, some are hearing but early signers because their parents and/or siblings were deaf, and others are late learners of the language who were not exposed in childhood.

The teaching strategies that have been employed have allowed for regular instruction of ASL to many adult hearing students, though the efficacy of those strategies has generally not been examined empirically. This situation encourages us to ask the following questions: What can the field of SLA learn from the instructional strategies of a community that places a primary focus on visual communication? What can the teaching of ASL learn from theories, models, and practices that have been used for spoken and written language instruction over the years? And, finally, what are the best ways to teach ASL so that adult hearing learners can make the most gains? These questions may serve as a guide for future evaluations of ASL pedagogies.

THE SOCIO-CULTURAL ENVIRONMENT OF ASL INSTRUCTION

One cannot consider linguistic aspects of ASL teaching without taking into account the unique history of ASL instruction over the years. The teaching of ASL is superposed on the socio-cultural history of the Deaf community—a history that has been influenced greatly by interactions between Deaf and non-Deaf (i.e., hearing) people. Deaf people have endured much oppression by hearing people over the years (whether or not the purported oppression has been deliberate or not), and the complex dynamics of the interactions between the two communities have involved issues of disability, social capital, and general power differentials (Ladd, 2003; Lane, 1999; Lane, Hoffmeister, & Bahan 1996; McDermid, 2009).[7] In many cases, Deaf instructors feel that they are subject to discrimination that is not evident in the experiences of their hearing colleagues (McDermid, 2009). An example of societal oppression against Deaf people, or what Lane (1999) has referred to as *audism* (the "hearing way of dominating, restructuring, and exercising authority over the deaf community", p. 43), can be evident in the fact that some hearing people want to learn ASL in order to help Deaf people, whether it be for professional, religious, or other reasons.[8] Whereas this might provide an internal motivation for hearing adult learners of ASL, it also likely plays a role in the beliefs that some hearing students have about ASL and the Deaf community and in the ways in which hearing people interact with their instructors. The socio-cultural history of the Deaf community has likely impacted general trends of ASL instruction.[9]

In addition to the general teaching of language, instructors of ASL have also been responsible for teaching the culture of the Deaf community—providing the proper environment for enculturation of the hearing learner and appropriate socialization into the community (Rutherford, 1988). One such example of Deaf culture is a primary focus on visual information and an avoidance of relying on sound or speech for communication. This facet of Deaf culture has influenced the degree to which spoken English is allowed, if at all, within the classroom; this is discussed later in this article. Certainly, other foreign languages also include the teaching of culture, but perhaps not to the extent that ASL instructors incorporate cultural material beginning with introductory level-courses. Students are often encouraged to attend Deaf community gatherings (e.g., regularly-scheduled informal meetings at restaurants) and events (e.g., school for the Deaf homecoming weekends or special activities at Deaf social clubs), which allows cultural knowledge (e.g., unspoken rules about interacting with others in ASL) to be gained outside of the classroom, as well.

Efforts to preserve ASL for the future have likely played an important role in the general investment of Deaf people in the teaching of the language. Deaf people have wanted to preserve their language and culture in spite of threats from members of the medical community (e.g., researchers and doctors who support the use of cochlear implants) and others to eradicate deafness or outlaw the use of signed language in the education of deaf children (Lane, Hoffmeister, & Bahan, 1996). Whereas instruction of an endangered spoken language might share this characteristic with ASL (i.e., instructors would be committed to supporting the vitality of their endangered languages), there are likely noteworthy differences between the teaching of ASL and many, if not most, spoken languages that are commonly taught. As one example, the teaching of ASL by Deaf to hearing people allows the Deaf to increase the population of those with whom they can communicate using their everyday language. Meaningful interaction between Deaf and hearing people is often constrained by hearing people's ability to use signed language fluently. ASL instructors have worked tirelessly to share their visual language with people who have previously been dependent on hearing for communication. Thus, the history of a linguistic and cultural minority has played a large part in the teaching of ASL. This fact cannot be overlooked when considering the methods of ASL instruction that may be most effective.

NOTEWORTHY DIFFERENCES BETWEEN SIGNED AND SPOKEN LANGUAGES

In order to address various points regarding ASL pedagogy, it may be useful to also make a couple points about the language explicit—especially those which may influence how it is taught vis-à-vis the teaching of spoken languages. First, ASL does not have a widely used writing system, although English words, or glosses, are sometimes used to represent ASL signs. Second, ASL structure is heavily influenced by the ability to display meaningful streams of information simultaneously. Both manual (i.e., the hand[s]) and non-manual (e.g., mouth/lip movements for adjectival and adverbial modifications of signs) articulators participate in the lexical, morphological, and syntactic constructs of the language. Such simultaneity differs from the highly sequential structure that is representative of spoken language, and this may have an effect on how adult hearing learners are able to process visual input. Additionally, aspects of the vocabulary and grammar of ASL and other signed languages have often been described as iconic. In general terms, iconic forms are those in which the form of a lexical item (or other linguistic process) resembles, in some way, some aspect(s) of the referent. Examples of this are provided in a later section, though it is important to note that iconicity is much more prevalent in signed languages than it is in spoken languages (see Taub, 2001).

IMPLICATIONS OF NOT HAVING A COMMONLY USED WRITING SYSTEM

One of the most notable characteristics of ASL is that there exists no commonly accepted written form of the language.[10] This fact has various implications for the teaching of ASL. For example, written homework would have to employ English words, or glosses, for representing ASL signs, and such glosses are not standardized for many lexical items. This makes it difficult to capture various aspects of the language such as grammatical inflections on particular signs that involve the use of the signing space and the use of non-manual signals. In addition, body movements (in the form of enactment to represent actions of depicted characters) and affective information (e.g., the emotions of characters) are aspects of ASL that are common in ASL discourse, yet there do not exist well-known and systematic ways for capturing such meaningful devices. Even so, according to one study, a method of glossing ASL sentences with English words is beneficial for pedagogical purposes (Buisson, 2007). The results of that study are reported at the end of this section.

There are various important contributions of a writing system to language learning. Writing allows for permanence that can be reviewed and altered; it allow one to refining a drafted sentence with multiple passes. In the absence of a writing system to capture an utterance or thought, a constructed segment is ephemeral—lasting only as long as it takes to articulate the sounds or gestures of the construction.

In the case of signed languages, one might suggest that recorded videos would serve the same purpose as a writing system (i.e., allowing for the documentation of phrases and sentences). Video recordings have been invaluable for capturing aspects of ASL and Deaf culture over the years, but they are not fully comparable to a writing system in various aspects. The process of creating, reviewing, and editing video differs significantly from writing (in terms of time and resources that are required to perform those tasks). Yet, it is also true that video can capture a wealth of information that is not present in written language (e.g., affective and mimetic displays by the signer). Some authors (e.g., Bienvenu, 2009) suggest that videos of signed productions of ASL could be used for regular homework assignments. Yet, for many students there exist technology challenges for the creation and editing of videos. Some of the issues include access to high-quality, user-friendly video equipment and editing software and knowledge of video editing and storage (e.g., on CD or DVD). However, the situation is changing rapidly with the advent of increasingly sophisticated technologies that are becoming widespread among high schools, colleges, and universities. An important aspect of employing the use of video-based assignments is to train students on current technologies for the creation of quality videos; Bienvenue sees this as an important step in utilizing this methodology.

Some ASL programs include regular homework assignments that require students to create videos of themselves producing ASL. Needless to say, this type of assignment requires that instructors take the time to critique the signed work. Some instructors (e.g., Bienvenu, 2009) have suggested that more time is required to evaluate video work than written work, but others feel that there may be no differences (Schornstein, 2005). One difference between video-based and written homework, Bienvenu argues, is that a video-based assignment requires the instructor to rewind or fast-forward to other segments of the video for comparison purposes, whereas different pages of a written document can quickly and easily be scanned when needed.

Writing systems also allow for the development of a culture's written literature, which provides a language learner with a wealth of opportunities for practice with learning language structure and lexical items. In the absence of a written literature, a culture may engage genres of oral discourse (e.g., oratory, folklore, and performance art) for passing on the culture's traditions and beliefs, and this is certainly true for ASL (Frishberg, 1988). A video-based literature that captures genres of oral discourse could perhaps provide the same benefits as a written literature, though the availability of a large and diverse set of resources for signed language instruction and learning may remain limited—at least when compared with written resources for the common spoken languages that are taught to adult speakers. One particular issue with a lack of a written literature is the lack of resources for advanced courses—the level of language learning where students are involved in regular reading and composition of self-generated samples of extended language production. As noted earlier, the vast majority of ASL instruction that occurs, as reported by the 2009 MLA report (Furman et al., 2010), focuses on introductory learning, though some advanced instruction is also available. The extent to which advanced ASL courses are limited, if at all, by a lack of a writing system has not been explored. This theme is an important one to remember when considering differences between the instruction of signed versus spoken language.

One recent study questioned whether a system for writing ASL signs and sentences would be useful for an ASL learner. Buisson (2007) investigated the efficacy of English glossing (or "written equivalents of ASL sentences", p. 331) for facilitating the learning of ASL grammar by beginning L2 learners. In a study of an online glossing program, a test group of 66 students from four universities was given lessons that provided step-by-step instructions of the glossing of ASL sentences. Then, the students were asked to identify various aspects of the glossing conventions such as: (a) the correct glossing rule to be used for a segment and/or its application, (b) the correctly glossed phrase or sentence that corresponds to an ASL segment, and (c) an ASL segment that corresponded to a glossed phrase or sentence. This experimental group was compared to a control group that did not learn the glossing conventions or participate in the glossing tasks but rather engaged in reading online articles about deaf education and answering multiple-choice questions about the content. All participants were given grammar pre-tests and post-tests for both English and ASL. The results revealed that the glossing lessons significantly improved the ASL grammatical knowledge of the beginning learners; they scored nearly two standard deviations higher in the ASL grammatical posttest when compared to the control group. Unfortunately, Buisson does not provide details about which aspects of grammar were successfully acquired using this method. Interestingly, the English grammar knowledge of the test participants also improved significantly vis-à-vis that of the control group. Buisson suggests that this result may be due to the purposeful focus on lessons that compared and contrasted the grammars of English and ASL; the opportunity for students to use English as a source of comparison allowed them to also improve their English skills. In short, the author claims that glossing lessons (in this case, delivered via the internet) can provide a bridge for the adult speaker of English in their acquisition of ASL. The implications from the Buisson study are that instructors should consider whether some type of a writing system for ASL constructions might be useful for the learning of aspects of ASL.

UNIQUE ASPECTS OF ASL STRUCTURE AND IMPLICATIONS FOR ASL INSTRUCTION[11]

There are certainly challenges involved in capturing signed language via a written form, and those are likely due, at least in part, to the possibility of using multiple articulators (e.g., the hands, the face, and the torso) simultaneously for encoding meaning creation. Lexical items that do not readily change in form (or meaning) such as common nouns (e.g. the ASL sign MOTHER or the compound FACE-STRONG) can be easily represented via their English translations (e.g. *mother or resemble*), but signs that can be inflected or otherwise modified in form to change the meaning of the sign present challenges. For example, the sign TO-GIVE can be inflected for person, number, and temporal aspect by moving the hand(s) in particular ways and in specific orientations within the signing space, which could result in a sign with the meaning: *I give to them repeatedly.* The signer could simultaneously add a particular mouth (i.e., non-manual) gesture to the inflected sign that would provide manner (i.e., adverbial) information such as: *I give to them repeatedly in a haphazard way.* The inflections are said to occur simultaneously with the verb—rather than sequentially such as the affixes that commonly characterize conjugated forms in spoken language. These simultaneously realized inflections are particularly difficult to capture via a writing system that generally represents meaningful items sequentially.[12] One of the challenges that lies ahead for curriculum developers is to investigate the best ways to teach simultaneously realized morphology and inflections to students who are accustomed to the sequential morphology (e.g., affixes) of spoken languages. Such research might also benefit the teaching of languages for which simultaneous structure (e.g., grammatical tonal contrasts) is a notable part of the grammar. For example, questions about the cognitive processing of simultaneous versus sequential information could be investigated.

In the early years of ASL instruction (primarily through the 1970s), the teaching of ASL focused mostly on the learning of lexical items rather than on the complex grammar of a visual-spatial language (Peterson, 2009). This was likely due, in part, to the lack of resources for representing the complexities of a visual-spatial language, though other factors may also have contributed to the practice.[13] Even so, it may be the case that the learning of individual signs may continue to be the focus of some instructors of ASL. Failure to highlight aspects of simultaneity within the grammar of ASL may lead many students to believe that learning ASL primarily means learning signs and sequencing them in accordance with English grammar. It has also been reported that students commonly use the curriculum materials as vocabulary books (Schornstein, 2005) rather than as guides for learning aspects of signed language grammar in addition to lexical material.

Some particularly difficult constructions for the L2 hearing learner of ASL involve *constructed action* and the so-called *classifiers* that are common in signed languages (Quinto-Pozos, 2005). Classifiers are signs that are used to describe the location, motion, and visual-geometric properties of objects and how they interact

(Schembri, 2003; Supalla 1986). Constructed action, on the other hand, is the use of the body in mimetic ways for describing the actions and/or appearance of characters (Metzger, 1995; Quinto-Pozos, 2007). These types of constructions require the manipulation of visual perspective for comprehension (i.e., understanding that the signer's visual perspective differs from the interlocutor's perspective) and involve the simultaneous and/or coordinated production of multiple meaningful units. They are often difficult for the signed language learner (Quinto-Pozos, 2005; Schornstein, 2005). In order to provide students with a more complete picture of ASL (including its signs and its grammar), curricula need to include the various types of constructions that are mentioned here. In addition, future research should examine the efficacy of teaching methods for these types of constructions, as noted in Quinto-Pozos (2005). Common ASL curricula are discussed later in this article.

As noted earlier, one other characteristic of signed languages that should be made explicit is the degree to which they employ iconicity within their lexical items and as part of their grammars. As an example, the ASL sign TREE is articulated with the forearm positioned vertically and all fingers of the hand are extended as if producing a gesture for the number five. In this rather iconic sign, people often liken the forearm to the trunk of a tree and the hand and fingers to the branches of the tree. Not all signs in ASL are iconic, of course, and natural linguistic processes seem to make iconic signs more arbitrary over time (Klima & Bellugi, 1979). In general, iconicity is not a feature of ASL that Deaf children take advantage of during acquisition (Meier, 1987; Meier, Mauk, Cheek, & Moreland, 2008), and even Deaf adult signers of ASL do not process iconic signs differently than non-iconic signs (Bosworth & Emmorey, 2010). However, the same may not be true for adults who could potentially capitalize on iconicity for memory reasons. This is an empirical question, of course, that could be examined within the context of L2 learning of ASL.

OTHER ASPECTS OF ASL INSTRUCTION

Some students take ASL because they think it will be an easy language to learn—perhaps because of its pictorial qualities or because they feel that it is simply English represented in the manual modality (Jacobowitz, 2005; Kemp, 1998; Peterson, 2009). In reality, certain aspects of ASL are quite difficult for the adult hearing person, and achieving fluency is not nearly as easy as many people think it may be. Jacobs (1996) analyzed ASL as a Category 4 language for English speakers, which means that it may be comparable to an adult L1 speaker of English learning Chinese or Japanese as an L2. A Category 4 language would be more difficult to learn than Spanish or French for a native English speaker. Unfortunately, some students who enroll in ASL do so because they have struggled with the learning of foreign spoken languages. In such cases, it is not clear if L2 language learning may be particularly difficult for such students, or if the challenge lies in learning languages that are spoken (and written). It may be the case that some students are better visual learners than auditory learners, and for those students ASL learning may, indeed, be easier for them to learn than a spoken language would be. However, no research has addressed this question. Because students often perceive ASL to be an easy language to learn, they may not expend the same effort to learn the language as they would to learn a spoken language. Future research could address possible differences between so-called auditory learners and visual learners and their abilities to acquire ASL.[14]

In spite of all the challenges of learning ASL for the adult learner, there are some learners who make notable progress with language learning. They achieve this in spite of having to learn how to use their hands, arms, and bodies in new ways and having to acquire a manual phonology as an adult.[15] This speaks to the dedication of the instructors of ASL—many of whom have not received training in formal programs that focus on the teaching of ASL and the formal study of SLA models and theories. There have been few programs for ASL instructors over the years, yet there exist many ASL instructors throughout the U.S. and Canada.[16] This means that many ASL instructors have had to refine their teaching methods mostly through trial and error—by improving lessons and activities after obtaining feedback from students and colleagues. Of course, there also exists a small minority of instructors who have advanced degrees in the teaching of ASL from one of the few accredited programs that have been in existence.

A few organizations have been established over the years to assist with the provision of learning opportunities for ASL instructors. One of them is the American Sign Language Teachers Association (ASLTA), which is a national professional organization of educators dedicated to improving the teaching of ASL. The ASLTA was established by the National Association of the Deaf (NAD); it hosts biennial national conferences, and there also exist regular regional, state, and local workshops that are organized for ASL instructors. Another organization that is important to mention is the Conference of Interpreter Trainers (CIT). Like the ASLTA, the CIT hosts national conferences every two years. Both of these organizations exist to provide ASL instructors with opportunities for improving their knowledge of pedagogical methods and tips for teaching content related to ASL.

The ASLTA helps to set standards for ASL instruction. One approach that they have taken is to produce position papers on various topics such as general guidelines for consideration when an instructor candidate is being considered for a position, the suggested enrollment limit for ASL courses, and a code of ethics for ASL instructors.[17] Incidentally, there has been considerable debate within the ASL teaching profession about who is qualified to teach the language. Some people feel that only Deaf and hard of hearing candidates are appropriate candidates for ASL instructor positions—presumably because they are core members of a community that uses ASL on a daily basis.[18] Another manner in which the ASLTA has worked to develop standards for ASL instruction is by drafting a proposed ASL version of the American Council on the Teaching of Foreign Languages (ACTFL) guidelines. The document contains proposals for defining proficiency in ASL—from kindergarten to post-secondary classrooms. As such, the document is intended to apply to the instruction of ASL for both Deaf and hearing students. The Standards for Learning American Sign Language (Ashton, Cagle, Kurz, Newell, Peterson, & Zinza, in press) adopts the view of the Standards for Foreign Language Learning that language proficiency should be demonstrated through five domains: Communication, Cultures, Connections, Comparisons, and Communities (National Standards, 2010). This effort to create a version of the National Standards for ASL, which was driven by the ASLTA, allows ASL to be understood alongside its spoken language peers, and it will likely be an important guiding force in the profession for years to come.

One of the topics of discussion within the field of ASL instruction over the years has been whether or not to allow the use of spoken language in the classroom. In many cases, the ASL instructors are Deaf individuals who prefer not to use spoken language (for various reasons, some of which concern accessibility issues; spoken language is generally not very accessible to Deaf people with little or no residual hearing). Some ASL programs adopt "no voice" policies in their classrooms, and instructors and students are expected to follow those policies throughout. As noted earlier, the no voice rules are in line with general norms of Deaf culture and are often espoused by Deaf instructors (McDermid, 2009). However, such rules are sometimes relaxed by hearing teachers in certain circumstances (e.g., during office hours, during a one-on-one encounter with a student, or even during class time if a student may not be understanding a key point made by the instructor). Some programs arrange for an interpreter to accompany the instructor for the first day of classes for beginning students; this facilitates communication during that class if the students have any questions about course requirements. It is important to note that not all programs follow this practice for various reasons (e.g., lack of available resources or beliefs that no speech should ever be used in the classroom at all because it will cause students to rely on that form of communication rather than on trying to make themselves understood in ASL). In general, "no voice" policies means that gesture is relied upon heavily, although written English is also employed by the instructor during lessons (e.g., writing on the board or in the form of handouts distributed to students). In addition, signing and speaking at the same time does not allow for a grammatically correct rendering of either the signed or the spoken language (see Tevenal & Villanueva, 2009), and engaging in speaking while signing likely presents an impediment to learning important aspects of the grammar of a signed language, as noted earlier. It should also be noted that some ASL instructors do use spoken English in the classroom. As suggested above, this practice is often looked upon negatively by Deaf signers of ASL, though it could be the case, in theory, that Deaf people who feel comfortable speaking may also employ the use of spoken English in the classroom. The practice likely occurs most often with hearing instructors. Whether or not the use of spoken English in certain situations (e.g., for clarifying confusion) allows students to more quickly acquire ASL is an empirical question that does not seem to have been addressed in the research literature. Notwithstanding the efficacy of using spoken English for ASL instruction, there lies a socio-cultural issue of allowing a means of communication that has often resulted in forms of oppression for members of the Deaf community over the years (Lane, Hoffmeister, & Bahan, 1996).

BEST PRACTICES TEACHING ASL

Current Curricula

Various curricula for teaching ASL have been developed over the years, and the majority of ASL programs in the United States utilize one or more of those resources.[19] Those curricula have only been in existence since about the 1980s, with prior materials either being structured primarily in dictionary formats with pictures and/or descriptions of signs with minimal information about grammar and culture (Peterson, 2009; Rosen, 2010). In the early decades of ASL teaching several conferences were held to discuss aspects of ASL linguistics and the teaching of ASL (as one example, see Caccamise & Hicks, 1978).

Rosen (2010) compares the most common curricula in use today for the teaching of ASL, including an analysis of the general theoretical assumptions about L2 language learning that underlie the various approaches. His analysis finds that common curricula for teaching ASL can be described in terms of various theories of language instruction that have been popular over the years, although no curriculum currently espouses content-based instruction (CBI) or task-based language teaching (TBLT), which he suggests are common in the current L2 teaching of spoken languages. A recurring theme in Rosen's writings is that instructors of ASL should become more knowledgeable about the theoretical underpinnings of the curricula that they utilize for teaching ASL; presumably this would help them to improve the effectiveness of their instructional approaches.

An early text, *A Basic Course in American Sign Language* (Humphries, Padden, & O'Rourke, 1980), often referred to as the *ABC* book, was perhaps one of the first books that contained substantial information about grammatical matters in addition to clear sketches of signs that have served as examples for ASL signs for countless students of ASL over the years. The language learning methods suggested within this text were formatted as language drills. A later curriculum by two of the authors, *Learning American Sign Language* (Humphries & Padden, 1992), expanded upon the earlier material and introduced a video accompaniment with examples of the lexical and grammatical content within the books. Rosen (2010) reported that this curriculum is used in nearly half (49%) of the 701 high schools throughout the country that completed his survey.[20]

Another pioneering curriculum in the field was simply named *American Sign Language* (Baker-Shenk & Cokely, 1980), though it has been affectionately known as the *Green Books* because of the color of the cover that was used for the three books within the set. This curriculum contained an extensive description of grammatical aspects of ASL, which have been referenced many times over the years—including citations by linguists who have been engaged in detailed studies of the structure of the language. Additionally, the Green Books were characterized by language drills, which were likely common within the pedagogical methods of the time in which it was developed. The curriculum contains video resources for students to view short dialogues between two fluent Deaf signers, and the dialogues—designed to be imitated by the language learner—constitute a notable portion of the material in the books. Rosen (2010) claims that the *Green Books* is a curriculum used in 30% of high school programs.[21]

The most common curriculum in use by high school programs today (83% of the programs, according to Rosen, 2010) had its beginnings in the late 1980s, and it emphasized a different methodology for ASL instruction: the functional-notional framework. The introduction of *Signing Naturally* (Smith, Lentz, & Mikos, 1988) to the field of ASL instruction is viewed by some as representing a watershed event for ASL instruction (Peterson, 2009). Of particular note is that the methodology encouraged language learning by focusing on common ways in which people interact (e.g., introductions, talking about where one lives and their family, and making requests); explicit grammatical instruction is not emphasized in this curriculum. The instructor is guided through the approach with curriculum guides for the three levels of the curriculum. Video texts in DVD format also accompanied this curriculum. In 2009, a second edition of the original Level I of the series was published, and the curriculum remains very popular for ASL programs—both at the secondary and post-secondary level.

Other curricula are also used for the teaching of ASL. *Bravo ASL!* (Cassell, 1996), which is used in less than 10 percent of high school programs (Rosen, 2010) has been in existence for 15 years. This curriculum takes the learner through the daily interactions of a Deaf man and his family and examples of the common types of daily activities that allow the learner to be exposed to ASL that is based on functions of interaction. As with the other curricula, *Bravo ASL!* contains a student workbook with grammatical information and cultural notes. A newer curriculum is *Master

ASL! (Zinza, 2006), which seems to be gaining in popularity. This curriculum covers introductory material for ASL learning, and it also contains workbooks with accompanying video resources (i.e., a DVD). A myriad of other curricula have also been developed in recent years, and some of them take advantage of Internet technologies for distribution. This brief review of common ASL curricula is not intended to be exhaustive, but rather to provide a snapshot of the types of resources that have been commonly used since the 1980s in ASL classrooms. See Rosen (2010) for a more comprehensive comparison of commonly used ASL curricula.

It appears that no study has looked at the efficacy of one curriculum over another. Thoryk (2010) also suggested this to be the case, and she noted that "instead of addressing efficacy, current ASL materials predominantly rely on generalized, short-phrase references to 'natural settings' or amorphous 'standards'; inclusion of anecdotal claims and testimonies; and vague references to 'field testing' without providing access to any real data" (pp. 100–101). Additionally, as Rosen (2010) pointed out, none of the curricula commonly in use today utilize the teaching philosophies that have been adopted most recently for the instruction of spoken languages (e.g., CBI and TBLT). However, he also notes that "there is no empirical study of the impact that pedagogies in ASL as a second language have on learning" (352). As one possible example, it may be the case that language learning in the visual modality, because of its strong tendency toward visual iconicity, might allow the learner to take advantage of other cognitive skills (e.g., visual-based memory and the management of non-linguistic spatial phenomena) for their acquisition of a signed language. This is only a possibility—one that must be explored with empirical studies that examine such skills and their role in each of the curricula that are used.

OTHER MATERIALS FOR THE ACQUISITION OF SPECIFIC SKILLS

In addition to the curricula that have been developed for the learning of ASL in the classroom, there also exist various extra-curricular learning resources that target specific aspects of the language. For example, fingerspelling, a system for representing the letters of an alphabet via handshapes and movements, is used regularly within ASL, and the majority of adult learners of ASL struggle with fingerspelling comprehension or production.[22] Because of these struggles, materials have been developed over the years in an effort to focus on the development of such skills.[23] Fingerspelling is covered in a few of the general curricula on the market, but not with the focus that the self-contained products have provided. There also exist videos and workbooks that focus solely on ASL numbers and various ways in which certain ASL signs can incorporate quantities (e.g., the single signs FIVE-DOLLARS for the meaning *five dollars* or TWO-WEEKS with downward movement of the hands for the meaning *every two weeks*).

There are various commercially available products for focusing on fingerspelling skills. Some of these materials contain extensive descriptions of fingerspelling in ASL—including the history of fingerspelling within the language and how some commonly fingerspelled words have become lexicalized over time and now appear more sign-like in nature. However, some of the materials only provide learners with video examples of fingerspelled words with which to practice their comprehension skills.

The methods for practicing fingerspelling production and comprehension often involve drills and activities that are designed to have the learner focus on the production or comprehension of fingerspelling. However, most of these methods for acquiring fingerspelling skills have not been assessed. This is not true, however, with respect to one such fingerspelling curriculum, which has been investigated by some of the limited research on the ASL pedagogical materials.

Thoryk (2010) investigated the efficacy of a particular curriculum resource for the acquisition of fingerspelling skills. The author tested a commercially-available teacher text and two accompanying DVDs that focus on the acquisition of fingerspelling skills by providing the instructor with various lessons for guiding students through the learning of fingerspelled words with various characteristics (e.g., common vs. uncommon words, common vs. uncommon letter combinations, and items that appear more sign-like vs. those that are characteristically more sequential in nature).

Students in ASL classes at a state-funded university and its regional campuses comprised the learners whose progress was evaluated by Thoryk (2010), with an experimental group being exposed to the curriculum by their instructors in addition to their regular ASL curriculum and a control group having only been exposed to fingerspelling via the regular ways in which students learn about that skill through their standard curricula.

The pre- and post-test scores showed that there was no measured improvement in the comprehension skills of the students across the two groups. The experimental group exhibited a mean gain of 10 points over the semester, whereas the control group improved, on average, by 12 points. In addition, Thoryk (2010) reported that the experimental group exhibited greater variation than the control group.

Thoryk's (2010) study showed that the fingerspelling curriculum that was employed was not effective in significantly improving a student's comprehension of fingerspelled items in comparison with the typical type of exposure that a student might receive by learning ASL through one or two of the most commonly used ASL curricula. This study was insightful, though the extent to which practice time, or frequency of exposure to the fingerspelling, might have an effect is not known. It is not clear whether more frequent exposure to the curriculum would result in better skills than not using the curriculum at all. Nonetheless, the study serves as an important example of the need to scrutinize curricula in order to determine their efficacy as learning materials. Instructors should be aware that some curricula may not be successful at improving students' skills in comparison with methods that do not employ the curricula. If such materials are used, instructors could consider taking steps to assess their usefulness.

RETHINKING HOW WE APPROACH A VISUAL-GESTURAL LANGUAGE

In addition to the availability of curricula and resources for teaching and learning various aspects of ASL, at least a couple works have been written about the teaching and learning of a signed language. Wilcox and Wilcox (1997) is geared toward "good teachers who need program and classroom guidelines for the teaching of ASL" (p. 3), whereas Peterson (2009) provides the student who is about to embark on ASL learning a general introduction to some of the points that should be considered before learning a signed language. The general goal of both of these works is clear: visual-gestural language learning may not conform to what hearing people expect from language learning experiences with spoken languages. Part of the title of the Wilcox and Wilcox book perhaps captures the essence of their

efforts: *Learning to See: Teaching American Sign Language as a Second Language.*
It appears that Wilcox and Wilcox (1997) was intended as a resource for ASL teachers who have had limited access to formal preparation for becoming ASL instructors. The authors point out that the increased popularity of ASL classes over the years has had an impact on the field of ASL instruction, which has been generally ill-prepared to respond to the need for increased enrollment. They note that there have been few teacher training programs, no standard curricula,[24] little or no literature on the L2 instruction of ASL, and no accreditation procedures for ASL programs and teachers. For these reasons, the authors provided a resource for instructors that addresses various topics such as: myths and misconceptions about ASL, discussions of language mode (e.g. spoken, written, signed) and how ASL and English are situated in the Deaf community taking into account language mode, information about the linguistic structure of ASL, various aspects of Deaf culture, and a myriad of points about teaching ASL (including curriculum and course design, evaluation and measurement, and general information about instructional materials). The book constitutes an important resource for novice teachers of ASL or those who have not had access to such information from formal education.

Whereas Wilcox and Wilcox (1997) present points about ASL instruction from a teacher's perspective, Peterson (2009) is interested in clarifying some of the myths and misconceptions that beginning students tend to have before embarking on their study of ASL. This theme of prevailing misunderstandings is an echo of the Wilcox and Wilcox (1997) discussion of the topic. However, Peterson's discussions are based on the results of a survey that was completed by 1,115 new university students of ASL. The size of that sample is impressive, and it provides Peterson with data to make his points about the lack of accurate information that many students have about ASL. The sample was primarily female (80%), mostly monolingual English speakers (80%), and primarily college-aged (67% were 18–24 years of age).

One of Peterson's (2009) interests lies in students' perceptions of ASL. He reported that nearly 68% of the students from his survey answered "yes" to the question "Is ASL is a visual-gestural form of English?" In addition, 60% of the students agreed to the statement "It will be easier to learn ASL if the teacher signs and speaks at the same time." Responses to both of these questions provide evidence that a particular misconception among hearing people is that ASL is simply a manual form of English. This may have contributed to the fact that more than half (53%) of the students felt that they would be fluent within two years, which aligns with the general belief (not from the survey) that a student can learn the language and how to interpret between that language and English within the time it takes to complete an Associate's or Bachelor's degree. Peterson's book, therefore, is an attempt at dispelling myths about ASL and the learning of the language in hopes of setting the stage for more efficient language learning. The writings of Wilcox and Wilcox (1997) and Peterson (2009) suggest that ASL instructors should carefully consider the preconceptions that hearing students bring to their experiences with the adult learning of ASL. Perhaps some of the differences between visual-gestural and auditory-oral languages should be made explicit to the language learner before they fully engage in the learning process. Whether this would result in more successful language learning is also a possible topic for future research.

SUGGESTED DIRECTIONS FOR RESEARCH

ASL instruction has gained a notable presence in secondary and post-secondary institutions within the last 15–20 years. Student enrollment has increased tremendously, the number of required instructors to meet student demand has multiplied, and the number of high schools, colleges, and universities that accept ASL as a language that fulfills a foreign language requirement has grown steadily. Yet systematic examination of the teaching resources and methodologies that have been used has mostly not occurred. In order for the field to move forward, this needs to change. Some possible themes for research could be the following: the socio-political history of the Deaf community in which ASL instruction is situated, linguistic differences between signed and spoken languages, and the use of video and computer-based technologies.

The ASL classroom is but one reflection of the Deaf community's interactions between Deaf and hearing people; however, in this case ASL is the expected language of interaction and the ASL-signing model (i.e., the instructor who is often a member of the Deaf community) is in charge. This dynamic is, in some ways, the opposite of what is encountered in everyday life for the students and even the instructor, if he/she is Deaf. Deaf and non-Deaf ideologies co-exist in this space, though the Deaf ones may be highlighted and supported in these classroom interactions. It is within this academic setting that hearing students begin to learn about what Deaf people value—in terms of communication. The dynamics of this setting likely influence the ways in which ASL is taught and what is expected from the students. Understanding the dynamics of this setting is an important step in being able to explain the uniqueness of ASL instruction. In general terms, what can be learned about instructors of ASL, about their position with respect to the larger Deaf community, and about how Deaf and non-Deaf ideologies have affected the way ASL is commonly taught? What are the specific effects on the teaching of ASL that come from cultural (i.e., Deaf culture) influences? This is an area of inquiry that may be particularly informative to SLA researchers who may not be aware of the intricacies of Deaf culture. In particular, what can the larger SLA community learn from teaching practices that have their roots in a rich and complex minority community? Within this line of research one should also examine the beliefs of ASL instructors about teaching and what they feel is effective. In other woulds, what would ASL instructors suggest (in terms of research) for how to move the field forward? Such work would allow ASL instructors to contribute to regular discussions of language pedagogy within the much larger field of SLA research and practice.

This area of research would also allow investigators to examine whether having beginning hearing students learn about the complexities of the sociocultural history of Deaf and non-Deaf communities early in their experience (e.g., with resources such as Peterson, 2009) allows them to be more successful ASL learners. It may be the case that allowing beginning students to learn about ASL and the Deaf community would also assist in their subsequent ASL learning.

In addition, there remains much work to be done in the area of classroom-based linguistic topics. For example, to what extent should English (whether it be written, spoken, or even signed) be used in the classroom and are there effective ways of incorporating English into the teaching of ASL (e.g., through glossing, written homework, fingerspelling certain items, etc.)? In terms of fingerspelling, when might be the best time to incorporate fingerspelling into the teaching of ASL and to what extent should it be explicitly taught? Are there influences from English that might be best to avoid in the classroom? Many adult learners of ASL have acquired English as a first language, and research on this topic is vital.

One could also consider various questions regarding the uniqueness of ASL when compared to spoken languages. For example, can visual iconicity serve as a bridge to ASL learning? Can a focus on the teaching of so-called classifiers and constructed action allow the adult hearing learner of ASL to rely less on English structure when learning ASL grammar? Does the learning of ASL for hearing adults present unique challenges for students who must acquire a manual phonology (i.e., a phonological system that uses hand configurations, movements and locations in the signing space for realization) while also becoming accustomed to new ways of motorically using their arms, hands, and bodies? Some of these questions can be captured by the larger query: What are the impacts of linguistic similarities and differences between signed and spoken languages on pedagogy?

Finally, what types of video and computer-based technologies might be successful teaching aids for a visual-gestural language? On the surface, this question might seem to only concern the teaching of ASL and other sign languages, but it is likely that the teaching of spoken language could benefit greatly from knowing more about how all learners utilize visual information (e.g., body language and gesture[25]) while they are learning a language. In other words, what is the role of multi-modal cues as part of L2 learning and the development of socio-pragmatic competence for a language learner? In the case of ASL, are there specific types of video technologies that are best for homework, student revisions of their signing, and ASL assessments? What are the best ways to deliver practice resources for students (e.g., fingerspelling exercises, lessons on grammar, and the presentation of lexical items)? Should video materials (e.g., Internet, DVDs, etc.) allow the student to control the speed at which the language is being produced? Should English translations be presented, side-by-side, with the ASL videos? Are classroom technologies that are designed for assisting with instruction (e.g., Smartboard) effective for facilitating the teaching and learning of ASL and other visual languages? It may be the case that such technologies actually hamper the visual communication strategies that are being acquired by the novice learner of ASL.[26] And, what are the types of video and computer-based resources that are effective for online teaching of a signed language?

Inquiry into these three broad areas would provide ASL instructors and curriculum designers with much needed information for continually improving methods of ASL instruction. In addition, such work could serve to highlight similarities and differences between the teaching of signed and spoken languages; this is information that all language professionals—instructors and researchers alike—may benefit from having. ASL instruction can learn a great deal from what has been done in the field of SLA, and instructors and researchers of spoken language could also benefit from understanding how visual-gestural language is most effectively taught. It is likely that the popularity of ASL will continue, and there is much work to be done.

ACKNOWLEDGMENTS

I would like to thank an anonymous reviewer, the editor of *ARAL*, and various colleagues for their feedback on earlier versions of this article. Among those colleagues are Carrie Lou Garberoglio, Richard P. Meier, and Keith Walters. Any errors in interpreting previous writings or oversights in the inclusion of particular works are my own.

NOTES

1 As is customary, the use of "Deaf" (with capitalized "D") refers to a cultural and linguistic minority that uses signed language for daily communication, whereas "deaf" (with lower-case "d") refers solely to audiological status.

2 As noted, ASL is also the signed language of English-speaking Canada. However, most of the statistics reported in this article come from data about the teaching of ASL in the U.S.

3 Welles (2004) reported that there was a 432% increase in enrollments between 1998 and 2002, but she also noted that that figure is partially a result of differences in reporting. In 2002, the survey asked specifically for ASL enrollments, whereas in 1998, ASL enrollments that were reported were included in the category labeled *other languages*.

4 This ratio includes courses in two- and four-year institutions, with an average mean for all languages reported at approximately five to one. The only language that approaches ASL in a similar comparison is Italian, listed at a ratio of 10 introductory courses for every advanced course.

5 The vast majority of adult learners of ASL are hearing individuals, though occasionally, deaf or hard-of-hearing students who have had limited or no exposure to ASL will take ASL foreign language courses alongside their hearing peers. This is sometimes done because the students find spoken/written foreign languages too difficult to learn or perhaps the students feel they would like to improve their ASL skills. In most cases, Deaf students have never taken an ASL course before, which is unlike the common practice of hearing students taking English (or another language) throughout their school career. This fact is changing, however, since some schools for the Deaf are beginning to offer ASL courses to their Deaf and hard-of-hearing students.

6 Internet searches revealed few mentions of ASL within SLA journals and at SLA conferences. However, research on the teaching of other signed languages to hearing adults is emerging (see Mertzani, 2010; Napier, Leigh, & Nann, 2007). Additionally, less-pedagogically oriented literature on SLA and sign languages has had an important impact on theoretical discussions—specifically with respect to the critical period hypothesis (e.g., see Mayberry, 1993; Newport, 1990).

7 Ironically, the writing of this manuscript by a hearing person who is a late learner of ASL and not by a Deaf instructor or researcher of ASL may be viewed as evidence of the types of power differentials that have existed—and continue to exist—between Deaf and hearing people for years.

8 *Audism*, according to various sources, was originally coined by Tom Humphries, an academic who is among the early developers of ASL curricula for hearing students.

9 Some may consider the dynamics between Deaf and hearing individuals as representative of socio-political factors as opposed to what has been described here as socio-cultural matters. In either case, the role of power differentials between Deaf and hearing individuals is a notable characteristic of such interactions.

10 A few systems for transcribing signed languages have been invented, but they are typically used for research purposes. One notable exception is SignWriting (www.signwriting.org), which is a system that uses visual symbols to represent various components of signs. The use of SignWriting appears to be more widespread than it was in the past (and it has been used to document material from various sign languages), though it is typically not used within the ASL L2 classroom for pedagogical purposes.

11 Whereas this section highlights ways in which signed languages might pattern in unique ways, there are also multiple linguistic similarities between signed and some spoken languages (e.g., aspects of word order, lack of copular constructions, and many null-subject realizations, to name a few). It might be useful to examine how pedagogies are similar across signed and spoken languages for the teaching of such devices.

12 The ability to inflect certain signs without the use of sequential affixes and the use of various parts of the body (i.e., the hands, the head, and the torso) for meaning creation not only represent differences between signed and spoken languages, but also may be the primary reasons why it is not entirely possible to faithfully produce a signed and spoken language simultaneously. Generally, spoken languages differ in aspects of their grammar (e.g., word order and morphological processes) from signed languages, and that is why signing and speaking at the same time results in ungrammatical or incomplete productions of one or both languages (e.g., Tevenal & Villanueva, 2009). If sequential phenomena were similar across modalities, the production timing of corresponding constructions from signed and spoken languages could presumably match up and serve as a way for hearing learners to use their L1 for learning the signed language. Unfortunately, signing and speaking results in signed segments that most closely match the spoken language word order but omit or incorrectly portray much needed grammatical information from the signed language.

13 For example, many people were unaware of the richness and complexity of ASL during the early years of ASL instruction. In addition, attitudinal factors that surrounded ASL and the Deaf community (e.g., see Lane, Hoffmeister, & Bahan, 1996) may have played a role in the ways in which ASL was taught.

14 Another related point is that ASL students who aim to become ASL-English interpreters are faced, during their training, with the dual task of learning ASL and learning how to interpret between two languages. Many interpreter training programs are found at community colleges though more four-year programs are now available, which means that some ASL students are exposed to little more than two years of ASL instruction before they find themselves in professional interpreting positions. To my knowledge, this situation is not mirrored in the field of spoken language interpretation or translation. Anecdotally speaking, the result for ASL is that many novice interpreters do not have the ASL skills to perform

adequately in their interpreting assignments. Unfortunately, the Deaf community has encountered this reality for decades.

15 Presumably, one potential benefit of having to learn a manual phonology as an adult is that students do not experience interference from their L1 phonology. However, if one considers vocabulary learning, a student would not have the benefit of capitalizing on cognates between languages for bootstrapping their acquisition of new words.

16 In the U.S. alone, if one considers that nearly 92,000 students are taking ASL at colleges and universities (Furman, Goldberg, & Lusin, 2010), and there are 701 high schools that offer ASL (Rosen, 2008), a conservative estimate of the number of ASL instructors throughout the U.S. would be 1,850. This figure represents one ASL teacher per high school and college/university instructors teaching four courses with 20 students in each course. However, this does not take into account part-time instructors who teach fewer than four classes at any one institution.

17 See www.aslta.org for more information about these matters.

18 Kanda & Fleischer (1988) put forth suggestions for the profiles of ASL instructors. Additionally, see www.aslta.org for information related to this topic.

19 Rosen (2010) notes that more than three-fourths of high schools throughout the country use more than one curriculum for instruction, and more than half of the teachers in his survey (from 701 public high schools) make their own materials. In most cases, the teacher-created materials are likely to augment existing curricula.

20 Rosen (2008) reported only on ASL instruction of ASL in high schools. Figures for college and university instruction are not currently available.

21 Presumably, Rosen's (2010) survey allowed respondents to indicate all the curricula that they use, which results in percentages that total more than 100%.

22 Fingerspelling is common in ASL, whereas it may not be use to the same extent in other signed languages. By some accounts, fingerspelled words comprise between 5–15% of the lexical items in discourse (Morford & MacFarlane, 2003; Padden & Gunsauls, 2003).

23 Another aspect of ASL that has received attention lately with respect to the development of resources for teaching and learning is the so-called classifiers of the language. As one example, TreeHouse Video has created various materials that focus on classifier constructions are designed to complement traditional ASL

curricula (Lessard, 2002).

24 Presumably, Wilcox and Wilcox (1997) were referring to not having curricula with measurable student outcomes that could be evaluated across language programs and schools.

25 There is growing interest in examining the use of co-speech gesture as a language learning resource. For example, see Gullberg (2010).

26 I thank an anonymous reviewer for commenting on the use of Smartboard, a topic that has been discussed in an online listserve of ASL instructors.

ANNOTATED BIBLIOGRAPHY

Mertzani, M. (Ed.). (2010). *Sign language teaching and learning.* Papers from the 1st Symposium in applied sign linguistics. Centre for Deaf Studies, University of Bristol, 24–26 September 2009. Bristol, UK: Centre for Deaf Studies, University of Bristol.

Mertzani presents a collection of writings from authors representing signed language teaching throughout Europe and other continents. The collection, representing talks given at the 1st Symposium in Applied Sign Linguistics held at the University of Bristol in 2009, highlights teaching methods and resources, teacher training, linguistic phenomena, and pedagogical approaches to teaching signed language (including online approaches). This work represents an important contribution to an emerging field of applied sign linguistics because of the diversity of perspectives that it includes, the multiple sign languages that it covers, and the possibilities for future research that it highlights.

Napier, J., Leigh, G., & Nann, S. (2007). Teaching sign language to hearing parents of Deaf children: An action research process. *Deafness and Education International, 9,* 83–100.

Napier and colleagues provide a detailed account of a program developed in Australia for teaching Australian Sign Language (Auslan) to hearing parents of Deaf children. This population of learners is often overlooked because many of them are not among the typical students enrolled in signed language courses at colleges and universities. An important facet of the Napier et al. study is the process used to develop their curriculum: they sought input from various groups of interested parties: professionals with expertise in Auslan and services for deaf individuals (e.g., early language intervention programs with hearing parents), teachers (of Auslan to hearing students and general educators of deaf children), and the parents of deaf children. The authors report on the program that was developed and some of the teaching resources that were produced as part of that process. Details of this work are invaluable and could be used for future research on the efficacy of such curricula.

Peterson, R. (2009). *The unlearning curve: Learning to learn American Sign Language*. Burtonsville, MD: Sign Media.

This book details Peterson's doctoral dissertation research: a look at various perceptions that hearing students have about the learning of ASL. The author argues that his results show that many students approach the learning of ASL with many misconceptions, and part of the process of learning, for those students, is modifying those preconceived notions in order to more successfully learn the language. Peterson used a survey approach, and his sample size is impressive (over 1,100 students). Additionally, Peterson brings years of experience interacting with the Deaf community and time as an administrator of ASL programs to his perspective about how ASL learners can be more successful. As with other suggested pedagogical approaches, in future research it would be worthwhile to compare students whose learning has been supported by learning *about* ASL (either before or early in the learning of the language) and those students who do not have the benefit of the material covered in this book.

REFERENCES

Ashton, G., Cagle, K., Kurz, K., Newell, W., Peterson, R., & Zinza, J. (in press). Standards for Learning American Sign Language (ASL) in the 21st Century. In *Standards for Foreign Language Learning in the 21st Century*. Yonkers, NY: National Standards in Foreign Language Education Project.

Baker-Shenk, C., & Cokely, D. (1980). *American sign language*. Washington, DC: Gallaudet University Press.

Bienvenu, M. J. (2009). Revolution at work: ASL curriculum re-visited. *Deaf Studies Digital Journal, 1*. Retrieved from http: //dsdj.gallaudet.edu/index.php?issue = 1

Bosworth, R. G., & Emmorey, K. (2010). Effects of iconicity and semantic relatedness on lexical access in American Sign Language. *Journal of Experimental Psychology: Learning, Memory, & Cognition, 36*, 1573–1581.

Buisson, G. J. (2007). Using online glossing lessons for accelerated instruction in ASL for preservice Deaf education majors. *American Annals of the Deaf, 152*, 331–343.

Caccamise, F., & Hicks, D. (1978). *American Sign Language in a bilingual, bicultural context.* Proceedings of the Second National Symposium on Sign Language Research and Teaching, Coronado, CA. Bethesda, MD: National Association of the Deaf.

Cassell, J. (1996). *Bravo ASL! Curriculum.* Eden Prairie, MH: Sign Enhancers.

Cooper, S. B., Reisman, J. I., & Watson, D. (2008). The status of sign language instruction in institutions of higher education, 1994–2004. *American Annals of the Deaf, 153*, 78–88.

Frishberg, N. (1988). Signers of tales: The case for literary status of an unwritten language. *Sign Language Studies, 59*, 149–170.

Furman, N., Goldberg, D., & Lusin, N. (2010). Enrollments in languages other than English in United States institutions of higher education, Fall 2010. Retrieved from http: //www.mla.org/2009_enrollmentsurvey

Gullberg, M. (2010). Methodological reflections on gesture analysis in second language acquisition and bilingualism research. *Second Language Research 26*, 75–102.

Humphries, T., & Padden, C.,(1992). *Learning American Sign Language.* Englewood Cliffs, NJ: Prentice Hall.

Humphries, T., Padden C., & O'Rourke T. (1980). *A basic course in American Sign Language.* Carrollton, TX: TJ Publishers.

Jacobowitz, E. L. (2005). American Sign Language teacher-preparation programs in the United States. *Sign Language Studies, 6*, 76–110.

Jacobs, R. (1996). Just how hard is it to learn ASL: The case for ASL as a truly foreign language. In C. Lucas (Ed.), *Multicultural aspects of sociolinguistics in deaf communities* (pp. 183–226). Washington, DC: Gallaudet University Press.

Kanda, J., & Fleischer, L. (1988). Who is qualified to teach American Sign Language? *Sign Language Studies, 59*, 183–194.

Kemp, M. (1998). Why is learning American Sign Language a challenge? *American Annals of the Deaf, 143*, 255–259.

Klima, E., & Bellugi, U. (1979). *The signs of language.* Cambridge, MA: Harvard University Press.

Ladd, P. (2003). *Understanding Deaf culture: In search of Deafhood.* Bristol, UK: Multilingual Matters.

Lane, H. (1999). *The mask of benevolence: Disabling the Deaf community.* San Diego, CA: Dawn Sign Press.

Lane, H., Hoffmeister, R., & Bahan, B. (1996). *Journey into the Deaf world.* San Diego, CA: Dawn Sign Press.

Lessard, P. (2002). *Classifiers: A closer look.* San Francisco, CA: Treehouse Video LLC.

Mayberry, R. I. (1993). First-language acquisition after childhood differs from second-language acquisition: The case of American Sign Language. *Journal of Speech and Hearing Research, 36,* 51–68.

McDermid, C. (2009). Two cultures, one programme: Deaf professors as subaltern? *Deafness and Education International, 11,* 221–249.

Meier, R. P. (1987). Elicited imitation of verb agreement in American Sign Language: Iconically or morphologically determined? *Journal of Memory and Language, 26,* 362–376.

Meier, R., Mauk, C., Cheek, A., & Moreland, C. (2008). The form of children's early signs: Iconic or motoric determinants? *Language, Learning, and Development, 4,* 1–36.

Mertzani, M. (Ed.). (2010). *Sign language teaching and learning.* Papers from the 1st Symposium in applied sign linguistics. Centre for Deaf Studies, University of Bristol, 24–26 September 2009. Bristol, UK: Centre for Deaf Studies, University of Bristol.

Metzger, M. (1995). Constructed dialogue and constructed action in American Sign Language. In C. Lucas (Ed.), *Sociolinguistics in deaf communities* (pp. 255–271). Washington, DC: Gallaudet University Press.

Morford, J. P., & MacFarlane, J. (2003). Frequency characteristics of American Sign Language. *Sign Language Studies, 3,* 213–225.

Napier, J., Leigh, G., & Nann, S. (2007). Teaching sign language to hearing parents of Deaf children: An action research process. *Deafness and Education International, 9,* 83–100.

National Standards of Foreign Language Education. (2010). Retrieved from http: //www.actfl. org/files/public/StandardsforFLLexecsumm_rev.pdf

Newport, E. L. (1990). Maturational constraints on language learning. *Cognitive Science, 14,* 11–28.

Padden, C., & Gunsauls, C. (2003). How the alphabet came to be used in a sign language. *Sign Language Studies, 4,* 10–33.

Peterson, R. (2009). *The unlearning curve: Learning to learn American Sign Language.* Burtonsville, MD: Sign Media.

Quinto-Pozos, D. (2005). Factors that influence the acquisition of ASL for interpreting students. In M. Marschark, R. Peterson, & E. A. Winston (Eds.), *Sign language interpreting and interpreter education: Directions for research and practice,* (pp.159–187). New York, NY: Oxford University Press.

Quinto-Pozos, D. (2007). Can constructed action be considered obligatory? *Lingua 117,* 1285–1314.

Rosen, R. S. (2008). American Sign Language as a foreign language in U.S. high schools: State of the art. *The Modern Language Journal, 92,* 10–38.

Rosen, R. S. (2010). American Sign Language curricula: A review. *Sign Language Studies, 10,* 348–381.

Rutherford, S. (1988). The culture of American Deaf people. *Sign Language Studies*, *59*, 129–146.

Schembri, A. (2003). Rethinking "classifiers" in signed languages. In K. Emmorey (Ed.), *Perspectives on classifier constructions in sign languages* (pp. 3–34). Mahwah, NJ: Lawrence Erlbaum Associates.

Schornstein, R. (2005). Teaching ASL in the university: One teacher's journey. *Sign Language Studies*, *5*, 398–414.

Smith, C., Lentz, E. & Mikos, K. (1988). *Signing naturally.* San Diego, CA: Dawn Sign Press.

Supalla, T. (1986). The classifier system in American Sign Language. In C. Craig (Ed.), *Noun classification and categorization* (pp. 181–214). Philadelphia, PA: John Benjamins.

Taub, S. F. (2001). *Language from the body. Iconicity and metaphor in American Sign Language.* Cambridge, UK: Cambridge University Press.

Tevenal, S. & Villanueva, M. (2009). Are you getting the message? The effects of SimCom on the message received by Deaf, Hard of Hearing, and Hearing students. *Sign Language Studies*, *9*, 266–286.

Thoryk, R. (2010). A call for improvement: The need for research-based materials in American Sign Language education. *Sign Language Studies*, *11*, 1.

Welles, E. B. (2004). Foreign language enrollments in United States institutions of higher education, Fall 2002. *ADFL Bulletin*, *35*, 1–20.

Wilcox, S. (2010). Universities that accept ASL in fulfillment of foreign language requirements. Retrieved from http: //web.mac.com/swilcox/UNM/univlist.html

Wilcox, S., & Wilcox, P. P. (1997). *Learning to see. Teaching American Sign Language as a second language.* Washington, DC: Gallaudet University Press.

Zinza, J. E. (2006). *Master ASL!* Burtonsville, MD: Sign Media.

SECTION C: TOPICS IN INTEGRATED APPROACHES

Research in Language-Literature Instruction: Meeting the Call for Change?

Kate Paesani

The purpose of this review is to assess whether recent scholarship on language-literature instruction—the deliberate integration of language development and literary study at all levels of the foreign language curriculum—within the context of U.S. institutions of higher education reflects shifts in thinking regarding the role of literature in foreign language curricula. These shifts have come in response to the 2007 Report of the Modern Language Association Ad Hoc Committee on Foreign Languages, which recommended replacing the traditional two-tiered program structure with more coherent curricula that merge language and content, and to the general questioning of communicative language teaching as a viable method for language instruction and adequate preparation for advanced-level work in a foreign language. Current approaches to language-literature instruction and foreign language curriculum design favor multimodal language development that places equal importance on oral and written language and interpretative interaction with literature to construct textual meaning and establish form-meaning connections. This review surveys empirical and classroom practice research on literature in language courses and language in literature courses and concludes with a consideration of larger curricular issues and areas for future research.

For more than a century, literature has been an important component of foreign language (FL) programs in U.S. institutions of higher education and a valuable tool for understanding language, culture, and history (see Paran [2008] for a discussion of the value of literature and research arguing for and against its use in FL learning). During the early part of the 20th century, literature was the primary object of study and the ultimate goal of FL study, in part because of the nearly exclusive focus on reading and writing. As a result, literature held a place of prestige in the academic community and served as a source of moral and ideational inspiration and content. Yet, with the advent of audiolingualism in the postwar years, the onset of communicative language teaching in the 1970s, and the increased focus on oral competence that resulted, the role of literature in FL study began to shift. Instead of solely serving as the end goal of FL study, literature had also become a way to provide an authentic look into target language cultures and a means of learning the language itself (Kramsch & Kramsch, 2000).

According to Nance (2010), the end of literature's unquestioned place of prestige at the end of the 20th century was due in part to the fact that literature instruction and curriculum structure continued to follow the same model that had been in place for decades: adherence to the literary canon and a textcentric, transmission model of literary interpretation. In contrast, multiple developments in language instruction took place over the years to respond to new findings in second language (L2) acquisition research. Today, informed by empirical and classroom practice research on language-literature instruction and literary scholarship extending well beyond the canon, the profession is rethinking the role of literature in FL programs. In particular, a recent report of the Modern Language Association (MLA) Ad Hoc Committee on Foreign Languages (hereinafter, MLA Report, 2007), "Foreign Languages and Higher Education: New Structures for a Changed World," which recommended creating articulated, coherent language-literature curricula, and related scholarship questioning the usefulness of communicative language teaching (CLT) as an approach to language development, have fueled discussions about reconfigured FL curricula and the role of literature in developing learners' ability to engage in multimodal language use and textual thinking. As such, in the 21st century, this reconfigured view has allowed literature to reclaim its primacy at all levels of FL instruction. Indeed, as Swaffar and Arens claimed,

> Increasingly, FL acquisition research suggests that literature is the necessary textual environment for creating strong readers, readers who have the cognitive strategies and linguistic resources to comprehend and interpret a work as well as an aesthetic object as a complicated act of communication within a culture. (2005, p. 79)

The purpose of this review is to assess whether recent empirical and classroom practice scholarship in language-literature instruction, defined as the deliberate integration of language development and literary study at all levels of the curriculum, reflects shifts in thinking regarding the role of literature in FL curricula. This review is restricted to FL instruction in U.S. institutions of higher education not only to reflect the content of current debates in the applied linguistics literature but also to avoid overlap with other recent review articles on language-literature instruction. These articles have focused on pedagogical research in English as a second language and English as a foreign language (ESL/EFL) contexts (Carter, 2007); empirical reports and their pedagogical implications in ESL and FL contexts (Paran, 2008); research developments across the history of one journal (Kramsch & Kramsch, 2000); language-literature instruction with a specific focus on poetry (Melin, 2010); and teaching reading, with literature as only a peripheral consideration (Bernhardt, 2005; Grabe, 2004). The research on language-literature instruction in ESL/EFL contexts, which reports on studies in the United Kingdom, the United States, Europe, and Asia, is considerable and touches on numerous issues such as English for academic purposes (e.g., Minkoff, 2006; Viswamohan & Torche, 2007), links between reading literature and writing (e.g., Hirvela, 2001, 2005), and literary stylistics (e.g., Watson & Zyngier, 2007).

THE LANGUAGE-LITERATURE DIVIDE

Starting in the mid-1980s and continuing through the 1990s, scholars in applied linguistics produced a large body of research on what is now known as the language-literature divide in university FL programs (e.g., Barnett, 1991; Bernhardt, 1995; Henning, 1993; Hoffman & James, 1986; Kramsch, 1985; Muyskens, 1983; Schultz, 1995). This divide is characterized by fixed lines of demarcation between language study in lower-level courses and literary study in upper-level courses, the assumption being that once students have completed lower-level language courses, they are ready to carry out the advanced-level tasks expected in literature courses. However, as Byrnes and Maxim (2004) demonstrated, this assumption has not been realized. In fact, lack of attention to literary texts in lower-level courses and to language development in upper-level courses has made advanced work in literature inaccessible to many undergraduate students

(Bernhardt, 1995; Schultz, 1995).[1]

The sources of the language-literature divide are numerous. In 1967, the MLA created the American Council on the Teaching of Foreign Languages (ACTFL), signaling a long-standing professional and symbolic rift between language and literature—and those who teach each subject—in FL departments (Donato & Brooks, 2004). This rift corresponded with a growing sense of decreased responsibility on the part of literature faculty toward language development (James, 2000) and the resultant administrative and personnel divisions that persist today (e.g., language courses staffed by graduate student or adjunct instructors, and few tenured or tenure-track faculty teaching introductory courses). In addition, different pedagogical goals grew out of this rift in each camp: functional, interactive language use on the one hand, and literary-cultural interpretation on the other. The view of literary analysis as the ultimate goal of language instruction compounded the problem and reinforced a number of assumptions: Literature should not be taught before students attain a high level of language proficiency; language is merely a tool for analyzing and appreciating literature; and students in literature classes deepen language knowledge passively by reading and listening to lectures (Barnett, 1991; Hall, 2005; Muyskens, 1983). Kramsch (1985) summed up the problem as follows: Communicative and literary goals in FL departments are at odds with one another; the former encourages two-way communication and negotiation, and the latter treats literary texts "as finished products, to be unilaterally decoded, analyzed, and explained or ... to illustrate grammatical rules and enrich the reader's vocabulary" (p. 356).

CALLS FOR CHANGE

Starting in the late 1990s, discussions about the language-literature divide began to shift toward a focus on larger curricular issues such as program redesign to promote development of advanced-level FL abilities through the study of texts, literary and otherwise (e.g., Byrnes, 1998; Byrnes & Maxim, 2004; Paesani, 2004; Scott & Tucker, 2002; Swaffar & Arens, 2005). This shift was punctuated by the MLA Report (2007), and the stream of responses to its recommendations (e.g., Geisler, 2008; Maxim, 2009; Pfeiffer, 2008; Pireddu, 2008; Porter, 2009; Walther, 2009; Wellmon, 2008). The report recommended "replacing the two-tiered language-literature structure with a broader and more coherent curriculum in which language, culture, and literature are taught as a continuous whole" (MLA Report, p. 3). Further, the report proposed that this reform be accomplished through development of students' "translingual and transcultural competence," or "the ability to operate between languages" (pp. 3–4), and increased emphasis on cultural narratives present in FL texts such as poetry, prose, film, and journalism. Within this proposed structure, literature, therefore, is one of many text types that comprise FL study.[2]

The call for curricular reform in the MLA Report and elsewhere has been coupled with a general questioning over the past decade of CLT as a viable method for language instruction and of communicative competence as adequate preparation for advanced-level work in a FL (e.g., Byrnes, 2006; Byrnes & Maxim, 2004; Schultz, 2009). CLT has come to be associated primarily with interactive, transactional, oral language use that encourages student recall of information rather than analysis and critical evaluation of that information (Schultz, 2009; Swaffar, 2006). However, this practice does not articulate well with the kind of language use that FL departments consider desirable to carry out their intellectual and academic missions. Indeed, as Byrnes (2006) argued, because of its propensity to separate language from literary-cultural content, a focus on CLT "may unintentionally sustain the long-standing bifurcation of FL programs into language courses and content courses with all the attendant negative consequences" (p. 244).

Following Swaffar's (2006) recommendation that FL programs redefine communicative competence as the ability to read, write, listen, speak, and reflect critically and intelligently about a culture's multiple facets, recent research has argued in favor of situating texts at the center of the curriculum and developing multimodal language abilities, such that reading, writing, listening, and speaking are viewed as complementary rather than separate skills (e.g., Byrnes, Crane, Maxim, & Sprang, 2006; Kern, 2008; Kern & Schultz, 2005; Maxim, 2008, 2009). Moreover, the text-centric transmission model of literary instruction, in which texts are seen as having a fixed interpretation, is slowly being replaced by approaches that encourage interpretative interaction with texts representing the literary canon and beyond and that highlight "the sociological, cultural, and historical dimensions of the literary" (Kern & Schultz, 2005, p. 383). These changes in curricular and pedagogical thinking are major advances in discussions about the language-literature divide and move the profession closer to a merging of the two sides. To determine whether these changes have been reflected to date in the research, I turn now to a critical summary of scholarship presenting empirical and classroom practice perspectives on the use of literature in language courses followed by a critical summary of the role of language in literature courses.[3] It should be noted from the outset that very little of the existing scholarship on language-literature pedagogy is empirical in nature; most published articles provide examples of pedagogical and curricular best practices and policy statements.

LITERATURE IN LANGUAGE COURSES

The traditional structure of language courses includes an orientation toward the development of communicative competence, a preference for oral versus written language use, explicit focus on language forms, reliance on language-oriented textbooks, and little systematic linking of form and meaning through the study of FL texts. However, as the research reviewed thus far suggests, the nature of collegiate language instruction is changing, and literature is seen as an important element in this change. Numerous scholars have argued over the past decade for the integration of literature from the very start of language study (e.g., Kern, 2008; Paesani, 2004, 2005; Walther, 2007). For instance, Walther (2007) suggested that literature be given a greater role in introductory-level courses to show how language works in context and to draw studentss' attention to connections between language and communicative intent. Likewise, Scott and Huntington (2007, 2008) argued that studying literature in introductory language courses can help students gain insight into FL cultures, understand differing cultural perspectives, develop critical thinking skills, and interpret textual content. Their empirical research investigated the role of literature within the *Standards for Foreign Language Learning in the 21st Century* (ACTFL, 2006).[4] Their first study (Scott & Huntington, 2007), which focused on the interpretive mode of communication, investigated students' interpretive processes when reading a Francophone poem in teacher-moderated versus student-centered small group discussions. Results showed that students were able to engage in interpretive communication and access the content of literature in teacher-moderated discussions. Their second study (Scott & Huntington, 2008), which focused on the cultures standard, compared students' understanding of and attitudes about Francophone culture after reading a fact sheet versus a Francophone poem. Results showed that the group who read the poem had more personal reactions to culture and were more likely to engage in discussions about cultural content. Both studies underscored the importance of incorporating literary texts in introductory FL courses.

Maxim (2006b) and Stewart and Santiago (2006) provided further empirical support for the integration of multimodal language use with textual thinking, literary analysis, and development of academic literacy. Maxim's study on the use of extensive reading in a first-semester German course showed that reading a novel as part of the curriculum did not interfere with students' linguistic development. Indeed, students who spent half of class time reading a novel and half of class time doing communicative development activities scored at least as well on departmental exams testing grammar and vocabulary as those students who only completed communicative development activities. Stewart and Santiago integrated a novel into intermediate-level language courses through an instructional unit shaped by the *Standards*. Their case study included two groups of students, one consisting of first language (L1) English learners of Spanish and one consisting of L1 Spanish learners of English who read a novel (in their respective L2) about a bicultural Puerto Rican American's search for identity in the United States. Stewart and Santiago found that the study of the literary text encouraged a complex level of cultural understanding and sensitivity and had a lasting and profound effect on both student groups.

In spite of such empirical support for more fully integrating multimodal language development with textual thinking and literary analysis, some attempts at integrating literature into the language classroom are instrumental in nature, wherein literature is viewed only as a tool for developing language proficiency. In such approaches, little attention is paid to the social, historical, and cultural content of literary texts or to the development of students' analytical and critical thinking skills. In their study of 16 course syllabi from first-and second-semester Spanish language courses and instructor questionnaire responses, Alvstad and Castro (2009) found that literature was indeed used instrumentally. In the syllabi examined—which included assignments, schedules, course descriptions, and objectives—the concepts of literature and culture were simplified or not clearly defined. Furthermore, the objectives for literature reflected the course objectives as a whole, such as development of grammatical and lexical knowledge and improved written and oral language skills. Two examples of instrumental uses of literature are evident in scholarship on classroom best practices as well. Paesani (2005) proposed a model of grammar instruction that uses literary texts as comprehensible input in introductory language courses. Although some of the activities in the sample lesson plan asked students to think about the content, themes, and role of narrative voice in a French poem, literature was used primarily as an inductive presentation of grammatical forms and as a model for student writing. Davidheiser (2007), who used fairy tales in introductory German courses to teach European culture and social practices, also presented an instructional sequence focused on students' language development. Through the reading of shortened and linguistically modified tales, Davidheiser suggested that learners engage in retelling activities for oral and written language development, sentence creation activities for grammar development, and true/false or yes/no question answering for listening development. Davidheiser also outlined an approach to fairy tales in advanced literature courses that, he claimed, integrates language development. However, the brief description of the approach does not make clear that language development is explicitly addressed.

Apart from these isolated examples, the majority of scholarship on literature in language instruction fully integrates textual thinking and literary analysis with multimodal language development across instructional levels. This work can be grouped into to two major pedagogical emphases: process-oriented and literacy-based.

Process-Oriented Approaches

Process-oriented approaches are concerned with the cognitive act of reading and the ways in which learners engage in both top-down and bottom-up reading processes. Process-oriented pedagogy seeks to engage learners in the act of reading through strategy instruction and structured lessons that include pre-reading activities to activate background knowledge; reading activities to focus on textual content, features, and organization; and postreading activities to expand on learners' knowledge and encourage creative language production. Scholarship on process-oriented best practices for literature instruction in language classes include Barrette, Paesani, and Vinall (2010) and Paesani (2006a, 2006b, 2009). Barrette et al. (2010) argued in favor of interweaving literary analysis, stylistics, and culture at all levels of the FL curriculum through the use of literature. They outlined an intermediate-level process-oriented lesson plan for a Spanish short story that develops multimodal language competence (reading, writing, and speaking) as well as analytical and critical thinking skills, and then provided suggestions for using the same story at introductory and advanced levels. The series of articles by Paesani (2006a, 2006b, 2009) focused on the integration of literature into advanced language courses, in which textual thinking is usually absent. In two articles, Paesani (2006a, 2009) explored the uses of Raymond Queneau's *Exercices de style* (1947), which tells the same story 99 times using various linguistic and stylistic devices, as a way to spiral literature into an advanced grammar course, develop critical thinking and analytical skills, and improve writing competence. In both cases, sample lesson plans focused on the study of grammar and stylistic features through text comparison and the development of a writing portfolio modeled on the literary texts studied. Similarly, in the third article, Paesani (2006b) presented a process-oriented instructional sequence whose goals were to heighten learners' awareness of language varieties, develop multimodal language competence, and incorporate cultural and literary content into a phonetics and pronunciation course. Several text types in addition to literature (music, film, maps, and images) were explored and compared in instructional activities.

The pedagogical approaches outlined in Maxim (2006a), making the case for reading and writing poetry in introductory courses to give learners a voice, and Maxim (2006b), arguing for the development of textual thinking and academic literacy through extensive reading, serve to segue between process-oriented and literacy-based literature instruction in language courses. Although not explicitly labeled as process-oriented, Maxim's (2006a) contextualized approach to poetry, modeled on Maley and Duff (1989), included prereading, reading, and postreading activities. Moreover, the approach is characterized by five tenets, many of which reflect a literacy orientation: development of students' creative self expression, de-emphasis of the native speaker model as the ultimate goal of language learning, recognition of students' multicompetence (in L1 and L2), encouragement of playfulness in language learning, and increased dialogue between students and instructor. Likewise, Maxim (2006b) outlined a pedagogy for the extensive reading of a novel, modeled on Swaffar, Arens, and Byrnes (1991), that begins with prereading and then proceeds with the following four reading and postreading steps: initial reading with attention to major events, their organization, and their linguistic expression; location of details and the language used to express them; reproduction of textual language through summary writing; and application of real-world knowledge to assess cultural implications in the text. In both articles, Maxim's focus on genre, on form-meaning connections, and on historically and culturally situated text interpretation further illustrates the literacy orientation of the pedagogical approaches, as well as their careful, process-oriented integration of language and literature.

Literacy-Based Approaches

Literacy-based approaches (e.g., Kern, 2000; New London Group, 1996; Swaffar & Arens, 2005) to FL instruction see texts as central to language development and promote "dynamic, culturally and historically situated practices of using and interpreting diverse written and spoken texts to fulfill particular social purposes" (Kern, 2000, p. 6). Unlike process-oriented approaches, which place primary importance on cognitive aspects of reading and strategies to encourage top-down and bottom-up text processing, literacy-based approaches place primary importance on the text itself, the sociocultural contexts that influence meaning, the form-meaning connections that contribute to interpreting textual messages, and the learner's interaction with the text to engage in meaning making. Reading and writing, often seen as separate skills in CLT and process-oriented approaches, are complementary and integral to meaning construction, which involves critical thinking about, and interpretation and transformation of discourse through, a variety of contexts and textual genres. Transmission models of literary analysis in which texts are viewed as having a fixed interpretation, therefore, do not figure into literacy-based instruction. Although a detailed discussion of literacy-based pedagogy is beyond the scope of this review, the brief description here and the summary of pedagogical practice research below make clear that literacy-based approaches aim to merge language and content in the ways recommended by the MLA Report (2007) and other calls for change.

Allen and Paesani (2010) explored the implications of the MLA Report recommendations for introductory FL courses and argued in favor of literacy-based pedagogy as a viable approach for implementing curricular reform. To support their position, they identified three challenges to realizing curricular change and fostering literacy in introductory courses—pedagogy, course content, and departmental buy-in—and proposed solutions to address each one. In addition, they proposed a sample literacy-based, second-semester French curriculum organized around literary and other texts and grounded in pedagogical activities designed to enhance students' linguistic development as well as their ability to think critically about textual content. Allen and Paesani concluded that in light of the changing landscape in U.S. higher education today, literacy-based approaches represent a means of keeping introductory FL courses relevant to students as well as the broader intellectual mission of the university.

Hoecherl-Alden (2006), Redmann (2008), and Schultz (2009) presented examples of pedagogical best practices for integrating literature into language courses through literacy-oriented instruction. Hoecherl-Alden (2006), for instance, argued for a multidimensional, workshop-style (i.e., student-centered) approach to intermediate language courses in which literary and cultural content form the basis of the curriculum, and language instruction is contextualized within discussions about literature and culture. Classroom activities in workshop-style courses may include dramatic readings of texts, cooperative tasks, peer evaluation and feedback, and reflective journaling. Such collaborative activities, Hoecherl-Alden argued, promote development of a classroom community that facilitates student-initiated analysis of and deeper connections with literary texts.

Redmann (2008), who also targeted intermediate-level language courses, developed a literacy-based approach with similar goals to Hoecherl-Alden (2006): to encourage textual analysis and interpretation, to make form-meaning connections, to create a discourse community in the classroom, and, ultimately, to help bridge the language-literature divide. She described a fourth-semester German course in which four young-adult novels complemented the regular textbook content. In her sample lesson plan, Redmann described activities such as a reading journal, summary writing, genre comparison, examination of linguistic features, creation of and responses to critical questions, and text reformulation that put literacy into practice.

Finally, Schultz (2009), whose sample intermediate-level language course was informed by the *Standards*, implemented a "literary approach to language learning" (p. 140). Her approach reflects a literacy orientation because it combines aspects of reader-response theory to promote individual, experiential interaction with texts and semiotic analysis to encourage form-meaning relationships. The French course she described, intended to meet the needs of students in a global studies course, is text-based and thematic. Students studied various genres, including literature, but applied strategies of literary analysis to all texts in an effort to bridge the language-literature divide and prepare them for more advanced FL study.

LANGUAGE IN LITERATURE COURSES

The traditional structure of literature courses includes an orientation toward the exclusive focus on literary analysis and the study of literary movements, themes, and genres, with little if any systematic or substantive focus on language development. Yet, as many researchers have pointed out (e.g., Allen, 2009a; Byrnes & Maxim, 2004; Maxim, 2008; Steinhart, 2006), it is unrealistic to expect that content be the sole focus of literature courses, given that students are still working toward advanced language abilities. According to Maxim (2008), attending to linguistic development only in language courses and failing to focus on language forms in literature courses "does not fully take into account the (con)textual nature of language use that permeates all levels of language use and that inherently requires grammar to be inextricably linked to meaning, and function to form" (p. 173). Indeed, because language is inherently meaning based, it must be studied in contextualized, discourse-length texts. Literature courses, therefore, seem an ideal venue for continued language development.

Empirical research on the nature of classroom discourse in literature courses underscores the need for continued attention to students' language development. Donato and Brooks (2004) studied classroom discourse in a fourth-year Spanish literature course to see whether literary discussions played a role in development of advanced language functions. They found that teacher talk dominated classroom discussions and that students did not have opportunities for elaborated responses. Donato and Brooks concluded that literature instructors should become aware of types of advanced-level speaking functions and provide opportunities for students to use them in a variety of discussion activities. Mantero (2006), in response to the findings in Donato and Brooks (2004) and Mantero (2002), proposed a theoretical model of instruction that provides opportunities for extended discourse and language learning in literature-based classrooms. Mantero's (2006) applied literacy in L2 education (ALL2E) model allows students to actively construct textual meaning through interactions with other students. As such, "an understanding and command of grammar emerges through dialogic interaction about and with the text" (p. 108).

Studies by Zyzik and Polio (2008) and Polio and Zyzik (2009) further support the need to develop students' speaking abilities and provide linguistic support in FL literature courses. Both examined form-focused classroom discourse in three fourth-year Spanish literature courses. Zyzik and Polio (2008) investigated the types and frequency of incidental focus on form (e.g., techniques that draw students' attention to language forms as problems arise) in classroom discourse and literature instructors' perceptions of its use. Polio and Zyzik (2009) investigated teacher and student perceptions of explicit focus on language development in literature classes. Similar to Donato and Brooks (2004), both studies found that teacher talk dominated classroom discussion and that students were not provided with adequate opportunities for negotiation or extended discourse. Zyzik and Polio (2008) and Polio and Zyzik (2009) concluded that pedagogical attention to advanced speaking functions with explicit linguistic support is necessary in literature courses and suggested several strategies for achieving this, including reading journals, vocabulary notebooks, weekly language-focused break-out sessions, and hybrid courses with online language support and development activities.

Given the empirical support for attention to language development in literature courses, it is important to see whether this need is addressed in scholarship on classroom practice. Overall, this scholarship reflects not only a focus on language development merged with literary study (as called for in the MLA Report [2007] and elsewhere) but also on interpretative interaction with texts. The majority of articles surveyed reflect literacy-based approaches to language in literature courses, however, a handful of articles share characteristics of process-oriented instruction. It is this latter group of articles to which I now turn.

Process-Oriented Approaches

The scholarship in this group presents a variety of models for integrating language in literature instruction: literary pragmatics (Warner, 2009), input-to-output (Weber-Fève, 2009), a *Standards*-based 3R (recognize, research, relate) model (McEwan, 2009), and literature for engagement (Nance, 2010). Although not all framed as process-oriented per se, the four approaches share a structure of prereading, reading, and postreading activities that focus on simultaneous engagement with literary language and content, as well as on strategy development and bottom-up/top-down text processing. Warner's (2009) model of literature instruction through literary pragmatics is the most explicitly language focused of the process-oriented approaches summarized here. According to Warner, literary pragmatics develops students' "critical linguistic awareness" (p. 162), or their understanding of complex aspects of culture and their relationship to language use. Warner's sample lesson plan for an intermediate-level German literature course integrates literary pragmatics and analysis. Activities include activation of students' knowledge about language conventions; recognition and discussion of text conventions; identification of the links connecting the narrator, conventions, and cultural meaning; and written responses to in-class discussion.

Weber-Fève (2009) proposed an input-to-output approach to literature instruction that combines reading, speaking, and writing activities with close reading to target language features. Although not focused on literary pragmatics, the types of activities Weber-Fève implemented in a third-year "introduction to French literature" course (e.g., activation of background information, focus on text conventions, and written responses to literary texts) share similarities with the activities presented in Warner (2009), as well as with process-oriented approaches to teaching literature.

Using the *Standards* as a general framework, McEwan (2009) proposed a 3R model of literature instruction to respond "to the call by postsecondary language instructors for greater precision in linguistic and literary analysis in standards-based instruction" (p. 146). The 3R model—recognize, research, relate—draws on both reader-response and schema theories. In the recognize (pre- and while-reading) stage, students identify linguistic and literary elements in a text that reflect the FL culture to reveal prior knowledge and areas for further investigation. In the research stage (while- and postreading), students identify and discuss underlying cultural perspectives in a text, link these to linguistic and literary elements, and choose a topic to investigate further. Finally, in the relate stage (postreading), students merge their newly acquired knowledge from the research stage with the linguistic and literary elements identified in the recognize stage to create a unique interpretation of the text. According to McEwan, this approach to literature promotes a multifaceted view of culture.

Although not explicitly focused on language forms, Nance (2010) proposed a four-stage pedagogy of teaching for engagement that responds to the mismatch between the structure of classroom discussion in language versus literature courses and develops students' speaking abilities. The first stage (prereading) is intended to activate students' prior knowledge and scaffold key terms and concepts. The activities in the second and third stages (while- and postreading) move from overall comprehension, summary, and observation to specific study of conventions, and finally to writing about literature by taking a position and formulating an argument. The final stage encourages students to read and discuss literature outside of the classroom context. Nance claimed that this pedagogy not only engages students in elaborated discourse, but it also encourages them to view the study of literature as a socially constructed intellectual endeavor.

Literacy-Based Approaches

As was the case with the pedagogical best practices scholarship on literature in language courses, literacy-based approaches are abundant in work on language in literature courses. Most of this work foregrounds the notion of genre, yet one exception is Redmann (2005), who proposed the use of interactive reading journals, an activity type consistent with literacy-based pedagogy, to bridge the language-literature divide, and discussed their use in intermediate and advanced literature courses. According to Redmann, interactive reading journals develop FL literacy because they require students to engage critically with literary texts and to interpret meaning individually and socially, all through the use of multiple language modalities (reading, speaking, writing). The multipart journal entries are carried out before, during, and after reading and discussion of literary texts and include tasks that activate background knowledge, develop summarizing skills, establish form-meaning connections, and encourage reflection.

Swaffar and Arens (2005), Kern and Schultz (2005), Bridges (2009), and Allen (2009c) explore in multiple ways the role of genre—understood broadly as the study of various culturally situated text types and the discourse conventions that characterize them—in literacy-based approaches to language in literature instruction. Swaffar and Arens (2005) proposed a holistic, genre-based curriculum that integrates language, literature, and various other genres across levels. Their literacy-based pedagogy is implemented through the reading matrix and the *précis*, structured reading tasks that lead from focused comprehension activities to specific language production activities through the identification of textual patterns and form-meaning connections. These genre-oriented activities facilitate the socially and culturally situated interpretation of texts and development of multimodal language abilities. Similarly, Kern and Schultz (2005) examined the role of literary analysis in the development of socially and culturally embedded FL literacy. They outlined a sample intermediate-level French reading and composition course focused on multimodal language development through the use of language in context. In the course, students derived meaning from literary texts and various other nonliterary genres such as film, newspaper articles, and paintings, and engaged in critical thinking, close reading, vocabulary building, and cultural and genre comparison activities. Bridges (2009) argued for an expanded definition of literature to include genres such as the graphic novel (see also Chute [2008], who made a case for the graphic novel as a form of literature in English curricula). Graphic novels, according to Bridges, are multimodal due to their visual and textual elements, contribute to students' advanced-level language development, and serve as a gateway to more traditional, canonical literary texts. Bridges incorporated a graphic novel into a third-year German literature course with a literacy-based approach; activities included brainstorming, completion of graphic organizers, genre analysis, directed reading, reflective journals, and story rewriting with the goal of encouraging students to make connections between language and its cultural context as they build textual meaning. Finally, Allen (2009c) used genre as a fundamental element in an advanced writing course organized around the reading and analysis of contemporary French texts, including various types of literature. In her integrated, multimodal approach, students examined rhetorical moves, discourse conventions, stylistic devices, and form-meaning connections, and then applied this knowledge to the development of a digital writing portfolio. In self-reporting of objectives from the beginning of the class and self-evaluation of achievement at the end of the class, half of students reported "that through completing reading and writing tasks in the course, they had greater awareness of how and why stylistic devices are used in texts," and two-thirds of students reported that class content and activities contributed to "new understandings of the relationships between reading and writing, reader and writer" (pp. 379–380).

Maxim (2008) and Eigler (2009) provided examples of language-literature instruction within the genre-based curriculum of the Georgetown University German Department.[5] Maxim (2008) explored the use of multiple genres, including literature, to develop advanced-level language abilities in a Level IV course on Berlin. An instructional unit in which students read a short story and scholarly analysis of the story is intended to develop students' skills in literary analysis, reading, and writing. In addition, Maxim argued, this merging of language and literary study prepares students for the type of work required in Level V courses such as that described by Eigler (2009), who demonstrated how the development of advanced speaking and writing abilities is integrated into literature instruction. Both sample courses employ a guided approach to literary texts, in which students develop FL literacy by activating appropriate background knowledge; reading and establishing a common understanding of the text through in-class discussion; examining word-, sentence-, and discourse-level patterns and form-meaning connections; and carrying out creative and elaborated writing tasks. This common instructional framework and complementary use of genre and activity types illustrate the curricular cohesion of this particular FL program. Indeed, Maxim and Eigler represent only two examples of a larger body of empirical, pedagogical, and policy-oriented scholarship documenting this innovative program that develops students' critical thinking, academic literacy, and multimodal language development across the 4-year undergraduate curriculum, and encompasses program goals, pedagogy, course sequencing, and assessment (e.g., Byrnes et al., 2006; Byrnes & Sinicrope, 2008; Rinner & Weigart, 2005; Sprang, 2008).

CONCLUSION

Taken together, the research on literature in language courses and language in literature courses demonstrates a move toward multimodal language development, interpretative interaction with texts, and the integration of language and literature at all levels of the collegiate FL curriculum. Indeed, this corpus of empirical and classroom practice articles on language-literature instruction reflects the calls for change outlined at the start of this review by confirming the importance of integrating literature and other text types from the start of language instruction, and of continued attention to language development until the end of students' course of study. Moreover, this scholarship demonstrates that a pedagogical focus on multimodal language development and critical engagement with texts across the curriculum, rather than an exclusive focus on CLT at lower levels and on text-centric literary interpretation at upper levels, contributes to carrying out the intellectual and academic missions of FL departments.

Literacy, in particular, emerges as the predominant framework for the type of curricular and pedagogical reform that effectively bridges the language-literature divide. As Kern (2004, p. 7) argued, "an overarching goal of literacy can provide a unifying focus by drawing students' attention to the interactions among form, context, and function in all their uses of language—whether they are speaking, listening, reading, or writing." Furthermore, as Swaffar and Arens (2005) claimed, a genre-based orientation facilitates the organization of a holistic, coherent curriculum anchored in texts, whose goal is the development of literacy. Yet, a literacy-based orientation need not be exclusive. A number of scholars have drawn links between literacy and the *Standards*, arguing that the vagueness in the *Standards* document regarding literature provides the flexibility to open up the narrow focus of literary studies through genre and to merge literature with other aspects of FL programs, namely, language and culture (Arens, 2008; Schultz, 2009). Indeed, Schultz (2009) claimed that this vagueness is a benefit, because it allows latitude regarding how to teach literary texts. She further argued that the connections and communities standards, in particular, relate to the interdisciplinary, multicultural, and global aspects of literature and, as such, to the MLA Report's (2007) notions of translingual and transcultural competence. Arens (2008) suggested the five content areas of the *Standards* serve as a heuristic for interactions among language, literature, and culture and proposed a reconfigured "Standards for Genre Learning" (pp. 46–48). Similarly, Kern (2004) claimed that literacy-based goals mesh well with the *Standards* framework and illustrated how the principles of literacy (cf. Kern, 2000) fall within the *Standards*' five content areas. Yet, in spite of this scholarship, it is not clear that U.S. institutions of higher educations are ready to embrace the *Standards* as an organizing framework (Scott, 2009). As Allen (2009a) noted, the *Standards* document decentralizes the role of literature, and this marginalization is troubling to FL departments, given the continued importance of literature in the curriculum and the literature-oriented research interests of many faculty members.

Regardless of whether FL programs organize curriculum and instruction around notions of genre and literacy or the five content areas of the *Standards*, further research is necessary to determine best practices for integrated language-literature instruction that moves students toward advanced-level FL abilities. As Carter (2007), Donato and Brooks (2004), and Kern and Schultz (2005) clearly stated, additional empirical research on the relationship between literature and FL acquisition is imperative. As the research reviewed here shows, important discoveries have emerged about the nature of classroom discourse and the importance of literature across the curriculum. Yet, there is still insufficient evidence regarding how students interact with literary texts to make sense of their cultural content, how literacy and literary thinking manifest themselves in language production tasks, and the role of assessment in language-literature instruction. Moreover, the body of research reviewed herein focuses on the implementation of language-literature instruction in just one course. To adequately document the long-term nature of developing L2 "advancedness" and determine best practices in language-literature instruction, longitudinal research implemented within a coherent curricular framework is essential. Although not specific to language-literature instruction, the research in Byrnes, Weger-Guntharp, and Sprang (2005) and Ortega and Byrnes (2008) provides examples of longitudinal investigations that employ a variety of data-gathering techniques (e.g., case study, qualitative, and quantitative). Similarly contextualized, longitudinal research specific to language-literature instruction will not only assess whether curricular and pedagogical change implemented in response to the MLA Report is effective and has a lasting impact on development of learners' academic literacy and multimodal language competencies, but it will also lend support to the findings of the single course studies presented here.

If FL programs are to implement the type of curricular and pedagogical change outlined in the publications reviewed here, then further research into language-literature instruction in precollegiate FL contexts is also needed. Such investigations are imperative for the creation of well-articulated, coherent secondary and postsecondary FL programs and for the advancement of students within those programs. Additionally, curricular and pedagogical change must be reflected in research and practice regarding graduate student teacher development. As several scholars have noted (e.g., Allen, 2009b; Maxim, 2005; Mills, 2011; Schechtman

& Koser, 2008; Wurst, 2008), graduate student teachers typically do not receive formal training in the teaching of FL literature or in the merging of language and literature across the curriculum. Moreover, graduate students are often socialized into the language-literature divide in their one methods course and subsequent teaching workshops, where the focus is on language instruction, and language and literature are presented as clearly distinct program elements. Although scholarship in this area is emerging, more empirical and classroom practice research is essential to bring about principled, theory-driven practice and to help FL departments make sound decisions regarding curriculum, instruction, and graduate student professionalization.

Finally, a consideration of the role of new technologies in language-literature instruction may also shed light on the development of FL literacy and advanced language abilities. A handful of studies have provided empirical support for the effectiveness of hybrid learning modules (Kraemer, 2008a, 2008b), electronic glosses and online dictionaries (Johnson, 2010), and collaborative online writing practice (Grossman, 2009) for integrating language and content and increasing student success and interest in reading literature. Future research might explore these and other technologies, such as computer-mediated communication with target language cultures to create communities of learning, or online collaborative text applications (e.g., eComma) to analyze and interpret literature. Technology has the potential to make literature relevant to today's students and to provide multimodal access to literature through sound, text, hypertext, images, and video. As such, this and other new research can keep discussions of language-literature instruction current and move collegiate FL programs more closely toward meeting the call for curricular and pedagogical change through the full integration of multimodal language development and interpretative interaction with literature at all levels of the curriculum.

NOTES

1 Although developing students' advanced-level capabilities is the goal of most FL programs, a clear characterization of "advancedness" remains to be determined. Several scholars have carried out important work in this area (e.g., Byrnes & Maxim, 2004; Byrnes et al., 2005; Ortega & Byrnes, 2008). However,

more research is needed.

2 As the references cited thus far suggest, this call for curricular change had already been made many times over in the applied linguistics and FL pedagogy literature. That this more recent call came from the MLA is therefore not without significance, particularly given the already established professional rift between scholars and practitioners in language and literary studies. Furthermore, nearly all the members of the ad hoc committee that authored the report represent the literature side of the aisle, further punctuating the seriousness of the divide and the urgent need for change.

3 In some respects, this distinction between literature in language courses and language in literature courses is artificial, given that these lines have started to blur; nonetheless, it serves as an efficient way to organize the review in order to investigate whether or not recent scholarship has indeed responded to the calls for change and shifts in thinking outlined here.

4 The *Standards* propose five content areas (communication, cultures, connections, comparisons, and communities) and related standards for FL curriculum organization, implemented through three modes of communication (interpersonal, interpretive, and presentational). Although the *Standards* are not an instructional approach per se, they have received attention in recent scholarship regarding their potential application outside of K–12 contexts to collegiate FL programs (e.g., Scott, 2009). Of particular interest in this research is how literature fits within the *Standards* framework and which of the standards might be met through literary study.

5 The well-documented innovations of the Georgetown University German Department (e.g., Byrnes et al., 2006; Byrnes & Kord, 2002) are an example of the type of curricular and pedagogical reform referred to throughout this article. Their genre-based curriculum is composed of five levels that integrate language and content throughout. Literary texts figure prominently in Levels IV and V but are also integral to Levels I–III as students gradually move from the study of primary (private) to secondary (public) discourses.

ANNOTATED BIBLIOGRAPHY

Kern, R., & Schultz, J. M. (2005). Beyond orality: Investigating literacy and the literary in second and foreign language instruction. *Modern Language*

Journal, *89*, 381–892.

This article argued for an approach to research in L2 acquisition and pedagogy that considers the development of socially and culturally embedded literacy and the relationship between literacy and literature. The authors called for increased qualitative and quantitative research to look at how students interact with texts and the classroom community to interpret cultural content and to explore how literacy and the literary manifest themselves through language production tasks. A sample course illustrates the authors' vision of literacy and the literary implemented through an approach that is multimodal, contextualized, and text-based.

Maxim, H. H. (2006b). Integrating textual thinking into the introductory college-level foreign language classroom. *Modern Language Journal*, *90*, 19–32.

This empirical study explored the development of textual thinking and academic literacy through extensive reading in a first-semester German course. Students in the experimental group spent half of class time doing communicative development activities and the other half reading a German novel. Students in the control group spent all of class time doing communicative development activities. Results showed that students in the experimental group scored at least as well as those in the control group on departmental exams. The author concluded that extensive reading is not only feasible in introductory courses, but it is also desirable for preparing students for advanced-level language tasks.

Modern Language Association Ad Hoc Committee on Foreign Languages. (2007). Foreign languages and higher education: New structures for a changed world. *Profession 2007*, 234–245.

The MLA Report recommended replacing the traditional two-tiered FL program structure with more coherent curricula that merge language, literature, and culture to develop students' translingual and transcultural competence (i.e., the ability to operate between languages and cultures). The report further recommended an increased emphasis on cultural narratives present in FL texts such as poetry, prose, film, and journalism, and changes to departmental governance that increase collaboration and ensure that all department members contribute to implementing a shared educational mission.

Polio, C., & Zyzik, E. (2009). Don Quixote meets *ser* and *estar*: Multiple perspectives on language learning in Spanish literature classes. *Modern Language Journal, 93*, 550–569.

This empirical study investigated student and instructor perspectives on language-focused instruction in advanced Spanish literature classes. Data revealed that whereas more than half of students stated language learning as a course goal, only one of three instructors stated language-oriented goals. Moreover, both groups reported minimal improvement in students' speaking abilities, and both viewed language learning in class as incidental rather than explicit. The authors concluded that pedagogical attention to advanced speaking functions with explicit linguistic support is necessary in literature courses and suggested several strategies for achieving this, including vocabulary notebooks, weekly language-focused breakout sessions, and hybrid courses with online language support and development activities.

Schultz, J. M. (2009). A Standards-based framework for the teaching of literature within the context of globalization. In V. M. Scott (Ed.), *Principles and practices of the Standards in college foreign language education* (pp. 128–143). Boston, MA: Heinle & Heinle.

This article situates the role of literature within the framework of the *Standards*, with a specific focus on connections and communities, which the author argued relates to the interdisciplinary, multicultural, and global aspects of literature. The proposed pedagogical approach to language-literature instruction develops higher-order critical thinking skills and combines aspects of reader-response theory to promote individual, experiential interaction with texts; semiotic analysis to encourage form-meaning relationships; and the connections and communities standards to situate texts outside of the individual. A sample text-based course illustrating the approach is provided.

Swaffar, J., & Arens, K. (2005). *Remapping the foreign language curriculum: An approach through multiple literacies*. New York, NY: Modern Language Association of America.

Swaffar and Arens argued in favor of literacy and genre as organizing principles for a holistic curriculum that eschews the language-literature divide and presents a coherent program anchored in texts. The authors developed a literacy-based pedagogy implemented through the reading matrix and the *précis*, and they defined learning outcomes for a genre-based curriculum. Several chapters focus specifically on the place of literature within the holistic curriculum and the types of genre-based activities that facilitate the socially and culturally situated interpretation of texts and the development of multimodal language abilities.

REFERENCES

Allen, H. W. (2009a). In search of relevance: The *Standards* and the undergraduate foreign language curriculum. In V. M. Scott (Ed.), *Principles and practices of the Standards in college foreign language education* (pp. 38–52). Boston, MA: Heinle & Heinle.

Allen, H. W. (2009b). Moving beyond the language-literature divide: Advanced pedagogy for tomorrow's foreign language professors. *ADFL Bulletin, 41*, 88–99.

Allen, H. W. (2009c). A multiple literacies approach to the advanced French writing course. *French Review, 83*, 368–385.

Allen, H. W., & Paesani, K. (2010). Exploring the feasibility of a pedagogy of multiliteracies in introductory foreign language courses. *L2 Journal, 2*, 119–142.

Alvstad, C., & Castro, A. (2009). Conceptions of literature in university language courses. *Modern Language Journal, 93*, 170–184.

American Council on the Teaching of Foreign Languages. (2006). *Standards for foreign language learning in the 21st century.* New York, NY: American Council on the Teaching of Foreign Languages (ACTFL) and the National Standards in Foreign Language Education Project.

Arens, K. (2008). Genres and the *Standards*: Teaching the 5 C's through texts. *German Quarterly, 81*, 35–48.

Barnett, M. A. (1991). Language and literature: False dichotomies, real allies. *ADFL Bulletin, 22*, 7–11.

Barrette, C. M., Paesani, K., & Vinall, K. (2010). Toward an integrated curriculum: Maximizing the use of target language literature. *Foreign Language Annals, 43*, 216–230.

Bernhardt, E. (1995). Teaching literature or teaching students? *ADFL Bulletin, 26*, 5–6.

Bernhardt, E. (2005). Progress and procrastination in second language reading. *Annual Review of Applied Linguistics, 25*, 133–150.

Bridges, E. (2009). Bridging the gap: A literacy-oriented approach to teaching the graphic novel *Der erste frühling. Die Unterrichtspraxis/Teaching German, 42*, 152–161.

Byrnes, H. (1998). Constructing curricula in collegiate foreign language departments. In H. Byrnes (Ed.), *Learning foreign and second languages* (pp. 262–295). New York, NY:

Modern Language Association of America.

Byrnes, H. (Ed.). (2006). Perspectives: Interrogating communicative competence as a framework for collegiate foreign language study. *Modern Language Journal, 90,* 244–266.

Byrnes, H., Crane, C., Maxim, H. H., & Sprang, K. A. (2006). Taking text to task: Issues and choices in curriculum instruction. *ITL: International Journal of Applied Linguistics, 152,* 85–110.

Byrnes, H., & Kord, S. (2002). Developing literacy and literary competence: Challenges for foreign language departments. In V. M. Scott & H. Tucker (Eds.), *SLA and the literature classroom: Fostering dialogues* (pp. 35–72). Boston, MA: Heinle & Heinle.

Byrnes, H., & Maxim, H. H. (2004). *Advanced foreign language learning: A challenge to college programs.* Boston, MA: Heinle & Heinle.

Byrnes, H., & Sinicrope, C. (2008). Advancedness and the development of relativization in L2 German: A curriculum-based longitudinal study. In L. Ortega & H. Byrnes (Eds.), *The longitudinal study of advanced L2 capacities* (pp. 109–138). New York, NY: Routledge.

Byrnes, H., Weger-Guntharp, H. D., & Sprang, K. (2005). *Educating for advanced foreign language capacities.* Washington, DC: Georgetown University Press.

Carter, R. (2007). Literature and language teaching, 1986–2006: A review. *International Journal of Applied Linguistics, 17,* 3–13.

Chute, H. (2008). Comics as literature? Reading graphic narrative. *PMLA, 123,* 452–465.

Davidheiser, J. C. (2007). Fairy tales and foreign languages: Ever the twain shall meet. *Foreign Language Annals, 40,* 215–225.

Donato, R., & Brooks, F. B. (2004). Literary discussions and advanced speaking functions: Researching the (dis)connection. *Foreign Language Annals, 37,* 183–199.

Eigler, F. (2009). From comprehension to production: Literary texts in the advanced foreign language classroom. *ADFL Bulletin, 41,* 24–34.

Geisler, M. E. (2008). The MLA report on foreign languages: One year into the future. *Profession 2008,* 229–239.

Grabe, W. (2004). Research on teaching reading. *Annual Review of Applied Linguistics, 24,* 44–69.

Grossman, K. M. (2009). Creating e-learning communities in language and literature classes. In I. Lancashire (Ed.), *Teaching literature and language online* (pp. 331–342). New York, NY: Modern Language Association of America.

Hall, G. (2005). *Literature in language education.* Basingstoke, UK: Palgrave Macmillan.

Henning, S. D. (1993). The integration of language, literature, and culture: Goals and curricular design. *ADFL Bulletin, 24,* 51–55.

Hirvela, A. (2001). Connecting reading and writing through literature. In D. Belcher & A. Hirvela (Eds.), *Linking literacies: Perspectives on L2 reading-writing connections* (pp.

109–134). Ann Arbor: University of Michigan Press.

Hirvela, A. (2005). ESL students and the use of literature in composition courses. *Teaching English in the Two Year College, 33*, 70–77.

Hoecherl-Alden, G. (2006). Connecting language to content: Second language literature instruction at the intermediate level. *Foreign Language Annals, 39*, 244–254.

Hoffman, E. F., & James, D. (1986). Toward the integration of foreign language and literature teaching at all levels of the college curriculum. *ADFL Bulletin, 18*, 29–33.

James, D. (2000). Kleiner mann, was nun? In R. M. Terry (Ed.), *Agents of change in a changing age* (pp. 237–270). Lincolnwood, IL: National Textbook.

Johnson, L. P. (2010). Electronic literary texts: A survey of tools and some strategies for developers. *CALICO Journal, 27*, 477–490.

Kern, R. (2000). *Literacy and language teaching.* Oxford, UK: Oxford University Press.

Kern, R. (2004). Literacy and advanced foreign language learning: Rethinking the curriculum. In H. Byrnes & H. H. Maxim (Eds.), *Advanced foreign language learning: A challenge to college programs* (pp. 2–18). Boston, MA: Heinle & Heinle.

Kern, R. (2008). Making connections through texts in language teaching. *Language Teaching, 41*, 367–387.

Kraemer, A. (2008a). *Engaging the foreign language learner: Using hybrid instruction to bridge the language-literature gap.* Unpublished doctoral dissertation, Michigan State University, East Lansing, MI.

Kraemer, A. (2008b). Happily ever after: Integrating language and literature through technology? *Die Unterrichtspraxis/Teaching German, 41*, 61–71.

Kramsch, C. (1985). Literary texts in the classroom: A discourse. *Modern Language Journal, 69*, 356–366.

Kramsch, C., & Kramsch, O. (2000). The avatars of literature in language study. *Modern Language Journal, 84*, 553–573.

Maley, A., & Duff, A. (1989). *The inward ear: Poetry in the language classroom.* New York, NY: Cambridge University Press.

Mantero, M. (2002). Bridging the gap: Discourse in text-based foreign language classrooms. *Foreign Language Annals, 35*, 437–456.

Mantero, M. (2006). Applied literacy in second language education: (Re)framing discourse in literature-based classrooms. *Foreign Language Annals, 39*, 99–114.

Maxim, H. H. (2005). Enhancing graduate student teacher development through curricular reform. *ADFL Bulletin, 36*, 15–21.

Maxim, H. H. (2006a). Giving beginning adult language learners a voice: A case for poetry in the foreign language classroom. In J. Retallack & J. Spahr (Eds.), *Poetry and pedagogy: The challenge of the contemporary* (pp. 251–259). New York, NY: Palgrave Macmillan.

Maxim, H. H. (2008). Developing advanced formal language abilities along a genre-based curriculum. In S. L. Katz & J. Watzinger-Tharp (Eds.), *Conceptions of L2 grammar: Theoretical approaches and their application in the L2 classroom* (pp. 172–188). Boston, MA: Heinle & Heinle.

Maxim, H. H. (2009). An essay on the role of language in collegiate foreign language programmatic reform. *Die Unterrichtspraxis/Teaching German, 42*, 123–129.

McEwan, E. K. (2009). Incorporating the *Standards* into a 3R model of literary and cultural analysis. In V. M. Scott (Ed.), *Principles and practices of the Standards in college foreign language education* (pp. 144–160). Boston, MA: Heinle & Heinle.

Melin, C. (2010). Between the lines: When culture, language, and poetry meet in the classroom. *Language Teaching, 43*, 349–365.

Mills, N. A. (2011). Teaching assistants' self-efficacy in teaching literature: Sources, personal assessments, and consequences. *Modern Language Journal, 95*, 61–80.

Minkoff, P. (2006). Talking it over in class. In A. Paran (Ed.), *Literature in language teaching and learning* (pp. 45–57). Alexandria, VA: Teachers of English to Speakers of Other Languages.

Muyskens, J. A. (1983). Teaching second-language literatures: Past, present and future. *Modern Language Journal, 67*, 413–423.

Nance, K. A. (2010). *Teaching literature in the languages: Expanding the literary circle through student engagement.* Upper Saddle River, NJ: Prentice Hall.

New London Group. (1996). A pedagogy of multiliteracies: Designing social futures. *Harvard Educational Review, 66*, 60–92.

Ortega, L., & Byrnes, H. (2008). *The longitudinal study of advanced L2 capacities.* New York, NY: Routledge.

Paesani, K. (2004). Using literature to develop foreign language proficiency: Toward an interactive classroom. In C. J. Stivale (Ed.), *Modern French literary studies in the classroom: Pedagogical strategies* (pp. 13–25). New York, NY: Modern Language Association of America.

Paesani, K. (2005). Literary texts and grammar instruction: Revisiting the inductive presentation. *Foreign Language Annals, 38*, 15–23.

Paesani, K. (2006a). *Exercices de style*: Developing multiple competencies through a writing portfolio. *Foreign Language Annals, 39*, 618–639.

Paesani, K. (2006b). A process-oriented approach to *Zazie dans le métro*. *French Review, 79*, 762–778.

Paesani, K. (2009). Exploring the stylistic content of *Exercices de style*. *French Review, 82*, 1268–1280.

Paran, A. (2008). The role of literature in instructed foreign language learning and teaching: An evidence-based survey. *Language Teaching, 41*, 465–496.

Pfeiffer, P. C. (2008). The discipline of foreign language studies and reforming foreign language education. *Modern Language Journal, 92*, 296–298.

Pireddu, N. (2008). Literature? *C'est un monde:* The foreign language curriculum in the wake of the MLA report. *Profession 2008*, 219–228.

Porter, C. (2009). The MLA recommendations: Can we get there from here? *ADFL Bulletin, 41*, 16–23.

Queneau, R. (1947). *Exercices de style*. Paris, France: Galimard.

Redmann, J. (2005). An interactive reading journal for all levels of the foreign language curriculum. *Foreign Language Annals, 38*, 484–493.

Redmann, J. (2008). Reading Kästner's *Emil und di Detektive* in the context of a literacy-oriented curriculum. *Die Unterrichtspraxis/Teaching German, 41*, 72–81.

Rinner, S., & Weigart, A. (2005). From sports to the EU community: Integrating curricula through genre-based culture courses. In H. Byrnes, D. Weger-Guntharp, & K. Sprang (Eds.), *Educating for advanced foreign language capacities* (pp. 136–151). Washington, DC: Georgetown University Press.

Schechtman, R. R., & Koser, J. (2008). Foreign languages and higher education: A pragmatic approach to change. *Modern Language Journal, 92*, 309–312.

Schultz, J. M. (1995). Making the transition from language to literature. In M. A. Haggstrom, L. Z. Morgan, & J. A. Wieczorek (Eds.), *The foreign language classroom: Bridging theory and practice* (pp. 3–20). New York, NY: Garland.

Scott, V. M. (2009). *Principles and practices of the Standards in collegiate foreign language education*. Boston, MA: Heinle & Heinle.

Scott, V. M., & Huntington, J. A. (2007). Literature, the interpretive mode, and novice learners. *Modern Language Journal, 91*, 3–14.

Scott, V. M., & Huntington, J. A. (2008). Reading culture: Using literature to develop C2 competence. *Foreign Language Annals, 35*, 622–631.

Scott, V. M., & Tucker, H. (2002). *SLA and the literature classroom: Fostering dialogues*. Boston, MA: Heinle & Heinle.

Sprang, K. A. (2008). Advanced learners' development of systematic vocabulary knowledge: Learning German vocabulary with inseparable prefixes. In L. Ortega & H. Byrnes (Eds.), *The longitudinal study of advanced L2 capacities* (pp. 139–162). New York, NY: Routledge.

Steinhart, M. M. (2006). Breaching the artificial barrier between communicative competence and content. *Modern Language Journal, 90*, 258–261.

Stewart, J. A., & Santiago, K. A. (2006). Using the literary text to engage learners in a multilingual community. *Foreign Language Annals, 39*, 683–696.

Swaffar, J. (2006). Terminology and its discontents: Some caveats about communicative competence. *Modern Language Journal, 90*, 246–249.

Swaffar, J., Arens, K., & Byrnes, H. (1991). *Reading for meaning: An integrated approach to language learning.* Englewood Cliffs, NJ: Prentice Hall.

Viswamohan, A., & Torche, U. (2007). Literature and media in an ESP classroom. In B. Beaven (Ed.), *IATEFL 2006 Harrogate Conference Selections* (pp. 104–105). Canterbury, UK: International Association of Teachers of English as a Foreign Language (IATEFL).

Walther, I. (2007). Ecological perspectives on language and literacy: Implications for foreign language instruction at the collegiate level. *ADFL Bulletin, 38*, 6–14.

Walther, I. (2009). Curricular planning along the fault line between instrumental and academic agendas: A response to the report of the Modern Language Association on Foreign languages and higher education: New structures for a changed world. *Die Unterrichtspraxis/Teaching German, 42*, 115–122.

Warner, C. (2009). Hey, you! The Germans! Using literary pragmatics to teach language as culture. *Die Unterrichtspraxis/Teaching German, 42*, 162–168.

Watson, G., & Zyngier, S. (2007). *Literature and stylistics for language learners.* New York, NY: Palgrave Macmillan.

Weber-Fève, S. (2009). Integrating language and literature: Teaching textual analysis with input and output activities and an input-to-output approach. *Foreign Language Annals, 42*, 453–467.

Wellmon, C. (2008). Languages, cultural studies, and the futures of foreign language education. *Modern Language Journal, 92*, 292–295.

Wurst, K. A. (2008). How do we teach language, literature, and culture in a collegiate environment and what are the implications for graduate education? *Die Unterricht-spraxis/Teaching German, 41*, 57–60.

Zyzik, E., & Polio, C. (2008). Incidental focus on form in university Spanish literature classes. *Modern Language Journal, 92*, 53–70.

Content-and-Language Integrated Learning: From Practice to Principles?

Christiane Dalton-Puffer

This article surveys recent work on *content-and-language integrated learning* (CLIL). Related to both content-based instruction and immersion education by virtue of its dual focus on language and content, CLIL is here understood as an educational model for contexts where the classroom provides the only site for learners' interaction in the target language. That is, CLIL is about either foreign languages or lingua francas. The discussion foregrounds a prototypical CLIL context (Europe) but also refers to work done elsewhere. The first part of the discussion focuses on policy issues, describing how CLIL practice operates in a tension between grassroots decisions and higher order policymaking, an area where European multi- and plurilingual policies and the strong impact of English as a lingua franca play a particularly interesting role. The latter is, of course, of definite relevance also in other parts of the world. The second part of the article synthesizes research on learning outcomes in CLIL. Here, the absence of standardized content testing means that the main focus is on language-learning outcomes. The third section deals with classroom-based CLIL research and participants' use of their language resources for learning and teaching, including such diverse perspectives as discourse pragmatics, speech acts, academic language functions, and genre. The final part of the article discusses theoretical underpinnings of CLIL, delineating their current state of elaboration as applied linguistic research in the area is gaining momentum.

Forms of instruction that combine content teaching and language teaching are not a new topic in the *Annual Review of Applied Linguistics* (see Crandall, 1992; Snow, 1998; Spanos, 1989; Stoller, 2004). Viewing these reports as a series, one notes a development from case reports and program descriptions to more general research questions, more classroom-based research, and an increasingly international perspective. This article will further develop this international perspective with a specific but not exclusive focus on content-and-language integrated learning (CLIL) research conducted in Europe over the last 5 or 6 years. Evidence for the global interest in CLIL can be gleaned from the numerous activities in this area: the establishment of an *Association Internationale de Linguistique Appliquée* research network on CLIL and immersion classrooms for the 2006–2011 period (www.ichm.org/clil/), a symposium at *American Association of Applied Linguistics Conference 2010* organized by Roy Lyster, the recent foundation of an association for CLIL at tertiary level (ICLHE—Integrating Content and Language in Higher Education; www.iclhe.org), a biennial series of CLIL conferences in Europe since 2004 (e.g., www.clilconsortium.jyu.fi/), the foundation of the *Latin American Journal of Content & Language Integrated Learning*, a new series of conferences in Latin America (www.clilsymposium.org), and many more.

CLIL: CHARACTERISTICS AND CONTRASTS

Widely advertised as a "dual-focused approach" that gives equal attention to language and content (e.g., Mehisto, Marsh, & Frigols, 2008, p. 9), CLIL can be described as an educational approach where curricular content is taught through the medium of a foreign language, typically to students participating in some form of mainstream education at the primary, secondary, or tertiary level.

Although the first "L" in CLIL is meant to stand for any language, it would be an extreme case of denial to claim that this is also the case in reality. CLIL languages tend to be recruited from a small group of prestigious languages, and outside the English-speaking countries, the prevalence of English as CLIL medium is overwhelming (see Eurydice Network, 2006; Fernández et al., 2008; Lim & Low, 2009). Therefore, most of the time in this article, CLIL effectively means CEIL, or content-and-English integrated learning.

Without a doubt, there are many characteristics that CLIL shares with other types of bilingual education, such as content-based instruction (CBI) and immersion education, which have been widely adopted in North American contexts (Brinton, Snow, & Wesche 1989/2008; Johnson & Swain, 1997; Lyster, 2007; Stoller, 2004). In fact, whether a concrete program is referred to as immersion or CLIL often depends as much on its cultural and political frame of reference as on the actual characteristics of the program. The following points exemplify what appears to be typical of CLIL programs in Europe, South America, and many parts of Asia (see also Lasagabaster & Sierra, 2009):

- CLIL is about using a foreign language or a lingua franca, not a second language (L2). That is, the language of instruction is one that students will mainly encounter in the classroom, given that it is not regularly used in the wider society they live in.
- The dominant CLIL language is English, reflecting the fact that a command of English as an additional language is increasingly regarded as a key literacy feature worldwide.
- CLIL also implies that teachers will normally be nonnative speakers of the target language. They are not, in most cases, foreign language experts, but instead content experts, because "classroom content is not so much taken from everyday life or the general content of the target language culture but rather from content subjects, from academic/scientific disciplines or from the professions" (Wolff, 2007, pp. 15–16).
- This means that CLIL lessons are usually timetabled as content lessons (e.g., biology, music, geography, mechanical engineering), while the target language normally continues as a subject in its own right in the shape of foreign language lessons taught by language specialists.
- In CLIL programs typically less than 50% of the curriculum is taught in the target language.
- Furthermore, CLIL is usually implemented once learners have already acquired literacy skills in their first language (L1), which is more often at the secondary than the primary level.

In short, CLIL could be interpreted as a foreign language enrichment measure packaged into content teaching.

LANGUAGE POLICY ISSUES

The global spread of CLIL, the pace of which "has surprised even its most ardent advocates" (Maljers, Marsh, & Wolff, 2007, p. 7) suggests looking into language policy in order to understand the driving forces behind it. As it happens, a recent conceptual reorientation in the study of language policy, expanding the view beyond deliberate central planning toward language practices and beliefs (Shohamy, 2006; Spolsky, 2004), provides an excellent foil for this undertaking. In most places, the implementation of CLIL has been fuelled from two directions: high-level policymaking and grass-roots actions, with the latter dovetailing parental and teacher choices. What we see above all is individuals reacting to what they rightly perceive as major shifts in society and economic life, with both becoming increasingly international, requiring ever better educated employees who know certain languages that are considered crucial in the job market (e.g., Ferguson, 2006). Parents believe that CLIL promises their children an edge in the competition for employment (Li, 2002), and teachers often take the initiative, adapting their language practices to teaching through the medium of English (e.g., Dalton-Puffer, Hüttner, Jexenflicker, Schindelegger, & Smit, 2008; Maljers et al. 2007). On the other end of the spectrum, high-level political agents, some of them supra-national, also began to recognize these advantages and have designed their language management activities accordingly. In the following I will mainly use Europe as a showcase, but analogous processes can be observed in Latin American and Chinese contexts, among others (e.g., *Latin American Journal of Content and Language Integrated Learning*; Li, 2002; Lim & Low, 2009; McDougald, 2009; Tollefson & Tsui, 2004; Tsui & Tollefson, 2007).

On the level of European language policy, CLIL has been featured in a series of declarations (European Commission, 1995, 2003, 2008) and has even been invested with "a major contribution to make to the Union's language learning goals" (European Commission, 2003, p. 8). These language-learning goals aim at creating multilingual citizens, which is not surprising given the extent of linguistic diversity of the European Union with its 23 official languages spoken by populations exhibiting a mostly monolingual habitus.

The European Union actively encourages its citizens to learn other European languages, both for reasons of professional and personal mobility within its single market, and as a force for cross-cultural contacts and mutual understanding. . . . The ability to understand and communicate in more than one language . . . is a desirable life-skill for all European citizens. Learning and speaking other languages . . . improves cognitive skills and strengthens learners' mother tongue skills; it enables us to take advantage of the freedom to work or study in another Member State. ("A Guide to Languages in the European Union," 2008)

Despite CLIL being cast in the role of an important language enrichment measure, precise learning goals and objectives are largely missing. Although a series of transnational expert groups has translated the high-level claims into conceptualizations, curricular guidelines, and model materials (e.g., www.clilcompendium.com, www.ccn-clil.eu, www.clilconsortium.jyu.fi, http://archive.ecml.at/mtp2/CLILmatrix/), few of the 27 national education systems have actually responded with substantial investments into CLIL implementation, teacher education, and research, leaving the impetus to the grassroots stakeholders (see Eurydice Network, 2006). Spain and the Netherlands are exceptions in this respect: in Spain, numerous research and development projects are being conducted (Eurydice Network, 2006; e.g., Escobar Urmeneta, 2010; Fernández Fontecha, 2009; Lasagabaster & Ruiz de Zarobe, 2010; Lorenzo, Casal, & Moore, 2005). In the Netherlands, a national accreditation system for CLIL schools has established explicit quality parameters and a supply of teacher and school development measures (www.europeesplatform.nl).

The situation in Asia is somewhat different because habitually monolingual populations and states are complemented by "riotously multilingual countries" (Bruthiaux, 2009, p. 124), while at the same time there seems generally little political pressure to deny the special role of English in the concert of languages in the 21st century. Association of Southeast Asian Nations, for instance, proclaimed English as its working language without much perceptible debate, a decision unthinkable in the European Union. Language and education policies in Latin America are different again, but reports on CLIL-related issues have only recently started to become accessible (e.g., Fernández et al., 2008; McDougald, 2009; Pistorio, 2009).

What appears to be shared by stakeholders across continents and circumstances is (a) the belief in the benefits of equipping every citizen with a knowledge of English and (b) the belief that CLIL is the way to transcend the perceived weaknesses of traditional foreign language teaching. Research is therefore called upon to verify in how far CLIL can fulfill these and other expectations (e.g., regarding the cognitive advantages mentioned in the policy quotation mentioned earlier), and I will return to these issues in the following sections.

LEARNING OUTCOMES

Considering that CLIL has even been cast in the role of "a catalyst for change in language education" (Marsh & Frigols, 2007, p. 33), it is not surprising that most of the research on outcomes is in the area of attainment in the CLIL language. In this regard it is important to note that the standard of comparison in such studies are not native speakers of the medium of instruction, but learners studying the target language in traditional foreign language classes, often attending the same school as the CLIL students and usually referred to as mainstream or non-CLIL students.

Given the fact that CLIL students nearly always continue with their regular foreign language program alongside their CLIL content lessons and thus have a time advantage over their peers, it is to be expected that their foreign language test scores surpass those of the mainstream learners. This expectation is clearly confirmed by recently published surveys (Admiraal, Westhoff, & de Bot, 2006; Lasagabaster, 2008; Lorenzo et al., 2005; Ruiz de Zarobe, 2008, 2010; Zydatiß, 2007), which deal with respondents of varying ages (approximately 10–16 years). Even so, the question of how much and in what respect CLIL students are better remains of interest, as does the question of why.

Studies concur that CLIL students' receptive and productive lexicon is larger overall, contains more words from lower frequency bands, has a wider stylistic range, and is used more appropriately (e.g., Jexenflicker & Dalton-Puffer, 2010; Lo & Murphy, 2010; Ruiz de Zarobe, 2010; Zydatiß, 2007), with statistical comparisons uniformly showing large effect sizes of CLIL instruction. A simple explanation that would see CLIL as the sole cause of this is, however, under-cut by other research results. The longitudinal study ($N = 1,305$) by Admiraal et al. (2006) showed CLIL students to already have better entry-level receptive vocabulary scores (see also Lo & Murphy, 2010), an advantage that remained stable across 4 years rather than increasing. One might have expected a faster growth rate for CLIL students, as has indeed been found by Lo and Murphy (2010) for their Hong Kong immersion learners. These authors also argued that the specific advantage of CLIL learners seemed to lie in academic vocabulary and words from the 5,000+ frequency range, attributing this to the special learning conditions of subject and content integration (see also Zydatiß, 2007). A further perspective on possible causalities was added by Sylvén's results from Sweden (2004; $N = 363$), showing that out-of-school reading behavior correlated more strongly with vocabulary scores than being in a CLIL class.

The skill that has recently received increased attention is writing, not least because the comparisons between CLIL and non-CLIL learners are more confounded in this area than in the other competence areas. Several studies comparing CLIL and non-CLIL writing (e.g., Jexenflicker & Dalton-Puffer, 2010; Ruiz de Zarobe, 2010) concur in finding that CLIL students had at their disposal a wider range not only of lexical but also morphosyntactic resources, which they deployed in more elaborate and more complex structures. What was not to be assumed outright given the focus on meaning (and not form) in CLIL classrooms is the fact that CLIL students also show a higher degree of accuracy, not only in inflectional affixation and tense use but also in spelling. The greater pragmatic awareness of CLIL students was shown in their better fulfillment of the communicative intentions of writing tasks. There were, however, dimensions of writing on which CLIL experience seemed to have little or no effect. These were the dimensions that reach beyond the sentence level (i.e., cohesion and coherence, discourse structuring, paragraphing, register awareness, genre, and style). With regard to the latter, significant insights have also been gained by comparing CLIL students' L2 writing with their subject writing in the L1 (Coetzee-Lachmann, 2009; Järvinen, 2010; Llinares & Whittaker, 2010; Lorenzo & Moore, 2010; Vollmer, Heine, Troschke, Coetzee, & Küttel, 2006), which, perhaps surprisingly, has not been found to necessarily surpass CLIL-L2 writing in these respects. Interesting practical as well as theoretical implications arise from this: Might we be justified in postulating some kind of general level of writing development that has an impact on how learners deal with a writing task independently of whether it is in their L1 or in L2? This is an issue that needs to be developed further with reference to current discussions on pluriliteracies (e.g., Prinsloo & Baynham, 2008).[1]

A note on morphosyntax should be added at this point: Although some studies showed that CLIL students outperformed their peers in some morphosyntactic components, such as sentence complexity, affixal inflection (Dalton-Puffer, 2007b, p. 281), or the use of placeholders, other properties, notably the use of null subjects, negation, and suppletive forms, seemed to remain unaffected (Martínez Adrián & Gutiérrez Mangado, 2009; Villarreal & García Mayo, 2009). Given the high variability of foreign language exposure between different CLIL programs, the critical amount of CLIL necessary to produce the automatization of low-level morphosyntactic processes remains an open question.

Finally, the area where a difference between CLIL students and mainstream learners is most noticeable is their spontaneous oral production. All the quantitative surveys so far (Admiraal et al., 2006; Lasagabaster, 2008; Ruiz de Zarobe, 2008; Zydatiß, 2007) show CLIL students to be ahead on all dimensions of their respective speaking constructs, a result that was underscored by self-reports obtained in student interviews where learners consistently mentioned greater fluency and speaking confidence (Dalton-Puffer et al., 2008). A range of studies (e.g., Hüttner & Rieder-Bünemann, 2010; Maillat, 2010; Mewald, 2007; Moore, 2009) concur in ascribing CLIL students greater flexibility and listener-orientedness, and they also appeared more self-assured in conveying their intended meanings in the L2 even if they momentarily lacked linguistic resources (see also Nikula, 2008). CLIL students also demonstrated more adeptness at dealing with the requirements of spontaneous conversational interaction and were more adept at implementing macro-level structuring devices as well as micro-level features like maintaining tense consistency in narratives. Regarding the phonetic component, however, the effects of CLIL instruction seem to be altogether more moderate (Admiraal et al., 2006; Gallardo del Puerto, García Lecumberri, & Gómez Lacabex, 2009). Overall the evidence is robust enough to warrant the verdict that CLIL definitely fosters spontaneous L2 speaking skills, with pronunciation being the least affected of the speaking dimensions.

Observations from several studies cited earlier feed into a pool of evidence suggesting that CLIL students are particularly strong in strategic competence, allowing them to successfully convey content notions at an early stage even though their linguistic resources are still limited (see also Lorenzo & Moore, 2010;

Moore, 2009).[2] However, this does not mean that there were no high scores among mainstream learners. Rather, CLIL classes showed a significantly broader band of students just below the top level. In other words, people with special language-learning aptitude may reach high proficiency levels via traditional foreign language classes, but CLIL significantly enhances the language skills of a broad group of students whose foreign language talents or interests are average (e.g., Mewald, 2007).

I will now turn to the question of content learning. It is a common concern of educators and parents how being taught in the foreign language will affect learners' knowledge, skills, and understanding of the subject. Because the medium of learning is less perfectly known than the L1, it is feared that this will lead to reduced subject competence as a result of either imperfect understanding or the fact that teachers preempt this problem and simplify content (see Hajer, 2000). Research on the issue has been difficult to carry out because relatively few countries conduct standardized testing in science and social studies subjects. Thus ready-made constructs of subject-specific competence in a particular area are hard to come by, making quantitative surveys and cross-country comparisons more problematic than those regarding language attainment.

Research findings on content-learning outcomes are altogether less conclusive than those on language-learning outcomes. On the positive side, some studies concur with results emerging from Canadian immersion contexts (e.g., Day & Shapson, 1996) that showed immersion students outperforming peer controls even when tested in the L1, a result that has been replicated for young CLIL mathematics learners in Belgium (van de Craen, Ceuleers, & Mondt, 2007). This, it has been claimed, may have to do with the fact that CLIL students work more persistently on tasks and show a higher tolerance of frustration, thus acquiring a higher degree of procedural competence in the subject (Vollmer et al., 2006). Additionally, Vollmer et al. also argued that linguistic problems, rather than leading to task abandonment, often prompted intensified mental construction activity (through elaborating and relating details and discovering contradictions), resulting in deeper semantic processing and better understanding of curricular concepts. This suggests that rather than being a hindrance, L2 processing actually has a strong potential for the learning of subject-specific concepts.

Critical voices, however, are beginning to make themselves heard. Until recently, such opinions have mostly been voiced in studies published in languages other than English, which makes them generally accessible only in condensed form (Lim Falk, 2008; Swedish studies reported in Sylvén, 2004; several Turkish publications briefly summarized in Kiraz, Güneyli, Baysen, Gündüz, & Baysen, 2010). One shared observation seems to be reduced active student participation in the classroom (as was also self-reported by students in interviews; Dalton-Puffer et al., 2008), which may lead to less learning. In a study by Lim Falk (2008), CLIL students used less relevant subject-based language in speech and writing than did the control students. Lim Falk argued that in content subjects, "English is an obstacle, and is also considered as such" (p. 5). Airey's qualitative data (Airey, 2009; Airey & Linder, 2006) also showed that some students have problems describing science concepts in English. Problems with the linguistic expression of academic concepts are also reported by Walker (2010) for late-immersion secondary students in Hong Kong.[3] In Europe, there is an incipient debate that CLIL might have adverse effects on advanced L1 academic language proficiency, but no research on this is available at the moment.

Positioned between these opposing views, three studies report neither a positive nor a negative effect of CLIL regarding content learning. Admiraal et al.'s (2006) quantitative survey in the Netherlands showed CLIL students' performance in L1 university entrance exams in history and geography to be neither better nor worse than their peers'. However, Admiraal et al. warned against hasty overgeneralization because of the pioneer effect of bilingual education in the Netherlands at the time of data collection, implying that particularly motivated students and teachers might have dealt exceptionally well with a difficult challenge. Jäppinen (2005) compared three age groups of Finnish CLIL and non-CLIL mathematics learners ($N = 669$), finding weak negative effects for the youngest age group (7–9), slightly positive effects in the middle group (10–12), and zero effects for the older learners (13–15). In Switzerland, Badertscher and Bieri (2009) conducted a qualitative longitudinal study of six fourth- to sixth-grade classes, combining oral subject-knowledge interviews with classroom observation. The study is theoretically and methodologically interesting because, due to the unavailability of standardized subject tests, the authors developed a discourse-based operationalization of the learners' conceptual declarative knowledge. In addition, it is one of the very few studies examining a context where languages other than English are used as CLIL languages (in this case, German and French). Summarizing their results, Badertscher and Bieri found that CLIL had neither positive nor negative effects on the students' performance in the subject-knowledge interviews. I concur with their opinion that the intriguing question regarding content outcomes is really this: How it is possible that learners can produce equally good results even if they studied the content in an imperfectly known language? The classroom and its pedagogical and linguistic practices should hold some answers.

CLASSROOM INTERACTION AND PEDAGOGICAL PRACTICE

CLIL instruction has at times been constructed as a kind of catalyst for change in classroom pedagogies, implying that it somehow causes a shift from (traditional) teacher-centered practices to (more innovative) student-centered learning arrangements. In Duff's study of Hungarian bilingual schools in the early 1990s, the appearance of new classroom genres was indeed empirically supported (e.g., Duff, 1995); however, such an effect is by no means guaranteed. In comparative classroom observations Badertscher and Bieri (2009) found no difference in overall lesson design between their Swiss CLIL and non-CLIL content classrooms, an observation that can also be made on the basis of Dalton-Puffer's Austrian data (2007b). Furthermore, there is evidence that even suggests increased teacher orientation in CLIL teaching because CLIL teachers' limited L2 competence may prompt them to adhere very closely to their preparation (Dalton-Puffer et al., 2008). In the 40 Austrian CLIL lessons studied by Dalton-Puffer (2007b) this resulted in whole-class discussions narrowly kept on track. In a case study of one Finnish biology teacher, Nikula (2010) examined the differences in that teacher's interactional behavior during biology lessons conducted in L1-Finnish and L2-English. Her findings indicate that the teacher's language use in the CLIL lessons was pragmatically less varied and less subtle, a fact that was echoed in CLIL teacher interviews in terms of "being largely divested of the possibility to use humor" (Dalton-Puffer et al., 2008). On the other hand, Nikula noted that in the CLIL lessons the students had "more room for active engagement in classroom discourse than non-CLIL settings" (2010, p. 120), suggesting that the CLIL teachers' status as

L2 users of English puts them on a more equal footing with the students, allowing the learners to claim a larger share of the discourse space (the same observation was made by Smit [2010] for tertiary learners). An additional dimension of the concept of discourse space is theorized by Maillat (2010), who observed that Swiss secondary students quite unexpectedly produced richer interactions in history and biology role plays conducted in L2 than those in L1. Maillat claimed that this is due to a mask effect inherent in the L2, as it allows a clear distinction between speaker and learner identities so that "the epistemic commitment of the speaker to the validity of her statements is reduced" (p. 51) because the learner's own personal beliefs are not engaged. Maillat explained that this pragmatic mask effect is unavailable in the language classroom given that the L2 functions as the focal point of learning. In sum, these studies show that CLIL classrooms differ from foreign language classrooms in some fundamental pragmatic parameters, which is of some importance in explaining the reduced foreign-language-speaking anxiety that is commonly observed in CLIL students (e.g., Dalton-Puffer et al., 2008; Maillat, 2010; Nikula, 2007) as caused by something beyond the mere lack of error correction (see later in this article about error correction).

A pragmatic stance has also been used to investigate the realization of speech acts in CLIL lessons, notably directives, due to their special frequency in classroom interaction (Dalton-Puffer, 2007b; Dalton-Puffer & Nikula, 2006; Moore, 2007). Findings show the impact of the situational context classroom in terms of a clear division between the instructional and regulative registers[4] with regard to norms of directness and indirectness: Given that questions for content are part of the core purpose of school lessons, directness is licensed in the instructional register in teacher-student and student-student interactions. In the regulative register, on the other hand, a stronger impact of the local matrix cultures emerges: A comparison of CLIL lessons from Finnish and Austrian German contexts (Dalton-Puffer & Nikula, 2006) showed an obvious difference in politeness forms (and presumably norms), with the Austrian classrooms exhibiting considerable amounts of indirectness features in teacher requests for actions (rather than for content information), whereas the Finnish requests were more direct overall. But even in a context like the Austrian one, where the students were exposed to numerous linguistic models for making polite requests in English, they had much less opportunity to produce a wide range of requests themselves.[5] That is, the use of speech acts that learners experience in CLIL classrooms may be far removed, pragmatically, from the linguistic contingencies in other settings, and it is clear that more research on speech acts and transfer to out-of-class settings is urgently needed.

On a more general pragmatic level, students' tendency to adopt a very informal style of speaking has been noted as well (Moore, 2007; Nikula, 2007). It is possible to argue that such a high level of informality corresponds to what Cummins (1984, 2000) called basic interpersonal conversational skills being enacted in the naturalistic environment, which would imply an understanding that students only master a rather colloquial way of using English and have no access to or awareness of more formal and more academic styles of speaking.[6] Nikula, however, interprets this fact as an indication that CLIL encourages participants to construct their roles in ways that are subtly different from the L1 content lessons. A good deal more research in different contexts is clearly needed before more general conclusions can be drawn.

Even though CLIL classrooms are widely considered as motivating, the actual commitment of participants to using the target language seems to vary enormously. Student behavior during group work has often been used as a measure in this respect, the most common observation being that students immediately switched to the L1 once they were among themselves (e.g., Canagarajah, 1995; Cromdal, 2005; Dalton-Puffer, 2007b; Tarone & Swain, 1995), a finding that was, however, not supported by Nikula's Finnish data. On the contrary, Nikula (2007) found her participants using the L2 even for social purposes, such as a student passing on greetings from one teacher to another. What can be said with some certainty is that the language choices of individual teachers have a significant impact in this regard, constituting something like house rules for the students (e.g., Dalton-Puffer, 2007b; Pessoa, Hendry, Donato, Tucker, & Lee, 2007). But apart from such local rules of use, one should also take into account the amount of CLIL in students' weekly timetables as well as the wider sociolinguistic context in terms of affecting the status of the target language.

Another important conceptual vantage point in studies of CLIL classroom discourse has been learning theories that focus on the negotiation of meaning. Most of the studies examine the language-learning potential of meaning negotiation (see Doughty & Williams, 1998), but in fact the negotiation concept provides an excellent basis for a content-and-language approach, given that school subjects are talked into being during lessons. One study that directly addresses this is Badertscher and Bieri's (2009) comparison between Swiss CLIL and mainstream teaching. Among others things, they found that (a) there are over twice as many negotiation sequences in the CLIL lessons than in the L1 lessons and (b) during CLIL lessons, teachers more reliably attended to obvious difficulties of understanding. Badertscher and Bieri interpreted these findings as constitutive for explaining the equally good learning results of the CLIL students even though they were studying through an imperfectly known language. Mariotti's (2006) study in Italy also revealed CLIL lessons to have a high rate of student-initiated negotiation sequences, an interesting partial result being that the presence of two teachers in the classroom discouraged such negotiations. Other studies (Badertscher & Bieri, 2009; Dalton-Puffer, 2007b), however, do not indicate such high rates of student-initiated negotiation sequences, although Badertscher and Bieri's comparison with mainstream L1 teaching did show a somewhat higher rate for the CLIL students. What has so far been overlooked in all but a few studies is the fact that it might be of great significance at what point in their CLIL careers a group's negotiation behavior is being observed, because there actually seems to be an increase over time. Badertscher and Bieri (2009) noted such an increase, an observation strongly supported by Smit's (2010) longitudinal ethnographic study of a tertiary level group, which revealed considerable growth in active student negotiating behavior combined with a clear shift of focus over time from phonetic intelligibility to coconstructing content. In other words, there are indications that the use of an L2 or lingua franca contributes to a learning group's development as a community of practice, which allows for an extension of the traditionally narrow student role. It is essential, though, to remember that transfer of insights from secondary and tertiary sectors must take account of the social and institutional differences prevailing at these levels of education.

It has also been noted that the pedagogic design of lessons (encouraging one-word answers or longer student contributions) has a strong impact on the likelihood of actual language errors and the ensuing necessity for implicit or explicit correction (Dalton-Puffer, 2007b; Pessoa et al., 2007). The two connected claims that students should be given the necessary interactional space to test their linguistic hypotheses while talking about subject content and that teachers should pay selective but explicit attention to instances of linguistic error or difficulty have become tenets that most CLIL researchers would underwrite (e.g., Pérez Vidal, 2009). In this connection, Lyster's (e.g., 1998, 2007) work on Canadian immersion classrooms has served as a foil for studies in European CLIL contexts (e.g., Dalton-Puffer, 2007b; Lochtmann, 2007; Smit, 2010), producing shared findings like teachers' preference for recasts rather than explicit correction and preference for attending to lexical rather than pronunciation or syntactic errors, as well as a largely intuitive approach to language-focused work as such (Krampitz, 2007).

Language focus can of course be understood in a broader sense than in the studies described earlier, which focused mainly on vocabulary, phonology, and sentence grammar. A recent wider focus of interest in this respect is academic language (see Chamot & O'Malley, 1994; Cummins, 1991; Mohan, Leung, & Davison, 2001) and its development via and use in CLIL lessons. The work on discourse functions such as explaining, hypothesizing, or defining (Dalton-Puffer, 2007a, 2007b; Lose, 2007; Smit, 2010) demonstrates the nonelaborate nature of student realizations of these functions, presumably encouraged by the high degree of contextualization and the informal nature of the classroom talk among familiar participants. Lose (2007) concluded that her secondary students' realization level of academic language functions clearly remained behind the level of L2 competence they demonstrated during their foreign language lessons. Teachers, though clearly capable of producing canonical realizations of these discourse functions, had no declarative knowledge concerning them and were therefore unable to attend explicitly to this issue. A study conducted by Kong (2009) in China contrasted language-trained with content-trained teachers doing science. Her findings indicate that teachers' depth of content knowledge reflected positively not only on the complexity of knowledge relationships co-constructed by the teacher and students but also on "the use of correspondingly complex language" (Kong, 2009, p. 254). Findings such as these thus seem to speak in favor of content-trained teachers, but these teachers' degree of L2 competence clearly remains an issue—and one that remains unsolved in many contexts.

A series of studies, conducted by Llinares and Whittaker (2009, 2010; Whittaker & Llinares, 2009) with Spanish lower-secondary students, showed that, through a carefully orchestrated progression of tasks from oral to written and the ensuing scaffolding, even beginning lower-secondary CLIL students could be guided toward taking first steps into truly subject-specific discourse. Morton's work on the same Spanish social science data (2010) demonstrated that a focus on classroom genres might be a particularly powerful instrument for promoting the development of oral and written academic literacy in CLIL learners. Although parallel work on university lectures (Dafouz, Núñez, & Sancho, 2007; Núñez Perucha & Dafouz Milne, 2007) naturally focused on aspects of lecturers' talk (such as stance, deictic pronouns, and discourse markers), the two strands concur in demonstrating that a genre focus might furnish the much sought-after analytical tool that captures content-and-language integration.[7] Even so, it is clear that much more work needs to be done conceptually and empirically across different contexts until the notions of discourse functions and genres in CLIL classrooms can be regarded as settled.

Generalizing over these and other classroom studies from different contexts (e.g., also, Bonnet, 2004; Llinares & Whittaker, 2009, 2010; Morton, 2010; Whittaker & Llinares, 2009), it can be said that language use in CLIL classrooms shows that the extent to which learners are required to verbalize complex subject matter either orally or in writing largely depends on the decisions and traditions of content-subject pedagogies. Clear differences are also visible between (national) educational cultures with regard to the emphasis on literacy practices in content teaching (central European subject didactics, for instance, seems to be particularly oracy-oriented; e.g., Dalton-Puffer, 2007b; Duff, 1995). On the whole, however, it would be fair to say that explicit attention to this aspect of content learning is rare in CLIL classrooms.

UNDERLYING ASSUMPTIONS AND THEORETICAL UNDERPINNINGS

As noted earlier, public expectations regarding CLIL center on its being efficient and effective for foreign language learning, expectations that are fueled by dissatisfaction with the outcomes of school-based foreign language learning and a somewhat stereotypical view of foreign language lessons as a series of mechanistic grammar drills. CLIL is thus believed to deliver the goods more reliably and with less pain for the learners. It is worth asking the question what assumptions lie behind such expectations.

What is at the center for stakeholders is the understanding that CLIL classrooms are an environment for naturalistic language learning, implying that the best kind of language learning proceeds painlessly, without formal instruction. These implicit baseline assumptions are in line with Krashen's (1985) monitor model, which continues to be the most prominent reception-based theory of language acquisition outside academic research circles. As is well known, the basic idea of the model is that if the language learner is exposed to comprehensible input, acquisition will occur, especially if the learning situation is characterized by positive emotions. The latter condition is widely thought to be fulfilled in CLIL by virtue of the fact that language mistakes are supposedly neither penalized nor corrected in CLIL classrooms.

Applied linguistic research into CLIL has, naturally, made use of a wider theoretical base than this, starting with a focus on interaction (see Long, 1996). Several studies of this kind and their diverse diagnoses regarding the extent of negotiation in CLIL classrooms were mentioned in the previous section. Another important theoretical influence has been Swain's output hypothesis (1995) and its claim that only the self-regulated production of utterances that encode learners' intended meanings forces them to actively process morphosyntactic aspects of the foreign language, thereby expanding their active linguistic repertoire and achieving deeper entrenchment of what they already know. In the CLIL context the implications of the output hypothesis have frequently served as a foil for those observed language behaviors in classrooms that appear conditioned by pedagogical practices restricting the active linguistic engagement of learners both in speech and writing. A further development has been focus on form, that is, paying attention at specific moments during the learning process to formal, lexicogrammatical aspects of language as carriers of meaning (see Doughty & Williams, 1998). An immersion-specific version of this has been formulated in Lyster's (2007) counterbalanced approach, which advocates giving equal weight to meaning focus and form focus in immersion education. Certainly with regard to Canadian immersion education, which was the prime conceptual reference point in (the beginnings of) European CLIL, we can detect a clear movement away from relying solely on the idea of the self-propelled, implicit language learner. In the CLIL scene there has been as yet little activity in this direction in the sense of doing observational (little) or experimental (none) research on form-focused activities during CLIL lessons. The observation tool for language-sensitive pedagogy of de Graaff, Koopman, Anikina, and Westhoff (2007) could serve as a good starting point for systematic study in this regard. For the time being, the definition of CLIL as a dual-focused approach has to be regarded as programmatic rather than factual, and practices that are "content-oriented but language sensitive" (Wolff, 2007, p. 17) cannot be regarded as firmly established.

An even more fundamental move away from the theorems underlying the natural approach is embodied in views of learning as contextual and socially distributed, as they are now widely accepted in education. Under these premises, human beings learn through interacting with other social beings, whereby language acts as a particularly powerful semiotic means for participating and performing in the activities and encounters of the social world.

In accord with the premises of this kind of learning theory, language itself is also conceived of as a process that is socially constructed (e.g., Lantolf, 2002; Lantolf & Thorne, 2006; Swain, 2000). As social encounters involve specific persons in specific roles at specific times and places, the context of situation becomes instrumental rather than coincidental in the language acquisition process and in learning in general. Content-based situations help steer learners' attention from language forms to things accomplished and meanings conveyed through language, and it may well be that it is here that the success of CLIL as a language-learning environment lies. But how far this catalyst role of CLIL will actually go and how necessary it is depend on the contingencies of individual contexts: Contrary to many people's expectations, CLIL is not a panacea.

Much CLIL research, then, while clearly following more sophisticated conceptual orientations than policy papers, still tends to share with those the position that CLIL classrooms are somehow fundamentally different from foreign language lessons. My account (section 4) has shown that there are indeed several such differences, but it must not be overlooked that both CLIL and EFL (English as a foreign language) happen via speech events called *lessons* in well-known institutions called *schools* or *universities*. What I want to underscore, then, is that CLIL classrooms are *classrooms* exhibiting the respective characteristics in terms of participant roles, goals, physical setting, temporal structure, and the like. It needs to be stressed that by virtue of these characteristics, CLIL classrooms share a great deal more with traditional language lessons than a partisan look would make one believe and that CLIL cannot therefore be expected to prepare learners for other situational contexts in any direct way.

What I would like to argue, however, is that this situation offers considerable potential. CLIL lessons are part of the learners' everyday experience of school, they take place within the same local, institutional, personal, and cultural context as all the other school lessons that CLIL learners experience. The lessons are thus well-embedded in the matrix culture of the L1 and possess a high degree of familiarity for the learners. The learners know the discourse of the classroom, and this well-established knowledge provides them with a mental schema or discourse domain for dealing with particular situations (Douglas, 2004). Over and beyond the authentic situation and the cognitively engaging material (Snow, 1998), I consider this familiarity to be a decisive asset in foreign-language CLIL. On entering target-language contexts in the so-called real world, whether they be with native speakers in the target culture or with other nonnatives in lingua franca contexts, L2 speakers are often challenged or even overwhelmed by having to attend to several demanding tasks simultaneously: trying to get hold of the ropes of the discourse, working with incomplete topic knowledge, and operating in an imperfectly known language code. Clearly, if such challenges can be simplified, the burden of the L2 learner can be lightened. As research has shown, being a topic expert significantly improves nonnative speakers' chances to successfully participate in mixed native speaker-nonnative speaker interactions (Zuengler, 1993). Learners in CLIL content classrooms are, by definition, not topic experts, but they are participating in a didactic discourse whose aim is to develop their topic knowledge rather than presuppose it. There are thus two bonuses deriving from the educational setting: the didactic nature of the interaction and the cultural familiarity with the domain of use and its rules. My claim, then, is that CLIL provides a space for language learners that is not geared specifically and exclusively to foreign language learning but at the same time is predefined and prestructured in significant ways by being instructional and taking place within the L1 matrix culture. This, I claim, is a significant source for the self-confident and self-evident use of the foreign language and its ultimate appropriation by many CLIL learners, which is regularly observed to be the most striking outcome of CLIL programs.

LOOKING AHEAD

Concerns with theorizing the interaction of language and content are currently becoming a focus of attention for CLIL researchers. Although the most frequently used wording tends to be that of "content and language integration," a more appropriate goal, I think, would be to transcend such an understanding that conceptualizes language and curricular content as separate reified entities and instead think of them as one process. Several of the approaches that applied linguists have embraced in doing ESL (English as a second language)/ CBI and CLIL research hold a good deal of promise for such an undertaking (constructivist-contextual and sociocultural theories of learning, or systemic functional linguistics)[8] and it will be the task of the research community over the next years to build the necessary bridges to general learning theories based on ideas of discursiveness and performativity ("being doing science"). A first approximation was formulated by Gajo (2007) who suggested that "the notion of integration [of language and content] implies precise reflection on the linguistic aspect of subject knowledge and on the role of discourse in the learning process" (p. 568). I suggest that Halliday's (1993) language-based learning theory is one good starting point for this undertaking.

Apart from the concern with theory, there is a clear empirical research agenda with regard to academic language abilities and requirements, namely, identifying subject-specific language use in terms of lexicon and genres for various content areas. This should lead to clarifying what academic language skills are generally and what they are specifically by subject (the Council of Europe has recently commissioned a project attempting to do this for mother tongue education; see www.coe.int/t/dg4/linguistic/Schoollang_EN.asp). On the theoretical level, this kind of work should lead to a deeper understanding of what *cognitive academic language ability* is (Cummins, 1991). By the same token, the relationship between language for specific purposes and CLIL has to be explored further: The connection was made very clearly before the notion of CLIL saw the light of day (Widdowson, 1980), but has, to my knowledge, not been systematically pursued since then.

Further points on the research agenda are furnished by current debates around CLIL in Europe: first, the already mentioned doubts regarding possible adverse effects on L1 advanced academic language proficiency; second, the continuation (or not) of foreign language classes alongside CLIL lessons; and third, the affordances and challenges of employing native speakers as content teachers as well as CLIL teacher qualifications in general. Although all these debates have a language policy dimension, the one that returns us to the language policy issues discussed at the outset most directly is the need to determine in how far the CLIL enterprise can and does contribute to the production of multilingualism and/or plurilingual individuals. In pursuing this research agenda it will be vital to keep in mind the realization that conceptualizations and findings based on the global lingua franca English as a CLIL medium need to be carefully examined for their transferability to other languages.

NOTES

1 These are relevant issues also in the development of ESL learners'academic literacy (see Schleppegrell & O'Hallaron, 2011—this volume).

2 Analogous findings have been reported for immersion students (e.g. Harley, Allen, Cummins, & Swain, 1990).

3 The problematicity of this is also discussed in Schleppegrell & O'Hallaron's article (2011—this volume) on the academic language development of ESL students in the United States.

4 *Instructional register* refers to talk dedicated to the immediate purpose of instruction and informing about the content taught. *Regulative register* refers to talk designed to organize instruction and learning (Christie, 2002).

5 Analogous findings were reported in the 1990 volume by Harley et al. and were at the core of Swain's output hypothesis (e.g., Swain, 1995).

6 This is another concern that CLIL shares with academic literacy development in ESL learners (cf. Schleppegrell & O'Hallaron, 2011—this volume).

7 See Paesani (2011—this volume) for a similar trend in language-and-literature integration.

8 With regard to CBI, compare to, for example, Gibbons (2002); Mohan & Beckett (2001); and Schleppegrell, Achugar, & Orteíza (2004).

ANNOTATED BIBLIOGRAPHY

Coyle, D., & Baetens Beardsmore, H. (Eds.). (2007). *International Journal of Bilingual Education and Bilingualism* [Special Issue on CLIL], 10.

In addition to a range of empirical studies, Coyle's introductory chapter "Towards a Connected Research Agenda for CLIL Pedagogies" (pp. 543–562) gives a good introduction into key issues and presents her influential 4Cs conceptualization of CLIL education (content, communication, cognition, culture). Another important contribution is de Graaf et al.'s "Observation tool for effective L2 pedagogy in CLIL" (pp. 603–624).

Coyle, D., Hood, P., & Marsh, D. (2010). *CLIL: Content and language integrated learning*. New York, NY: Cambridge University Press.

A comprehensive and accessible introduction to CLIL as an educational approach that covers important theoretical and pedagogical background in addition to providing sound guidelines for implementation. Manages to address both educators and scholars.

Dale, L., Van der Es, W., & Tanner, R. (2010). *CLIL skills*. Leiden, the Netherlands: University of Leiden, Expertisecentrum mtv.

This handbook combines the expertise of experienced classroom teachers and teacher educators from the Netherlands. Strong not only on activities but also featuring a well-thought out general concept and background knowledge on each topic area. It is designed not only for CLIL teacher education courses but also for self-study.

Dalton-Puffer, C. (2007b). *Discourse in content and language integrated learning (CLIL) classrooms*. Amsterdam, the Netherlands: John Benjamins.

The book is a comprehensive study based on a corpus of 40 secondary level CLIL lessons taught in Austria, providing a detailed analysis of the discourse produced in CLIL classrooms and a discussion of its contribution to language learning processes. Topics discussed include construction of content knowledge, influence of questions on classroom interaction, classroom directives, repair work, and academic language functions.

Dalton-Puffer, C., Nikula, T., & Smit, U. (Eds.). (2010). *Language use and language learning in CLIL*. Amsterdam, the Netherlands: John Benjamins.

This is a collection of 12 empirical studies on classroom interaction as well as learning outcomes that includes a new research focus on writing in CLIL contexts. The final chapter by the editors discusses several problematic issues around CLIL that have so far remained underexposed and underdiscussed.

Hansen-Pauly, M. A., Bentner, G., Llinares, A., Morton, T., Dafouz, E., Favilli, F., Novotna, J., et al. (2009). *Teacher education for CLIL across contexts*. Brussels, Belgium: European Commission, Directorate General for Education and Culture. Retrieved from http: //clil.uni.lu

This publication is the product of a 3-year multilateral European project involving 14 coauthors. It consists of two parts: (a) a conceptual framework developed from classroom observation and relevant research in selected areas of bilingual education and learning to scaffold curriculum development for CLIL teacher education and (b) a booklet of tasks and activities for use in teacher development.

Marsh, D., & Wolff, D. (Eds.). (2007). *Diverse contexts—converging goals. CLIL in Europe*. Frankfurt am Main, Germany: Lang.

Twenty-eight contributions from across the European Union cover classroom practice, evaluation, research, and program management. Wolff's opening chapter "CLIL: Bridging the Gap Between School and Working Life" (pp. 15–25) is an excellent first text for novices on CLIL training courses, summarizing the basic assumptions in a positive light but without undue oversimplification.

Pérez Vidal, C. (2009). The integration of content and language in the classroom: A European approach to education (the second time around). In E. Dafouz & M. Guerrini (Eds.), *CLIL across educational levels* (pp. 3–16). Madrid, Spain: Richmond.

This is a compact, article-length introduction and overview. It includes a short history of CLIL in Europe, but is particularly strong on revealing underlying educational, psycholinguistic, and pedagogical thinking.

REFERENCES

Admiraal, W., Westhoff, G., & de Bot, K. (2006). Evaluation of bilingual secondary education in the Netherlands: Students' language proficiency in English. *Educational Research and Evaluation, 12*, 75–93.

Airey, J. (2009). Estimating undergraduate bilingual scientific literacy in Sweden. *International CLIL Research Journal, 1*, 26–35.

Airey, J., & Linder, C. (2006). Language and the experience of learning university physics in Sweden. *European Journal of Physics, 27*, 553–560.

Badertscher, H., & Bieri, T. (2009). *Wissenserwerb im content-and-language integrated learning*. Bern-Stuttgart-Wien, Switzerland: Haupt.

Bonnet, A. (2004). *Chemie im bilingualen Unterricht. Kompetenzerwerb durch Interaktion*. Opladen Germany: Leske+Budrich.

Brinton, D. M., Snow, M. A., & Wesche, M. B. (2008). *Content-based second language instruction*. Ann Arbor: University of Michigan Press. (Original work published 1989)

Bruthiaux, P. (2009). Multilingual Asia: Looking back, looking across, looking forward. In L. Lim & E.-L. Low (Eds.), *Multilingual, globalizing Asia* (pp. 120–130). Amsterdam, the Netherlands: John Benjamins.

Canagarajah, S. A. (1995). Functions of code switching in ESL classrooms: Socialising bilingualism in Jaffna. *Journal of Multilingual and Multicultural Development, 6*, 173–195.

Chamot, A. U., & O'Malley, M. (1994). *The CALLA handbook: Implementing the Cognitive Academic Language Learning Approach*. Reading, MA: Addison-Wesley.

Christie, F. (2002). *Classroom discourse analysis. A functional perspective*. London, UK: Continuum.

Coetzee-Lachmann, D. (2009). *Assessment of subject-specific task performance of bilingual geography learners* (Unpublished doctoral thesis). University of Osnabrück, Germany.

Coyle, D., Hood, P., & Marsh, D. (2010). *CLIL: Content and language integrated learning*. New York, NY: Cambridge University Press.

Crandall, J. (1992). Content-centered learning in the U.S. *Annual Review of Applied Linguistics, 13*, 110–126.

Cromdal, J. (2005). Bilingual order in collaborative word processing: On creating an English text in Swedish. *Journal of Pragmatics, 37*, 329–353.

Cummins, J. (1984). *Bilingualism and special education*. Clevedon, UK: Multilingual Matters.

Cummins, J. (1991). Conversational and academic language proficiency in bilingual context. *AILA Review, 8*, 75–89.

Cummins, J. (2000). *Language, power, and pedagogy: Bilingual children in the crossfire*. Clevedon, UK: Multilingual Matters.

Dafouz, E., Núñez, B., & Sancho, C. (2007). Analyzing stance in a CLIL university context: Non-native speaker use of personal pronouns and modal verbs. *International Journal of Bilingual Education and Bilingualism, 10*, 647–662.

Dalton-Puffer, C. (2007a). Academic language functions in a CLIL environment. In D. Marsh & D. Wolff (Eds.), *Diverse contexts—converging goals* (pp. 201–210). Frankfurt, Germany: Peter Lang.

Dalton-Puffer, C. (2007b). *Discourse in content and language integrated learning (CLIL) classrooms*. Amsterdam, the Netherlands: John Benjamins.

Dalton-Puffer, C., Hüttner, J., Jexenflicker, S., Schindelegger, V., & Smit, U. (2008). *Content and language integrated learning an Österreichs Höheren Technischen Lehranstalten. Forschungsbericht.* Vienna, Austria: Universität Wien & Bundesministerium für Unterricht, Kultur und Kunst.

Dalton-Puffer, C., & Nikula, T. (2006). Pragmatics of content-based instruction: Teacher and student directives in Finnish and Austrian classrooms. *Applied Linguistics, 27*, 241–267.

Day, E. M., & Shapson, S. M. (1996). *Studies in immersion education*. Clevedon, UK: Multilingual Matters.

de Graaff, R., Koopman, G. J., Anikina, Y., & Westhoff, G. (2007). An observation tool for effective L2 pedagogy and language integrated learning (CLIL). *International Journal of Bilingual Education and Bilingualism, 10*, 603–624.

Doughty, C., & Williams, J. (Eds.). (1998). *Focus on form in classroom second language acquisition*. Cambridge, UK: Cambridge University Press.

Douglas, D. (2004). Discourse domains: The cognitive context of speaking. In D. Boxer & A. Cohen (Eds.), *Studying speaking to inform second language learning* (pp. 25–48). Clevedon, UK: Multilingual Matters.

Duff, P. (1995). An ethnography of communication in immersion classrooms in Hungary. *TESOL Quarterly, 29*, 505–537.

Escobar Urmeneta, C. (2010). Pre-service CLIL teacher-education in Catalonia. Expert and novice practitioners teaching and reflecting together. In Y. Ruiz de Zarobe & D. Lasagabaster (Eds.), *CLIL in Spain: Implementation, results and teacher training* (pp. 188–218). Newcastle upon Tyne, UK: Cambridge Scholars.

European Commission. (1995). *White paper on education and training. Teaching and learning: Towards the learning society.* Retrieved from http: //europa.eu/documents/comm/ white_papers/pdf/com95_590_en.pdf

European Commission. (2003). *Promoting language learning and linguistic diversity: An action plan 2004–2006*, 1–29. Retrieved from http: //ec.europa.eu/education/ doc/official/ keydoc/actlang/act_lang_en.pdf

European Commission. (2008). Multilingualism: An asset for Europe and a shared commitment. *Communication of the European Commission*, 1–15. Retrieved from http: //ec.europa.eu/education/languages/pdf/com/2008_0566_en.pdf

Eurydice Network. (2006). *Content and language integrated learning (CLIL) at school in Europe*. Brussels, Belgium: Retrieved from http: //eacea.ec.europa.eu/education/eurydice/thematic_studies_archives_en.php

Ferguson, G. (2006). *Language planning and education*. Edinburgh, Scotland: Edinburgh University Press.

Fernández, D. J. et al. (Eds.). (2008). *Proceedings selection from XXXIII FAAPI Conference: Using the language to learn. Learning to use the language: What's next in Latin America*. Santiago del Estero, Argentina: British Council.

Fernández Fontecha, A. (2009). Spanish CLIL: Research and official actions. In Y. Ruiz de Zarobe & R. M. Jiménez Catalán (Eds.), *Content and language integrated learning: Evidence from research in Europe* (pp. 3–21). Bristol, UK: Multilingual Matters.

Gajo, L. (2007). Linguistic knowledge and subject knowledge: How does bilingualism contribute to subject development? *International Journal of Bilingual Education and Bilingualism, 10*, 563–579.

Gallardo del Puerto, F., García Lecumberri, M., & Gómez Lacabex, E. (2009). Testing the effectiveness of content and language integrated learning in foreign language contexts: Assessment of English pronunciation. In Y. Ruiz de Zarobe & R. M. Jiménez Catalán (Eds.), *Content and language integrated learning: Evidence from research in Europe* (pp. 215–234). Bristol, UK: Multilingual Matters.

Gibbons, P. (2002). *Scaffolding language, scaffolding learning: Teaching second language learners in the mainstream classroom*. Portsmouth, NH: Heinemann.

A guide to languages in the European Union. (2008, September). *EUBusiness.com*. Retrieved from: http: //www.eubusiness.com/topics/Languages/eu-languages-guide/

Hajer, M. (2000). Creating a language-promoting classroom: Content-area teachers at work. In J. K. Hall & L. Stoops Verplaetse (Eds.), *Second and foreign language learning through classroom interaction* (pp. 265–285). Mahwah, NJ: Erlbaum.

Halliday, M. A. K. (1993). Towards a language-based theory of learning. *Linguistics and Education, 5*, 93–116.

Harley, B., Allen, P., Cummins, J., & Swain, M. (Eds.). (1990). *The development of second language proficiency*. Cambridge, UK: Cambridge University Press.

Hüttner, J., & Rieder-Bünemann, A. (2010). A cross-sectional analysis of oral narratives by children with CLIL and non-CLIL instruction. In C. Dalton-Puffer, T. Nikula, & U. Smit (Eds.), *Language use and language learning in CLIL classrooms* (pp. 61–80). Amsterdam, the Netherlands: John Benjamins.

Jäppinen, A.-K. (2005). Thinking and content learning of mathematics and science as cognitional development in content and language integrated learning (CLIL): Teaching through a foreign language in Finland. *Language and Education, 19*, 148–169.

Järvinen, H.-M. (2010). Language as a meaning making resource in learning and teaching content: Analysing historical writing in content and language integrated learning. In C. Dalton-Puffer, T. Nikula, & U. Smit (Eds.), *Language use and language learning in CLIL classrooms* (pp. 145–168). Amsterdam, the Netherlands: John Benjamins.

Jexenflicker, S., & Dalton-Puffer, C. (2010). The CLIL differential: Comparing the writing of CLIL and non-CLIL students in higher colleges of technology. In C. Dalton-Puffer, T. Nikula, & U. Smit (Eds.), *Language use and language learning in CLIL classrooms* (pp. 169–190). Amsterdam, the Netherlands: John Benjamins.

Johnson, K., & Swain, M. (Eds.). 1997. *Immersion education: International perspectives.* Cambridge, UK: Cambridge University Press.

Kiraz, A., Güneyli, A., Baysen, E., Gündüz, S., & Baysen, F. (2010). Effect of science and technology learning with foreign language on the attitude and success of students. *Procedia: Social and Behavioral Sciences, 2*, 4130–4136.

Kong, S. (2009). Content-based instruction: What can we learn from content-trained teachers' and language-trained teachers' pedagogies? *Canadian Modern Language Review, 66*, 233–267.

Krampitz, S. (2007). Spracharbeit im bilingualen Unterricht. Ergebnisse einer Befragung von LehrerInnen und Lehrern. In D. Caspari, W. Hallet, A. Wegner, & W. Zydatiß (Eds.), *Bilingualer Unterricht macht Schule: Beiträge aus der Praxisforschung* (pp. 133–146). Frankfurt am Main, Germany: Peter Lang.

Krashen, S. (1985). *The input hypothesis. Issues and implications.* London, UK: Longman.

Lantolf, J. P. (2002). Sociocultural theory and second language acquisition. In R. B. Kaplan (Ed.), *Oxford handbook of applied linguistics* (pp. 104–114). Oxford, UK: Oxford University Press.

Lantolf, J. P., & Thorne, S. L. (2006). *Sociocultural theory and the genesis of second language development.* Oxford, UK: Oxford University Press.

Lasagabaster, D. (2008). Foreign language competence in content and language integrated learning. *Open Applied Linguistics Journal, 1*, 31–42.

Lasagabaster, D., & Ruiz de Zarobe, Y. (Eds.). (2010). *CLIL in Spain: Implementation, results and teacher training.* Newcastle upon Tyne, UK: Cambridge Scholars.

Lasagabaster, D., & Sierra, J. M. (2009). Language attitudes in CLIL and traditional EFL classes. *International Journal of CLIL Research, 1*, 4–17.

Li, D. C. S. (2002). Hong Kong parents' preference for English-medium education: Passive victims of imperialism or active agents of pragmatism? In A. Kirkpatrick (Ed.), *Englishes in Asia: Communication, identity, power, & education* (pp. 29–62). Melbourne, Australia:

Language Australia.

Lim, L., & Low, E.-L. (Eds.). (2009). Multilingual, globalizing Asia: Implications for policy and education. *AILA Review, 22*.

Lim Falk, M. (2008). Svenska i engelskspråkig skolmiljö. Ämnesrelaterat språkbruk i två gymnasieklasser [Swedish in an English classroom environment. Language use in two grammar school classes]. Stockholm, Sweden: Eddy. (Reprinted from *Acta Universitatis Stockholmiensis* [Stockholm Studies in Scandinavian Philology], *46*)

Llinares, A., & Whittaker, R. (2009). Teaching and learning history in secondary CLIL classrooms: From speaking to writing. In E. Dafouz & M. Guerrini (Eds.), *CLIL across educational levels: Experiences from primary, secondary and tertiary contexts* (pp. 73–88). Madrid, Spain: Richmond.

Llinares, A., & Whittaker, R. (2010). Writing and speaking in the history class: A comparative analysis of CLIL and first language contexts. In C. Dalton-Puffer, T. Nikula, & U. Smit (Eds.), *Language use and language learning in CLIL classrooms* (pp. 125–144). Amsterdam, the Netherlands: John Benjamins.

Lo, Y.-Y., & Murphy, V. A. (2010). Vocabulary knowledge and growth in immersion and regular language-learning programmes in Hong Kong. *Language and Education, 24*, 215–238.

Lochtmann, K. (2007). Die mündliche Fehlerkorrektur in CLIL und im traditionellen Fremdsprachenunterricht: Ein Vergleich. In C. Dalton-Puffer & U. Smit (Eds.), *Empirical perspectives on CLIL classroom discourse—CLIL: Empirische Untersuchungen zum Unterrichtsdiskurs* (pp. 119–138). Frankfurt, Germany: Lang.

Long, M. H. (1996). The role of the linguistic environment in second language acquisition. In W. C. Ritchie & T. K. Bahtia (Eds.), *Handbook of second language acquisition* (pp. 413–468). New York, NY: Academic Press.

Lorenzo, F., Casal, S., & Moore, P. (2005). *Orientaciones para la elaboración del currículo integrado de las lengaus en los centros bilingües*. Seville, Spain: Consejería de Educación (Junta de Andalucía).

Lorenzo, F., & Moore, P. (2010). On the natural emergence of language structures in CLIL: Towards a theory of European educational bilingualism. In C. Dalton-Puffer, T. Nikula, & U. Smit (Eds.), *Language use and language learning in CLIL classrooms* (pp. 23–38). Amsterdam, the Netherlands: John Benjamins.

Lose, J. (2007). The language of scientific discourse: Ergebnisse einer empirisch-deskriptiven Interaktionsanalyse zur Verwendung fachbezogener Diskursfunktionen im bilingualen Biologieunterricht. In D. Caspari, W. Hallet, A. Wegner, & W. Zydatiß (Eds.), *Bilingualer Unterricht macht Schule: Beiträge aus der Praxisforschung* (pp. 97–107). Frankfurt am Main, Germany: Peter Lang.

Lyster, R. (1998). Negotiation of form, recasts, and explicit correction in relation to error types and learner repair in immersion classrooms. *Language Learning, 48*, 183–218.

Lyster, R. (2007). *Learning and teaching languages through content: A counterbalanced approach.* Amsterdam, the Netherlands: John Benjamins.

Maillat, D. (2010). The pragmatics of L2 in CLIL. In C. Dalton-Puffer, T. Nikula, & U. Smit (Eds.), *Language use and language learning in CLIL* (pp. 39–60). Amsterdam, the Netherlands: John Benjamins.

Maljers, A., Marsh, D., & Wolff, D. (Eds.). (2007). *Windows on CLIL. Content and language integrated learning in the spotlight.* The Hague, the Netherlands: European Platform for Dutch Education.

Mariotti, C. (2006). Negotiated interactions and repair. *VIEWS Vienna English Working Papers, 15*, 33–41. Retrieved from http: //anglistik.univie.ac.at/views/archive/

Marsh, D., & Frigols, M.-J. (2007). CLIL as a catalyst for change in language education. *Babylonia, 3*, 33–37.

Martínez Adrián, M.,& Gutiérrez Mangado, M. J. (2009). The acquisition of English syntax by CLIL learners in the Basque country. In Y. Ruiz de Zarobe & R. M. Jiménez Catalán (Eds.), *Content and language integrated learning: Evidence from research in Europe* (pp. 176–196). Clevedon, UK: Multilingual Matters.

McDougald, J. S. (2009). The state of language and content instruction in Colombia. *Latin American Journal of Content & Language Integrated Learning, 2*, 44–48.

Mehisto, P., Marsh, D., & Frigols, M. J. (2008). *Uncovering CLIL: Content and language integrated learning in bilingual and multilingual education.* Oxford, UK: Macmillan.

Mewald, C. (2007). A comparison of oral language performance of learners in CLIL and mainstream classes at lower secondary level in Lower Austria. In C. Dalton-Puffer & U. Smit (Eds.), *Empirical perspectives on CLIL classroom discourse* (pp. 139–178). Frankfurt, Germany: Peter Lang.

Mohan, B., & Beckett, G.H. (2001). A functional approach to research on content-based language learning. *Canadian Modern Language Review, 58*, 133–155.

Mohan, B., Leung, C., & Davison, C. (Eds.). (2001). *English as a second language in the mainstream.* London, UK: Pearson Education.

Moore, P. (2007). Enhancing classroom discourse: A modeling potential for content teachers. *Revista Española de Lingüística Aplicada. Ejemplar: Models and Practice in CLIL, 1*, 141–152.

Moore, P. (2009). *On the emergence of L2 oracy in bilingual education: A comparative analysis of CLIL and mainstream learner talk* (Unpublished doctoral thesis). Universidad Pablo de Olavide, Sevilla, Spain.

Morton, T. (2010). Using a genre-based approach to integrating content and language in

CLIL: The example of secondary history. In C. Dalton-Puffer, T. Nikula, & U. Smit (Eds.), *Language use and language learning in CLIL classrooms* (pp. 81–104). Amsterdam, the Netherlands: John Benjamins.

Nikula, T. (2007). Speaking English in Finnish content-based classrooms. *World Englishes, 26*, 206–223.

Nikula, T. (2008). Learning pragmatics in content-based classrooms. In E. Alcón Soler & A. Martínez Flor (Eds.), *Investigating pragmatics in foreign language learning, teaching and testing* (pp. 94–113). Clevedon, UK: Multilingual Matters.

Nikula, T. (2010). On effects of CLIL on a teacher's language use. In C. Dalton-Puffer, T. Nikula, & U. Smit (Eds.), *Language use and language learning in CLIL classrooms* (pp. 105–124). Amsterdam, the Netherlands: John Benjamins.

Núñez Perucha, B., & Dafouz Milne, E. (2007). Lecturing through the foreign language in a CLIL university context: Linguistic and pragmatic implications. *VIEWS Vienna English Working Papers, 16*, 36–42. Retrieved from http: //anglistik.univie.ac.at/views/archive/

Paesani, K. (2011). Research in language-literature instruction: Meeting the call for change? *Annual Review of Applied Linguistics, 31*, this volume.

Pérez Vidal, C. (2009). The integration of content and language in the classroom: A European approach to education (the second time around). In E. Dafouz & M. Guerrini (Eds.), *CLIL across educational levels* (pp. 3–16). Madrid, Spain: Richmond.

Pessoa, S., Hendry, H., Donato, R., Tucker, R. G., & Lee, H. (2007). Content-based instruction in the foreign language classroom: A discourse perspective. *Foreign Language Annals, 40*, 102–121.

Pistorio, Maria Inés. (2009).Teacher training and competences for effective CLIL teaching in Argentina. *Latin American Journal of Content and Language Integrated Learning 2*(2), 37–43.

Prinsloo, M., & Baynham, M. (Eds.). (2008). *AILA Applied Linguistics: Series 2. Literacies, global and local.* Amsterdam, the Netherlands: John Benjamins.

Ruiz de Zarobe, Y. (2008). CLIL and foreign language learning: A longitudinal study in the Basque country. *International CLIL Research Journal, 1*, 60–73.

Ruiz de Zarobe, Y. (2010). Written production and CLIL: An empirical study. In C. Dalton-Puffer, T. Nikula, & U. Smit (Eds.), *Language use and language learning in CLIL classrooms* (pp. 191–212). Amsterdam, the Netherlands: John Benjamins.

Schleppegrell, M., Achugar, M., & Orteíza, T. (2004). The grammar of history: enhancing content-based instruction through a functional focus on language. *TESOL Quarterly 38*, 67–93.

Schleppegrell, M., & O'Hallaron, C. (2011). Teaching academic language in L2 secondary settings. *Annual Review of Applied Linguistics, 31*, this volume.

Shohamy, E. (2006). *Language policy: Hidden agendas and new approaches*. London, UK: Routledge.
Snow, M. A. (1998). Trends and issues in content-based instruction. *Annual Review of Applied Linguistics, 18*, 243–267.
Spanos, G. (1989). On the integration of language and content instruction. *Annual Review of Applied Linguistics, 10*, 227–240.
Spolsky, B. (2004). *Language policy*. Cambridge, UK: Cambridge University Press.
Stoller, F. L. (2004). Content-based instruction: Perspectives on curriculum planning. *Annual Review of Applied Linguistics, 24*, 264–283.
Swain, M. (1995). Three functions of output in second language learning. In G. Cook & B. Seidlhofer (Eds.), *Principle and practice in applied linguistics* (pp. 125–144). Oxford, UK: Oxford University Press.
Swain, M. (2000). The output hypothesis and beyond: Mediating acquisition through collaborative dialogue. In J. P. Lantolf (Ed.), *Sociocultural theory and second language learning* (pp. 97–114). Oxford, UK: Oxford University Press.
Sylvén, L. K. (2004). *Teaching in English or English teaching? On the effects of content and language integrated learning on Swedish learners' incidental vocabulary acquisition* (Unpublished doctoral dissertation). Göteborg University, Göteborg, Sweden.
Tarone, E., & Swain, M. (1995). A sociolinguistic perspective on second-language use in immersion classrooms. *Modern Language Journal, 79*, 166–178.
Tollefson, J. W., & Tsui, A. B. M. (Eds.). (2004). *Medium of instruction policies: Which agenda? Whose agenda?* Mahwah, NJ: Erlbaum.
Tsui, A. B. M., & Tollefson, J. W. (Eds.). (2007). *Language policy, culture and identity in Asian contexts*. Mahwah, NJ: Erlbaum.
van de Craen, P., Ceuleers, E., & Mondt, K. (2007). Cognitive development and bilingualism in primary schools: Teaching maths in a CLIL environment. In D. Marsh & D. Wolff (Eds.), *Diverse contexts—converging goals: CLIL in Europe* (pp. 185–200). Frankfurt am Main, Germany: Lang.
Villarreal, I., & García Mayo, M. (2009). Tense and agreement morphology in the interlanguage of Basque-Spanish bilinguals: Content-based learning vs. the learning of English as a school subject. In Y. Ruiz de Zarobe & R. M. Jiménez Catalán (Eds.), *Content and language integrated learning: Evidence from research in Europe* (pp. 215–234). Bristol, UK: Multilingual Matters.
Vollmer, H. J., Heine, L., Troschke, R., Coetzee, D., & Küttel, V. (2006, August). *Subject-specific competence and language use of CLIL learners: The case of geography in grade 10 of secondary schools in Germany*. Paper presented at the ESSE8 Conference, London, UK.
Walker, E. (2010). Evaluation of a support intervention for senior secondary school English

immersion. *System, 38*, 50–62.

Whittaker, R., & Llinares, A. (2009). CLIL in social science classrooms: Analysis of spoken and written productions. In Y. Ruiz de Zarobe & R. M. Jiménez Catalán (Eds.), *Content and language integrated learning. Evidence from research in Europe* (pp. 215–234). Bristol, UK: Multilingual Matters.

Widdowson, H. (1980). *Reading and thinking in English 1–4*. Oxford, UK: Oxford University Press.

Wolff, D. (2007). CLIL: Bridging the gap between school and working life. In D. Marsh & D. Wolff (Eds.), *Diverse contexts—converging goals. CLIL in Europe* (pp. 15–25). Frankfurt am Main, Germany: Peter Lang.

Zuengler, J. (1993). Encouraging learners' conversational participation: The effect of content knowledge. *Language Learning*, 43, 403–432.

Zydatiß, W. (2007). *Deutsch*-Englische Züge in Berlin (DEZIBEL). Eine Evaluation des bilimgualen Sachfachunterrichts in Gymnasien: Kontext, Kompetenzen, Konsequenzen. Frankfurt am Main, Germany: Peter Lang.

Corpus Research Applications in Second Language Teaching

Ute Römer

Over the past few decades, corpora have not only revolutionized linguistic research but have also had an impact on second language learning and teaching. In the field of applied linguistics, more and more researchers and practitioners treasure what corpus linguistics has to offer to language pedagogy. Still, corpora and corpus tools have yet to be widely implemented in pedagogical contexts. The aim of this article is to provide an overview of pedagogical corpus applications and to review recent publications in the area of corpus linguistics and language teaching. It covers indirect corpus applications, such as in syllabus or materials design, as well as direct applications of corpora in the second language classroom. The article aims to illustrate how both general and specialized language corpora can be used in these applications and discusses directions for future research in applied corpus linguistics.

Over the past few decades, corpora, corpus tools, and corpus evidence have not only revolutionized linguistic research but have also had an impact on second language learning and teaching—probably a use that "the compilers [of corpora] may not have foreseen" (Johansson, 2007, p. 17). John Sinclair's work with COBUILD (Collins Birmingham University International Language Database),[1] Tim Johns's data-driven learning (DDL), and Dieter Mindt's empirical grammar research can be considered particularly groundbreaking developments in the context of pedagogically oriented English corpus linguistics in the 1980s (see Johns, 1986, 1991; Mindt, 1981, 1987; Sinclair, 1987, 1991). In the field of applied linguistics, more and more researchers and practitioners value what corpus linguistics has to offer to language pedagogy, and the number of publications on related topics has increased steadily. (See, e.g., Ädel, 2006; Aijmer, 2009; Aston, 2001; Braun, Kohn, & Mukherjee, 2006; Campoy, Belles-Fortuño, & Gea-Valor, 2010; Gavioli, 2006; Granger, Hung, & Petch-Tyson, 2002; Kettemann & Marko, 2006; Lombardo, 2009; Reppen, 2010; Römer, 2005; Scott & Tribble, 2006; Sinclair, 2004a; and the proceedings of the first seven events in the Teaching and Language Corpora [TaLC] conference series: Aston, Bernardini, & Stewart, 2004; Botley, Glass, McEnery, & Wilson, 1996; Burnard & McEnery, 2000; Frankenberg-Garcia, Flowerdew, & Aston, 2011; Hidalgo, Quereda, & Santana, 2007; Kettemann & Marko, 2002; Wichmann, Fligelstone, McEnery, & Knowles, 1997).[2] Also, there is now a wide range of fully corpus-based reference works (including dictionaries and grammars) available to learners, and a number of dedicated researchers and teachers have made concrete suggestions on how concordances and exercises directly derived from corpora could be used in the second language (L2) classroom.

I would, however, still be hesitant to say that corpora and corpus tools have been fully implemented in pedagogical contexts and would argue that much work still remains to be done in bridging the gap between research and practice. The practice of English language teaching (ELT) to date, at least, seems to be only marginally affected by the advances of corpus research, and comparatively few teachers and learners know about the availability of useful resources and get their hands on corpus computers or concordances themselves (see Mukherjee, 2004). In addition, current language-teaching materials still differ considerably from actual language use as captured in corpora (e.g., Römer, 2005). Despite the obvious and recognized strengths of corpus use in a pedagogical context, for example that corpora highlight what lexical items and collocations are typical in the language, and that they provide us with large amounts of natural language examples (see Hunston, 2002; Römer, 2005), it seems that there is still a lack of awareness of corpora and, in some cases, resistance toward corpora from students, teachers, and materials writers.

The aim of this article is to provide an overview of pedagogical corpus applications and to review recent publications in the area of corpus linguistics and language teaching. It aims to illustrate how both general language corpora, such as the British National Corpus (BNC) or the Corpus of Contemporary American English (COCA), and specialized corpora, such as the Michigan Corpus of Academic Spoken English (MICASE) or the International Corpus of Learner English

(ICLE), can be used in these applications. This article also discusses how much has been achieved so far in the field and points toward future research in applied corpus linguistics.

When we refer to applications of corpora in L2 teaching, this includes both the use of corpus *tools*, that is, the actual text collections and software packages for corpus access, and corpus *methods*, that is, the analytic techniques that are used when we work with corpus data. In classifying pedagogical corpus applications, that is, the use of corpus tools and methods in a language teaching and language learning context, a useful distinction (going back to Leech, 1997) can be made between direct and indirect applications (see Figure 1). This means that, indirectly, corpora can help with decisions about *what* to teach and *when* to teach it. Indirect corpus applications thus have an effect on the teaching syllabus and the design of teaching materials. Corpora can also be accessed directly by learners and teachers in the L2 classroom, and so "assist in the teaching process" (Fligelstone, 1993, p. 98). Direct applications mainly affect *how* something is taught and learned. They actively involve the learner and teacher in the process of working with corpora and concordances. The following sections will feature a few important lines of research and developments in both areas as presented in Figure 1. As the figure shows, we can identify different types of direct and indirect applications, depending on whom

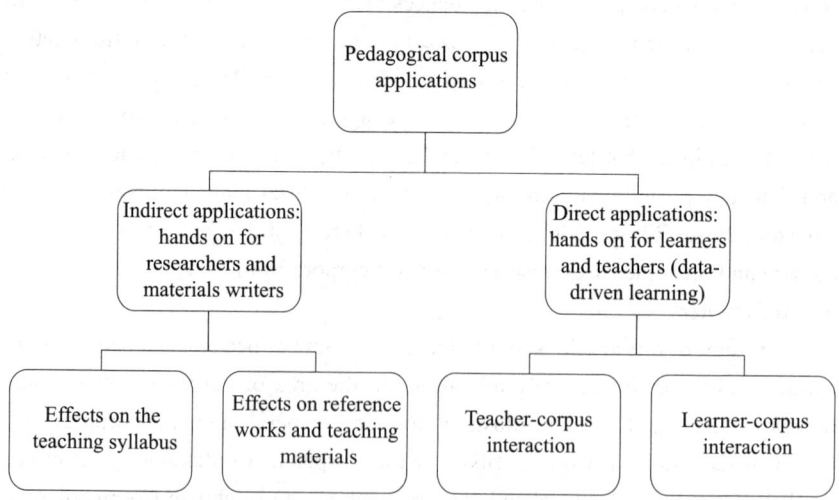

Fig. 1. The use of corpora in second language learning and teaching.

or what is affected by the use of corpus methods and tools. In the discussions below, I will consider these distinctions and refer throughout to the pedagogical uses of general corpora as well as specialized corpora. The focus will be on applications of English language corpora with occasional reference to studies which use corpora of other languages. This reflects the current state of the art where considerably more corpora of English than other languages are publically available and used in pedagogical contexts.

INDIRECT APPLICATIONS OF CORPORA AND CORPUS RESEARCH IN SECOND LANGUAGE TEACHING

As Barlow (1996) observed, "[t]he results of a corpus-based investigation can serve as a firm basis for both linguistic description and, on the applied side, as input for language learning" (p. 32). This implies that corpora and the evidence derived from them can greatly affect course design and the content of teaching materials. Existing pedagogical descriptions are evaluated in the light of "new evidence" (Sinclair, 2004c, p. 271), and new decisions are made about the selection of language phenomena, the progression in the course, and the presentation of the selected items and structures (cf. Mindt, 1981; Römer, 2005).

Corpus Research and Selecting What to Teach

Corpora have proven to be an invaluable resource in the design of language teaching syllabi that emphasize communicative competence (see Hymes, 1972, 1992) and give prominence to those items that occur frequently in the language and that learners are hence most likely to encounter in real-life communicative situations. In the context of computer corpus-informed ELT syllabi, the first and probably most groundbreaking development was the design of the *Collins COBUILD English Course* (CCEC) (Willis & Willis, 1989), an offshoot of the pioneering COBUILD project in pedagogically oriented lexicography (see Sinclair, 1987). The contents of this new, corpus-driven "lexical syllabus" are "the commonest words and phrases in English and their meanings" (Willis, 1990, p. 124). With its focus on lexis and lexical patterns, the CCEC responds to some of the most central findings of corpus research, namely, that language is highly patterned in that it consists of an immense degree of repeated word combinations, and that lexis and grammar are inseparably linked. Also worth mentioning is a much earlier attempt to improve the teaching of English vocabulary that was made long before the advent of computers and electronic corpora. In 1934, Michael West organized a conference "to discuss the part played by corpus-based word lists in the teaching of English as a foreign language" (Kennedy, 1992, p. 327). About 20 years later, West's (1953) *General Service List of English Words* (GSL) was published and has since then exerted great influence on curriculum design (cf. Kennedy, 1992; Willis, 1990). As the title indicates, West's GSL suggests a syllabus that is based on words rather than on grammatical structures. It is also based on frequently occurring words rather than on rare ones. Of course, frequency of occurrence is not the only criterion that should influence decisions about the inclusion of items in the teaching syllabus; there are other relevant criteria, such as "range, availability, coverage, and learnability (Mackey, 1965, p. 188)" (Kennedy, 1992, p. 340; see also Nation, 1990), but it is certainly an immensely important one (see also Leech, 1997). It can be safely assumed that learners will find it easier to develop both their receptive and productive skills when confronted with the most common lexical items of a language (and the patterns and meanings with which these items typically occur) than when the language-teaching input they get gives high priority to infrequent words and structures that the learners rarely encounter in real-life situations.

Another current strand in applied corpus research, which aims to inform the teaching syllabus and stresses the importance of frequency of occurrence, examines language items in actual language use and compares the distributions and patterns found in general reference corpora (of speech and/or writing) with the presentations of the same items in teaching materials (course books, grammars, and usage handbooks). The starting point for these kinds of studies usually includes language features that are known to cause perpetual problems for learners—for example, for German, discourse particles (Jones, 1997), modal verbs (Jones, 2000), the passive voice (Jones, 2000), and prepositions (Jones, 1997); and, for English, future time expressions (Mindt, 1987, 1997), *if*-clauses (Römer, 2004a), irregular verbs (Grabowski & Mindt, 1995), linking adverbials (Conrad, 2004), modal verbs (Mindt, 1995; Römer, 2004b), the present perfect (Lorenz, 2002; Schlüter, 2002), progressive verb forms (Römer, 2005, 2007), and reflexives (Barlow, 1996). For all these phenomena, researchers have found considerable mismatches between naturally occurring German and English and the type of German or English that is put forward as a model in the examined teaching materials. They have, as a consequence, called for corpus-inspired adjustments in the language-teaching syllabus (particularly as far as selection and progression are concerned) and for revised pedagogical descriptions that present a more adequate picture of the language as it is actually used. A case in point here is the misrepresentation of the functions and contextual patterns of English progressive forms in EFL (English as a foreign language) teaching materials used in German schools. Progressives that refer to repeated actions or events, for example, are considerably more frequent in authentic English than in textbook English, where the common function of repeatedness is neglected and the focus is on single continuous events (cf. Römer, 2005, pp. 261–263).

Specialized corpora, for example, those capturing a particular language for special or specific purposes (LSP), can also influence syllabus design for LSP courses. As Gavioli (2006) pointed out, in English for specific purposes (ESP), "working out basic items to be dealt with is a key teaching problem" (p. 23). A keyword analysis based on a corpus that contains the specific text or discourse type in question (e.g., English business letters, medical research articles, or newspaper editorials) can help solve this problem and assist teachers in "focus[ing] their efforts in terms of selection of language contents" (Pérez-Paredes, 2003, p. 1). An important issue for ESP teachers (who may or, what is more likely, may not be experts in the specific discourse they teach) is that they should give priority to teaching those words and expressions that their learners will need later on to be able to handle texts in their subject area. For instance, having access to a corpus of biology readings and lectures, to give just one example of a science course in English described by Flowerdew (1993), can enable teachers to successfully address this issue and make informed decisions about item and text selection for their course. Another example of how corpora can impact general EAP (English for academic purposes) teaching is Coxhead's (2000) Academic Word List (AWL). The AWL, based on a corpus of academic writing, contains the vocabulary items that are most relevant and useful to EAP learners. Simpson-Vlach and Ellis (2010) have taken Coxhead's idea from word to phrase level and devised an Academic Formulas List (AFL), which consists of word combinations that occur significantly more often in academic than in nonacademic speech and writing. Both studies

(AWL and AFL) take an indirect approach to using specialized corpora in language teaching and contribute to improving the teaching of EAP through informing syllabus design, for example, by helping with the selection of items to be included in the course.

Studies on learner corpora, that is, systematic computerized collections of the language produced by language learners, are also highly relevant for syllabus design (cf. Aston, 2000; Granger, 2002, 2009) since they provide insights on "the needs of specific learner populations" (Meunier, 2002, p. 125) and help to test teachers' intuitions about whether a particular phenomenon is difficult or not (Granger, 2002, p. 22). Nesselhauf (2005), for example, identified unidiomatic verb-noun collocations in German learner English (e. g., *reach an aim*, *drive a bike*), indicating that combinations such as *achieve an aim* or *ride a bike* may deserve particular attention in teaching materials designed for learners with first language (L1) German.

Corpus Research and Designing Teaching Materials

The results of the comparisons between corpora and course books mentioned earlier not only inform the language-teaching curriculum but also help with decisions about the presentation of items and structures in reference works and teaching materials. Corpora research has exerted a huge influence on reference publishing and has led to a new generation of dictionaries and grammar books. Nowadays, "people who have never heard of a corpus are using the products of corpus research" (McEnery, Xiao, & Tono, 2006, p. 97). In the context of ELT, the publications in the Collins COBUILD series constitute a major achievement. Based on real English and compiled with the needs of the language learner in mind, the COBUILD dictionaries, grammars, usage guides, and concordance samplers (see Capel, 1993; Carpenter, 1993; Goodale, 1995; Sinclair, 1990, 1992, 2001) offer teachers and learners more reliable information about the English language than any of the more traditional reference grammars or older non-corpus-based dictionaries. Two major advantages of the COBUILD and other corpus-based reference works for learners (e. g., Biber & Conrad, 2009; Biber, Leech, & Conrad, 2002; Bullon, 2006; Carter & McCarthy, 2006; Hornby, 2005; Peters, 2004; Rundell, 2007) are that they incorporate corpus-derived findings on frequency distribution and register variation, and that they contain genuine instead of invented examples. Particularly worth mentioning here is the student version of the entirely corpus-based *Longman Grammar of Spoken and Written English* (Biber et al., 2002). The importance of presenting learners with authentic language examples has been stressed in a number of publications (e.g., Fox, 1987; Kennedy, 1992; Römer, 2004a, 2005; Sinclair, 1991, 1997). Kennedy (1992), for instance, cautioned that "invented examples can present a distorted version of typicality or an over-tidy picture of the system" (p. 366), and Sinclair (1991) called it an "absurd notion that invented examples can actually represent the language better than real ones" (p. 5). Thanks to the corpus revolution, language learners can today choose from a range of reference works that are thoroughly corpus-based and that offer improved representations of the language they want to study. While course books and other materials used in the language teaching classroom have long been lagging behind this development and have been rather unaffected by advances in corpus linguistics (at least as far as the English as a foreign language market is concerned), the first attempts are now being made to produce textbooks that draw on corpus research and are fully based on real-life data, that is, on language that has in fact occurred (e. g., Barlow & Burdine, 2006; Carter, Hughes, & McCarthy, 2000; McCarthy, McCarten, & Sandiford, 2005). Some particularly innovative developments are currently taking place in Japan, where Yukio Tono of the Tokyo University of Foreign Studies hosts the world's first corpus-based English conversation program on television (watched by a million Japanese language learners) and publishes a series of accompanying textbooks that have become best sellers in Japan (Tono, 2011). Each unit of the program focuses on one of 100 keywords (selected from a BNC frequency list) and its most common collocation patterns. Model skits and exercises illustrate the use of these collocations.

Another branch of general corpora research that has exerted some influence on the design of reference works and, to a lesser extent, teaching materials is the area of phraseology and collocation studies. Scholars like Biber, Johansson, Leech, Conrad, and Finegan (1999); Hunston and Francis (2000); Kjellmer (1984); Lewis (1993, 1997, 2000); Meunier and Gouverneur (2007); Nattinger (1980); Pawley and Syder (1983); and Sinclair and Renouf (1988) have emphasized the importance of recurring word combinations and prefabricated strings in a pedagogical context because of their great potential in fostering fluency, accuracy, and idiomaticity. Although corpus-based collocation dictionaries (e. g., Benson, Benson, & Ilson,

2010; Hill & Lewis, 1997; Lea, 2002) are available, and although information on phraseology (i.e., about the combinations that individual words favor) is implicitly included in learner dictionaries in the word definitions and the selected corpus examples—and sometimes even explicitly described, for example, in the grammar column in the COBUILD dictionaries and in the *COBUILD Grammar Patterns* reference books (e.g., the "V *over* n" pattern for the verb argue; Francis, Hunston, & Manning, 1996, 1998)—such information and exercises on typical collocations are as yet largely missing from language-teaching course books (or they are inadequate; cf. Meunier & Gouverneur, 2007). Like Hunston and Francis (2000), I see a necessity in and "look forward to [more] information about patterns being incorporated in language teaching materials." (p. 272)

It has also been demonstrated in recent publications (e. g., Aijmer, 2002; Altenberg & Granger, 2001; Herriman & Boström Aronsson, 2009; Leńko-Szymańska, 2007; Nesselhauf, 2005) how the findings of studies based on learner corpora such as the ICLE can "enrich usage notes" in learners' dictionaries (Granger, 2002, p. 24), or how they "can provide useful insights into which collocational, pragmatic or discourse features should be addressed in materials design" (Flowerdew, 2001, pp. 376–377).

DIRECT APPLICATIONS OF CORPORA AND CORPUS RESEARCH IN SECOND LANGUAGE TEACHING

While the indirect approach centers on the impact of corpus evidence on syllabus design or teaching materials and is concerned with corpus access by researchers and—although to a lesser extent—materials designers, the direct approach is more teacher- and learner-focused. Instead of having to rely on the researcher as mediator and provider of corpus-based materials, language learners and teachers get their hands on corpora and concordance tools themselves and find out about language patterning and the behavior of words and phrases in an "autonomous" way (Bernardini, 2002, p. 165). Tim Johns, who pioneered direct corpus applications in grammar and vocabulary classes at the University of Birmingham (UK) in the 1980s, suggested to "confront the learner as directly as possible with the data, and to make the learner a linguistic researcher" (Johns, 2002, p. 108). Johns (1997) also referred to the learner as a "language detective" and formulated the motto "Every student a Sherlock Holmes!" (p. 101). This method, in which there is either an interaction between the learner and the corpus or, in a more controlled way, between the teacher and the corpus, is now widely known under the label *data-driven learning* (DDL; see Johns, 1986; 1994).

Examples of Direct Pedagogical Corpus Applications

Following Johns's example, a number of researchers have discussed ways in which corpora and concordances can be used by language learners. Bernardini (2002), for example, described the positive effects of what she calls corpus-aided discovery learning with the BNC, and described corpora as "rich sources of autonomous learning activities of a serendipitous kind" (p. 165; see also Bernardini, 2000b; 2004a). She envisioned the learner in the role of a "*traveller* instead of a *researcher*" (Bernardini, 2000a, p. 131; italics in original), and was less "interested in the starting or end point of a learning experience" than in what the learner experiences in between, on her or his journey (Bernardini, 2000a, p. 142). Kettemann (1995), too, stressed the exploratory aspect of DDL and considered concordancing in the ELT classroom "motivating and highly experiential" for the learner (p. 30).

To give a concrete example of a possible DDL task, learners could be asked to compile concordances of a pair of near-synonyms (such as *speak* and *talk*; see concordance samples in Figure 2) and work out the differences in the collocational and phraseological behavior of these words. Further examples of DDL activities are described in Aston (1997, 2001, 2009); Bennett (2010); Fligelstone (1993); Gavioli (2001, 2006); Hadley (2001); Johns (1991, 2002); Kaszubski (in press); O'Keeffe, McCarthy, and Carter (2007); Oksefjell-Ebeling (2009); Reppen (2010); Sripicharn (2004); and especially in Tribble and Jones (1997). Also worth mentioning are some materials and tools for the creation of DDL exercises that are available online, for example, exercises based on MICASE (see http: //micase.elicorpora.info/, links to "ESL/EAP Teaching Materials" and "ESL Self-Study Activities"), Tom Cobb's "Compleat Lexical Tutor" (http: //www.lextutor.ca/), a tool collection "[f] or data-driven language learning on the web" (Web site blurb), and a module on "Using concordance programs in the modern foreign languages classroom" of the Information and Communications Technology for Language Teachers, http: //www.ict4lt.org/en/en_mod2–4.htm.

The DDL method of using learner-centered activities with the teacher as a facilitator of these activities has, up to now, mainly been discussed with reference to ELT and English language corpora. Some of the few studies that deal with other languages include Whistle (1999) and Chambers (2005), who report on introducing DDL activities to the teaching of French in order to supplement other CALL (computer-assisted language learning) tasks; Dodd (1997) and Jones (1997), who show how corpora of written and spoken German can be exploited "to give students a richer language-learning experience in the foreign language environment" (Dodd, 1997, p. 131); and Kennedy and Miceli (2001, 2002, 2010) who suggest corpus consultation for learners of Italian.

```
1  ery? Can I think. .. Well I'd like to    speak about the gallery I like to speak for m
2  d morning. Hello! Yeah, I'd like to      speak about the squeeze on the benefits.
3  ught people might be less willing to to  speak at the meeting if they knew it was bein
4  d pointing. And er when you get up to    speak at the conference, you have to give yo
5  re's not quite as bad as when I had to   speak for Amnesty on Radio Essex last year an
6  ke to speak about the gallery I like to  speak for myself and er just the visual arts
7  't got a word . you're not allowed to    speak for the rest of the week. he's hiding
8  Well football fans? well David I ca n't  speak on behalf of Hibs, all I can say Mm. i
9  a member of the public I'm not here to   speak on behalf of the theatre at all. I migh
10 rhaps people could as actually come and  speak to me afterwards, if they, if they thi
11 e will if you'd like to come along and   speak to him individually afterwards he will
12 hat, then. When do you start again? I    speak to Stella now Do you speak, do you star
13 e appropriate way of doing it. Shall I   speak to Paula about that then? Yeah. Paula,
14 er Okay. I'll speak to Simon. I'll       speak to Simon erm about borrowing his P C at
15 ot to go  home and do? Are you sure?     Speak to me Yes Okay, right, one person from
16 rt is to go back one step, not just to   speak to people who are experiencing hurt, bu
17 ikey. Speak up loud, you've got ta be    speak up loud and clear. No. Uniform. Unifor
18 I think that they may be frightened to   speak up and that they're scared that if the
19 of talking about. Excuse me could you    speak up just a little bit? Yes yes er Thank
20 first floor. Oh I'm sorry! Can you       speak up then? Oh sorry! Have I Mm mm. Have

1  ney. All of that being said and Mr will  talk a bit more about the figures when he com
2  have an M P here on the phone line and   talk about this er proposed pay rise. They ca
3  ? Mm. . Erm I just want to go back and   talk about a few things we just touched on ea
4  are? Erm Without drawing it, try and     talk about a square. What would happen? Erm
5  Mm. Like we had you know, who could      talk about experiences you know, in a, in a
6  ey include Gerry Addams and we we could  talk about the other side, we could talk abo
7  ot , you know, I'm not er gon na even    talk about the disaster at airport things, yo
8  Mm. And basically, again can we just     talk about what we're trying to achieve? My
9  on, and Mr I know in a minute we'll      talk about the number of people who attend co
10 Becky. No, Becky. Becky . And we'll      talk about this in committee and let you kn
11 ople or all about that I do n't want to  talk about that I want to talk I want to talk
12 get them around the table and begin to   talk about those sort of things. Show a bit
13 bit, we just have done. We started to    talk about the solar system. How far have we
14 them anyway. Right. What else did we     talk about and we need to know, we have n't g
15 ber of possible pieces there, Did we     talk about this? We did. Ah, right, yes. So
16 . They look tired and worn out. They     talk quietly amongst themselves sometimes fin
17 s boss, the professor to come along and  talk to us, and let, some of their time is
18 than then, because as a kid they do n't  talk to you about them things do they like, y
19 going to talk to somebody who will not   talk to you, who will not s possibly even sm
20 how nice the man was when he started to  talk to Jason oh I'll go and help you how fr
```

Fig. 2. Concordance samples of "speak" and "talk," based on the spoken part of the BNC.

The Effectiveness of Direct Pedagogical Corpus Applications

Advantages of corpora work with learners have been suggested by scholars like Sinclair (1997), who noted that, for the learner, "[c]orpora will clarify, give priorities, reduce exceptions and liberate the creative spirit" (p. 38). Likewise, many researchers and teachers in the TaLC tradition are convinced that DDL can empower learners to find out things for themselves, that a data-driven approach raises the learners' language awareness, and that corpora have great pedagogic potential. The effectiveness of DDL has actually been indicated in studies on the teaching and learning of grammar and vocabulary by Boulton (2009); Cobb (1997); Cresswell (2007); Granath (2009); Johns, Hsingchin, and Lixun (2008); and Yoon (2008). As Yoon (2008) observed in a study on the influence of corpora use on L2 academic writing, "students assumed more responsibility for their writing and became more independent writers" (p. 31). On a similar note, Johns et al. (2008) found that "CALL activities [including DDL] did have a positive impact on students' English learning" (p. 503), and Boulton (2009) noted that in his empirical study "corpus samples led to more successful results than traditional pedagogical resources" such as bilingual dictionaries or usage manuals (p. 50). Concordancing has not only been shown to be a useful way "to mimic the effects of natural contextual learning" (Cobb, 1997, p. 314), but researchers have recently also highlighted its use and usefulness in translation teaching (Bernardini, 2004b; Kübler, 2011) and for error correction in foreign or second language writing (cf. Bernardini, 2004a; Chambers, 2005, 2007; Gaskell & Cobb, 2004). These descriptive empirical studies demonstrate that corpora nicely complement existing reference works, and that they may provide information that a dictionary or grammar book may not provide. They are based on experiments in which groups of students use corpora, corpusderived exercises, and/or concordances in the classroom, while control groups of students use traditional teaching materials.

Although according to Granath (2009), "advanced students definitely benefit from working with corpora" (p. 59), it is not clear whether this is also the case for beginning learners of a foreign language. Dealing with concordances based on large collections of native-speaker conversations, newspaper texts, research articles, or novels that contain many unknown words and complex sentence constructions may be too challenging a task for beginners, and not all learners may feel comfortable working with computers in language learning. A further limitation may be that it initially takes time for teachers to familiarize themselves and/or their students with online corpora or offline corpus tools. However, once they have been given basic training in corpus use, teachers should be able to create simple concordance exercises tailored to their learners' needs and access information about collocation and language patterning. Teachers could, for example, access the COCA interface (http: //www.americancorpus.org/) to search for a word or phrase and retrieve concordance samples and lists of collocations for this word or phrase. As a recent survey on teachers' needs has shown (see Römer, 2009a), teachers of a language that is not their L1 often require native-speaker advice on language points. Computer corpora that have been described as "tireless native-speaker informant[s], with rather greater potential knowledge of the language than the average native speaker" (Barnbrook, 1996, p. 140), can offer help in such situations.

UNRESOLVED ISSUES AND DIRECTIONS FOR FUTURE DEVELOPMENT

Despite the progress that has unquestionably been made in the field of applied corpus linguistics, there is still considerable room for development. A number of tasks can be formulated to enhance pedagogical corpus applications and help corpora make a stronger contribution to improving language learning and teaching. The tasks and future developments I envisage are grouped under three topics and discussed in turn in the following paragraphs: (a) focusing on learner and teacher needs, (b) fostering indirect uses of corpora in L2 teaching, and (c) fostering direct uses of corpora in L2 teaching.

While many corpus researchers (including myself) claim that corpus linguistics has an immense potential to help improve language pedagogy, I would argue that they do not always make sufficient efforts to reach practitioners with what could be called the corpus mission and to find out about what teachers actually want and need. My suggestion would therefore be to focus our attention more on language teachers and their needs and see how we could support them in their work. A survey of 78 practicing English language teachers (Römer, 2009a) brought to light that a number of wishes and everyday problems of German EFL teachers could actually be addressed by applied corpus linguists. Among the things the teachers who participated in this survey called for were, for example, better teaching materials, support in creating materials, and native-speaker advice. One possible response to these wishes would be to introduce more teachers to corpus resources that are already freely available online. If teachers received basic training in working with corpora and had access to computers with a good Internet connection and hence to online corpora (e.g., COCA, MICASE, and MICUSP [Michigan Corpus of Upper-Level Student Papers]),[3] they could design the required materials themselves whenever they needed them—for example, a worksheet on the most frequent nouns in the newspaper subsection of COCA or an exercise around a concordance of the common phrase *on the other hand* in the academic student papers included in MICUSP. They would also see that corpora, as large collections of native or expert speaker/writer output, can replace, for example, the "always available native speaker informant" they asked for, and that questions like "What prepositions go with that verb?" can easily be answered by looking at a right-sorted concordance of the verb in question.

Another task on our list should be to pay more attention to the needs of learners and consider which groups of learners may profit most from which type of materials. Related to this issue are questions centering around the learners' willingness and ability to deal with computer corpora, online search interfaces, and concordance exercises prepared by their teachers. DDL may work well with the computer-savvy student who is ready to explore larger amounts of language data, but it may not be the best solution for the techno-phobic student who prefers a teacher-centered, controlled type of instruction. For the latter type of learner, a good compromise solution may be an approach to DDL without computers. Boulton (2010), for example, described the benefits of using paper-based DDL materials and called for more DDL worksheets that are readily downloadable for teachers from Internet sources. The needs of learners will probably also vary considerably not only by learner type but also by learner level, course type, and learner objectives. As discussed earlier, working with large corpora that capture complex material with long sentences and low-frequency vocabulary items might intimidate beginning or intermediate learners who have a limited vocabulary. Two ways of addressing this problem could be to use a corpus of children's literature (see Johns et al., 2008) or a corpus consisting of "graded reader texts which contain a limited number of headwords" (Allan, 2009, p. 25). Depending on whether we are dealing with intermediate or more advanced learners, for instance, our focus in designing corpus-derived materials may shift to more specialized vocabulary and its preferred patterns of usage. Similarly, participants in a business English class or international students of mechanical engineering will probably profit most from working with materials that are tailored to their specific needs and discourse in their field of study. That means that when making decisions on what to teach and how to teach it, it is important to consider the learners' language background and what discourse community they eventually want to be a member of and be able to communicate with.

In terms of fostering indirect uses of corpora in language learning and teaching, more work probably has to be put into the creation of reliable corpus-based language descriptions for learners and teachers, especially descriptions of specialized discourses, such as academic English or business English. This implies that there is a need for more large specialized corpora that can be used as bases for creating dictionaries, usage guides, and grammars tailored to the needs of different groups of learners. Also, most available corpora consist predominantly of written language material—which does not come as a surprise given the amount of work that goes into transcribing and encoding speech data for computer-based analysis. In terms of helping learners develop their communicative competence, spoken corpora may, however, be the better basis of pedagogical language descriptions. Generally, I see more scope for research activities that are inspired by the needs of learners and teachers and that take the learners' communication needs and common learning problems into account. For example, language points that tend to be particularly difficult for learners could be identified through comparative analyses of corpora capturing learner (or novice) and native-speaker (or expert) performance data, or through contrastive linguistic analyses based on parallel corpora of the learners' native and target languages (e.g., Granger, 2004). Further comparative studies of lexical-grammatical features in corpora and course books (as already described) could also provide valuable insights into mismatches between real language and school language that need to be remedied. In selecting language points worth analyzing, I would suggest a shift in focus from individual words or empty grammatical structures to phraseological items (e.g., formulas, n-grams, phrase-frames, lexical bundles). Recent research in corpus linguistics has provided massive evidence for the inseparability of lexis and grammar (see, e.g., Biber, Conrad, & Cortes, 2004; Hoey, 2005; Hunston & Francis, 2000; Meunier & Granger, 2008; Römer, 2009b, 2010; Römer & Schulze, 2009; Sinclair, 1991, 2004d; Stubbs, 2001), so it appears only reasonable to provide learners with a more integrated perspective and offer them a view on the language that highlights frequently used phrases that function as important meaning-carrying units in the discourse.

In terms of fostering direct uses of corpora in language learning and teaching, corpus researchers would do well to help create more DDL exercises and corpus-derived teaching materials in general. In the future, I would hope to see more publications (similar to Tribble & Jones [1997] or Barlow & Burdine [2006]) that contain ready-made exercises based on authentic speech and writing from different text types and language varieties and focused on language items that are of central importance and/or troublesome for learners. Another important step we need to accomplish if we want DDL to gain more ground is create a DDL-friendly environment that encourages learner and teacher involvement. Teachers and learners have to be provided with access to corpora that are available on the Internet or to offline corpora and easy-to-use software packages for corpus analysis. A popularization of corpora and their pedagogical use also requires some basic training in accessing corpora and in working with concordances or collocation lists. Such training is crucial because concordance output, at first glance, may seem hard to handle, and because "a corpus is not a simple object, and it is just as easy to derive nonsensical conclusions from the evidence as insightful ones" (Sinclair, 2004b, p. 2). The good news is that, in most cases, only a few hours of orientation are required before learners and teachers can "enter the world of the corpus" and start exploring language patterns (Sinclair, 2004c, p. 297).

CONCLUSION

This article has focused on the relationship between corpus research and L2 teaching. It has discussed a range of developments in the emerging field of applied corpus linguistics and sketched avenues for future research activities that may positively impact L2 teaching. I hope to have shown that corpus resources and methods have great potential to improve pedagogical practice and that corpora can be used in a number of ways, indirectly to inform teaching materials and reference works and directly as language learning tools and repositories for the design of data-intensive teaching activities. I have also tried to make clear that a lot still remains to be done in research and practice before corpora will eventually arrive in the classroom. Communication between corpus researchers and practitioners has to be improved considerably so that teachers and learners get the support they need and deserve.

In a questionnaire he sent out to language teachers, teacher educators, and applied linguistic researchers in 2008, Christopher Tribble referred to the (direct) use of corpora in language teaching as "a minority sport." [4] One purpose of this article was to describe the potential of pedagogical corpus applications and to provide ideas on what can be done to foster direct and indirect corpus use in L2 teaching and to bring corpora and corpus tools to a larger group of learners and teachers. If we take up some of the ideas mentioned here, and if we are successful in improving communication among researchers, teachers, and materials designers, we can get more people involved in DDL and related activities and thus perhaps make applied corpus linguistics more of a majority sport.

NOTES

1 COBUILD is a project in pedagogically oriented lexical computing started in the 1980s.

2 TaLC conferences take place every other year in different European countries. TaLC conferences 1 through 9 were held in Lancaster (in 1994 and 1996), Oxford (in 1998), Graz (in 2000), Bertinoro (in 2002), Granada (in 2004), Paris (in 2006), Lisbon (in 2008) and Brno (in 2010). Since 1999, conferences with a similar focus to TaLC, organized by the American Association for Applied Corpus Linguistics (now the American Association for Corpus Linguistics [AACL]), have been held in North America (Ann Arbor, MI, in 1999 and 2005; Flagstaff, AZ, in 2000 and 2006; Boston, MA, in 2001; Indianapolis, IN, in 2002; Montclair, NJ, in 2004; Provo, UT, in 2008; and Edmonton, Alberta, Canada, in 2009).

3 MICUSP is freely accessible through a user-friendly search and browse interface at http: //search-micusp.elicorpora.info/. The URLs for COCA and MICASE are http: //www.americancorpus.org/ and http: //quod.lib.umich.edu/cgi/c/corpus/corpus, respectively.

4 A copy of the survey is available at http: //www.surveyconsole.com/console/ TakeSurvey?id=463263.

ANNOTATED BIBLIOGRAPHY

Sinclair, J. M. (Ed.). (2004a). *How to use corpora in language teaching.* Amsterdam, The Netherlands: John Benjamins.

This collection offers a useful state-of-the art overview of central research topics and practical applications in applied corpus linguistics. It is a book for teachers and applied linguists who are looking for guidance in how to include corpora and corpus evidence in their teaching and research. The book brings together 13 valuable contributions on topics including corpora use in the classroom, corpora as support tools for teachers, the availability of learner corpora, contrastive analyses of corpus data and textbooks, and central steps in corpus analysis. In his opening and closing chapters, John Sinclair, arguably the father of modern corpus linguistics, sets the scene and takes a look into the future of pedagogical applications of corpora.

Aijmer, K. (Ed.). (2009). *Corpora and language teaching.* Amsterdam, The Netherlands: John Benjamins.

This edited volume can be seen as a follow-up publication to Sinclair's (2004a) collection in that it provides an account of developments in pedagogical corpus applications 5 years on. It contains 12 chapters, offering mainly European scholars' perspectives on topics such as the relationship between corpus analysis and L2 language acquisition, applications of learner corpora in language teaching, DDL, and the compilation and use of new types of pedagogical corpora (consisting of textbook materials and spoken learner language).

Reppen, R. (2010). *Using corpora in the language classroom.* Cambridge, UK: Cambridge University Press.

Reppen's book provides a brief and practical introduction to the direct use of corpora in language teaching. The book focuses on creating corpus-derived teaching materials and on using corpus Internet resources in language teaching. Written in a very accessible style and filled with concrete examples and hands-on activities, it is an ideal resource for teachers who wish to bring corpora into their classrooms.

Simpson-Vlach, R. C., & Ellis, N. C. (2010). An academic formulas list: New methods in phraseology research. *Applied Linguistics, 31*, 487–512.

This article discusses the development of a corpus-derived, psycholinguistically and pedagogically validated list of formulaic sequences in academic speech and writing. This list, the Academic Formulas List (AFL), consists of sequences of words (e.g., *in terms of, on the other hand, due to the fact that*) that are frequent across genres and disciplines in spoken and/or written academic language, occur more commonly in academic than in nonacademic texts, and express a range of functions that are central in academic discourse. The article constitutes a wonderful example of how pedagogically inspired corpus work can result in a resource that is bound to positively affect the teaching and learning of (academic) English.

REFERENCES

Ädel, A. (2006). *Metadiscourse in L1 and L2 English.* Amsterdam, The Netherlands: John Benjamins.

Aijmer, K. (2002). Modality in advanced Swedish learners' written interlanguage. In S. Granger, J. Hung, & S. Petch-Tyson (Eds.), *Computer learner corpora, second language acquisition and foreign language teaching* (pp. 55–76). Amsterdam, The Netherlands: John Benjamins.

Allan, R. (2009). Can a graded reader corpus provide "authentic" input? *ELT Journal, 63*, 23–32.

Altenberg, B., & Granger, S. (2001). The grammatical and lexical patterning of MAKE in native and non-native student writing. *Applied Linguistics, 22*, 173–195.

Aston, G. (1997). Enriching the learning environment: Corpora in ELT. In A. Wichmann, S. Fligelstone, T. McEnery, & G. Knowles (Eds.), *Teaching and Language Corpora* (pp. 51–64). London, UK: Longman.

Aston, G. (2000). Corpora and language teaching. In L. Burnard & T. McEnery (Eds.), *Rethinking language pedagogy from a corpus perspective* (pp. 7–17). Frankfurt, Germany: Peter Lang.

Aston, G. (2001). *Learning with corpora.* Houston, TX: Athelstan.

Aston, G. (2009). Using BNC-XML in the classroom. In L. Lombardo (Ed.), *Using corpora to learn about language and discourse* (pp. 163–198). Frankfurt, Germany: Peter Lang.

Aston, G., Bernardini, S., & Stewart, D. (Eds.). (2004). *Corpora and language learners.* Amsterdam, The Netherlands: John Benjamins.

Barlow, M. (1996). Corpora for theory and practice. *International Journal of Corpus Linguistics, 1*, 1–37.

Barlow, M., & Burdine, S. (2006). *American phrasal verbs* (CorpusLAB Series). Houston, TX: Athelstan.

Barnbrook, G. (1996). *Language and computers. A practical introduction to the computer analysis of language.* Edinburgh, UK: Edinburgh University Press.

Bennett, G. R. (2010). *Using corpora in the language learning classroom.* Ann Arbor: University of Michigan Press.

Benson, M., Benson, I., & Ilson, R. F. (2010). *The BBI combinatory dictionary of English.* Amsterdam, The Netherlands: John Benjamins.

Bernardini, S. (2000a). *Competence, capacity, corpora. A study in corpus-aided language learning.* Bologna, Italy: CLUEB.

Bernardini, S. (2000b). Systematising serendipity: Proposals for concordancing large corpora with language learners. In L. Burnard & T. McEnery (Eds.), *Rethinking language pedagogy from a corpus perspective* (pp. 225–234). Frankfurt, Germany: Peter Lang.

Bernardini, S. (2002). Exploring new directions for discovery learning. In B. Kettemann & G. Marko (Eds.), *Teaching and learning by doing corpus analysis* (pp. 165–182). Amsterdam, The Netherlands: Rodopi.

Bernardini, S. (2004a). Corpora in the classroom: An overview and some reflections on future developments. In J. M. Sinclair (Ed.), *How to use corpora in language teaching* (pp. 15–36). Amsterdam, The Netherlands: John Benjamins.

Bernardini, S. (2004b). Corpus-aided language pedagogy for translator education. In K. Malmkjaer (Ed.), *Translation in undergraduate degree programmes* (pp. 97–112). Amsterdam, The Netherlands: John Benjamins.

Biber, D., & Conrad, S. (2009). *Real grammar. A corpus-based approach to English.* London, UK: Pearson Longman.

Biber, D., Conrad, S., & Cortes, V. (2004). If you look at. . . : Lexical bundles in university teaching and textbooks. *Applied Linguistics, 25,* 371–405.

Biber, D., Leech, G., & Conrad, S. (2002). *Longman student grammar of spoken and written English.* London, UK: Longman.

Biber, D., Johansson, S., Leech, G., Conrad, S., & Finegan, E. (1999). *Longman grammar of spoken and written English.* London, UK: Longman.

Botley, S., Glass, J., McEnery, T., & Wilson, A. (Eds.). (1996). *Proceedings of Teaching and Language Corpora 1996.* Lancaster, UK: University Centre for Computer Corpus Research on Language.

Boulton, A. (2009). Testing the limits of data-driven learning: Language proficiency and training. *ReCALL, 21,* 37–54.

Boulton, A. (2010). Data-driven learning: Taking the computer out of the equation. *Language Learning, 60,* 534–572.

Braun, S., Kohn, K., & Mukherjee, J. (Eds.). (2006). *Corpus technology and language pedagogy*. Frankfurt, Germany: Peter Lang.

Bullon, S. (Ed.). (2006). *Longman dictionary of contemporary English* (4th ed.). London, UK: Longman.

Burnard, L., & McEnery, T. (Eds.). (2000). *Rethinking language pedagogy from a corpus perspective*. Frankfurt, Germany: Peter Lang.

Campoy, M. C., Belles-Fortuño, B., & Gea-Valor, M. L. (Eds.). (2010). *Corpus-based approaches to English language teaching*. London, UK: Continuum.

Capel, A. (1993). *Collins COBUILD concordance samplers 1: Prepositions*. London: HarperCollins.

Carpenter, E. (1993). *Collins COBUILD English guides 4: Confusable words*. London: HarperCollins.

Carter, R., Hughes, R., & McCarthy, M. (2000). *Exploring grammar in context. Grammar reference and practice*. Cambridge, UK: Cambridge University Press.

Carter, R., & McCarthy, M. (2006). *Cambridge grammar of English*. Cambridge, UK: Cambridge University Press.

Chambers, A. (2005). Integrating corpus consultation in language studies. *Language Learning and Technology*, *9*, 111–125.

Chambers, A. (2007). Popularising corpus consultation by language learners and teachers. In E. Hidalgo, L. Quereda, & J. Santana (Eds.), *Corpora in the foreign language classroom* (pp. 3–16). Amsterdam, The Netherlands: Rodopi.

Cobb, T. (1997). Is there any measurable learning from hands-on concordancing? *System*, *25*, 301–315.

Conrad, S. (2004). Corpus linguistics, language variation, and language teaching. In J. M. Sinclair (Ed.), *How to use corpora in language teaching* (pp. 67–85). Amsterdam, The Netherlands: John Benjamins.

Coxhead, A. (2000). A new academic word list. *TESOL Quarterly*, *34*, 213–238.

Cresswell, A. (2007). Getting to "know" connectors? Evaluating data-driven learning in a writing skills course. In E. Hidalgo, L. Quereda, & J. Santana (Eds.), *Corpora in the foreign language classroom* (pp. 267–288). Amsterdam, The Netherlands: Rodopi.

Dodd, B. (1997). Exploiting a corpus of written German for advanced language learning. In A. Wichmann, S. Fligelstone, T. McEnery, & G. Knowles (Eds.), *Teaching and language corpora* (pp. 131–145). London, UK: Longman.

Fligelstone, S. (1993). Some reflections on the question of teaching, from a corpus linguistics perspective. *ICAME Journal*, *17*, 97–109.

Flowerdew, J. (1993). Concordancing as a tool in course design. *System*, *21*, 231–244.

Flowerdew, L. (2001). The exploitation of small learner corpora in EAP materials design.

In M. Ghadessy, A. Henry, & R. L. Roseberry (Eds.), *Small corpus studies and ELT. Theory and practice* (pp. 363–380). Amsterdam, The Netherlands: John Benjamins.

Fox, G. (1987). The case for examples. In J. M. Sinclair (Ed.), *Looking up: An account of the COBUILD project in lexical computing* (pp. 137–149). London, UK: Collins ELT.

Francis, G., Hunston, S., & Manning, E. (1996). *Collins COBUILD grammar patterns 1: Verbs*. London, UK: HarperCollins.

Francis, G., Hunston, S., & Manning, E. (1998). *Collins COBUILD grammar patterns 2: Nouns and adjectives*. London, UK: HarperCollins.

Frankenberg-Garcia, A., Flowerdew, L., & Aston, G. (Eds.). (2011). *New trends in corpora and language learning*. London, UK: Continuum.

Gaskell, D., & Cobb, T. (2004). Can learners use concordance feedback for writing errors? *System, 32*, 301–319.

Gavioli, L. (2001). The learner as researcher: Introducing corpus concordancing in the classroom. In G. Aston (Ed.), *Learning with corpora* (pp. 108–137). Houston, TX: Athelstan.

Gavioli, L. (2006). *Exploring corpora for ESP learning*. Amsterdam, The Netherlands: John Benjamins.

Goodale, M. (1995). *Collins COBUILD concordance samplers 4: Tenses*. London, UK: HarperCollins.

Grabowski, E., & Mindt, D. (1995). A corpus-based learning list of irregular verbs in English. *ICAME Journal, 19*, 5–22.

Granath, S. (2009). Who benefits from learning how to use corpora? In K. Aijmer (Ed.), *Corpora and language teaching* (pp. 47–65). Amsterdam, The Netherlands: John Benjamins.

Granger, S. (2002). A bird's-eye view of learner corpus research. In S. Granger, J. Hung, & S. Petch-Tyson (Eds.), *Computer learner corpora, second language acquisition and foreign language teaching* (pp. 3–33). Amsterdam, The Netherlands: John Benjamins.

Granger, S. (2004). Computer learner corpus research: Current status and future prospects. In E. Connor & T. A. Upton (Eds.), *Applied corpus linguistics. A multi-dimensional perspective* (pp. 123–145). Amsterdam, The Netherlands: Rodopi.

Granger, S. (2009). The contribution of learner corpora to second language acquisition and foreign language teaching. A critical evaluation. In K. Aijmer (Ed.), *Corpora and language teaching* (pp. 13–32). Amsterdam, The Netherlands: John Benjamins.

Granger, S., Hung, J., & Petch-Tyson, S. (Eds.). (2002). *Computer learner corpora, second language acquisition and foreign language teaching*. Amsterdam, The Netherlands: John Benjamins.

Hadley, G. (2001). *Concordancing in Japanese TEFL: Unlocking the power of data-driven learning.* Retrieved from http: //www.nuis.ac.jp/ ~ hadley/publication/ jlearner/jlearner.htm

Herriman, J., & Boström Aronsson, M. (2009). Themes in Swedish advanced learners' writing in English. In K. Aijmer (Ed.), *Corpora and language teaching* (pp. 101–120). Amsterdam, The Netherlands: John Benjamins.

Hidalgo, E., Quereda, L., & Santana, J. (Eds.). (2007). *Corpora in the foreign language classroom.* Amsterdam, The Netherlands: Rodopi.

Hill, J., & Lewis, M. (1997). *LTP dictionary of selected collocations.* Hove, UK: Language Teaching.

Hoey, M. P. (2005). *Lexical priming. A new theory of words and language.* London, UK: Routledge.

Hornby, A. S. (Ed.). (2005). *Oxford advanced learner's dictionary* (7th ed.). Oxford, UK: Oxford University Press.

Hunston, S. (2002). *Corpora in applied linguistics.* Cambridge, UK: Cambridge University Press.

Hunston, S., & Francis, G. (2000). *Pattern grammar. A corpus-driven approach to the lexical grammar of English.* Amsterdam, The Netherlands: John Benjamins.

Hymes, D. (1972). On communicative competence. In J. B. Pride & J. Holmes (Eds.), *Sociolinguistics* (pp. 269–293). Harmondsworth, UK: Penguin.

Hymes, D. (1992). The concept of communicative competence revisited. In M. Pütz. (Ed.), *Thirty years of linguistic evolution. Studies in honour of René Dirven on the occasion of his sixtieth birthday* (pp. 31–57). Amsterdam, The Netherlands: John Benjamins.

Johansson, S. (2007). Using corpora: From learning to research. In E. Hidalgo, L. Quereda, & J. Santana (Eds.), *Corpora in the foreign language classroom* (pp. 17–30). Amsterdam, The Netherlands: Rodopi.

Johns, T. F. (1986). Microconcord: A language-learner's research tool. *System, 14*, 151–162.

Johns, T. F. (1991). Should you be persuaded—Two samples of data-driven learning materials. In T. F. Johns & P. King (Eds.), *Classroom concordancing. ELR Journal, 4*, 1–16.

Johns, T. F. (1994). From printout to handout: Grammar and vocabulary teaching in the context of data-driven learning. In T. Odlin (Ed.), *Perspectives on pedagogical grammar* (pp. 27–45). Cambridge, UK: Cambridge University Press.

Johns, T. F. (1997). Contexts: The background, development and trialling of a concordance-based CALL program. In A. Wichmann, S. Fligelstone, T. McEnery, & G. Knowles (Eds.), *Teaching and language corpora* (pp. 100–115). London, UK: Longman.

Johns, T. F. (2002). Data-driven learning: The perpetual challenge. In B. Kettemann & G. Marko (Eds.), *Teaching and learning by doing corpus analysis* (pp. 107–117). Amsterdam, The Netherlands: Rodopi.

Johns, T. F., Hsingchin, L., & Lixun, W. (2008). Integrating corpus-based CALL programs in teaching English through children's literature. *Computer Assisted Language Learning, 21,* 483–506.

Jones, R. L. (1997). Creating and using a corpus of spoken German. In A. Wichmann, S. Fligelstone, T. McEnery, & G. Knowles (Eds.), *Teaching and language corpora* (pp. 146–156). London, UK: Longman.

Jones, R. L. (2000). Textbook German and authentic spoken German: A corpus-based comparison. In B. Lewandowska-Tomaszczyk, P. J. Melia (Eds.), *PALC'99: Practical Applications in Language Corpora* (pp. 501–516). Frankfurt, Germany: Peter Lang.

Kaszubski, P. (2011). IFAConc-a pedagogic tool for online concordancing with EFL/EAP learners. In A. Frankenberg-Garcia, L. FLowerdew, & G. Aston (Eds.), *New trends in corpora and language learning* (pp. 81–104). London,UK: Continuum.

Kennedy, G. (1992). Preferred ways of putting things with implications for language teaching. In J. Svartvik (Ed.), *Directions in Corpus Linguistics: Proceedings of Nobel Symposium 82 Stockholm, 4–8 August 1991* (pp. 335–373). Berlin, Germany: Mouton de Gruyter.

Kennedy, C., & Miceli, T. (2001). An evaluation of intermediate students' approaches to corpus investigation. *Language Learning & Technology, 5,* 77–90. Retrieved from http://llt.msu.edu/vol5num3/kennedy/

Kennedy, C., & Miceli, T. (2002). The CWIC project: Developing and using a corpus for intermediate Italian students. In B. Kettemann & G. Marko (Eds.), *Teaching and learning by doing corpus analysis* (pp. 183–192). Amsterdam, The Netherlands: Rodopi.

Kennedy, C., & Miceli, T. (2010). Corpus-assisted creative writing: Introducing intermediate Italian learners to a corpus as a reference resource. *Language Learning & Technology, 14,* 28–44. Retrieved from http: //llt.msu.edu/vol14num1/kennedymiceli.pdf

Kettemann, B. (1995). On the use of concordancing in ELT. *Arbeiten aus Anglistik und Amerikanistik, 20,* 29–41.

Kettemann, B., & Marko, G. (Eds.). (2002). *Teaching and learning by doing corpus analysis.* Amsterdam, The Netherlands: Rodopi.

Kettemann, B., & Marko, G. (Eds.). (2006). *Planing, gluing and painting corpora. Inside the applied corpus linguist's workshop.* Frankfurt, Germany: Peter Lang.

Kjellmer, G. (1984). Some thoughts on collocational distinctiveness. In J. Aarts & W. Meijs (Eds.), *Corpus linguistics. Recent developments in the use of computer corpora in English language research* (pp. 163–171). Amsterdam, The Netherlands: Rodopi.

Kübler, N. (2011). Working with corpora for translation teaching in a French-speaking setting. In A. Frankenberg-Garcia, L. Flowerdew, & G. Aston (Eds.), *New trends in corpora and language learning* (pp. 62–80). London, UK: Continuum.

Lea, D. (2002). *Oxford collocations dictionary for students of English.* Oxford, UK: Oxford University Press.

Leech, G. N. (1997). Teaching and language corpora: A convergence. In A. Wichmann, S. Fligelstone, T. McEnery, & G. Knowles (Eds.), *Teaching and language corpora* (pp. 1–23). London, UK: Longman.

Leńko-Szymańska, A. (2007). Past progressive or simple past? The acquisition of progressive aspect by Polish advanced learners of English. In E. Hidalgo, L. Quereda, & J. Santana (Eds.), *Corpora in the foreign language classroom* (pp. 253–266). Amsterdam, The Netherlands: Rodopi.

Lewis, M. (1993). *The lexical approach.* Hove, UK: Language Teaching.

Lewis, M. (1997). *Implementing the lexical approach.* Hove, UK: Language Teaching.

Lewis, M. (2000). *Teaching collocation. Further developments in the lexical approach.* Hove, UK: Language Teaching.

Lombardo, L. (Ed.). (2009). *Using corpora to learn about language and discourse.* Frankfurt, Germany: Peter Lang.

Lorenz, G. (2002). Language corpora rock the base: On standard English grammar, perfective aspect and seemingly adverse corpus evidence. In B. Kettemann & G. Marko (Eds.), *Teaching and learning by doing corpus analysis* (pp. 131–145). Amsterdam, The Netherlands: Rodopi.

McCarthy, M., McCarten, J., & Sandiford, H. (2005). *Touchstone student's book 1.* Cambridge, UK: Cambridge University Press.

McEnery, T., Xiao, R., & Tono, Y. (2006). *Corpus-based language studies. An advanced resource book.* London, UK: Routledge.

Meunier, F. (2002). The pedagogical value of native and learner corpora in EFL grammar teaching. In S. Granger, J. Hung, & S. Petch-Tyson (Eds.), *Computer learner corpora, second language acquisition and foreign language teaching* (pp. 119–141). Amsterdam, The Netherlands: John Benjamins.

Meunier, F., & Gouverneur, C. (2007). The treatment of phraseology in ELT textbooks. In E. Hidalgo, L. Quereda, & J. Santana (Eds.), *Corpora in the foreign language classroom* (pp. 119–140). Amsterdam, The Netherlands: Rodopi.

Meunier, F., & Granger, S. (Eds.). (2008). *Phraseology in foreign language learning and teaching.* Amsterdam, The Netherlands: John Benjamins.

Mindt, D. (1981). Angewandte Linguistik und Grammatik für den Englischunterricht. In P. Kunsmann & O. Kuhn (Eds.), *Weltsprache Englisch in Forschung und Lehre: Festschrift für Kurt Wächtler* (pp. 175–186). Berlin, Germany: Schmidt.

Mindt, D. (1987). *Sprache—Grammatik—Unterrichtsgrammatik. Futurischer Zeitbezug im Englischen I.* Frankfurt, Germany: Diesterweg.

Mindt, D. (1995). *An empirical grammar of the English verb. Modal verbs.* Berlin, Germany: Cornelsen.

Mindt, D. (1997). Corpora and the teaching of English in Germany. In A. Wichmann, S. Fligelstone, T. McEnery, & G. Knowles (Eds.), *Teaching and language corpora* (pp. 40–50). London, UK: Longman.

Mukherjee, J. (2004). Bridging the gap between applied corpus linguistics and the reality of English language teaching in Germany. In E. Connor & T. A. Upton (Eds.), *Applied corpus linguistics. A multi-dimensional perspective* (pp. 239–250). Amsterdam, The Netherlands: Rodopi.

Nation, P. (1990). *Teaching and learning vocabulary*. Boston, MA: Heinle & Heinle.

Nattinger, J. R. (1980). A lexical phrase grammar for ESL. *TESOL Quarterly, 14*, 337–344.

Nesselhauf, N. (2005). *Collocations in a learner corpus*. Amsterdam, The Netherlands: John Benjamins.

O'Keeffe, A., McCarthy, M., & Carter, R. (2007). *From corpus to classroom: Language use and language teaching*. Cambridge, UK: Cambridge University Press.

Oksefjell-Ebeling, S. (2009). *Oslo interactive English*: Corpus-driven exercises on the Web. In K. Aijmer (Ed.), *Corpora and language teaching* (pp. 67–82). Amsterdam, The Netherlands: John Benjamins.

Pawley, A., & Syder, F. H. (1983). Two puzzles for linguistic theory: Native-like selection and native-like fluency. In J. C. Richards & R. W. Schmidt (Eds.), *Language and Communication* (pp. 191–226). London, UK: Longman.

Pérez-Paredes, P. (2003). Small corpora as assisting tools in the teaching of English news language: A preliminary tokens-based examination of Michael Swan's *Practical English Usage* news language wordlist. *ESP World, 6*. Retrieved from http: //www.esp-world.info/articles_6/pascual.htm

Peters, P. (2004). *The Cambridge guide to English usage*. Cambridge, UK: Cambridge University Press.

Reppen, R. (2010). *Using corpora in the language classroom*. Cambridge, UK: Cambridge University Press.

Römer, U. (2004a). Comparing real and ideal language learner input. The use of an EFL textbook corpus in corpus linguistics and language teaching. In G. Aston, S. Bernardini, & D. Stewart (Eds.), *Corpora and language learners* (pp. 151–168). Amsterdam, The Netherlands: John Benjamins.

Römer, U. (2004b). A corpus-driven approach to modal auxiliaries and their didactics. In J. M. Sinclair (Ed.), *How to use corpora in language teaching* (pp. 185–199). Amsterdam, The Netherlands: John Benjamins.

Römer, U. (2005). *Progressives, patterns, pedagogy. A corpus-driven approach to English progressive forms, functions, contexts and didactics*. Amsterdam, The Netherlands: John Benjamins.

Römer, U. (2007). Looking at *looking*: Functions and contexts of progressives in spoken English and "school" English. In W. Teubert & R. Krishnamurthy (Eds.), *Corpus linguistics. Critical concepts in linguistics* (Vol. 4, pp. 3–14). London, UK: Routledge. (Reprinted from *The changing face of corpus linguistics* by A. Renouf & A. Kehoe, Eds., 2006, Amsterdam, The Netherlands: Rodopi)

Römer, U. (2009a). Corpus research and practice: What help do teachers need and what can we offer? In K. Aijmer (Ed.), *Corpora and language teaching* (pp. 83–98). Amsterdam, The Netherlands: John Benjamins.

Römer, U. (2009b). The inseparability of lexis and grammar: Corpus linguistic perspectives. *Annual Review of Cognitive Linguistics*, *7*, 140–162.

Römer, U. (2010). Establishing the phraseological profile of a text type: The construction of meaning in academic book reviews. *English text construction*, *3*, 95–119.

Römer, U., & Schulze, R. (Eds.). (2009). *Exploring the lexis-grammar interface*. Amsterdam, The Netherlands: John Benjamins.

Rundell, M. (Ed.). (2007). *Macmillan English dictionary for advanced learners* (2nd ed.). Oxford, UK: Macmillan.

Schlüter, N. (2002). *Present Perfect. Eine korpuslinguistische Analyse des englischen Perfekts mit Vermittlungsvorschlägen für den Sprachunterricht*. Tübingen, Germany: Narr.

Scott, M., & Tribble, C. (2006). *Textual patterns. Key words and corpus analysis in language education*. Amsterdam, The Netherlands: John Benjamins.

Simpson-Vlach, R. C., & Ellis, N. C. (2010). An academic formulas list: New methods in phraseology research. *Applied Linguistics*, *31*, 487–512.

Sinclair, J. M. (Ed.). (1987). *Looking up: An account of the COBUILD project in lexical computing*. London, UK: Collins ELT.

Sinclair, J. M. (Ed.). (1990). *Collins COBUILD English grammar*. London, UK: HarperCollins.

Sinclair, J. M. (1991). *Corpus concordance collocation*. Oxford, UK: Oxford University Press.

Sinclair, J. M. (Ed.). (1992). *Collins COBUILD English usage*. London, UK: HarperCollins.

Sinclair, J. M. (1997). Corpus evidence in language description. In A. Wichmann, S. Fligelstone, T. McEnery, & G. Knowles (Eds.), *Teaching and language corpora* (pp. 27–39). London, UK: Longman.

Sinclair, J. M. (Ed.). (2001). *Collins COBUILD English dictionary for advanced learners*. London: HarperCollins.

Sinclair, J. M. (Ed.). (2004a). *How to use corpora in language teaching*. Amsterdam, The Netherlands: John Benjamins.

Sinclair, J. M. (2004b). Introduction. In J. M. Sinclair (Ed.), *How to use corpora in language teaching* (pp. 1–10). Amsterdam, The Netherlands: John Benjamins.

Sinclair, J. M. (2004c). New evidence, new priorities, new attitudes. In J. M. Sinclair (Ed.),

How to use corpora in language teaching (pp. 271–299). Amsterdam, The Netherlands: John Benjamins.

Sinclair, J. M. (2004d). *Trust the text. Language, corpus and discourse.* London, UK: Routledge.

Sinclair, J. M., & Renouf, A. (1988). A lexical syllabus for language learning. In R. Carter & M. McCarthy (Eds.), *Vocabulary in language teaching* (pp. 140–158). London, UK: Longman.

Sripicharn, P. (2004). Examining native speakers' and learners' investigation of the same concordance data and its implications for classroom concordancing with EFL learners. In G. Aston, S. Bernardini, & D. Stewart (Eds.), *Corpora and language learners* (pp. 233–245). Amsterdam, The Netherlands: John Benjamins.

Stubbs, M. (2001). *Words and phrases: Corpus studies of lexical semantics.* Oxford, UK: Blackwell.

Tono, Y. (2011). TALC in action: Recent innovations in corpus-based English language teaching in Japan. In A. Frankenberg-Garcia, L. Flowerdew, & G. Aston (Eds.), *New trends in corpora and language learning* (pp. 3–25). London,UK: Continuum.

Tribble, C., & Jones, G. (1997). *Concordances in the classroom. A resource book for teachers.* Houston, TX: Athelstan.

West, M. (1953). *A general service list of English words.* London, UK: Longman.

Whistle, J. (1999). Concordancing with students using an "off-the-Web" corpus. *ReCALL, 11,* 74–80.

Wichmann, A., Fligelstone, S., McEnery, T., & Knowles, G. (Eds.). (1997). *Teaching and language corpora.* London, UK: Longman.

Willis, D. (1990). *The lexical syllabus. A new approach to language teaching.* London, UK: HarperCollins.

Willis, D., & Willis, J. (1989). *Collins COBUILD English course.* London, UK: HarperCollins.

Yoon, H. (2008). More than a linguistic reference: The influence of corpus technology on L2 academic writing. *Language Learning & Technology, 12,* 31–48. Retrieved from http://llt.msu.edu/vol12num2/yoon.pdf

Teaching Multimodal and Digital Literacy in L2 Settings: New Literacies, New Basics, New Pedagogies

Heather Lotherington and Jennifer Jenson

Globalization and digitization have reshaped the communication landscape, affecting how and with whom we communicate, and deeply altering the terrain of language and literacy education. As children in urban contexts become socialized into communities of increasing cultural and communicational connectivity, complexity, and convergence (Jenkins, 2004), and funding for specialist second language (L2) support declines, classrooms have become linguistically heterogeneous spaces where every teacher is a teacher of L2 learners.

This article has two purposes: The first is to give an overview of the concept of multimodal literacies, which utilize diverse media to represent visual, audio, gestural, spatial, and tactile dimensions of communication in addition to traditional written and oral forms (Cope & Kalantzis, 2009a). Since the New London Group's manifesto on multiliteracies in 1996, which merged language and literacy education agendas in L2 teaching, language arts, media literacy, and cultural studies, new basics have developed that apply to all classrooms and all learners. Second, this article reviews and reports on innovative pedagogical approaches to multimodal literacies involving L2 learners. These are grounded theoretically (Cope & Kalantzis, 2009a, 2009b; Kress, 2003, 2010; New London Group, 1996) and epistemologically (de Castell & Jenson, 2003; Gee, 2009, 2010; Kellner, 2004; Lankshear & Knobel, 2003, 2006).

Multimodal literacies transcend the alphabetic world that is the focus of classroom literacy instruction. A generation ago, the world of literacy was based on paper. Now, literacy engages people in texts and discourses that traverse space and time on screens in which we can access and mix semiotic resources that include a multiplicity of languages. We do this instantaneously and ubiquitously, using new media in constant evolution.

Multimodal communication is not new. Face-to-face communication is inherently multimodal, and even the pinnacle of modern literate achievement, the book, has used visual modes to accompany alphabetic print for centuries, including resources such as illustrations, photographs, diagrams, charts, and maps.

Though multimodality does not necessarily utilize digital technologies, digital technologies enable "modes to be configured, be circulated, and get recycled in different ways" (Jewitt, 2009a, p. 1), thus intensifying multimodal possibilities. Digital media have been designed, engineered, and popularized in devices of ever-decreasing size at a dizzying rate over the past two decades, dramatically changing the media of communication, scope and speed of interactions, nature of discourse, and materiality of texts.

On the street, in public transport, and in shops and cafes, people are physically connected to portable digital devices for varied communicative purposes: Shoppers speak into hands-free cellular telephones; commuters listen to MP3 files, thumb-type on smartphones, or whiz through iconic applications on smartphones; and children (and others) play games on pocket-sized gaming consoles and smartphones—even a baseline cell phone has games on it. These accessories directly insert the individual into a digitally mediated multimodal world, creating new schema for participation and meaning making.

The affordances of new media have revolutionized social literacy practices: New orthographic and discourse conventions are proliferating, authorship is moving from individual construction to collaborative remix, and genres such as games have become canvasses for complex literacy practices. Kress (2009a) maintained that in this era, linear, alphabetic writing is no longer the primary carrier of literate meaning. So why is it that the interactive screen-based media of the 21st century have taken a back seat in the classroom, where print literacies continue to predominate? This is a new frontier for second language (L2) instruction where the old basics simply do not fit. Assumptions about learners, language form and format, text types, and social discourses must all be reexamined.

NEW WAYS OF UNDERSTANDING LITERACY

New Dimensions in Literacy

We have moved from "telling the world to showing the world" (Kress, 2003, p. 140). At a recent scholarly meeting, Lotherington (2010) proposed the idea of two-dimensional (2D) literacies to metaphorically capture the static, linear, paper-based reading and writing agendas of school language and literacy curricula and assessment. Digitally mediated, multimodal communication is dynamic, adding a third dimension of space, in that the reader can enter the text in new and exciting ways (e.g., as cowriter in collaborative texts, actor in augmented reality contexts, or avatar in virtual games); and it is interactive, adding the fourth dimension of time. In this metaphorical view, classroom literacies are flat: They are lifted off the page only in the mind of the reader—surely the aim of reading the statically encoded information therein. Literate engagement in the interactive, multimodal genres created in digital space engages the participant in dynamic, multidimensional communication, (potentially) involving

- social interaction,
- haptic activation,
- physical coordination,
- visual design,
- modal complexity (e.g., multiple language engagement, musical accompaniment, and animation),
- dynamic, collaborative text construction, and
- alphabetic literacy.

These new possibilities reshape how we understand, teach, and test language and literacy in the classroom.

In L2 teaching contexts, whether characterized as second, foreign, or international language education, teachers have been hesitant to acknowledge and engage these new dimensions of literacy. Valdés (2004) pointed to L2 teachers' tendency to conceptualize language in their teaching as an abstract linguistic system, detached from a broader socially constructed multimodal perspective:

The view that there are multiple literacies rather than a single literacy, and that these literacies depend on the context of the situation, the activity itself, the interactions between participants, and the knowledge and experiences that these various participants bring to these interactions, is distant from the view held by most L2 educators who still embrace a technocratic notion of literacy and emphasize the development of decontextualized skills. (p. 79)

Reducing L2 learning to the flat literacies of paper-based resources in the classroom raises questions of authenticity in L2 learning. If teachers are to meaningfully engage L2 learners in communication as it exists in the social world, these brave new dimensions of literacy must be woven into classroom learning.

Language, Culture, and Convergence

New media are built from old media (Bolter & Grusin, 1999; McLuhan, 1964). Proliferating digital technologies do not displace older communication technologies, but merge cultural forms and practices (Buckingham, 2003). According to Henry Jenkins (2006), we are living in a *convergence culture*, where the media, including those who control, consume, and produce it, have converged. This is most evident in the semantic capabilities of Web 2.0, which allow greater production and user control than previous media.

For Jenkins (2006), convergence is not necessarily technologically driven; it is an artifact of new production and consumption practices. Jenkins offers a positive example in a *Harry Potter* fan fiction (or *fanfic*) community, where a young girl created her own online school newspaper for the mythical magic school, Hogwarts, attended by the students in the *Harry Potter* series. Children from around the world participated and were offered help with their contributions to the paper. Whereas the convergence piece appears to be driven largely by popular culture and by the consumption of the *Harry Potter* enterprise in this example, underscoring Lemke's (2006) observation that media convergence is blatant in commercial media where pop culture artifacts have tentacles in multiple media franchises, Jenkins argued that this need not be read simply as an artifact of mass market global capitalism. It is a positive example of children becoming apprenticed in creative expression, in this case, through writing. In sites such as this, culture and language are converging, whether the sites are connected with novels; are based mostly on alphabetic input;

are game-based sites involving language, image, and movement (e. g., *Club Penguin* or *Farmville*); or are game-based sites with massively multiplayer online role-playing games (MMORPG), which immerse the player in image, written dialogue, sound, action, and animation (e. g., *World of Warcraft*).

Thorne, Black, and Sykes (2009) commented that creative apprenticeship in digital activities can benefit L2 learners:

> In many new media contexts, from literary gestures in fan fiction communities to language mediated coordination among players in an online game, specific language competencies develop in interaction within particular genres (i.e., fan fiction) and routine interactional scenarios (i.e., gaming contexts). (p. 815)

Black (2005) described how fan fiction provided L2 learners unconfident in their written English with opportunities to meaningfully participate in the fanfic community, whose members reviewed fictions as "unofficial beta-readers" (p. 125) or proofreaders, providing holistic critiques and suggestions for rewording.

In the convergence culture of the 21st century, the individual has become simultaneously creator and consumer of mediated communication. The collaborative authorship and digitally connected knowledge communities created by participatory culture are new basics that educational infrastructures must accommodate. All teachers, especially those in the L2 classroom, must understand that single authorship is now an option, not a model in writing, and that the physical classroom extends beyond its brick walls, connected digitally to resources and learning partners.

Epistemological Shifts in Digital Literacies

Changes in the relative value of knowledge (i.e., what counts as knowledge and how one comes to know) is as Lyotard (1984) anticipated, a condition of postmodernity. Jewitt (2009a) ascribed the 21st-century turn to multimodalism to postmodern influences; the increasing democratization of knowledge in the networked society has challenged modern configurations of truth and authority. This is evident in the ways in which traditional notions of literacy are being reshaped by digital forms. An example of this is the *wiki*, which is a democratically produced text, accessed and edited collaboratively by multiple users (e.g., Wikipedia). Though these changes have been brought about through the proliferation of computer-based and screen-based technologies, these same technologies, in the not-so-distant future, could disentangle from the screen altogether and be broadcast without aid of a screen through new pixel technologies. What these technologies have brought about is a new understanding of what it means to know, including how it means to know multimodally.

Lankshear and Knobel (2008) viewed the shift to digital literacies as one that is "shorthand for the myriad social practices and conceptions of engaging in meaning making mediated by texts that are produced, received, distributed, exchanged, etc. via digital codification" (p. 5). These texts (e.g., images, movies, podcasts, blogs, and online social networking sites) encode knowledge very differently, and both what is produced and how one knows and comes to know are different from these processes in traditional print-based literacies. What it is to know under these conditions, then, in multiple languages in L2 contexts is central to this review.

Multimodality and Literacy

The New London Group, in their 1996 manifesto introducing the concept of *multiliteracies*, theorized changing the " 'what' of literacy pedagogy" (p. 65) to include six design elements in the meaning-making process: linguistic, visual, audio, gestural, and spatial meaning, and multimodal interplay. This formative theorizing of multiliteracies in the era of the static Web, or Web 1.0, however, lacked the interactive, participatory capabilities of Web 2.0. Theoretical and practical exploration of multimodal literacies has since mushroomed from multiple perspectives, including systemic functional linguistics (Kress, 2003, 2010; Unsworth & Cléirigh, 2009), digital epistemology (Jenson & de Castell, 2004; Kellner, 2004; Lankshear & Knobel, 2003, 2006), new literacies (Street, Pahl, & Rowsell, 2009), critical multimedia (Lemke, 2006), visual literacy (Jewitt, 2002, 2008; Kress & Van Leeuwen, 2006; Unsworth, 2006), videogaming (Beavis, 2002; de Castell & Jenson, 2009; Gee, 2003; Peterson, 2010; Zheng, Wagner, Young, & Brewer, 2009), and multilingual/multicultural inclusion in literacy education (Cummins, 2006; Dagenais, Toohey, & Day, 2006; Gutiérrez, 2008; Kenner, Al-Azami, Gregory, & Ruby, 2008; Kenner, Ruby, Jessel, Gregory, & Arju, 2008; Lotherington, 2008, 2009, 2011; Lotherington, Sotoudeh, Holland, & Zentena, 2008; Martin-Jones &

Saxena, 2003). Most, but not all, theorists—or practitioners—work with digital mediation.

Kress framed multimodality as a "domain of inquiry," (2009b, p. 54), noting that particular media offer different modal possibilities; these capabilities include the combination of audio, visual, linguistic, gestural, and spatial modalities to convey rich meanings. Kress (2010) demonstrated how even the traditional textbook has undergone significant changes in both appearance and content, becoming increasingly image-centered, and moving away from the linear toward a more modular design framework. Cope and Kalantzis (2009a) described changes in reading from page to screen, noting that Web sites are read more like images than linear text.

Researchers are showing the ways in which multimodal forms of knowing and coming to know are being pushed by the affordances of digital technologies, which are, in turn, changing the ways in which we think of curriculum and pedagogy (Hull & Nelson, 2005; Jewitt, 2006; Kress, 2003; Lotherington, 2009; Mills, 2010). The move toward multimodal literacies in the classroom, though, is a rocky one, and L2 learning contexts are notoriously resistant in adapting (Tan & McWilliam, 2009; Valdés, 2004; Warschauer, 2008). Indeed, even where technological hardware is available, school contexts have been shown to be underutilizing the creative potential of such technologies for the purposes of L2 teaching and learning (Ware, 2008).

NEW BASICS IN EDUCATION

From the 3 Rs to Multidimensional Worlds

The new literacy movement to refocus literacy as social practice began decades ago with the work of anthropological researchers, such as Shirley Brice Heath (1983), Ruth Finnegan (1988), and Brian Street (1984, 1995), who framed textual practices within a wider sphere of social communication. The New London Group's (1996) collaboration to discuss "what was happening to meaning making and representation in the worlds of work, citizenship and personal life that might prompt a reconsideration of our approaches to literacy teaching and learning" (Cope & Kalantzis, 2009b, p. 166) propelled creative conversations about literacy pedagogy as multimodal. With increasing population mobility, the social practice orientation of new literacy scholars has converged with the concerns of applied linguists and sociolinguists working in L2 learning and language policy; and with rapidly evolving information and communications technologies, these concerns have increasingly involved those of contemporary media scholars working with digital multimedia.

New basics apply to new literacies. Modes, according to Kress (2009b), are realized through semiotic resources, which are culturally negotiated, so they are not static or universal. Cope and Kalantzis (2009a) framed a grammar of multimodality around core modes of expression—linguistic, visual, spatial, gestural, and audio—based on questions of meaning, leaning conceptually on systemic functional grammar (Halliday, 1994). Cope and Kalantzis explained, "some of the differences in meaning potential afforded by the different modes are fundamental. . . . writing's intrinsic temporality orients it to causality; image to location" (p. 264). Their grammatical dimensions are the following:

- Representational—What do the meanings refer to?
- Social—How do the meanings connect the persons they involve?
- Organizational—How do the meanings hang together?
- Contextual—How do the meanings fit into the larger world of meaning?
- Ideological—Whose interests are the meanings skewed to serve? (p. 365)

Sinclair (2010) visualized students as knowledge makers in contemporary education who need room for digital play. Sinclair revised the fundamental 3 Rs of modern education (viz., reading, writing, arithmetic) to 4 Rs for the digital era that are fundamentally ludic and collaborative: *reuse* (backup), *revise* (adapt), *remix* (combine), and *redistribute* (share). These practices are basic to digitally mediated multimodal text creation in which information is understood as recombinant (Sinclair, 2010).

The significance of this shift to a multimodal approach to learning is that it presumes first and foremost that the primary mode of transmission and production is digital, which opens up possibilities beyond just one approach. Multimodal learning supports collaborative authorship, including the search for, creation, and layering of modes that parallel, extend, and expand textual production, bringing L2 learners together in pursuit of communicative objectives and supporting contextualized acquisition of coded target language forms.

A Ludic Perspective: Play as Work; Work as Play

As *Homo Ludens* author Johan Huizinga (1960) noted decades ago, *play* is an essential part of what it means to be human, not to mention that play is one of the key ways children learn (Piaget, 1951; Singer & Singer, 2005). And yet, in schools, play is something that is consistently relegated to the playground. It is something that occurs outside of the hard work of learning and of classrooms, sometimes in the gym or the art room or the music class (though less and less as governments continue to cut back funding to the humanities and physical education). As an outsider to the serious business of learning and work, play is also something that is very much associated with childhood; freedom of movement; creativity and permission to construct new rules; and experimenting with status quo, inversion, and irony. Play is elemental to meaningful engagement with digital technologies—including schoolwork, language learning, and engaging in language play (Derrida, 1978). For example, when tasked with creating a comic-like piece, students in the Joyce Public School project in Toronto, Canada, described in this article literally played with text size, type, font, color, image placement, and word choice to produce the effects they wanted, including irony and word play. The hard work of producing the kinds of multimodal, multilingual digital objects we explore in this article are also ludic (viz., *play* in Latin) activities.

NEW PEDAGOGIES: MULTIMODAL LITERACIES IN L2 CONTEXTS

Extended Classroom Borders

What is an L2 teaching and learning context in the second decade of the 21st century? This article reviews a variety of contexts for L2 teaching and learning where multiple media offer a panorama of communicative possibilities, calling into question the applicability of familiar dichotomized constructs.

The L2 classroom has traditionally relied on polarized binaries, boxing language into pairs of productive-receptive skills (i.e., reading-writing, speaking-listening), and dividing learners into L1 (first language) and L2—native speakers and nonnative speakers. These concepts are epistemologically grounded in the social and linguistic worlds of speech communities and flat literacies. Many online communities of practice do not acknowledge the binary distinctions that mark insiders and outsiders in physical speech communities, where sociopolitical concepts such as *second language* and *foreign language* have explanatory power. Zheng et al. (2009), describing social interaction in a virtual world, explained: "In online interaction, learners do not have many opportunities to perceive social, cultural, and linguistic cues directly through embodiment" (p. 505). Though this degree of anonymity is not universal in digital space, it is certainly the case with MMORPG and virtual world environments where players interact through avatars (created online personae).

Though multimodality does not necessarily involve the digital, increasingly this is the case, and certainly it is the way of this century. However it is realized, multimodal learning approaches learners and learning differently. In this review, we group multimodal pedagogies as intergenerational, digitally mediated interactional, and ludic, though these categories are neither static nor exclusive, and some projects fit into all three.

Intergenerational Connections

As Dooley (2008) pointed out, a multiliteracies approach guides diversity into rather than out of literacy education. As an example of this, the creation of dual language books and materials—multimodal resources utilizing multiple languages and modes oriented to supporting children's L1 in L2 learning environments—has blossomed in different social and cultural contexts. Cummins (2006), in discussing a dual language book project involving a host of immigrant languages in suburban Toronto (see Schecter & Cummins, 2003), explained the concept of "identity text" (p. 59): stories written bilingually in home and school languages, as self-affirming student identity investments that maximize conditions for learning. McCarty and Bia (2002), describing decades-long work in the evolution of an indigenous education program at Rough Rock Community School in Arizona, compared the relatively unstructured Navajo literacy materials created in-house to the regimented, skill-oriented English as a second language (ESL) curriculum. Kenner, Al-Azami, et al. (2008) described a bilingual poetry project in a Bangladeshi community in

East London where, with intergenerational support, children learned a poetic range spanning generations, languages, and cultures. In addition, Naqvi (2008), working with Pakistani immigrants, reported on bicultural minority language resources for children in schools in western Canada.

Though these projects involved primarily alphabetic literacies (though not necessarily the same alphabets), they incorporated the languages of families split by acculturation into old and new countries in ways that were less rigid and more fun than timetabled L2 classes. Some of these projects used the Web as a publishing venue, though these were sites of display rather than interactivity (e.g., http://thornwood.peelschools.org/Dual).

Similar bilingual and multilingual resources for schoolchildren have been developed as dynamic digital objects. Khvtisiashvili (2010) described a University of Utah project to preserve indigenous languages through film animation of traditional stories. The stories were scripted as action sequences, with the characters' lines voiced by native community members in vernacular translation. The animated stories utilized both indigenous and majority languages, facilitated intergenerational cultural and linguistic transmission, and offered opportunities to craft and animate characters, as well as to create and edit video. Though these multimodal activities were intended to support and archive indigenous languages, by linking English speakers with indigenous elders to make a collaborative intellectual product, the animated traditional legends project offered a splendid participatory pedagogy for teaching multimodal literacies using any languages.

Digitally Mediated Interactional Spaces

In an interesting genealogical take on digital literacies in a context understood as foreign language learning, Bo-Kristensen and Meyer (2008) examined the language laboratory. Long considered a pedagogical dinosaur, the language lab is the ancestor of technologically mediated L2 learning, an example of remediation (Bolter & Grusin, 1999) in educational innovation. In the context of a military college in Denmark, Bo-Kristensen and Meyer looked at the relationship between L2 pedagogy and technologically mediated pathways for learning in the contexts of English as a foreign language (EFL), and Danish as a second language (DSL) in

Denmark. They found traditional audio-lingual and behavioral language teaching methodology simply reinscribed in the remediated EFL digital lab. However, in the virtual language laboratory where the affordances of Web 2.0 mediated the experience of language learning, a sense of immediacy was effected by the temporal-spatial flexibility, fostering more informal EFL learning and answering more closely the students' needs. Here, the teacher assumed much more agency in assembling dynamic resources in the target language, such as film and radio archives, and Web sites that the learners could access instantaneously. The latest incarnation of the language lab, the mobile language lab, linked learners (in the adult DSL context researched) through mobile devices such as cell telephones and facilitated authentic, relevant content, as did the virtual lab. However, the mobile lab gave more agency to learners who could produce their own authentic learning content by capturing and uploading communication scenarios and materials themselves.

This comparative study reveals that the more portable the digital technology used in the context of L2 teaching—moving from the large, fixed language lab to the virtual lab to linked mobile devices—the more agentive, participatory learning was enabled. More agency was given to the student for locating and contributing relevant and authentic language content, extending the walls of the classroom and the reach of teaching materials to include learner-selected language data in oral, written, and other visual forms (e.g., gestural) that were meaningful and authentic to the learning context.

Using the affordances of digital texts to implement French as a foreign language instruction at the college level in the United States, Williams (2009) found novel ways of comparatively teaching the grammatical forms, *tu and vous*, which are socially differentiated forms of the second person pronoun (viz., you) in French that have no direct parallels in English, and as such present socially perplexing learning to Anglophones. Using the Coca-Cola France Web site (www.coca-colafrance.fr) to stimulate critical framing (following Kern, 2000; New London Group, 1996), Williams described how even the nuisance pop-up window survey could be used to analyze when and where formal and informal pronominal use was preferred. Interactional patterns included typical class and small group discussions in addition to interaction with and on the site itself. Analytical framing in class also included semiotic resources affecting the perceived formality of pronominal use on the Web site, such as font color, size, and pronominal choice in embedded video clips.

Ware (2008) observed 20 ELL (English language learner) students over the course of a year in an intermediate ESL program at a technologically rich, urban American middle school to qualitatively capture their digital literacies during and after school. She found that the laptops students carried were used shockingly seldom for school activities, taking up about an hour a week in class time, and that those activities centered on PowerPoint presentations and word processing. Though she defends the complexities of navigating the Web for information retrieval and critique, we note that these activities do not reach the literacies of this century, which engage the interactive potential of the semantic Web. Nor are they in any sense ludic.

As a component of this research, Ware (2008) instituted an after school multimedia project with ELL students to explore digital storytelling, which, though time-consuming, was highly motivating to the students. The digital storytelling project engaged the students in a collaborative learning model for multimodal learning and presentation, but it did not incorporate their home languages. Ware suggested that multimodal activities can provide ELL students with visual and verbal alternatives in text creation and recommended positive potential for L2 learning in mode-switching activities, addressing what Jewitt (2009b) described as intersemiotic relationships in multimodality: "the interplay between modes" (p. 25). Ware (2008) offered examples of L2 learning opportunities embedded in mode-switching activities such as students translating textbook materials into comic strips or choosing endings in branched hyperlinked stories, but cautioned, "multimedia literacy practices certainly broaden the breadth of those experiences, but we still have little empirical evidence of the depth in which students develop their linguistic repertoire when moving across textual, visual, and aural modes" (p. 49).

Ludic Approaches

In the world of digital gaming, Zheng et al. (2009) studied artifacts from Chinese L2 learners' engagement with American players in the virtual world, *Quest Atlantis*, to examine how their environmental interaction supported English language acquisition. The problem-solving nature of games coupled with the immersive environment of a virtual world creates the conditions for embodied interaction wherein players collaboratively problem solve. Though interaction in a virtual world is distinguished from real-world interactions in that avatars provide an anonymous shield, and their virtual behavior is ontologically regulated by the virtual world they inhabit, which might allow them to fly, for example, the game leaves a trace that learners can track and follow, read, critique, and learn from. Zheng et al. (2009) claimed that the embodied learning enabled by playing *Quest Atlantis* supported the L2 learners' real-world English language development, by requiring them to "coordinate in-the-moment actions" (p. 489) using English.

Digital gaming encourages the learner by eradicating the fatality of the right-wrong, pass-fail assessment of static literacies (de Castell & Jenson, 2003). The mechanical reboot-restart mechanism of digital games makes failing to make the grade or not finding the clue or, as an avatar, losing the battle or even getting killed, a certain kind of learning, motivating the player to retry, promoting critical evaluation. This could be viewed as a foundational building block of the New London Group's (1996) initial theorizing of the *how* of multiliteracies, as well as creative thinking and problem solving.

Virtual games provide a kind of identity building milieu. The player creates an avatar's superficial physical characteristics, and then learns to interact in the game ontology, acquiring and building the avatar's linguistic, sociocultural, and pragmatic competence. Cummins (2006) discussed the importance of supporting L2 learners' positive, self-affirming identity building to facilitate learning a new language. In the *Olifantsvlei fresh story* project (Stein, 2006, 2008) that we review next, the aim was children's real-world identity building in postapartheid South Africa.

Stein's (2006, 2008) *Olifantsvlei fresh story* project demonstrated the ludic principle in pedagogical development without the intervention of digital mediation. The storytelling project took place in the early part of the decade in a rural South African context of very high social and economic need and manifest multilingualism. This multimodal storytelling project welcomed young children's languages, which included both local and foreign African languages into a ludic space, despite the reservations of teachers in their English-medium school. Stories were created around homemade dolls that were constructed in a "semiotic chain of narrative" (Stein, 2008, p. 119), as character representatives of the children's lifeworlds for the purpose of developing "a body of imaginative, local 'fresh stories'based on and arising from the children's lives and local experiences" (Stein, 2008, p. 98).

Children developed homemade dolls that were repurposed for school after teachers' attempts to create papier mâché dolls failed. In fact, the teachers' artistic failure created an educational juncture for children's agency in creating dolls from local materials that, in themselves, told stories. The dolls were used in improvisational storytelling, and stories were invited in any language. The project extended children's semiotic resources for communicating in a playful, agency-building context that tapped their local knowledge, welcomed their input in multiple languages, and created opportunities for self-affirming identity building in postapartheid education.

One of the objectives of this project was to move from the controlled spaces of the classroom; rules for language use and ways of learning were rejected for more improvisational learning, inviting playful engagement with objects, and thereby with the meanings ascribed to those objects through language(s). Similarly, in the next example from our own work, we show how play can be harnessed to create provocative learning.

In Toronto, the teachers at Joyce Public School have been working with researchers at York University to codesign flexible, ludic (de Castell & Jenson, 2003, 2009), culturally sensitive projects in the primary and junior grades (K–5) that include children's home and community language networks and the digital literacies that are an ineluctable component of fundamental literacy in the 21st century. The ongoing collaborative community of practice has as its goal the creation of experimental multiliteracies pedagogies (Cope & Kalantzis, 2000, 2009b; New London Group, 1996) that create projects welcoming community languages, cross-curricular learning, multimodal expression, and digital play into the elementary language and literacy classroom (Lotherington, 2008, 2009, 2011). The agenda is approached from a grassroots perspective based on a supportive learning community comprising university researchers and elementary school teachers for the theoretical and practical advancement of project-based multimodal literacies education. Our orientation to work within a professional development platform circumvents criticisms researchers have made about multimodal literacies paradigms lacking adequate teacher preparation (Tan, Bopry, & Guo, 2010).

The Joyce project approached multimodal literacies in terms of

- sharing responsibility for education beyond classroom walls to open pathways for language support and inclusion;
- playful engagement with and development of digitally supported, multilingual projects that instantiate Courtney Cazden's (1981) notion of "performance before competence" (p. 7);
- supporting multilingualism in dynamic modal communication; and
- ludic epistemology (de Castell & Jenson, 2009).

In this work in particular, we sought not just the modalities of text and image, but the modality of play. As a modality, play can be activated and learned from and used to frame and develop ideas by playful engagement with digital media.

Imagine a World

This teacher-directed, student-supported project, called Imagine a World, was implemented in the fall of 2009. It was developed in support of a schoolwide initiative focused on developing student understandings of similarity and difference at all grade levels, and for the upper grades in the school, this generally fell under the theme of respect. For grade 4 and 5 students, this meant a yearlong, cross-subject inquiry that attempted to familiarize students with the range of differences present in their own schools and families as well as the world more generally. Topics covered included family structure, race, ethnicity, class, religion, immigration stories, languages, sexual orientation, gender (masculinities and femininities), and individual difference within those categories. To begin this yearlong inquiry, the four grade 4 and 5 teachers involved (including one special education teacher) decided that the best way to begin to talk about difference was to look at similarities; they used, across all their classes, a beautifully illustrated book by Mem Fox (1997), entitled *Whoever You Are*, that specifically addressed the question of what makes people similar.

After reading the book, the teachers asked students to fill in the phrase, "We are all. . . ." Students individually contributed up to three written responses. The second part of the activity involved the students refining the phrases and redeploying them to create a collagraph print, which uses glue and other materials (much like a collage) to create a three-dimensional (3D) image in a mirrored state, which is then transferred from plate to paper for printing. The next activity was to focus on difference in language, in contrast to the similarities that were being displayed in the images, and students and their parents were invited to rewrite the English phrases in their home languages. Finally, a multimedia, multilingual talking book including eight languages and a printed artifact was produced from the collaborative student, teacher, and parent work.

What is significant here in terms of modalities is that multiple languages, play, sound, text, and 3D image making (collagraph print) are intertwined. The hybrid intersection of these pieces created a multimodal, multilingual digital artifact that showed not only the powerful similarities of humanity (see Figure 1, which depicts the commonalities of human fertilization and the perceived opportunities in life) but also the richness of linguistic differences (both spoken and written) present in one small community and accessed by all 70 students, incorporating L2 students' abilities as assets to the process, in print as well as narrative voice-over. The artifact represents a deep engagement not only with the phrases invoked in multiple languages but also in representing those complex ideas through sound and image, showing the complexity of abstract thought in creatively attempting to find similarities that cross cultures, languages, and generations.

Hurdles in Multimodal Literacy Education

In 2002, Venezky and Davis, reporting on the transformation of schooling in the networked world, gave a generally failing grade:

> In most schools ICT [Information and communication technology] has not become routinised; even in the most successful cases reported here, pockets of teachers remain who have yet to accept a need for integrating ICT into their teaching or to be prepared to do this. Among those who have begun these tasks, further professional development is often needed. In addition, many infrastructures are inadequate for the applications desired, and budgets for expansion are not currently available. (p. 36)

Fig. 1. A page from multimodal project, *Imagine a World*,
by grade 4 and 5 students at Joyce Public School.

We are now so socially enmeshed in digital literacy practices that the concept of optional extrication from the digital world is not realistic, yet language and literacy instruction continues to resist digitized multimedia and multimodal literacy practices as optional or secondary to flat textual practices. Pockets of resistance reside in the complexities of the educational system, in teachers' socialization and professional expectations, and in assessment paradigms. Warschauer (2008) queried whether the educational establishment understands the point of language and literacy learning to prepare students for civic engagement, higher education, and employment possibilities—or to improve test scores.

Street et al. (2009) signaled that not including multimodal resources in the classroom undermines what children bring to the learning task by ignoring the modes children already use to make meaning. However, Dooley (2008) pointed out that there are deep epistemological differences in ways of knowing English (as an L2) in digitally mediated popular culture worlds and in historically entrenched school literacies, noting that the former facilitate procedural literacies, invented identities, and performance epistemologies marked by spontaneity and hybridity, whereas the latter focus on propositional knowledge, archival identities, and reproducing social texts. Dooley suggested that migrating pop culture into the classroom is a colonizing act, if youth cultures are inserted into epistemologies of modern print. This is precisely what Lotherington, Neville-Verardi, and Sinitskaya Ronda (2009) showed with high school students, who, though scathing toward the mandatory provincial literacy tests they had written, were resistant to a revised version incorporating digital pop culture content.

In L2 education, there has been a tendency for researchers to focus on the digital or the multilingual, sidestepping the complexities of intersecting contemporary literacies in the classroom. Much research on multimodal literacies in the classroom still focuses on the dual modalities of text and image to the exclusion of the myriad modalities that construct learning and understanding in this digital age. Though good teaching and learning have resulted from multimodal pedagogies that do not incorporate digital mediation, avoiding the digital world is another thing altogether. One reason for avoidance of digital technologies in multimodal learning is evident in Tan and McWilliam's (2009) comparative description of the relative success of two educational initiatives to implement a digital literacies program in Queensland, Australia. One of these contexts was a public reception school specializing in English language instruction for newly arrived migrants and refugees of diverse cultural and linguistic origins and educational backgrounds. Tan and McWilliam described how well-meaning ESL teachers deferred to traditionally held basics in print literacy, adhering to an understanding of print as central to L2 learning and expressing a concern that students might be overloaded by digital demands. Meanwhile these students were observed to be actively using their personal iPods during school lessons to download and share music files. In fact, it was observed to be the teachers who were struggling to understand how they might incorporate technologies that were new to them—not to the students. This is unsurprising if one surveys core courses in teacher education and L2 certification programs, which, like educational institutions, have been slow in providing opportunities to learn about and explore new technologies for language teaching.

A brick wall facing many educators is the standardized testing culture that functions as a watchdog over flat literacy practices. Even in cases where there is political will to transform ELL education, the teachers themselves may manifest resistance. Tan et al. (2010) ascribed the reluctance of a teacher in a Singaporean secondary school to move on from traditional ELL expectations to tensions between a transformative critical multiliteracies approach and the power of traditional assessment practices:

> Although Alicia had shifted her pedagogical practices to include reading and designing of multimodal texts, she remained adamant about critical multimedia literacies being less important than conventional literacy. We note that this could be the influence of the language-dominant assessment that was still in place in the education system. (p. 14)

As Lankshear and Knobel (2006) aptly put it, the point here is not that these are new forms of *letteracy*, nor is the central importance the construction of written texts, but in the everyday lives of many, the production and consumption of multimodal, digital artifacts. That means very different kinds of knowing—the difficulty, as McLuhan (1967/2001) foresaw, is figuring out what the nature of those differences are. The challenge in education policy and practice is that testing still typically tests the former, under conditions that are no longer simply print-based, monocultural, or first and foremost local.

CONCLUSION: MULTIMODAL VISTAS IN L2 EDUCATION

Digitally mediated communication is creatively multimodal, engaging "multipurpose, multifunctional technologies that involve layers of complexity and application in L2 learning that are unique among the technologies of the modern world" (Levy, 2009, p. 779). We would venture to say digital technologies are dominant communication media in a postmodern world. As Kellner (2004) suggested, education urgently requires "revision [that] involves both critically seeing the past and present and imagining a different future" (p. 10).

This article has given an overview of theoretical perspectives on multimodality and digital epistemologies, and described pedagogical projects that implement different kinds of multimodal teaching practices in a variety of international L2 contexts. Appropriate teacher education, assessment practices, the pedagogical space to experiment with multimodality, and respect for the varying (multiple) language competencies of all members of a learning context, no matter how configured, are critical directions for creating the conditions for successful multimodal L2 teaching.

Sinclair (2010) cut through the typical binary of physical and virtual worlds—online and offline—to present a more realistic continuum of worlds as physical→augmented→hybrid→mixed/blended→virtual, exposing the digital native-digital immigrant paradigm (Prensky, 2001; Tunsbridge, 1995) as overgeneralized and naïve. Sinclair offered as a more useful description of acculturation in the continuously digitizing world the following spectrum: digital aliens, immigrants, adaptives, natives, and avatars. Wherever teachers pose themselves on this continuum, it does not define the worlds of others, notably their students, no matter which languages they bring into the classroom. Nor does it accommodate the shifting landscape of teaching and learning under rapidly changing conditions.

ANNOTATED BIBLIOGRAPHY

Gee, J. P. (2003). *What video games have to teach us about learning and literacy.* New York, NY: Palgrave Macmillan.

Gee is one of the first scholars to make the argument that videogames train their players in ways that could be profitably recognized by educational specialists. Gee argued that good video games in general can be shown to enact 36 learning principles, which include, for example, that learning in videogames is not accomplished through the delivery of content, understood as abstracted facts; rather, meaning and significance arise through the player's activation and negotiation of images, objects, and events in context. Gee challenged classrooms to imagine similar kinds of teaching.

Jenkins, H. (2006). *Convergence culture: Where old and new media collide.* New York, NY: New York University Press.

For Jenkins, convergence culture signals the movement of production from mainstream media into the hands of what had once been seen as its consumers. His argument is that local sites of production have meaningfully shifted the consumption/production dichotomy to one that recombines these relations, giving consumers more and more access to the means of production, resulting in a convergence of media practices.

Lankshear, C., & Knobel, M. (2006). *New literacies: Everyday practices and classroom learning.* Maidenhead, UK: McGraw Hill/Open University Press.

Lankshear and Knobel's second edition so substantially revises their 2003 text that it has a subtitle change. They tackled new literacies both ontologically and chronologically, demystifying the fundamental concept of remix and introducing some of the mushrooming new literacies popping up in Web 2.0 forums that stretch literate practices into creative, dynamic, interactive forms, such as blogging and fanfiction.

Lyotard, J. (1984). *The postmodern condition: A report on knowledge.* Minneapolis: University of Minnesota Press.

The Postmodern Condition is a definitive text on the epistemic and cultural changes brought about by the shift from modernism to postmodernism. Central to this work is the argument that postmodernism puts an end to singular claims about truth and instead relies on local conditions and contexts and a multiplicity of truths. In turn, what counts as knowledge and what that knowledge is worth under conditions of computerization are discussed.

New London Group. (1996). A pedagogy of multiliteracies: Designing social factors. *Harvard Educational Review, 66,* 60–92.

The New London Group was a collection of 10 eminent scholars who met in New London, New Hampshire, in 1994 to discuss how literacy education could be reimagined in a rapidly changing world. They wrote this now classic article collaboratively—anticipating the participatory Web before it had been created—in which they grappled with how global connection, which encouraged local cultural diversity, and multimodality could be factored into understanding literacy and literacy education. In this discussion, they coined the term multiliteracies.

REFERENCES

Black, R.W. (2005). Access and affiliation: The literacy and composition practices of English language-learners in an online fanfiction community. *Journal of Adolescent and Adult Literacy, 49,* 118–128. doi: 10.1598/JAAL.49.2.4

Beavis, C. (2002). Reading, writing and role-playing computer games. In I. Snyder (Ed.), *Silicon literacies* (pp. 47–61). London, UK: Routledge.

Bo-Kristensen, M., & Meyer, B. (2008). Transformations of the language laboratory. In T. Hansson (Ed.), *Handbook of research on digital information technologies: Innovations, methods, and ethical issues* (pp. 27–36). Hershey, PA: IGI Global.

Bolter, J. D., & Grusin, R. (1999). *Remediation: Understanding new media.* Cambridge, MA: MIT Press.

Buckingham, D. (2003). *Media education: Literacy, learning and contemporary culture.* Cambridge, UK: Polity Press.

Cazden, C. (1981). Performance before competence: Assistance to child discourse in the zone of proximal development. *Quarterly Newsletter of the Laboratory of Comparative Human Cognition, 3,* 5–8.

Cope, B., & Kalantzis, M. (2000). Introduction. Multiliteracies: The beginnings of an idea. In B. Cope & M. Kalantzis (Eds.), *Multiliteracies: Literacy learning and the design of social futures* (pp. 3–8). London, UK: Routledge.

Cope, B., & Kalantzis, M. (2009a). A grammar of multimodality. *International Journal of Learning, 16,* 361–425. doi: 10.1080/15544800903076044

Cope, B., & Kalantzis, M. (2009b). Multiliteracies: New literacies, new learning, *Pedagogies: An International Journal, 4,* 164–195. doi: 10.1080/15544800903076044

Cummins, J. (2006). Identity texts: The imaginative construction of self through multiliteracies pedagogy. In O. Garcia, T. Skutnabb-Kangas, & M. E. Torres-Guzmán (Eds.), *Imagining multilingual schools: Languages in education and glocalization* (pp. 51–68). Clevedon, UK: Multilingual Matters.

Dagenais, D., Toohey, K., & Day, E. (2006). A multilingual child's literacy practices and contrasting identities in the figured worlds of French immersion classrooms. *International Journal of Bilingual Education and Bilingualism, 9,* 205–218.

de Castell, S., & Jenson, J. (2003). Serious play. *Journal of Curriculum Studies, 35,* 649–665. doi: 10.1080/0022027032000145552

de Castell, S., & Jenson, J. (2009, December). *Digital hermeneutics.* Paper presented at the National Reading Conference, Albuquerque, NM.

Derrida, J. (1978). *Writing and difference* (A. Bass, Trans.). Chicago, IL: University of Chicago Press.

Dooley, K. (2008). Multiliteracies and pedagogy of new learning for students of English as an additional language. In A. Healey (Ed.), *Multiliteracies and expanding landscapes: New pedagogies for student diversity* (pp. 102–125). South Melbourne, Australia: Oxford University Press.

Finnegan, R. H. (1988). *Literacy and orality: Studies in the technology of communication.* Oxford, UK: Blackwell.

Fox, M. (1997). *Whoever you are.* Orlando, FL: First Voyager Books.

Gee, J. P. (2003). *What video games have to teach us about learning and literacy.* New York, NY: Palgrave Macmillan.

Gee, J. P. (2009). Reflections on Reading Cope and Kalantzis' "'Multiliteracies' : New literacies, new learning." *Pedagogies: An International Journal, 4*, 196–204. doi: 10.1080/15544800903076077

Gee, J. P. (2010). *New digital media and learning as an emerging area and "worked examples" as one way forward.* Cambridge, MA: MIT Press.

Gutiérrez, K. D. (2008). Developing a sociocritical literacy in the third space. *Reading Research Quarterly, 43*, 148–164.

Halliday, M. A. K. (1994). *An introduction to functional grammar* (2nd ed.). London, UK: Edward Arnold.

Heath, S. B. (1983). *Ways with words: Language, life and work in communities and classrooms.* Cambridge, UK: Cambridge University Press.

Huizinga, J. (1960). *Homo ludens: A study of the play-element in culture.* Boston, MA: Beacon Press.

Hull, G., & Nelson, M. (2005). Locating the semiotic power of multimodality. *Written Communication, 22*, 224–261. doi: 10.1177/0741088304274170

Jenkins, H. (2004). The cultural logic of media convergence. *International Journal of Cultural Studies, 7*, 33–43. doi: 10.1177/1367877904040603

Jenkins, H. (2006). *Convergence culture: Where old and new media collide.* New York, NY: New York University Press.

Jenson, J., & de Castell, S. (2004). "Turnitin" : Technological challenges to academic ethics. *Communication and Information, 4*, 245–267.

Jewitt, C. (2002). The move from page to screen: The multimodal reshaping of school English. *Visual Communication, 1*, 171–195.

Jewitt, C. (2006). *Technology, literacy and learning: A multimodal approach.* Abingdon, UK: Routledge.

Jewitt, C. (2008). Multimodality and literacy in school classrooms. *Review of Research in Education, 32*, 241–267. doi: 10.3102/0091732 × 07310586

Jewitt, C. (2009a). Introduction. In C. Jewitt (Ed.), *The Routledge handbook of multimodal analysis* (pp. 1–7). Abingdon, UK: Routledge.

Jewitt, C. (2009b). An introduction to multimodality. In C. Jewitt (Ed.), *The Routledge handbook of multimodal analysis* (pp. 14–27). Abingdon, UK: Routledge.

Khvtisiashvili, T. (2010, April). *Animation, a tool for language revitalization.* Paper presented at Preserving the Future: Sustainability of Language, Culture and Nature, University of Iceland, Reyjavik.

Kellner, D. M. (2004). Technological revolution, multiple literacies and the revisioning of education. *E-Learning, 1*, 9–37.

Kenner, C., Al-Azami, S., Gregory, E., & Ruby, M. (2008). Bilingual poetry: Expanding the cognitive and cultural dimensions of children's learning. *Literacy, 4*, 92–100.

Kenner, C., Ruby, M., Jessel, J., Gregory, E., & Arju, T. (2008). Intergenerational learning events around the computer: A site for linguistic and cultural exchange. *Language and Education, 22*, 298–319. doi: 10.1080.09500780802152572

Kern, R. (2000). *Literacy and language teaching.* Oxford, UK: Oxford University Press.

Kress, G. (2003). *Literacy in the new media age.* London, UK: Routledge.

Kress, G. (2009a, November). *The future of language.* Public lecture given at Languages of the Wider World, School of Oriental and African Studies and University College London Centre for Excellence in Teaching and Learning, London, UK.

Kress, G. (2009b). What is a mode? In C. Jewitt (Ed.), *The Routledge handbook of multimodal analysis* (pp. 54–67). Abingdon, UK: Routledge.

Kress, G. (2010). *Multimodality: A social semiotic approach to contemporary communication.* London, UK: Routledge.

Kress, G., & Van Leeuwen, T. (2006). *Reading images: The grammar of visual design* (2nd ed.). London, UK: Routledge.

Lankshear, C., & Knobel, M. (2003). *New literacies: Changing knowledge and classroom learning.* Buckingham, UK: Open University Press.

Lankshear, C., & Knobel, M. (2006). *New literacies: Everyday practices and classroom learning.* Maidenhead, UK: McGraw Hill/Open University Press.

Lankshear, C., & Knobel, M. (Eds.). (2008). *Digital literacies: Concepts, policies and practices.* New York, NY: Peter Lang.

Lemke, J. (2006). Towards critical multimedia literacy: Technology, research and politics. In M. McKenna, L. Labbo, R. Kieffer, & D. Reinking (Eds.), *International handbook of literacy & technology* (Vol. 2, pp. 3–14). Mahwah, NJ: Erlbaum.

Levy, M. (2009). Technologies in use for second language learning. *Modern Language Journal, 93*, 769–782.

Lotherington, H. (2008). Digital epistemologies and classroom multiliteracies. In T. Hansson (Ed.), *Handbook of research on digital information technologies: Innovations, methods, and ethical issues* (pp. 261–280). Hershey, PA: IGI Global.

Lotherington, H. (2009). Glocalization, representation and literacy education. *e-Learning, 6,* 274.

Lotherington, H. (2010, March). *Language and the "physics" of literacy: Reassessing 3D communication in 2D curricula.* Invited presentation given at New Directions in Language Policy: Four conversations, Glendon College, York University, Toronto, Ontario, Canada.

Lotherington, H. (2011). *Pedagogy of multiliteracies: Rewriting Goldilocks.* New York, NY: Routledge.

Lotherington, H., Neville-Verardi, D., & Sinitskaya Ronda, N. (2009). English in cyberspace: Negotiating hypertext literacies. In L. B. Abraham & L. Williams (Eds.), *Electronic discourses in language learning and language teaching* (pp. 11–42). Amsterdam, the Netherlands: John Benjamins.

Lotherington, H., Sotoudeh, S., Holland, M., & Zentena, M. (2008). Project-based community language learning: Three narratives of multilingual storytelling in early childhood education. *Canadian Modern Language Review, 65,* 125–145.

Lyotard, J. (1984). *The postmodern condition: A report on knowledge.* Minneapolis: University of Minnesota Press.

Martin-Jones, M., & Saxena, M. (2003). Bilingual resources and funds of knowledge for teaching and learning in multiethnic classes in Britain. *International Journal of Bilingual Education and Bilingualism, 6,* 267–282.

McLuhan, M. (1964). *Understanding new media: The extensions of man.* New York, NY: New American Library.

McLuhan, M. (2001). *The medium is the massage: An inventory of effects.* Berkley, CA: Gingko Press. (Original work published 1967)

McCarty, T., & Bia, F. (2002). *A place to be Navajo: Rough Rock and the struggle for self-determination in indigenous schooling.* Mahwah, NJ: Erlbaum.

Mills, K. A. (2010). "Filming in progress" : New spaces for multimodal design. *Linguistics and Education, 21,* 14–28.

Naqvi, R. (2008). From peanut butter to Eid . . . Blending perspectives: Teaching Urdu to children in Canada. *Diaspora, Indigenous, and Minority Education, 2,* 154–164. doi: 10.1080.15595690801894269

New London Group.(1996). A pedagogy of multiliteracies: Designing social factors. *Harvard Educational Review, 66,* 60–92.

Peterson, M. (2010). Computerized games and simulations in computer-assisted language learning: A meta-analysis of research. *Simulation & Gaming, 21,* 72–93. doi: 10.1177/1046878109355684

Piaget, J. (1951). *Play, dreams and imitation in childhood* (C. Gattegno & F. M. Hodgson,

Trans.). London, UK: Routledge and Kegan Paul.

Prensky, M. (2001). Digital natives, digital immigrants. *On the Horizon*, *9*, 1–6.

Schecter, S., & Cummins, J. (Eds.). (2003). *Multilingual education in practice: Using diversity as a resource.* Portsmouth, NH: Heinemann.

Sinclair, G. (2010, May). *Exploring Canada's digital future.* Featured "Big Thinking" lecture at the Congress of the Humanities and Social Sciences, Concordia University, Montréal, Québec, Canada.

Singer, D., & Singer, J. L. (2005). *Imagination and play in the electronic age.* Cambridge, MA: Harvard University Press.

Stein, P. (2006). The Olifantsvlei fresh stories project: Multimodality, creativity, and fixing in the semiotic chain. In C. Jewitt, & G. Kress (Eds.), *Multimodal literacy* (pp. 123–138). New York, NY: Peter Lang.

Stein, P. (2008). *Multimodal pedagogies in diverse classrooms: Representation, rights and resources.* London, UK: Routledge.

Street, B. (1984). *Literacy in theory and practice.* Cambridge, UK: Cambridge University Press.

Street, B. (1995). *Social literacies: Critical approaches to literacy in development, ethnography and education.* London, UK: Longman.

Street, B., Pahl, K., & Rowsell, J. (2009). Multimodality and new literacy studies. In C. Jewitt (Ed.), *The Routledge handbook of multimodal analysis* (pp. 191–200). Abingdon, UK: Routledge.

Tan, L., Bopry, J., & Guo, L. (2010). Portraits of new literacies in two Singapore classrooms. *RELC Journal*, *41*, 5–17. doi: 10.1177/0033688210343864

Tan, J. P.-L., & McWilliam, E. (2009). From literacy to multiliteracies: Diverse learners and pedagogical practice. *Pedagogies: An International Journal*, *4*, 213–225. doi: 10.1080/15544800903076119

Thorne, S. L., Black, R. W., & Sykes, J. M. (2009). Second language use, socialization, and learning in Internet interest communities and online gaming. *Modern Language Journal*, *93*, 802–821.

Tunsbridge, N. (1995). The cyberspace cowboy. *Australian Personal Computer*, *12*, 64–70.

Unsworth, L. (2006). Towards a metalanguage for multiliteracies education: Describing the meaning-making resources of language-image interaction. *English Teaching: Practice and Critique*, *5*, 55–76.

Unsworth, L., & Cléirigh, C. (2009). Multimodality and reading: The construction of meaning through image-text interaction. In C. Jewitt (Ed.), *The Routledge handbook of multimodal analysis* (pp. 151–169). Abingdon, UK: Routledge.

Valdés, G. (2004). The teaching of academic language to minority second language learners.

In A. F. Ball & S. W. Freedman (Eds.), *Bakhtinian perspectives on language, literacy and learning* (pp. 66–98). Cambridge, UK: Cambridge University Press.

Venezky, R. L., & Davis, C. (2002). *Quo vademus? The transformation of schooling in a networked world* (OECD/CERI Report, version 8C). Retrieved from OECD Web site: http://www.oecd.org

Ware, P. (2008). Language learners and multimedia: Literacy in and after school. *Pedagogies: An International Journal, 3,* 37–51. doi: 10.1080/15544800701771598

Warschauer, M. (2008). Technology and literacy: Introduction to the special issue. *Pedagogies: An International Journal, 3,* 1–3. doi: 10.1080/15544800701771564

Williams, L. (2009). Navigating and interpreting hypertext in French. In L. B. Abraham & L. Williams (Eds.), *Electronic discourses in language learning and language teaching* (pp. 43–64). Amsterdam, the Netherlands: John Benjamins.

Zheng, D., Wagner, M. M., Young, M. F., & Brewer, R. A. (2009). Negotiation for action: English language learning in game-based virtual worlds. *Modern Language Journal, 93,* 489–511.

SECTION D: INSTRUCTION IN SPECIFIC SKILL AREAS

Best Practices in Teaching Logographic and Non-Roman Writing Systems to L2 Learners

Michael E. Everson

The past few decades have witnessed a growing interest in how second language (L2) learners come to read in languages employing non-alphabetic writing systems such as Chinese and Japanese and languages employing non-Roman alphabetic systems such as Arabic and Hebrew. Indeed, with efforts afoot to begin more programs in these languages at the K-12 and collegiate levels, in immersion and bilingual settings, and with stated goals for students to eventually attain high levels in reading proficiency, an understanding of this research is critical if program development is to go forward in a principled way. This article discusses some of the theoretical developments that have helped illuminate the cross-orthographic reading process and reports on the relevant research in L2 cross-orthographic reading that has shaped our understanding of the issues involved in learning to read in languages that employ non-Roman alphabetic, logographic, and syllabary systems of writing. The article will also discuss teaching implications, strategies, and classroom practice put forth by reading practitioners, many of which have yet to find consensus.

There has been a recent upsurge of interest in languages generally thought of as less commonly taught in traditional world language education. In the United States, for example, languages such as Chinese, Japanese, and Arabic, while still only a small part of the foreign language educational landscape, have begun to experience steady or growing enrollments in schools (Modern Language Association, 2007), and are beginning to be attractive alternatives as curricular offerings at all educational levels. Aside from the enrollment trends, there is interest in expanding instruction in less commonly taught languages such as Chinese in the lower grades, with the eventual goal to have longer articulated learning sequences (Asia Society, 2010).

With selected U.S. states developing roadmaps to meet the demands of diverse populations, there is a new importance placed upon the nurturing of heritage language learners, or those who grow up speaking a second language at home but who often do not develop literacy skills in these languages. Within the American context, heritage learners are now considered an important priority in maintaining national language capacity (Brecht & Rivers, 2000; Brecht & Walton, 1993) with specific instructional needs that must be addressed (He, 2008; Koda, Zhang, & Yang, 2008; Kondo-Brown, 2010; Montrul, 2010). To meet these challenges, states are also beginning programs (Asia Society, 2010; Falsgraf & Spring, 2007) in the early grades that employ immersion and bilingual models of language education whereby content is learned in the target language, thus providing alternatives to more traditional foreign language education models.

As well, the Flagship language initiative makes a variety of less commonly taught languages such as Chinese, Hindi, Urdu, Korean, Persian, and Russian available with the goal of taking students to superior levels of proficiency, levels that have not been attainable through traditional sequences of language exposure offered in university settings. As less commonly taught languages begin their ascent, initiatives designed to prepare teachers have begun with programs such as STARTALK, a U.S. government initiative which over the past three years has begun summer programs nationwide to train teachers in Chinese, Arabic, Hindi, Swahili, Turkish, Persian, and Urdu.

The majority of these languages are also of interest for educators and researchers because they share something in common that is different from the more traditional foreign language offerings of Spanish, French, and German— they do not employ the Roman alphabet, but instead use a totally different alphabetic system as in the case of Arabic and Hebrew, a non-alphabetic logographic system in Chinese, or a mix of native syllabary systems with borrowed Chinese characters, in the case of Japanese. If these languages are ever to take their place as more commonly taught languages in world languages education, it will be essential that we come to understand how these languages are mastered by students of different ages, who come from different literacy backgrounds, and who learn them in a variety of different learning settings.

To this end, this article will highlight some of the theoretical issues that underpin the reading of selected languages employing non-Roman orthographies. While there are many languages that employ such writing systems, this article will highlight the languages of Chinese, Japanese, Arabic, and Hebrew. The selection of these languages is not entirely arbitrary—Chinese employs a writing system that is non-alphabetic in nature, a system that has been responsible for transmitting through its written artifacts a culture that goes back millennia. Japanese, while also employing Chinese characters, employs syllabary systems that make it one of the most unique multi-script writing systems in the world. Arabic and Hebrew, on the other hand, employ non-Roman alphabets that share the characteristic of vowels being sometimes, but not always, marked in text, thus presenting unique challenges in the learning of these languages. Arabic is also unique in that its diglossic nature employs a written language that is different from the dialects commonly spoken across the Arab world. These languages were chosen also because of burgeoning research traditions that have developed to investigate reading in these writing systems as second languages (L2), among learners of different ages who are learning these languages in different types of settings. This article, then, includes short summaries of research to illustrate some of the methodologies used to investigate various topics. The article will then discuss the search for best practices for teaching learners to read in these languages, practices that have yet to find consensus among their practitioners.

THE ORTHOGRAPHIC VARIABLE

Researchers have been able to document that certain languages take American learners longer to learn. For example, Jackson and Malone (2010) report that State Department employees are enrolled in highly intensive daily instruction for almost 6 months (600 class hours) in a Western European language (e.g., French, Dutch, or Spanish), about 10 months (1100 class hours) for a so-called hard language (e.g., Russian, Hindi, or Thai), and 2 years for the most challenging languages (Arabic, Chinese, Japanese, and Korean) in order to attain professional competence. These expectations would be much lower in secondary and post-secondary language programs where the intensity of instruction as well as the number of contact hours would be much less. While languages such as Chinese, Japanese, and Arabic differ linguistically and culturally in a number of ways from languages such as French and Spanish, the writing systems employed in many of the languages stated above are either non-alphabetic in nature, or employ non-Roman alphabets that present special challenges for learners whose first language (L1) employs the Roman alphabet.

The Chinese writing system, for example, is often termed a logography because its primary unit, the character, has been thought in its structure to represent meaning instead of sound, although characters do often contain phonetic cues, with phonology thought to play an important role in Chinese character recognition and reading (Perfetti & Dunlap, 2008; Perfetti & Liu, 2005; Perfetti, Liu, & Tan, 2002, 2005). In fact, approximately 85% of all Chinese characters are termed *compound* characters (Zhu, 1988), whereby they contain a component that contains a radical conveying semantic information, and a phonetic element that hints at how the entire character is pronounced. For instance, the left hand part of each of the following characters is a semantic radical termed "three dot water" in Chinese, and classifies each of these characters as having something to do with water: 海 [hǎi] meaning *sea*, 洋 [yáng] meaning *ocean*, and 池 [chí] meaning *pond*. With regard to phonetic elements, the character 工 in Chinese by itself is pronounced [gōng], and is found in the following characters as the phonetic element, giving a hint as to the pronunciation of the entire character: 空 [kōng] *empty*, 贡 [gòng] *contribute*, and 红 [hóng] *red*. Unfortunately, this phonetic element is not very reliable in giving a systematically precise pronunciation of the overall character.

In the Chinese writing system, the character constitutes the smallest pronounceable unit in the written language (Cheung, McBride-Chang, & Chow, 2006) with each character pronounced as a syllable with generally only one pronunciation per character. Chinese is also written using the Roman alphabet, termed *romanization*. Although there have been many romanization systems in use to either transcribe or teach Chinese to foreign language learners, the pinyin system is currently the most often used for foreign language teaching purposes in America. Consequently, the topic of how students who come from an alphabetic system in English to learn Chinese characters has received a great deal of research attention, as researchers are interested in knowing whether or not phonological processing strategies brought from their first reading experience transfer when learning a writing system whereby phonology is less systematically portrayed in the actual written unit.

Japanese, on the other hand, employs multiple scripts, thus offering a series of different challenges to American foreign language learners. Two of the scripts are syllabary systems whereby sound maps onto the printed symbol at the syllable level. These two syllabaries consist of 46 basic symbols and also have somewhat specialized functions, with one (*hiragana*) being used primarily for function words such as case-marking particles, and the other (*katakana*) being used for words borrowed from other languages. To complicate matters, Japanese also uses Chinese characters termed *kanji*. These characters operate differently in Japanese than in Chinese, however, in that a character can be pronounced with more than one syllable, and with different pronunciations depending upon the contextual use of the specific *kanji*. Japanese can also be written using the Roman alphabet, called *romaji*, which is used for road signs, as well as introducing foreign language learners to Japanese vocabulary before the native writing systems are introduced. To give an example, the sentence: ジョンスミスは私のアメリカ文学の教授である means "John Smith is my American literature professor.": ジョソスミス and アメリカ are foreign words meaning "John Smith" and "America," so are written in *katakana*. 私, 文学 and 教授 are written in *kanji*, and mean "I," "literature" and "professor." The other symbols are *hiragana*, serving the grammatical functions of subject marker, possessive marker, and verb. Consequently, similar research questions have been asked about how foreign language learners approach the learning of Chinese characters, as well as the syllabary scripts that are more finite.

Non-Roman alphabets such as Hebrew and Arabic also present their own sets of challenges. Hebrew, for example, is written right to left, with 22 letters, most of which denote consonants and an ancillary system of 13 vowel diacritic marks (Ravid, 2006). Texts designed for proficient readers of Hebrew omit vowels, but texts designed to teach reading to children and L2 learners include the vowels, as they provide a transparent pronunciation of syllables involving very few exceptions in terms associated with specific letter strings, position in a word, and vowel combinations (Geva & Wade-Woolley, 1998), facilitating accurate word decoding even by novice learners (Geva & Siegel, 2000).

Challenges in learning to read Modern Standard Arabic (MSA) stem from the fact that MSA is the literary language of the Arab-speaking world, with newspapers, most books, and magazines written in MSA. Children will learn MSA in school, but in their homes grow up speaking one of the many spoken dialects of Arabic which are generally not written. MSA, therefore, can serve as a means of oral communication between educated Arabic speakers whose regional or national dialects are mutually unintelligible. It is also used for certain television shows such as news broadcasts, and the formal language of education such as school lectures. The downside of learning MSA for Arab children is that they generally have no oral/aural experience with MSA when they begin learning it in school, making it more akin to learning a second language (Fender, 2008). To complicate matters, the Arabic writing system as used in texts for proficient readers, does not represent short vowels, meaning that the reader will be aided by the surrounding context to determine the proper pronunciation. Children learning to read MSA, however, are helped with this process, as diacritics are used in the text to mark the presence of short vowels, thus giving learners the means to phonologically decode words. As children develop more proficiency in MSA, these diacritics are dropped so that their materials resemble those more commonly used by experienced MSA readers. Foreign language learners of Arabic whose first language writing system is alphabetic, then, may be aided in learning vowelled Arabic given their L1 experience in deriving phonology from print. Vowelled Arabic will also be something foreign language learners and Arab children have in common, as they both are learning to read in a language they are also just learning to speak. Consequently, similar to Hebrew learners, the support they receive from diacritical vowel markings, and the support Chinese learners receive from romanization such as pinyin, will be a necessary component of best practice.

Because the theoretical frameworks that support foreign language reading are usually based on L2 learners who have already learned to read in their first language (L1), theoretical underpinnings have arisen largely from data derived from post-secondary learners of Chinese and Japanese, and often deal with various aspects of how students learn to read and the strategies they employ to cope with Chinese and Japanese scripts. That is, even though there are studies that involve learning to read Chinese and Japanese beyond the character and/or word level (Chang, 2010; Everson & Ke, 1997; Lee-Thompson, 2008; Warnick, 2001), many of the findings center on the character or word. In her review of word recognition, Koda (1996, 2008) discusses frameworks stemming from connectionist theories that stress the importance of the effects of L2 processing experience, thus focusing on the effect of different proficiency levels as a variable of interest. Processing experience takes into account not only linguistic knowledge but also processing efficiency, factors that may develop separately. The other important framework takes into consideration L1 and L2 orthographic distance effects, or the theory that the extent to which the L2 shares orthographic properties with the learner's L1 may aid the development of word recognition efficiency in the L2.

These theoretical foundations are important for a number of reasons when examining post-secondary school learners of these languages. First, they have focused much of the research on script-specific topics, such as whether or not learners who come from L1 alphabetic backgrounds access the phonological aspects of print in orthographies such as Chinese that have been heretofore conceptualized as being more meaning-based scripts that do not lend themselves to phonological access by their readers. Second, they have encouraged a line of research investigating the strategies that learners employ to memorize, access, and infer the meaning of Chinese characters, as well as investigating the value placed on characters by both teachers and learners. Third, these foundations have taken into account the development of reading proficiency in studies involving mostly beginning but some advanced learners as research subjects. Lastly, it should be noted that this research has spotlighted the importance of word recognition and lower-level processing in an era of foreign language research that has been dominated by more schema-theoretic perspectives that emphasize the role of factors such as background knowledge in comprehension processing. One of the major contributions of this research, then, is that it has been able to document the difficulties L1 readers of English experience at the more micro-level of the reading process when learning to read in writing systems that are not alphabetically-based.

RESEARCH ON CHINESE

Given this backdrop of how the writing systems used in Chinese and Japanese differ so dramatically from the Roman alphabet learned in school by native English speakers, it should come as no surprise that much of the research has investigated how students of these languages learn Chinese characters. This is testimony to the complexity of the task facing foreign language learners of Chinese when they begin to learn characters, as their rudimentary knowledge of the spoken language combined with a yet undeveloped sense for how the orthography, morphology, and phonology operate, all contribute to making the task of learning Chinese characters a burgeoning area of research.

McGinnis (1999), for example, surveyed first year college-level students of Chinese about the strategies they employed to learn characters, and found that initially learners preferred repeated practice and character-specific mnemonic aids in the form of personal stories to memorize a character's sound, meaning, or shape. At this stage, students did not deconstruct characters into their radical or phonetic elements, but focused on memorizing characters as holistic units. In a similar study, however, Ke (1998) found that as beginning students progressed, those who perceived the learning and use of character components as more important strategies performed better in tasks of character recognition and production. These learners also felt that practicing characters in context so that they were combined to form multi-character words was more effective than learning the characters individually. It seems, then, that students early on in the character learning process develop an understanding of how Chinese characters are composed and the need to look for recurring elements such as radicals and phonetics, but due to the sheer number of recurring components in Chinese characters, have not yet learned enough characters to generate rules that will help them decompose characters systematically. As their orthographic awareness increases, however, learners become more reliant on their knowledge of character component structures, a finding corroborated by Shen (2005) who determined through survey research that the use of strategies whereby students used character components as aids to figure out character pronunciation and meaning was among the most heavily replied upon by beginning learners.

A number of other studies corroborated this research and lent more evidence to the importance of radical knowledge as an aid in a variety of character identification tasks. Taft and Chung (1999), for example, found that novice learners of Chinese used their knowledge of Chinese radicals as an aid to recall the meanings of characters that were newly learned, especially when the target characters were initially presented to the learners with more explanation about the meanings and use of radicals. As well, Jackson, Everson, and Ke (2003) found that students completing their first year of Chinese were able to guess the meaning of unfamiliar characters in a multiple-choice format based on the meaning of the character's semantic radical. In other words, early on in their experience, beginning learners of Chinese who knew the meaning of a Chinese radical by itself could apply the radical to guessing the meaning of characters they had not yet formally learned, though this ability was somewhat variable.

Wang, Liu, and Perfetti (2004) also found that beginning learners learned the structure of Chinese orthography early in their learning experience, perhaps due to their scrutiny of the characters to compensate for their inability to readily access the pronunciation of the characters, and that explicit instruction hastened the learning process. These findings were extended by Shen and Ke (2007), who investigated learners' awareness of radicals and this effect on word acquisition among students of three levels of Chinese proficiency. They discovered a moderate correlation across all levels between their overall Chinese character vocabulary and their ability to apply knowledge of radicals. As with the previously cited research, they also found that radical knowledge developed early among beginning learners, yet also found that it advanced rapidly during their first year of study, and that an overwhelming amount of their participants (93%) found the knowledge of radicals to be helpful in learning characters.

The finding that knowledge of radicals was helpful in learning characters was also found in Shen (2010) who investigated the learning of individual radicals by beginning learners of Chinese. Her findings indicated that learners considered the sounds and shapes of individual radicals to be more difficult to learn than their meanings, and that aural-oral practice and repetition was a learning technique most favored by the students.

In addition to this research that investigated the students' ability to infer the meanings of Chinese characters, studies employing think aloud protocols have discovered the need for students to attempt to recover the pronunciation of the characters when they are reading (Everson & Ke, 1997; Lee-Thompson, 2008) or learning characters (Winke & Abbhul, 2007). In his book decrying specific myths about Chinese, DeFrancis (1984) referred to one as "the ideographic myth," (p. 133) or the notion that Chinese as a writing system was able to bypass the intermediary of speech, a theory that DeFrancis (1989) disputed. He even called for Chinese to be termed a logographic phonetic, instead of a logography to underscore the importance of the phonological aspects of Chinese characters. DeFrancis stated that there is no writing system that is read without phonology, a view shared by

Perfetti, Zhang, and Berent (1992) who have put forth the universal phonological principle in reading which states that there is no writing system that is read without phonology and that Chinese is no exception.

The think-aloud protocol evidence of laborious vocal decoding when Chinese learners read different authentic texts in Chinese led Everson (1998) to conduct a study that confirmed the importance for CFL learners of achieving a sound-symbol match when pronouncing and identifying the meaning of two character words. In this study, learners who had completed one year of Chinese were given a naming task whereby they would pronounce in Chinese a series of two-character words displayed to them on a computer monitor that were part of their first-year curriculum that they had already studied. Later, they were required to give the meaning for these and other words so that the relationship between the two tasks could be correlated. The results indicated that when learners could identify the meaning of a Chinese two-character word, there was about a 90% likelihood that they also could pronounce it, suggesting that the retrieval of meaning for these learners is not exclusively a visual process, and that learners use their spoken language resources to anchor the meaning of the characters. Lee-Thompson (2008) found a common strategy among her intermediate learners when reading Chinese text was to write pinyin by the characters they were reading as an aid to recovering and remembering their pronunciation.

It should be noted that when involved in reading at the text level, intermediate level students (Everson & Ke, 1997: Lee-Thompson, 2008) experienced difficulty isolating meaningful word units in the text, with students explaining in their think-aloud protocols or as witnessed by their marking of the text that the lack of spacing between characters and words in running text presents major challenges to students even at the intermediate level. That is, the lack of visible boundaries between words was a significant hurdle for students in processing the overall text. Follow-up research by Shen (2008) in which learners were asked to judge whether or not certain characters in a text went together as words indicated that these learners used a variety of strategies for determining which characters went together, while providing evidence that for even advanced learners, this is a difficult task. Bassetti (2005) puts forth the explanation that what constitutes a word in Chinese for Chinese language learners is not straightforward, possibly due to their L1 perceptions of what words are in English, and the effect of the complex system of word morphology that the Chinese language and orthographic system impose upon them as L2 learners. In a task where both third- and forth-year learners of Chinese as well as L1 readers of Chinese were asked to circle the characters that formed words in a text, her results indicated that the L2 learners and L1 readers of Chinese differed in their perceptions of what constitutes a word in Chinese, with many L2 learners expressing difficulty in the task due to the qualitative differences between English and Chinese word formation.

While more research is needed that investigates reading beyond the word and sentence level, data from advanced learners engaged in think-aloud protocols indicated that they possess a greater depth of understanding of Chinese orthography, morphology, and language use in general, with evidence that they could more easily isolate problems in word identification and text comprehension, thus making less random decisions than the less advanced learners about how to remedy problematic situations (Everson & Ke, 1997). Again, advanced learners used a strategy of attempting to pronounce characters they did not recognize, while also employing surrounding context, text structure, background knowledge of the topic and the visual make-up of the unknown characters, thus testifying to an impressive repertoire for working through problems in both textual understanding and word recognition.

RESEARCH ON JAPANESE

Given that Japanese employs two syllabary scripts in the form of *katakana* and *hiragana* as well as Chinese characters, it is no wonder that much of the research in Japanese as a foreign language investigates how learners deal with a multi-script orthography. Early research involving beginning learners indicated that symbol identification speed distinguished good from poor readers (Koda, 1990), and that lower level processing skills contributed significantly to successful text comprehension (Koda, 1992), findings that set the stage for more research in this area. Such findings were important to start investigation into so-called lower level processing as much of the research to date at that time emphasized the importance of top down processing and not attention to the character or word level.

As with Chinese, an early strand of research investigated the extent to which learners use the phonological information available to them when recognizing words (Matsunaga, 1995, 1996, 2001), harkening back to the theory that readers whose L1 reading experience was with alphabetic languages, would be disadvantaged in reading languages whose orthographies are non-alphabetic, and therefore do not portray phonological information in a systematic, accessible manner.

Chikamatsu (1996), for example, investigated the word recognition strategies of Chinese and American learners of Japanese. Her purpose was to determine whether or not these learners employed strategies more akin to those used in their L1 (i.e., phonological processing for the American learners and visual processing for native speakers of Chinese). In this study, the subjects were shown a series of words from their vocabulary experience written in varying forms of *kana*, the Japanese syllabary scripts, and asked whether or not these were legal words. Her results indicated that the Chinese students employed more visual strategies and the American students, more phonologically-based strategies. Chikamatsu (2006) replicated this experiment with American L2 learners of varying proficiency levels, and found that the higher proficiency L2 learners of Japanese employed more visual information than the beginning level learners who, again, tended to use phonological information to a higher degree. This was interpreted to mean that beginning learners of Japanese whose L1 was English transferred their L1 processing strategies to the L2, but that this interference dissipated as proficiency in the L2 increased.

The predominance of L1 phonological strategies was also documented by Mori (1998) in a test designed to determine whether American learners would differ from Chinese and Korean learners in a short-term memory task when presented with pseudo-*kanji* characters that differed in the degree to which phonological elements were presented as pronunciation aids in the characters. Her results indicated that the American learners were hampered when the pseudo-characters prevented the learners from using a phonological analysis to remember the characters, whereas Korean and Chinese learners employed Chinese characters exclusively or partially in the Chinese and Korean writing systems.

As with the research in both L1 and L2 Chinese, researchers of L2 Japanese are also interested in how well learners can figure out unknown *kanji* encountered in isolation or in running text (Kondo-Brown, 2006b; Mori, 2002; 2003; Mori & Nagy, 1999; Toyoda, 2000). Mori and Nagy (1999), for example, set up varying contextual conditions whereby students could guess the meanings of unknown (two) *kanji* word combinations. In their study, the learners employed an integrated strategy of inferring meaning from the composition of the *kanji* themselves, as well as the surrounding context. But when only one of these sources was available to the subjects, their ability to guess the meanings of the *kanji* decreased significantly. It also seemed that the learners' strategy of using the clues within the *kanji* and their ability to use context was not correlated, indicating that the ability to extract information derived from morphological analysis of the *kanji*, and the ability to extract information derived from context may entail different processing skills.

Further investigation (Mori, 2002) indicated that these two sources of information were additive, thus giving inferencing advantage to students who could integrate both sources of information. In a further study (Mori, 2003), these results were borne out when students' guesses with actual *kanji* meanings were compared. Mori (1999) indicated that the strategies readers chose for this task seemed to be related to their beliefs about learning in general, and their beliefs about language learning in particular. Kondo-Brown (2006b) also investigated the inferencing of unknown *kanji* among two groups of Japanese learners, finding that inferencing ability improved with proficiency, although even among the higher proficiency group, inferencing ability was variable.

Inferencing ability also improved when learners could retrieve partial or full phonological renderings of one of the characters. In a study conducted by Toyoda (2000), the researcher had beginning learners of Japanese guess either the pronunciation or meaning of two-*kanji* word combinations they had not yet learned after undergoing several training sessions designed to heighten their awareness as to the purpose of Chinese character components. Her analysis indicated that even at this beginning stage, learners showed evidence of using their knowledge of the meaning and pronunciation components of *kanji* to make successful guesses, though they were more successful at inferring meaning than pronunciation.

Another interesting line of research has sought to determine attitudes both teachers and learners of Japanese have towards *kanji* learning, and how these attitudes may be related to learning strategies. Shimizu and Green (2002) investigated the beliefs of Japanese teachers' views of learning and teaching *kanji*, employing a principle component analysis that revealed six similar dimensions accounting for the variance. Teachers' beliefs centered around factors dealing with beliefs that *kanji* were (a) useful in the Japanese reading process; (b) difficult; (c) embedded with cultural meaning; (d) potentially motivating to the students' learning experience; (e) required a specific aptitude for learning; and (e) were not about to be replaced by a phonological script. Their analysis indicated that belief systems surrounding the importance of teaching *kanji* are complex and possibly influence their choice of *kanji* teaching strategies. The overall analysis indicated that the preferred strategies for teaching *kanji* were rote learning (strategies emphasizing drill and practice and repeated writing of *kanji*), memory strategy learning (linking the learning of new *kanji* with *kanji* already taught), and context strategy learning (emphasizing that the meaning of *kanji* in authentic reading situations is largely context-dependent). Particularly interesting findings were indications that teachers who emphasized the utility and cultural meaning of *kanji*, and who enjoy teaching *kanji* to students who enjoy learning them, seem less likely to emphasize rote learning strategies to their students.

Mori and Shimizu (2007) employed a similar measurement instrument used in the previous study to investigate students' attitudes and beliefs towards learning *kanji* as well as their self-reported *kanji* learning strategies, and again found that these belief systems were complex and multi-dimensional. In summary, their analysis yielded six attitudinal factors (*kanji* is fun; *kanji* is difficult; *kanji* has cultural value; *kanji* has a future; *kanji* is useful; *kanji* learning requires special abilities) and six strategy belief factors (morphological analysis, rote memorization, context-based strategies, association strategies, metacognitive strategies, and helplessness). The complexity of the students' belief systems is reflected in the different dimensions captured in the study, from attitudinal factors as to how difficult and enjoyable *kanji* are to learn to the students' beliefs as to how useful their learning strategies seem to be, all the way working towards an appreciation of *kanji* as a purveyor of culture over time. Although correlational in nature, there were indications that certain relationships existed between belief systems and strategy use. For example, students who exhibited an appreciation of the cultural value of *kanji* seemed to have a more comprehensive view of effective learning strategies and were less likely to feel lost in the *kanji* learning process. There also was a relationship between enjoyment of learning *kanji* and belief in the efficacy of morphological analysis and the use of creativity in coming up with imaginative memorization strategies. On the other hand, perceptions of *kanji* difficulty were associated with strategies of rote memorization and a sense of feeling lost in the *kanji* learning process. Overall, however, students considered rote memory of *kanji* to be the most effective strategy for learning, and metacognitive strategies the least effective, indicating that students may in the end feel that *kanji* learning is a question of brute-force memorization, repeated writing and practice, and that ultimately, the overall structure of the character and/or its surrounding context, are not all that important in deriving *kanji* meaning. The researchers speculated that this might be due to teachers falling back on the way they learned to write Japanese, which potentially exerts a powerful influence on the way their students approach *kanji* learning. Attitudes and strategies were also the focus of a study (Mori, Sato, & Shimizu, 2007) investigating learners' ability to use context and morphological information to learn novel *kanji* words. Their results indicated a significant relationship between belief in the effectiveness of their learning strategies and their success in employing morphological analysis, thus highlighting the power of task-specific beliefs and metacognitive awareness in the word recognition process.

RESEARCH ON HEBREW AND ARABIC

Much of the research involving learning to read in Hebrew and Arabic focuses on children learning these languages in bilingual settings, both in FL and L2 settings, and some studies involving L1 Arabic learners of Hebrew. The research has also been framed in terms of the script dependent hypothesis (Geva & Siegel, 2000) and orthographic depth hypothesis (Katz & Frost, 1992) which state that orthographies differ in how regularly they portray sound-to-symbol relationships, thus facilitating reading development in languages that employ more shallow orthographies. The reading of Hebrew and Arabic, therefore, presents unique opportunities for research in that Hebrew and Arabic orthographies are considered shallow when vowels in words are marked in text for beginning L1 and L2 learners, and deep when presented without vowels in texts designed for proficient readers.

From the viewpoint of L1 Arabic reading development, Abu-Rabia (2002) has highlighted the vowelling of text and the presentation of words in context as critical components of L1 Arabic reading development. Studies investigating the role of vowelling and context among good and poor L1 readers of Arabic (Abu-Rabia, 1997), and reading employing different text types (Abu-Rabia, 1998b) were influenced by whether or not the texts were vowelled. Abu-Rabia (2001) also found among L1 Arabic readers of L2 Hebrew performing reading tasks in both languages, that vowelling affected isolated and contextual word recognition as well as silent reading comprehension in both languages.

An alternative view termed the central-processing hypothesis states that skilled reading is not influenced by the orthographic system involved, but instead depends on linguistic and cognitive skills such as working memory, naming speed, and lexical processing, without which reading development will be difficult regardless of the orthographic system (Baluch, 2006). Much of the research testing these theories, then, is characterized by testing bilingual or trilingual (Abu-Rabia & Siegel, 2003; Schwartz, Geva, Share, & Leikin, 2007) learners of various ages in varying learning contexts (Abu-Rabia, 1998a, 1999) over a variety of reading performance and intelligence measures.

Researchers have found evidence that supports both of these frameworks, leading some to state that these hypotheses are not either/or, but in fact complementary. Abu-Rabia and Siegel (2002), for instance, tested the reading, memory, and language skills of heritage language children aged 9–14 whose home language was Arabic and whose language of school instruction was English but who also learned to write Arabic in a heritage language school program. The researchers found significant correlations between reading skills, syntactic awareness tests, and working memory tests, indicating that these qualities were not language specific. Geva and Siegel (2000) tested children in grades 1–5 learning to read concurrently in their L1 English and L2 Hebrew. General intelligence tests, L1 and L2 memory tasks, and word recognition and pseudoword recognition tasks were administered in both languages. Profiles in word and pseudo-word decoding indicating steeper development in English than in Hebrew along with orthographic-specific decoding errors supported the script dependent hypothesis. The researchers, however, argued for a complementary relationship between these two hypotheses, as individual differences in memory explained a small portion of the variance between L1 and L2 reading measures.

Geva, Wade-Woolley, and Shany's (1997) longitudinal study of children learning to read simultaneously in L1 English and L2 Hebrew during grades 1 and 2 found that the speed and accuracy of letter naming, word reading, and reading of these words in text across languages was highly correlated, though in the early stage of language acquisition, text reading was not more efficient than reading of isolated words. The researchers believe that orthographic depth and morphosyntactic complexity may interact with L2 proficiency effects in determining L2 reading development, and that the steps associated with L1 reading efficiency (accuracy before speed) may apply to L2 word recognition development although these steps may not emerge concurrently.

Other studies (Leikin, Share, & Schwartz, 2005; Schwartz, Laikin, & Share, 2005; Schwartz, Share, Leikin, & Kozminsky, 2008) were conducted comparing performance on a number of reading measures among immigrant first grade Russian speaking children learning Hebrew bilingually, and immigrant first grade Russian speaking children who were also literate in Russian. The studies also included a sample of monolingual/monoliterate Hebrew-speaking children. One study (Leikin, Swartz, & Share, 2010) found that (a) the bi-literate bilinguals outperformed mono-literate bilingual and monolingual peers on measures of phonemic awareness, word identification and pseudoword decoding accuracy; (b) Russian speaking children not literate in this language were indistinguishable from monolingual counterparts on Hebrew phonemic awareness, decoding, and spelling skills; and (c) mono-literate bilinguals were inferior to their bi-literate peers on Russian phonemic awareness measures. The researchers concluded that Russian literacy impacted both Russian (L1) and Hebrew (L2) literacy skills and highlights the relationship between literacy acquisition and explicit phonemic awareness, with transfer involving the interplay between Russian syllabic complexity, the nature of the Russian script, and the training that typically accompanies the onset of literacy acquisition in this language. Phonological processing skills were also found to be correlated with word recognition skills in English and Arabic among Canadian-Arabic bilinguals (Abu-Rabia & Siegel, 2002).

TOWARDS BEST PRACTICE

In his review of research-based implications for L2 reading, Grabe (2004, 2009) cites several areas that need to be considered in L2 reading instruction: (a) ensure fluency in word recognition, (b) emphasize the learning of vocabulary, (c) activate background knowledge, (d) ensure acquisition of linguistic knowledge and general comprehension, (e) teach recognition of text structures and discourse organization, (f) promote development of strategic readers rather than mechanical application of strategy checklists, (g) build reading fluency and rate, (h) promote extensive reading, (i) develop intrinsic motivation for reading, and (j) contribute to a coherent curriculum for student learning. Grabe states that there is empirical support for each of these implications, although at the same time he emphasizes the need for additional research to further identify aspects of effective L2 reading instruction in particular settings. It is hoped that this article has provided some of this additional research so as to highlight that while these areas apply to reading in the languages covered in this review, orthographic issues particular to these languages require unique awareness and attention on the part of their educational practitioners.

INTRODUCING CHARACTERS

For example, one enduring controversy among Chinese and Japanese pedagogues is when the native scripts should be introduced to learners. Because learners are unable to determine the pronunciation of Chinese characters, they begin their study of Chinese by learning vocabulary through romanization, or systems that present the language using the roman alphabet, with diacritics to represent the tone of the word. Although there are a number of systems in use, pinyin has become the romanization system of choice for most textbooks used in the United States. As an example, the word "friend," is a two-character word written 朋友 in Chinese, and is presented as *péngyou* for beginning learners in pinyin, with the diacritic over the first syllable indicating the rising tone. One school of thought contends that it is best to introduce vocabulary words, written dialogues, and spoken drills in pinyin until learners acquire a significant amount of spoken language through this medium, thereby giving the student a firm base of spoken proficiency upon which to associate the written characters, much the way a child learns to read after learning to hear and speak the spoken language. As a learner's proficiency advances, new vocabulary will be introduced in both characters and pinyin, but reading texts will be exclusively written in Chinese characters. An opposing view is that students should be introduced to characters immediately, as characters are a motivating factor for learners of Chinese, and represent the Chinese language in the most authentic way. The concern, of course, is that overwhelming the student with characters is demotivating and so labor intensive that Chinese character learning becomes the primary purpose of the course, resulting in dispirited and demoralized students not learning to speak the language who end up dropping the course (For more discussion on the use of romanization in learning Chinese and Japanese, see Christensen & Warnick, 2006; Nara, 2003; Unger, 2001; Xing, 2006).

More recent theory pointing to the need to develop a metalinguistic understanding of the linguistic structure of the language that the new script will map onto, as well as learning the properties of the script itself, seems to call for a firm foundation of spoken language to be taught to the learner. This has led some to temper the enthusiasm for exclusive use of authentic texts to beginning learners, recommending that pedagogical reading materials designed around what students can say in the spoken language also have their place (Everson, 2009). Encouraging in this regard is the study by Hitosugi and Day (2004) that demonstrated that through the use of Japanese children's books, even beginning learners of Japanese can make progress in reading in as little as ten weeks through a structured reading program employing texts that were well within the proficiency range of the learners, while also improving learners' attitudes towards the learning of Japanese.

In Japanese, there has also been controversy about when to introduce the *kana* scripts as well as the *kanji*, the Chinese characters. Japanese learners are aided by the fact that any words in Japanese can be written in *hiragana* or *katakana*, two systems that have a relatively small number of symbols and can be learned by students in a relatively short time. Therefore, vocabulary can be introduced to students in the native scripts of *hiragana* and *katakana* almost immediately, and *kanji* can be introduced at the teacher's discretion. A study in Chinese (Packard, 1990) compared two groups of Chinese language learners in the same program, one which learned Chinese characters immediately, and one which started learning characters after a lag of three weeks. The lag group did better on tests of phonetic discrimination after one semester, and measures of oral production after one year. A similar study in Japanese (Hatasa, 2002) compared one group that learned the *kana* scripts immediately, to a group learning Japanese first in *romaji* and introducing *kana* scripts eight weeks later. In this study, there was no significant difference in terms of achievement between the groups. In a similar study, Dewey (2004) found that how students value the introduction of the writing systems is related to how the teacher views this issue, thus indicating a loyalty to the teacher influencing the learning views of novice learners. In-service and pre-service training of teachers, therefore, will need to highlight these findings so that teachers can learn to develop a sense of balanced instruction between learning to speak and learning to read in these languages.

TEACHING THE COMPONENTS OF CHINESE CHARACTERS

In line with this recommendation is the amount of research already cited in this review that suggests that learning the structural properties of Chinese characters facilitates a learner's word recognition development and ultimate reading achievement. This impacts a number of the categories presented by Grabe (2004, 2009) such as fluency in word recognition, and enabling the learner to acquire vocabulary. More specifically, the research among foreign language learners of Chinese indicates that they develop an appreciation of the component parts of Chinese characters as aids to character and word recognition early on in their learning experience (Ke, 1998; Taft & Chung, 1999; Wang, Liu, & Perfetti, 2004) with students reporting their heavy reliance upon this strategy (Shen, 2005; Shen & Ke, 2007). This ability to use the phonetic and semantic elements of the Chinese character seems to advance rapidly among beginning learners, and is used as an aid for both recall and inferencing unknown characters (Jackson, Everson, & Ke, 2003; Shen, 2005). Perhaps because of their limited control of the spoken language, and consequent inability to access phonological properties of the characters (Wang, Liu, & Perfetti, 2004), the ability to exploit the semantic elements of characters develops before an ability to attend to the phonetic components of characters, although learners demonstrate a need to recover the pronunciations of character when they read (Everson & Ke, 1997; Lee-Thompson, 2008), identify (Everson, 1998), and learn characters (Winke & Abbhul, 2007).

For best practice, then, we must ask about the best way to present Chinese character instruction in both our classes and in our learning materials so that students can develop strategies that facilitate both the initial learning and use of Chinese characters in the reading process. As well, given the variable nature of students ability to actually use these components successfully, it appears this is no longer nice-to-know information to be taught from a cultural or historical perspective, but information that must be woven systematically into the fabric of

Chinese reading classroom pedagogy.

A number of research studies suggest that how these principles are taught can make a difference in how students learn characters, with some researchers (Shen, 2004) recommending that class time be used to introduce characters by highlighting their etymological background and the various components making up the characters. This leads to the learner appreciating and exploring characters in a concept-driven way, an approach that may be more powerful for retention than rote memory-type strategies, strategies still used by students and advocated by some teachers. It should also be noted that technological advances that provide the capability to animate characters, rapidly deconstruct the characters into their component parts through animation and the use of color, and supply the pronunciation through audio files, can highlight etymological and character components more as primary information and less as historical or background information, as has been done with the teaching of characters through traditional textbooks (Fan, 2010). Textbooks, then, should include more of this information so that students can begin to view characters as forms not composed of random strokes, but instead as a principled orthographic system.

It should be noted, however, that much of our research involves beginning learners of Chinese, a more plentiful subject pool of students just beginning to learn characters. While initial results indicate the need to continue teaching strategies that build upon our learners' proficiency as they move into more advanced levels (Chang, 2010; Warnick, 2001), more research needs to be conducted to understand the reading strategies and perception of character components by advanced learners. Indeed, Koda (2001) has argued that perhaps a better way to view this complex issue is not to concern ourselves with when to introduce characters, but instead to determine how to enhance the learning of Chinese characters for learners at different levels of proficiency.

JAPANESE *KANJI* LEARNING: CHARACTER COMPONENTS, STRATEGIES, AND BELIEFS

Investigating the role of the component parts of Japanese *kanji* is as central to the Japanese L2 research and pedagogical community as it is to those who research and teach Chinese. *Kanji* present different challenges to Japanese learners, for although they often present the same semantic meaning as their Chinese counterparts, they can be pronounced in multiple ways, and unlike the general monosyllabic pronunciation of characters by speakers of Chinese, they can be pronounced with more than one syllable. Yet, there are some similarities on what the research has revealed concerning learners of Japanese that are similar to the findings from Chinese learners.

Researchers have found, for example, that learners in some studies prefer a very rote approach to memorizing characters, and that their strategic orientation to learning characters is related to their beliefs linked to their perceptions of *kanji* (Mori & Shimizu, 2007), and even to the beliefs of their teacher (Shimizu & Green, 2002). Different types of *kanji* are perceived by learners to be easier to learn than others (Yamashita & Maru, 2000), with learners attending to basic construction principles and meanings before sound (Toyoda, 2009). While beginning students can be taught the basics of inferencing unknown characters (Toyoda, 2000), inferencing *kanji* is thought to be a complex process involving not only the component elements of the *kanji*, but also the use of the character's surrounding context (Mori, 2002, 2003; Mori & Nagy, 1999). Given these findings where inferencing seems to require a balance between use of the context as well as the morphological properties of the Chinese characters, best practice calls for reading exercises that develop in the learner a heightened awareness of the different sources that are available in a text that will help them construct meaning as they read, thus pointing to Grabe's (2004, 2009) categories of text structure and discourse organization as important areas of best practice. Research employing think-aloud protocols among advanced learners (Everson & Ke, 1997) indicates they employ a highly orchestrated and fluent system of exploiting both linguistic and contextual elements when reading text and solving word identification problems. Instead of trusting that these abilities will develop in our students on their own, best practice must reserve a place in the curriculum for explicitly developing these skills through exercises that teach the importance of contextual information in reading, as well as teaching our learners that morphological and phonological information derived from the characters themselves are potentially useful in retrieving meaning.

It seems as well that there is a complex relationship between attitudes towards learning Chinese characters and the strategies students employ to learn them, with research evidence suggesting that positive attitudes and knowledge about characters interact in a powerful way to inspire learning. The evidence also suggests that teachers serve as powerful purveyors of both language and culture, and can influence students' views that their difficulties in learning *kanji* are not because they are somehow ill-equipped for the learning task which is somehow beyond them (Mori, Sato, & Shimizu, 2007). The classroom, then, should also be a place where teachers take an active role in getting the students to examine and develop their learning strategies (Gamage, 2003), with the role of the teacher also being as a builder of student confidence in addition to one who imparts content knowledge. This expanded role for the teacher of developing strategic readers (Grabe, 2004, 2009) will then also need to be included as part and parcel of pre-service and in-service teacher development so as to increase teacher awareness of their multi-faceted role in the classroom when teaching reading. As well, best practices should include being aware of our students' attitudes, as there seems to be connections between how our students view themselves as readers and their interest in reading in Japanese (Kondo-Brown, 2006a), indicating that getting to know our students and how they feel about learning these languages and what they believe the difficulties are will be helpful to remedy these problems.

It should also be emphasized that with all of the attention that is paid to the teaching of characters in the Chinese and Japanese curriculum, the ultimate goal of our reading programs should be to where our learners actually get to the point to where they can read Chinese and Japanese texts. All too often, teachers run the risk of focusing their reading instruction on selected aspects of reading without providing and guiding their students with opportunities to read extended texts. In other words, best practice dictates that students be provided opportunities to read more materials that are not far above their proficiency level, thus pointing to Grabe's (2004, 2009) recommendation that students be given plentiful opportunities for extended reading. All too often, our learners spend too much time in translation or other tasks that do not require them to actually read, but often decode their way through densely written texts containing far too many unknown words.

While there is rightfully an emphasis placed upon our students learning to read authentic materials, learning to read in different orthographic systems requires pedagogical interventions that take into consideration the learners' relative unfamiliarity with the new orthography they are learning, as well as the language system that underlies it. It has been noted that Hitosugi and Day (2004) devised an extensive reading curriculum for second semester university students of Japanese that employed books designed for Japanese children that started with texts employing the *kana* systems of Japanese writing, and slowly progressing to texts employing *kanji*. An integral part of their program was explaining to the students the purpose for extensive reading, and to give them the opportunity to read texts that were specifically designed to be at their reading level. In this particular program, evidence suggests that those participating in this extensive reading exhibited gains in reading proficiency, as well as positive attitudes towards reading in Japanese. Such pedagogical interventions hold promise for remedying some of the problems typically associated with reading in Chinese and Japanese—a lack of automaticity when processing both *kana* and Chinese characters, an inability to develop reading fluency, and opportunities to read texts within one's proficiency level so as to develop the beginnings of the stamina necessary down the road if one is to read authentic materials for longer periods of time. Clearly, if our goals dictate that we want to take our learners beyond the intermediate levels of reading, our classrooms will need to provide opportunities for our learners to develop into extensive readers, with pedagogy designed to take into consideration their current level of reading proficiency.

THE ROLE OF WRITING

A final word should be given to the role of requiring students to learn to write Chinese characters from memory. It should come as no surprise that research among foreign language learners of Chinese indicates that there is a strong relationship between the ability to recognize characters and the ability to write them from memory (Ke, 1998). Yet, a high price is paid in time and effort to attain this proficiency, with evidence indicating that for learners of Japanese at the end of their second year of study, there is a considerable gap between learners' ability to recognize and produce *kanji* (Chikamatsu, 2005). Moreover, with the proliferation of affordable Chinese and Japanese word processing programs that show promise in helping learners to be more accurate writers (Chikamatsu, 2005), and the need to handwrite beyond basic character formation being questioned as unauthentic, some have dismissed this part of the curriculum as being a waste of time (Allen, 2008).

While the importance of being able to reproduce characters correctly with proper balance and stoke order is not questioned, an emphasis on writing characters from memory by hand may be reserved for students whose professional needs dictate the development of this special ability. Yet, it should be noted that the idea of abandoning handwriting will most likely be contested among native teachers of Chinese, as the writing of characters is not only viewed by them as useful for communication, but as a gateway into Chinese and much of Asian culture, where people have been learning Chinese characters this way for thousands of years. Or as Walker (1989) has pointed out, for native teachers of languages such as Chinese, Japanese, and Korean, "... the writing system often embodies the very image of their language" (p. 119).

An important cornerstone, then, is for teachers and program directors to be aware of how best practice addresses the pedagogical cultures that reside in the minds of teachers who come to the classroom as native or non-native speakers of the language. Current reading pedagogy stresses that we strive to make our learners strategic readers by developing a complex array of skills that goes beyond a curriculum that spends inordinate amounts of time having our learners memorize how to write characters from memory. With time as a resource that no teacher can afford to squander, teachers will need to reevaluate the goals of their particular programs to determine the extent to which writing characters from memory will be addressed.

HEBREW AND ARABIC

Lastly, research in learning to read in Arabic and Hebrew takes us to a somewhat different dimension in L2 learning, as much of the research investigates the reading development in these languages among children. In this regard, the bilingual context of this learning indicates a complex relationship between L1/L2 language proficiency, orthographic depth with vowelled and unvowelled text, learner age, and contextual settings of language use and instruction (Saiegh-Haddad & Geva, 2010). In her synthesis of research, Geva (2006) asserts the need to give L2 learners sustained and systematic opportunities to develop proficiency in their L2 oral proficiency, while not overlooking the fact that students experiencing difficulty may be having problems in the acquisition of basic literacy skills. As with Chinese and Japanese, this need also falls within a number of categories referred to in Grabe's (2004, 2009) synthesis, especially the need to ensure the acquisition of linguistic knowledge. The importance of vowelled texts in Hebrew and Arabic for beginning learners also draws upon the need for developed language resources among our learners, not only to take advantage of their experience with alphabetic reading if their L1 is represented by alphabets, but also to facilitate and harness the power of phonological processing derived from more explicit phonological representation provided by marking vowels.

As the demand for opportunities to learn Arabic increases, there are some in the Arabic teaching profession who support moving towards proficiency-based instruction, yet note the challenges accompanying an effort to teach a diglossic language where a literary-based written language (MSA, or Modern Standard Arabic) and a host of Arabic spoken dialects reside side-by-side. In its attempt to move towards standardized instruction of Arabic, members of the Arabic teaching community in the United States have written that to prepare learners of Arabic, "teachers of Arabic disagree on whether their students should be taught only MSA or a dialect or a mixture of both. . ." , though there is "undisputed agreement by teachers and scholars that a thorough understanding of MSA is important" (Standards, 2006, p. 115). There is a likelihood, then, that Arabic reading programs will be standardized in teaching their students to read in MSA, though how and what variant of the spoken language other than MSA will be taught (if at all) might vary from program to program. For those interested in how language fields develop and meet the instructional challenges facing their members (Brecht & Walton, 1993), Arabic will provide a compelling case study for evaluating the evolution of best practice.

CONCLUSION

This article has provided a summary of research done in selected languages that employ non-Roman orthographic writing systems, such as Arabic, Chinese, Hebrew, and Japanese. As such, it presents only a summary of findings, and does not include other languages that are beginning to gain research attention. It is hoped that even though research in these languages was not addressed in this review, researchers will find the theoretical underpinnings and thoughts on best practice presented here as helpful in framing their own research agendas and pedagogical methods. This article, then, concludes with a plea for more and continuing research investigating how people read in these languages. A review of the reference list indicates a critical mass of researchers who specialize in this area, a list that must be expanded if we are to understand the reading process in languages that many believe are the wave of the future for L2 learning and instruction.

ANNOTATED BIBLIOGRAPHY

Cook, V., & Bassetti, B. (Eds.) (2005). *Second language writing systems.* Clevedon, UK: Multilingual Matters.

This book features a particularly strong first chapter framing L2 reading and writing in different writing systems, along with research findings in these areas. Chapters include data-based studies in EFL/ESL as well as languages such as Chinese and Japanese as foreign languages. Chapters putting forth implications for pedagogy are also featured.

Everson, M.E., & Xiao, Y. (Eds.). (2009). *Teaching Chinese as a foreign language: Theories and applications.* Boston, MA: Cheng & Tsui.

This volume was compiled to meet the need for a resource to aid the many student teachers enrolling in teacher development programs. The volume has articles written by a number of experts dealing with a number of pedagogical issues, including reading.

Koda, K., & Zehler, A. M. (Eds.). (2008). *Learning to read across languages: Cross-linguistic relationships in first- and second-language literacy development.* New York, NY: Routledge.

This volume is an excellent resource for those interested in first- and second-language reading in languages employing non-Roman alphabets or logographs. As such, it describes the writing systems used in Chinese, Arabic, Hebrew, Khmer, and Korean and discusses how reading skills in these diverse languages differ from one another, and how reading in a first language transfers to learning to read in a second language. Excellent chapters on the theoretical underpinnings of prior literary experience are examined, as are research findings in second language reading by first language readers of these five languages.

Nara, H., & Noda, M. (2003). *Acts of reading: Exploring connections in pedagogy of Japanese*. Honolulu, HI: University of Hawai'i Press.

Most books dealing with the learning of Chinese and Japanese for foreign language learners take a four skills approach and discuss reading, speaking, listening, and writing. This volume is an exception, treating reading exclusively, and explores reading in Japanese from both a first and second language approach. While giving an abundance of information about reading theory, Japanese language practitioners will appreciate the third section of the book that deals with the design, implementation, materials selection and evaluation of a reading program in Japanese.

AUTHOR NOTE

The author wishes to thank the editor and two anonymous reviewers for their suggestions and comments during the writing of this article.

REFERENCES

Abu-Rabia, S. (1997). Reading in Arabic orthography: The effect of vowels and context upon reading accuracy on poor and skilled native readers of Arabic. Social and cognitive factors influencing the reading comprehension of Arab students learning Hebrew as a second language in Israel. *Reading and Writing: An Interdisciplinary Journal, 9*, 65–78.

Abu-Rabia, S. (1998a). Social and cognitive factors influencing the reading comprehension of Arab students learning Hebrew as a second language in Israel. *Journal of Research in Reading, 21*, 201–212.

Abu-Rabia, S. (1998b). Reading Arabic texts: Effects of text type, reader type, and vowelization. *Reading and Writing: An Interdisciplinary Journal, 10*, 105–113.

Abu-Rabia, S. (1999). Towards a second-language model of learning in problematic social contexts: The case of Arabs learning Hebrew in Israel. *Race Ethnicity and Education, 2*, 109–126.

Abu-Rabia, S. (2001). The role of vowels in reading Semitic scripts: Data from Arabic and Hebrew. *Reading and Writing: An Interdisciplinary Journal, 14*, 39–59.

Abu-Rabia, S. (2002). Reading in a root-based-morphology language: The case of Arabic. *Journal of Research in Reading, 25*, 299–309.

Abu-Rabia, S., & Siegel, L. S. (2002). Reading, syntactic, orthographic, and working memory skills of bilingual Arabic-English speaking Canadian children. *Journal of Psycholinguistic*

Research, 31, 661–678.

Abu-Rabia, S., & Siegel, L. S. (2003). Reading skills in three orthographies: The case of trilingual Arabic-Hebrew-English-speaking Arab children. *Reading and Writing: An Interdisciplinary Journal, 16*, 611–634.

Asia Society. (2010). Meeting the challenge: Preparing Chinese language teachers for American schools. New York, NY: Asia Society.

Allen, J. R. (2008). Why learning to write Chinese is a waste of time: A modest proposal. *Foreign Language Annals, 41*, 237–251.

Baluch, B. (2006). Persian orthography and its relation to literacy. In R. M. Joshi & P. G. Aaron (Eds.), *Handbook of orthography and literacy* (pp. 365–376). Mahwah, NJ: Lawrence Erlbaum Associates.

Bassetti, B. (2005). Effects of writing systems on second language awareness: Word awareness in English learners of Chinese as a foreign language. In V. Cook & B. Bassetti (Eds.), *Second language writing systems*, (pp. 335–356). London, UK: Multilingual Matters.

Brecht, R. D., & Rivers, W. P. (2000). *Language and national security in the 21st century.* Dubuque, IA: Kendall/Hunt Publishing Company.

Brecht, R. D., & Walton, A. R. (1993). National strategic planning in less commonly taught languages. Washington, D.C.: The National Foreign Language Center.

Chang, C. (2010). See how they read: An investigation into the cognitive and metacognitive strategies of nonnative readers of Chinese. In M. E. Everson & H. H. Shen (Eds.), *Chinese Language Teachers Association Monograph Series: Vol. 4. Research among learners of Chinese as a foreign language* (pp. 93–116). Honolulu, HI: University of Hawai'i, National Foreign Language Resource Center.

Cheung, H., McBride-Chang, C., & Chow, B. W-Y. (2006). Reading Chinese. In R. M. Joshi & P. G. Aaron (Eds.), *Handbook of orthography and literacy* (pp. 421–438). Mahwah, NJ: Lawrence Erlbaum Associates.

Chikamatsu, N. (1996). The effects of L1 orthography on L2 word recognition. *Studies in Second Language Acquisition, 18*, 403–432.

Chikamatsu, N. (2005). L2 Japanese kanji memory and retrieval: An experiment on the tip-of-the-pen (TOP) phenomenon. In V. Cook & B. Bassetti (Eds.), *Second language writing systems* (pp. 71–96). London, UK: Multilingual Matters.

Chikamatsu, N. (2006). Developmental word recognition: A study of L1 English readers of L2 Japanese. *The Modern Language Journal, 90*, 67–85.

Christensen, M. B., & Warnick, J. P. (2006). *Performed culture: An approach to East Asian language pedagogy.* Columbus, OH: The Ohio State University, National East Asian Languages Resource Center.

DeFrancis, J. (1984). *The Chinese language: Fact and fantasy.* Honolulu, HI: University of

Hawaii Press.

DeFrancis, J. (1989). *Visible speech: The diverse oneness of writing systems*. Honolulu, HI: University of Hawaii Press.

Dewey, D. P. (2004). Connections between teacher and student attitudes regarding script choice in first-year Japanese language classrooms. *Foreign Language Annals, 37*, 567–577.

Everson, M. E. (1998). Word recognition among learners of Chinese as a foreign language: Investigating the relationship between naming and knowing. *The Modern Language Journal, 82*, 194–204.

Everson, M. E. (2009). Literacy in Chinese as a foreign language. In M. E. Everson & Y. Xiao (Eds.), *Teaching Chinese as a foreign language: Theories and applications* (pp. 97–112). Boston, MA: Cheng & Tsui.

Everson, M. E., & Ke, C. (1997). An inquiry into the reading strategies of intermediate and advanced learners of Chinese as a foreign language. *Journal of the Chinese Language Teachers Association, 3*, 1–20.

Falsgraf, C., & Spring, M. K. (2007). Innovations in language learning: The Oregon Chinese flagship model. *Journal of the National Council of Less Commonly Taught Languages, 4*, 1–16.

Fan, M. H. (2010). *Developing Chinese orthographic awareness: What insights into characters do beginning level Chinese as a foreign language textbooks provide?* Berlin, Germany: Lambert Academic Publishing.

Fender, M. (2008). Arabic literacy development and cross-linguistic effects in subsequent L2 literacy development. In K. Koda & A. M. Zehler (Eds.), *Learning to read across languages: Cross-linguistic relationships in first- and second-language literacy development* (pp. 101–124). New York, NY: Routledge.

Gamage, G. H. (2003). Perceptions of kanji learning strategies: Do they differ among Chinese character and alphabetic background learners? *Australian Review of Applied Linguistics, 26*, 17–31. Retrieved from http: //ro.uow.edu.au/artspapers/69

Geva, E. (2006). Learning to read in a second language: Research, implications, and recommendations for services. In R. E. Tremblay, R. G. Barr, & R. D. Peters (Eds.), *Encyclopedia of early childhood development* (pp. 1–12). Montreal, Quebec: Centre of Excellence for Early Childhood Development. Retrieved from http: //www.child-encyclopedia.com/pages/PDF/second_language.pdf

Geva, E., & Siegel, L. S. (2000). Orthographic and cognitive factors in the concurrent development of basic reading skills in two languages. *Reading and Writing: An Interdisciplinary Journal, 12*, 1–30.

Geva, E., & Wade-Woolley (1998). Component processes in becoming English-Hebrew biliterate. In A. Y. Yucesan Durgunoglu & L. Verhoeven (Eds.), *Literacy development in a multilingual context: Cross-cultural perspectives* (pp. 85–110). Mawah, NJ: Lawrence Erlbaum Associates.

Geva, E., Wade-Woolley, L., & Shany, M. (1997). Development of reading efficiency in first and second language. *Scientific Studies of Reading, 1*, 119–144.

Grabe, W. (2004). Research on teaching reading. *Annual Review of Applied Linguistics, 24*, 44–69.

Grabe, W. (2009). Epilogue: Reflections on second language reading research and instruction. In Z. H. Hong & N. J. Anderson (Eds.), *Second language reading research and instruction: Crossing the boundaries* (pp. 192–205). Ann Arbor, MI: The University of Michigan Press.

Hatasa, Y. A. (2002). The effects of differential timing in the introduction of Japanese syllabaries on early second language development in Japanese. *The Modern Language Journal, 86*, 349–367.

He, A. (2008). Chinese as a heritage language: An introduction. In A. W. He & Y. Xiao (Eds.), *Chinese as a heritage language: Fostering rooted world citizenry* (pp. 1–12). Honolulu, HI: University of Hawai'i, National Foreign Language Resource Center.

Hitosugi, C. I., & R. R. Day. (2004). Extensive reading in Japanese. *Reading in a Foreign Language, 16*, 20–30.

Jackson, N. E., Everson, M. E., & Ke, C. (2003). Beginning readers' awareness of the orthographic structure of semantic-phonetic compounds: Lessons from a study of learners of Chinese as a foreign language. In C. McBride-Chang & H. C. Chen (Eds.), *Reading development in Chinese children* (pp. 141–153). Westport, CT: Greenwood Press.

Jackson, F. H., & Malone, M. E. (2010). *Building the foreign language capacity we need: Toward a comprehensive strategy for a national language framework.* Washington, D.C.: Center of Applied Linguistics. Retrieved from http: //www.cal.org/resources/pubs/building-the-foreign-language-capacity-we-need.html

Katz, L., & Frost, R. (1992). The reading process is different for different orthographies: Theorthographic depth hypothesis. In: R. Frost & L. Katz (Eds.), *Orthography, phonology, morphology, and meaning* (pp. 67–84). Amsterdam, the Netherlands: Elsevier.

Ke, C. (1998). Effects of strategies on the learning of Chinese characters among foreign language students. *Journal of the Chinese Language Teachers Association, 33*, 93–112.

Koda, K. (1990). The use of L1 reading strategies in L2 reading, *Studies in Second Language Acquisition, 12*, 293–410.

Koda, K. (1992). The effects of lower-level processing skills in FL reading performance: Implications for instruction. *The Modern Language Journal, 76*, 502–12.

Koda, K. (1996). L2 word recognition research: A critical review. *The Modern Language Journal, 80*, 450–460.

Koda, K. (2001). Development of kanji knowledge among adult JFL learners. In H. Nara (Ed.),

Advances in Japanese language pedagogy (pp. 1–21). Columbus, OH: The Ohio State University, National East Asian Languages Resource Center.

Koda, K. (2008). Impacts of prior literacy experience on second language learning to read. In K. Koda & A. M. Zehler (Eds.), *Learning to read across languages: Cross-linguistic relationships in first- and second-language literacy development* (pp. 68–96). New York, NY: Routledge.

Koda, K., Zhang, Y., & Yang, C. (2008). Literary development in Chinese as a heritage language. In A. W. He & Y. Xiao (Eds.), *Chinese as a heritage language: Fostering rooted world citizenry* (pp. 137–149). Honolulu, HI: University of Hawai'i, National Foreign Language Resource Center.

Kondo-Brown, K. (2006a). Affective variables and Japanese L2 reading ability. *Reading in a Foreign Language*, *18*, 55–71.

Kondo-Brown, K. (2006b). How do English L1 learners of advanced Japanese infer unknown *kanji* words in authentic texts? *Language Learning*, *56*, 109–153.

Kondo-Brown, K. (2010). Curriculum development for advancing heritage language competence: Recent research, current practices, and a future agenda. *Annual Review of Applied Linguistics*, *30*, 24–41.

Lee-Thompson, L. C. (2008). An investigation of reading strategies applied by American learners of Chinese as a foreign language. *Foreign Language Annals*, *41*, 702–721.

Leikin, M., Schwartz, M., & Share, D. L. (2010). General and specific benefits of bi-literate bilingualism: A Russian-Hebrew study of beginning literacy. *Reading and Writing*, *23*, 269–292.

Leikin, M., Share, D. L., & Schwartz, M. (2005). Difficulties in L2 Hebrew reading in Russian-speaking second graders. *Reading and Writing: An Interdisciplinary Journal*, *18*, 455–472.

Matsunaga, S. (1995). The role of phonological coding in reading *kanji:* A research report and some pedagogical implications (Tech. Rep. No. 6). Honolulu, HI: University of Hawaii, Second Language Teaching and Curriculum Center.

Matsunaga, S. (1996). The linguistic nature of kanji reexamined: Do kanji represent only meanings? *Journal of the Association of Teachers of Japanese*, *30*, 1–22.

Matsunaga, S. (2001). Subvocalization in reading *kanji:* Can Japanese text be comprehended without it? In H. Nara (Ed.), *Advances in Japanese language pedagogy* (pp. 30–46). Columbus, OH: The Ohio State University, National East Asian Languages Resource Center.

McGinnis, S. (1999). Student goals and approaches. In M. Chu (Ed.), *Mapping the course of the Chinese language field* (pp. 151–188). Kalamazoo, MI: The Chinese Language Teachers Association.

Modern Language Association. (2007). Enrollments in languages other than English in United States institutions of higher education, Fall 2006. Retrieved from http: //www.mla.org/2006_

flenrollmentsurvey

Montrul, S. (2010). Current issues in heritage language acquisition. *Annual Review of Applied Linguistics, 30*, 3–23.

Mori, Y. (1998). Effects of first language and phonological accessibility on *kanji* recognition. *The Modern Language Journal, 82*, 69–81.

Mori, Y. (1999). Beliefs about language learning and their relationship to the ability to integrate information from word parts and context in interpreting novel *kanji* words. *The Modern Language Journal, 83*, 534–545.

Mori, Y. (2002). Individual differences in the integration of information from context and word parts in interpreting unknown *kanji* words. *Applied Psycholinguistics, 23*, 375–397.

Mori, Y. (2003). The roles of context and word morphology in learning new *kanji* words. *The Modern Language Journal, 87*, 404–420.

Mori, Y., & Nagy, W. (1999). Integration of information from context and word elements in interpreting novel *kanji* compounds. *Reading Research Quarterly, 34*, 80–101.

Mori, Y., Sato, K., & Shimizu, H. (2007). Japanese language students' perceptions on *kanji* learning and their relationship to novel kanji word learning ability. *Language Learning, 57*, 57–85.

Mori, Y., & Shimizu, H. (2007). Japanese language students' attitudes toward *kanji* and their perceptions on *kanji* learning strategies. *Foreign Language Annals, 40*, 472–490.

Nara, H. (2003). Designing a reading program. In H. Nara & M. Noda (Eds.), *Acts of reading: Exploring connections in pedagogy of Japanese.* Honolulu, HI: University of Hawai'i Press.

Packard, J. L. (1990). Effects of time lag in the introduction of characters into the Chinese language curriculum. *The Modern Language Journal, 74*, 167–175.

Perfetti, C. A., & Dunlap, S. (2008). Learning to read: General principles and writing system variations. In K. Koda & A. M. Zehler (Eds.), *Learning to read across languages: Cross-linguistic relationships in first- and second-language literacy development* (pp. 13–38). New York, NY: Routledge.

Perfetti, C. A., & Liu, Y. (2005). Orthography to phonology and meaning: Comparison across and within writing systems. *Reading and Writing: An Interdisciplinary Journal, 18*, 193–210.

Perfetti, C. A., Liu, Y., & Tan, L. H. (2002). How the mind can meet the brain in reading: A comparative writing systems approach. In H. S. R. Kao, C. K. Leong, & D. G. Gao (Eds.), *Cognitive neuroscience studies of the Chinese language* (pp. 35–60). Hong Kong: Hong Kong University Press.

Perfetti, C. A., Liu, Y., & Tan, L. H. (2005). The lexical constituency model: Some implications of research on Chinese for general theories of reading. *Psychological Review, 112*, 43–59.

Perfetti, C. A., Zhang, S., & Berent, I. (1992). Reading in English and Chinese: Evidence for a "universal" phonological principle. In R. Frost & I. Katz (Eds.), *Orthography, phonology, morphology, and meaning* (pp. 227–248). Amsterdam, the Netherlands: Elsevier.

Ravid, D. (2006). Hebrew orthography and literacy. In R. M. Joshi & P. G. Aaron (Eds.), *Handbook of orthography and literacy* (pp. 339–364). Mahwah, NJ: Lawrence Erlbaum Associates.

Saiegh-Haddad, E., & Geva, E. (2010). Acquiring reading in two languages: An introduction to a special issue. *Reading and Writing: An Interdisciplinary Journal, 23*, 263–267.

Schwartz, M., Geva, E., Share, D. L., & Leikin, M. (2007). Learning to read in English as a third language: The cross-linguistic transfer of phonological processing skills. *Written Language and Literacy, 10*, 25–52.

Schwartz, M., Leikin, M., & Share, D. L. (2005). Bi-literate bilingualism versus mono-literate bilingualism: A longitudinal study of reading acquisition in Hebrew (L2) among Russian-speaking (L1) children. *Written Language and Literacy, 8*, 179–206.

Schwartz, M., Share, D. L., Leikin, M., & Kominsky, E. (2008). On the benefits of bi-literacy: Just a head start in reading or specific orthographic insights? *Reading and Writing: An Interdisciplinary Journal, 21*, 905–927.

Shen, H. H. (2004). Level of cognitive processing: Effects on character learning among non-native learners of Chinese as a foreign language. *Language and Education, 18*, 167–183.

Shen, H. H. (2005). An investigation of Chinese character learning strategies among nonnative speakers of Chinese. *System, 33*, 49–68.

Shen, H. H. (2008). An analysis of word decision strategies among learners of Chinese. *Foreign Language Annals, 41*, 501–524.

Shen, H. H. (2010). Analysis of radical knowledge development among beginning CFL learners. In M. E. Everson & H. H. Shen (Eds.), *Research among learners of Chinese as a foreign language* (Chinese Language Teachers Association Monograph Series: Vol. 4), (pp. 45–65). Honolulu, HI: University of Hawai'i, National Foreign Language Resource Center.

Shen, H. H., & Ke, C. (2007). Radical awareness and word acquisition among nonnative learners of Chinese. *The Modern Language Journal, 91*, 97–111.

Shimizu, H., & Green, K. E. (2002). Japanese language educators' strategies for and attitudes toward teaching *kanji*. *The Modern Language Journal, 86*, 227–241.

Standards for foreign language learning in the 21st century (2006). National Standards in Foreign Language Education Project (3rd Edition). Lawrence, KS: Allen Press.

Taft, M., & Chung, K. (1999). Using radicals in teaching Chinese characters to second language learners. *Psychologia: An International Journal of Psychology in the Orient, 42*, 243–251.

Toyoda, E. (2000). English-speaking learners' use of component information in processing unfamiliar *kanji*. *Australian Review of Applied Linguistics, 23*, 1–14.

Toyoda, E. (2009). An analysis of L2 readers' comments on *kanji* recognition. *Electronic Journal of Foreign Language Teaching, 6*, 5–20.

Unger, J. M. (2001). The first framework: getting down to basics. In H. Nara (Ed.), *Advances in Japanese language pedagogy* (pp. 336–428). Columbus, OH: The Ohio State University, National East Asian Languages Resource Center.

Walker, G. (1989). The less commonly taught languages in the context of American pedagogy. In H. S. Lepke (Ed.), *Shaping the future: Challenges and opportunities* (pp. 111–137). Middlebury, VT: Northeast Conference.

Wang, M., Liu, Y., & Perfetti, C. (2004). The implicit and explicit learning of orthographic structure and function of a new writing system. *Scientific Studies of Reading, 4*, 357–379.

Warnick, J. P. (2001). Reading as socio-cultural performance. In H. Nara (Ed.), *Advances in Japanese language pedagogy* (pp. 137–180). Columbus, OH: The Ohio State University, National East Asian Languages Resource Center.

Winke, P. M., & Abbuhl, R. (2007). Taking a closer look at vocabulary learning strategies: A case study of a Chinese foreign language class. *Foreign Language Annals, 40*, 697–712.

Yamashita, H., & Y. Maru (2000). Composition features of *kanji* for effective instruction. *Japanese Language and Literature, 34*, 159–178.

Xing, J. Z. (2006). *Teaching and learning Chinese as a foreign language: A pedagogical grammar.* Hong Kong: Hong Kong University Press.

Zhu, D. X. (1988). Dynamic account of the functions of phonetic radicals in modern Chinese character. In X. Yuen (Ed.), *Written language and culture.* Beijing, China: Beijing Guanming Daily Publishing House.

Collaborative Writing in L2 Contexts: Processes, Outcomes, and Future Directions

Neomy Storch

Collaborative writing is the joint production of a text by two or more writers. Despite the widespread use of collaborative writing in the world outside the second language (L2) classroom, the use of collaborative writing tasks in L2 classes, to date, seems relatively limited. The overarching aim of this article is to suggest that collaborative writing activities, if carefully designed and monitored, may form an optimal site for L2 learning. The article begins by providing a brief theoretical rationale for collaborative writing, drawing on both cognitive and sociocultural theories. It then reviews the small number of published studies that have investigated collaborative writing in different L2 contexts. This review provides empirical evidence that working jointly on producing a written text provides opportunities for language learning, but that factors such as task type, L2 proficiency, and the relationships that the learners form affect these opportunities and may also affect language-learning gains. The chapter then considers new directions in implementing collaborative writing: online collaboration via wikis. The article concludes by highlighting the factors that need to be considered in order to maximize the language-learning potentials of collaborative writing in face-to-face and online modes.

Collaborative writing may be defined as the joint production or the coauthoring of a text by two or more writers. Note that the defining trait of collaborative writing is the joint ownership of the document produced. Thus collaborative writing is distinguished from the group-planning or peer-feedback activities that are often manifest as part of the process approach to writing instruction.

The use of collaborative writing tasks is quite common in university courses. For example, group assignments are increasingly assigned in university courses because they are believed to reflect the team writing often undertaken in the real world (Strauss, 2001). There have been a number of studies documenting the advantages (as well as the potential difficulties) of such team writing projects (e.g., Dias, Freedman, Medway, & Pare, 1999; Mirel & Spilka, 2002). In addition, leading composition scholars such as Kenneth Bruffee (1993) have written about the benefits of collaborative writing such as the fostering of reflective thinking and a greater awareness and understanding of audience.

Yet in second language (L2) classrooms, the use of collaborative writing tasks has been relatively rare. Although the 1980s and 1990s saw growth in the use of pair and small-group work in the language classroom, informed by interaction hypothesis of Long (1996) and communicative approaches to L2 instruction, most of these peer-interaction activities employed oral tasks (e.g., information gap tasks) rather than writing tasks. Numerous studies based on the interaction hypothesis (for a review, see Mackey & Gass, 2006) have shown that when learners work in small groups (and more commonly in pairs), they engage in negotiations of meaning with the goal of making their output comprehensible and more target-like. These negotiations are said to facilitate L2 learning. Ortega (2007) noted that although researchers informed by cognitive-interactionist theories of second language acquisition (SLA) have focused mainly on oral interaction, the same type of interaction may occur in other modalities, such as writing.

The use of writing tasks in pair work activities began more earnestly following the seminal work of Swain (1985, 1993, 1995) on the importance of output for L2 development. Swain (1993, 1995) argued that the need to produce output is more likely to encourage learners to process language more deeply, notice gaps in their interlanguage, and reflect on language use. Although Swain referred to both oral and written output, writing may in fact provide greater opportunities for testing hypotheses, receiving and noticing feedback, and focusing on accuracy. Weissberg (2000), in his longitudinal study, found that adult L2 learners were more likely to produce new syntactic forms in their writing than in their speaking tasks. Writing is less ephemeral than speaking and does not require online processing; hence, the provision and subsequent noticing of corrective feedback are more feasible with writing (Cumming, 1990; Harklau, 2002). Furthermore, writing is more likely to encourage learners to reflect on their language use, drawing on their explicit knowledge of the language (Adams & Ross-Feldman, 2008; Williams, 2008). Weissberg (2006) suggested that tasks that integrate speaking and writing, as is the case in collaborative writing tasks, may be more conducive to language learning than solitary writing. As Weissberg pointed out, collaborative writing provides learners with a multitude of roles not available during solitary writing: that of tutors, coauthors, sounding boards, and critical readers.

Swain's subsequent work (2000, 2006, 2010) expanded on the advantages of collaborative writing, specifically in her writing on collaborative dialogue and languaging. Collaborative dialogue (Swain, 2000) is defined as the talk that emerges when learners engage in a problem-solving activity. *Languaging* (Swain, 2006, 2010) is the process of using language in an attempt to make meaning; that is, it is a means through which thinking is articulated and thus brought into existence. When engaged in writing, learners *language* about language; that is, they deliberate about how to best express their intended meaning. Although languaging can occur with oneself, when one is composing individually, such languaging is usually subvocal (thinking), which is speech directed to oneself. The benefit of collaborative writing is that it encourages other-directed talk, that is, talk that is vocalized. Once thoughts are vocalized, they are transformed into artefacts. These artefacts, together with the written text, can be further explored, that is, languaged further.

Swain's work on collaborative dialogue is very much informed by Vygotsky's (1978) sociocultural theory. The underlying premise of sociocultural theory is that all learning is fundamentally a social process, the result of interaction among humans in the social milieu. Vygotsky's work focused on children's cognitive development, particularly the development of higher-order cognitive functions such as voluntary attention and intentional memory. Furthermore, the interaction was generally conceived as between an adult and a child. The adult (expert) provides carefully attuned assistance (scaffolding) to the child (novice). However, in the field of SLA, a number of researchers have subsequently shown that scaffolding can also be provided by peers in pair or group work, where the role of the expert is fluid (Ohta, 2001) or shared by learners pooling their expertise, a process referred to as collective scaffolding (Donato 1994; Storch, 2002, 2009). In this sense, jointly constructed performance can outstrip individual competence (Swain, 2000).

While collaborative writing seems well supported theoretically, the number of empirical studies that have investigated collaborative writing in L2 classes is relatively small. Three strands can be discerned in this body of research. The first strand comprises studies that have focused on the nature of the cognitive processes that collaborative writing engenders. These studies have also considered the impact of factors such as task type and L2 proficiency grouping on these processes. The second strand includes studies that have looked more closely at the outcome of collaborative writing, whether it be in terms of the text produced compared to texts produced by students writing individually or in terms of evidence of language learning attributable to collaboration. The third strand includes studies that consider collaborative writing as it unfolds in computer-mediated communication and, in particular, the use of wikis.

COLLABORATIVE WRITING: COGNITIVE PROCESSES

Since collaborative writing is said to encourage learners to language, that is, to reflect on language use in the process of producing language, a number of researchers have examined the nature of languaging that occurs during such activities, and the factors that may impact on it. The two factors that have received the most research attention are task type and L2 proficiency grouping. Languaging in these studies has been operationalized as language-related episodes (LREs). These episodes are segments in the learners' dialogues where they deliberate about language (grammatical form, lexical choices, mechanics) while trying to complete the task (Swain & Lapkin, 2001).

Building on earlier work by Storch (2001) and by Swain and Lapkin (2001), de la Colina and García Mayo (2007) compared attention to language generated by three types of tasks: jigsaw, text reconstruction, and dictogloss. Unlike the earlier studies, de la Colina and García Mayo's study was conducted in an EFL (English as a foreign language) setting (English language learners in a university in Spain) and with low-proficiency L2 learners. The study found that all three collaborative writing tasks were effective in drawing learners' attention to language, but that the more structured task (text reconstruction) elicited more LREs than the other two tasks. Although the data (LREs) showed that even these low-proficiency L2 learners were able to provide one another mutual scaffolding, the researchers noted that many of these LREs were resolved incorrectly, suggesting that such tasks may not be suitable for low-proficiency L2 learners.

Storch and Wigglesworth's (2007) study examined, among other issues, the attention to language generated by two types of meaning-focused writing tasks: a data commentary report (based on a graphic prompt) of about 150–200 words and an argumentative essay of about 250–300 words. The participants in this study were advanced ESL (English as a second language) learners. Given the longer text requirement of the essay, the participants were given more time to complete it, and hence it was perhaps not surprising that the essay elicited more LREs than the data commentary report. Being meaning-focused tasks, both elicited more attention to lexical choices (lexical LREs) than to accuracy (form-focused LREs). Storch and Wigglesworth suggested that this greater attention to lexis could also be attributable to the fact that the participants were fairly advanced L2 learners and hence had less need to deliberate about grammatical accuracy. Furthermore, unlike de la Colina and García Mayo's (2007) study, most of the LREs in this study were resolved correctly. However, the authors also noted variation between pairs not only in terms of attention to language (i.e., how many LREs were elicited) but also in terms of the nature of pair work. Although most pairs collaborated, one pair formed a dominant-passive relationship in which one participant contributed very little to the languaging activity (for patterns of dyadic interaction, see Storch, 2002, 2009).

Clearly, the L2 proficiency of learners may affect the quantity and quality of the LREs. One of the early studies to consider the impact of proficiency pairing on attention to language use was by Leeser (2004). In Leeser's study, 10 Spanish L2 learners were assigned to pairs of similar proficiency (two high-high and two low-low pairs) and mixed proficiency (one pair) and asked to complete a dictogloss task. The pair talk was analyzed for the number and type of LREs (whether lexical or form focused) and their resolution. The study found that L2 proficiency had an impact on the number of LREs produced: the high-high pairs produced the greatest number of LREs, followed in descending order by the high-low and low-low pairs. The focus of the LREs also seemed to be affected by L2 proficiency: the high-high pairs focused mainly on grammatical forms; the low-low pairs mainly on lexis. Although most LREs were resolved correctly across all proficiency pairings, the highest proportion of unresolved LREs was found in the data of the low-low pairs, again suggesting that languaging may not be as successful among low-proficiency pairs.

Building on Leeser's work, subsequent studies investigated the effect of not only the learners' L2 proficiency pairing but also the relationship that they formed when working in pairs of similar and mixed proficiency. In a novel research design, Watanabe and Swain (2007) compared the nature of attention to form of individual learners when interacting with both more and less proficient interlocutors. That is, the study investigated whether the occurrence of LREs differed when the same four English L2 learners interacted with lower- and with higher-level interlocutors. Although the study involved learners in a multistage task (writing and responding to feedback), of most relevance here is the learners' languaging in the writing stage. The researchers found that the learners produced more LREs when they interacted with a higher-level interlocutor. Drawing on the model of dyadic interaction developed by Storch (2002, 2009), the researchers analyzed the relationships formed by the dyads and found that learners who collaborated produced more LREs than other patterns of interaction, thus suggesting that it is the pattern of interaction that may be more important than the relative L2 proficiency of the interlocutors.

Kim and McDonough (2008), using a research design similar to that of Watanabe and Swain (2007), paired eight intermediate Korean L2 learners with fellow intermediate interlocutors and then with advanced interlocutors. The task used was a dictogloss. The results showed that when interacting with an advanced peer rather than with an intermediate peer, learners produced more LREs in total (grammatical and lexical) and a greater proportion of these LREs were lexical. Furthermore, a greater proportion of LREs were left unresolved or were resolved incorrectly when learners worked with fellow intermediate peers rather than with more advanced peers. In terms of patterns of interaction, the study found that learners who were collaborative with an intermediate interlocutor tended to be more passive with an advanced interlocutor, whereas learners who were dominant with an intermediate interlocutor were more collaborative with an advanced interlocutor. However, it is not clear whether these patterns of pair interaction affected the number of LREs produced.

The importance of the relationships pairs formed was also one of the key finding in Aldosari's (2008) doctoral research. Aldosari's study, conducted in EFL classes in Saudi Arabia, set out to investigate the effect of proficiency grouping, task type, and the relationships learners formed on the quantity and type of LREs that collaborative writing tasks elicited. Three tasks were used: jigsaw, composition, and an editing task. Eighteen students participated in the study, forming six pairs each of high-high, high-low, and low-low pairs (based on their EFL instructor's assessment). The study found that task type affected the type of LREs, with more meaning-focused tasks (jigsaw and composition) eliciting more attention to lexis; whereas the editing task generated more grammar LREs. However, in terms of the number of LREs, the main determinant was the relationships the pairs formed rather than their proficiency grouping or type of task. Learners who formed collaborative pairs generated more LREs than those who formed asymmetrical patterns of interaction (expert-novice or dominant-passive). Furthermore, collaboration tended to occur mainly among the similar proficiency pairs (low-low and high-high) rather than the mixed proficiency pairs, where the more proficient learner tended to dominate the interaction.

COLLABORATIVE WRITING: OUTCOMES

The data (LREs) of the studies reviewed showed that when collaborating on a writing task, the learners deliberated about language choices; articulated their uncertainties; provided suggestions, countersuggestions, and explanations; and gave and received feedback. Swain and Lapkin (2001) claimed that LREs represent language learning in progress. A number of researchers have set out to verify this claim by investigating the outcomes of collaborative writing activities.

Storch's (2005) classroom-based study compared the writing produced by two groups of fairly advanced ESL learners who were given the choice to work on a writing task (data commentary task) individually or in pairs. Eighteen students chose to work in pairs, and five elected to work individually. All the texts produced were analyzed using a range of quantitative and qualitative measures. Quantitative measures included measures of fluency (total number of words), accuracy (percentage of error-free clauses, errors per words) and complexity (e.g., proportion of dependent clauses to clauses). The texts were also assessed globally using a 5-scale scheme that took into consideration content, structure, and task fulfillment. The study found that pairs tended to produce shorter texts, but that the texts were more accurate and the language more syntactically complex. Furthermore, pairs tended to produce texts that had a better structure and clearer focus. However, given the relatively small-scale nature of the study, it is not surprising that the differences were not statistically significant.

In a larger-scale experimental study, Wigglesworth and Storch (2009) compared texts produced by 48 pairs with texts produced by 48 learners working individually. All the participants were advanced ESL learners. The texts produced were compared using only quantitative measures, similar to the measures used in the Storch (2005) study. The researchers found that there were no statistically significant differences between the texts produced by pairs and by individuals in terms of fluency and complexity. However, the texts produced by pairs were more accurate than the texts produced individually, a difference that was statistically significant. Based on an analysis of the pair talk, Wigglesworth and Storch attributed these findings to the focus on language use and to the availability of collective scaffolding and mutual feedback that collaborative writing activities provided the learners.

The preceding two studies have shown that collaboration tends to result in more accurate texts. However, perhaps a more pertinent question is: Do collaborative writing activities, and the LREs thereby generated, lead to language learning? The following studies attempted to address this question.

Kim (2008) compared the effectiveness of collaborative and individual tasks on the acquisition of L2 vocabulary by learners of Korean as a second language. The task used was a dictogloss, and language gains were measured by comparing scores on a pretest and two posttests. This study had 32 participants: 16 learners completed a dictogloss in pairs (8 pairs), and 16 completed the same task individually. In this study the learners who completed the dictogloss task individually engaged in think-aloud protocols. The study found that the number of LREs produced by the pairs and by the individuals was similar, but fewer LREs were resolved incorrectly or remained unresolved in the pair work, because of the opportunity to pool knowledge in the pair work condition. More importantly, pairs performed significantly better on the vocabulary posttests (immediate and delayed) than the learners who completed the tasks individually. However, it should be noted that the tests assessed the learners' knowledge of word meanings rather than their ability to use the vocabulary; and hence the gains only represent one aspect of vocabulary learning.

Watanabe and Swain's (2007) study, discussed earlier, used the participants' initial joint writing task as a pretest and their subsequently individually written task (after receiving reformulation feedback and processing it collaboratively) as the posttest to assess language gains resulting from collaborative activity. The posttest was scored by noting whether each participant got the reformulated items right or wrong. The findings suggested that collaborative activity led to language learning (retention of feedback) but that the patterns of pair interaction greatly influenced the posttest performance. When the learners formed a collaborative pattern of interaction, they were more likely to achieve higher posttest scores regardless of their partner's proficiency level.

Brooks and Swain (2009) examined not only whether learning occurred as a result of collaborative activity but also the most effective source of learning. In their study, two pairs of adult ESL learners participated in four sessions. In the first session, the pairs coauthored a text. In the second session, the noticing session, the learners compared their version of the text to a reformulated version. In the third session, the stimulated recall session, the participants reflected on their noticing session (using a video recording of the noticing session) and were also given an opportunity to ask the researcher further questions about the reformulations. The students were then asked to revise their jointly produced text individually. This revised version was used as a posttest, to assess the learning that took place as well as the source of the learning, given that the learners had three different sources of expertise: peers, the reformulation, and interactions with the researcher in the recall session. The researchers traced any changes made in the posttest to the source of the expertise. Perhaps the most interesting finding of this study was that the most effective source of expertise was the peers. A very high proportion of the solutions to language problems that the learners discussed and resolved during the coauthoring session were maintained in the posttest. In contrast, some of the language errors, which were reformulated, discussed with peers and with the researcher, reappeared in the final version. The researchers explained their results in terms of the learners' zone of proximal development (Vygotsky, 1978). That is, the reformulations and assistance provided by the researcher dealt with structures that were perhaps beyond the learners' developmental stage. Peers, on the other hand, provided one another with assistance that was more attuned to their needs and developmental stage.

Storch (2008) noted that earlier studies on collaborative writing tended to consider only the quantity of LREs rather than their quality, and she suggested that depth of engagement evident in the LREs may affect subsequent language development. In her study, 22 ESL advanced learners completed two similar versions of a text reconstruction task: The first version was completed in pairs and the next version individually. The data analysis of the transcribed pair talk showed that pairs attended to a range of grammatical and lexical items, but that the nature of their attention ranged from elaborate to simple. Guided by the work of Kuiken and Vedder (2002), elaborate attention was operationalized as instances where learners deliberated and discussed language items and simple attention where one learner made a suggestion and the other repeated, acknowledged, or did not respond to the suggestion. Analysis of learner performance on a set of items that were common to the two versions of the text reconstruction task suggested that although attention, whether elaborate or simple, tended to lead to learning or consolidation of the structures focused on, it was elaborate attention that was more beneficial to both members of the pair than simple attention. Elaborate attention, where learners deliberated over alternatives, and questioned and explained their suggestions, led to consolidation or learning more so than simple attention. Tocalli-Beller and Swain's (2005) study, on the processing of feedback (reformulations), also found that where students engaged with the reformulations, either disagreeing with or questioning the reformulations, this verbalization advanced their understanding of the suggested changes. However, it should be noted that depth of engagement does not necessarily involve learners articulating grammatical rules. Gutiérrez (2008) argued that lack of ability to articulate language knowledge does not necessarily reflect lack of knowledge. The claim made by Storch (2008) is that it is not language knowledge per se but the depth of attention and engagement that may be important in collaborative writing tasks and subsequently for L2 development.

To date, the number of studies on the outcomes of collaborative writing, particularly studies showing evidence of L2 learning, are few in number and small scale. More research is clearly needed to provide evidence to support the claim that collaborative writing tasks result in L2 learning and, if so, whether they are equally beneficial for all linguistic features.

COLLABORATIVE WRITING: ONLINE COLLABORATION

In the past 20 years, the field of computer-mediated interaction has greatly diversified in scope. Warschauer and Grimes (2007) described the various forms of interaction facilitated by the latest features of computer technology, often referred to as Web 2.0, including blogs, wikis, and social networks. These new developments provide opportunities for new types of interactions and collaborative activities.

Of particular relevance is the use of wikis, a new form of collaborative writing activities. Wiki refers to a special type of Web site that allows all users to contribute or edit within the site, and a record of all contributions is kept. One of the major advantages of the wiki is that whereas group collaboration on a document in the past could only be achieved by individual asynchronous editing, which then necessitated coordinating the edits, wikis allow all group members to have equal access to the most recent version of the document. Thus group members can build on one another's ideas. Unlike traditional face-to-face collaborative writing, wikis usually involve a group of writers rather than pairs, and the writing activity takes place over a long term.

There has been a growing awareness of the educational possibilities of wikis, and reports on their use have increased. In the field of general education, there have been reports describing the use of wikis with young learners (e.g., Wilkoff, 2007), university students (e.g., Elgort, Smith, & Toland, 2008) and teacher trainees (e.g., Arnold & Ducate, 2006; Matthew, Felvegi, & Callaway, 2009; Wheeler, Yeomans, & Wheeler, 2008). For example, Matthew et al.'s study was part of an ongoing large-scale project investigating the potential of a class wiki to enhance teacher trainees' learning of course content. The learners' reflective diary entries suggested that the wikis contributed to the students' learning by encouraging them to read one another's contributions and synthesize the various sources of information. However, both the Wheeler et al. and the Elgort et al. studies suggested that wiki collaborative activity may evoke new notions of authorship. Wheeler et al.'s study found that although students were happy to post their contributions to a wiki space for other group members to read, they were resistant to having their contributions altered or deleted by other group members. Elgort et al. reported that wikis seemed to encourage posting contributions and some limited synthesis of information but very little evaluation.

To date, there seems to be little published research on the use of wikis in L2 learning contexts. Most of the available research is quite descriptive, reporting on teachers' and learners' experiences of wikis implemented in L2 writing classrooms. For example, Mak and Coniam (2008) described how Year 7 (age 11) ESL students in an English-medium secondary school in Hong Kong produced a text using wikis over a 6-week period. In an in-depth case study of one group of four students, the researchers show that initially students' contributions were merely additions (not necessarily cohesive) to other students' contributions. However, as the project progressed and the students became more accustomed to the wiki environment, they began to edit one another's work as well as add to the content that had been written. Mak and Coniam noted that the amount of each student's contributions varied a great deal over time for individual students and among students. Furthermore, most of the contributions made by the students were in terms of adding to the content, with very few instances of error corrections (own or peers'). Mak and Coniam attributed this lack of attention to accuracy to the fact that Hong Kong students tend to spend little time on proofreading and correcting their work and are averse to amending their peers' work, as they do not wish their peers to lose face.

However, Kessler's (2009) larger study, conducted with 40 EFL adult learners in Mexico, also reported on students' lack of attention to language use when involved in a wiki project. Kessler's study, which moved beyond a description of how wikis were implemented, investigated ESL learners' attention to accuracy in a long-term (16-week) wiki project. As in the case of Mak and Coniam's (2008) study, here too, analysis of the learners' revisions for LREs showed that most of the revisions made were to content and style (font size, color, etc.) rather than to form. When corrections to form were made, they tended to focus on word choice and spelling rather than grammatical accuracy. An interesting observation was that students often spent a great deal of time altering the style of sentences yet ignored the errors in the sentences. In fact, there were slightly more errors that were overlooked than errors that were attended to. Despite instructions about the need to produce a grammatically accurate wiki text, the students seemed to often ignore grammatical errors that they later (when shown in subsequent interviews) demonstrated an ability to correct. Interviews with the students suggested that one reason for these findings is that the students clearly perceived this collaborative writing activity as meaning rather than language focused; another reason is that they felt that the errors did not impede comprehension of the content.

The findings of these studies thus suggest that the mode of communication may affect attention to language in collaborative writing tasks. A study by Tan, Wigglesworth, and Storch (2010), which compared face-to-face and computer-mediated collaborative writing by the same pairs of Chinese L2 learners in an Australian university, found that whereas students tended to engage with one another's contributions when composing texts in the face-to-face mode, in the computer-mediated mode the style of interaction was cooperative. That is, in the computer-mediated mode the learners contributed equally to the task completion, taking turns to propose a sentence. However, they often did not engage with one another's contribution by building on it or providing feedback. Thus wikis or other forms of computer-mediated collaborative writing tasks may not be optimal for a focus on grammatical accuracy.

Kessler and Bikowski (2010), in a reanalysis of Kessler's (2009) data, considered the nature of the participants' contributions to content revisions (rather than language revisions). The authors reported that the participants added, deleted, and elaborated on one another's contributions. However, the authors also found that willingness to contribute to the wiki text and the nature of the contribution changed over time. In the first 2 weeks of the project, very few students participated, and the pattern of contribution was deletion and replacement of entire extant texts. In subsequent weeks, more students began to contribute, and the pattern of contribution changed. The deletions were minor amendments rather than whole text deletions, and there were also many instances of elaborations on one another's contributions. These findings confirm those of Mak and Coniam's (2008) study and suggest that willingness to contribute to and collaborate in a coauthoring activity may take time to develop. However, these findings also suggest that perhaps in large-group projects (40 participants), a sense of text ownership may be elusive.

CONCLUSION

Collaborative writing tasks may be conducive to language learning because they provide learners with opportunities not only for language practice but also to language. That is, collaborative writing avails learners with opportunities to deliberate about their own and their peers' language use as they attempt to create meaning. Although learners engage in languaging when writing individually (see Kim, 2008), perhaps one of the greatest advantages of collaborative writing is that it affords learners opportunities to pool their linguistic resources when encountering problems. Languaging about language is one of the ways to gain new knowledge about a language or consolidate existing L2 knowledge. This collaboration leads to the production of more accurate texts and may lead to language learning gains.

However, the studies reviewed show that in implementing collaborative writing tasks, the nature of the task, the L2 proficiency of the learners, and the mode of communication (whether face-to-face or via computer-mediated interaction) need to be taken into consideration. Some collaborative writing tasks (e.g., text reconstruction) may not be suitable for low-proficiency L2 learners. L2 proficiency is a factor not only in selecting the most appropriate collaborative writing task but also in assigning students to form pairs. This is particularly pertinent in classes with learners of varying L2 proficiencies. The research suggests that collaborative tasks may not be suitable for low-proficiency L2 learners, unless they are paired with higher-proficiency learners (Leeser, 2004), and the nature of the relationship formed by pairs of unequal proficiency needs to be monitored (Aldosari, 2008).

Wiki collaborative writing may encourage participation, but it may not encourage attention to language use. Thus, although wiki-produced texts may be highly collaborative writing activities, unlike face-to-face collaboration, they may not encourage learners to language and the texts produced may not be as accurate as those produced in face-to-face collaborative writing. As with any new technology or approach, the use of wikis engenders issues and challenges for teachers. There is still a lack of clarity of the nature of wiki collaboration and a lack of knowledge on how to best structure such collaborative activities, including the optimal group size.

Research on collaborative face-to-face tasks suggests that the relationship learners form when completing collaborative tasks is important, as research has shown that not all pair work is necessarily collaborative, and it is collaboration that creates the conditions conducive to language learning rather than pair work per se (Aldosari, 2008; Storch, 2002, 2009). The longitudinal nature of wiki projects may be an advantage: It may allow learners to develop the trust and group cohesion that seems necessary for successful collaboration.

Reported teacher observations and surveys suggest a persistent reluctance on the part of learners to engage in coauthoring (e.g., Peretz, 2005) and of teachers to implement such activities, particularly in EFL settings (McDonough, 2004). Students' reluctance to engage in collaborative writing may be related to past experiences of group work. Watanabe's (2008) study shows that students' attitudes toward collaborative activity are very much influenced by their actual experience of collaboration. Watanabe found that learners reported positive attitudes to collaborative activity if they engaged in collaborative pair work. Conversely, those who experienced noncollaborative pair work were negatively disposed to collaborative activity. Thus there is clearly a need to monitor students' collaborative writing activity and perhaps even to train them before implementing collaborative writing tasks.

Learners' reluctance to engage in collaborative writing activities may abate with the advent of collaborative computer-mediated tasks. Research on web-based collaborative writing (wikis) (e.g., Kessler, 2009) seems to suggest that learners embrace collaboration much more readily perhaps because wikis are so intrinsically collaborative. This bodes well for the future of collaborative writing tasks in L2 classrooms.

ANNOTATED BIBLIOGRAPHY

Storch, N. (2009). *The nature of pair interaction. Learners' interaction in an ESL class: Its nature and impact on grammatical development.* Saarbrücken, Germany: VDM Verlag.

This book reports on a longitudinal investigation of pair work in an ESL context. A model of dyadic patterns of interaction is presented together with lengthy excerpts that illustrate the distinct nature of the four patterns identified. This model has informed the work of a number of researchers investigating the nature of pair work.

Swain, M. (2006). Languaging, agency and collaboration in advanced second language learning. In H. Byrnes (Ed.), *Advanced language learning: The contribution of Halliday and Vygotsky* (pp. 95–108). London, UK: Continuum.

The chapter presents a cogent rationale for collaborative writing from a sociocultural theoretical perspective. Drawing on Vygotsky's insights into the relationship between language and thought, Swain developed the key concepts of languaging and agency and explained their contribution to the development of advanced L2 proficiency. The examples provided enhance the discussion of these fairly complex concepts.

Watanabe, Y., & Swain, M. (2007). Effects of proficiency differences and patterns of pair interaction on second language learning: Collaborative dialogue between adult ESL learners. *Language Teaching Research, 11,* 121–142.

This study, based on Watanabe's master's thesis, presents a novel approach to investigating the impact of L2 proficiency pairing on the nature of collaborative talk and on the learning outcomes that result from collaboration with lower- and higher-proficiency peers.

REFERENCES

Adams, R., & Ross-Feldman, L. (2008). Does writing influence learner attention to form? The speaking-writing connection in second language and academic literacy development. In D. Belcher & A. Hirvela (Eds.), *The oral/literate connection: Perspectives on L2 speaking, writing, and other media interactions* (pp. 210–225). Ann Arbor: University of Michigan Press.

Aldosari, A. (2008). *The influence of proficiency levels, task type and social relationships on pair interaction: An EFL* context (Unpublished doctoral dissertation). University of Melbourne, Australia.

Arnold, N., & Ducate, L. (2006). Future foreign language teachers' social and cognitive collaboration in an online environment. *Language Learning & Technology, 10,* 42–66.

Brooks, L., & Swain, M. (2009). Languaging in collaborative writing: Creation of and response to expertise. In A. Mackey & C. Polio (Eds.), *Multiple perspectives on interaction: Second language research in honor of Susan M. Gass* (pp. 58–89). New York, NY: Routledge.

Bruffee, K. (1993). *Collaborative learning: Higher education, interdependence and the authority of knowledge.* Baltimore, MD: Johns Hopkins University Press.

Cumming, A. (1990). Metalinguistic and ideational thinking in second language composing. *Written Communication, 7,* 482–511.

Dias, P., Freedman, A., Medway, P., & Pare, A. (1999). *Worlds apart: Acting and writing in academic and workplace contexts.* Mahwah, NJ: Erlbaum.

de la Colina, A. A., & García Mayo, M. P. (2007). Attention to form across collaborative tasks by low-proficiency learners in an EFL setting. In M. P. García Mayo (Ed.), *Investigating tasks in formal language learning* (pp. 91–116). London, UK: Multilingual Matters.

Donato, R. (1994). Collective scaffolding in second language learning. In J. P. Lantolf & G. Appel (Eds.), *Vygotskian approaches to second language research* (pp. 33–56). Norwood, NJ: Ablex.

Elgort, I., Smith, A., & Toland, J. (2008). Is wiki an effective platform for group course work? *Australasian Journal of Educational Technology, 24,* 195–210.

Gutiérrez, X. (2008). What does metalinguistic activity in L2 learners' interaction during a collaborative writing task look like? *Modern Language Journal, 92*, 519–537.

Harklau, L. (2002). The role of writing in classroom second language acquisition. *Journal of Second Language Writing, 11*, 329–350.

Kessler, G. (2009). Student-initiated attention to form in wiki-based collaborative writing. *Language Learning & Technology, 13*, 79–95.

Kessler, G., & Bikowski, D. (2010). Developing collaborative autonomous learning abilities in computer mediated language learning: Attention to meaning among students in wiki space. *Computer Assisted Language Learning, 23*, 41–58.

Kim, Y. (2008). The contribution of collaborative and individual tasks to the acquisition of L2 vocabulary. *Modern Language Journal, 92*, 114–130.

Kim, Y., & McDonough, K. (2008). The effect of interlocutor proficiency on the collaborative dialogue between Korean as a second language learners. *Language Teaching Research, 12*, 211–234.

Kuiken, F., & Vedder, I. (2002). The effect of interaction in acquiring the grammar of a second language. *International Journal of Educational Research, 37*, 343–358.

Leeser, M. J. (2004). Learner proficiency and focus on form during collaborative dialogue. *Language Teaching Research, 8*, 55–81.

Long, M. (1996). The role of the linguistic environment in second language acquisition. In W. C. Ritchie & T. K. Bhatia (Eds.), *Handbook of research on language acquisition: Vol. 2. Second language acquisition* (pp. 413–468). New York, NY: Academic Press.

Mackey, A., & Gass, S. (2006). Introduction. *Studies in Second Language Acquisition, 28*, 169–178.

Mak, B., & Coniam, D. (2008). Using wikis to enhance and develop writing skills among secondary school students in Hong Kong. *System, 36*, 437–455.

Matthew, K., Felvegi, E., & Callaway, R. (2009). Wiki as a collaborative learning tool in a language arts methods class. *Journal of Research on Technology in Education, 42*, 51–72.

McDonough, K. (2004). Learner–learner interaction during pair and small group activities in a Thai EFL context. *System, 32*, 207–224.

Mirel, B., & Spilka, R. (Eds.). (2002). *Reshaping technical communication: New directions and challenges for the 21st century.* Mahwah, NJ: Erlbaum.

Ohta, A. S. (2001). *Second language processes in the classroom: Learning Japanese.* Mahwah, NJ: Erlbaum.

Ortega, L. (2007). Meaning L2 practice in foreign language classrooms: A cognitive-interactionist SLA perspective. In R. M. DeKeyser (Ed.), *Practice in second language: Perspectives from applied linguistics and cognitive psychology* (pp. 180–207). New York, NY: Cambridge University Press.

Peretz, A. (2005). Teaching scientific/academic writing: A place for new technologies. *Electronic Journal of e-Learning, 3*, 55–66.

Storch, N. (2001). Comparing ESL learners' attention to grammar on three different collaborative tasks. *RELC Journal, 32*, 104–124.

Storch, N. (2002). Patterns of interaction in ESL pair work. *Language Learning, 5*, 119–158.

Storch, N. (2005). Collaborative writing: Product, process and students' reflections. *Journal of Second Language Writing, 14*, 153–173.

Storch, N. (2008). Metatalk in pair work activity: Level of engagement and implications for language development. *Language Awareness, 17*, 95–114.

Storch, N. (2009). *The nature of pair interaction. Learners' interaction in an ESL class: Its nature and impact on grammatical development*. Saarbrücken, Germany: VDM Verlag.

Storch, N., & Wigglesworth, G. (2007). Writing tasks: Comparing individual and collaborative writing. In M. P. García Mayo (Ed.), *Investigating tasks in formal language learning* (pp.157–177). London, UK: Multilingual Matters.

Strauss, P. (2001). "I'd rather vomit up a live hedgehog" —L2 students and group assessment in mainstream university programs. *Prospect, 16*, 55–66.

Swain, M. (1985). Communicative competence: Some roles of comprehensible input and comprehensible output in its development. In S. Gass & C. Madden (Eds.), *Input in second language acquisition* (pp. 235–253). Rowley, MA: Newbury House.

Swain, M. (1993). The output hypothesis: Just speaking and writing aren't enough. *Canadian Modern Language Review, 50*, 158–164.

Swain, M. (1995). Three functions of output in second language learning. In G. Cook & B. Seidlhofer (Eds.), *Principle and practice in applied linguistics: Studies in honor of H.G. Widdowson* (pp. 125–144). Oxford, UK: Oxford University Press.

Swain, M. (2000). The output hypothesis and beyond: Mediating acquisition through collaborative dialogue. In J. Lantolf (Ed.), *Sociocultural theory and second language learning* (pp. 97–114). Oxford, UK: Oxford University Press.

Swain, M. (2006). Languaging, agency and collaboration in advanced second language learning. In H. Byrnes (Ed.), *Advanced language learning: The contribution of Halliday and Vygotsky* (pp. 95–108). London, UK: Continuum.

Swain, M. (2010). "Talking-it-through" : Languaging as a source of learning. In R. Batstone (Ed.), *Sociocognitive perspectives on language use/learning* (pp. 112–130). Oxford, UK: Oxford University Press.

Swain, M., & Lapkin, S. (2001). Focus on form through collaborative dialogue: Exploring task effects. In M. Bygate, P. Skehan, & M. Swain (Eds.), *Researching pedagogic tasks: Second language learning, teaching, and testing* (pp. 99–118). New York, NY: Longman.

Tan, L., Wigglesworth, G., & Storch, N. (2010). Pair interactions and mode of communication:

Comparing face-to-face and computer mediated communication. *Australian Review of Applied Linguistics*, *33*, 27.1–27.24.

Tocalli-Beller, A., & Swain, M. (2005). Reformulation: The cognitive conflict and L2 learning it generates. *International Journal of Applied Linguistics*, *15*, 5–28.

Warschauer, M., & Grimes, D. (2007). Audience, authorship, and artifact: The emergent semiotics of Web 2.0. *Annual Review of Applied Linguistics*, *27*, 1–23.

Watanabe, Y. (2008). Peer-peer interaction between L2 learners of different proficiency levels: Their interactions and reflections. *Canadian Modern Language Review*, *64*, 605–635.

Watanabe, Y., & Swain, M. (2007). Effects of proficiency differences and patterns of pair interaction on second language learning: Collaborative dialogue between adult ESL learners. *Language Teaching Research*, *11*, 121–142.

Weissberg, R. (2000). Developing relationships in the acquisition of English syntax: Writing versus speech. *Learning and Instruction*, *10*, 37–53.

Weissberg, R. (2006). *Connecting speaking and writing.* Ann Arbor: University of Michigan Press.

Wheeler, S., Yeomans, P., & Wheeler, D. (2008). The good, the bad and the wiki: Evaluating student-generated content for collaborative learning. *British Journal of Educational Technology*, *39*, 987–995.

Wigglesworth, G., & Storch, N. (2009). Pairs versus individual writing: Effects on fluency, complexity and accuracy. *Language Testing*, *26*, 445–466.

Wilkoff, B. (2007, May 10). Safety vs. panic [Web log post]. *Discourse about discourse* [blog]. Retrieved from http: //yongesonne.edublogs.org/2007/05/10/safety-vs-panic/

Williams, J. (2008). The speaking-writing connection in second language and academic literacy development. In D. Belcher & A. Hirvela (Eds.), *The oral/literate connection: Perspectives on L2 speaking, writing, and other media interactions* (pp. 10–25). Ann Arbor: University of Michigan Press.

Vygotsky, L. S. (1978). *Mind in society: The development of higher psychological processes.* Cambridge, MA: Harvard University Press.

Teaching Pragmatics: Trends and Issues

Naoko Taguchi

Theoretical, empirical, and practical interest in pragmatic competence and development for second language (L2) learners has resulted in a large body of literature on teaching L2 pragmatics. This body of literature has diverged into two major domains: (a) a group of experimental studies directly testing the efficacy of various instructional methods in pragmatics learning and (b) research that explores optimal instructional practice and resources for pragmatic development in formal classroom settings. This article reviews literature in these two domains and aims at providing a collective view of the available options for pragmatics teaching and the ways that pragmatic development can best be promoted in the classroom. In the area of instructional intervention, this article reviews studies under the common theoretical second language acquisition paradigms of explicit versus implicit instruction, input processing instruction, and skill acquisition and practice. In the area of classroom practice and resources, three domains of research and pedagogical practices are reviewed: material development and teacher education, learner strategies and autonomous learning, and incidental pragmatics learning in the classroom. Finally, this article discusses unique challenges and opportunities that have been embraced by pragmatics teaching in the current era of poststructuralism and multiculturalism.

An emergence of communicative competence models (Bachman, 1990; Bachman & Palmer, 1996; Canale & Swain, 1980) marked a shift in the view of second language (L2) learning from simply a mastery of grammatical forms to the acquisition of functional and social use of these forms as well. Since then, pragmatic competence, namely, the ability to communicate and interpret meaning in social interactions, has become an essential component of L2 proficiency, distinct from grammatical, discourse, and strategic competencies. Perhaps the most widely used definition of pragmatics is found in the relationship between *pragmalinguistics* and *sociopragmatics*. Pragmalinguistics refers to the linguistic resources available to perform language functions, and sociopragmatics refers to the language user's assessment of the context in which such resources are implemented (Leech, 1983; Thomas, 1983). Pragmatic development entails acquisition of both of these knowledge bases, as well as efficient control of them in real-time communication. For instance, learners need to know what syntactic forms and lexis they should use in order to refuse an invitation from someone. At the same time they need to be able to determine whether such refusal is acceptable within a particular situation in the target culture, and if so, what to say in order to refuse whom and under what circumstances. To this end, pragmatics extends beyond grammar. It entails knowledge of forms, as well as their functional possibilities, and contextual requirements that determine form-function mappings.

The teaching of pragmatic competence has gained greater attention as pragmatics in the communicative competence models has begun to gain explicit recognition. This is evidenced in the dozen book-length publications that have appeared on this topic since 2000. Some of these publications are edited volumes of empirical papers that describe instructional methods and learning opportunities in the classroom (Alcón-Soler & Martínez-Flor, 2008; Martínez-Flor & Alcón-Soler, 2005; Martínez-Flor, Usó-Juan, & Fernández-Guerra, 2003; Rose & Kasper, 2001; Taguchi, 2009; Yoshimi & Wang, 2007). Others are teachers' guides and resource books with ready-made lesson plans and teaching tips (Bardovi-Harlig & Mahan-Taylor, 2003; Houck & Tatsuki, 2011; Ishihara & Cohen, 2010; Ishihara & Maeda, 2010; Tatsuki & Houck, 2010), and still others are research monographs that document the process of pragmatic development in formal settings, in turn informing us about instructional activities and practice that are optimal for pragmatic growth (Ohta, 2001; Taguchi, in press). Collectively, these books have helped us recognize the interconnectedness among theory, research, and practice in pragmatics. They have given us an opportunity to explore the theoretical construct of pragmatic competence and its central features, along with instructional methods and materials through which these features can be taught. Empirical studies, either as laboratory experiments or classroom implementations, have served to assess learning outcomes of target pragmatic features and generate an array of implications for teaching in the classroom as well as in less traditional learning environments (e.g., computer-mediated forums and online social media outlets).

This article reviews a selection of the existing literature and discusses diverse issues related to pragmatics teaching and learning in the following two categories: (a) experimental studies that directly test the effectiveness of specific instructional methods of pragmatics learning and (b) literature that addresses optimal instructional materials and resources for pragmatic development in formal classroom settings. In the area of instructional intervention, this article reviews studies that have applied the common second language acquisition (SLA) frameworks of explicit versus implicit learning, input processing instruction, and skill acquisition and practice. In the domain of instructional practice and resources, literature in three areas is reviewed: material development and teacher education, learner strategies and autonomous learning, and incidental pragmatics learning in classroom. Finally, this article discusses unique challenges faced by interlanguage pragmatics in the era of poststructuralism and multiculturalism and the ways in which these challenges translate into pragmatics teaching.

INSTRUCTIONAL INTERVENTION STUDIES IN INTERLANGUAGE PRAGMATICS

Pragmatic competence involves the ability to manage a complex interplay of language, language users, and context of interaction. Given this complexity, one would naturally wonder whether pragmatic competence is indeed teachable. Gabriele Kasper's plenary talk at the TESOL Convention in Orlando, Florida, in 1997, entitled "Can Pragmatic Competence Be Taught?" (Kasper, 1997) inspired growth in applied empirical studies on the teaching of pragmatics. As a result of the dominance of morphosyntax studies in instructed SLA, the teachability of pragmatics was a genuine question at that time, motivating researchers to explore the ways that formal instruction could be translated to the area of sociocultural and sociolinguistic abilities. Following this call, early studies produced in the 1990s showed that most aspects of pragmatics are amenable to instruction, meaning that instruction is better than noninstruction for pragmatic development (for a review, see Kasper & Rose, 1999; Rose, 2005).

Having established the benefits of instruction, the field later evolved around a question of efficacy: What instructional methods could best enhance the learning of pragmatics? This question was taken up by a line of instructional intervention studies that implemented a planned pedagogical action directed toward the acquisition of select pragmatic features. These studies compared the effects of certain teaching methods over others by measuring the degree of learning from pre- to post-instruction (Kasper, 2001; Kasper & Roever, 2005; Martínez-Flor & Alcón-Soler, 2005; Roever, 2009). Later studies largely followed cognitively oriented SLA theories in experiment design, which, in turn, has strengthened the connections between interlanguage pragmatics and SLA at large. By far, the SLA theory that has provided the strongest impetus for pragmatics intervention studies is Schmidt's (1993, 2001) noticing hypothesis, which claims that learners must notice L2 features in input for subsequent development to occur in their acquisition of these features. Hence, speakers' attention to linguistic forms, functional meanings, and relevant contextual features is a necessary condition for pragmatics input to become intake.

Previous instructional studies have applied this theoretical paradigm by designing interventions in such a way that noticing of the target form-function-context mappings is facilitated through various instructional methods such as explicit metapragmatic information, input enhancement, consciousness raising, and repeated processing of pragmalinguistic forms. A group of studies that compared the effect of explicit versus implicit approaches can serve as representative of these methods. Explicit approaches involve direct explanation of target pragmatic features followed by practice, while implicit approaches with-hold explanation but provide input and practice opportunities where learners can develop implicit understanding of pragmatic forms and their uses (Kasper & Rose, 2002). Recently, researchers have argued that selection of explicit and implicit conditions represents a continuum between absolutely explicit and implicit extremes rather than a dichotomy (Jeon & Kaya, 2006; Takahashi, 2010a, 2010b).

Alcón-Soler (2007) is an example of an intervention study that compared the effect of explicit and implicit treatment on Spanish EFL (English as a foreign language) learners' acquisition of request forms in English. The explicit group received metapragmatic information regarding requests. Then they were asked to identify examples of requests in provided scripts and to justify their choices. The implicit group was given awareness-raising tasks that featured input enhancement (i.e., requests and related sociopragmatic factors placed in bold type or capitalization) but received no metapragmatic explanation. In the posttest, both groups outperformed the control group, but no significant differences were detected between the two experimental groups; however, the explicit group maintained learning up to the delayed posttest given 3 weeks after the treatment.

These studies are discussed in more detail in Takahashi (2010a). There she reviewed 49 intervention studies in L2 pragmatics published since the 1980s, which were divided into three groups: studies that explored the effectiveness of explicit intervention ($k = 26$), studies that focused on the effectiveness of implicit intervention ($k = 2$), and studies that compared explicit and implicit conditions in terms of their instructional effects ($k = 21$). Several generalizations were drawn from this review. First, echoing Jeon and Kaya's (2006) metaanalysis, the robustness of explicit instruction was largely confirmed, reiterating the crucial role of metapragmatic explanation for promoting pragmatic development. Second, instructional treatments that showed strong durability effects in delayed posttests were often characterized as having cognitively demanding tasks, by, for example, having participants engage in a comparison between their performance and target-like performance and/or promoting their discovery of target pragmatic conventions. Takahashi argued that the superiority of explicit instruction found in Alcón-Soler's study, cited above, can be attributed to learners' greater cognitive involvement in the explicit condition; unlike implicit conditions in which learners simply identified request forms that were directed by researchers through input enhancement, learners in the explicit condition were required to find target request forms on their own. Takahashi also emphasized that, while the nature of intervention does play a decisive role, L2 proficiency, instructional targets, length of instruction, and methods of assessment also moderate observed learning benefits.

Although the noticing hypothesis and related concepts of consciousness and attention have long permeated the pragmatics instructional practice, recently the field of interlanguage pragmatics has welcomed two new theoretical paradigms as guiding frameworks for pragmatics instruction—input processing and skill acquisition theories. Under the assumption that language acquisition is a by-product of comprehension, the input processing theory aims to describe cognitive mechanisms that operate when the learner is processing input (VanPatten, 1996, 2007). The model makes a number of claims about strategies that learners use to understand form-meaning connections or to parse sentences. Derived from various insights of the input processing model, a teaching model called processing instruction aims to teach learners how to process input so that target grammatical structures are processed to comprehend meaning. To achieve this, the processing instruction engages learners in structured input activities in which learners have to rely on grammatical forms in order to get meaning.

Input processing theory and processing instruction have recently been applied to pragmatics instruction in a study by Takimoto (2009), which investigated the effects of input processing instruction on learning request forms in L2 English. Takimoto compared three types of input-based interventions: (a) structured input tasks with explicit metapragmatic information, (b) structured input tasks without explicit information, and (c) problem-solving tasks (a type of inductive activity). In structured input tasks, learners first listened to a dialogue containing target request forms and then evaluated their appropriateness. Four productive and receptive tasks assessed the instructional outcomes: a discourse completion task, a role-play task, a written appropriateness judgment task, and a listening appropriateness judgment task. The three experimental groups out-performed the control group in all measures, but no significant differences were found among the treatment groups in the posttest. A delayed posttest revealed the sustained effect of structured input tasks and problem-solving tasks for all measures, although the explicit group failed to maintain their gains on the listening measure. Takimoto's studies lend support to the effectiveness of processing instruction found in morphosyntax studies (e.g., VanPatten & Oikkenon, 1996): Comprehension-based instruction could prove effective in both production and comprehension-based tasks.

These findings were further confirmed in a more recent study by Takimoto (2010), but this time, he examined the effects of repetition of input processing tasks on learning request forms in English. He compared two task repetition conditions: same task and similar task repetition. The former group repeated exactly the same input structured activities, while the latter group repeated these activities using slightly different scenarios. The control group received no instruction. Two measures of learning outcomes were used: an acceptability judgment test evaluating target request forms and a discourse completion test that elicited requests. Although no difference was found between the two treatment conditions on the judgment task, the same task group outperformed the similar task group on production of requests. Findings were attributed to the deeper-level perceptual processing involved in the same task condition. The same task repetition allows learners to familiarize themselves with the activity content more easily, consequently freeing up their memory and directing their attention to target forms. Takimoto's study brought new insights into pragmatics by incorporating some key concepts of current SLA literature—repetition, practice, and frequency (e.g., Collins & N. Ellis, 2009; DeKeyser, 2007).

More recently, the role of repetition and practice, together with insights drawn from input processing theory and processing instruction, have been applied to the teaching of Chinese pragmatics. Li's (in press) study examined effects of explicit metapragmatic information and structured input tasks on learning accurate, speedy comprehension, and production of Chinese request forms. Building on the cognitive theory of skill acquisition, specifically the ACT-R model (Anderson, 1993), Li conceptualized acquisition of pragmatic rules as involving a transition from the stage of declarative knowledge to procedural knowledge. Declarative knowledge refers to the knowledge of *what*, which is conscious and analyzable. Procedural knowledge refers to the knowledge of *how* and involves the state in which one's knowledge is executed in actual behavior. Skill acquisition is a process in which declarative knowledge becomes proceduralized via repeated practice of rules. The endpoint of skill acquisition is a stage in which rule application becomes automatic and unconscious, leading to fluent, accurate performance.

Li investigated whether or not different amounts of practice could yield differential effects in the development of accurate and speedy performance of the speech act of requests. Learners of Chinese were assigned to three groups: an intensive training group, a regular training group, and a control group. The intensive and regular training groups received explicit explanation on request forms and then practiced them through structured input activities modeled after Takimoto's studies (2009, 2010). The intensive group practiced twice as much as the regular group. The control group received metapragmatic explanation but had no practice. Two measures assessed learning outcomes: a listening appropriateness judgment task and an oral discourse completion task. In the former task, judgment accuracy and response times were analyzed. In the latter task, production accuracy and fluency (measured by planning time and speech rate) were analyzed. Results revealed no group difference on accurate judgment of request forms in the listening task, probably due to a ceiling effect: All groups did well after metapragmatic instruction, leaving little room to improve through practice. As to response times, the intensive group's response speed became significantly faster after practice, whereas no such effect was found in the other two groups. Analyses of the oral production of requests also revealed mixed findings. There was no significant practice effect on fluency, but there was on accuracy: The intensive group outperformed the other two groups after practice. The findings are in part consistent with skill acquisition theory in that declarative knowledge (as measured by accuracy) is shared across different skill domains (e.g., listening and speaking), but procedural knowledge (as measured by fluency) requires skill-specific practice (DeKeyser, 2007). Following this principle, comprehension-based practice might improve performance accuracy in both comprehension and production tasks, but the effect may not transfer across modalities in fluency.

Other than House (1996), Li's study is probably the only instructional study that extends the usual measure of pragmatic performance accuracy to performance fluency, thereby expanding the conceptualization of pragmatic competence. Following Kasper's (2001) claim that pragmatic development involves acquiring pragmatic knowledge and gaining automatic control in processing this knowledge in real time, several recent studies examined the development of the combination of processing speed and fluency in pragmatic performance (e.g., Taguchi, 2008a, 2008b). These studies showed that accuracy and fluency are distinct components of L2 pragmatic performance and do not develop in parallel, which further reiterates the importance of conjoined analysis of pragmatic knowledge and processing capacity in pragmatic development.

Although empirical efforts to measure pragmatic fluency are relatively recent, the knowledge-processing dichotomy is hardly new and goes back to the 1980s, as seen in Faerch and Kasper's (1984) original model of pragmatic competence. They conceptualized pragmatic knowledge as involving declarative and procedural components. Declarative knowledge consists of resources needed for pragmatic performance (e.g., linguistic and sociocultural knowledge, knowledge of discourse). Procedural knowledge refers to knowledge used in selecting and combining parts of declarative knowledge for the purpose of achieving communicative goals. Whether or not instruction helps promote development of procedural knowledge as well as declarative knowledge, indicated in fluency and accuracy respectively, is an original question that should be explored further in future research. This direction will help situate interlanguage pragmatics in a wider field, composed of SLA, cognitive psychology, and psycholinguistics.

In summary, the last two decades have seen a rapid expansion of intervention studies in interlanguage pragmatics. Like grammar and lexis, pragmatic competence was found to be profitably enhanced through instruction under the common SLA frameworks of noticing and explicit/implicit instruction, input processing, and skill acquisition and practice. Some of the recent developments are seen more explicitly in connection with cognitive theories that intend to reveal the underlying mechanisms that operate in registering and retaining form-function-context mappings. Another recent development is seen in the target of instruction, which has also expanded its scope from pragmatic knowledge to processing efficiency in using this knowledge.

An accumulation of empirical findings suggests several directions for future pragmatic instructional studies. First, future research should explore more dynamic examination of learnability, pragmatic targets, instructional methods, and learning outcomes. Although previous pragmatics studies targeted a range of proficiency groups from beginning level to advanced, very few studies have aimed at comparing learning success of learners with different proficiency levels nor measured their linguistic competence for instructional readiness specific to target pragmalinguistic forms. These observations have been made in recent reviews (Roever, 2009; Takahashi, 2010a, 2010b). Takahashi suggested that future research should explore how learners with different proficiency levels cope with the same pragmatic interventions, based on the premise that learners whose linguistic competence is still underdeveloped may not be able to fully benefit from instruction. Similarly, Roever (2009) suggested considering a three-way interaction among pragmatic targets, types of interventions, and learners: namely, exploring what kinds of target features (e.g., speech acts, formulae) should be taught to what kinds of learners (in terms of proficiency or developmental level) using what kinds of methods (e.g., implicit or explicit, input-based or output-based). This direction of research will advance our understanding of the relationship between pragmatic learnability and instructional intervention. Empirical data might tell us that instructional effect is mediated through learners' readiness; learners' linguistic maturity and complexity of pragmalinguistics forms and sociopragmatic factors are important variables to consider when understanding effects of particular instructional methods.

Another direction for future research relates to transfer of learned pragmatic knowledge, in response to a question on whether learning one pragmatic feature can facilitate learning of another pragmatic feature. This question is pertinent, considering that most previous studies limited their instruction to one or two pragmatics features (e.g., speech acts, address terms, and routines), consequently reinforcing a view of pragmatic competence as a constellation of bits of isolated pragmatic features that have to be taught independently from one another. Future research could be more creative in identifying commonalities across pragmatic features and targets, and devising an instructional method that promotes transfer of learned pragmatic knowledge from one area to another knowledge domain. For instance, syntactic and lexical mitigations in requests (e.g., hedging) could also be used as softeners in disagreements. Hence, it would be interesting to examine whether learned knowledge about requests can help promote performance of another speech act, disagreements. Similarly, formal versus informal address terms can be taught and measured within speech acts of different levels of formality so that sociopragmatic knowledge of form-context associations gets strengthened over different domains of pragmatic resources. Because the exchange of pragmatics resources across different pragmatic acts has not been attested, while learners' overgeneralization of specific pragmatic forms is certainly a consideration, future research in this direction could help us see connections among seemingly separate pragmatic targets, thereby presenting a possibility for a more comprehensive curriculum of pragmatic instruction.

INSTRUCTIONAL RESOURCES AND PRACTICE FOR PRAGMATICS LEARNING

Materials for Pragmatics Teaching and Teacher Education

As shown in the previous section, instructional studies in interlanguage pragmatics have long centered around debates on their effects on pragmatic learning. As a by-product of these studies, a variety of materials and activities have been generated for teaching pragmatics in classrooms. Because pragmatics entails linguistic resources for both performing communicative acts and discerning social perceptions of these acts, teaching materials inevitably involve several key elements: social context, functional language use, and interaction. Therefore, activities and tasks have been designed in a way to incorporate these components. For example, consciousness-raising tasks typically have learners listen to conversations either through video or audio, with attention directed to the target pragmatic features and sociolinguistic variables of particular speech events (e.g., setting, participant relationships) (e.g., K. Ishida, 2009). Similarly, receptive-skills tasks expose learners to pragmatic input but have them act on this input by evaluating the appropriateness of the target pragmatic forms on a rating scale or by selecting appropriate forms from a list of expressions (e.g., Takimoto, 2009). Productive-skills tasks have taken a variety of formats, including role-playing activities, structured conversations, discourse completion tests, and cloze tests. In role-playing activities, students typically practice speech acts by assuming specific roles in hypothetical scenarios and interacting with peers (e.g., Pearson, 2006). These activities and tasks are presented in resource books and textbooks targeted at pragmatics, as well as in teachers' guides (e.g., Bardovi-Harlig & Mahan-Taylor, 2003; Ishihara & Cohen, 2010; Ishihara & Maeda, 2010; Tatsuki & Houck, 2010).

Martínez-Flor and Usó-Juan (2006) proposed a comprehensive framework for facilitating development of pragmatic and intercultural competencies. The model consists of six stages: (a) researching, (b) reflecting, (c) receiving, (d) reasoning, (e) rehearsing, and (f) revising. The first two stages expose learners to pragmatic concepts (e.g., speech acts of requests and apologies), and have them gather first language (L1) pragmatic data and analyze these data according to social variables (e.g., gender, social status). In the third and fourth stages, learners receive explicit instruction on the L2 version of these pragmatic acts and are then expected to analyze these acts using L2 data. The last two stages provide opportunities for learners to practice their knowledge in communicative activities and to receive feedback. This model brings together several critical elements of pragmatics teaching: cultural comparisons, explicit pragmatic information, awareness-raising of pragmalinguistic forms and their situational variations, focused practice, and feedback.

More recently, technology has brought exciting new venues for materials and formats used in pragmatics teaching (Taguchi & Sykes, in preparation). This is because some of the key instructional features endorsed by technology—for example, input, interaction, simulation, and multimedia environment—are indeed key conditions for pragmatics learning. There are several Web sites dedicated to L2 pragmatics (for a review, see Cohen, 2008). These Web sites provide interactive multimedia modules where learners can watch video clips of conversations that include speech acts and verbal explanations of these speech acts, find cultural tips, and complete exercises. Computer-assisted language learning (CALL) has also expanded our options for pragmatics instruction. Ward, Rafael, Bayyari Yaffa Al, and Thamar (2007), for example, developed a computer program in which learners of Arabic practice using backchannels by producing them in response to prerecorded utterances. A computer then analyzes the timing and frequency of their backchannels and provides corrective feedback. Using CALL, several instructional intervention studies have been conducted (Saita, 2001; Utashiro & Kawai, 2009). Utashiro and Kawai developed an original computer-based course called DiscourseWare and examined its effect on the learning of Japanese reactive tokens (i.e., backchannel signals; e.g., *sodesuka*, meaning "I see" ; *honto*, meaning "really"). Learners of Japanese received computer-delivered instruction on different reactive tokens over a period of 2 weeks. They watched video clips of native speaker conversations and identified and practiced the reactive tokens that appeared in previous conversations. Instruction was sequenced according to three stages to promote a blended learning experience: self-paced/computer-based, instructor-led, and interaction-based learning. Results revealed significant gains in their receptive and productive tasks at all stages. Learners'awareness of reactive tokens also improved after instruction, and this gain was retained at the time of the delayed posttest, 1 week after the instruction. Findings suggest the importance of explicit instruction in the use of reactive tokens and the potential benefit of a blended learning experience when using CALL for pragmatics learning.

Synchronous and asynchronous computer-mediated communication (CMC) is another instructional tool available for pragmatics learning (see Belz, 2008, for a review). Previous studies have demonstrated the effectiveness of CMC in teaching apology speech acts, interactional particles, and modal particles (e.g., Gonzalez-Lloret, 2008; Kakegawa, 2009; Sykes, 2005; Vyatkina & Belz, 2006; Wishnoff, 2000). CMC offers learners an authentic context for communication by having them engage in online dialogues with native speakers. Given that target pragmatic features appear in a contextualized manner, with written, unmoving input, it is easier for learners to notice pragmatic targets. These benefits were revealed in Kakegawa's (2009) study that examined the development of Japanese learners' use of sentence final particles through their e-mail correspondence with native speakers. In this study, Japanese learners in the United States received explicit instruction about the use of particles and exchanged e-mails with native speakers in Japan for 10 weeks. Over time, learners increased the frequency of particles and used a greater variety of them in a productive manner, suggesting that the combination of e-mail exchange and explicit instruction proved effective in learning these particles.

Another emerging technological option for pragmatics learning is virtual social platforms (e.g., *Second Life*). Examining language socialization in online communities is a growing interest among SLA researchers. Social networking, Internet interest communities and forums, three-dimensional multiuser virtual worlds, and online games are increasingly considered as alternative venues for language learning (e.g., Lafford, 2009). This trend is also seen in pragmatics. A series of publications by Sykes (Sykes, 2009, 2011; Sykes, Oskoz, & Thorne, 2008) describe her work on a virtual online space that simulates a Spanish study-abroad environment created for pragmatics learning. Sykes developed *Croque-landia*, a three-dimensional, graphically rich space that emulates real Spanish-speaking worlds where learners engage in goal-directed activities with avatars and practice speech acts. Advantages of these immersive spaces for pragmatics learning are summarized in Sykes et al. (2008). One major advantage involves situated roles and identities in immersive environments. Learners can simulate numerous participant roles and practice pragmatic functions in diverse social settings, which could help them to understand the impact of their language use in social interaction. Another advantage is that learners can feel emotional connection in response to the virtual environments and their collaborative partners, which could lead to motivation in learning. Finally, immersive spaces provide authentic interactional environments for low-risk practice. Learners can gain extensive opportunity to practice pragmatic acts in a nonthreatening environment with elements built into the spaces.

Effects of virtual environments in pragmatics learning were reported in Sykes (2009, 2011). In her study, Spanish learners completed five request speech acts with computer-generated avatars in *Croquelandia*. A discourse completion task consisting of request-making scenarios was administered at pre- and posttests, and request expressions types were then coded and compared. Results revealed very little change from pre- to posttest in terms of expression choice, but there was evidence of increased pragmatic awareness. Lack of improvement in pragmalinguistics was interpreted as incongruence between the outcome measure (i.e., discourse completion test) and the types of learning that occurred in the virtual environment.

Although empirical data are still limited, use of immersive worlds suggests a number of profound transformations to traditional approaches in terms of pragmatic learning. This type of instructional arrangement brings together the key elements of pragmatics teaching: context, functional language use, and interaction, with added values of authenticity, self-discovery, and experiential learning. However, as Sykes (2009, 2011) cautioned, a great deal of work needs to be done in order to understand how interactions in virtual spaces may facilitate pragmatics learning. For instance, this unique setting necessitates more empirical investigation into learners' behavioral data as virtual environments involve multimodal processing of written, oral, and gestural communication modes in tasks and in-game exploration features (e.g., area map and navigation tools, written and voice chats, feedback mechanisms, help centers, and hidden tips). Analysis of learners' use of these symbolic resources will help us understand how goal-oriented tasks and content delivery in virtual spaces compare to those in CMC or face-to-face interaction, and what aspects of these contexts may carry significant considerations for pragmatics learning. Afterwards, an experiment can be conducted to determine whether these features specific to immersive environments could prove effective for pragmatic development.

Up to this point I have discussed available resources and practice for pragmatics teaching in traditional and nontraditional learning contexts. As the body of materials and options for pragmatics learning grows, emerging research in pragmatics teaching is significant for practitioners and consumers of these materials. To this end, teacher training is critical because it inevitably influences the ways in which instructional methods and materials are utilized. Despite this importance, the knowledge and beliefs held by teachers about sociocultural aspects of language and effective techniques for teaching pragmatics have rarely been addressed (Cohen, 2008; Eslami-Rasekh, 2005). According to a nationwide survey conducted by Vasquez and Sharpless (2009), many of the 104 MA TESOL programs in the United States reported the teaching of pragmatics theories, but actual training on methods for teaching and assessing pragmatic competence was largely inconsistent. There was large variation among programs in their beliefs and attitudes toward the importance of the pragmatics-component in teacher preparation education. Some programs stated that pragmatics should be integrated throughout the curriculum, while others expressed that pragmatics is addressed as questions come up. The findings indicate a discrepancy between theoretically and empirically grounded needs for pragmatic teaching and teachers' preparedness and willingness in dealing with pragmatics in the classroom.

Learner Strategies and Autonomous Learning

Another emerging instructional option for pragmatics is strategy instruction, which could be profitably combined with technology-based materials that provide an array of opportunities for autonomous, independent learning. Cohen (2005) recently developed a set of taxonomies of speech act strategies consisting of three categories: strategies for the initial learning of speech acts (e.g., identifying target speech acts and gathering information about them), strategies for using speech act material that has already been learned (e.g., using a memory aid to remember speech act expressions), and learners' metapragmatic considerations (e.g., monitoring their own speech acts for appropriateness; see Ishihara & Cohen [2010] for an update). To date, there have been only a few preliminary findings on the effectiveness of strategy-based instruction in pragmatic development (Cohen & Shively, 2007; Cohen & Sykes, in press).

Recently Shively (2010) proposed a pedagogical framework that promotes strategy instruction in pragmatics teaching in a study-abroad context. Her framework is informed by previous models that combine explicit instruction and awareness raising of pragmatic features with data-driven activities (e.g., Martínez-Flor & Usó-Juan, 2006). She extends these models by taking advantage of the affordances that an immersion context and technology offer. In Shively's model, after explicit pragmatic instruction at the predeparture stage, learners are introduced to fieldwork methods for pragmatic data collection. The class instructor provides specific guidance as to how to look for pragmatic features in naturalistic data, as well as how to analyze, interpret, and reflect upon pragmatic behaviors in relation to larger communicative patterns in the host culture. Learners then engage in communicative practice of pragmatic features and receive feedback from the instructor. Taking advantage of the immersion context, practice consists of assigning learners to participate in the speech activity they are currently studying through authentic social interaction in the host community (e.g., inviting their host family to social events). At the post-study-abroad stage, learners could continue their learning of language and culture by staying connected with friends they made in the host country through technology (e.g., chat, blogs, and social networking sites).

Strategy instruction in pragmatics learning has several benefits. For one, it helps develop learners' autonomy, helping them take initiative and responsibility for their learning. Pragmatic knowledge developed in class or through pedagogical intervention can also transfer to real-life situations outside of the classroom. In addition, independent learning accommodates individual differences in learning styles because learners prefer different ways of learning—some prefer direct engagement with materials, whereas others prefer more abstract applications of them. By having learners self-guide their learning process, teachers can appreciate individual preferences in cultivating knowledge, which will essentially maximize learning outcomes. For these reasons, Cohen's strategy taxonomies serve as useful guidelines. They echo earlier claims made about the benefits of autonomous learning where learners act as amateur ethnographers and collect information about pragmatics (Bardovi-Harlig, 1992) and expand these benefits in a more systematic manner. Whether strategy training proves a useful option for pragmatics teaching remains a question for future empirical investigation.

Incidental Pragmatics Learning in the Classroom

A general consensus in the literature is that classroom learning is poor in opportunities for pragmatics learning. This results from the lack of both a range of representations of communication situations and registers within classroom discourse, as well as information about pragmatic norms of the given language in textbooks, and instead the presence of inauthentic language samples based on intuitions of textbook writers (Bardovi-Harlig, 2001; Kasper, 2001; Vellenga, 2004). However, there is also a small amount of evidence that learners do pick up pragmatic features through incidental exposure to input and repeated use of the target features in classroom, even when pragmatic features are not intended learning targets, suggesting that naturalistic development of pragmatic competence is possible in a formal classroom without explicit instruction (R. Ellis, 1992; Kanagy, 1999; Nikula, 2008; Ohta, 2001; Taguchi, in press; Tateyama & Kasper, 2008). A good example of this phenomenon is Ohta's (2001) study on acquisition of acknowledgment and alignment expressions in L2 Japanese. Acknowledgment is a feedback signal used to show attentiveness in conversations (e.g., *sodesuka desu ka*, meaning "oh really"), and alignment is an emphatic feedback signal (e.g., *ii desu ne*, meaning "That's great, isn't it?"). Naturalistic recordings of classroom interactions revealed that through recycled use of these expressions in peer conversations, learners gradually developed appropriate production. Collaborative peer-peer interaction created a range of opportunities for students to use targets that were not available in teacher-fronted exchanges. These findings tell us about the potential of opportunities for and outcomes of incidental pragmatics learning in various classroom practice and activities.

Although Ohta (2001) is perhaps the only existing study that explicitly links classroom resources to pragmatic-related learning outcomes. Several recent classroom observational studies have analyzed classroom discourse to identify opportunities for pragmatics learning. Tateyama and Kasper's (2008) analysis of naturally occurring requests in classroom revealed that, compared with interactions with students, requests from a class instructor to a native speaker classroom guest reflected a wider range of interactional sequences, linguistic resources, and speech styles. These different styles associated with requests potentially provided learners with opportunities to observe how request speech acts are structured differently in various situations. In another study, Nikula (2008) used the discourse-pragmatic approach to analyze pragmatic language use in a content-based L2 English classroom in Finland. Seventh-grade physics and biology lessons taught in English were recorded and analyzed for instances representing negotiation of misunderstandings, disagreements, and initiations. Although students' linguistic repertoire used to perform these functions was not as versatile as that of native speakers, they clearly attempted to monitor degrees of directness in potentially face-threatening situations. Students showed pragmatic proficiency not only in terms of avoiding threats to face but also in terms of recognizing how to participate in classroom interactions while also attending to interpersonal relationships. Various interactional accomplishments observed among students illustrate the nature of content-based classrooms as potential environments for practicing conversational participation.

Taguchi's (in press) study, which examined the development of pragmatic comprehension and production among Japanese learners of English in an immersion setting, provided a rich opportunity to analyze the impact of classroom discourse in this environment. Quantitative data on learners' pragmatic gains were analyzed with qualitative data on their sociocultural experiences collected through interviews, classroom observations, journals, and field notes. The body of triangulated data generated an interesting portrayal of opportunities for pragmatic practice, learners' stance in accessing such opportunities, and context-specific factors that facilitated or constrained this access. For instance, class observation revealed a number of jokes, expressions of sarcasm, and indirect communication, all of which assumed shared context and background knowledge between teachers and students. These opportunities for nonliteral communication seemed to contribute to the learners' steady progress in the ability to comprehend implicature. In contrast, their ability to produce formal, high-imposition speech acts did not progress much over time. It was speculated that this resulted from learners' lack of attention to the sociocultural aspects of language use, reinforced through interactions with classroom instructors. Teachers rarely corrected students' inappropriate language use, putting politeness considerations behind encouragement of direct interaction. As a result, students seemed to have developed an inaccurate assessment of target form-function-context mappings, which constrained their progress in appropriately using formal speech acts.

As summarized above, observational classroom studies have revealed that pragmatics learning can be constructed through classroom interactions. Future research would benefit from focusing on a systematic analysis of classroom discourse and practice (i.e., teacher talk, routines, and peer-peer interaction) from a pragmatic perspective. This could unveil the facilitative potential of opportunities for incidental pragmatics learning within various classroom practice and activities. When linked with formative and summative assessment, such an analysis should yield meaningful information about which aspects of pragmatic competence develop naturally along with resources that are present in a given classroom, and which aspects do not progress quickly and thus require instructional intervention.

PRAGMATICS TEACHING IN THE ERA OF POSTSTRUCTURALISM AND MULTICULTURALISM

Although the framework of communicative competence has immensely influenced our understanding and practice of pragmatics in L2 teaching, the wave of poststructuralism that the applied linguistics field has embraced in the last decade, together with the surge of transnationalism and multiculturalism, has inevitably challenged the traditional notion of pragmatic competence. In the current society, multiple ethnic groups and languages form a demographic makeup of one place. People develop diverse perspectives through varieties of experiences stemming from racial and ethnic differences. In this new era, knowledge of socially appropriate language use (Bachman & Palmer, 1996; Canale & Swain, 1980), which is the defining characteristic of the communicative competence models, is open to debate, as seen in the recent reconceptualization of communicative competence into interactional competence (Lee, 2006; Young, 2002; Young & He, 1998) and symbolic competence (Kramsch & Whiteside, 2008). The central problem in these definitions of communicative competence models relates to the homogeneous native speaker norms assumed in expressions like *socially appropriate language use* and *language functions appropriate to situations*. By whose criteria is appropriateness determined in a given language, and to what extent are these criteria valid? Do native speakers of different backgrounds operate under identical standards in judging and projecting appropriateness of behaviors? If the assumption of idealized native speakers is in question, can teachers still transmit ideological beliefs about community norms to students, and are students expected to conform to these norms? These questions have yet to be answered in the current era of globalization and multiculturalism.

Take English, the most researched language in pragmatics, for example. Only about 7% of the world population is composed of native English speakers. The vast majority of interactions involving English take place in the absence of native speakers, and English as a lingua franca is increasingly used as a means of international communication. House (2010) revealed that speakers of lingua franca bring their own pragmatic norms in communication, and various interactional norms, standards of politeness and directness, and cultural conventions are constantly negotiated among speakers. Speakers develop their own discourse strategies and communicative styles in their use of English as a lingua franca. In this communication venue, monolingual norms do not exist, nor are they relevant to evaluation of pragmatic competence, yet studying monolingual norms remains the mainstream practice in traditional interlanguage pragmatics research.

An equally important consideration in native speaker norms is learners' subjectivity in the emulation of and resistance to the norms in social interaction (Ishihara, 2010). Some learners may want to conform to the pragmatic norms of the given culture, but others elect not to use these forms, perhaps signaling a desire to maintain their identity. Recent studies provide empirical support for this observation Davis (2007) study. In Davis's study, Korean learners of English in Australia showed a preference toward routines in American English over their counterparts in Australian English because of the fascination with American culture that they developed in their home country. Ishihara and Tarone (2009) found that learners of Japanese tended to resist pragmatic use of honorifics or gendered language because of their beliefs in egalitarian social relationships coming from their home culture norms.

These findings reiterate the uniqueness of pragmatics. Learning pragmatics involves learning linguistic behaviors that are reflective of values and norms of a given culture. When learners' L1 and L2 cultures do not operate under the same values and norms, or when learners do not agree with L2 norms, linguistic forms that encode target norms are not easily acquired. While in terms of grammar and lexis, those cases are treated as instances of negative transfer or L1 interference that are largely unconscious, in pragmatics, learners are considered to make conscious decisions on whether to accept or resist target pragmalinguistic forms and sociopragmatic norms, and these decisions are thought to be guided by their subjectivity, beliefs, and experiences in their L1. These characteristics of pragmatics bring about a range of unique challenges in pragmatics teaching. For instance, echoing Ishihara and Tarone (2009), we need to assess who the students are in the classroom and what needs they have for their language study in order to take into consideration individuals' subjectivity in making pragmatic choices. Similarly, possible consequences of selecting pragmatic behavior should be made clear to learners, although the selection should be left to them according to their own learning goals (Judd, 1999). Adding to Judd, however, we should recognize that learners' pragmatic choice reflects not only their goals, but also their level of

L2 proficiency, which might constrain their ability to perform pragmatic functions.

The poststructuralist movement is also an impetus in the shifting view of pragmatic competence as a monolithic trait within individual learners to an emergent state jointly constructed among participants in discourse. Traditionally, pragmatic competence has been operationalized as the ability to use appropriate speech act formulae, comprehend indirect meaning, or choose proper speech styles, and these features have been considered target features in instruction. However, such practice begs the question of whether pragmatics can be reduced to a set of isolated linguistic systems used to index social functions and other styles and behaviors associated with politeness. This reductionist view has been challenged by the recent poststructuralist perspective, which argues that pragmatic acts are dynamic in nature, constructed and negotiated through interaction among participants (Kasper, 2006). Under poststructuralism, language is considered fundamentally unstable and subject to change across settings and through interaction. Meaning is produced within discourses and regulated by all forms of semiotic activity, including texts, images, gestures, and spaces (e.g., Pennycook, 2001). This poststructuralist perspective has recently been adopted for pragmatics. Corresponding to Kasper's (2001) approach to discursive pragmatics, an increasing number of recent studies have applied conversation analysis (CA) to the analysis of action, meaning, and context in pragmatic acts. CA utilizes the *emic* approach in analyzing talk-in-interaction to reveal how participants coconstruct actions sequentially turn-by-turn and design their turns to jointly accomplish the activity at hand. Together with CA, an emerging body of studies in interactional linguistics and discourse-functional linguistics has focused on analyzing ongoing social activities and sequential contexts where specific linguistic forms are used (e.g., M. Ishida, 2009; Mori, 2006). These studies have revealed how particular linguistic forms emerge from the "moment-by-moment unfolding of talk-in-interaction, in conjunction with other types of multimodal semiotic resources available for interactional participants" (Mori, 2009, p. 344).

The challenge of future pragmatics teaching then involves reconceptualizing the goal of instruction to reflect this new epistemology. Pragmatic competence could be promoted in more authentic, less structured dialogic activities where learners have choices to adapt their pragmatic resources to ongoing interactions. Likewise, in identifying target pragmatic features, we can apply performance-based analysis that involves examination of wide-ranging features of interactional competence, without limiting these to traditional linguistic elements such as directness of syntactic forms and semantic strategies. Some interactional features we could analyze include fluency, discourse, and conversation-management skills; the ability to accomplish mutual understanding; and the ability to recover from communicative breakdowns. These features are suggested in recent literature that proposed application of CA-informed materials to pragmatics instruction (Felix-Brasdefer, 2007; Huth & Teleghani-Nikasm, 2006).

CONCLUSION

Thanks to the rapidly growing literature in L2 pragmatics over the last few decades, we have witnessed a rich array of empirical studies that have collectively presented a variety of options for pragmatics teaching and learning in formal classrooms as well as in less traditional learning environments (e.g., online social media). A veritable explosion of instructional intervention studies in the last two decades has certainly helped us situate pragmatics teaching within the larger scope of SLA research, while also drawing explicit connections to psycholinguistic-oriented theories that explicate cognitive underpinnings for pragmatics learning. Research in the same period on pedagogical resources has continuously expanded options of pragmatics teaching from teacher-directed instruction toward more individualized, self-paced learning through use of technology and strategy training. Studies under the social constructivist view have taken an ecological approach to data by adapting rich, qualitative analyses of classroom input and interaction in terms of resources for pragmatics learning. A recent addition to this area is the expressed consideration to the practitioners of pragmatics teaching or teachers who inevitably influence how instructional methods and materials are implemented.

Whether we refer to instructional methods, materials, or classroom opportunities, a body of select literature reviewed here suggests a variety of possibilities and challenges involved in teaching pragmatics. Pragmatics addresses a wide range of elements—forms, functions, contexts, social relationships, cultural conventions, and norms—and this complexity has made teaching pragmatics a demanding task. Likewise, in the era of transnationalism and poststructuralism, pragmatics has identified additional issues to consider, such as target pragmatic norms for instruction, learners' subjectivity in emulating norms, and pragmatics as a discourse activity. Although these assorted issues have generated more questions than answers in terms of optimal instructional conditions for pragmatic development, the unique challenges and opportunities that are inherent to the nature and practice of pragmatics will continue to expand future scholarship in the area of interlanguage pragmatics and in the wider field of applied linguistics.

ANNOTATED BIBLIOGRAPHY

Belz, J. (2008). The role of computer mediation in the instruction and development of L2 pragmatic competence. *Annual Review of Applied Linguistics, 27*, 45–75.

This article discusses the role of computer mediation in pragmatic teaching and the development of L2 pragmatic competence. Based on existing literature, potential contributions of CMC to pragmatic instruction are examined in four areas identified as problematic or unexplored in pragmatics pedagogy: authenticity of instructional materials, opportunities for meaningful interactions, longitudinal documentation of pragmatic competence, and efficacy of CMC-based pedagogical intervention. This article also reviews a range of options for technology-aided pragmatic teaching, including self-accessible Web sites, use of corpora, and synthetic immersive environments and virtual spaces.

Ishihara, N., & Cohen, A. (2010). *Teaching and learning pragmatics: Where language and culture meet.* Harlow, UK: Pearson Longman.

This 16-chapter resource book provides comprehensive guidelines for teachers about how to deal with pragmatics issues in classroom. The book begins with an introspective analysis of teachers' knowledge about pragmatics and then moves on to a variety of practical tips for teaching pragmatics: gathering pragmatic data to be used for classroom purposes, understanding common causes of students' pragmatic failures, understanding benefits of an awareness-raising approach, developing lesson plans and assessment tools for pragmatic skills, and analyzing textbook materials for pragmatic use. Hands-on activities and discussion questions embedded throughout the book are designed to equip teachers with practical techniques on pragmatics teaching, which can assist them in making informed instructional decisions in the classroom.

Taguchi, N. (2009). *Pragmatic competence*. Berlin, Germany: Mouton de Gruyter.
This book is an edited collection of empirical studies that examine pragmatic competence in Japanese as a second language. This volume offers insights about pragmalinguistics and sociopragmatics related to Japanese language and culture. By documenting use of pragmatic forms and norms by learners of Japanese, the book informs practitioners about potential ease and difficulties related to learning Japanese pragmatics and presents pedagogical implications in terms of dealing with these pragmatic targets in the classroom.

REFERENCES

Alcón-Soler, E. (2007). Fostering EFL learners' awareness of requesting through explicit and implicit consciousness-raising tasks. In M. de Pilar Garcia Mayo (Ed.), *Investigating tasks in formal language learning* (pp. 221–241). Bristol, UK: Multilingual Matters.

Alcón-Soler, E., & Martínez-Flor, A. (2008). *Investigating pragmatics in foreign language learning, teaching and testing*. Bristol, UK: Multilingual Matters.

Anderson, J. R. (1993). *Rules of the mind*. Hillsdale, NJ: Erlbaum.

Bachman, L. F. (1990). *Fundamental considerations in language testing*. New York, NY: Oxford University Press.

Bachman, L. F., & Palmer, A. S. (1996). *Language testing in practice: Designing and developing useful language tests*. Oxford, UK: Oxford University Press.

Bardovi-Harlig, K. (1992). Pragmatics as a part of teacher education. *TESOL Journal, 1*(3), 28–32.

Bardovi-Harlig, K. (2001). Evaluating the empirical evidence: Grounds for instruction in pragmatics? In K. Rose & G. Kasper (Eds.), *Pragmatics in language teaching* (pp. 13–32). Cambridge, UK: Cambridge University Press.

Bardovi-Harlig, K., & Mahan-Taylor, R. (2003). *Teaching pragmatics*. Washington, DC: Office of English Programs, U.S. Department of State.

Belz, J. (2008). The role of computer mediation in the instruction and development of L2 pragmatic competence. *Annual Review of Applied Linguistics, 27*, 45–75.

Canale, M., & Swain, M. (1980). Theoretical aspects of communicative approaches to second language teaching and testing. *Applied Linguistics, 1*, 1–47.

Cohen, A. (2005). Strategies for learning and performing L2 speech acts. *Intercultural Pragmatics, 2–3*, 275–301.

Cohen, A. (2008). Teaching and assessing L2 pragmatics: What can we expect from learners? *Language Teaching, 41*, 213–235.

Cohen, A., & Shively, R. (2007). Acquisition of requests and apologies in Spanish and French: Impact of study abroad and strategy-building intervention. *Modern Language Journal, 91,* 189–212.

Cohen, A., & Sykes, J. (in press). Strategy-based learning of pragmatics: An example of intercultural language learning. In F. Dervin & A. J. Liddicoat (Eds.), *Linguistics for intercultural education in language learning and teaching.* Amsterdam, The Netherlands: John Benjamins.

Collins, R., & Ellis, N. (Eds.). (2009). Input and second language construction learning: Frequency, form, and function [Special issue]. *Modern Language Journal, 93*(3), 329–470.

Davis, J. (2007). Resistance to L2 pragmatics in the Australian ESL context. *Language Learning, 57,* 611–649.

DeKeyser, R. (2007). *Practice in a second language: Perspectives from applied linguistics and cognitive psychology.* Cambridge, UK: Cambridge University Press.

Ellis, R. (1992). Learning to communicate in the classroom: A study of two learners' requests. *Studies in Second Language Acquisition, 14,* 1–23.

Eslami-Rasekh, Z. (2005). Raising the pragmatic awareness of language learners. *ELT Journal, 59,* 199–208.

Faerch, D., & Kasper, G. (1984). *Strategies in interlanguage communication.* Harlow, UK: Longman.

Felix-Brasdefer, C. (2007). Teaching the negotiation of multi-turn speech acts: Using conversation-analytic tools to teach pragmatics in the FL classroom. In L. F. Bouton (ed.) *Pragmatics and language learning: Vol. 1* (pp. 167–197). Manoa: Second Language Teaching and Curriculum Center at University of Hawaii.

Gonzalez-Lloret, M. (2008). Computer-mediated learning of L2 pragmatics. In E. Alcón-Soler & A. Martínez-Flor (Eds.), *Investigating pragmatics in foreign language learning, teaching and testing* (pp. 114–134). Bristol, UK: Multilingual Matters.

Houck, N., & Tatsuki, D. (2011). *Pragmatics from research to practice: New directions.* Alexandria, VA: TESOL.

House, J. (1996). Developing pragmatic fluency in English as a foreign language. *Studies in Second Language Acquisition, 18,* 225–252.

House, J. (2010). The pragmatics of English as a lingua franca. In A. Trosborg (Ed.), *Handbook of pragmatics: Vol. VII* (pp. 363–387). Berlin, Germany: Mouton de Gruyter.

Huth, T., & Teleghani-Nikasm, C. (2006). How can insights from conversation analysis be directly applied to teaching L2 pragmatics? *Language Teaching Research, 10,* 53–79.

Ishida, K. (2009). Indexing stance in interaction with the Japanese desu/masu and plain forms. In N. Taguchi (Ed.), *Pragmatic competence* (pp. 41–68). Berlin, Germany: Mouton de Gruyter.

Ishida, M. (2009). Development of interactional competence: Changes in the use of *ne* in L2 Japanese during study abroad. In H. Nguyen & G. Kasper (Eds.), *Talk-in-interaction: Multilingual perspectives*. Honolulu: University of Hawaii, National Foreign Language Resource Center.

Ishihara, N. (2010). Maintaining an optimal distance: Nonnative speakers' pragmatic choice. In A. Mahboob (Ed.), *Non-native speakers of English in TESOL: Identity, politics, and perceptions* (pp. 35–53). Newcastle upon Tyne, UK: Cambridge Scholars.

Ishihara, N., & Cohen, A. (2010). *Teaching and learning pragmatics: Where language and culture meet*. Harlow, UK: Pearson Longman.

Ishihara, N., & Maeda, M. (2010). *Advanced Japanese: Communication in context* [Kotoba to bunka no kousaten]. London, UK: Routledge.

Ishihara, N., & Tarone, E. (2009). Emulating and resisting pragmatic norms: Learner subjectivity and pragmatic choice in L2 Japanese. In N. Taguchi (Ed.), *Pragmatic competence* (pp. 101–128). Berlin, Germany: Mouton de Gruyter.

Jeon, Eun-Hee, & Kaya, T. (2006). Effects of L2 instruction on interlanguage pragmatic development. In N. John & L. Ortega (Eds.), *Synthesizing research on language learning and teaching* (pp. 165–211). Philadelphia, PA: John Benjamins.

Judd, E. (1999). Some issues in the teaching of pragmatic competence. In E. Hinkel (Ed.), *Culture in second language teaching and learning* (pp. 152–166). Cambridge, UK: Cambridge University Press.

Kakegawa, T. (2009). Development of the use of Japanese sentence final particles through email correspondence. In N. Taguchi (Ed.), *Pragmatic competence* (pp. 301–334). Berlin, Germany: Mouton de Gruyter.

Kanagy, R. (1999). Interactional routines as a mechanism for L2 acquisition and socialization in an immersion context. *Journal of Pragmatics, 31*, 1467–1492.

Kasper, G. (1997). *Can pragmatics be taught?* Plenary speech presented at the Annual TESOL Convention (March, the 32nd conference, international), Orlando, Florida.

Kasper, G. (2001). Classroom research on interlanguage pragmatics. In K. Rose & G. Kasper (Eds.), *Pragmatics in language teaching* (pp. 33–62). Cambridge, UK: Cambridge University Press.

Kasper, G. (2006). Introduction. Multilingua, 25, 243–248.

Kasper, G., & Roever, C. (2005). Pragmatics in second language learning. In E. Hinkel (Ed.), *Pragmatics in language teaching and learning* (pp. 317–328). Mahwah, NJ: Erlbaum.

Kasper, G., & Rose, K. (1999). Pragmatics and SLA. *Annual Review of Applied Linguistics, 19*, 81–104.

Kasper, G., & Rose, K. (2002). *Pragmatic development in a second language*. Oxford, UK: Blackwell.

Kramsch, C., & Whiteside, A. (2008). Language ecology in multilingual settings: Towards a theory of symbolic competence. *Applied Linguistics, 29*, 645–671.

Lafford, B. (Ed.). (2009). Technology in the service of language learning: Update on Garrett (1991). *Modern Language Journal Focus Issue, 93*, 673–887.

Lee, J. (2006). Towards respecification of communicative competence: Condition of L2 instruction or its objective? *Applied Linguistics, 27*, 349–376.

Leech, G. (1983). *Principles of pragmatics*. Harlow, UK: Longman.

Li, S. (in press). The effect of input-based practice on pragmatic development in L2 Chinese. *Language Learning*.

Martínez-Flor, A., & Alcón-Soler, E. (2005). Pragmatics in instructed language learning [Special issue]. *System, 33*(3), 381–536.

Martínez-Flor, A., & Usó-Juan, E. (2006). A comprehensive pedagogical framework to develop pragmatics in the foreign language classroom: The 6Rs approach. *Applied Language Learning, 16*, 39–64.

Martínez-Flor, A., Usó-Juan, E., & Fernández-Guerra, A. (2003). *Pragmatics competence and foreign language teaching*. Castellon, Spain: Servei de Publications de la Universitat Jaume I.

Mori, J. (2006). The workings of the Japanese token *hee* in informing sequences: An analysis of sequential context, turn shape, and prosody. *Journal of Pragmatics, 38*, 1175–1205.

Mori, J. (2009). The social turn in second language acquisition and Japanese pragmatics research: Reflection on ideologies, methodologies and instructional implications. In N. Taguchi (Ed.), *Pragmatic competence* (pp. 335–338). Berlin, Germany: Mouton de Gruyter.

Nikula, T. (2008). Learning pragmatics in content-based classrooms. In E. Alcón-Soler & A. Martínez-Flor (Eds.), *Investigating pragmatics in foreign language learning, teaching, and testing* (pp. 94–113). Bristol, UK: Multilingual Matters.

Ohta, A. (2001). A longitudinal study of the development of expression of alignment in Japanese as a foreign language. In K. Rose & G. Kasper (Eds.), *Pragmatics and language teaching* (pp. 103–120). New York, NY: Cambridge University Press.

Pearson, L. (2006). Patterns of development in Spanish L2 pragmatic acquisition: An analysis of novice learners' production of directives. *Modern Language Journal, 90*, 473–495.

Pennycook, A. (2001). *Critical applied linguistics: A critical introduction*. Mahwah, NJ: Erlbaum.

Roever, C. (2009). Teaching and testing pragmatics. In M. H. Long & C. J. Doughty (Eds.), *Handbook of language teaching* (pp. 560–577). Malden, MA: Wiley-Blackwell.

Rose, K. R. (2005). On the effects of instruction in second language pragmatics. *System, 33*, 385–399.

Rose, K., & Kasper, G. (2001). *Pragmatics in language teaching*. Cambridge, UK: Cambridge University Press.

Saita, I. (2001). *Aizuchi and cut in-focusing on a situation and setting where a problem concerning cross-cultural communication often occurs. A study on two-way distance learning system of Japanese language* (Research outcome report. Grant-in-aid scientific research report 1999–2000). (C) (2), 9–21.

Schmidt, R. (1993). Consciousness, learning and interlanguage pragmatics. In G. Kasper & S. Blum-Kulka, (Eds.), *Interlanguage pragmatics* (pp. 43–57). New York, NY: Oxford University Press.

Schmidt, R. (2001). Attention. In P. Robinson (Ed.), *Cognition and second language instruction* (pp. 3–32). Cambridge, UK: Cambridge University Press.

Shively, R. (2010). From the virtual world to the real world: A model of pragmatics instruction for study abroad. *Foreign Language Annals, 45*, 105–137.

Sykes, J. (2005). Synchronous CMC and pragmatic development: Effects of oral and written chat. *CALICO Journal, 22*, 399–432.

Sykes, J. (2009). Learner request in Spanish: Examining the potential of multiuser virtual environments for L2 pragmatics acquisition. In L. Lomika & G. Lord (Eds.), *The second generation: Online collaboration and social networking in CALL* (pp. 199–234). San Marcos, TX: CALICO.

Sykes, J. (2011). Teaching through multi-user virtual environments: User-driven design and implementation for language learning. In G. Vicenti & J. Braman (Eds.), *Teaching through multi-user virtual environments: Applying dynamic elements to the modern classroom* (pp. 283–305). Hershey, PA: IGI Global.

Sykes, J., Oskoz, A., & Thorne, S. (2008). Web 2.0, synthetic immersive environments, and mobile resources for language education. *CALICO Journal, 25*, 528–546.

Taguchi, N. (2008a). Cognition, language contact, and development of pragmatic comprehension in a study-abroad context. *Language Learning, 58*, 33–71.

Taguchi, N. (2008b). The role of learning environment in the development of pragmatic comprehension: A comparison of gains between EFL and ESL learners. *Studies in Second Language Acquisition, 30*, 423–452.

Taguchi, N. (2009). *Pragmatic competence.* Berlin, Germany: Mouton de Gruyter.

Taguchi, N. (in press). *Context, individual differences, and pragmatic development.* Bristol, UK: Multilingual Matters.

Taguchi, N., & Sykes, J. M. (in preparation). *Technology in interlanguage pragmatics research and teaching.* Philadelphia, PA: John Benjamins.

Takahashi, S. (2010a). Assessing learnability in second language pragmatics. In A. Trosborg (Ed.), *Handbook of pragmatics: Vol. VII* (pp. 391–421). Berlin, Germany: Mouton de Gruyter.

Takahashi, S. (2010b). The effect of pragmatic instruction on speech act performance. In A.

Martínez-Flor & E. Usó-Juan (Eds.), *Speech act performance: Theoretical, empirical and methodological issues* (pp. 127–144). Amsterdam, The Netherlands: John Benjamins.

Takimoto, M. (2009). The effects of input-based tasks on the development of learners' pragmatic proficiency. *Applied Linguistics, 30,* 1–25.

Takimoto, M. (2010). Evaluating the effects of task repetition on learners' recognition and production of second language pragmatic chunks. Paper presented at the International Conference of Malaysian English Language Teaching Association, Selangor, Malaysia. June

Tateyama, Y., & Kasper, G. (2008). Talking with a classroom guest: Opportunities for learning Japanese pragmatics. In E. Alcón-Soler & E. Martínez-Flor (Eds.), *Investigating pragmatics in foreign language learning, teaching, and testing* (pp. 45–71). Bristol, UK: Multilingual Matters.

Tatsuki, D., & Houck, N. (2010). *Speech acts and beyond: New directions in pragmatics.* Alexandria, VA: TESOL.

Thomas, J. (1983). Cross-cultural pragmatic failure. *Applied Linguistics, 4,* 91–111.

Utashiro, T., & Kawai, G. (2009). *Blended learning for Japanese reactive tokens: Effects of computer-led, instructor-led, and peer-based instruction.* In N. Taguchi (Ed.), *Pragmatic competence* (pp. 275–300). Berlin, Germany: Mouton de Gruyter.

VanPatten, B. (1996). *Input processing and grammar instruction in second language acquisition.* Norwood, NJ: Ablex.

VanPatten, B. (2007). Input processing in adult second language acquisition. In B. VanPat-ten & J. Williams (Eds.), *Theories in second language acquisition: An introduction* (pp. 115–135). Mahwah, NJ: Erlbaum.

VanPatten, B., & Oikkenon, S. (1996). Explanation versus structured input in processing instruction. *Studies in Second Language Acquisition, 18,* 495–510.

Vasquez, C., & Sharpless, D. (2009). The role of pragmatics in the master's TESOL curriculum: Findings from a nationwide survey. *TESOL Quarterly, 43,* 5–28.

Vellenga, H. (2004). Learning pragmatics from ESL & EFL textbooks: How likely? *TESOL-EJ, 8.* Retrieved from http: //www/writing.berkeley.edu/tesl-ej/ej30/a3.html

Vyatkina, N., & Belz, J. (2006). A learner corpus-driven intervention for the development of L2 pragmatic competence. In K. Bardovi-Harlig, C. Félix-Brasdefer, & A. S. Omar (Eds.), *Pragmatics and language learning: Vol. 11* (pp. 293–329). Manoa: Second Language Teaching and Curriculum Center at University of Hawaii.

Ward, N., Rafael, E., Bayyari Yaffa Al, B., & Thamar, S. (2007). Learning to show you're listening. *Computer Assisted Language Learning, 20,* 385–407.

Wishnoff, J. (2000). Hedging your bets: L2 learners' acquisition of pragmatic devices in academic writing and computer-mediated discourse. *Second Language Studies, 19,* 127–157.

Yoshimi, D., & Wang, H. (2007). *Selected papers from pragmatics in CJK classrooms:*

The state of the art. Manoa: University of Hawaii at Manoa, National Foreign Language Resource Center.

Young, R. (2002). Discourse approaches to oral language assessment. *Annual Review of Applied Linguistics, 19*, 105–132.

Young, R., & He, A. W. (1998). *Talking and testing: Discourse approaches to the assessment of oral proficiency.* Amsterdam, The Netherlands: John Benjamins.

CONTRIBUTOR BIODATA

Martha Bigelow is an associate professor at the University of Minnesota in the Department of Curriculum and Instruction. Her research interests span the fields of education, applied linguistics, and cultural studies, with a focus on the language learning and schooling experiences of adolescent refugees from East Africa. Her work in teacher education and with schools seeks to cultivate pedagogies that support equity and access in education. She recently published a book entitled *Mogadishu on the Mississippi: Language, racialized identity and education in a new land* with Wiley Blackwell.

Robert J. Blake is a professor of Spanish at the University of California, Davis and founding director of the University of California Consortium for Language Learning & Teaching. He publishes in the fields of Spanish linguistics, second language acquisition, and computer-assisted language learning. He co-authored *Tesoros Online*, a multimedia program for introductory Spanish (http: //www.tesoros.es). He also co-authored *Al corriente: Curso intermedio de español*, 4th Edition (McGraw-Hill Companies). He was the PI for the development of "Arabic without walls" an online course taught through UC Irvine. In 2008, he published *Brave new digital classrooms: Technology and foreign language learning* (Georgetown). In 2004, Professor Blake was inducted into the North American Academy for the Spanish Language.

Yuko Goto Butler is an associate professor of language and literacy in education at the Graduate School of Education at the University of Pennsylvania. Her research interests are primarily focused on the improvement of second and foreign language education among young learners in both the U.S. and Asia in response to the diverse needs of an increasingly globalizing world. She has been interested in identifying effective ESL/EFL teaching methods and strategies that take into account the relevant linguistic and cultural contexts in which instruction takes place. She is also interested in how best to assess children's second/foreign language proficiency.

Christiane Dalton-Puffer is an associate professor of linguistics at the English Department of the University of Vienna, where she teaches in the TEFL program and directs the Centre for English Language Teaching. Her current research is in content and language integrated learning (CLIL) and classroom discourse.

Other research interests include learner and teacher attitudes and lay theories, pronunciation teaching and learning, as well as language teacher education. She is the author of *Discourse in content and language integrated learning (CLIL) classrooms* (Benjamins 2007) and co-convenor (with Tarja Nikula and Ute Smit) of the AILA Research Network on CLIL.

Jelena Mihaljević Djigunović is a professor of second langauge acquisition and TESOL at Zagreb University's English Department. Her main research interests centre around the age factor, teaching modern languages to young learners, individual differences, and L2 teacher education. She has been involved in a number of large scale research projects on L2 learning and teaching, the latest one being the *Early language learning in Europe* (ELLiE). She has published extensively in national and international journals. Her publications include two research books on affective learner factors and over 100 papers, as well as a number of ESL teaching materials.

Michael E. Everson is an associate professor of foreign language and ESL education at the University of Iowa. His primary research interest is how second language students learn to read in cross-orthographic reading situations. His scholarship has appeared in a number of journals and book collections, with his most recently co-edited publications being *Teaching Chinese as a foreign language: Theories and applications* (with Yun Xiao) and *Research among learners of Chinese as a foreign language* (with Helen H. Shen). Professor Everson has served on a number of boards to promote less commonly taught language education initiatives, and is a former president of the National Council of Less Commonly Taught Languages.

Jennifer Jenson is an associate professor of pedagogy and technology in the Faculty of Education at York University, Canada. She has published on games and learning, educational technology policies and practices, and gender and technology.

Celeste Kinginger is a professor of applied linguistics at the Pennsylvania State University where she is involved in the education of language learners, teachers, and researchers. Her recent publications include: *Language learning in study abroad: Case studies of Americans in France* (Modern Language Journal Monograph, 2008); *Language learning and study abroad: A critical reading of research* (Palgrave/Macmillan, 2009); and *Contemporary study abroad and foreign language learning: An activist's guidebook* (Pennsylvania State University Center for Advanced Language Proficiency Education and Research, 2009). Her current projects include an edited volume entitled *Social and cultural aspects of cross-border language learning* (John Benjamins).

Ewa Kuśmierczyk is a PhD candidate in the School of Linguistics and Applied Language Studies at Victoria University, New Zealand. She has an MA in Applied Linguistics and has been a tutor in Applied Linguistics courses at Victoria University since 2007. Her current project is looking at multimodal approaches to construction of professional identity in job interviews. The analysis of speech in conjunction with gesture, bodily movements, and document use aims at gaining a better understanding of how interview participants interact to create positive interview outcomes.

Heather Lotherington is a professor of multilingual education at York University where she teaches in the Faculty of Education, and in the Graduate Program in Linguistics and Applied Linguistics. Her research focuses on multimodal literacies, multilingual inclusion and pedagogical innovation. Since she spearheaded a collaborative research venture between York University and Joyce Public School in Toronto in 2003, researchers and teachers have been continuously engaged in co-designing multimodal literacies projects (see www.multiliteracies4kidz.ca). Their award winning research has been widely published. Professor Lotherington's most recent book is *Pedagogy of multiliteracies: Rewriting Goldilocks* (Routledge, 2011).

Marianne Nikolov is a professor of English applied linguistics at the University of Pécs, Hungary. Her research interests include early learning and teaching of modern languages, assessment of processes and outcomes in language education, individual differences (especially language learning aptitude and motivation of all age groups), teacher education, and language policy. Her most recent large-scale project is on developing diagnostic tests of English as a foreign language for children in grades 1 to 6. Presently, she is a fellow at the Center for Advanced Study in the Behavioral Sciences at Stanford University, California. For more information see: http://englishdepartments.btk.pte.hu/index.php?p=contents&cid=12.

Jonathan Newton is a senior lecturer in the School of Linguistics and Applied Language Studies, Victoria University of Wellington, New Zealand. His research focuses on language teaching for the workplace, classroom-based SLA research, and intercultural language teaching. His articles have appeared in journals such as *Second Language Research*, *System*, *Journal of Pragmatics*, *English Language Teaching Journal*, and *Modern English Teacher*. He has papers forthcoming in *Language Learning* and *The Journal of Second Language Writing*. He recently co-authored two books, *Teaching ESL/EFL listening and speaking* (with Paul Nation, Routledge, 2009), and a second, *Workplace talk in action: An ESOL resource* (with Nicky Riddiford, VUW, 2010).

Catherine O'Hallaron is a doctoral student in Literacy, Language, and Culture in the School of Education at the University of Michigan, Ann Arbor. She received her MA in Teaching English as a Second Language from Universidad Interamericana and taught college-level English as a foreign language to native Spanish speakers in Puerto Rico for four years. She has also worked in teacher education, preparing undergraduate students to teach Spanish at the elementary level. Her current research interests include linguistic approaches to studying English learners' writing development and the use of functional linguistic pedagogy in enhancing teachers' reading and writing instruction.

Kate Paesani is an associate professor of French and director of basic French courses at Wayne State University. Her research interests include literacy-based approaches to language instruction, the role of literary texts in the undergraduate curriculum, and foreign language teacher development. Her work has appeared in journals such as *Foreign Language Annals*, *The French Review*, and *L2 Journal*. She is also co-editor of the volumes *Language program articulation: Developing a theoretical foundation* (Heinle & Heinle, 2005) and *The syntax of nonsententials: Multidisciplinary perspectives* (John Benjamins, 2006).

David Quinto-Pozos is an assistant professor in the department of linguistics at the University of Texas, Austin. David's research focuses on signed languages, and he works on register variation, language contact, the interaction of language and gesture, and developmental signed language disorders. He has directed the American Sign Language (ASL) programs at the University of Pittsburgh, the University of Illinois at Urbana-Champaign and currently co-directs the program at UT-Austin. He teaches courses on bilingual first language acquisition and signed language linguistics. David is also a certified ASL-English interpreter and currently President of *Mano a Mano*, a national organization for trilingual (Spanish-English-ASL) interpreters.

Ute Römer is currently the director of the applied corpus linguistics unit at the University of Michigan English Language Institute where she manages the Michigan Corpus of Academic Spoken English and the Michigan Corpus of Upper-level Student Papers projects. Her primary research interests and areas in which she has published include corpus linguistics, phraseology, and the application of corpora in language learning and teaching. Her current research focuses on student academic writing and on how corpus tools and methods can be used to identify meaningful units in specialized discourses.

Mary Schleppegrell is a professor of education at the University of Michigan, Ann Arbor. Her research explores the relationship between language and learning with a focus on students for whom English is a second language. She is the author of *The Language of schooling* (Erlbaum, 2004); co-author, with Zhihui Fang, of *Reading in secondary content areas: A language-based pedagogy* (University of Michigan Press, 2008); and co-editor, with Cecilia Colombi, of *Developing advanced literacy in first and second languages: Meaning with power* (Erlbaum, 2002). Her work has appeared in *Linguistics and Education*, *TESOL Quarterly*, and other journals and edited volumes.

Neomy Storch is a senior lecturer in ESL and applied linguistics at the School of Languages and Linguistics, the University of Melbourne, Australia. Her research has focused on issues related to ESL pedagogy. These issues have included the nature of peer collaboration, the role of L1 in L2 classes, the development of academic writing and the contribution of feedback to such development. She has published widely on her research in leading journals in the field of second language teaching and applied linguistics.

Naoko Taguchi is an associate professor in the Modern Languages Department at Carnegie Mellon University where she teaches courses on SLA, pragmatics, and Japanese language and culture. As a Fulbright scholar, she completed her Ph.D. in Applied Linguistics at Northern Arizona University, and she is the recipient of the 2004 MLJ-ACTFL Emma Birkmaier Dissertation Award. She edited the volume *Pragmatic competence* with Mouton de Gruyter and is co-editing the volume *Technology in interlanguage pragmatics research and teaching* with John Benjamins. Her research monograph, Context, *individual differences, and pragmatic development*, is forthcoming from Multilingual Matters. Her publications appeared in *Modern Language Journal, Applied Linguistics, Language Learning, TESOL Quarterly,* and *Studies in Second Language Acquisition,* among others. She is currently on the editorial board for *Japanese SLA.*

Patsy Vinogradov began teaching in Russia in 1994, and since then she has worked in the field of language education in a variety of settings. She specializes in teaching English as a Second Language to adult immigrants and refugees with limited formal schooling. Her research interests include literacy instruction and curriculum design for adult learners with low first language literacy, as well as professional development for instructors. She teaches at Hamline University in St. Paul, Minnesota, and she is a doctoral student in Education at the University of Minnesota.

图书在版编目(CIP)数据

剑桥应用语言学年度评论.2011:第二语言教育研究＝Annual Review of Applied Linguistics 2011 · Topics in Second Language Pedagogy:英文／(美)查伦·波利奥(Charlene Polio)主编. —北京:商务印书馆,2016
(剑桥应用语言学年度评论)
ISBN 978－7－100－12611－3

Ⅰ.①剑… Ⅱ.①查… Ⅲ.①应用语言学—研究—英文 Ⅳ.①H08

中国版本图书馆 CIP 数据核字(2016)第 239025 号

所有权利保留。
未经许可,不得以任何方式使用。

剑桥应用语言学年度评论 2011 · 第二语言教育研究
Annual Review of Applied Linguistics
2011 · Topics in Second Language Pedagogy
主编　〔美〕Charlene Polio
导读　张　琳

商 务 印 书 馆 出 版
(北京王府井大街36号　邮政编码100710)
商 务 印 书 馆 发 行
北京市松源印刷有限公司印刷
ISBN 978－7－100－12611－3

2016 年 12 月第 1 版　　开本 880×1230　1/32
2016 年 12 月北京第 1 次印刷　印张 15⅛
定价:45.00 元